BROADWAY

W9-BSX-938

Prof. Wyman

Prof. Louis Agassiz

ARD

J.C. Fiske

Geo. P. Sanger

Prof. Lane

Emory Washburn

EGE

Est. of B. Curr

Prof. Cooke

Mrs. C. R. Lowell

HALL

Henry James

Lith

President Eliot

A. L. Moering

Anna L.

Moering

A. P. Prof. Peabody

PRESCOTT ST.

QUINCY ST.

Plympton Heirs

Holmes

Mrs. Anna L.

PARK

E. S. Carr

Estate

J. H. Holt Torry Heirs

Wm. Torrey

EN ST.

WALNUT ST.

Geo Holl

Dd. Mullin

CAMBRIDGE
1873

William James

Books by Robert D. Richardson

HENRY THOREAU: A LIFE OF THE MIND

EMERSON: THE MIND ON FIRE

WILLIAM JAMES: IN THE MAELSTROM
OF AMERICAN MODERNISM

William James

In the Maelstrom of American Modernism

A BIOGRAPHY

Robert D. Richardson

HOUGHTON MIFFLIN COMPANY
BOSTON · NEW YORK
2006

For information about permission to reproduce selections
from this book, write to Permissions, Houghton Mifflin Company,
215 Park Avenue South, New York, New York 10003.

Visit our Web site: www.houghtonmifflinbooks.com.

Library of Congress Cataloging-in-Publication Data
Richardson, Robert D., 1934– .
William James / Robert D. Richardson.
p.   cm.
Includes bibliographical references and index.
ISBN-13: 978-0-618-43325-4
ISBN-10: 0-618-43325-2
1. James, William, 1842–1910. 2. Philosophers — United
States — Biography. I. Title.
B945.J24R53 2006
91 — dc22   2005037776

Printed in the United States of America

Book design by Robert Overholtzer

MP 10 9 8 7 6 5 4 3 2 1

For ANNIE, who wrote,
"We have less time than we knew
and that time buoyant, and cloven,
lucent, missile, and wild."

If this life be not a real fight, in which something is eternally gained for the universe by success, it is no better than a game of private theatricals from which one may withdraw at will. But it *feels* like a real fight — as if there were something really wild in the universe which we, with all our idealities and faithfulnesses, are needed to redeem.

—WILLIAM JAMES

CONTENTS

II. THE ACTION OF CONSCIOUSNESS

III. THE PRINCIPLES OF PSYCHOLOGY

PREFACE

THIS IS AN intellectual biography of William James. That is to say, it seeks to understand his life through his work, not the other way around. It is primarily narrative, aiming more to present his life than to analyze or explain it. As with my previous books on Thoreau and Emerson, I have tried to read what James read and to show how his reading is reflected in his writing.

The James family is one of the most unusual of all American families, and it has become impossible to separate William James from his unorthodox and talented family, especially from his famous brother Henry, the novelist. My intention, however, has been to concentrate as much as possible on William himself, on the man who made major contributions to at least five fields — psychology, philosophy, religious studies, teaching, and literature — and whose leading ideas are still so fresh and challenging that they are not yet fully assimilated by the modern world they helped to bring about.

William James believed not just that our minds are active rather than passive but that mind *is* activity. Nothing in our experience, for James, is really passive — not sleep, not hypnotic trance, not habit, not instinct, and least of all temperament. Active, it will be seen, does not mean orderly. Much of James's best work is a protest not only against dualism but against what Ian Hacking calls "dynamic nominalism"; that is, our habit of creating and naming categories into which we then sort ourselves. Once ADHD had been described, suddenly we saw it in every other child. James's strength of mind, his resistance to easy labeling, and his focus on experience itself rather than words for experience give his work its continuing explanatory power. James thought, for example, that "our beliefs and attention are the same fact." He was supremely interested in how the mind actually works. For that reason he began with chemistry and physiology — especially the latter, with its emphasis on the processes of the body. Where Freud insisted on the importance of the unconscious, James, who knew Freud's work before he met him, insists on the importance of consciousness, which he understood as a stream, a process. James indicates the road to modernism, and even to postmodernism, when he overcomes the ancient distinction between mind and body and proposes that the furthest we may be able to get is to say that "the thought itself is the thinker."

James maintained that one's philosophy is fundamentally an expression of one's temperament. James's own quicksilver temperament is the key to his life, his thought, and his style. It was Nabokov who pointed out that the most interesting part of a writer's biography is the biography of his style.

Alfred North Whitehead said, "In western literature there are four great thinkers, whose services to civilized thought rest largely on their achievements in philosophical assemblage; though each of them made important contributions to the structure of philosophic system. These men are Plato, Aristotle, Leibniz, and William James." John McDermott says, "William James is to classic American philosophy as Plato was to Greek and Roman philosophy, an originating and inspirational fountainhead." James is famous for pragmatism (which he sometimes felt he should have called humanism), though he should be remembered for his radical empiricism (which could have been called phenomenology); that is, his belief that reality is confined to what we experience, with the crucial proviso that nothing we experience can be excluded.

His book *The Will to Believe* was about the right to believe, and his *Varieties of Religious Experience* made religion possible for many educated moderns who are uncomfortable with the authority of churches and dogmas. The book is also a cornerstone of the modern field of comparative religion. Though it is nearly a hundred years since James died, his thought is still very much alive. "I find him visibly and testably right," says Jacques Barzun. "He is for me the most inclusive mind I can listen to, the most concrete and the least hampered by trifles."

Biography begins in the mysteries of temperament, lives in narrative, but aims beyond it, as the historian Jules Michelet understood, to resurrection. In telling the story of James's life I have tried to honor his love of spontaneity and activity and his positive fondness for chaos and chance. It was James himself who said, "Individuality is founded in feeling; and the recesses of feeling, the darker, blinder strata of character, are the only places in the world in which we catch real fact in the making, and directly perceive how events happen, and how work is actually done."

I have been beyond fortunate in my teachers and friends. Jack Bate, the biographer of Keats and Johnson and my teacher in college and graduate school, first suggested that I write a life of William James. Jack liked to quote Whitehead about how education was impossible apart from "the habitual vision of greatness." Jack was, and is, my vision of greatness. So is Justin Kaplan, the biographer of Twain and Whitman, who showed me the Cambridge Cemetery and stood beside me at the grave of William James. I am proud to say that John J. McDermott, who writes "for those among us who believe in intellectual passion rather than settling for intellectual inquiry," considered me worth trying to educate. He also read the entire manuscript and helped at every turn. Annie Dillard believed in both my subject and me through thick and thin.

For substantial help and encouragement I am also grateful to Wendy Doniger, who helped with WJ and Sanskrit, to Gerald Holton, who called my attention to Ernst Mach's and Niels Bohr's interest in WJ, to Stanley Hauerwas for his spirited critique of WJ, to Tracy Kidder for his interest in voluntary poverty, to Joan Mark for WJ and Mary Austin, to Brenda Wineapple for her work on WJ and Gertrude Stein, and to Carol Zaleski for calling my attention to James's interest in attention. I also owe more than I can acknowledge in a short space to the wide learning and good sense of the late Burton Feldman, of Victor Gourevitch, and of Jere Surber. The friendly kindness and enthusiasm of Deirdre Bair, Lyndall Gordon, Jerry Loving, James Maraniss, Jay Martin, Robert Stone, and Ann Warner helped keep me going. The students in my James family seminar at Chapel Hill provided important education. My colleagues in the Seekers Forum of Key West — truly the Metaphysical Club South — gave me the openhearted but rigorous hearing we all hope for.

For reading all or part of this book in manuscript and for valuable — often crucial — suggestions I thank Bobby Baird (who gave the book an especially searching reading), Wendy Doniger, John J. McDermott, and Phil Kowalski. For help with research and bibliography I am indebted to Nathan Eddy, who with Megan Carnes pulled together a huge bibliography of James's reading; to Bryan Sinche and Karah Rempe, who assembled a publishable secondary bibliography of work on James from 1974 on; and to Phil Kowalski, who is the best all-around research assistant I have had.

Among librarians I wish to thank particularly Peter Drummey and Nick Gordon of the Massachusetts Historical Society Library, Jack Eckert of the

Countway Library at Harvard Medical School, David Emerson of the Conway (New Hampshire) Public Library, and Linda Blair of the Lake Placid Public Library. Most of the work for this book was necessarily done at the Houghton Library at Harvard, which is the model of what a rare book and manuscript library can be. The knowledge and competence of Leslie Morris, curator of manuscripts, and the reading room staff—Susan Halpert, Jenny Rathbun, Betty Folsey, Tom Ford, Emily Walhout, and their colleagues—and the superb service ethic of the place make working at the Houghton one of the great pleasures of scholarly life in America. My agent, Tim Seldes, both stood behind and advanced the entire project. His contribution is enormous and priceless, as is that of my superb editor, Deanne Urmy. Larry Cooper, my manuscript editor, improved everything he touched. For the shortcomings of the book, I have myself to thank.

William James

Prologue

H E H A D N O T B E E N sleeping well in Palo Alto all semester — he suffered from angina and had recently been much troubled by gout — and so William James was lying awake in bed a few minutes after five in the morning on April 18 when the great earthquake of 1906 struck. James was sixty-four, famous now as a teacher and for his work in psychology, philosophy, and religion. He was spending the year as a visiting professor at Stanford University, twenty-five miles south of San Francisco. His mission was to put Stanford on the map in philosophy.

Jesse Cook, a police sergeant on duty that morning in the San Francisco produce market, first noticed the horses panicking, then saw the earthquake start. "There was a deep rumble, deep and terrible," said Cook, "and then I could actually see it coming up Washington Street. The whole street was undulating. It was as if the waves of the ocean were coming toward me."[1] John Barrett, city desk news editor of the *Examiner*, was already in his office when he heard "a long low moaning sound that set buildings dancing on their foundations." Barrett and his colleagues suddenly found themselves staggering. "It was as though the earth was slipping . . . away under our feet. There was a sickening sway, and we were all flat on our faces." Looking up, Barrett saw nearby buildings "caught up in a macabre jig . . . They swayed out into the street, then rocked back, only to repeat the movement with even more determination."[2]

James Hopper, a reporter for the *Call*, was home in his bed. He rushed to his window. "I heard the roar of bricks coming down," he wrote, "and at the same time saw a pale crescent moon in the green sky. The St Francis hotel was waving to and fro with a swing as violent and exaggerated as a tree in a tempest. Then the rear of my building, for three stories upward,

1

fell. The mass struck a series of little wooden houses in the alley below. I saw them crash in like emptied eggs, the bricks passing through the roofs as though through tissue paper. I had this feeling of finality. This is death."[3]

Out in the streets, "trolley tracks were twisted, their wires down, wriggling like serpents, flashing blue sparks all the time." Barrett saw that "the street was gashed in any number of places. From some of the holes water was spurting; from others gas." Astonished guests in the Palace Hotel looked out one of its few intact windows and saw a woman in a nightgown carrying a baby by its legs, "as if it were a trussed turkey."[4]

In the first moments after the quake there was total silence. "The streets," Hopper recalled, "were full of people, half clad, disheveled, but silent, absolutely silent."[5]

In San Jose, south of Palo Alto, along the line of the rip, the buildings of the state asylum at Agnews collapsed with a roar heard for miles, killing a hundred people, including eighty-seven inmates. Some of the more violent survivors rushed about, attacking anyone who came near. A doctor suggested that since there was no longer any place to put them, they should be tied up. Attendants brought ropes and tied the inmates hand and foot to those (small) trees that had been left standing.

In Palo Alto the stone quadrangle at Stanford was wrecked. Fourteen buildings fell; the ceiling of the church collapsed. The botanical garden was torn up as if by a giant plow. A statue of Louis Agassiz fell out of its niche and plunged to the pavement below, where it was photographed with its head in the ground and its feet in the air. Stanford was still on Easter vacation. Almost all the students were gone. One, however, was staying on the fourth floor of Encina Hall, a large stone dormitory. He sprang out of bed but was instantly thrown off his feet. "Then, with an awful, sinister, grinding roar, everything gave way, and with chimneys, floorbeams, walls and all, he descended through the three lower stories of the building into the basement." The student, who later told all this to James, added that he had felt no fear at the time, though he had felt, "This is my end, this is my death."[6]

The first thing William James noticed, as he lay awake in bed in the apartment he shared with his wife, Alice, on the Stanford campus, was that "the bed [began] to waggle." He sat up, inadvertently, he said, then tried to get on his knees, but was thrown down on his face as the earthquake shook the room, "exactly as a terrier shakes a rat." In a short piece of writing about the quake, written twenty-three days later, James recalled that "everything that was on anything else slid off to the floor; over went bureau and chiffonier with a crash, as the fortissimo was reached, plaster cracked, an awful roaring noise seemed to fill the outer air, and in an instant all was still again, save the soft babble of human voices from far and near."[7]

The thing was over in forty-eight seconds. James's first unthinking response to the quake was, he tells us, one of "glee," "admiration," "delight," and "welcome." He felt, he said, no sense of fear whatever. "Go it," I almost cried aloud, "and go it stronger." The Marcus Aurelius whom James admired, and who had prayed, "O Universe, I want what you want," could scarcely have improved on James's unhesitating, fierce, joyful embrace of the awful force of nature. It was for James a moment of contact with elemental reality, like Thoreau's outburst on top of Mount Katahdin, like Emerson's opening the coffin of his young dead wife, or like the climax of Robert Browning's poem "A Grammarian's Funeral" (one of James's favorites), in which the funeral procession of the outwardly unremarkable but deeply dedicated scholar — whose patient work has ignited the renaissance of learning — climbs from the valley of commonplace life to the heroic alpine heights where his spirit belongs: "Here — here's his place, where meteors shoot, clouds form, / Lightnings are loosened, / Stars come and go! Let joy break with the storm."

James's second response was to run to his wife's room. Alice was unhurt, and had felt no fear either. Then James went with a young colleague, Lillien Martin, into the devastation of downtown San Francisco to search for her sister, who was also, it turned out, unhurt. James's active sympathy and quick mobilization were characteristic, as was his third response to the event, which was to question everyone he saw about his or her feelings about the quake. His diary for the next day, April 19, says simply, "Talked earthquake all day."[8] It was also entirely characteristic that he next wrote up and published a short account of the experience, in which he noted that it was almost impossible to avoid personifying the event, and that the disaster had called out the best energies of a great many people.[9]

James's care for his wife, his concern for his colleague, and his writing up what he learned seem usual enough; it is his initial, unexamined, unprompted response that opens a door for us. James possessed what has been called a "great experiencing nature"; he was astonishingly, even alarmingly, open to new experiences. A student of his noted that he was at times a reckless experimenter with all sorts of untested drugs and gasses. This risk-taking, this avidity for the widest possible range of conscious experience, predisposed him to embrace things that many of us might find unsettling. It has been suggested that the earthquake experience was for James the near equivalent of a war experience. It may have been that, and it may have been even more than that. He no longer believed — if he ever had — in a fixed world built on a solid foundation. The earthquake was for him a hint of the real condition of things, the real situation. The earthquake revealed a world (like James's own conception of consciousness) that was pure flux having nothing stable, permanent, or absolute in it.

James had four years to live after the earthquake of 1906, and his work was far from done. In 1909 he was still trying to make sense of some of his most challenging and sweeping ideas in a book called *A Pluralistic Universe*. Here he firmly rejects what he calls the "stagnant felicity of the absolute's own perfection." He rejects, that is, the idea that everything will finally be seen to fit together in one grand, interlocked, necessary, benevolent system.[10] For James there are many centers of the universe, many points of view, many systems, much conflict and evil, as well as much beauty and good. It is, he said, "a universe of eaches."[11]

James's universe is unimaginably rich, infinitely full and variegated, unified only in that every bit of it is alive. Citing the German thinker Gustav Fechner for protective intellectual cover — a common maneuver for the canny enthusiast whose intoxicated admiration extended outward to writers and thinkers in all directions — James speaks approvingly of "the daylight view of the world." This is the view that "the whole universe in its different spans and wave-lengths, exclusions and envelopments, is everywhere alive and conscious."[12] In *Pragmatism*, published a year after the quake, he wrote, "I firmly disbelieve, myself, that our human experience is the highest form of experience extant in the universe. I believe rather that we stand in much the same relation to the whole of the universe as our canine and feline pets do to the whole of human life. They inhabit our drawing rooms and libraries. They take part in scenes of whose significance they have no inkling. They are merely tangent to curves of history the beginnings and ends and forms of which pass wholly beyond their ken. So we are tangent to the wider life of things."[13]

James's understanding of how each of us operates in the world is like George Eliot's description of the pier glass and the candle in *Middlemarch*. "Your pier glass or extensive surface of polished steel," Eliot writes, "rubbed by a housemaid, will be minutely and multitudinously scratched in all directions; but place now against it a lighted candle as a centre of illumination and lo! The scratches will seem to arrange themselves in a fine series of concentric circles round that little sun. It is demonstrable that the scratches are going everywhere impartially, and it is only your candle which produces the flattering illusion of a concentric arrangement, its light falling with an exclusive optical selection. These things are a parable," she concludes. "The scratches are events, and the candle is the egoism of any person." For William James, too, the world as a whole is random, and each person makes a pattern, a different pattern, by a power and a focus of his own. There is no single overarching or connecting pattern, hidden or revealed. "We carve out order," James wrote, "by leaving the disorderly parts out; and the world is conceived thus after the analogy of a forest or a block of marble from which parks or statues may be produced by eliminating irrelevant trees or chips of stone."[14]

Eliot's image also suggests something important about James's own life. Just as his early career plans careened wildly from civil engineering to painting to chemistry to being a naturalist to becoming a physician or a researcher in physiology, so any biography that undertakes to locate or exhibit the central James, the real James, the essential James, or that tries to make a shapely five-act play out of his life, runs the risk of imposing more order than existed — like the medieval hagiographer who gave the world what a modern scholar summarized as "all and rather more than all that is known of the life of St. Neot."

We have at least three main reasons to remember William James. First, as a scientist, a medical doctor, and an empirical, laboratory-based, experimental physiologist and psychologist, he was a major force in developing the modern concept of consciousness, at the same time that Freud was developing the modern concept of the unconscious. James was interested in how the mind works; he believed mental states are always related to bodily states and that the connections between them could be shown empirically.

Second, as a philosopher (psychology, in James's day, was a branch of philosophy and taught in the philosophy departments of universities), James is famous as one of the great figures in the movement called pragmatism, which is the belief that truth is something that happens to an idea, that the truth of something is the sum of all its actual results. It is not, as some cynics would have it, the mere belief that truth is whatever works for you. It must work for you *and* it must not contravene any known facts. James was interested more in the fruits than in the roots of ideas and feelings. He firmly believed in what he once wonderfully called "stubborn, irreducible facts." Written in readable prose intended for both the specialist and the general reader, James's books, in the words of one colleague, make "philosophy interesting to everybody."[15]

Third, James is the author of *The Varieties of Religious Experience,* the founding text of the modern study of religion, a book so pervasive in religious studies that one hears occasional mutterings in the schools about King James — and they don't mean the Bible. James's point in this book is that religious authority resides not in books, bibles, buildings, inherited creeds, or historical prophets, not in authoritative figures — whether parish ministers, popes, or saints — but in the actual religious experiences of individuals. Such experiences have some features in common; they also vary from person to person and from culture to culture. *The Varieties of Religious Experience* is also, and not least, the acknowledged inspiration for the founding of Alcoholics Anonymous. It is James's understanding of conversion that AA has found especially helpful.[16]

In trying to specify the groundnote of James's thought, his gifted student, colleague, and biographer Ralph Barton Perry pointed to "the one germinal idea from which his whole thought grew, . . . the idea of the essentially active and interested character of the human mind."[17] The mind was never for James an organ, a "faculty," or any kind of fixed entity. There is a good deal of truth to the comment of Paul Conkin that if psychology lost its soul with Kant, it lost its mind with James.[18] Mind for James was a process of brain function, involving neural pathways, receptors, and stimuli. Mind does not exist apart from the operations of the brain, the body, and the senses. Consciousness is not an entity either, but an unceasing flow or stream or field of impressions. James was convinced that no mental state "once gone can recur and be identical with what was before . . . There is no proof that an incoming current ever gives us just the same bodily sensation twice." James proposed that the elementary psychological fact . . . [is] not thought or this thought or that thought, but my thought."[19]

The process of mind, the actual stream of consciousness, is all there is. James throws down his challenge to Platonism: "A permanently existing 'idea' which makes its appearance before the footlights of consciousness at periodic intervals is as mythological an entity as the Jack of Spades."[20]

In place of the mythological world of fixed ideas, James has given us a world of hammering energies, strong but evanescent feelings, activity of thought, and a profound and relentless focus on life now. For all his grand accomplishments in canonical fields of learning, James's best is often in his unorthodox, half-blind, unpredictable lunges at the great question of how to live, and in this his work sits on the same shelf with Marcus Aurelius, Montaigne, Samuel Johnson, and Emerson. James's best is urgent, direct, personal, and useful. Much of his writing came out of his teaching, and it has not yet lost the warmth of personal appeal, the sound of the man's own voice. In one of his talks to teachers he said, "Spinoza long ago wrote in his *Ethics* that anything that a man can avoid under the notion that it is bad he may also avoid under the notion that something else is good. He who acts habitually *sub specie mali,* under the negative notion, the notion of the bad, is called a slave by Spinoza. To him who acts habitually under the notion of good he gives the name of freeman. See to it now, I beg you, that you make freemen of your pupils by habituating them to act, whenever possible, under the notion of a good."[21]

James's life, like all lives lived with broad and constant human contact, was marked by losses and tragedy, which he felt as deeply as anyone. Yet death moved him, most often, not to speculate on the hereafter but to redouble his energies and mass his attentions on the here and now. He remarked in *Pragmatism* that "to anyone who has ever looked on the face of a dead child or parent" — and he had done both — "the mere fact that matter could have taken for a time that precious form, ought to make matter sacred ever after. It makes no difference what the principle of life may be, material or immaterial, matter at any rate co-operates, lends itself to all life's purposes. That beloved incarnation was among matter's possibilities."

It is not hard to see how the writer of such sentiments became a much-loved person. How he came to be such a writer and such a man in the first place is more difficult to understand, and that is what this book is about.

James's life, especially his early life, was full of trouble, but the keynote of his life is not trouble. He is a man for our age in his belief that we are all of us afflicted with a certain blindness "in regard to the feelings of creatures and people different from ourselves." He understood, and he said repeatedly, how hard it is to really see things, to see anything, from another's point of view. He had a number of blindnesses himself. But he did not abandon the effort to understand others, and he proposed that wherever some part of life "communicates an eagerness to him who lives it," there is where the life becomes genuinely significant. He himself looked for what he called the "hot spot" in a person's consciousness, the "habitual center" of his or her personal energy. James understood the appeal of narrative, and so it is with a narrative that he made his point about joy. He tells a story, taken from an essay by Robert Louis Stevenson, in which Stevenson describes a curious game he and his school friends used to play as the long Scottish summers ended and school was about to begin.

"Towards the end of September," Stevenson writes, "when school time was drawing near and the nights were already black, we would begin to sally forth from our respective [houses], each equipped with a tin bull's eye lantern."

> ... We wore them buckled to the waist upon a cricket belt, and over them, such was the rigor of the game, a buttoned top-coat. They smelled noisomely of blistered tin; they never burned aright, though they would always burn our fingers; their use was naught, the pleasure of them merely fanciful; and yet a boy with a bull's eye lantern under his top-coat asked for nothing more.
>
> When two of these [boys] met, there would be an anxious "Have you got your lantern?" and a gratified "Yes!" . . . It was the rule to keep our glory contained, none could recognize a lantern bearer, unless (like the polecat) by the smell. Four or five would sometimes climb into the belly of a fishing boat or choose out some hollow of the links where the wind might whistle overhead. There the coats would be unbuttoned and the bull's eyes discovered, and in the checkering glimmer, under the huge windy hall of the night, and cheered by the rich steam of the toasting tinware, these fortunate young gentlemen would crouch together in the cold sand of the links or the scaly bilges of the fishing boat and delight themselves with inappropriate talk.

But the talk, says Stevenson, was incidental. "The essence of this bliss was to walk by yourself on a black night, the slide shut, the top-coat buttoned, not a ray escaping . . . a mere pillar of darkness in the dark, and all the while, deep down in the privacy of your heart, to know you had a bull's eye at your belt, and to sing and exult over the knowledge."

"The ground of a person's joy," says James, is often hard to discern. "For to look at a man is to court deception . . . and to miss the joy is to miss all. In the joy of the actors lies any sense of the action. That is the explanation, that is the excuse. To one who has not the secret of the Lanterns, the scene upon the links is meaningless."[22]

The great Hasidic masters say that we each have a tiny spark in us waiting to be blown into a fire. Jean-Paul Sartre said there are really no individuals, only universal singulars. William James would say that each of us is alone, but each of us has a lantern. Without the lantern, the interior spark, we are in the position of the old man who was observed by a reporter, a few minutes after the San Francisco earthquake, standing in the center of Union Square, and who was, "with great deliberation, trying to decipher the inscription of the Dewey monument through spectacles from which the lenses had fallen."[23]

I. GROWING UP ZIGZAG

1. Art Is My Vocation

A T THE AGE OF EIGHTEEN, well past the time when other young American men he knew were off to college, William James found himself going to school in Bonn, Germany, and locked in conflict with his imperious, mercurial father, Henry James Sr. Father wanted William to learn German; he chose the school in Bonn; he accompanied William there and saw him installed. Then Father fled the country, unable to understand or make himself understood in the language.

He had refused to allow William to go to an American college, fearing he would be corrupted there. Father wanted him to become a scientist; he thought science would bear out his views of religion. William's interest in science came and went; his interest in religion was nil. What he wanted to be was an artist. On August 19, 1860, after he had been in Bonn for about a month, William sent his father an unusually strong — in fact cheeky — letter. "I wish you would as you promise set down as clearly as you can on paper," he wrote, "what your idea of the Nature of Art is."[1]

Henry James Sr. was the author of a long procession of unwanted and unread books, published at his own expense. In this context, William's saying "as clearly as you can" seems almost taunting. The family style was brash, teasing, and reckless, but there was real trouble here. It was, as usual in the James family, complicated, and it had been simmering for some time. Father had just agreed to take the family (Mother, Father, Aunt Kate, William — Willy in the family — Harry, Wilky, Bob, and Alice) back to America from Europe so that Willy could resume his painting with William Morris Hunt in Newport, Rhode Island. Father had agreed to go back, though, typically, he continued to grumble about the reason for going back. Henry Senior despised painters, and had brought the family to Europe the year before precisely to discourage William's growing interest in art. Now, while he had agreed to let William return to America to study painting, he was haranguing the boy with his views on the danger posed by painting to one's spiritual well-being. It was not that art was too unworldly for Father; it was for him far too worldly.[2]

The letter his father sent him in reply has not survived, but William's exasperated response five days later is that of a still angry and upset young man: "What I wanted to ask you for at Mrs. Livermore's" — this, apparently, was where Father, but not William, got it all out in the open — "were the reasons why I should not be an 'artist.' I could not fully make out from yr. talk there what were exactly the causes of your disappointment at my late resolve, what your view of the nature of art was, that the idea of my devoting myself to it should be so repugnant to you."[3]

Despite, or more likely because of, his father's opposition, William's resolve was at the moment quite firm. Early in August he had written his friend Tom Perry with the great news. "We are to return to Newport!!" William announced. "I have come to the conclusion that 'Art' is my vocation."[4] William had not wanted to go abroad at all this most recent time. Back in September 1858, then sixteen and enjoying drawing with Hunt in Newport, he had protested against the proposed move to Europe in a letter to a friend: "Father took it into his head the other day that it was absolutely necessary for our moral and intellectual welfare to return immediately to Europe."[5] William's tone was light as he went on to rail happily against "such turpitude on the part of a being endowed with a human heart," but the edge of real opposition was already apparent.

Yet if William held back little, Father held back nothing. Two months later, in November 1858, William's younger brother Wilky, then not quite thirteen, had come home with a white and black greyhound pup, the care of which had fallen to William. His father thought William "ineffectual and pusillanimous" in his failure to discipline the puppy effectively after it jumped on the bed and tore the buttons off the sofa. William wrote his friend Ed Van Winkle, "Father said the other day with tears in his eyes: 'Never, never before did I so clearly see the utter and lamentable inefficiency and worthlessness of your character: never before have I been so struck with your perfect inability to do anything manly or . . . a . . . good!'"[6] Sixteen-year-old William was enjoying his outrage — exaggerating for comic effect — but the antagonism was there, and even a touch of malice. Ed Van Winkle would have known what to make of those series of dots. William's father had a pronounced stutter.

By the spring of 1859, Father had concluded, as he told a family friend, that William felt "a little too much attraction to painting . . . Let us break that up we said." So Father hauled the family abroad in the fall of 1859, going first to Geneva for the better part of a year and then to Bonn in July 1860. Father's main motive for the trip was not just to get William away from art, but to get him into science.[7]

William James had turned eighteen in January 1860. He was thin, almost slight. Just over five feet eight inches, he weighed less than 140 pounds, sometimes less than 130. He looks a little wild in early photographs. His dark hair covers the tops of his ears, and he has a boyish mustache barely distinguishable from a smudge on the photographic plate. He has dark eyebrows, which direct attention to his lively eyes, which have a piercing and moody intensity.

He was a flashy dresser. George Santayana noted years later that there was an "afterglow of Bohemia" about him. He wore white suits, or jackets fastened only by the top button, large floppy bow ties, a straw boater in summer. In his early pictures he never smiles, and the dandified dress is in odd contrast to the brooding young man who stares out at us. He positively reveled in his non-Victorian appearance. "I have got a neat yellow alpaca coat," he wrote his sister, "white damask vest, blue cravat, and a pair of splendid cinnamon coloured pantaloons, with straps, very tight, and a broad black strap running down them."[8]

He was all energy. He took stairs two or three at a time until he was past fifty. "He was always around the corner and out of sight," his brother Harry recalled. "We were never in the same schoolroom, in the same game, scarce even in step together . . . When our phases overlapped . . . it was only for a moment — he was clear out before I got well in." The same brother saw Willy as "vividly bright," "charged with learning," and he marveled over "the abundance, the gaiety and drollery, the generous play of voice and fancy" in Willy's letters, which could touch the "contemporary scene and hour into an intensity of life . . . the great sign of that life my brother's signal vivacity and cordiality, his endless spontaneity of mind."[9]

Above all, in these years, Harry remembered William drawing, "his head critically balanced and his eyebrows working. Willy was "drawing and drawing, always drawing, especially under the lamplight of the Fourteenth Street back parlor [in New York City] . . . always at the stage of finishing off, his head dropped from side to side, and his tongue rubbing his lower lip."[10]

As he moved from America to Europe and back, from school to school and subject to subject, always with his extraordinary "intensity of animation and spontaneity of expression," supplying for any company the "motive force" of imagination "in any quantity required," he gave his brother Harry the sense that there was "for him no possible effect whatever that mightn't be more or less rejoiced in as such." What all this animation and liveliness seemed like to William himself is suggested in a comment he made later. "The constitutional disease from which I suffer," he wrote, "is what the Germans call Zerrissenheit or torn-to-pieces-hood. The days are broken in pure zig-zag and interruption."[11]

Despite the unconventional and often exasperating zigzagging of his education, and perhaps because he sometimes yearned for ordinariness, William's intellectual interests at sixteen were not much different from those of many young men of his sort who were vaguely headed for college. In a letter of March 1, 1858, to Ed Van Winkle, William fretted about choosing a profession. He solemnly quoted Coleridge's "Rime of the Ancient Mariner" on the same subject: "He prayeth well, who loveth well both man and bird and beast." He mentions, smoothly enough, Rousseau, Newton, Michelangelo, Geoffroy Saint-Hilaire, Shakespeare, Galileo, Cuvier, and Brunel, as he writes about hoping himself to do something comparably useful. He feels drawn to the idea of becoming a naturalist, cites poetry easily (he invokes Longfellow's up-and-at-'em "Psalm of Life"), is dubious about engineering (Ed's declared interest), and rounds out the account of his current studies by emphasizing algebra, spherical trigonometry, and descriptive geometry. He is careful not to commit himself; he is equally careful not to seem directionless. "We will see what will turn up," he wrote. "I will be prepared for everything."[12]

If the above suggests a young man — a boy, really — following well-worn ways but guardedly holding back from any firm commitment, some observations made the following winter by his friend Tom Perry show William out finding new and interesting things in the intellectual world and bringing them back for others. Perry recalled William bringing home a volume of Schopenhauer and reading "amusing specimens of his delightful pessimism."[13] It is perfectly characteristic of the volatile William James that he later came to loathe Schopenhauer's pessimism, which he took as equivalent to determinism, and that he came rather delightedly to abuse the author of *The World as Will and Idea*. Schopenhauer's pessimism, James wrote twenty-five years later, is "that of a dog who would rather see the world ten times worse than it is, than lose his chance of barking at it."[14]

And one evening in February 1859, says Perry, William told his friends about Ernest Renan. Renan was known then for two volumes of essays, one of which had just appeared, and as a frequent and lively contributor to the *Revue des Deux Mondes*. His great *Vie de Jésus* was still ahead of him, but he was already known to be skeptical of the divine inspiration of the Bible and of what Emerson called "historical Christianity." William's feelings about Renan were mixed. A little over a year after this February evening, in May of 1860, William was making fun of a young friend's enthusiasm for Renan, but he knew the French author well enough to quote his saying, "I think, myself, that there is not any intelligence superior to man's in the universe."[15]

William had been working on his German with a tutor back in Newport. His French was already excellent. He had studied it as a child and had gone to school in Paris and Boulogne. In the fall of 1859, when the family went back abroad, this time to Geneva, William enrolled in the Geneva Academy, the precursor to the University of Geneva, where he plunged into the study of anatomy. This included going to see a drowned man dissected. The smell was not too bad, Harry told a friend, though one student fainted and another turned bright green.[16] William also studied math and, on his own, osteology.

This is the science curriculum of the dutiful son, and it represents serious university-level work, but a notebook James began in Geneva in November 1859 is what really shows the already impressive breadth of this seventeen-year-old's interests. He lists, among many others, Hallam, Fergusson, Orbigny, Siebold, Milnes, Edwards, Villon, Rabelais, Sir Thomas Browne, Mill, Butler, Browning, and Pascal. Another section of the list includes Carlyle, Confucius, Zoroaster, Epictetus, the *Imitation of Christ*, Persian poetry, *Gulistan* of Saadi, Heine, Goethe, and Breton poetry. Some of the names are lightly lined through, as though ticked off the list when sampled, but there is nothing yet to show that he actually read all this, and it may be mostly an inventory of interests.

There are more specific entries — reading notes — in the same notebook. Since this was his year in Geneva, most of the books are in French, whatever their subject. There is a surprising emphasis on Indic literature and religion: the *Vishnu Purana, Chef d'Oeuvres du Théâtre Indien, Fragments du Mahabarata, Selections from Mahabarata, Nala: Episode du Mahabarata,* and *La Sakountala: Drame Hindou* all appear on the list. The bare list of names cited above also includes Aristotle, Plato, Bacon, Descartes, and Locke. The more specific book list includes less routine figures and books, such as Jeremy Taylor's *Holy Living and Holy Dying,* Vico's *Science Nouvelle,* Condorcet's *Éloge* of Haller, and a French edition of Plotinus's *Enneades.* James was also interested in the national epics, which had first become widely known only in the early nineteenth century. He specifies the *Kalevala,* the *Chanson de Roland,* the *Cid, Le Roman de la Table Ronde,* as well as the *Mahabarata.*

But what brings alive for us the young man who kept this ambitious notebook is, first, the signature of his young sister, Alice, then eleven, on the title page, as though she were to be co-keeper of the notebook, and the two pages of mottoes and quotations that begin the notebook's entries. By turns serious, strenuous, warm, and bleak, they convey a golden ardor of youth glorying in expression, any expression.

> I am; what I am
> My dust will be again.
>
> The rain it raineth every day.
>
> 'Tis writ on Paradise's gate
> Wo to the dupe who yields to fate
>
> The understanding's copper coin
> counts not with the gold of love.

The Schopenhauer mood is on display here with "Earth equals host who murders his guests," and the young man's terror at premature professional narrowing is expressed with this: "Here is the sum, that when / one door opens another shuts."[17]

William's intellectual mood swings are related to his emotional weather. One cannot reduce one to the other, but neither can be safely ignored. William's general mood was often up this year in Geneva. "Willie is in a very extraordinary state of mind," Alice wrote their father, "composing odes to all the family."[18] Alice was eleven and a half when she wrote this. She was precocious and articulate, and might well have found William's mood extraordinary; the ode he had written her was about his proposing "to join myself to thee / By matrimonial band," her turning him down, and his subsequent despair. "I'll drown me in the Sea, my love, / I'll drown — me in — the Sea!" It was all — or almost all — high spirits and good-natured fun. Willy wrote their absent father with evident glee, "Alice took it very cooly."[19]

William found the Geneva winter appalling. He wrote to a friend back in the States: "A sort of early twilight continues all day long for days and days together. A low black pall of thick clouds spread over the whole heavens uniformly, prevents the view of the mountains and makes the ground appear as luminous as the sky, while a strong cutting bleak wind blows steadily and chills your very bones." One book that touched James during the summer of 1860, just as his struggles with his father were coming out in the open, was Goethe's *Sorrows of Young Werther*. He told his new Swiss friend Charles Ritter (he whose enthusiasm for Renan William had recently mocked) that this tale of a young man who literally kills himself for love was "an extraordinary book and much more worthy of attention than I had been led to believe."[20]

He was writing now from Bonn, no longer from Geneva, but it was still heavy weather inside and out. Bonn was on the Rhine. "The water is all yellow," he wrote Ritter, "and the current is so rapid that it makes the most laborious effect possible to watch the steamships go back upstream, they go so very slowly."[21]

William was fighting his own way upstream against his benevolent, controlling, and ever-changeable father. He was now making just enough progress so that Henry Senior booked passage for the family to start the return trip to America in early September 1860.

2. Growing Up Zigzag

WILLIAM JAMES WAS BORN on January 11, 1842, at the Astor House in New York City. He was the first child of Henry and Mary Walsh James, both thirty-one; they had just bought a house at 5 Washington Place but had returned to the hotel for the lying-in. On March 3, Ralph Waldo Emerson, then thirty-eight and just beginning to be known outside eastern Massachusetts, gave the first of a series of lectures, called "The Times," at the New York Society Library. Among his hearers was the new father, Henry James, who was instantly impressed, writing Emerson a warmly appreciative letter and inviting him to his home.

Emerson was at this time trying to recover from the devastating loss of his own firstborn, Waldo, who had died of scarlatina on January 22 at the age of five. Emerson and Henry James quickly became friends, and James family tradition has it that Emerson went up to see and give his blessing to the new infant. Mythological coincidings should never be swallowed whole or dismissed out of hand. There is no doubt that Emerson came to have an effect on William, but there is also no doubt that Emerson's immediate — and enormous — effect was on William's father. The biographer of Henry James Sr. says that Henry's letters to Emerson are "the richest emotional outpouring he left behind." He further says that Emerson wholly changed the direction of James's thinking, turning him from being "entrenched in a remote and embattled redoubt of the Scotch-Irish Presbyterian mind" to the "larger contemporary, non-sectarian intellectual world."[1]

When William was fifteen months old, his brother Henry, known first as Harry, then as Henry Junior, was born, on April 15, 1843. Their father took the family, with the two small boys, to England in October of the same year. Crossing the Channel to France, two-year-old William was seasick and "screamed incessantly to have the 'hair taken out of his mouth.'"[2]

When Willy was two and a half and Harry just thirteen months old, their father had another life-changing experience; this one was shattering. They were living in a place called Frogmore Cottage, near Windsor Castle. Looking back from thirty-five years later, Henry Senior wrote:

> One day . . . towards the close of May [1844], having eaten a comfortable dinner, I remained sitting at the table after the family had dispersed, idly gazing at the embers in the grate, thinking of nothing, and feeling only the exhilaration incident to a good digestion, when suddenly — in a lightning flash as it were — "fear came upon me, and trembling, which made all my bones to shake." To all appearance it was a perfectly insane and abject terror, without ostensible cause, and only to be accounted for, to my perplexed imagination, by some damned shape squatting invisible to me within the precincts of the room, and raying out from his fetid personality influences fatal to life. The thing had not lasted ten seconds before I felt myself a wreck.[3]

James added that the depression he felt in the wake of this experience took him two years to pull out of, and that he came to see it as representative of what everyone had to go through in his or her development. It was a sort of second birth.

What life was like for the small boys while their father struggled out from under his "vastation" (a common seventeenth-century variant of "devastation," an archaism by the 1840s) can only be imagined. Reliable details of William's early life are scarce. We know that he called his father and mother "Henwy" and "Mawy" about this time; his father wished to avoid the more formal names and relationships, and he taught his sons to use first names before they could even pronounce them. It was an early example of what would now be seen as Henry Senior's extraordinary parental narcissism. He also seems to have been genuinely fond of his children, and it is obvious that he got great pleasure from his systematic nonconformity. William, predictably, fought with his father and, equally predictably, had moments of tenderness toward his mother, though she always preferred his brother Henry. There is a curious sentence in a letter William wrote to the family from England in 1880 in which he said, "I found myself thinking in a manner unexampled in my previous life, of Father and Mother" — so much for Henwy and Mawy — "in their youth coming to live there as a blushing bridal pair, with most of us children still unborn, and all the works unwritten; and my heart flowed over with a kind of sympathy, especially for the beautiful, sylphlike, and inexperienced mother."[4]

During the summer of 1845, Henry and Mary James took their little family back to America, where it continued to expand. When William was three and a half, Wilky (Garth Wilkinson James) was born. When he was four and a half, Bob (Robertson) was born, and when he was six and a half, in the summer of 1848, Alice was born. The next year Mary James suffered a miscarriage, after which she had no more children. As the family grew, it also moved about. William had lived in at least eighteen different houses by the time he was sixteen; this does not count the numerous long residences in hotels, which led his brother Henry to say that the young Jameses were "hotel children."

It was mainly the father who moved the family around. For impulses that he called reasons, he sent and withdrew his children to and from school after school, starting with, and later interspersed with, stretches of home tutoring. Until William was ten he was taught at home, by a variety of tutors, mostly young women. When he was ten, he attended a New York school called the Institute Vergnes, on lower Broadway near Bond Street, learning French among "infuriated ushers," as his brother Harry recalled it, "of foreign speech and flushed complexion, the tearing across of hapless 'excersizes' and dictees, and the hurtle through the air of dodged volumes."[5]

Between the ages of ten and sixteen, William attended at least nine different schools, with various interludes of schooling at home. After the Institute Vergnes, the year William was eleven and twelve, he and Henry went to a school kept by one Richard Pulling Jenks. Jenks was "bald, rotund, of ruddy complexion" and was also, said Harry, "one of the last of the whackers." This school was also on Broadway, near Fourth Street, and consisted of two upper rooms. William did Latin and Greek with Mr. Jenks, penmanship with Mr. Dolmidge, and drawing with Mr. Coe. The next year, 1854–55, it was yet another school, this one run by Messrs. Forest and Quackenbos, at the corner of Fourteenth Street and Sixth Avenue. William was in the "classical department," which meant learning Latin with George Quackenbos.[6]

Formal education apart, life in the James family in New York was instructive in its own inimitable way. The boys went to some sort of theater almost every weekend. It might be Barnum's Great American Museum or the dancer Lola Montez; they went to many different versions of *Uncle Tom's Cabin*. In 1854 they saw *A Midsummer Night's Dream*, and in 1855 *The Comedy of Errors*. Pictures — that is, paintings — figured prominently as well. A large view of Florence by Thomas Cole hung in their home. They went to see Emanuel Leutze's *Washington Crossing the Delaware*, which was displayed "in a wondrous flare of projected gaslight."[7]

Among the childhood books William later remembered fondly was Caroline Sturgis Tappan's *Rainbows for Children*, which came out when he was six. His brother remembered that Hawthorne's *Wonder-Book* "had helped to enchant our boyhood." Harry also recalled later how Rodolph Toepffer's two-volume *Voyages en Zigzag* was carefully perused by himself and by Willy, who evidently became lastingly fond of the term. Dickens's *David Copperfield* was read aloud in the downstairs parlor. When the part about the Murdstones' heartless treatment of young Davy was read, the parlor table, which was covered with a cloth, began to tremble and shake. Under the table was little Harry, sobbing uncontrollably, having sneaked down after his bedtime to listen. *Uncle Tom's Cabin*, published in 1852 when Willy was ten, was a great family favorite, "much less a book," Harry wrote later, "than a state of vision, of feeling, and of consciousness."[8]

William also read the boys' adventure books of Mayne Reid, beginning with *Rifle Rangers* in 1850 and *Scalp Hunters* in 1851. These are florid, swaggering, irresistible books, full of excitement and danger and violence. Reid, who was born in Ireland, came to America at twenty, traveled and traded on the Red River and the Missouri, wandered the American West and Mexico, became a journalist in Baltimore (where he knew Poe), fought in the Mexican War in 1846, and tried to fight in Hungary in 1849 before retiring to England at thirty-one to start writing up his adventures.

This is how *Scalp Hunters* starts: "Unroll the world's map, and look upon the great northern continent of America. Away to the wild west, away toward the setting sun, away beyond many a far meridian, let your eyes wander. Rest them where golden rivers rise among peaks that carry the eternal snow. Rest them there." Mayne Reid had a big impact on James, giving him his first real tilt toward the outdoor life. Years later he recalled how Reid "was forever extolling the hunters and field-observers of living animals' habits, and keeping up a fire of invective against the 'closet naturalists,' as he called them, the collectors and classifiers, and handlers of skeletons and skins."[9]

In 1855 Father took the family abroad again, intending, as he playfully wrote his friends Edmund and Mary Tweedy, to "educate the babies in strange lingoes." They went to Geneva, where Willy, then thirteen, attended first the Institution Haccius, then the Pensionnat Roediger. Though he made some progress in German and, especially, French, his father soon concluded that Swiss schools were overrated, and he promptly moved the family to Paris. Then, in late November, he packed them off to London, where they continued to traipse from one address to another while being tutored at home in Latin and in the "ordinary branches of English education" by Robert Thomson (who later and quite coincidentally had Robert Louis Stevenson as a student).[10]

Willy got a microscope for Christmas in 1855. He was nearly fourteen, and his interests were in both science and art. In June 1856 Father shepherded the family back across the Channel to Paris. William wrote his friend Ed Van Winkle in New York, describing the cities he had recently lived in with colorful language that tells us something about his frame of mind. "Geneva," he wrote, "is a queer old city . . . The old part is black, the streets are black, the houses are black, the people are black. It's a regular 15th century place. In it is Calvin's church with the very canopy under which he preached." London he liked as little: "It is a great huge unwieldy awkward colorless metropolis with a little brown river crawling through it." He liked Paris: "The sky is blue, the houses are white and everything else is red. There is a general red hue about the population which comes, I suppose, from the red trowsers of the soldiers. The sun and the white plaster and the bright colors are all very dazzling." But New York was where William really wanted to be. "Taken as a whole," he wrote, Paris "is not to be compared to New York."[11]

In Paris, in the fall of 1856, in a house Harry remembered as having "the merciless elegance of tense red damask," William did Virgil, German, and math with a tutor, a poet named Lerambert, who was "spare and tightly black-coated, spectacled, pale and prominently intellectual." On days when M. Lerambert did not appear, William studied history and geography with his father. He had no companions except his brothers, and he was not allowed to play in "these nasty narrow French streets" any more than he had been allowed to play in the streets of London. After a short while, William's father put him in a language school called the Institution Fezandié in Paris, run by a follower of the utopian thinker Charles Fourier.[12]

During the winter of 1857, the fifteen-year-old William was accepted into the atelier of the painter Léon Cogniet. Cogniet, then in his sixties, was a famous and honored painter who had run drawing schools in Paris since 1830. His *Marius Meditating Among the Ruins of Carthage,* which hung in the Luxembourg Gallery, "impressed us the more," Harry recalled, "in consequence of this family connection." Cogniet had been a friend of Théodore Géricault, whose *Raft of the Medusa* hung (still hangs) in the Louvre. In this titanic canvas of the remnants of a ship's company on a disintegrating raft, the wretchedness of the ragged and the dying still assaults and washes over the viewer with a power like that of the sea itself.

Cogniet also knew Eugène Delacroix, who was William's favorite painter. "I remember his [William's] repeatedly laying his hand on Delacroix," Harry recalled, "whom he found always and everywhere interesting — to the point of trying effects with charcoal and crayon, in his manner." William particularly admired *La Barque du Dante,* in which Dante is surrounded by the tormented souls in hell. William liked paintings, of whatever size, that were full of vivid violence or moody desolation.[13]

Nothing ever suited Henry James Sr. for long. In June 1857 he moved the family to Boulogne and enrolled William in the Collège Impériale there. This, Willy explained to a friend, was more a high school than what Americans thought of as a college. One of William's instructors told his father that William was "an admirable student, and that all the advantages of a first-rate scientific education which Paris affords ought to be accorded to him." So back to Paris they all went. Henry Senior seems to have moved the family around more to facilitate William's education than for any other single reason. But financial worries arose in Paris. So back to Boulogne they all went, where it was cheaper to live and where, as it happened, William was happier than anywhere else in Europe. "We . . . got to have a real home feeling there," he wrote Ed Van Winkle. There were lots of English-speaking boys at his school. He had a camera now, a "big cumbrous camera," his brother recalled, "involving prolonged exposure, exposure mostly of myself, darkened development, also interminable, and ubiquitous brown blot." Willy also had galvanic batteries, administered shocks to anyone willing, and made the family careful to examine anything before they sat on it. He collected "marine animals in splashy aquaria" and went in for the "finely speculative and boldly disinterested absorption of curious drugs."[14]

Perhaps he was already interested in various states of consciousness. What fifteen-year-old isn't? Certainly he was, temperamentally, a risk taker all his life. His student and biographer Ralph Barton Perry says, "He 'tried' things, nitrous oxide gas, mescal, Yoga, Fletcherism, mental healers." His experiment with mescal (when he was fifty-four) was a failure. He had a terrible hangover the next day, and declared, "I will take the visions on trust." He said of alcohol that it excited the "yes" function in people, but his own nervous constitution made drinking unpleasant, and he came to regard it as a problem. "Beware of the enemy, your enemy, — alcohol, of course," he wrote one friend. Coffee and tobacco also affected him adversely, and he (mostly) avoided them.[15]

William did well at school; Harry read voraciously and, it was now noticed, wrote all kinds of stories. The youngest brother, Bob, remembered only humiliation at the end of the school year in Boulogne. Writing to Alice many years later, Bob recalled "the college municipale and its stone vaulted ceiling where Wilky and I went and failed to take prizes . . . I see yet the fortunate scholars ascend the steps of his [the mayor's] throne, kneel at his feet, and receive crown or rosette, or some symbol of merit which we did not get. The luck had begun to break early." The father, eyes fixed mainly on William, saw only that his eldest son behaved very decently in Boulogne toward his brothers, being "perfectly generous and conciliatory . . . always disposed to help them and never oppress."[16]

By the end of spring 1858, with William sixteen, Harry fifteen, Wilky almost thirteen, Bob almost twelve, and Alice almost ten, Father and Mother took the family back to America, to Newport. But a year in Newport revived disillusionment in Henry Senior. He did not want to go back to New York, he didn't want to stay in Newport, and he couldn't find a house he liked in Cambridge — he said he wanted to get Willy into the Lawrence Scientific School at Harvard. But he took the whole family abroad once again, this time to Geneva, then to Bonn, and finally, in response to William's revolt, home again to America.

When Henry James the novelist, many years later, looked back on this time, he found the family's ceaseless comings and goings, the redoublings back and yet again forth, to be a narrative impossibility. In his memoir he simply omitted any mention of the year spent in Newport between European trips. William would probably have preferred to omit the whole European venture of 1859–60. There were parts he had loved, particularly in Boulogne. But recalling the stay in London and the long stay after it in Paris, William "denounced" it all to his brother Harry as "a poor and arid and lamentable time, in which missing such larger changes and connections as we might have reached out to, we had done nothing he" — Harry is here reporting what William told him — "and I but walk about together in a state of direst propriety, little 'high' black hats and inveterate gloves, the childish costume of the place and period, to stare at grey street scenery . . . dawdle at shop windows and buy water-colors and brushes."

William's rejection of his European schooling was not just the judgment of later years. Sixteen-year-old William sent this conclusion to Ed Van Winkle at the time: "We have now been three years abroad. I suppose you would like to know whether our time has been well spent. I think that as a general thing, Americans had better keep their children at home."[17]

3. Newport and the Jameses

BY THE FIRST OF OCTOBER 1860 the Jameses were back in Newport. A nostalgic letter from William to his brother Bob in 1876 suggests something of the particular appeal of the place. "The elements at Newport are as rare as ever," William wrote. "I sailed over to the dumplings and lay there a couple of hours and walked out to a new settlement north of the fort whence a steam ferry now goes to Newport. I spent an afternoon at Lily pond and another at Paradise — and everywhere there was the same magic mildness and blondness in the light and colour and the same softness in the air. It is a charmed spot."[1]

A hundred and sixty-five miles from New York and seventy from Boston, Newport was already a fashionable watering place. It was still a picturesque seaport town, not the yachting center it would become, and it had Revolutionary memories, not the egregious baronial "cottages" of the Vanderbilts and Astors. The cosmopolitan air of the place owed something to the English Friends who had settled there in 1656, and to the synagogue, the oldest in America, built by Portuguese Jews in 1762. The Redwood Library, used by William and his family, went back to a philosophical society that may have had an early association with Bishop Berkeley, the English idealist philosopher who lived there from 1729 to 1731. Newport was the summer home of well-to-do southerners, such as the Middletons of South Carolina, and it was the winter home of old Yankee families, some of them Quaker, like the Perrys. The town was hospitable to Europeanized, semi-émigrés such as the Jameses, the Tweedys (the Jameses' chief social connection in Newport), John La Farge, and William Morris Hunt. With its impermanent, seasonally changing population, Newport was, as Linda Simon aptly notes, a "place of emotional quarantine for Americans returning from expatriation."[2]

The Jameses were essentially centered in Newport from 1858 to 1864. The family had been from the Hudson River valley. They became a New York City family, then were Americans abroad, before moving to Newport. They were, in their restless and frequent moves, American to the core, but they were also, it has been said, a sort of nation unto themselves. William and Henry and Wilky and Bob and Alice were, first and last, citizens of the James family.[3]

The grandfather, William of Albany, known as Old Billy James, had come to America in 1789, aged eighteen, from Bailieborough, in Cavan County, the southernmost part of Ulster. He had been a friend of Thomas Addis Emmet, whose younger brother Robert was hanged by the British in 1803. The family may have come originally from Wales around 1700. A portrait of Old Billy shows a beefy, powerful man, still youngish, who had, we are told, "a great and righteous and truly formidable anger." He was an enormously successful businessman, with many interests and ventures. In 1824 he bought, for thirty thousand dollars, the village of Syracuse, New York, then a place so desolate as "to make an owl weep to fly over it."

Old Billy became one of the wealthiest men in America. Of his many children, the one who gave him the most trouble was Henry, who became the father of Willy and Harry. (Readers and family members alike have been annoyed by the Jameses' stubborn recirculation of a handful of first names.) Young Henry drank, did badly at school, and ran up huge unauthorized bills for cigars and oysters. Old Billy called his son a swindler — his exact word — and tried to disinherit him. Old Billy also tried to cheat his third wife, Catharine Barber James, out of the share of his wealth to which she was legally entitled. In 1832 Old Billy was holding the buildings and grounds of Union College in Schenectady as collateral for a loan needed by the college to pay the winners of the state lottery it had been franchised to run. The college paid off the loan on December 4. On December 15 Old Billy suffered a stroke; four days later he was dead.[4]

The general tone of life in his son's family in Newport in the early 1860s was one of energetic uproar. The Newport house was a lively, busy place, a hubbub of physically active, vehemently articulate people, with the father at the center of everything. "There could not be a more entertaining treat," wrote E. L. Godkin, the founder and editor of *The Nation* (to which William later attributed his basic political education), "than a dinner at the

James house, when all the young people were at home. They were full of stories of the oddest kind, and discussed questions of morals or taste or literature with a vociferous vigor so great as sometimes to lead the young men to leave their seats and gesticulate on the floor. I remember, in some of the heated discussions, it was not unusual for the sons to invoke humorous curses on their parent, one of which was that 'his mashed potatoes might always have lumps in them.'"[5]

Edward Emerson, Ralph Waldo's son, came to visit in Newport during spring vacation in 1860. He was not yet sixteen, was younger than Willy and Harry, but older than Wilky, Bob, and Alice. Edward remembered how "'the adipose and affectionate Wilkie,' as his father called him, would say something, and be instantly corrected by the little cock-sparrow Bob, the youngest, but good-naturedly defend his statement, and then Henry (Junior) would emerge from his silence in defence of Wilkie. Then Bob would be more impertinently insistent, and Mr. James would advance as moderator, and William, the eldest, join in. The voice of the Moderator presently would be drowned by the combatants and he soon came down vigorously into the arena, and when in the excited argument, the dinner knives might not be absent from eagerly gesticulating hands, dear Mrs. James, more conventional, but bright as well as motherly, would look at me, laughingly reassuring, saying 'Don't be disturbed, Edward; they won't stab each other. This is usual when the boys come home.' And the quiet little sister ate her dinner, smiling, close to the combatants." When Edward's sisters, Ellen and Edith Emerson, came to visit in July 1862, Ellen wrote home about it: "The funniest thing in the world is to see this delectable family together all talking at once. Edith and I spend all dinner in convulsions."[6]

This air of gleeful anarchy and uninhibited high-toned hilarity was set by the witty father. Full of what his second son called "apostolic energy," he was an undisciplined, impulsive, and affectionate man, a vituperative controversialist, and, in his writing (says his biographer) a "blocked and monomaniacal hierophant." He had a wooden leg, the result of a boyhood accident, and he needed pavements. He lived, therefore, in towns and cities. Edward Emerson recalled him limping along on his wooden leg "with some activity." He did not use a cane, and this had consequences too. Occasionally he wrenched his back; at least once he took a bad fall. Jane Carlyle and her husband, Thomas, met him when he was thirty-two. "One awaits in horror," she wrote, "to see him rush down amongst the tea-cups, or walk out thro' the window glass, or pitch himself headforemost into the grate! From which and the like imminent dangers he is only preserved by a continual miracle."[7]

His restless physical energy was matched by similar qualities of mind. "No tradition had a brighter household life with us than our father's head-long impatience," wrote his son Harry. "He moved in a cloud, if not rather a high radiance, of precipitation . . . a chartered rebel against cold reserves." He was a man of immense charm. More than one acquaintance noted how "he would give other men a warm pat on the back, almost caressingly." He enjoyed the company of women, and he paid attention to Marianne Mott, Caroline Tappan, Annie Fields, Anna Barker, and many other women who were prominent in Boston's social and intellectual scene. He kissed Caroline Dall — the diarist and an early admirer of Margaret Fuller — once with enough deliberation and emphasis that she recorded the moment in her diary: "Henry James — Apr 25 1866 — kiss."[8]

Henry James Sr. was a superb conversationalist. James Russell Lowell thought him the "best talker in America." He was not, by most accounts, a good lecturer, but in less formal situations he could be vivacious, colorful, and irreverent. One day he drew E. L. Godkin aside and asked him if he had read Dante. Godkin said no. "Ah," said James with relief, "then I have a brother yet." He told Godkin he thought Dante a "dear dismal old" poet, a man of the past, of no interest except to "those d — d literary fellows" — he meant Longfellow and Longfellow's friends — "who are all memory, being shut up to it as a miser to his money-bags." James's stutter led Thomas Carlyle to remark that "a stuttering man is never a worthless one." Once past the stutter, he had a bantering flow of words. One time, as William noted in a journal, his father tried to bring up the name Birckbear. Before he got it right, he ran through "Beauclerk, Backhouse, Brickbat, Bedrid, Bedbug, Bankrupt, Buckwheat, Blackguard, and Beaukard."[9]

He devoted a great deal of time and energy to his family: "He talked to, laughed with, embraced and kissed his children." Aunt Kate (Catharine Walsh, the sister of Mary Walsh James) thought Henry James Sr.'s affection for William "was very deep, a peculiar thing in its expression, but something unlike his feeling for his other children."[10]

The whole family lived and communicated in a blizzard of pet names and nicknames, egged on by the gleeful parents. Garth Wilkinson James, the next-to-youngest brother, was Wilky, Wilkie, Wilk, and Wilkums. Robertson, the youngest brother, was Bob, Bobbins, Robby, Bobby, and Hoppergrass Bob. Thirteen-year-old Wilky addressed a letter home to "Dearest of the Daddybusses and Mommybusses on earth." Harry addressed his friend Thomas Sergeant Perry as Peri, Faithless Tom, Mein leiber schonster Peri, My best of Peris, Sargey, and My dear Child, before settling down to Sarge. Alice had the most pet names, many of them showered on her by her older brother Willy. He called her Sweetlington, Sisterkin, Cherie de Soeur, Cherie de Jeune Bal, Beautlet, my Dearest darling Alice, the noiseless Alice, most kissworthy Alice, you lovely Babe, Dearest Child, la seule que j'aime, Cherie, charmante de Bal, and countless others. It is impossible to overstate the family's tone of verbal bravado and panache, the uncorked exuberance and reckless affection flung indiscriminately across rooms and through the mails. Nineteen-year-old William once wrote Kitty Temple this response to the photograph of her that had fallen out of her envelope. "Wheeeeew! oohoo! a ha! la la!" — here he drew a musical staff and a flourish — "boisteroso triumphissimo. Chassez to the right, cross over, forward two, hornpipe and turn summerset. Up came the fire engines, but I proudly waved them aside."[11]

This constant funning and badinage may have been more or less decodable in actual social settings. Sometimes one can clearly catch the tone as it lies on the page, but not always. Even within the family, someone could mistake the tone of a letter. In the late 1880s, after Alice had been living abroad for some time, William, who had always been very close to Alice, went abroad to see her, she having been ill. He reported the meeting in a letter: "She was witty and animated and curious about everything, and the tone of invective and sarcasm which I have always read as shrill and forced in her letters, is uttered in the softest most laughing way in the world, and gives an entirely different impression." William's candid admission is a standing warning not to be too sure we have really gotten exactly the intended tone of all this remarkable family's utterances.[12]

4. The Father

HENRY SENIOR WAS a fond father, but he could be a puzzling and even an appalling one. Harry recalled that "he used to spoil our Christmasses so faithfully for us, by stealing in with us, when Mother was out, to the forbidden closet and giving us a peep the week or so before." One acquaintance called him Absolute James; he once referred to himself as Saint James the Less. In his own eyes he may have been a minor apostle, but he never doubted that he *was* an apostle. His bottomless princely indulgences extended to his whole flock. Ice cream was his universal cure. In 1860, on the trip to Bonn that was to be so short, the father said — and William, who plainly adored the parent he was learning to oppose, wrote down, perhaps partly for its metrical lilt — "My children shall live upon ices in Bonn, whenever they are in ill health."[1]

He worked at his writing table at home in full view of the family, turning out one long book after another, each a theological tirade in a private, sealed language interspersed with brilliant flashes of insight and imagery. Harry later looked back on the dreadful — and moving — futility of his father's intellectual labors, on "the pathetic tragic ineffectualness of poor father's lifelong effort, and the silence and oblivion that seems to have swallowed it up."[2] William's comment at the time was to draw, one night, a frontispiece for his father's book; it showed a man beating a dead horse.

The elder Henry James's life had been cut in two by a boyhood accident in Albany when he was thirteen. He and his friends were accustomed to playing with hot-air balloons, which were, like modern ones, open at the bottom. Beneath the open hole, on a platform that hung by strings from the balloon canopy, sat a ball of tow or rough twine, saturated with turpentine and set afire. The heat from the burning tow would cause the balloon to rise. Sometimes the balloon caught fire, the ropes holding the platform would burn through, and the flaming ball of tow would fall to earth, where the boys would kick it around. One day when young Henry James "had a sprinkling of this [turpentine] on his pantaloons, one of those balls went through the open window of Mrs. Gilchrist's stable. [James,] thinking only of conflagration, rushed to the hayloft and stomped out the flame, but burned his leg."[3]

The burned leg did not heal, and a doctor amputated it. Anesthesia had not yet been invented. What remained of the leg refused to heal; the doctor performed a second amputation. James carried the scars, inner as well as outer, of this accident all his life. In 1858, when he was forty-seven, he wrote an essay attacking surgery and those who maintain that "surgery is good . . . it often saves lives." His answer was "Doubtless; but at the expense of making the patient limp horribly all his days. It is the devil's method of dealing with disease — the method of the knife and cautery, the method of force . . . For my individual part, I would vastly rather die at once."[4]

It may have been this boyhood episode, as much as anything else, that gave edge and heat and immediacy to the elder James's stinging and lifelong sense of evil. It forms the subject of some of his most vivid writing, and his sense of the reality of evil was communicated in one way or another to all of his children. "Every man who has reached even his intellectual teens," he wrote in 1863, "begins to suspect this; begins to suspect that life is no farce; that it is not genteel comedy even; that it flowers and fructifies on the contrary out of the profoundest tragic depths, the depths of the essential dearth in which its subject's roots are plunged . . . The natural inheritance of everyone who is capable of spiritual life is an unsubdued forest where the wolf howls and every obscene bird of night chatters." Evil was for him a daily and practical matter. The one great evil in the universe was, he thought, "the principle of selfhood, the principle of independence in man." He once told his youngest son, Bob, that "to seek our own private pleasure, this precisely is our conception of the devil."[5]

As a boy and as a young man, Henry had rebelled wildly against his father, Old Billy. At the age of ten, well before the accident, he was drinking gin or brandy every morning on the way to school. He did wretchedly at Union College, from which he eventually dropped out. His drinking got worse. He rejected everything his father stood for, except money. Even after Old Billy's death, young Henry kept up his revolt, abandoning his studies altogether, leaving Albany and falling in with professional gamblers, before finally coming to his senses and turning a corner in 1835.

Henry Senior's adult convictions were — are — strong, idiosyncratic, and not easily located in the history of thought. His originality is at least partly owing to the strange and lonely road by which he had come. He started out attending the First Presbyterian Church in Albany, the family church. At the age of eight he entered Albany Academy, where he was a student for five years and where he first came in contact with Joseph Henry, the self-educated physicist, co-discoverer with Michael Faraday of electrical induction, and later the first director of the Smithsonian Institution. After his college years, broken only by a short stint of working in Boston for the *Christian Examiner,* the leading Unitarian journal of the time, Henry hit bottom, experienced a turnaround, and appealed to his older brother William for help. "I want drilling and disciplining — I want advice and support in study," he wrote to his brother.

William was a moderate, literary Presbyterian minister in Rochester, New York, whose eager enemies brought Charles Grandison Finney, the great revivalist, to town as a rebuke to the old-fashioned, sedate, intellectual William. Henry became active in the Presbyterian church in Albany in 1835, at age twenty-four, then went almost immediately as a student to Princeton Theological Seminary, a Presbyterian school then in the midst of intense factional debate. The so-called New School faction pulled out of Princeton and started Union Theological Seminary in New York City in 1836, the year after Henry James went to Princeton. Princeton had strong antitranscendental Calvinists such as James W. Alexander, and moderate "school of conciliation" theologians such as Charles Hodge. It was Hodge who said of Princeton, "I am not afraid to say that a new idea never origi-nated in this seminary."

Dissatisfied with Princeton, and with Hodge in particular, Henry turned next to the tiny sect of Sandemanians, who believed, with the Englishman Robert Sandeman (1718–1771), that there was no basis in Scripture for pas-toral authority. The radically anticlerical Sandemanians were Calvinists, and Henry found a temporary home with a group of these primitive Christians in New York City. The group was headed by a layman, James Buchanan, who called on everyone "to come out from every system of worship in which the authority of man in any manner or way, has place."[6]

In 1838 Henry went to England and met Michael Faraday, the self-made scientist who was also the world's most eminent practicing Sandemanian. Returning to New York, Henry fell in love with Mary Walsh and married her in 1840, not in a church, to be sure, but in a civil ceremony. By then Henry had shifted his spiritual allegiance from the Sandemanians to John Walker of Ireland and a small sect called Separatists. Walker was an ad-mirer of Jonathan Edwards, and one can see a strong thread of Calvinism in Henry's odyssey. It is perhaps most helpfully thought of as personal Cal-vinism, meaning no clergy, no churches, no liturgy, just the always inade-quate individual living in a meaningless and vicious chaos called Nature. That was one side; an unknowable God was on the other side.[7]

Sometime around 1842, James met and came under the influence of William Henry Channing, nephew of the famous Boston Unitarian preacher William Ellery Channing. William Henry was then a Christian socialist, and has been described as "a self-tormented creature, earnest, hy-persensitive, torn by doubts, a 'concave man'" — Thoreau's phrase — who was "convinced, as a friend remarked, that 'Christ did not understand his own religion.'"[8] Channing and Emerson were together responsible for turning Henry James Sr. from sectarian theology to philosophical theol-ogy, from church reform to social reform, and from salvationism to utopi-anism. In 1843 Henry Senior wrote his old teacher Joseph Henry, pressing the idea that "all the phenomena of physics are to [be] explained and grouped under laws exclusively spiritual, that they are in fact only the ma-terial expression of spiritual truth — or as Paul says the visible forms of in-visible substance." This conviction helps explain why Henry Senior had wanted to meet Faraday and why he wanted a scientific education for his own son.[9]

In 1844, while living in England, James suffered his breakdown — his vastation — from which he recovered only after being introduced by Sophia Chichester to the writings of Emanuel Swedenborg. James was soon drawn to Swedenborg's vast enterprise of showing that every single thing in the physical world is an expression of something in the far more basic spiritual world, that the physical and the spiritual are what we might now call parallel universes, with minute, point-by-point parallel details connecting every rock, plant, and animal. For Swedenborg, as for James, the spiritual universe is the real one, the one that matters and that gives direction to the merely physical universe.

Within two years, as more children came and the household grew more numerous and complicated, Henry became interested in Fourierist socialism — called in America at that time Associationism — which is a sort of Swedenborgianism applied to the political and social worlds. Fourier envisioned a world free of sexual repression and boring, repetitive factory labor. In a Fourierist community each person would be encouraged to have a full range of sexual relationships and would also be able to work at half a dozen different tasks a day, each one engaging and freely chosen.

With five children, his wife and her sister, and five serving girls in the house, Henry became sharply critical of monogamous marriage and interested in the free and spontaneous expression of affections. He wrote against marriage and also against the new women's movement. His cut-and-thrust newspaper articles stirred up small storms of heated rhetoric. He abandoned the Swedenborgians. Institutionalized religion was at an end, he thought; the Swedenborgians had not understood this and had simply set up a new institution. With his gaudy gift for scatological invective, James grumbled about the "stagnant slipslop" of the papers that opposed him. He wrote to the *New York Tribune* that Christ had salvaged and recycled the "excrementitious product of human history," and he blasted the poor Swedenborgian church for "emptying itself of all . . . struggle . . . against established injustice in order to concentrate its energy and prudence upon the washing and dressing, upon the larding and stuffing, upon the embalming and perfuming of its own invincibly squalid little corpus."[10]

Even the gentle Bronson Alcott got so riled up during a public confrontation with Henry Senior that he lost his composure and called the one-legged patriarch of the James clan "damaged goods" to his face. But there was always more to Henry than battle relish and vituperative glee. And in the mid-1850s he found his true subject, which he set forth in a book called *The Nature of Evil.* James's treatment of this subject caught and held the attention of the philosopher Charles S. Peirce, who must therefore be considered James's greatest follower. In a piece called "Evolutionary Love," written in 1893, Peirce credited Henry James Sr. with having disclosed "for the problem of evil its everlasting solution," and he quoted the following from Henry Senior's volume *Substance and Shadow:* "It is no doubt very tolerable finite or creaturely love to love one's own in another, to love another for his conformity to one's self: but nothing can be in more flagrant contrast with the creative love, all whose tenderness *ex vi termini* [to the farthest limit of one's strength] must be reserved only for what intrinsically is most bitterly hostile and negative to itself."[11]

When Thoreau's friend the poet Ellery Channing met him in the early 1840s, Henry James the elder was in New York, married, with two small children. Channing described him as "a little fat rosy Swedenborgian amateur, with the look of a broker, and the brains and heart of a Pascal." Photographs show a self-satisfied man with a lively direct gaze, an uneven mouth, and a crooked, enigmatic little smile.[12]

5. *Newport and the Jameses, Continued*

THERE WAS, OF COURSE, more to family life than the father, and time has not staled but, if anything, only increased our interest in all the Jameses, beyond even the warm and protective attention Harry threw back over them from the rosy retrospect of 1913, from another century and from the edge of an even more disastrous war than the one bearing down on America in 1860, when the mother and the father, the brothers and the sister, were all gone and there was no one left but Harry. "We were," he wrote on page two of his autobiography, in what was essentially its founding statement, "to my sense, the blest group of us, such a company of characters and such a picture of differences, and withal so fused and united and interlocked, that each of us, to that fond fancy, pleads for preservation, and . . . I shall be ashamed, as of a cold impiety, to find any element altogether negligible."[1]

The mother, Mary Robertson Walsh, was Scottish on her mother's side, Irish on her father's. She met Henry James through her brother Hugh, who was a student with Henry at Princeton Theological Seminary. Mary had long talks with Henry, who persuaded her to leave her family's Presbyterian church (because the Gospels do not require ministers) and persuaded her also to marry him. The ceremony was performed on July 28, 1840, by the mayor of New York, Isaac Varian. Mary was thirty, Henry twenty-nine.

When Henry had his vastation Mary was thirty-four. In 1846, two years later, she wrote a friend about her enthusiasm for the utopian ideas of Charles Fourier, read to her by "my hopeful, loving Henry."[2]

By 1848 she had five children, the oldest of whom was six and a half. About the time Alice was born in that year, Henry Senior was beginning to write and publish in the New York newspapers against the institution of marriage. In 1849 Mary had a miscarriage, a severe hemorrhage, and for a time her life was in great danger.

Mary ran the household, which in 1850 consisted of at least thirteen persons: the five children, herself, her husband, her sister Catharine — Aunt Kate — and five Irish servant girls between the ages of twenty and twenty-four. Her husband was against the women's movement. He thought that a woman should serve as "man's patient and unrepining drudge, his beast of burden, his toilsome ox, his dejected ass." Henry Senior's conflicted attitudes must have affected his children. Certainly they affected William. Henry Senior had the utopian's dislike of all institutions. He indulged in high-minded — one might say overtheorized — denunciations of marriage, yet he himself stayed comfortably, parasitically, sybaritically within a relationship from which, if he ever thought seriously of leaving it, no trace of that thought has survived.[3]

Mary tolerated it all. She was the emotional and workaday center of the family, the rock that made it all possible. And whatever her irrepressible husband wrote or said, he was, like the children — like the *other* children, one wishes to say — utterly dependent on her. Alice found in her "the essence of divine maternity, from which I was to learn great things, give all but ask nothing." In this way Mary made herself indispensable and, as Jean Strouse observed, put everyone permanently in her debt.

The 1850s saw the promulgation by the Vatican of the dogma of the Immaculate Conception of Mary and the publication of Coventry Patmore's *The Angel in the House.* Women were being unrealistically adored and unreasonably subordinated at the same time. Mary's favorite child was Harry; he gave her the least trouble. He spoke later of "her gathered life in us, and of her having no other . . . We simply lived by her." He went on to say, "Nothing was in the least worth while without her," and he never forgot "the mere force of her complete availability." She saw things clearly and spoke her mind. She thought, as she said in 1874, that the trouble with William was "that he must express every fluctuation of feeling, and especially every unfavorable symptom." She offered advice; she wrote warm letters. "My Darling Will," she would start out, even when darling Will was thirty-two.[4]

For all the family's reckless expressiveness and rebelliousness and its often indictable teasing, Mary's place at its emotional center was completely secure. She knew it and seems, after a fashion, to have flourished in it. The following scrap of correspondence, written by Mary to her husband thirty years after they were married, when they were both sixty, is not the voice of a shattered or broken woman. She is away from home, tending to Alice. He is home, ill. "My heart melts with tenderness toward you, my precious one," she writes, "but my prayer is that we may both be saved from the great folly and wickedness of anxiety about each other — your loving wifey."[5]

Harry, her second son, was seventeen and a half when the family returned to America and to Newport in September 1860. A photograph of about this time shows a self-possessed, clean-shaven, fashionably dressed young man with a full head of dark hair. He is standing easily and looking straight at the camera. William usually did not. Harry's eyes, which do not pierce or otherwise call attention to themselves, are already those of the artist, on whom, as he once said, "nothing is lost." He was a good enough student, and he was an omnivorous reader. He had written letters, stories, and plays while abroad. After returning to Newport, he took art lessons from William Morris Hunt, as did his brother William, but his talent and his interest in this direction were less than William's, and his real life was in reading, reading, and yet more reading. And, of course, in writing. In Newport this year he did some translations of plays by Alfred de Musset and tales by Prosper Mérimée. None of this was published.

Harry, most often paired with Willy, although sometimes with Wilky, was close now to his elder brother — though William, always and unforgettably the oldest, was beginning to move in a sphere by himself. Nevertheless, Harry was the nearest observer of his brother William's entire life, and over the years, despite lapses, disagreements, and moments of devilment and pique, Harry was in the main William's closest confidant, with the important exception of his wife, Alice. Because so much of what is known about William, especially in his youth, comes to us filtered by and through Henry, Henry must be considered the co-author of any serious account of William's early life. But their closeness began to change in Newport as William's choices led him to places where Henry did not care to follow, and where Henry was no longer obliged by their father to do so.

Wilky turned fifteen in the fall of 1860. (He used the "ie" ending; friends and family often wrote "Wilky.") Frequently paired with Harry from Geneva (1855) on, he wore his hair like Harry's, but he had a fuller, heavier face. He was, Nathaniel Hawthorne's son Julian recalled, "of middle height, broad shouldered and symmetrical." As a boy, he was healthy, robust, and very sociable. Once in Europe, in the mountains, when he was quite young, he was bitten by a snake, and his younger brother, Bob, recalled many years later how a village priest "thrust a heated knife into Wilkie's adder-bitten finger and saved him from death."[6]

Wilky was the only member of the family who disliked reading, an activity, Harry noted, that was "inhuman and repugnant to him." When the family arrived in Newport in September 1860, the father took Wilky and Bob to Concord and enrolled them in the progressive school opened there by Frank Sanborn, a friend of Emerson and Thoreau and a close ally of the abolitionist John Brown. Wilky was a great favorite at the school; he was "incomparable," said Julian Hawthorne. "Besides being the best dressed boy in the school, and in manner and talk the most engaging, his good humor was inexhaustible." He soon had a visible crush on a girl named Grace Mitchell. From Julian's point of view, Wilky just "could not preserve his poise in Grace's presence."[7]

Bob, a year younger than Wilky, was fourteen the year of the return to Newport. In later life Bob remembered his childhood as meager and sad, filled with disappointment and neglect, and disfigured by awful portents. "I developed such an ability for feeling hurt and wounded that I became quite convinced by the time I was twelve years old that I was a foundling," he wrote. A photograph taken a year and a half after the return shows a good-looking young man, all dressed up, slumping in his chair and staring straight ahead with a troubled frown. Other evidence from this time suggests there was another side. When he was nine, his father thought he had "ten times the go-ahead of all the rest of his children." We have Julian Hawthorne's word that at the Sanborn school Bob was "robust and hilarious, tough, tireless as hickory, great in the playground, not much of a scholar . . . full of fun and audacities . . . He was hugely popular in the school." Bob stayed only one year at Sanborn's, though Wilky came back for a second. Bob's year at home and subsequent stays at home were unhappy. Moody and self-pitying, he was a trial to his parents. His plan in 1860 was to go into dry goods and make a lot of money.[8]

When twenty-three-year-old Ellen Emerson and her twenty-year-old sister, Edith, visited Newport for three glorious weeks in July 1862, Bob James had been out of school and at home for over a year. Wilky, Bob, and Alice came in their small sailboat — called, one might have guessed, the *Alice* — to take Ellen and Edith sailing. Wilky sailed the boat at first, then handed the tiller to Ellen. Bob instantly came to Ellen's side, to be helpful, as she reported in detail in a letter. "'Take care, Miss Ellen,' he had said. 'That way Miss Ellen . . . No, no this way now.' At last there came a very exciting moment. 'So! So! No, the other way! Look out for heads! Here! Let me,' and he seized the helm and screamed something to Wilky by the mast and the sail whirled across the boat which went up on one side and down on the other, turned half-way round, and we recovered ourselves and picked up our hats and laughed all but Robby who was quite shocked." At home in the evenings Robby — Bob — was quieter and, Ellen wrote, "by his piquant silence and dancing eyes kept us in a chronic fever of curiosity." Bob was not quite sixteen.[9]

Alice, the youngest, the brilliant sister, had just turned twelve when they all came back to Newport. In later years she was haunted, says her biographer, by a sense of deprivation, of "there not being enough love in her own family to go around." There is not much from the early years to refute this. A photograph of her at six shows a sad little girl, all but extinguished by her long black dress, heavy black cape with geometrical trim, and tight white lace collar. A photo of her at nine shows her in Paris, bearing up stoically beneath a large spreading dress and a voluminous, fancy-cut three-quarter-length coat. Her eyes, in all her photographs, are focused on something in the distance. Her repose seems distant too. At eleven we see her studying at home under her father's eye, "reducing decimal fractions to their lowest possible rate of subsistence." Back in Newport, at twelve and a half, she is the quiet smiling sister at the table dominated by boisterous older boys. In July 1862, now almost fourteen, she goes with her father to call on Miss Ellen and Miss Edith, goes sailing with them in the boat named after her, and makes funny conversation with Robby.[10]

William wrote her fond, playful, hyperbolical, adoring letters for years; it was a long, teasing, brotherly flirtation, an ironical but affectionate courtship that has a modern reader wondering at its excesses. Alice must have found William's attention both flattering and a burden. There is no question that there was a strong current of feeling between sister and brother. The most direct and revealing single image that survives of William James is a pencil sketch he did of himself when he was about twenty-four and Alice was seventeen or eighteen. Harry remembered him drawing it, sitting in front of a mirror. So he is not looking at us, but at himself. Or perhaps at Alice, to whom he gave the sketch. She kept it all her life, between the pages of a book, where her companion Katharine Loring found it after Alice James's death.[11]

Life among the Jameses was a perpetual tussle for control. Partly because there was so much unconventionality and gleeful disorder in the family, control was a strategy and a goal for most of the members. Unable ever to control himself for long, the father tried to control the family. His hectic moving them about is only the most obvious of his many controlling behaviors. His wife, Mary, exercised control by being the opposite of her husband, the calm and predictable center, the one who kept track of money and correspondence and who presided over family relations. Alice learned how to use her poor health to make and dominate a space for herself, creating conditions of exclusive and extensive personal needs. William had a prolonged and disorderly youth, as had his father, and, like his sister, William found ways to use his neurasthenia and precarious health to get his way. Henry Junior became famous for his control over his language, his point of view, his life, and his papers. Bob cultivated misfortune and aggressive resentment as ways of asserting an identity and making a place for himself. Wilky, whose inability to handle money was even worse than his father's, was perhaps the one James offspring who never developed a successful way of controlling others.

Connecting the natural setting and the social liveliness of Newport, and giving expression to both, was the studio of William Morris Hunt, where William diligently went every day to prepare himself for a life of art. Hunt, now thirty-six, had been born in Brattleboro, Vermont. He went to Harvard, contracted tuberculosis, and traveled to Europe, where he stayed twelve years, during which time he studied with Jean-François Millet, who was then living in poverty in a basement in a village called Barbizon, near Paris. After buying Millet's *The Sower* and many of his drawings, Hunt returned to America in 1856, settling at Newport in a house called Hill Top, with a large studio behind it.

Hunt was, in Harry's description, "all muscular spareness and brownness and absence of waste [with a] long arch of handsome nose, upwardness of strong eyebrow, and glare, almost, of eyes that both recognized and wondered." Here he taught, to John La Farge, William and Henry James, and perhaps a dozen others, the painting methods of Thomas Couture (a teacher of Manet's) and "the universal humanistic significance of Millet's treatment of rural subjects." La Farge recalled how Hunt introduced him to "the teachings, the sayings, and the curious spiritual life which a great artist like Millet opens to his devotees." Hunt's studio was dominated by the spirit of Millet. "Every day some remark of Millet was quoted, some way of his was noticed, some part of his life was told. He was in this way, in those studios, a patron saint."[12]

"Interest once shed upon a subject is liable to remain always with the subject," William James later wrote in his *Talks to Teachers,* and his own early interest in Delacroix, Millet, Hunt, and La Farge remains visible in the paintings and drawings by James that survive. He did a portrait of Kitty Temple (she of the "Wheeeeew!" letter) that is strong and competent. His drawings show real mastery and power. With few exceptions they are studies of human figures, especially of heads, above all of faces. They are particularized and individuated, as are his drawings of animals, almost all of which convey tension, energy, and motion. Painting and drawing, not just for the professional artist but for anyone, are ways of paying attention to particular things. The habit of attention, the ability to regard every single thing and person with what Ruskin called a "separate intention of the eye," is the most lasting and important thing William James got from his time as an apprentice artist.[13]

Hunt's studios were attractive too because of the presence of Hunt's most gifted student, John La Farge, a tall, darkly handsome American, born in New York but deeply and exotically Europeanized. Harry remembered La Farge as "jacketed in black velvet or clad from top to toe in old fashioned elegances of cool white, and leaning much forward with his protuberant and over-glazed, his doubting yet all seeing vision." William had met La Farge at Hunt's early in the summer of 1859, and had run to Harry and friends and burst out, "There's a new fellow come to Hunt's class. He knows everything. He has read everything. He has seen everything — paints everything. He's a marvel!" La Farge, who would go on to a great career as a painter and decorative artist — he was the discoverer of the opalescent stained glass that Louis Tiffany took over, which made Tiffany famous — was, in Harry's view as well, "quite the most interesting person we knew."[14]

It was Harry's judgment, much later, that there was "no stroke of it" — William's drawing — that did not show "his possible real mastery of the art." La Farge, who was as well or better qualified to say, told an interviewer that William drew "beautifully," "repeating the word three or four times." Later he wrote that William had showed an "extraordinary promise of being a remarkable, perhaps a great painter."[15]

But William decided against a life as an artist, and around April 1861 he quit drawing and painting, with a suddenness that Harry never forgot, the same kind of suddenness that marked so many of his father's decisions. Perhaps his father's disapproval finally got to him; perhaps it was Hunt's telling him that America did not value its artists; perhaps he convinced himself that he would never be more than a mediocre painter; perhaps it was the eye trouble and the nervous indigestion he was beginning to complain of. Many years later he would tell his son that the year in the studio had pretty much quenched his desire to be an artist. More startling and unexpected is his comment in *The Principles of Psychology* in which he called aesthetics the study of the useless.

Whatever the exact mixture of reason, rationale, and disinclination that propelled William's decision, it must be noted that April 1861 was a troubling, exciting, decisive time of large changes in American life. The Confederates fired on Fort Sumter on April 12. Three days later President Lincoln issued a call to arms. Two days after that, on the seventeenth, Rhode Island militiamen marched off to fight. William James and Tom Perry went to see them off. That night a fire broke out in Newport, and Harry was injured while working at one of the huge, heavy pumping machines helping to put the fire out. Apparently he hurt his back; he would be years getting over it, and it would disqualify him for military service. Eight days after Harry's accident, on April 26, William signed up as a ninety-day recruit in the Newport Artillery Company, a state militia unit. On the following day, Tom Perry noted, "we made bandages all evening." Next morning, "after breakfast we all rolled bullets." William Morris Hunt himself was swept up in the war and would soon move to Boston. Small wonder that the world of painting suddenly seemed inadequate.[16]

The charmed life at Newport did not collapse all at once. When Ellen and Edith Emerson visited in the summer of 1862, more than a year later, they had a glorious season, which appears to us as something far back, an age of unreachable innocence. "We are . . . having the best time in the world," wrote Ellen, "taking walks on the Cliff, drives on the Avenue, baths on the beaches and going to parties in the evening." They went for a picnic; it was like life in a wonderful painting. "The table was set in the valley under a tall ash-tree," Ellen wrote. "Edith and I on the back and William and Wilky on the front seat of 'the Tilbury' drove over there 7 miles in the afternoon, having a grand time and laughing all the way. Our drive home was the best however," she said, "through a thick fog and the boys singing."

The moment seems all the more fragile because, as none of those young people could forget for very long, the guns had been firing for the past fifteen months; it was not just one wagonful of young people whose youth and innocence were driving off into the fog and the night.[17]

6. Harvard, 1861

ALTHOUGH WILLIAM JAMES signed up as a ninety-day recruit in the Newport Artillery Company just two weeks after the firing on Fort Sumter, he did not actually serve in the Union army. He wanted to go; at least a letter of his father's says he wanted to go: "I have had a firm grasp for three days past upon the coat-tails of my Willy and Harry, who both vituperate me beyond measure because I won't let them go off." Something changed William's mind. Perhaps it was his father's opposition; perhaps it was the eye trouble and stomach trouble he was experiencing; or perhaps it was the fact that in May 1861 the U.S. War Department changed the terms of enlistment for federal service from ninety days to three years. He may have struck a bargain with his father: he would not go to war if he could go to college. However it came about, William did go to school, to Harvard, that fall of 1861.[1]

His father did not want any of his children to go to college, and, strictly speaking, not one of them did. Back when William was sixteen and eager to attend Union College, his father "would not hear of my going to any College whatsoever," Willy wrote Ed Van Winkle. "He says that Colleges are hot beds of corruption, where it [is] impossible to learn anything." Father's blank opposition may have stemmed from his own misspent years at Union, but he may also have been well informed about current conditions at Harvard College. Father may have relented now, three years later, but only to the extent of allowing Willy to enroll in the Lawrence Scientific School, which was part of Harvard University but distinctly separate from Harvard College.[2]

Harvard College in the 1860s was at or near the lowest point ever reached in its already long history. Charles W. Eliot, who became the president of Harvard in 1869, thought the college "struck bottom" in 1853, the year he graduated. The great preacher Phillips Brooks thought the low point had come in 1855, the year *he* graduated. It was in any case a small and stagnant place, then and for the next dozen years or so. Even in 1868 there were only 529 undergraduates and 23 teachers in the college. There were schools of medicine, law, divinity, and science, but they were not graduate schools, did not require or expect an entering student to have a college degree, had no admission standards or exams to speak of, and no written exams at all. The modern university, with graduate and professional schools built neatly atop a firm undergraduate base, did not exist in America, though Cornell, Michigan, and Yale were all groping, as was Harvard, for something better than they had, something more like the German than the English model.

Reforms were widely opposed lest they drive away students. The curriculum in the college had been retreating from the partially elective system of earlier years. Few American students were going to college at all. In 1869 one half of one percent of the population attended college.

At Harvard the practice of hazing was at its height. The first Monday of fall term was called Bloody Monday, and we are told that "the average freshman was literally afraid for his life . . . for the sophomores took care to spread horrifying accounts." The sophomores rounded up the freshmen, forced them to fight, hosed down their rooms and belongings, rolled them in blankets, took them to the riverside, and tossed them into the Charles. There were all sorts of silly rules. Freshmen could not sport a cane before Christmas, wear a high hat, smoke a cigar, or frequent Leavitt and Pierce's smoke shop and billiard parlor. The humorist Artemus Ward said that Harvard College was located in the Parker House bar in downtown Boston.[3]

The curriculum was largely fixed and uninteresting, consisting mainly of the classics, taught by rote and examined by recitation. The boys considered it bad form for a student to talk to a teacher unless it was absolutely unavoidable. Frederic Hedge, a transcendentalist minister and friend of Emerson's, observed in 1866 that the college was not really a college at all but "a more advanced school for boys," the principle of which was coercion, the professors taskmasters and police officers, and the president the "chief of the College police." Religion — that is, Protestantism — ruled. The future historian John Fiske was docked sixty-four merit points in 1861–62, his junior year (and the year William James first arrived in Cambridge), for reading the work of Auguste Comte during Sunday service in Christ Church. President C. C. Felton wrote Fiske's parents, threatening to expel the boy if he tried to spread his "infidel" opinions.[4]

The early career of Francis James Child — whom William met and warmed to almost as soon as he came to Cambridge — shows how Harvard was squandering the talents of its faculty. Child started teaching there in 1846, became the Boylston Professor of Rhetoric and Oratory in 1851, and began publishing his great *English and Scottish Popular Ballads* in 1857. He was famous on both sides of the Atlantic but was still, in 1867–68, teaching almost nothing but freshman composition, which he loathed. In 1868 he was finally allowed to offer an elective in Old English and *The Faerie Queen* and Shakespeare. "Until then," says Henry James III, William's oldest son and biographer of Charles W. Eliot, "and so far as the students of Harvard College were concerned, Child's unusual knowledge and gifts were largely wasted." In the opinion of Eliot himself, then a young chemist in the Lawrence Scientific School, "the college was more or less wasting four precious years of the lives" of the young men who went there. If Henry Senior distrusted Harvard College, he had reason to.[5]

In any case, when William went to Cambridge it was to attend not the college but the Lawrence Scientific School. The school had been started in 1847. Louis Agassiz, who had just arrived in America from Switzerland, was appointed to its chair of natural history and he wanted it to be a place for "individual study and research in Geology and Zoology." Agassiz possessed immense charm; he had political and scientific connections at the highest levels. His head was startlingly large, his energy inexhaustible. He dominated any gathering; he radiated immense personal force. Agassiz got his way on practically everything except evolution, an idea he wagered his entire life and career against.

As a result of Agassiz's influence, the Lawrence Scientific School had a very narrow, European-style research focus. If one enrolled in the chemistry department, as William James did, one did not study in any other department. In the year James arrived, a young teacher was working on a proposal to broaden the school by offering students introductory courses in a variety of scientific fields. When, some years later, that young teacher, Charles W. Eliot, became president of Harvard, he found his old proposal filed away, forgotten, in a drawer of the president's desk. There were no requirements for admission to the Lawrence Scientific School beyond a vague proof of good character. No specific attainments were needed, not even a high school diploma. The college, which required a knowledge of Greek and Latin for admission, naturally looked down its nose at the scientific school.

But if Harvard College and the Lawrence Scientific School were small, sparsely attended, poorly equipped, and thinly staffed, they had nevertheless already attracted a number of exceptional, scientifically minded persons. Harvard also continued to "produce" remarkable men even during its worst years. It requires some agility to reconcile these things, and the answer may lie in Macaulay's observation, about English universities at a comparable low period, that the "defenders of our universities commonly take it for granted that we are indebted to them for all the talent which they have been unable to destroy." Still, the place attracted gifted men. The comparative anatomist Jeffries Wyman, the botanist Asa Gray, and the mathematician Benjamin Peirce were all teaching at Harvard. The 1850s saw the professionalization of science, in both Europe and America, and the word "scientist" first began to be common.[6]

The end of the decade and the early 1860s were great days for science. Darwin's *Origin of Species* appeared in England in November 1859. It reached America shortly thereafter; it was being discussed at the dinner table in Concord by Henry Thoreau and his friends in early January 1860. The essence of Darwin's argument for natural selection had already been communicated by him two years earlier, in 1857, in a letter to Asa Gray, who, like Agassiz, did not teach in the college but in the Lawrence Scientific School.

The late 1850s also saw the discovery that all organic compounds are derived from inorganic elements. Spectrum analysis — flame spectrometry — was first used in 1859; this led to the discovery of new elements. When the first international meeting of scientists was held, in 1860, it was an international congress of chemists. The same year, Gustav Fechner published his *Elemente der Psychophysik,* the founding statement of the new psychology, conceived by him as a natural or exact science. Fechner held that everything in what we call the mind is simply a matter of physical sensation and that precise measurement of reaction time is the proper method of psychology.

Positivism ("to measure is to know") was riding high. Auguste Comte had laid it down in a six-volume work, published from 1830 to 1842. Comte there identified what he called the law of the three ages of thought. By 1860 it seemed clear to a growing number of young people interested in science that the first and second ages, the age of theology and the age of metaphysics, had passed or were passing away, and that the third age, the age of positive knowledge, was coming to maturity. And for all the shortcomings of the disorganized cluster of schools at Harvard, Cambridge was one of the places where the new excitement was beginning to be felt.

New ideas were in the air when nineteen-year-old William James arrived in late August 1861 and signed up to study chemistry with Assistant Professor Eliot (the title had been invented for him) at the Lawrence Scientific School. Just why William chose chemistry is not clear, but it was a rapidly advancing field. New elements were being found: cesium in 1860, thalium and rubidium in 1861. There was the international meeting of chemists. The ringed structure of benzene would be discovered in 1865, and Professor Eliot himself would produce the first textbook in English on inorganic chemistry in 1867.[7]

Eliot was just eight years older than James; he had entered Harvard in 1849 and worked in the chemistry laboratory of Josiah P. Cooke. When William arrived, Eliot was teaching chemistry and running the laboratory. Eliot believed in new methods of teaching; his students did not just listen to lectures, they learned by doing. William was expected, for example, to analyze fifty unlabeled substances between Thanksgiving and the end of the term in mid-January.

William liked studying chemistry, but he had early doubts about Eliot. "I don't believe he is a very accomplished chemist," he wrote home in mid-September 1861, adding carefully, "but can't tell yet." On the other hand, he told his brother Harry, "Prof. Eliot is a fine fellow, I suspect, a man who if he resolves to do a thing will do it. I find analysis very interesting so far." William stuck with it for two years, and when, much later, he would insist on the reality of "stubborn, irreducible fact," he would be speaking in part from the analytical chemist's deeply grounded respect for the discernible differences between one substance and another.[8]

One chemical substance proved too much for him. Eliot assigned his students experiments to be done on themselves. At the start of James's second year of chemistry, his project was to observe the effects of eating bread made with a new baking powder that contained phosphates. There was a bit of a phosphorus craze in the 1850s and 1860s; it was thought that ingesting it would improve brain function. The bread made James sick, however, and he asked for his project to be transferred to someone else. (Perhaps the someone else had better digestion. Baking powder today commonly contains phosphates).[9]

Cambridge offered James more than chemistry. He rented two rooms, one of them a small sleeping chamber, from Mrs. John Pascoe, whose house was on the corner of Linden and Harvard streets. He took his meals at Catharine Upham's, near the corner of Oxford and Kirkland streets, on the present site of Lowell Lecture Hall. He loved the food: "'Fish, roast beef, veal cutlets or pigeons?' says the splendid tall noble looking white armed black eyed Juno of a handmaid, as you sit down." And there were always "three, three" desserts. His daily routine, he reported home, was "up at 6, breakfast and study till 9, when I go to School, till one, when dinner a short loaf and work again till 5 then Gymnasium or walk till tea and after that visit, work, literature, correspondence etc. Etc till ten." His day, like his prose, didn't have enough commas.

He kept careful track of money; money was always an issue in the James family. William's term bill came to $117.56. On September 4 he spent $4.25 for a bathtub, 25 cents for a sponge, and 10 cents for a towel. A week's board was $3.50. Extras included 18 cents for ginger nuts and soda water, an extravagance for which he apologized. On the first of November he had $1.34 in hand, and he noted, with a scrupulousness that may have been satiric, that 3 cents of what he had was "unaccounted for." The way money worked in the James family was that Father spent impulsively, and often without consulting his wife, who then wrote letters trying, politely and indirectly, to find out where the money was going. The result, with William, was his slightly defensive, amused, and satirically precise accounting to his mother. One account notes 20 cents for paper, 6 cents for soda water, and $1.87 for a copy of Holbein's *Dance of Death*.[10]

He wrote good letters home. He told Harry that after a week he had "not for one minute the feeling of being at home here." By mid-December he felt "as if I came here only a week ago for the first time," but by March 1862 he was, as he wrote home, beginning to feel settled. Wilky, Harry, and Bob all visited him at different times during his first term. Harry had also wanted to go to Harvard that fall, but Father had said no. William saw old friends such as Tom Perry and Edward and Ellen Emerson. He visited families known to his family: the Wards, the Tappans, the Forbeses. He met new families, was invited to a dance; he had, he wrote home, invitations to tea — he called them "tea-fights" — at the Atkinsons', the Hoopers', the Ameses', the Livermores', the Gaffields'. A few students, but only a few, left Harvard that fall to go to war. He became good friends with Francis James Child. Most important, within a month of coming to Cambridge he met young Charles Sanders Peirce, whose father, Benjamin Peirce, taught mathematics. It was Benjamin Peirce who in 1864 read a paper to the American Academy for the Advancement of Science on linear associative algebra, a paper remarkable for its bright, terse opening definition of mathematics as "the science which draws necessary conclusions." Charles would aim to do something similar in philosophy.[11]

Looking back on this era from the vantage point of 1893, Charles Peirce insisted that the years from 1846 through 1859 had been "the most productive period of equal length in the entire history of science from the beginnings till now." With offhand brilliance, or what Anne Carson calls "inadvertent lucidity," Peirce went on to say that "the idea that chance begets order, which is one of the cornerstones of modern physics . . . was at that time put in its clearest light." In saying "chance begets order," he is pointing to the 1846 *Letters on the Application of Probability to the Moral and Political Sciences*, by L.A.J. Quetelet, as the beginning, and Darwin's *Origin of Species* as the culmination. Quetelet's work, enthusiastically reviewed by the astronomer Herschel, uses statistics to predict crime in specific areas of

Paris. Darwin applied Quetelet's ideas to nature. It is one of the few occasions when a scientific revolution has been fueled by the social sciences.[12]

By mid-November of his first term, James's seriocomic plan for the future was "1 year study Chemistry, then spend one term at home, then 1 year with Wyman, then a medical education, then 5 or 6 years with Agassiz, then probably death, death, death with inflation and plethora of knowledge." The time scheme didn't work out precisely and there were some missing pieces, but for all his clowning William already had a rough plan of his next seven or eight years.[13]

James soon found Cambridge congenial. No known letter or journal expresses the slightest shade of regret about coming. Indeed his life there quickly blew into a windstorm of activity; intellectually he was expanding so fast it could almost be thought of as an explosion. As he explained to Tom Perry in May 1862:

> What with my dictionary of Sciences, Cosmical and Anorganistic, wh. occupies most of my spare time, The Correspondences from the "war's seat" wh. I am writing as a casus belli for several of our daily newspapers . . . and my private studies in Pantology, Botany, History, orthography (including researches into the Atheism of Spinoza, Pythagoras, Pocahontas, and other great opera-writers), Sk'ahnah'a nevheen & oriental languages, biethylenotriphenylammoniadiamine, my naturally historical studies, billiards, shaving, three affaires of the heart (1 blonde, 1 brunette, 1 albino), Gymnastics, exercise, fasting, prayer, charity, social enjoyment, music, dancing, buttoning, unbuttoning, musing, biting my nails, knitting (my brows) and darning my stockings, wringing my hands (there being no bell), digesting & riding in the cars, besides sleeping and loafing and utile cum dulce, . . . I have small time for writing letters.

In this tumbling cascade of nonstop nonsense we get a comic index to both the outer and the inner delights of William's new life. As much for the students Harvard attracted — and the books, courses, lectures, museums, and performances available in Boston and Cambridge — as for its faculty, Cambridge in the early 1860s was already a good place for a young man who wanted to live all-out.[14]

7. Science and the Civil War

IN HIS EARLIEST DAYS in Cambridge, and just as he was immersing himself in chemistry with Professor Eliot, James went to Boston to hear the first of Louis Agassiz's twelve lectures titled "Methods of Study in Natural History." These lectures, which began on September 10 and which William continued to attend, were, from the opening remarks to the final sentence, a single-minded attack on the work of Charles Darwin and on the idea that one species can, over time, transform itself into another. "It is my belief," Agassiz starts out, "that naturalists are chasing a phantom in their search after some material gradation among created beings by which the whole Animal Kingdom may have been derived by successive development from a single germ or from a few germs."[1]

Darwin's *Origin of Species* proposed "descent with modification" as the explanation of how new species originate out of earlier ones. For Agassiz, however, it was not Darwin but Baron Cuvier (1769–1832) who had "found the key." Agassiz quotes Cuvier: "We shall find that there exist [in the animal kingdom] four principal forms, four general plans . . . in accordance with which all animals seem to have been modeled." These four plans or structural conceptions, sometimes called types or archetypes, are the vertebrate, the mullusk, the articulate, and the radiate. All departures from Cuvier's great fundamental principle of classification are, says Agassiz with magisterial simplicity, "errors."

Agassiz marshaled a lifetime of research, collecting, observing, teaching, and writing to prove that no member of any one of the four orders ever exhibits a single characteristic of any of the other orders. Each order is complete in nature. The vertebrate order, for example, includes four classes: fishes, reptiles, birds, and mammals. Some species show up earlier in the fossil record, some later. This demonstrated to Agassiz that the entire order, with all its classes, subclasses, and species, existed as a plan from the beginning.

Agassiz was what would now be called a creationist. Different species were created at different times and places in a choreographed fulfillment of a complex and preordained master plan. Agassiz observed many correspondences between animals. For him these correspondences did not suggest descent or transformation. Rather, they were proof of "correspondences of thought, — of a thought that is always the same, whether it is expressed in the history of the type through all time or in the life of the individuals that represent the type at the present moment, or in the growth of the germ of every being born into that type today . . . In other words," Agassiz goes on, "the same thought that spans the whole succession of geological ages controls the structural relations of all living beings as well as their distribution over the earth." In finding the four great structural principles of all living beings, Cuvier had come upon God's blueprint for creation. It remained only to fill in the details. Darwin's transformation theory was muddying the waters.[2]

Agassiz's views were disseminated as widely as he could manage. His lectures were printed in the *Atlantic Monthly,* then gathered in 1863 into a book, *Methods of Study in Natural History,* which went through nineteen editions by 1889. Agassiz left himself no room to change his mind, which was fixed and immutable on the subject of speciation. Almost single-handedly Agassiz held up scientific recognition of evolution in America for decades. William James's immediate comment on Agassiz in the fall of 1861 takes no position on the issue, but it does show that he was attracted to the great teacher in Agassiz. "He is an admirable, earnest lecturer, clear as day and his accent" — Agassiz was Swiss — "is most fascinating. I should like to study under him."[3]

William also went over to Harvard College in mid-September to sit in on Jeffries Wyman's course in the comparative anatomy of vertebrates. Wyman was tall, slender, bespectacled, and overstudious (too many hours in unventilated laboratories); he had more than a theoretical grasp of his subject, being capable of leaping with a knife onto the back of a huge wounded alligator in the St. Johns River in Florida and killing it, "with anatomist's security," by driving the knife between the base of the skull and the first vertebra. Wyman embraced evolution cautiously, though he inclined toward a theistic version not greatly different from Cuvier's. He was a skilled field naturalist, the first to describe the gorilla and the first to call attention to the Indian shell mounds in Florida. He was initially sympathetic to the idea of spontaneous generation, but he was a meticulous laboratory technician, and his experiments eventually brought him to the same conclusion as Pasteur's, that spontaneous generation could not be demonstrated. When asked by the college students, whose questions he encouraged despite prevailing custom, "What do you believe about evolution?" Wyman replied, "The evidence is not all in. We must suspend judgment until it is, and hold our minds open." In September, James thought

Wyman's lectures "promise to be very good, prosy perhaps a little and monotonous, but plain and packed full and well-arranged." By November he was hoping to spend a year studying with Wyman.[4]

The year went swiftly. Wilky visited William in September; Harry came in October. Wilky came again in early December, and Bob showed up two days before Christmas. January 15 to March 1, 1862, was vacation. William moved in March to a room in a house on Trowbridge Street near what is now Massachusetts Avenue. The James family also moved this spring, to a new house in Newport at the corner of Spring Street and Lee Avenue. In May William took time to go hear John Wilkes Booth act in *Richard III, Hamlet,* and *Romeo and Juliet.* "Rant! Rant! Rant! of the most fearful kind," he wrote home. "The worst parts most applauded — but with any amount of fire and energy in the passionate parts." The summer of 1862 was the summer of Ellen and Edith Emerson's magical visit to Newport.[5]

In the fall of 1862 William went back to Cambridge for his second year of chemistry. Harry, now nineteen, went as well, entering not the college or the scientific school but the law school. Tom Perry came and entered the college. Two weeks later Wilky, now seventeen, enlisted through a Newport recruiting station in the 44th Massachusetts Regiment. Father was trying to get an appointment at the naval academy for Bob, who was just sixteen at the end of August. Wilky traveled, for his forty days of basic training, to Camp Meigs, near Dedham, Massachusetts, a short distance south and west of Boston, within easy reach of Cambridge by train. Although William had a busy life in Cambridge, he found time to go down by train at least seven times to visit Wilky at the camp. Wilky also came up to Cambridge when he could, and William paid for some military photographs of Wilky on October 22, the day Wilky shipped out.[6]

In addition to working on chemistry, William attended Agassiz's public lectures on introductory geology and Joseph Lovering's physics course over in the college, on "Acoustics, Electricity, Magnetism, Optics and Heat from a mechanical point of view." Lovering talked about pipe organs; he did research on the aurora borealis. His wry tone may have caught William's ear. Lovering let drop things like, "The reason why the undulatory theory of light is now universally accepted is that the people who formerly believed in the corpuscular theory are all dead."[7]

On the opening page of a notebook he started this fall of 1862, William copied down comments that show his new interest in the nature of force. William Grove's *Correlation of Forces* maintains that each of the forces of nature — light, heat, and electricity are given as examples — can be converted into any other. James comments: "Mr. Grove I suppose considers our modern 'forces' light magnetism etc to be no more physical entities than we now consider Bacon's 'forms' are." William had also been reading Michael Faraday's *Experimental Researches in Chemistry and Physics*. On the same page where he practiced his signature and relocated himself from "William James Newport R.I." to "William James Cambridge Mass.," he quoted Faraday: "For my own part, many considerations urge my mind towards the idea of a cause of gravity which is not resident in the particles of matter merely, but conjointly in them and in all space." James, from now on, had a marked interest in physics, especially in questions of energy and force, an interest he encapsulated some time later as "matter is motion, motion is force, force is will." Even his language could take on the swift elegance of mathematical demonstration.[8]

On January 1, 1863, Lincoln's Emancipation Proclamation went into effect. Francis Child, the Harvard professor, who took his meals at the same boarding house as Willy and Harry James, and with whom William had quickly become friends, had recently drafted a paper describing the aims of the new Boston Educational Commission's Committee on Correspondence, of which he was a member. The commission had in 1862 sent thirty-five people to Port Royal, South Carolina, to help educate newly released slaves. Port Royal, an island north of Hilton Head and south of Charleston, had been in Union hands since early in the war. Now, in January 1863, both William and Henry James applied for places at a similar mission. Their applications may have been rejected, since neither of them went.[9]

William's third Harvard term ended on January 15. He did not return for the spring semester. Instead he started a program of reading and note taking on his own. In early February William was feeling, he said, "apathetic and indisposed for work." But he roused himself to efforts at organization. He made regular entries in a notebook in a neat hand for two whole weeks. He constructed chronologies, working from pre-Socratic times and thinkers to the French Revolution. Apart from his study of science at the Lawrence School and his work earlier at the academy in Geneva, William James was largely self-educated. The German literary historian Georg Gervinus once said of Goethe (in a book James read about this time) that "his home education prevented his ever thoroughly appreciating history." Gervinus means this as a limitation, yet it can also be a liberation. What James did not get from his spotty formal schooling he was obliged to get for himself. John Dewey would later remark that James's lack of formal education was one of his greatest assets, "since it protected his mind against academic deadening."[10]

James formed a plan to write abstracts of what he read, and he started with Friedrich Max Müller's *Lectures on the Science of Language*. Müller was trying to "explain the rise and development of all the types of language and languages we know by the laws, inductively ascertained, of 1) dialectic regeneration and 2) phonetic decay." In this volume, and in Frederic Farrar's *Origin of Language*, which he read and made an abstract of the following week, William was trying to grasp yet another broad field of study in a new and avowedly scientific light.[11]

The Civil War keeps intruding in the notebook. Archy Pell, a Newport friend, came home on February 8, 1863: "He calls himself now an abolitionist and disbelieves in McClellan" (the commander of the Union army who so exasperated Lincoln by his inactivity). Years later, William told his wife about a dinner party at the Wards', in Boston during the war: "When I came out under the frosty stars with the refrain of the John Brown song in my head, 'He captured Harper's Ferry with his 19 men so few, / And he frightened old Virginny till she trembled through and through,' the contrast between the two kinds of life smote into me." William said little about the war, but it was very much on his mind.

William kept stubbornly at his reading. He read Thomas Buckle's essay on John Stuart Mill, noting that "Buckle's noble enthusiasm for truth is inspiring." Buckle was a historian and radical positivist who believed that facts and measurement alone matter, and his outlook had been sharply influenced by Quetelet's social statistics. Buckle believed that "to a philosophical mind, the action of an individual counts for little." Great men, he insists, are "only to be regarded as tools by which that work was done, which the force and accumulation of preceding circumstances had determined should be done." Individuals, he says, are "in the great average of affairs, inoperative for good; they are also, happily for mankind, inoperative for evil." James's enthusiasm for Buckle's enthusiasm was temporary, but it shows just how far into the positivist camp James had advanced at age twenty-one. Still, on the other side, he never stopped reading literature, no matter how busy he was. He read Balzac's *Lys dans la Vallée*, which he found "wonderful," and he vowed, "I will read all Balzac."[12]

In early April he set himself to read and summarize Jonathan Edwards's *Great Christian Doctrine of Original Sin Defended*. William read little theology at this time, but Edwards was one of the few religious writers his father approved of by name, and William was just now coming to grips with his father's views. William's notes on Edwards cover eleven closely written pages. He cannot get through Edwards's opening section on "arguments which prove . . . that we sin all and justly are accursed" without bursting in to say, "There is no proof that it is just we should be born to sin except 2 or

3 texts . . . I do not understand." But after this one objection, William makes no further comments of his own.

It may be that he rejected Edwards's entire argument, and that the rest of the synopsis represents a cold, dutiful slog through arguments he did not accept. It is also possible, and perhaps more likely, that he came increasingly to respect Edwards's abilities and the profound power of the subject. James's objection, after all, is not to the fact of human sinfulness, only to the claims that it is just, and that the justice can be proven. James goes on to summarize what we are to make of the corruption of the Catholic Church and the subsequent quick dimming of the Reformation. "Surely all this being true, it is a paradox to say that men have ability, light and means to do their whole duty. How has the gospel been so misunderstood? If obscure, how is the possession of such a dark thing an advantage? It must be that we have a native blindness. If a soil obstinately abound in weeds so that we cannot suppress them, we must think such a produce agreeable to the nature of that soil." No matter how much he might disagree with Edwards, or with Father, about the cause and nature of evil, William James was already coming to share Edwards's and Father's sense that evil is real.[13]

Another of the things James was learning by making abstracts of his reading was style. A comparison of James's summary with Edwards's original does not always come out in Edwards's favor. And like Edwards, James came to prefer the concrete example; the soil bearing weeds despite all our care is the kind of illustration that Edwards was good at, and that James was becoming good at.

After wrestling with Edwards for ten days, James turned next to Epictetus, the Stoic philosopher whose crucial initial teaching in his *Encheiridion* urges us to give our attention and energy to those things within our control and to let the rest go. From his opening sentence — "Some things are under our control, some things are not" — Epictetus wants us to take as our starting point not Adam's fall but our own situation. James's summary of section 20 of the *Encheiridion:* "I am in his power who can gratify my wishes and inflict my fears. Not to be a slave, then, I must have neither desire nor aversion for anything in the power of others."

James in his early years frequently goes back to the Stoic line, to Epictetus and even more frequently to Marcus Aurelius. James saw Stoicism as a way to freedom. In this he differed sharply from his brother Henry, who dismissed Stoicism in an early review as a philosophy fit only for slaves, since it taught men to embrace the given. But as the Civil War came ever closer to William's world, one hears a note somewhere between determination and desperation as he records Epictetus's insistence that the first care of a philosopher "should be the ease and quiet of his own breast." It is "a less evil for you that your servant or child should be vicious than that yourself should be perpetually unhappy with an anxious care to prevent it."[14]

Almost as he was writing these words, the tide of war was rising around him. In March 1863 a federal draft act went into effect. It applied to all northern men between the ages of twenty and thirty-five, and to unmarried men up to the age of forty-five. In late March Wilky was back in Massachusetts, having been recommended by his colonel for a place in the newly forming black regiment, the 54th Massachusetts. In April, as William was working on Jonathan Edwards and Epictetus, his own name appeared on the certified enrollment list for the state militia for Ward 5 in Newport. On May 1 his cousin Willy Temple — son of a younger sister of Henry James Sr. — was killed at Chancellorsville. Three weeks later, on May 21, Bob James enlisted in the 45th Massachusetts. He was underage, but his hoped-for appointment to the naval academy had not come through. Four days later, Willy Temple was buried in Albany.

Three days after the burial, Wilky's new regiment, the 54th Massachusetts, under the command of Colonel Robert Gould Shaw, arrived at Boston's South Station from Camp Meigs on its way to war. The regiment, composed of one thousand black soldiers, including Charles and Lewis Douglass, sons of Frederick Douglass, and thirty white officers, including Wilky James, marched through the streets of Boston surrounded by tumultuous throngs of spectators. With its twenty-five-year-old boy colonel out in front on his horse, the regiment went past the house of Wendell Phillips on Essex Street, where William Lloyd Garrison stood watching, holding in his arms a bust of John Brown. As Shaw rode by, he turned in his saddle and saluted the old abolitionist, who had tears running down his face.

As the regiment passed the house of Dr. Oliver Wendell Holmes, out came Holmes and his friend Henry James Sr. "to say Godspeed to his boy." Moving down State Street, the regiment was met with both cheers and hostility. At one point a group of toughs tried to attack the soldiers, but was held off by a large force of police. After marching in review on Boston Common in front of Governor John Andrew and other dignitaries, the 54th set off again, heading to Battery Wharf and singing "The Battle Hymn of the Republic" with a thousand voices.[15]

William James was in the crowd that day, and just as Charles Russell Lowell, one of the 54th's new officers, was passing on his horse, Lowell's fiancée — Colonel Shaw's nineteen-year-old sister, Josephine — came "whirling up on horseback" and reined in beside Lowell, just behind where William was standing. William knew Josephine; he had met her in Newport. As he described the scene many years later to Josephine's daughter, William wrote, "I looked back and saw their faces and figures against the evening sky, and they looked so young and victorious, that I, much gnawed by questions as to my own duty of enlisting or not, shrank back — they had not seen me — from being recognized. I shall never forget the impression they made."[16]

At such a moment, and in a scene right out of Delacroix, it might have seemed to William as though everyone were signing up and marching off, but it was not so. Of the 776,829 names called up in the three national drafts of 1863 and 1864, only 46,347 men were held for military service, or about one out of sixteen. At Harvard the percentage was higher. During the war, 1,311 Harvard men enlisted in the Union army and navy; they were decimated: 138, or 10.5 percent, were killed or died in the war. It was far worse for the 250 Harvard men who enlisted in the Confederate army and navy. Of them 64, or an appalling 25 percent, died or were killed in the war. Even so, Samuel Eliot Morison says that "college life went on much as usual, and with scarcely diminished attendance. Public opinion in the north did not require students to take up arms as it did in the World War; there was no mass movement into the army or navy; draftees who hired a substitute were not despised." Wilky and Bob James went, as did cousins Gus Barker and Willy Temple. Archy Pell and Oliver Wendell Holmes Jr. went, as did Robert Shaw and Charles Russell Lowell. On the other hand, neither William nor Henry James went, nor did Edward Emerson, Julian Hawthorne, Tom Perry, or Charles S. Peirce.[17]

The war was nevertheless inescapable. Bob James was now an officer in Massachusetts's second black regiment, the 55th, though he was still only sixteen. He was caught up in the Boston draft riots in July 1863. Bob was among a dozen soldiers who, along with General R. A. Pierce, were trapped in a room over Read's Gun Store — which had just been looted and gutted — in Dock Square, waiting for reinforcements to deliver them from the newly armed mob in the streets below. The mob had been spreading terror for three days, "hunting down any man in certain localities of it wearing the uniform of our army." During the hours he was shut up, Bob said, "The life of black soldiers in certain streets . . . was not worth five minutes purchase." A bit later, patrolling North Street near Dock Square with another officer, he found himself surrounded by a mob, pulled out his large navy revolver, and fired it. The rabble made way, and "quite without expecting it we were borne beyond the reach of the crowd."[18]

In early July came the Battle of Gettysburg. On July 10, Wilky and the 54th were shipped to James Island, outside Charleston Harbor. The next day Harry was drafted, though he did not get the notice for a few days. At almost the same time, Bob's regiment was ordered to New Bern, North Carolina. On July 17, Wilky's regiment attacked Fort Wagner as part of the attempt to capture Charleston. The attack was disastrous; half the regiment was killed. Fourteen of the remaining 24 officers fell (the regiment had already seen fierce fighting), as did 256 of the remaining 600 men. The assault failed. During the fight Wilky was wounded in the side and the foot. He dragged himself to the water's edge, where he was found by ambulance men and put on a stretcher. On the way back behind the lines, "a round shot blew off the head of the stretcher bearer in my rear," Wilky recalled later, "and we all fell down together."[19]

Wilky was found by accident in a field hospital by the father of a fellow officer in the regiment. Both wounds were by then severely infected. The metal was dug out of Wilky's foot on the ship that took him back north. He was brought home and put, on his stretcher, just inside the door of the Jameses' Newport house, where he lay for days, too sick to be moved to a bedroom, too weak to turn himself over. One of the best of William's surviving drawings is the one he did of Wilky at this time. It is a tender portrait, an image of the gravely wounded brother, a memorial that does not fade the way pain itself fades and is forgotten. The following February, in 1864, William wrote his cousin Jeannette Barber about the old pleasant days in Newport, adding with a simplicity that spoke volumes, "Wilky put an end to everything last summer."[20]

8. Comparative Anatomy and Medical School

FATHER'S NEW BOOK, *Substance and Shadow,* came out in June 1863; it posed the philosophical question of what is real. Wilky, lying near death just inside the door of the family home, posed the same question. Two weeks after Wilky came home, Bob's regiment was ordered to Morris Island, near Charleston Harbor, to help build an artificial island as an emplacement for a huge cannon, called the Swamp Angel, which eventually hurled a few of its two-hundred-pound shells into the city of Charleston, five miles distant, before the great gun burst. At the end of the same month, August, Harry was declared exempt from military service by reason of physical disability; in all likelihood it was his bad back.[1]

William returned to Cambridge in September 1863. He was still at the Lawrence Scientific School, but he had shifted from chemistry to anatomy and physiology, under Professor Wyman. (Charles W. Eliot was no longer teaching at Harvard; his five-year appointment had ended in March, he was not promoted, and neither he nor James was present for the spring term of 1863.) William was now more interested in comparative anatomy. It was much closer to what was already perceived as one of the great issues of the day, that of speciation, raised by Darwin and by the unconnected co-discoverer, Alfred Russel Wallace. By mid-September William was writing his sister, "I work in a vast museum, at a table all alone, surrounded by skeletons of mastodons, crocodiles and the like." Occasionally, he told Alice, when people visited the museum, a little girl would peep into the room and whisper, "Is folks allowed here?"[2]

There was a new urgency to William's studies. As he told his cousin Kitty Prince — a daughter of Henry Senior's oldest brother — in mid-September, "I am obliged before the 15th of January [the end of the fall semester] to make finally and irrevocably the choice of a profession." He had, he told Kitty, four possibilities: natural history, medicine, printing, and beggary. He preferred natural history, but he knew it was unlikely to pay much, and "I have to consider lucre." His father was well-off, being the son of a very wealthy man, but with Father's lavish way of living, his losses in the Panic of 1857, and the fact that the remaining money would eventually have to be split five ways, it was already clear that the younger generation of Jameses would have to paddle their own canoes.[3]

As William returned to the world of Cambridge and science, one of his early interests was the reading of *On the Origin of Species*, almost certainly during the early days of September. His notebook for this period has many ripped-out pages; all that remains of his notes on Darwin is one sentence from the next-to-last chapter: "The less any part of the organization is concerned with special habits, the more important it becomes for classification." The chapter that contains this statement is titled "Mutual Affinities of Organic Beings . . . ," and in it Darwin challenges both Lamarck and Agassiz on points of comparative anatomy. Darwin is skeptical about calling any system of classification the "plan of creation," because "unless it be specified whether order in time or space, or both, or what else is meant by the plan of the Creator, it seems to me that nothing is thus added to our knowledge." Darwin proposes "descent with modification" as the explanation of how new species come about. The entire chapter reads like a direct challenge to Agassiz's *Methods of Study in Natural History*. Darwin dismisses Cuvier's four great types or archetypes and proposes instead that "community of descent is the hidden bond which naturalists have been unconsciously seeking, and not some unknown plan of creation."[4]

Darwin and Agassiz differed on how creation works. Stretching a point, we could say they differed over the logic of creation, which is perhaps why William went out this fall and bought, not his father's most recent book, but his earlier one of 1857, *Christianity. The Logic of Creation*. In the view of Henry Senior, creation was not a physical but a spiritual act. One of his best commentators observes that "this denaturalizing of creation was an indispensable preliminary to his other views. The origin of all his thinking was his perturbation over the problem of evil . . . If creation is the result of an arbitrary physical act of God, then he alone must be held responsible for the existence of evil." Henry Senior had to find a way around this, so he made creation a spiritual, not a natural, act. He denied the authority of natural law, and he denied too "the final reality of the natural world." The real world is the world of spirit. It follows that "science is not, cannot be final truth."[5]

Almost everything William James was engaged in this fall was pressing him in the opposite direction. As William entered the big, confident world of modern science — his father's precise wish for him — Father was always present to him as a great antipodal figure, an invisible sparring partner. By late 1863 William no longer found it helpful to think of things in the old terminology of spirit versus substance. He was learning the new ways of talking about force — or energy — and matter. By mid-September he was reading Ludwig Büchner's *Kraft und Stoff* and laying out a synopsis of the opening chapter for himself with swift logic and clarity. "Force and Matter are inseparable. It is impossible to think of a pure force antecedent to matter creating matter; or existing independently after the creation of matter; or of a force springing into existence creating matter and then merging itself in that matter. Therefore," Büchner's argument goes, "matter can never have been created and is eternal." It is impossible to frame a position further removed from that taken by Henry James Sr.[6]

Just because he takes notes on a book or quotes it does not mean that James believes or accepts the book or the quotation. It is clear from the above that he is, in late 1863, moving fairly comfortably in the straight corridors of positivist thought. But James's early intellectual life is not an orderly, step-by-step construction of his later, mature views. What we are watching is often the assembly of new playing pieces, the acquisition of new vocabularies, new ways to know, as much as the acquisition of new information.

James now is reading books the conclusions of which he may or may not retain, but the style of which will have a permanent effect on his own writing. Among these indistinct prefigurings is James's reading this fall of Sydney Smith's dryly titled *Elementary Sketches of Moral Philosophy.* Moral philosophy, in Smith's view, covers everything not included under natural philosophy. Smith was a controversialist, a follower of the Scottish philosopher Dugald Stewart, a proponent of Catholic emancipation; he was the wittiest of the Scottish Common Sense philosophers and the best writer among them. He was one of the founders, and the first editor, of the *Edinburgh Review,* for which he proposed the motto *Tenui musam metitamur avena* (We cultivate literature on a little oatmeal).

Smith was an ardent believer in the association of ideas, in the notion, first given its full form by David Hartley, that "complex mental phenomena are formed from simple elements derived ultimately from sensation." The belief that everything mental has a physical explanation and origin — one of the rocks on which positivism is built — is put forward by Smith by way of an attack on metaphysics, "a word of dire sound and horrible import," says Smith. "A great philosopher," he says, "may sit in his study and deny the existence of matter: but if he takes a walk in the street he must take care to leave his theory behind him." Smith makes his point not so much with the abstraction as with the following: "Pyrro said there was no such thing as pain; and he saw no proof that there were such things as carts, and wagons; and he refused to get out of their way: but Pyrro had, fortunately for him, three or four stout slaves, who followed their master, without following his doctrine; and whenever they saw one of these ideal machines approaching, took him up by the arms and legs, and without attempting to controvert his arguments, put him down in a place of safety." Smith writes, "We may believe anything for a moment, but we shall soon be lashed out of our impertinences by hard and stubborn realities."[7]

Smith's final chapters are on habit, which he accounts for on the principle of association, and which he believes to be the strongest force in our lives. Examples tumble out; the abstract argument suddenly becomes as tangible as a bag of potatoes. "In Minorca Governor Kane made an excellent road, the whole length of the island, and yet the inhabitants adhered to the old road, though not only longer but extremely bad. The merchants of Bristol have an excellent and commodious Exchange, but they always meet in the street. There is hardly any convenience of life or any notion of utility or beauty which may not be entirely changed by habit; it is needless to multiply the instances." There is almost nothing, according to Smith, that habit cannot accomplish. "There is no degree of disguise or distortion which human nature may not be made to assume from habit; it grows in every direction in which it is trained, and accommodates itself to every circumstance which caprice or design places in its way . . . There is not a single principle of our nature, which may not be cherished to the complete exclusion and subjugation of all the rest."

Smith's pitch for habit is the rhetorical and substantive peak of his book. And it is at this culminating point that James extracts the observation that "it is only the great passions which, tearing us away from the seductions of indolence, endow us with that continuity of attention to which alone superiority of mind is attached." So James is already interested in the power of habit, in the way in which attention defines and limits — indeed constitutes — our interests, and in the importance of emotions or passion for an explanation of human behavior. But more important perhaps than any of these ideas for James is the long shadow cast by Smith's bright style, his vivid examples, and, above all, his neatly phrased and blunt respect for "hard and stubborn realities."[8]

In mid-December 1863, William wrote his cousin Kitty Prince: "I have at last made choice of that 'profession' which has made so great a figure in this correspondence. It is, to wit, — 'médecine.'" As William came to his decision, Wilky had just resigned from his regiment for reasons of health. Bob, seventeen years old, had received a battlefield promotion to captain, and Harry's first publication, a story called "A Tragedy of Error," was about to appear in the *Continental Monthly*. Alice was fifteen. The elder Jameses now sold their Newport house, committing themselves to a serious search for a house in Boston or Cambridge.[9]

William moved to a room in Harvard's Divinity Hall in Cambridge and began attending lectures at Harvard Medical School in Boston in early February. If he expressed little enthusiasm for this new educational direction, it may have been partly because Harvard Medical School at that time did not inspire confidence, let alone enthusiasm. The medical school was in the worst condition of any part of the university. It was poorly equipped; its faculty, Eliot claimed, had the most bad blood, and, he added with a slap, "it has always been so." Neither a high school diploma nor a college degree was required for admission. "No applicant for instruction," writes one historian of the school, "who could pay his fees or sign his note was turned down."

Harvard Medical School was a moneymaking operation, designed to supplement the apprentice system. It was openly and intentionally hostile to science, which it understood as taking time away from the all-important practical aspects of medicine. The school was located on North Grove Street, near Massachusetts General Hospital and the Charles River. It was run by the professors, all of whom were part-time, and it had only nominal ties to Harvard. There were no grades and no written exams, either in courses or at the end. Students bought tickets for the annual winter lectures as though to a concert series. A complete set of lecture tickets cost fifty dollars. As Professor Oliver Wendell Holmes explained, "Medical visits in the country were worth only twenty-five cents apiece," and with prospects for future earnings so dim, "the ambitious student could not afford to make an expensive outlay for his future work." The faculty, led by the professor of surgery Henry J. Bigelow (who had treated the wounded Wendell Holmes, sticking a carrot in his wounded foot to keep it open), resisted reforms for fear of driving away paying students. Bigelow was also skeptical about current students' ability to benefit from increased requirements. Large numbers "could hardly sign their names to the register, and had difficulty in deciphering the simplest writing," says another historian. Bigelow opposed written exams, for example, on the grounds that "more than half of them [the students] can barely write."[10]

Students were expected to attend lectures for two terms, perform a few recitations, make a few visits to hospitals, and present a brief thesis. It was possible to get through the whole thing in a year. When a candidate had completed the two terms, had a short thesis in hand, and had paid a fee of thirty dollars, he took his one and only examination. The fee, it has been explained, was the only qualification "with which the student could effect no kind of compromise." The exam was brief, oral, and covered nine subjects. A student who passed five out of the nine got an M.D. degree and a license to practice. New doctors could thus be set loose on the public lacking basic knowledge of almost half the subjects of their profession. "The ignorance and general incompetence of the average graduate of American Medical Schools," wrote William's former chemistry professor Charles Eliot at this time, "is something horrible to contemplate."[11]

Why was William James attracted to such a course of study at such a place? He was neither a fool nor a knave; indeed he was one of the "minority [which] successfully wrung a measure of good from the vicious system which they were powerless to destroy." He was not seriously thinking of practicing medicine as a career, although he had looked into it enough to know that he was most interested in the branch just beginning to be called psychiatry, or psychological medicine. James probably saw an M.D. as an insurance policy. He was, as he repeatedly said, inclined more toward natural history than anything else, but he was constantly aware of the difficulty of making a living thereby. His teachers, Louis Agassiz, Jeffries Wyman, and the equally prominent Asa Gray, all had taken medical degrees. Wyman and Gray had both practiced medicine, and James would have understood from their example if not their advice that the degree gave him a prudent fallback position, an income-producing occupation that could be pursued part-time while he worked on other things that interested him more.[12]

Accordingly, in February 1864 James began attending lectures in materia medica, chemistry, practice, obstetrics, and anatomy. He began dissecting a cadaver, which he called "the dear old 'subject,'" and absorbing the medical knowledge of the time. He took careful notes on, for example, leeches, which he learned were to be applied for mumps (if the swellings turned hard) and for dysentery (to the abdomen). For spinal meningitis it was leeches and cupping to the spine, for rheumatism it was leeches to the affected joints, and for "passive hyperaenemia of the liver" one applied leeches to the anus. In this context, William's occasional caustic comments about medicine seem understandable.[13]

The James family moved from Newport to Boston in May 1864. The new address was 13 Ashburton Place, on Beacon Hill, right next to the statehouse. Alice began attending a Boston school kept by a Miss Clapp. Harry was writing stories and reviews. Wilky was home for most of 1864; Bob was still in the army, but was restless and ready to quit. Only a boy officer, he was already inclined (like his father) toward drinking, womanizing, and self-loathing. William now moved to the Boston house, from which it was a short walk down the back side of Beacon Hill to the medical school. During the summer, William went for a week's vacation to Newport. Harry, whose back was still giving him a great deal of pain, went to Northampton for Mr. Denniston's water cure.[14]

In the fall, while waiting for the start of medical lectures in early November, William James turned his attention to the idea of writing book reviews. Harry had not only had a story published back in February, he had a review coming out in the October issue of the *North American Review*, edited by Charles Eliot Norton. William saw it as a way of making a little money, and perhaps a way of keeping up with his younger brother. He may also have felt that it was time to step forward, modestly, on the public stage. He proposed, and Norton accepted, a longish review of Thomas Huxley's *Lectures on the Elements of Comparative Anatomy.*

Comparative anatomy, especially as it concerned arguments for and against Darwin's transmutation theory, was something James had been hearing, reading, and thinking about since his first week in Cambridge three years earlier. It is not surprising that he had views on the subject; what is surprising is his already marked opposition to Agassiz. (Reviews in Norton's magazine were unsigned, providing cover for the authors, but not infallibly so. Editors and insiders knew who wrote what.)

James says that Huxley "inclines generally to that view of the phenomena of life which makes them result from the general laws of matter, rather than from the subordination of those laws to some principle of individuality, different in each case." It is clear that James shares this view of the dependence of everything on physical laws. He is critical of Cuvier, Agassiz's idol, and approves of Huxley's early endorsement of Darwin, "provided it shall be found compatible with the fact of sterility between animals of different species." James is impressed that so many scientists are coming over to Darwin's view, adding, "We may well doubt whether it may not be destined eventually to prevail." He notes that the new hypothesis of "the Self-Competency of Nature" is taken by many people to lead to "atheism." He admits that we can no longer speak, with Richard Owen, of a "special adaptive force by which the Sovereign of the universe attains his ends," nor can we speak, with William Whewell, of "a purpose in many other parts of Creation." But James balks at positivism pure and simple, and he takes pains in this review to keep a door open. "Is it likely," he asks, "that then any better than now we shall be able utterly to stifle our idea of final cause, or go off satisfied with an answer to How, when the question we asked was Why? May it not be," he goes on, warming to the subject, "that, finding Nature a great closed sack, as it were, *tota, teres atque rotunda* [a smooth and rounded whole], without any *partial* inlets to the Supernatural, without any *occasional* Ends *within* her bosom, we shall be driven to look for final causes on some deeper plane underlying the whole of Nature at once, and there shall find them?"[15]

James concludes with a list of Huxley's primary divisions and classes of animals, which is a clear contradiction of Cuvier. No one reading this review can miss the writer's tempered approval of Darwin or the tacit divergence from Agassiz. But the review is not openly insistent; it concludes, indeed, with a caution like Wyman's: "We think all this is still somewhat problematical."

In November, as the medical term got under way, James bought a large, hardbound, blank indexed notebook with several pages for each letter of the alphabet, and he began making entries, mostly concerning his reading, in this new encyclopedic format.[16]

In December, General Sherman took Savannah. Wilky was mustered in again and shipped south to take part in the attack on Charleston. Henry James Sr. gave his wittiest and most successful talk ever, on Carlyle, at the Concord Lyceum. As Charleston and Fort Sumter fell to the Union in February 1865, William worked on a second review, this one a short notice of an article by Alfred Russel Wallace. In that piece, Wallace is at pains to answer the questions "Has variation ceased?" and "Why do we not observe it?"

Wallace's answer is that, in the case of humans, natural causes of variation are no longer active. Society has learned that the physically weak have contributions to make and must be protected too. Wallace here undercuts the social Darwinists, who defended, for example, the low status of the working person on the grounds of simple survival of the fittest individuals. Wallace emphasizes instead man's social and communal side, the fact that "all the members of a community profit by the gift of any one member," and he applies the idea of natural selection not to individuals but to whole communities. He claims that natural selection "singles out for preservation those communities whose social qualities are the most complete."

James's admiration for this turn of thought is clear. He calls Wallace's theory "obvious," adding that "in this case as in the case of Darwin's original law, what most astonishes the reader is the fact that the discovery was made so late." James had thus reached a fairly full acceptance of Darwin's transmutation theory and rejected the most insidious argument of social Darwinism by the time he was twenty-three.[17]

James's medical studies seem to have started well enough. His reading was invigorating; he was deeply involved in Darwin's thought and in the implications of Darwin's work. He was writing bold, clear reviews. But he found it hard to settle down. So when an opportunity arose to go with Agassiz (who, whether you agreed with him on all points or not, was after all the most famous scientist of his day) on a scientific expedition to Brazil and up the Amazon River, James jumped at the chance. Leaving medical school abruptly, he went to New York, where he boarded the steamship *Colorado* on March 29, 1865, bound for Rio de Janeiro.

9. *The Gulls at the Mouth of the Amazon*

A GASSIZ HAD A HUGELY ambitious plan for the South American expedition. "The origin of life is the great question of the day," he wrote, and he made it clear that he was after nothing less than the great answer. "How did the organic world come to be as it is? . . . How did Brazil come to be inhabited by the animals and plants now living there? . . . The first step must be to ascertain the geographical distribution of the present animals and plants." Darwin's *Origin of Species* had conceded that science knew very little about the dispersion and distribution of species. Agassiz moved into this large gap (as had Henry Thoreau in his own way), and he picked out Brazil for the testing ground.[1]

"I am often asked what is my chief aim in this expedition to South America," Agassiz wrote. "The conviction which draws me irresistibly, is that the combination of animals on this continent, where the faunae are so characteristic and so distinct from all others, will give me the means of showing that the transmutation theory" — that is, Darwin's theory — "is wholly without foundation in fact." The general plan was to examine first the fishes in the Rio São Francisco, a river system quite isolated from others in Brazil, rising in the high country behind Rio de Janeiro and flowing north to the Atlantic at Neopolis, south of Recife (then Pernambuco). Next the expedition would gather fish from the Amazon; Agassiz confidently expected them to be wholly distinct, not just slightly different, from those in the Rio São Francisco.[2]

Agassiz was fifty-eight. His reputation as America's leading scientist was enormous. The Brazil trip, intended to demonstrate his case against Darwin, was also a revisiting, in a way, of his now distant youth, when he had published, at the age of twenty-two, *The Fishes of Brazil,* a work based on specimens that he had not himself gathered but that had been turned over to him by a naturalist named Martius. Now, more than thirty-five years later, Agassiz was going to Brazil to see for himself, taking along six other professional naturalists and six unpaid volunteers, including Steven Thayer (son of the major backer of the expedition, Nathaniel Thayer), Tom Ward (son of Samuel Gray Ward, another major backer of the expedition), Newton Dexter (a Harvard senior), Walter Hunnewell, and William James. Agassiz; his wife, Elizabeth; his brother-in-law, a Dr. Cotting; and Cotting's wife brought the number to seventeen.

The passage was miserable for James. As the ship left New York and passed Sandy Hook it began to "jump about lively." James felt the deck heaving beneath his feet and wrote a last few lines home, to be mailed by the harbor pilot. "One feels oneself growing heavy and light alternately," he wrote. He quickly became seasick, "actively nauseous," for a day and a half, and thereafter, "for 12 mortal days, I was, body and soul, in a more indescribably hopeless, homeless and friendless state than I ever want to be in again." He spent much of the voyage out planning how to get home.[3]

Agassiz gave lectures every day on the ship; he offered detailed instructions on methods of collecting, preserving, and transporting specimens. One preserving method, for larger animals, involved an injection of wax, tallow, and red lead. Reptiles, fish, and very large insects were to be preserved in alcohol. Smaller specimens would be kept in a special fluid made of common salt, alum, and "corrosive sublimate." Small insects would be packed dry, in layers, with paper moistened with alcohol and camphor. Everything they collected would be put in boxes, kegs, or barrels for the journey home to the museum at Harvard.[4]

The *Colorado* anchored at Rio de Janeiro on April 22, after a twenty-two-day trip. During the voyage, the Civil War had come to an end and Lincoln had been assassinated, but none of this was known to those aboard the *Colorado.* William found Rio and its approaches so overpoweringly grand that "no words of mine . . . can give any idea of [the] magnificence of this harbor and its approaches." But he tried nevertheless. Rio, he wrote, has "the boldest, grandest mountains, far and near, the palms and other trees of such vivid green as I never saw anywhere else." His mood was so exultant that he wrote his parents, "Yesterday [his first day ashore] was I think the day of my life on which I had the most outward enjoyment."[5]

A laboratory was soon set up on land, over a Mr. Davis's store. Agassiz lavished time and attention on the emperor Dom Pedro II de Alcantara and his suite, who were collectively referred to by the sailors of the *Colorado* as "them kings." The emperor was a great patron of science and of Agassiz; he provided free passage, placed a steamer at Agassiz's disposal, put him in touch with local naturalists, and arranged help in innumerable ways large and small. William found the conditions unpleasant. "Unlimited perspiration," he wrote Harry, "unlimited itching of the skin caused by fleas and mosquitoes, and worst of all on both cheeks and one side of neck by virulent ring-worms which appeared on board ship and which 'still wave' with undiminished fire." While Agassiz and others explored inland,

James was assigned to collect polyps, jellyfish, and all other marine life except fish in the bay area of Rio.[6]

Two weeks after his arrival, James came down with varioloid, or variola minor, a mild form of smallpox but enough to put him in the hospital. By June 3 he was writing to his father, "My coming was a mistake . . . I shall learn next to nothing of Natural History as I care about learning it. My whole work will be mechanical, finding objects and packing them, and working so hard at that and in travelling, that no time at all will be found for studying their structure." He said, with premature confidence, "I am convinced now, for good, that I am cut out for a speculative rather than an active life." He felt, as he often had and often would, overwhelmed. "The grit and energy of some men are called forth by the resistance of the world," he wrote his father. "But as for myself I seem to have no spirit whatever of that kind, no pride which makes me ashamed to say 'I can't do that.'" He still believed — though he was by now twenty-three — that things would come to him by themselves, that his true talent would reveal itself without effort on his part, that we simply cannot force our talent. He decided to return home. He would not even consider a sailing ship, but he declared himself willing to travel via Bordeaux or Southampton if that was the only way he could get home by steamship.

Yet despite his freely expressed (in letters home) and rather smug doubts about Agassiz (too much the politician, too much the charlatan, too fixed in his anti-Darwinism), the more he came to know the man, the more he admired him. "He is an extraordinary being," he wrote his family, "having with all his foibles, a greater personal fascination than any one I know." Agassiz radiated such warmth that it was said of him, "One has less need of an overcoat in passing by Agassiz's house than by any other in Cambridge." In his indecision, James stayed — temporarily, as he thought — with the expedition, which, after many delays and disappointments, finally headed north on July 25, 1865, on a dirty, crowded steamer, the *Cruzeiro do Sul*, for the sixteen-day coastal voyage to Pará (now Belém), at the mouth of the Amazon. Here the great part of the trip began.[7]

Everything about the Amazon staggers the imagination. As one approaches Pará from the Atlantic, the banks of the southern, smaller mouth of the river are 150 miles apart. The island of Marajo, one of several in the mouth, is half the size of Ireland. The province of Pará, with a capital city also called Pará and with a population then of fifteen thousand, is the size of western Europe. The Amazon, with a flood-stage discharge ten times that of the Mississippi, has the greatest flow of any river on earth, accounting for 20 percent of all the water that runs into the oceans. It is so large that most of the lower river seems not like a river at all but like a freshwater sea. For a hundred miles inland the river is indistinguishable from the ocean except for its calmness and its discolored water. There is little visible current; the slope of the lower river is a fifth of an inch per mile. Three hundred and fifty miles up, the Amazon is still forty miles wide. It is four thousand miles long, with a thousand tributaries, some of which are themselves a thousand miles long, and several are twenty miles wide where they meet the main river.

Agassiz's project was on the same scale as the Amazon. With a new steamer, the *Icamiaba,* provided by the emperor, and with the help of many local guides and helpers, Agassiz planned to examine the fish in the river and in all the main tributaries. Not only that, he also wanted to send parties up and down and back and forth, so that he would be able to collect fish from each location at different times. The ultimate aim was to demonstrate not only that the fish of the Rio São Francisco and its isolated basin were different from the fish of the Amazon, but also that the fish in each part of the Amazon system were completely different from the fish in any other part.

Within two weeks of arriving at Pará, James was with Agassiz on the first major north-flowing tributary west of the province, the Xingu. Agassiz had found forty-six new species in his first fourteen days, and he was jubilant. James reported home that Agassiz already had "a total number of fishes greater than the collection which Spix and Martius made in the whole 4 years of their sojourn!" James was feeling better now, and on July 23 he told Agassiz he would not go home but would see the Amazon expedition through.[8]

One contemporary book about the Amazon tries to suggest the scope of this vast watery part of the world in its title, *Fifteen Thousand Miles on the Amazon and Its Tributaries.* William James, while he was not the expedition leader and was on the river for only five months, nevertheless covered at least five thousand miles, most of it by steamer, but for two of those months and perhaps a thousand miles he went by small boats that used oars and by canoe. His tropical odyssey took him two thousand miles up the Amazon, all the way to the Peruvian border, and two thousand miles back. On the way he spent considerable time on six major tributaries (these were the small-boat and canoe excursions); he traveled the Xingu and the Tapajos (both south of the Amazon, running north) on the way up the great river. He went into the Içá and the Jutaí when he was high on the upper Amazon (then called the Solimões) and into the Rio Negro, Lake

Manacapuru, and the Rio Trombetas on the return trip. The whole adventure bears comparison not so much with Twain's *Life on the Mississippi* or Thoreau's *Week on the Concord and Merrimack Rivers*, but rather with Melville's time in Polynesia, for the Amazon, like the Marquesas and the Tuamotus, is a world overrun by water.

It was a physically demanding trip, but after the varioloid in Rio, James's condition improved dramatically, and he soon was reveling in his almost suspiciously good health, in his exhilarating outdoor tropical life, and in his picturesquely rundown appearance. He wrote his sister that he wore nothing but "shirt and trowsers, both in a frightfully dilapidated state. With shaven head and fuzzy chin and hacked up hands, and sunburnt feet and cheeks bloated with the remains of my small pox." There are photos of William in Brazil. In one, a studio shot, he is dressed in a loose-fitting coat. He wears baggy pants that sag in huge wrinkles to the floor. He wears a Panama hat and a short beard running along his entire jaw line; he has black-lensed glasses. He is thin, he looks serious, and his whole form slopes forward and left.[9]

He was a delightful traveling companion, as Elizabeth Agassiz reported. "You know," she wrote her daughter, "how bright, intelligent, cultivated, he is, a fellow of vivid keen intellect. He works hard and is ready to turn his hand to anything for your father." His moods over the next five months went up and down, as usual, but in general as the trip progressed James went from frustration to satisfaction, from sick to well, from complaint to admiration. Even his drawings, it has been argued, show a mood of calm replacing one of earlier anger. By October, late in the trip, he reported home, "My health at present is probably better than it ever was in my life . . . I never felt in better spirits, nor more satisfied than I do now with the way in which I am spending my time. I feel that I am gaining a great deal in every way." James's enthusiasm here was in part meant to reassure the family, which had been alarmed by his earlier reports of illness.

Despite, or perhaps because of, the lack of books, he felt himself growing intellectually. He gave most of the credit to Agassiz. Instead of making snide little cracks about bringing his daily catch to "the principal light of modern science," James began to appreciate how much Agassiz actually knew and how good a teacher he was. He reported to his mother with some delight, "This morning he [Agassiz] said I was 'totally uneducated.' He has done me much good already and will evidently do me more before I have got through with him."[10]

Buoyed by the spectacular results of the first two weeks, Agassiz rushed upriver while deploying small side trips — fishing excursions — left and right. James was struck by the forests, which he found "not as grand and tangled as those about Rio, but more soft and smiling and much more penetrable." It was, he said, "very beautiful, and the evenings, after dinner, when the fresh breeze blows and the moon grows bright, and the herons fly along the shore, are not to be forgotten."

Agassiz dispatched James in a large canoe, with Dexter, a Brazilian named Talisman, and a local boat crew of four Indians with a white captain, up the Tapajos, which empties into the Amazon four hundred miles from the sea. The Amazon is still forty miles wide at this confluence. The Tapajos itself was so wide that James reported the opposite shore to be visible as a mere blue line, and after paddling seventy miles up the Tapajos "there was no apparent narrowing of the stream." They slept on the beach or in hammocks; they fished by day and by night — night fishing was especially productive — and they used nets, bows and arrows, poison (this worked best in lakes and ponds), hook and line, and spears. Eight days later James's party returned to the Amazon, joined with another side-trip party, and headed upriver together for Manáos, a good-sized town a thousand miles from the ocean.[11]

Agassiz could barely contain his excitement as the number of new species rapidly grew. The whole expedition moved swiftly up the upper Amazon to Tabatinga, on the Peruvian border. James recalled, thirty years later, one particular night on the river, probably from this stage of the trip. "I well remember," he said, "at night, as we all swung in our hammocks in the fairy-like moonlight, on the deck of the steamer that throbbed its way up the Amazon between the forests guarding the stream on either side, how he [Agassiz] turned and whispered, 'James, are you awake?' and continued, 'I cannot sleep; I am too happy; I keep thinking of these glorious plans.'"[12]

From Tabatinga, which James described as "5 houses, 5 hovels, a flagstaff and a cannon," Agassiz aimed to go on "as far as Urimaguas in the Peruvian steamer, and from thence by canoe, horseback, and foot to Rioco, high up on the front Cordillera beyond Mayobomba." Shortly after their arrival at Tabatinga, however, Agassiz changed his plans and decided to send James instead. James's excitement now matched that of Agassiz. Of his new and demanding assignment he wrote home, "Hooray!"

But a revolution had erupted in Peru, making travel there unsafe. Agassiz shifted gears once again, heading downriver instead and sending out side trips far into the interior. Just before leaving Tabatinga for the long trip back to the sea, Agassiz's crew took aboard the remains of a Spanish expedition that had come down from Ecuador on the Rio Napo to the upper Amazon, and James and the others saw what they themselves might well have looked like if the hour had struck for them as it had struck for the Spanish. "They have been all through the Andes, been shipwrecked, are the most shabby, bearded, jaundiced looking set of roughs you ever saw. Beside their voyage ours seems like a holiday excursion. By Jove, I honor them." They showed up on "2 rafts with palm leaf houses built on them covered with monkeys and parrots and sich" — James is joshing here; he means "such" — "with a smudge smoking in the evening at the front to drive off mosquitoes."[13]

Agassiz's plan now was for James to lead a small expedition for fish, first on the Putumayo, or Içá, a river that runs into the upper Amazon from the north and west, and then on the Jutaí, which comes up from the south. These were little-known rivers, James was the leader, his morale was at its peak, and Agassiz expected important results. "This dispersion of parties to collect simultaneously in different areas, divided from each other by considerable distances," wrote Agassiz, "will show how the fishes are distributed, and whether their combinations differ in these localities as they have been found to do in the lower Amazon."

Agassiz liked to overstate things, but it remains true that at least a part of his main argument against Darwin was now in William James's hands. James did not have much alcohol for preserving specimens, and Agassiz was worried, we learn from his wife, about James's judgment of which species to preserve. But James, still only twenty-three, came through. "The commission could not have been better executed," Agassiz wrote, "and the result raises the number of species from the Amazon water to more than 600, every day showing more clearly how distinctly the species are localized, and that this immense basin is divided into numerous zoological areas, each one of which has its own combination of fishes."[14]

James had thrown himself into the spirit of Agassiz's quest, and his results seemed to cement the conclusion Agassiz had been after all along. It was the high point of James's Amazon voyage. The Rio Içá represents the farthest James reached from the sea; he was in charge, and he carried out his charge handsomely. It was, he wrote home, "a most original month and one which from its strangeness I shall remember to my dying day."[15]

James's trip up the Amazon involved a lot of hard work, monotony, and even boredom. "I hate collecting," he wrote home. But there was also a measure of magic, a thread of romance as in a Mayne Reid novel. His crew slept on beaches, "fraternized with the Indians," and, said James, there was, "running through all, a delightful savor of freedom and gypsyhood." Once they saw two "wild Indians . . . naked at a distance on the edge of the forest." They called out to the Indians in "Lingoa Geral," but they ran away. "It gave me a very peculiar and unexpected thrilling sensation to come thus suddenly upon these children of nature."

There were also alluring young women in some of the towns and villages. At Obydos, on the north bank, "the damsels were very pretty with splendid soft black hair . . . In their combs they wear two kinds of white flowers, of the most wildly melodious perfume." This is all in a letter to Alice. "We danced a regular home quadrille and polka with another stiff awkward 'square' dance whose name I have forgotten. We talked, gesticulated, fraternized in short, and passed a very merry evening . . . Ah Jesuina, Jesuina, my forest queen, my tropic flower, why could I not make myself intelligible to thee?" This is James's habitual teasing tone with his sister, with its familiar note of self-mockery. James's "forest queen" understood, he wrote, "absolutely nothing" of his talk. He tells the story on himself, then goes on with the mock romancing: "She now walks upon the beach with her long hair floating free, pining for my loss."

But if some of James's Brazilian memories sound like the amorous South Sea idylls that Bougainville brought back and made popular, Brazil also broke open some of James's previously unexamined stereotypes. On first seeing Rio, he noted that "almost everyone is a negro or a negress, which words I perceive we don't know the meaning of with us." On the Amazon he remarked on "the beautiful brown color" of the Indians, adding, "Their skin is dry and clean looking, and they perspire very little so that on the whole I think they are better looking in that respect than either negroes or white men, who in this climate are always sweaty and greasy looking."[16]

For most of his time on the Amazon, James felt, he said, "a perfect disinclination to write," but he did make two brief attempts to record parts of the trip. One was an account of his great month on the upper Amazon, the Içá, and the Jutaí; the other was an account of the fishing trip to Lake Manacapuru. It is sobering to see how inept these bits of failed narrative are. One tails off into an overdetailed description of monkey manners, the other manages to convey, without intending to, a sense of the dead weight of routine expeditionary journal-keeping. For a rather short piece, it is a seemingly endless, undifferentiated, monochromatic chronicle. For a man who would come to understand narrative as central to writing, he still had everything to learn about telling a story.[17]

If he did not learn anything about narrative from Agassiz, and if he did not come to accept Agassiz's argument against Darwin, James did learn something of enormous value that stayed with him. He came to appreciate the man who once said, "I feel within myself the strength of a whole generation," and whose "hungry heart" aimed at "nothing less than an acquaintance with the whole of animated nature." Above all, James grasped the reason for Agassiz's limitless interest in fact and detail. "No one," he wrote his father, "sees farther into a generalization than his own knowledge of details extends, and you have a greater feeling of weight and solidity about the movement of Agassiz's mind, owing to the continual presence of this great background of special facts, than about the mind of any other man I know."[18]

James's small but real contribution to the Thayer expedition is nicely phrased in a letter Agassiz sent James toward the end of the trip, as James was heading downstream to catch a steamer for home, taking with him a good part of what had been collected. Agassiz wrote: "If Dexter, Thayer, yourself and Bourget are at all successful [on the final set of side trips] and I have good luck also . . . I look forward to land in Para with over 2000 species [of fish]. This will be double the number of the Mediterranean or any other circumscribed marine basin; and yet thus far the sea has been looked upon as the real home of the fishes and the freshwater as containing comparatively few. All the ideas now prevailing upon the intensity of life in the waters will have to be modified."[19]

The Amazon voyage was a benchmark experience for James. His major finding, like that of Agassiz, was a negative one. Agassiz had intended to disprove Darwin's notion that species evolved and changed over time. He expected to find that each section of the Amazon River system had a wholly different and distinct population of fish, each species of which had been created specifically in and for the place it occupied. He proved no such thing, but he did show that the reigning assumption that the sea was the home of the majority of species was perhaps wrong. The great river systems such as the Amazon might well have more. What William James learned was that he did not after all want to be a field naturalist. Though he discovered new strengths and abilities, he also lost something on the great, slow, wandering river, namely his sense of direction. He had started medical school to give himself a bit of insurance when he became a naturalist. Now he was facing a return to a largely pointless program.

James always looked back on this trip with two emotions. One was a sense of sadness or melancholy. As he wrote to Elizabeth Agassiz a few years later, when her book on the Brazilian expedition came out, "To me the peculiar feature which at all times of the day and everywhere made itself felt, was the sadness and solemnity produced by the flood of sun and the inextricable variety of vegetable forms . . . On those side rivers at dawn when the forests used to reveal themselves standing as if painted the soberness was particularly striking." The trip seemed only half real even at the time. "Do you remember," Elizabeth Agassiz wrote him much later, "the afternoon when you and I passed each other in our separate boats, as I floated out of the Igarape into the sunset glow over the great river and you floated into the hidden water-way in the forest. It was a wonderful scene and as you rowed by me you said "is it real or a dream?"[20]

But the image that stayed with him longest, and that rose before his mind's eye during the winter darkness of Berlin or Cambridge, was of a sunnier mood. "While a Northeaster of December is raging here," he wrote his brother Bob years later, "at this very moment the sunlit waves are dancing and sparkling and the gulls skimming and the flowers blooming down at the mouth of the Amazon."[21]

10. Tea Squalls and a Life According to Nature

AS SOON AS HE was back in Boston, the twenty-four-year-old William flung himself into social life, which meant girls. He was extremely fond of the company of young women. While in Brazil he had letters from Clover Hooper and her cousin Mary Louisa Shaw; he sent butterflies and beetles home to Ellen Tappan, Ellen Sturgis Hooper, and his sister Alice. Almost as soon as he got home he went to a musical evening to hear Ellen Hooper play the piano, and declared, "She is by far the nicest girl to me in all Boston."[1]

Almost immediately after this, William's cousins Minnie and Ellie Temple and Ellie Van Buren (daughter of another sister of Henry Senior) came for a two-week stay. William escorted them to parties and other events "nearly every night." The consequences, he wrote Tom Ward, "were a falling in love with every girl I meet."[2]

He met quite a few. There was Ellen Washburn, sick now and bound for Europe for a change of air. There was Fanny Dixwell of Cambridge; she was lively, direct, beautiful, a talented artist, and a new acquaintance this year. William told his brother Wilky in March 1866 that she was "about as fine as they make 'em . . . A1, if anyone ever was." The trouble was that Wendell Holmes, the doctor's son, pretty much monopolized her. But when Wendell went to England in May, William stepped up his attentions to Fanny. Holmes's mother wrote her son to say that Fanny was "living quietly in Cambridge with the exception of visits from Bill James, who appears to go there at any time from 9-o-clock in the morning — I told her to let me know how the flirtation got on — she says he is a person who likes to know his friends very well. I had a little fun with her about him and told her I should write to you about it." Wendell got the message. By June 8 William had learned that Fanny "couldn't be mine."[3]

Another favorite of William's was Sara Sedgwick. She too went on to marry someone else, in this case Charles Darwin's son William. Others, who were probably more Alice's friends than his, included Mary Lee and Fanny Morse, and Silvy and Mary Watson, usually encountered at what William liked to call "tea-fights" or "tea-squalls." The Temple sisters, Minnie, Ellie, and Kitty, were always in and out of the Jameses' house. Usually it was Minnie who provoked a little emphasis in Willy's letters, but in January 1867 it was Kitty whom he found "growing upon me very much," as he told Alice. He flirted with and teased his sister as always, calling her "loved one" and "beloved" and asking her to "find out some handsome, spirited and romantic creature who I can fall in love with in a desperate fashion." William was frequently exuberant and given to overstatement and general skylarking, but his interest in these young women was not just manufactured to entertain correspondents. In a letter of 1867, William's mother wrote him to "beware of the fascinations" of yet another new acquaintance, a Miss Clara Schmidt, "or any other such artless charmer. You know your extreme susceptibility, or rather I know it, so I say beware."[4]

When James came back from Brazil, he resumed his medical studies. He took time to help Louis Agassiz's son, Alexander (who was becoming an increasingly important scientist in his own right), unpack some of the barrels of specimens from the Amazon. James was now studying microscopy, probably with Oliver Wendell Holmes Sr., and he made sketchy, desultory notes on what he saw in urine, liver cells, and breast cysts.[5] During the summer vacation he obtained an appointment as acting house surgeon at Massachusetts General Hospital, but by December he was applying for a position on the "medical side" of the hospital. A hint of self-loathing crept into the account he wrote his sister: "The present time is a very exciting one for ambitious young men at the medical school who are anxious to get into the hospital. Their toadying the physicians, asking them intelligent questions after lectures, offering to run errands for them etc this week reaches its climax; they call at their residences and humbly solicit them to favor their appointment, and do the same at the residences of the 10 trustees. So I have 16 visits to make. I have little fears," he added sarcastically, "with my talent for flattery and fawning, of a failure."[6]

After his return from the expedition, William had found the family scattered and unsettled, uncertain about the future, and physically fragile. His mother and father were living in Boston with Harry and Alice, but they wanted to relocate and were looking at houses in Concord and Cambridge. Harry was writing steadily and by June 1866 had published four stories. Alice, now eighteen, was delicate but sociable. Bob, who had disliked the army and had started drinking heavily while still in it, had been mustered out in September 1865, at the age of nineteen. Thanks to John Murray Forbes, Bob had gone in December to Burlington, Iowa, to work on the railroad, but after a few months he wrote his parents proposing to come home and study architecture.

Wilky had just returned to his Florida venture of attempting to create successful plantations with newly freed blacks. Somewhere between twenty and fifty thousand northerners tried their hands at planting in the South just after the war. Only 5 percent of them were farmers, and Wilky was not one of them. Between 1866 and 1869 Wilky bought forty thousand dollars' worth of land in Gordon, Florida, about ten miles north of Gainesville in Alachua County. Most of this money came from Henry James Sr., though Aunt Kate and, at first, Forbes, invested as well. It was the biggest single investment the elder Henry James ever made. In May the family moved to a rented house in Swampscott, Massachusetts, a seaside town north of Boston.

William's closest friendship now was with Wendell Holmes, son of the Dr. Oliver Wendell Holmes with whom William was studying at the medical school. He and Wendell had become friends after Wendell was mustered out of the Union army in July 1864. Though the war was not over, Wendell had served his three years. William's trip to Brazil intervened, and then, when James returned to Boston in early 1866 the friendship deepened. Holmes was ten months older than James. He had gone to Harvard College, graduating in 1861, despite being fined twice as a freshman for defacing the rooms of faculty members, docked sixty-five points as a senior for "repeated and gross indecorum in the recitation of Professor Bowen," and fined and publicly admonished, also when he was a senior, for breaking windows in a freshman's room.

This undergraduate troublemaker had also discovered Emerson, whom he called a "firebrand," and he always, in later days, credited Emerson's writings with providing the spark that "started a flame in him." From Emerson's *Representative Men* the seventeen-year-old Holmes discovered

Plato, read up on him, then wrote an essay about him. Young Holmes had not been entirely satisfied with Plato; he found his logic faulty, his classification of ideas "loose and unscientific." He showed the essay to Emerson, who returned it saying, "I have read your piece. When you strike at a king you must kill him." To Holmes's considerable credit, he told this story on himself in later years with relish and admiration for Emerson's sally.[7]

Holmes was over six feet tall, slender, lanky, and clean-shaven. Coming home one day in late July 1861 from the Boston Athenaeum with Hobbes's *Leviathan* under his arm, he ran into an acquaintance who told him his first lieutenant's commission with the 20th Massachusetts Volunteer Infantry Regiment had come through. Holmes returned the book to the library unread. During the war he was wounded three times: in the chest at Ball's Bluff, in the neck at Antietam, and in the foot at Fredericksburg. He had a grimly realistic view of war. He was not at all sure the Union could win, and he was highly critical of what he took to be his father's too sudden conversion from anti-abolitionist to northern jingoist. In war, the younger Holmes wrote, much later, "you come down to Truth." He had felt, he said, when he heard the sabers jingle and the "command of the bugle," that he had "touched the blue steel edge of actuality for half an hour."[8]

Wendell's struggle with his father was sharper and much longer-lived than William's with his. Wendell continued to dislike his father after his father's death. The older Holmes once asked the older James — they belonged to some of the same Boston clubs — if his sons despised him. Being told no, Holmes unheedingly went on to outline his theory that "each generation strangles and devours its predecessor." We learn with no surprise that one of Wendell's favorite plays was Aeschylus's *Prometheus Bound,* in which the hero is chained to a rock by a vengeful and fatherly Zeus. When Wendell came back from the war, as he told Harold Laski many years later, "my father asked me what I was going to do and I told him I was going to Harvard Law School." "Pooh," the older Holmes is supposed to have said. "What's the use of going to the Harvard Law School? A lawyer cannot be a great man."[9]

The older Holmes — poet, novelist, wit, doctor (discoverer of the means of transmission of puerperal fever), teacher, editor, and inventor of the hand-held stereopticon — was the most photographed man in America at midcentury. He stood five feet three. After having dinner at the Holmeses' one evening, William James declared there was no love lost between father and son. If the older Holmes was contemptuous of the law, the younger Holmes thought his father had squandered his talents and failed to concentrate his energies to make one lasting contribution. The older Holmes published a piece in the *Atlantic Monthly* called "My Search for the Captain," which quickly became famous. It was about searching for his wounded son during the Civil War. Wendell was embarrassed by the piece; the war was a sore subject between them. Wendell was capable of an angry and scornful tone toward his father, who he thought underestimated the unity and determination of the South. "I think you are hopeful" about the North's winning the war, he wrote home, "because (excuse me) you are ignorant."[10]

By late March 1866, James was writing Tom Ward that "the only fellow here I care anything about is Holmes, who is on the whole a first rate article, and one which improves by wear." They were a somewhat unlikely pair, the robust, romantic war hero and the thin, sickly medical student. Holmes's personality was cool, detached, and self-contained. James's was warm, impulsive, and outgoing. He was a giver; Holmes was not. But they shared a consuming interest in ideas. Holmes knew almost nothing about biology or chemistry, but he had read Darwin and was sympathetic to positive science. He liked drawing and had read a lot of Ruskin. He was vaguely interested in medicine but enormously interested in philosophy.

William and Wendell saw each other often and argued everything out. One day Holmes got off on materialism, which he was against and which he seems to have accused William of favoring. James's response came to him only after they had parted for the day, so James wrote out what he had to say and mailed it. They both agreed that humans are biologically determined, and one can see in the following bit, addressed by James to Holmes, the critical temper, the eagerness to unmask, they also shared at this time. "If the end of all," James wrote, "is to be told that we must take our sensations as simply given, or as preserved by natural selection for us, and interpret this rich and delicate overgrowth of ideas, moral, artistic, religious, and social, as a mere mask, a tissue spun in happy hours by creative individuals and adopted by other men in the interests of their sensations — how long is it going to be well for us not to 'let on' all we know to the public?"[11]

In a note to Holmes just before a pending trip, James wrote to the man he was now calling Wendyboy, "I will go in [to Boston] tomorrow night and we will evolve cosmos out of chaos for positively the last time." It is just a phrase, of course, like Holmes's referring to their talks as "twisting the tail of the cosmos"; it has a little biblical echo, but it is also a neat summary of what modern statistics and modern science were now doing in their excited pursuit of the idea, as Charles Sanders Peirce would formulate it, that "chance begets order," that "chance was no enemy of science but its tool." We may smile at these young men and their overheated discussions, but they already had their hands on some of the intellectual levers of the age, and they felt their own power growing within them.[12]

William James's working philosophy this summer of 1866, his actual beliefs (taking "belief" to mean what Alexander Bain said it meant, "that upon which a man is prepared to act"), was still that of the classical Stoicism of Marcus Aurelius. During June James was reading George Long's translation of the *Meditations*. He read it slowly and carefully, at the rate of two or three pages a day, and he wrote to his old Brazilian friend Tom Ward about it. He had been "in a pretty unsettled theoretical condition," he told Ward, increasingly aware that "every man's life . . . is a line that continuously oscillates on every side of its direction." Ward was in similar straits. James offered his newly compact Stoicism as advice to Ward. As William's brothers were all too aware, William was perfectly comfortable giving advice, whether asked for or not. "Much of your uneasiness comes from . . . your regarding each oscillation as something final," James told Ward. "I think we ought to be independent of our moods, look upon them as external for they come to us unbidden, and feel if possible neither elated or depressed, but keep our eyes upon our work, and if we have done the best we could in that given condition, be satisfied."[13]

Marcus Aurelius "certainly had an invincible soul," he went on, "and it seems to me that any man who can, like him, grasp the love of a 'life according to nature' ie a life in which your individual will becomes so harmonized to nature's will as cheerfully to acquiesce in whatever she assigns to you, knowing that you serve some purpose in her vast machinery which will never be revealed to you, any man who can do this will, I say, be a pleasing spectacle, no matter what his lot in life." His plan now, he wrote Ward, was to drive his "physicking trade like any other tenth-rate man" and live "my free life in my leisure hours entirely within my own breast as a thing the world has nothing to do with."[14]

It sounds hollow as well as bitter. It sounded hollow to James as he wrote it — he apologized to Ward for his "conceited irrelevance" and his "crudities." Then in November he and his Stoic equilibrium plunged like a high-wire artist who has missed his footing. The cause was William's loss of direction, which in turn has to be seen against a screen of family trouble. The six months in Swampscott had pleased no one, and the family had moved into a rented house at 20 Quincy Street in Cambridge, across the street from the college.

Life there, said Harry, was "about as lively as an inner sepulcher." All of William's siblings were struggling. Wilky was spending huge sums of money in Florida on the farming venture. Bob was in Florida, in Boston, and out west, unable to make up his mind on one place or one course of action. Harry, suffering from his bad back and from constipation, tried ice as well as massage. Then, in early November, Alice, who was just eighteen, had a terrifying collapse. As she looked back on it, she said this was when "I broke down first, acutely, and had violent turns of hysteria." The experience, in some ways similar to her father's vastation, was similarly shattering, and Alice went off to New York, where for six months she underwent Dr. Charles F. Taylor's "movement" cure.[15]

Meanwhile William, who was already having trouble with his eyes, his digestion, and sleeplessness, had been working as acting house surgeon at Massachusetts General Hospital during August and September. Medicine was proving, like Brazil, a professional dead end. Since he no longer wanted to become a field naturalist, his main motive for studying medicine was now gone. It should not then be a surprise that somewhere around the middle of November 1866, "almost without perceptible exciting cause, during a dissecting session," William's own back went out. It was apparently a sudden episode of acute low-back pain with muscle spasm, an incapacitating injury often today associated with overexertion, strain, trauma, or stress. For James it was a physical correlative of the breakdown of his career plans. "Medicine is busted," he told a friend.[16]

Barely able to walk or work, he fell into a deep depression. He said nothing in his letters to Alice, Bob, and Wilky, but his condition could not be concealed from those at home: Mother, Father, and Harry. William soldiered on somehow at the medical school, but even while going through the motions of applying in December for a hospital position, he was already thinking of escaping to Europe. He kept his impending trip a secret from all but Harry, Mother, Father, and Holmes until about two weeks before his departure. When he did tell Alice, he reassured her that he would stop and see her in New York before he sailed.

It was a miserable and broken-down young man of twenty-five who sailed from New York for Brest, ostensibly to continue his studies, as he told Emerson when requesting a letter of introduction, but in reality to "fly from a home which had become loathsome," as he later confessed to Tom Ward. Loathsome is a strong word, but even that only hints at the depth of William's despair this spring.[17]

11. *We Must Be Our Own Providence*

WILLIAM EMBARKED ON April 17, 1867, on the *Great Eastern*, bound from New York to Brest. The steamer, nicknamed "the great iron ship," was at the time, and for the next forty-five years, the largest ship afloat. It was twice as long and four times as heavy as most ships of that era. Launched in 1858, this huge vessel had three separate means of propulsion. One set of engines turned side paddlewheels, another set turned an enormous four-bladed propeller, and if need be, the crew could set an acre and a half of sail on the ship's six masts. It had not been designed for the North Atlantic trade, where it was now in service. It was proving to be a great iron failure. It had, just now, few passengers, no cargo, and it rolled abominably. James was, miraculously, not seasick, and he noted with some pride that he had kept his place in the dining room, though the other tables were "pretty empty for three or four days."[1]

James quickly made his way to Paris, where he was to deliver some of Agassiz's Brazilian fish specimens to the Jardin des Plantes. In Paris he was overwhelmed by "the strange and old sights and sounds and smells," and he felt "there is at first something terrible about this city." He soon proceeded to Dresden, where there was a colony of Americans and where it would have been easy for him to make connections. In his current state of mind he was unhappy and displeased wherever he was, and he seems to have felt pleasure or hope only when he looked backward or forward. So not until he reached Dresden could he praise "the immensity and magnificence of Paris." Dresden he found utterly devoid of the romantic or the picturesque. It was hardly even foreign, he said; going there was like going to Chicago.[2]

In Dresden James lived with the scholar Christian Semler, an "open hearted excellent man," and his wife, "a sickly miserly petty-spirited nonentity." He wrote long, newsy, detailed letters to Boston. We have, therefore, a richly documented account of a remarkably quiet half year. His physician, a Dr. Carus, recommended repose. James described his daily routine in a letter home: "Read all the morning, go out for a walk and a lounge in a concert garden in the afternoon, and read after tea." For mental repose Dr. Carus prescribed French novels. James read Le Sage's *Gil Blas*, Erckmann and Chatrian's *L'Ami Fritz* and *Le Jouer de Clarinette*. He wrote and sent home a review of Herman Grimm's novel *Unueberwindliche*

Mächte (*Unconquerable Power*). He wrote home — deceptively — that his back was better, he eyed the young ladies at the windows of the boarding school opposite, he worked on his German, and he told charming stories. Five-year-old Anna Semler dropped a book one day and exclaimed, "Herr Je-sus." The shocked Frau Semler said to her, "Ach! Das sagen Kinder nicht, Anna!" ("Children don't say that!") To which the chastened Anna said to herself, sotto voce, "Nicht für Kinder."[3]

William ignored his doctor's orders long enough to read Hegel and Goethe. He read Hegel's chapter on epic poetry in the *Lectures on Aesthetics* and told his mother and father, "The truly monstrous sentences therein were quite a revelation to me." He liked Goethe's *Italienische Reise* (*Italian Journey*) better, especially the early chapters, in which Goethe — like James now — was outward bound. Goethe's great flash of insight in the gardens of Palermo was his realization that all the parts of the plant are discernible in the leaf and that there must be one archetypal leaf and one archetypal plant from which all plants derived.

James had experienced no such moment of insight. He could not feel, as the homeward-bound Goethe had felt, that he had "attained to the possession of some substantial knowledge, which gives him a permanent character from which he is ready to fight." What spoke to James in his present condition was the first part of Goethe's book, in which "he was all receptive — what he had was nothing — what he was in the act of getting, everything."[4]

In August William went to Teplitz, in Bohemia (now in the western part of the Czech Republic), because his doctor wanted him to try the baths there. They were supposed, James wrote, to be "a sovereign remedy for rheumatism, neuralgia, gout, old wounds, and all sorts of old stiffnesses such as mine." He writes his sister, "I have been greatly reinvigorated by my stay here and consider myself a well man." He had, he said, twice "walked 3 miles or more without any sensation in my back, so I conclude I am, if I continue prudent, safely out of the woods."[5]

But these hopeful statements do not tell the real story. In a letter to his father dated September 5, 1867, and marked "Private," he revealed his true situation. "The state of my back ever since I have been here has been very much worse than before I left home." He conceded that the baths at Teplitz had finally improved his back, but he told his father he was also suffering from "a chronic gastritis of frightful virulence and obstinacy." He added that he had severe dyspepsia, that he had been confined to his room, had been in a "half-starved and weak condition . . . making me irritable and tremulous in a way I have never before experienced." Just a few months earlier he had been secretive and reticent about his ailments, enjoying what Marilynne Robinson calls "the poor, imperfect, deeply welcome comforts of evasion and concealment." Now, at the other extreme, and with some small evidence of improvement in hand, he reveled in pouring it all out, though from a safe distance. Describing his condition to his father, he said, with self-pitying melodrama, "Thoughts of the pistol, the dagger and the bowl began to usurp an unduly large part of my attention," and he insisted that when he first tried the baths, out of desperation, they only made both back and stomach worse.[6]

By insisting on his sick and desperate condition, and by talking, even jokingly, about suicide, James was doing more than just reporting. He was either playing for sympathy or trying to jolt his father into seeing this depression for what it was. Even if it was not what would now be called full clinical depression, the episode was nearly overwhelming. It was nine months later when he finally admitted to his friend Tom Ward that he had spent the previous winter "on the continual verge of suicide."[7] His depression and suicidal thoughts may well have been literarily amplified by his interest in Hamlet and young Werther, but they were real enough, and they seem to have been linked not only to his struggle to find a career — something to *do* with himself — but also to his continuing struggle with his father.

In the second half of William's extraordinary letter home he returned to his long engagement with his father's ideas. William's own views were now, and had been for some time, almost diametrically opposed to those of Henry Senior. Father believed that just the spiritual was real; he had so little use for what he thought of as "low information" that he would not read his friend Wilkinson's biography of Swedenborg, believing as he did that a narrative can be valuable only when read symbolically. William believed that the natural and the physical were what was real. Father had a private language in which he defined words such as "moralism" to mean what he said they meant, no more, no less. William was trying to master the accepted languages and methods of science and philosophy and was already interested in expressing things in terms that could be understood by others. Father was convinced that "the one great evil in the universe [is] the principle of self-hood, the principle of independence in man." William would build his psychology, his philosophy, and his understanding of religion on the exact principles Father rejected. Father so despised "the subjective element in us, the personal element," that he thought we needed to "defecate ourselves of private or subjective ambitions" because "the subjective element (the me) is a purely phenomenal or waste element in consciousness." (This is typical Henry Senior. He could hardly open his mouth without sounding like a waiter falling down stairs with a tray full of dishes. He denigrated individualism with a scatological intensity that just calls renewed attention to his own individual — and outrageous — self.) William would build everything on the opposite assumption, that all consciousness to which we have access is personal and subjective. Father was an unqualified monist, believing that "God is the only being in the universe." William took the opposite line, the pluralist line, that every single separate thing in the universe is alive and valuable.[8]

Professionally defeated by the Amazon expedition and, increasingly, by medical school, William turned, in the autumn of his twenty-fifth year, to a serious reconsideration of his father's writings and, at the same time, of his father himself. It was a tangle: even while complaining to Father about "the darkness which to me has always hung over what you have written," he could end a letter, "Good night, my dear old Daddy." He could also say to him, "You live in such mental isolation that I cannot help often feeling bitterly at the thought that you must see in even your own children strangers to what you consider the best part of yourself."[9]

It has been observed that of Henry's five children William alone made a serious and sustained effort to come to terms with their father intellectually.[10] William's turn, this fall of 1867, to reading and arguing by mail with his father may have something to do with Charles Peirce's lectures on the logic of science, which William had attended in Cambridge back in October and November 1866. In one of those lectures, given a month or so before William's back trouble, Peirce had mentioned Henry James Sr. along with Jonathan Edwards and Ralph Waldo Emerson as among New England's "philosophers of genius." William may not have understood or accepted his father's views, just as he would concede jauntily that he had not understood a word of Peirce's lectures on logic; but he admired Charles Peirce, who was more or less his own age — and Peirce did understand and accept Father's ideas. At the very least, Father's ideas could no longer be simply ignored or dismissed with a smile.

Now, in 1867, William squared up to an affectionate but urgent confrontation. Father's *Substance and Shadow* and a number of articles and letters to the editor concerned what Henry Senior called "the physics of creation," and this is what William was trying, without success, to understand. Darwin had given the subject of the methods of creation a whole new life and importance, with a concreteness and a vocabulary that had excited William but was completely opaque to his father. William and his father wrote back and forth all fall. After William had objected to his father's isolation, to his logic, and to his use of language, and with due admission that his own position might appear to his parent "most pitiful and bald," he came at last to the point. He could not, he said, "attain to any such inexpugnable testimony of consciousness to my spiritual reality" as his father spoke of, and his own position was to reject the "spiritual" and the "divine." "Practically," he wrote, "it seems to me that all tendencies must now a days unite in Philanthropy: perhaps an atheistic tendency more than any, for sympathy is now so much developed in the human breast, that misery and undeveloped-ness would all the more powerfully call for correction when coupled with the thought, that from nowhere else than from us could correction possibly come, that we ourselves must be our own providence."[11]

12. A Dead and Drifting Life

IN SEPTEMBER 1867, at the same time that he was squaring off philosophically with his father, William shifted his German perch from Dresden to Berlin. He took rooms with his old friend Tom Perry, he worked on his German, and he met the philosopher Wilhelm Dilthey, who was then writing a life of Friedrich Schleiermacher (1768–1834), whose work strongly prefigured that of James himself. (This meant so little to James at the time that he couldn't remember Dilthey's name when he wrote home about him.) His letters insist that he was drifting and loafing, but by the end of October he was at least behaving like a man with a purpose, attending a heavy schedule of lectures in physiology at the University of Berlin.

William's year and a half in Germany, from April 1867 to November 1868, is complicated and difficult to keep in focus, partly because William was an increasingly complicated person. He wrote later that a person "has as many social selves as there are individuals who recognize him and carry an image of him in their mind." One self was the quick-witted and high-spirited brother and son, full of bounce and sass, who wrote "conversash" for "conversation," "orflings" for "orphans," "Bosting" for "Boston," who called his father's new book "Substance and Shadder," called Potsdam "Potsd—m," who said "suspish" for "suspicion," "condish" for "condition," who could call an acquaintance "the very Poetry of general imbecility," and would observe that "Spring is whanging through the fertile country of Bohemia in fine style."

But living in the same skin at the same time was a sickly young man with a dark, self-absorbed, despondent streak. After he told Tom Ward that medicine was out for him, "much to my sorrow," he added, "The future is very uncertain." He complained about the "gloomy dripping November day[s]," about his lack of education, about his lack of money, about his endless reading leading "to nothing at all." "I shall hate myself," he wrote, "till I get some special work." He complained about being in the "dismallest of dumps," about "living down this foreignness," about the "accursed thing in my back." His mood, which had been low when he left home, drifted further downward while he was in Germany. By March 1868 he felt he was in a "permanent depression."[1]

Behind the cheerful banter lay illness and despondency and complaint; behind or beneath that there was yet another, a third self — or at least there was something else going on. For all his protestations about his lack of direction, his drifting and empty life, and his inability to study, he was nursing a plan for the future, and he was doing it with a surprising clarity and steadiness. Medicine — meaning the practice of medicine — may have been out, as he told Ward in September 1867, but he had set his sights on the related fields of physiology and psychology, not with the idea of practicing, but more with an eye to the study and perhaps the teaching of those fields. To Ward he wrote, "I am going to try to stick to the study of the nervous system and psychology."[2]

Physiology is the study of how the body actually works. It is not concerned primarily with taxonomy or surgery or pharmacology as such. It is the science that studies the physical processes of living. For the old-school medical professors of the late 1860s physiology was an unwelcome intruder into the curriculum, a science that deflected student interest and energy from the healing arts. But physiology was the entering wedge of the movement that would soon remake the study of medicine entirely. After about 1900 biology would become the catchall word for the life sciences; before 1900 the general word was physiology.[3]

James's interest in physiology did not begin with this trip to Germany; his American medical school notebook for 1866–67 is dominated by physiological details, processes, and hypotheses. But by November 1867 he was doing little else. He told Ward he was attending five courses by three physiologists in Berlin. He was going to eleven lectures a week.[4] He wrote that he was blocking out "some reading in physiology and psychology which I hope to execute this winter." Starting in November, then, James's focus was increasingly on the field of psychology, which was just being reborn as a hard science, grounded firmly in physiology. "It seems to me," he wrote Ward, "that perhaps the time has come for Psychology to begin to be a science — some measurements have already been made in the region lying between the physical changes in the nerves and the appearance of consciousness — (in the shape of sense perceptions) and more may come of it."[5]

In late December James confirmed all this in a letter to his father. Though he was careful to hedge and protest ("ultimate prospects . . . pretty hazy . . . health . . . so uncertain"), he nevertheless declared, boldly enough, "As a central point of study I imagine that the border ground of physiology and psychology, overlapping both, would be as fruitful as any, and I am now working on to it."[6]

By his mid-twenties William James already had a remarkable capacity to convert misery and unhappiness into intellectual and emotional openness and growth. It is almost as though trouble was for him a precondition for insight, and accepting trouble was the first step in overcoming it. In January 1868, as his twenty-sixth birthday rolled past and he did his annual stocktaking, he wrote Holmes that he was in the dismalest of dumps, unable to understand "how it is I am able to take so little interest in reading this winter." He could not have known that it would be a little over two years before he really hit bottom. But as he was complaining about not reading, and about his back, and his loneliness, and the "inhuman blackness of the weather," and about the fact that all the brothers except him were now working productively, he was, at the same time, becoming fluent in German, reading — apparently with huge enjoyment — a great deal of poetry, and launching again into the writing of reviews and soliciting editorial help with them from Harry.[7]

James once noted that Darwin gave up reading poetry for years and then, finding it impossible to pick it up again, wished that he had not let it go. James himself read poetry — actively read poetry — all his life. Now he found Shakespeare's twenty-ninth sonnet, "When in disgrace with fortune and men's eyes," speaking to him. He told Ward to look at the closing lines of Emerson's "Give All to Love" and Christopher Cranch's "Stanzas" ("Thought is deeper than all speech / Feeling deeper than all thought") and recommended particularly Robert Browning's "A Grammarian's Funeral." "It always strengthens my backbone to read it," he wrote. He admired the poem's advice to just do your work, day by routine day, and leave to posterity or eternity the troublesome task of justifying or recognizing the work.

This was helpful to a young man who wanted to write but found writing difficult and uncongenial. Plunging in, he wrote a review of Ernest Aimé Feydeau's *La Comtesse de Chalis, ou Les Moeurs du Jour* and sent it to Harry, requesting him to "take care of" it and "smooth if possible the style." Writing the review at all was a positive step; sending it to Harry, who was now successfully writing and selling reviews and stories, must have cost William something in pride, acknowledging as it did that he had something to learn from his younger brother. The review itself is an ill-tempered tirade. "As a work of edification," James sniffed, "we consider [the book] a total failure. Viewed as a work of art it is not much better." Harry did an excellent, if radical, job of editing, cutting away most of Willy's long diatribe against French culture. Later in the month William sent another review, this one of Quatrefages's anthropology text, to Harry with a similar request for whatever editing might be needed.[8]

The exact process by which James turned trouble into insight and self-loathing into energy is pretty well hidden. In March, as he was admitting to a "permanent depression," catching the flu, and groaning about "one of the emptiest years of my life," he sent Harry a letter of backhanded thanks for his editing. He complained that his authorial pride, his "schrift-stellerisches selbtsgefuhl," was "naturally rather mangled by the mutilations you had inflicted on my keen article on Feydeau," and went on to comment on some of Harry's recently published stories with retaliatory relish. William had praised an earlier story, "Poor Richard," as "good much beyond my expectations; story, character and way of telling excellent in fact." But now he said, at length and behind a disingenuous cover ("I suppose you want to hear in an unvarnished manner . . ."), that "the material of your stories (except 'Poor Richard') has been thin," that the treatment was "rather dainty and disdainful," that the stories had a "want of blood," and he advised him, preposterously, "to select some particular problem, literary or historical to study on . . . then you could write stories by the way for pleasure and profit." There was in William some of his father's willingness to let fly, to unload snap judgments; at the same time he backpedaled a bit, admitting his taste to be "rather incompetent in these matters." In a later letter he apologized for his "law-giving tone," and went on, "I hope it did not hurt you in any way or mislead you as to the opinion I have of you as a whole, for I feel as if you were one of the 2 or 3 sole intellectual and moral companions I have."

He had been, of course, prescribing for himself. One way William responded to depression was to get angry — at himself, at the French, at Harry's style. Another way was to work. There was a certain resiliency deep inside him; no matter how overwhelming his circumstances, a hidden spring would free some Queequeg's coffin, which would pop to the surface and save him, at least temporarily.[9]

While feeling down this spring, he read Darwin's *Variation of Animals and Plants Under Domestication* and wrote a review of it. In this book, Darwin returned to the subject with which *On the Origin of Species* begins. The enormous changes that can be wrought in a short time by selective breeding — making the ears of cocker spaniels longer and longer by choosing and mating those with the longest ears in each litter, for example — prove that variation is possible, that selection can take place, and that a species of animal can change. The *Origin* had then moved on to the subject of natural, as opposed to artificial — that is, human — selection. In revisiting the question of variation under domestication, Darwin was focusing on the nature and limits of inheritance. William observed in his notice for the *North American Review* that Darwin "comes to the conclusion that every character of the parent, whether new or old, tends to be reproduced in the offspring either in a patent or a latent form." James was so interested in this book that he wrote a second review, and while he said in both notices that the general reader would probably prefer *On the Origin of Species,* he came back again to the same points about inheritance he discussed in the first review. He credited Darwin with discovering the "curious law" that "when two individuals which have diverged from a common parent stock are mated, there is a tendency in their offspring to take on features of that stock that may have been absent for great numbers of generations."

Inheritance was a live subject in the James family. If William ever glanced back at his own family, at his father's siblings and their children, at the illnesses, intemperance, instability, and early deaths of so many uncles, aunts, and cousins, to say nothing of the debilitating conditions that afflicted himself, Harry, and Alice, he could hardly have forgotten his own discovery, via Darwin, that in crossbreeding "itself we have a direct cause of reversion to a character long extinct."[10]

James's talk of depression was replaced in April and May by talk of being totally demoralized, yet April and May of 1868 were months of intellectual and emotional vitality for him, and he registered solid gains. He went back to Teplitz for the baths, then again to Dresden. Lacking the structure the physiology lectures had given his life in Berlin, he started a diary at the beginning of April. He stepped up his reading, and in letters and diary he began to write with a newly energetic feeling of intellectual engagement. He looked at paintings (by José Ribera, Guido Reni, Rubens, and Bellini), he visited a museum full of plaster casts of Greek sculpture, he studied Homer, and in early April he wrote Harry an extraordinary letter about it all.

His point of entry into Homer was his own Brazilian voyage. "My South American indians keep rising before me now as I read the O[dyssey]," he wrote, "just as the Iliad rose before me as I went with the Indians." The subject with Father had been creation; now the subject with Harry was evil. William suddenly found himself open to a whole new view of the world, a view that constellated for him around the question of evil. He admired "the health! the brightness, and the freshness!" of the Greeks, and marveled at the "total absence of almost all that we consider peculiarly valuable in ourselves." What most struck him was "the cool acceptance by the bloody old heathens of everything that happened around them, their indifference to evil in the abstract, their want of what we call sympathy, the essentially definite character of their joys, or at any rate of their sorrows (for their joy was perhaps coextensive with life itself)." What James was finding and working out for himself was that the Greeks simply didn't have the sense of the world as pervaded by evil that, say, Father had. "The Homeric Greeks 'accepted the universe,' their only notion of evil was its [the universe's] perishability — we say the world in its very existence is evil — they say the only evil is that everything in it in turn ceases to exist."

William's excited letter to Harry circles again and again to the same point in different ways. "To the Greek a thing was evil only transiently and accidentally and with respect to those particular unfortunates whose bad luck happened to bring them under it." In other words, evil was not a deliberate and inevitable condition of life, willed or sanctioned by an all-powerful and inscrutable force or deity. "Bystanders could remain careless and untouched — no after brooding, no disinterested hatred of it in se, and questioning of its right to darken the world, such as now prevail . . . Are you free? — exult! Are you fettered or have you lost anything? — Lament your impediment or your loss and that alone." This is not a Pollyanna move: to deny evil is not to deny suffering; all it does is remove the comfort — or the utter horror — of there being a cosmic or providential reason for the suffering.

Liberating himself from the concept of evil paradoxically permitted James to accept all the more fully the present reality of sadness and suffering. It is itself "ultimate," he said. And he added, "There is no 'reason' behind it, as our modern consciousness restlessly insists." What the Greeks gave James was one of the great acceptances that enabled him, both now and later, to embrace, to deal with, to get past trouble, though not without a certain cost. He summed it up for Harry: "This sad heroic acceptance (sans arrière pensée) of death seems to me the great tragic wind that blows through the Iliad, and comes out especially strong in Achilles."[11]

One such moment of insight would suffice many people for a month or a year, but James's intellectual and emotional openness, which was in some ways helped, not blocked, by his physical vulnerability, gave him one good moment after another during April and May this year. He went to see a performance of *Hamlet*. He was familiar with the play but had never felt the power of it before, "the endless fulness of it — how it bursts and cracks at every seam." He responded particularly to the darkly brooding, romantically introspective, and emotionally brimming figure of Hamlet while at the same time recognizing how completely different Hamlet is, as a type, from Achilles.[12]

Yet a week after his conversion to the Homeric worldview of action, acceptance, and bright, clear expression, James could voice an equally convincing description — if not quite acceptance — of the opposite point of view. "Hamlet," he wrote in his diary, "is about as big an example as can be found of the Germanic way I spoke about here last night" — he had written then of a spirit of "unquenchable longing" — "the fulness of an emotion becomes so superior to any possible words, that the attempt to express it adequately is abandoned, and its vastness indicated by the slipping aside into some fancy, or counter sense — so does action of any sort seem to Hamlet inadequate and irrelevant to his feeling."[13]

"Despair lames most people, but it wakes others fully up," James would write in his lecture "The Energies of Men." James himself was one of the latter. His seemingly contradictory but actually fruitful combination of physical discouragement and mental excitement continued into April and May, and he seems to have been aware of his own complex condition. In April he went for the third time to the baths at Teplitz and wrote in his diary that he was "in a queer state of weakheadedness from bathing and a sort of inward serenity and joy derived from reading Goethe and Schiller." He was particularly struck by Schiller's famous essay "Naive and Sentimental Poetry," and he reformulated Schiller's distinction for himself in his diary: "In the first, harmony is given us immediately, the poet is Nature; in the second the harmony is a reflection, the poet seeks a nature which is lost."[14]

He read a great deal of Goethe, including the *Roman Elegies, Wilhelm Meister's Apprenticeship,* Eckermann's *Conversations with Goethe,* the

Goethe-Schiller correspondence, *Hermann und Dorothea, Wahrheit und Dichtung, Egmont,* and more, and he told Tom Ward that he was "just beginning to break through the skin of Goethe's personality and to grasp it as a unity." He was unable to summarize or pinpoint it; what he kept coming back to was not this or that idea but his sense of Goethe's point of view. "The man lived at every pore of his skin, and the tranquil clearness and vividness with which every thing printed itself on his sensorium, and found a cool nook in his mind without interfering with any of the other denizens thereof, must have been one of the most exquisite spectacles ever on exhibition on this planet." What he was learning from Goethe, he wrote Ward, was respect for the world outside himself. He thought Goethe "had a deep belief in the reality of Nature as she lies developed and a contempt for bodiless formulas. Through every individual fact he came in contact with the world, and he strove and fought without ceasing ever to lay his mind more and more wide open to Nature's teaching." Goethe's natural gifts could not be communicated, James knew, but his enthusiasm could, and James rated that enthusiasm as "one of the important experiences of my own mind."[15]

Goethe had many gifts for this particular young American. There was the figure of Faust, who, confronting the problem of creation and the problem of one's personal starting point, turns to the opening of the Gospel according to John: "In the beginning was the word." Rejecting "word" because there must be a mind before there can be a word, Faust rewrites John: "In the beginning was the mind [*sinn*]." But now Faust rejects "mind" too, since there must be some force or energy or power that creates mind. "In the beginning was the power [*kraft*]." But power is nothing until it is exerted; as Emerson understood, "Power ceases in the moment of repose." So Faust comes at last, but not to rest, with "In the beginning was the act." The German word here is *tat*, the Greek, *pragma.*[16]

James responded most to Goethe's openness to life, and the result was that he was more open to life himself. Friendship mattered intensely to him. Isolated and lonely as he often felt, he wrote long letters to Ward, to Arthur Sedgwick, to Henry Bowditch, to Wendell Holmes, and, always, to Alice and Harry. "I have grown into the belief," he wrote Holmes, "that friendship (including the highest half of that which between the two sexes is united under the single name of love) is about the highest joy of earth and that a man's rank in the general scale is well indicated by his capacity for it."[17]

He longed for a practical focus. "Much would I give," he wrote the thoroughly focused Holmes in his new Germanic English, "for a constructive passion of some kind." On May 22 he had another of his now frequent turning points or crises. As he listened to the musical performance, the "magic playing," of a Miss Havens, "my feelings came to a sort of crisis. The intuition of something here in a measure absolute gave me such an unspeakable disgust for the dead drifting of my own life." He struggled to turn the moment to some use. "It ought to have a practical effect on my own will — a horror of waste life since life can be such." He yearned for "an end to the idle idiotic sinking into Vorstellungen [ideas, notions, images] disproportionate to the object."[18]

Though he despaired of ever being able to do laboratory work in physiology because of his back, he nevertheless pulled himself together and went to Heidelberg, where the great physiologists Hermann von Helmholtz and Wilhelm Wundt were laying the experimental, laboratory-based groundwork for the emerging science of physiological psychology. James left for Heidelberg on June 26, but the venture was a total failure. He simply funked it. He seems to have had no letters of introduction, no entrée to the homes or the classes of the great men. Overwhelmed, perhaps, by feelings of inadequacy or insignificance, he fled back to Berlin, where his mood of course darkened horribly. He felt himself sunk in "blue despair"; he tormented himself by asking how much money his younger brother Harry had made in the past year; he conducted a conversation with himself in his diary, in French, that begins, "Tu veux mourir, hein?" (So — you want to die?) Still, he concluded that even if all that was alive in him were fragments of a man, it was better to have fragments than nothing at all.[19]

He went back to reading novels; he listed George Sand's *Daniella,* her *Beaux Messieurs de Bois-Doré,* Wilkie Collins's *Woman in White,* Théophile Gautier's *Caprices et Zigzags,* and his *Capitaine Fracasse,* "one or two Balzacs, [and] a volume of tales by Mérimée." His back not improving, he tried blisters, which he recommended to Harry for his back.[20] "The application is uncomfortable but will pay. Blisters (strong) the size of a 50 cent piece. One every night on alternate sides of the spine. Empty bubble in morning. Dress with cloth covered with cerate" — a thick ointment made of wax or lard — "kept in place by straps of adhesive plaster. After each dozen blisters, omit a fortnight and recommence."[21] He continued to feel, as he told Henry Bowditch, that he was "tossing about Europe like a drowned pup about a pond in a storm." He also said, revealingly, to Bowditch, "I have talked with no one about scientific matters since leaving home."

He did not feel much like studying, but as he told his father, he managed "to keep something dribbling all the while." And in October he turned to confront a book he had been working himself up to for almost a year. He had read Johann Schultz's *Commentary on Kant's "Critique of Pure Reason"* in November 1867. In April 1868 he had read Victor Cousin on Kant. His friend Charles Peirce had read Kant years before, virtually committing the *Critique of Pure Reason* to memory when he was in college. Now even Wendell Holmes had read it. With all this preparation and with his new facility in German, James turned at last to the book itself, the mere reading of which felt like a triumph or a culmination. He wrote his father that Kant's book "strikes me so far as almost the sturdiest and honestest piece of work I ever saw. Whether right or wrong, (and it is pretty clearly wrong in a great many details of its Analytik part — however the rest may be) there it stands like a great snag or mark to which everything metaphysical or psychological must be referred. I wish I had read it earlier."[22] He also read a piece by Charles Renouvier, of whom he had not heard before, and was impressed by Renouvier's taking his stand on Kant and by his "vigor of style and compression."

James had been abroad for a little more than a year and a half, during much of which he had drifted, feeling in low spirits, albeit with a general intention to pursue the nascent field of physiological psychology. It takes time to turn a large ship around, but by November 1868 the ship seems indeed to have turned. Instead of drifting away from the career problem, James steered into it, bringing himself to return to America, to go back to medical school, and, for once, to finish something he had begun. He confirmed again to Tom Ward that "my only ideal of life is a scientific life," and on November 7, 1868, he left Europe on the *Ville de Paris,* bound home, through heavy gales, to Cambridge and to one last push toward his medical degree.

13. *Minnie Temple*

THE *VILLE DE PARIS* arrived in New York on November 18, 1868; James headed north. He wrote Henry Bowditch that he had six weeks in which to write his thesis if he wished to take the exam in March. He had decided to do it on the physiological effects of cold, and it was to take him nearly six months. The thesis almost certainly was suggested by the occasional improvements in his own condition that James experienced after therapeutic applications of ice or cold water on his back and by his new decision to pursue physiology. "The coldness of the water," he had written his father from Germany, "must be accommodated to the power of reaction of the subject, but if he can react the colder the better." The thesis, he told Bowditch — who was now in Europe — would "not contain any experiments or original suggestions. Time is too short and I only aim at squeezing through."[1]

He told people that he was unable or unsuited to do experimental work. He was maddeningly unspecific, but one gathers that the problem was partly the bad back, partly eye trouble, partly nerves, partly a general feeling of being "run down," and partly a temperamental impatience with laboratory routine. He consulted such published sources as E.N.J. Onimus's *De la Théorie Dynamique de la Chaleur dans les Sciences Biologiques*, L.J.D. Fleury's *Traite Pratique et Raisonné d'Hydrothérapie*, and Konrad Eckhard's *Experimental Physiologie des Nervensystems*. Somewhat to his surprise, he found himself enjoying reading for his thesis and for his exam, which he soon decided to put off until July.

He was, as usual, living, working, and thinking on many fronts. As January and his twenty-seventh birthday came around, he was reading new work that promised to treat even religion scientifically: Émile Burnouf's "Science of Religion," in *Revue des Deux Mondes*, and Étienne Vacherot's *La Religion*. He was having at least one good talk a week with Holmes now, and he was reading Charles Peirce's articles in the new *Journal of Speculative Philosophy*, which was the work of the St. Louis Hegelians and the first periodical in English to specialize in philosophy. Peirce, now thirty, had just published the papers that became known as his "Cognition Series" in the journal; they were "Questions Concerning Certain Faculties Claimed for Man," "Some Consequences of Four Incapacities," and "Grounds of Validity of the Laws of Logic." James told Bowditch that Peirce's articles were "exceedingly bold, subtle, and incomprehensible and I can't say that his vocal elucidations helped me a great deal to their understanding, but they nevertheless interest me strangely."[2]

Well they might; these papers are now recognized as "constituting the modern founding of semiotics, the general theory of signs."[3] Peirce would be recognized as early as 1877, by the English mathematician and philosopher W. K. Clifford, as "the greatest living logician, and the second man since Aristotle who has added to the subject something material, the other man being George Boole, author of *The Laws of Thought*."[4] Peirce's work was, and is, austere, rigorous, and laced with brilliance. It is clear that one part of James was strongly attracted to the Burnoufs and Peirces who were trying to understand everything in terms of science and mathematics, just as another part of him was engaged by those like Holmes, who would one day say, "The life of the law has not been logic, it has been experience."[5]

James was now also becoming reacquainted with the most spirited person he had ever known, Minnie Temple, who had turned twenty-three in December 1868, a few weeks after William's return from Germany. She was a first cousin; William James had an astounding thirty-six of them, nineteen on his father's side and seventeen on his mother's. Minnie's mother, Catharine James, was one of Henry Senior's sisters. Catharine had married Colonel Robert Emmet Temple; they had had six children, many of whom, including and especially Minnie, were in and out of the Jameses' home all through childhood. Minnie was orphaned at nine, a circumstance that made her seem much more interesting, said Harry, than his own conventionally supplied family.

Minnie had dark hair, large eyes, and a direct, unsettling gaze. She was pretty enough, but it was her animation, her wildness, and her avidity for life that made her irresistible. In one photograph, though her eyes are downcast, her face shows much feeling. Her hair has been cut close, and determination is evident in the line of her chin. In another photo, her eyes are open wide and she looks so restless and full of energy that it seems she can't sit still. She was in all things a free spirit. She was, William said later, "unique and without analogue in all my subsequent experience of people."

Harry observed that Minnie was "absolutely afraid of nothing she might come to by living with enough sincerity and enough wonder."[6] He also appreciated her "restlessness of spirit, the finest reckless impatience," and he much admired Minnie's rule of life, which was that the remote possibility of the best thing is better than the "clear certainty of the second best."[7] "I will write you as nice a letter as I can," she wrote John Gray, a young man a few years older than William James and later a well-known Boston lawyer, "but would much rather have a talk with you. As I can't have the best thing I am putting up with the second best, contrary to my pet theory."[8] She had, said Henry, "beyond any equally young creature I have known a sense for . . . play of life in others."[9] She loved gaiety and parties. "The whole world of old New York, that of the early dancing years, shimmers out for me from the least of her allusions," Harry wrote. And Minnie wrote John Gray, "We all went on a spree the other night, and stayed at the Everett House: from which, as a starting point, we poured ourselves in strong force upon Mrs. Gracie King's ball — a very grand affair, given for a very pretty Miss King, at Delmonico's. Our raid consisted of thirteen Emmets and a moderate supply of Temples and the ball was a great success."[10]

There was, in her freedom, a touch of old Albany, of Old Billy James, about her too, which made her such "a vivid exception to rules and precedents."[11] She craved above all things freedom of talk. "No one had ever seen a creature with such lightness of forms, a lightness all her own, so inconsequently grave at the core." She was eager to meet George Eliot, whose novels she loved. She could barely wait to hear what her friends had to say about Browning's new novel in verse, *The Ring and the Book*. Harry thought her "lovely unrest" more vivid than mere worldly success.[12]

Minnie Temple was the real-life prototype for Henry James's most interesting American girls, for Daisy Miller, Isabel Archer, and Milly Theale, and it was this provocative and irresistible Minnie — charged to the lips with life — who broke in upon William James's turbulent, unfixed, unsatisfied existence when he returned home from Germany. "Everyone was supposed, I believe, to be more or less in love with her," Harry wrote William some time later, adding that he, Harry, never was, though he admitted to William that he had "enjoyed pleasing her almost as much as if I had been."[13] Tom Perry kept a valentine poem Minnie had written to him. Holmes had been attracted to her; John Gray was deeply interested — so was William. As Harry said, they all were in love with her, more or less, and they all said so, more or less freely, later. As to whom *she* was in love with, rumor said Gray, Gray said Holmes, and Holmes — who was at the time the closest to William and in the best position to know — said it was William that Minnie had her eye on, and it was William who was in love with her.

In her letter to Gray of January 7, 1869, the letter in which she describes the ball at Delmonico's, Minnie pokes fun at the men of the moment in New York society as "a lot of feeble-minded boys," and she goes on to ask, by way of contrast, "Have you seen much of Willy James lately? That is a rare creature and one in whom my intellect (if you will pardon the misapplication of the term) takes more solid satisfaction than in almost anybody."[14]

Three weeks later, writing again to the good, steady Gray, the "almost" has disappeared. After giving Gray her health report (not good: the "old enemy" tubercular hemorrhages had reappeared; she had had seven big ones and several minor ones in the past week), she goes back to the subject of Willy: "I did not mean you to infer from my particularizing Willy James's intellect, that the rest of him was not to my liking. He is one of the very few people in the world that I love — 'and no mistake.' He has the largest heart as well as the largest head — and is thoroughly interesting to me — and he is generous and affectionate and full of sympathy."[15] This seems unambiguous; certainly it is free of irony or satire. But even more revealing are some of Minnie's shorter, less self-conscious bits. Writing again to Gray, she closes her letter by asking who, "by simply thinking out a religion" — she is referring here to Phillips Brooks — "has ever arrived at anything that did not leave one's heart empty? Do you ever see Willy James? Goodbye."

Willy was, it appears, a little slow to come around. We know that he *was* slow and that he *did* come around from a letter he wrote Harry later this year, in December 1869. A great deal of the record of the life and affections of Minnie Temple has disappeared. Many James family letters of this period are missing; a large number of pages were cut out of William's diary. Surviving documents must be approached with care, since, as Alfred Habegger reminds us, "interpretation has already been built into the documents the Jameses allowed to survive."[16]

William was a complicated, self-tormenting young man in his midtwenties, full of self-distrust and self-loathing, unable to accept himself, and therefore unlikely to be able to accept real affection or approval from another. When one combines these qualities with those mentioned by Minnie; when one remembers the quite real and — by William — fully appreciated problem of first-cousin romance; when one remembers his nervous ill health and her advanced tuberculosis; and when one remembers William's habitual exaggeration and self-denigration, it is all but impossible to be sure one is hearing his tone aright. His comment to Harry reads in full:

> What can I tell you of our common home? M. Temple was here for a week a fortnight since. She was delightful in all respects, and, although very thin, very cheerful. I am conscious of having done her a good deal of injustice for some years past, in nourishing a sort of unsympathetic hostility to her. She is after all a most honest little phenomenon, and there is a true respectability in the courage with which she keeps "true to her own instincts" — I mean it has a certain religious side with her. Moreover she is more devoid of "meanness," of anything petty in her character than any one I know, perhaps either male or female. *Je tiens à* [I insist on] telling you this, as I recollect last winter abusing her to you rather virulently. She sails this bright cold day for California. I trust the voyage won't be too hard upon her.[17]

This may not sound quite like the letter of a man in love, but it is. William had just seen an old and seemingly settled relationship transmute into something new. He had recognized a former blindness in himself, and he was standing on the threshold of a feeling that was stronger than cousinly affection. He was not in the habit of revealing his real feelings for a woman to his brother — or indeed to anybody except the woman involved. The wonder is not that his new feeling for Minnie was not more forcefully expressed, but that it was expressed at all.

Events curved cruelly now. Minnie's world was closing in on her. Hemorrhages were frequent. Doctors urged bed rest. Her longed-for European trip had never materialized, and the California trip William and she expected to be imminent was canceled at the last minute by the Emmet cousins Minnie was supposed to be going to visit.

In February 1869 Harry went abroad. At Oxford, as he stood within the precincts of Magdalen College, he wrote William that he "thought that the heart of me would crack with the fulness of satisfied desire."[18] This is the remark of a man in love. If William expressed too little, Henry expressed too much. Back in the American Cambridge, William read and admired D. F. Strauss's funeral oration for his brother Wilhelm. Wilhelm's life, Strauss said, illustrated two apparently opposite truths, the first of which was "that a man is nothing in the face of fate, that a breath of fate's power is enough to blow down, like a house of cards, the proudest towers of our projects and dreams." But Wilhelm's life also showed "that other, too often forgotten truth that, faced with a clear and serene spirit, and a straight, firm will, fate is at last impotent."[19]

William did not now possess a clear or serene spirit or a straight, firm will, but he knew what he wanted. His own life swirled on, parts of it muddied and obscured for us by excisions and mysteries, lost or burned letters and papers, and unrecoverable moments. In late March he told Tom Ward he had "had a little while ago an experience of life which woke up the spiritual monad within me as has not happened more than once or twice before in my life." What this experience may have been is anyone's guess. One guess is that it had everything to do with Minnie Temple.[20]

The term "spiritual monad" covers a lot of ground. It includes intense inner life, and it certainly doesn't exclude romance. It probably doesn't even exclude ghosts. This same month William published a review of a book on communicating with spirits, he read *The Ring and the Book* with great admiration, and he came to a sober and confining conclusion about nature. The book he reviewed was *Planchette, or The Despair of Science: Being a full account of modern spiritualism, its phenomena, and the various theories regarding it* . . . James thought the treatment of the subject "feeble"; he argued that "one narrative vouched for and minutely controlled" would be worth more than a hundred of the anecdotes and secondhand reports that filled the book. He objected to the overeager dismissal of the subject by eminent scientists, and he was equally critical of the overeager credulousness of the spiritualists. About the "phenomena" themselves he was noncommittal. "It is certain," he wrote, "that, if once admitted, they [the spirit phenomena] must make a great revolution in our conception of the physical universe."

This question would interest him off and on for the rest of his life. But he now thought those phenomena no different from any others. He refused to posit a supernatural. The spirit phenomena — he closed by saying — "would seem to have no more claim on the attention of each particular individual, than any of the special problems of organic chemistry, for instance, or of pathological anatomy." And no less a claim.[21]

James also kept up his general reading; he listed as read James Russell Lowell's *Under the Willows,* H. Steffans's *Was Ich Erlebte,* a French translation of Turgenev's *Fathers and Sons.* He found *The Ring and the Book* "magnificent." Browning had been a favorite of William's since Newport days; even his most complex work was easy reading for James. *The Ring and the Book,* a four-volume novel in verse, tells of the murder by Count Guido Franceschini of his seventeen-year-old wife, Pompilia. The plan of the book, anticipating Lawrence Durrell's *Alexandria Quartet* by ninety years, is to tell the same story from ten different points of view. There are ten dramatic monologues, each by a different person. The basic facts are not in dispute, but those facts add up to utterly different interpretations. Each new viewpoint both enlarges the reader's sympathetic horizon and diminishes his certainty about motive and meaning. As the tragic setting expands, the tragedy itself narrows and deepens. Perhaps James's reading, just six months earlier, of Wilkie Collins's *Woman in White,* another novel about a terrible mismatch, also told in a modern manner from multiple points of view, is significant here.

Minnie's relation to William James can itself be seen from many points of view, but the crucial ones are half obscured or simply excised. No letter from William to Minnie has been found, and only a few scraps of her letters to him survive. It was neither a match nor a mismatch exactly, but whatever it was, it was growing in intensity and swinging toward tragedy.

14. William James, M.D.

HARVARD ANNOUNCED the election of Charles W. Eliot as its president in March 1869. William wrote Harry that he knew more bad than good about Eliot, but he reserved judgment about the appointment. William's back was worse. Letters from Harry emphasized his own poor health, now centered in severe constipation, which Harry found painful and demoralizing to the point of panic and near despair.

Feeling at the mercy of his body, William was more than ever convinced of the mechanistic, deterministic view of life. "I'm swamped in an empirical philosophy," he wrote to Ward. "I feel that we are Nature through and through, that we are wholly conditioned, that not a wiggle of our will happens save as a result of physical laws." The only mitigation or offset of this view was James's feeling that, wholly conditioned as we are, we are still somehow "en rapport with reason." He really couldn't see his way through it. "It is not that we are all nature but [there is] some point which is reason," he went on; it is rather "that all is Nature and all is reason too. We shall see, damn it, we shall see."[1] He seemed to be getting nowhere. He felt once more (as he confessed a few months later) that the bottom had fallen out. Cambridge seemed no better than Germany.

At the time Eliot became president, despite the impressive number of first-rate minds in Cambridge, Harvard as an educational institution was moribund. Its best historian writes, "Harvard College was hidebound, the Harvard Law School senescent, the Medical School ineffective, the Lawrence Scientific School the resort of shirks and stragglers."[2] Enrollment was declining at Harvard, at Union College, and elsewhere; a smaller percentage of Americans was going to college than had gone in 1838. The fixed, mostly classical curriculum seemed increasingly irrelevant to the fast-moving country. Graduate education was almost nonexistent. The first American Ph.D. had been granted at Yale in 1861, and Yale had made the first serious steps toward a coherent scheme of graduate education with the establishment of its graduate department of philosophy and the arts, which offered advanced instruction in philology, philosophy, and pure science.[3] Nevertheless, there was in 1868–69 a total of thirteen resident graduate students enrolled in all fields in the entire Ivy League. The following year there were seven. Americans in search of a serious graduate education went to Germany. Three hundred went during the 1860s, a thousand during the 1870s.

Eliot issued fair warning that he intended to change things. He wrote a pair of articles for the *Atlantic Monthly* called "The New Education." He sympathized with modern parents who wanted a practical education to enable their sons to follow "business or any other active calling." He wanted to educate students for careers in "the workshops, factories, mines, forges, public works and counting rooms." Eliot expected little help from the older faculty. "To have been a schoolmaster or college professor thirty years only too often makes a man an unsafe witness in matters of education," Eliot said, and he used a railroad metaphor to explain: "There are flanges on his mental wheels which will only fit one gauge." The existing gauge, the classical schools and colleges, did not offer what was wanted.

The new scientific schools that had sprung up since the late 1840s (Sheffield Scientific School at Yale, Chandler Scientific School at Dartmouth, School of Mines at Columbia, Lawrence Scientific School at Harvard) were at least moving in the right direction, toward "a system of education based chiefly upon the pure and applied sciences, the living European languages and mathematics, instead of upon Greek, Latin, and mathematics, as in the established college system." But even the scientific schools had unacceptable limitations. The one at Harvard was only "a group of independent professorships, and each student was essentially just "the private pupil of some one of the professors, and the other professors are no more to him than if they did not exist." The range of study was, therefore, "inconceivably narrow," and one could take a B.S. degree "without a sound knowledge of any language, not even his own, and without any knowledge at all of philosophy, history, political science, or any of the natural or physical sciences, except the single one to which he has devoted two or three years at the most."[4]

Eliot's goal was to change the system from the top. If graduate and professional study could be reformed, everything leading up to it would have to change. That there was a demand for graduate education was proved by the Americans flocking to Germany. Eliot would try first to institute graduate-level lectures in philosophy and literature. He aimed to reform the law school and the medical school by making them graduate schools, which required their students to complete college degrees before entrance. Onto the existing — mainly English — system of recitations, lectures, and tutorials, Eliot grafted the German system, which was based on the strong department, the seminar, the specialized library, the laboratory, the monograph, and the learned journal.[5]

But the old order had not yet passed. Two days after Eliot became president, on May 21, 1869, William James handed in his medical thesis on the physiological effects of cold on the human body. One month later, on June 21, he took his final and only exam, the traditional ninety-minute oral exam, which William's son later described as "rather like the mad tea-party in *Alice in Wonderland*."[6]

It took place in one room. The professors of the nine required subjects stationed themselves at nine small tables around the room. The subjects were anatomy and physiology, surgery, chemistry, theory and practice of physic, midwifery and medical jurisprudence, materia medica, physiology and pathology of the nervous system, clinical medicine, and pathological anatomy. Nine students at a time were let into the room; each went up to a professor, who then administered a ten-minute oral test. A person in the middle of the room rang a bell at ten-minute intervals. At the bell, each of the nine students moved along to a different examiner. After ninety minutes of medical musical chairs, the dean called for votes. As he read out each student's name, all nine professors, without consultation, thrust forward their voting paddles simultaneously. Each paddle was white on one side and had a black spot on the other. Any student with no more than four black spots passed. The diploma conferred an M.D. degree and was also the license to practice. The system thus released on society as certified doctors men who, in some cases, were deficient in almost one half of the subjects.

James had taken the exam more seriously than some of his comments suggest, and he had done a great deal of studying. He carefully counted up the weeks he had spent on his medical education and came up with a total of three years and two or three months. He had, in fact, a good deal of medical knowledge, as such knowledge was understood at the time. Physiology, his area of study, was the subject that above all others would transform medicine from an art into a science. For all his professed distaste for medicine, then, James was part of this leading edge of change.

When it was Dr. Holmes's turn to examine William James at the mad tea party, Holmes asked a couple of questions about the nervus petrosis superficialis minor. When James answered, Holmes said, "If you know that you know everything," then asked for news of William's family. "I passed my examination with no difficulty," James wrote Bowditch, "and am entitled to write myself MD if I choose." He did not so choose; he saw the degree as the end of something, not the beginning, and he wrote Bowditch, "So there is one epoch of my life closed."[7]

15. *Treading Water*

D
URING THE SUMMER OF 1869, with his medical degree in
hand, William James experienced a little upturn in his health and
spirits. He spent July and August with the family, boarding in a
farmhouse in Pomfret, Connecticut, a town in the northeast corner of the
state, handy to the old New York and New England Railroad. He lolled in a
hammock, read Browning, and became reacquainted with some friends
from Newport days who were also staying in Pomfret, Lizzie Boott and her
father, Francis. Francis, born in 1813, was a composer, a Bostonian who had
spent most of his life in Florence. He was one of the models Henry James
used for Gilbert Osmond in *The Portrait of a Lady*.

William found Lizzie "one of the very best members of her sex I ever
met." She had grown up in Europe, knew Italian, French, and German, was
well educated, had "a great talent for drawing," and was hard at work becoming a painter. Minnie Temple kept an eye on things, noting to a friend,
"Lizzie Boott has been at Pomfret with the Jameses for a month and has
fallen quite in love (or should I say into love) with them, especially Uncle
Henry and Willy." William found Lizzie interesting because, as he told
Henry Bowditch, "she is in just about the same helpless state in which I
was when I abandoned the art." He also admitted to Bowditch that he
hadn't "realized before how much a good education . . . added to the
charms of a woman."[1]

There was quite a lot William hadn't realized about women. In this, as in
other respects, he took a long time to grow up. He had great difficulty in
breaking away from home, and his idea of a wife, when he thought about
such a thing, was strongly influenced by the example of his mother, the
selfless, always available woman who lived for her husband and children.
Virginia Woolf wrote of such a person, "When there was chicken she took
the wing, when there was a draught, she sat in it."

In August 1869 James read John Stuart Mill's new book, *On the Subjection of Women*. He was a little shaken up by it, finding it "strangely startling and suggestive," but he could not agree with Mill that the "actual
characters" of men and women could and would change over time in response to changes in "the generally accepted ideal of what they ought to
be." Mill objected to the present "swallowing up of the woman in the

man," and to the current ideal of marriage in which the woman was subordinate. James conceded that there was "an enormous deal to be said on both sides," but he insisted that there was "a strong presumption from use against Mill."[2]

William was attracted to strong, creative, educated young women, women not much like his mother. He was also attractive to such women, but he did not consider himself fit for marriage (health, nerves), and the whole question seems to have been an abstract one for him at this time. He now wrote a review of two books on women for the *North American Review*, Mill's book and Horace Bushnell's *Women's Suffrage: The Reform Against Nature*. James summarized but stopped short of endorsing Bushnell's argument that "society should . . . make a resolute stand against admitting [women] to share in any sort of government." What bothered James was Bushnell's recommendation of self-sacrifice for women. He spotted Bushnell's piously empty gallantry — though he was unable to see the same attitude in himself — and he objected to the idea that "suffering is a higher vocation than action." James was willing to admit that such a doctrine had done "much good in its day," saving slaves from despair and consoling the sick. "But," he added firmly, "there has probably not been an unjust usage in Christendom which has not at some time sought shelter under its wings. No well man or free man ever adopted it for his own use." For this and other weaknesses, James rejected Bushnell's book, saying "it certainly will add nothing in any circle to Dr. Bushnell's reputation either as a thinker or as an advocate."[3]

Mill was a different matter, and James was uneasy about what he took to be Mill's main point, his "thorough hostility to the accepted sentimental idea of the personal intercourse of man and wife." Mill insisted that the only acceptable ideal of marriage was one of independent equals, "each party being able to subsist alone, and seeking a mate not to supply an essential need, but to be enjoyed as a mere ally." James thought representative American men had a different ideal: "However he might shrink from expressing it in naked words, the wife his heart more or less subtly craves is at bottom a dependent being." Because a man's position in the outer world must be reconquered every day, and because "life is a struggle where success is only relative," James's American man "longs for one tranquil spot where he shall be valid absolutely and once for all; where, having been accepted, he is secure from further criticism." Wife and home are to be support and refuge. James could not accept Mill's "fervid passion for absolute equality, 'justice' and personal independence as the summum bonum for everyone." Unsure of himself, unequal to the ordinary demands of work and career, William James was now a long way from feeling complete in himself. He could not, at this point, even imagine such a feeling.[4]

The fall of 1869 went badly. William was still living with his parents and Alice at 20 Quincy Street in Cambridge. He had moved back in with his family in November 1866, which was, perhaps not coincidentally, the month he hurt his back in the dissecting room, setting in motion the discouraging and debilitating train of ills and complaints that was still going on three years later. He wrote Harry, who was now in Italy, that his health had caved in at Pomfret toward the end of August. Since then he had felt "great fatigue," and the "old weakness" had returned. He intended to try galvanism — that is, electrotherapy. He felt, as he said, "very much run down in nervous force," and he had resolved to read little and study not at all in the months to come.[5]

What exactly was wrong with William James? He reminds one of the neurotic invalid Mr. Fairlie in *The Woman in White*, whose condition is described by one of the narrators, the admirable Marian Holcomb: "I don't know what is the matter with him, and the doctors don't know what is the matter with him, and he doesn't know himself what is the matter with him. We all say it's on the nerves, and we none of us know what we mean when we say it."[6]

The news from Henry was both good and bad. He adored Rome. "At last —" he wrote, "for the first time — I live! It beats everything: it leaves the Rome of your fancy — your education — nowhere . . . I went reeling and moaning thro' the streets, in a fever of enjoyment." He was also reeling and moaning in the grip of massive, painful, intractable constipation. He poured himself out in letters to William; he detailed his agonies and cried out piteously, frantically, that "something must be done." He was demoralized, it was a "grievous trial," he was in a "wretched state," unable or unwilling, as his father might have seen it, to "eliminate his private or subjective ambition." With his bowels stopped up as with cement, the back problem that had kept him out of the war returned. He was utterly miserable, and hoped by his "frank and copious" letters to elicit medical help from William. "I palpitate to hear more," he wrote, "and invoke the next mail with tears in my eyes." William replied quickly and vigorously, recommending croton oil, senna, Epsom salts, electrotherapy, the English climate, and the "diet of Malvern." In a second letter he proposed grapes and figs before breakfast, lots of butter and fat, aloes, rhubarb, and tincture of colchicum.[7]

In October 1869 William read Father's new book, *The Secret of Swedenborg*, published in July. William still resisted his father's ideas, but he kept grappling with them, and indeed Henry Senior now exerted the steady pressure of a prevailing wind on his eldest son's mental course. Henry Senior's judgments might be outrageous, but they were not easily forgotten. Concerning Kant, he held a "hearty conviction" that the German philosopher was "consummately wrong, wrong from top to bottom, wrong through and through, in short, all wrong." Henry Senior hated the God of the orthodox churches, calling him the "obscene and skulking god of the nations," and he foamed over with Ahab-like vehemence: "Against this lurid power — half-pedagogue, half-policeman, but wholly imbecile in both respects, I . . . raise my gleeful fist." Swedenborg had come not to found a new denomination but to announce that institutional religion had ended. It was not all negative. Henry Senior believed that "Swedenborg's ontological doctrine is summed up in the literal veracity of creation, meaning by that term the truth of God's Natural Humanity, of the most living and actual unition of the divine and human natures."[8]

Henry Senior had first come to Swedenborg shortly after his crippling breakdown, or vastation, in May 1844, when he found in Swedenborg a vision of regeneration. In the first volume of his *Arcana Coelestia*, Swedenborg explains vastation as a necessary stage the twice-born person must pass through. The (far-fetched) explanation is contained in his gloss on the second verse of Genesis: "And the earth was without form, and void, and darkness was upon the face of the deep. And the Spirit of God moved upon the face of the waters." Swedenborg took "the face of the waters" to mean "the lusts of the unregenerate man," and the verse as a whole to signify "the vastation of man frequently spoken of by the prophets, which precedes regeneration: for before man can know what is true, and be affected by what is good, there must be a removal of such things as hinder and resist their admission; thus the old man must needs die before the new man can be born."[9]

William was able this fall to concede to Harry that "Father is a genius certainly — a religious genius," but he still had massive problems with that genius.[10] On one side William told Harry there were "many points which before were incomprehensible to me because doubtfully fallacious — [which] I now definitely believe to be entirely fallacious." On the other side were certain unspecified "great and original ideas." What most irritated William — and also Charles Peirce, who reviewed *The Secret of Swedenborg* at length — was his father's "ignorance of the way of thinking of other men, and his cool neglect of their difficulties."[11]

Both William and Harry now felt themselves to be marking time, if not slipping backward. Harry was disappointed not to be mastering German.

He wrote William, "Here I am at 26 with such a waste of lost time behind me and such an accumulated ignorance of so many of the elements and rudiments of my own tongue, literature, etc piled up in my track." William wrote Harry, urging him not to worry about trying to do justice to every country he visited. "We all learn sooner or later that we must gather ourselves up and more or less arbitrarily concentrate our interests, throw much overboard to save any."[12]

16. *The End of Youth*

MINNIE TEMPLE paid two visits to the Jameses in Cambridge in November 1869. One visit was before November 7, the other was from the twelfth to the nineteenth.[1] In the middle of Minnie's second visit, William wrote a long letter to his brother Bob, who had just become engaged to marry his first cousin Catharine Barber Van Buren.[2] William was aghast; he told Bob about the problems associated with "consanguineous marriages," dwelt on the awful "risk of generating unhealthy offspring," and declared that he himself was "fully determined never to marry with anyone" for fear of transmitting his own "dorsal trouble" to the next generation. Minnie reported on cousinly relations in a much brighter tone in a letter to her sister: "I have just returned from a visit to Cambridge of a week. I had a delightful time . . . Mr. Holmes was as nice as ever, Willy James, nicer than ever."[3]

Something happened, during this second visit, between William and Minnie. Two days after her happy report to her sister, Minnie wrote to John Gray, telling him, with notable emphasis, that she had enjoyed her visit to the Jameses "far more than I expected." She spoke of "the settling down and shaking up — the dissipating of certain impressions that I had thought fixed, and the strengthening of others I had not been so sure of etc etc. An epoch in short . . . in which a great deal of living was done in a short time." Nine days later she wrote Gray again: "In my next I will tell you a proposal that has been made to me, not of matrimony, but better."[4] Five days after this, William wrote Harry with his long account of changing his mind about Minnie, about how delightful she was "in all respects," and going as far as to comment, without irony, on her courage having a certain religious side to it.

Minnie Temple and William James did not fall in love this November. It was something more than that, and something less, and it was terribly complicated. She had been strongly, newly attracted to him for almost a year. He had been involved with other things and people, but in November when she visited William and his family twice, the two seem to have recognized and acknowledged a more than cousinly kinship, a profound bond with a solid religious basis. The scraps of Minnie's letters to William that survive have a seriousness of tone and an intimacy that are unique is his correspondence up to now.

And yet marriage was out of the question. As we have seen, William had strong feelings about first-cousin marriage; Minnie was desperately ill, and William believed that he was far too unhealthy to think of marriage, let alone children. But they were in some ways similar spirits, restless, yearning, hungry for life, ambitious, scornful of second best, sensitive, ironic, and outgoing, and there now arose between them a strange attraction, a cousinship of the spirit, the sort of thing Lyndall Gordon calls, in another context, an "uncategorized ferment of inward possibilities."[5] They were suddenly able to understand each other, drawn simultaneously to each other's avidity for life, each other's stoic, ironic acceptance, and each other's sad, tragic side. Minnie Temple was the first woman William had ever been able to accept as a complete equal, and the first person he could talk with about his deepest religious and spiritual concerns. They came, during November and December, to a difficult, exalted, doomed intimacy, deadly serious at times and too intense to maintain or to be good for Minnie, whose health was, of course, much the worse of the two.

Whatever the new understanding with Minnie really was, whatever the proposal that was better than matrimony (spiritual partnership? soulmating? some Werther-like love in death?), it only increased William's unhappiness. In the same letter to Harry in which he praised Minnie, he also praised some "extracts from a Persian poet" that Charles Eliot Norton had sent to the *North American Review*. These extracts were from *The Rubáiyát of Omar Khayyám*. Norton was reviewing Edward FitzGerald's translation; his long, old-fashioned piece comprises mostly excerpts and is essentially a first American edition, reprinting as it does seventy-six of the quatrains and giving a fair representation of the work as a whole. William found the quatrains "mighty things," and he urged Harry to read them. Minnie read them too.[6]

> Ah Love! Could you and I with fate conspire
> To grasp this sorry scheme of things entire

Would we not shatter it to bits, and then
Remold it nearer to the heart's desire!

William's mood darkened. On December 21 he wrote in the diary he reserved for moments of crisis, "I may not study, make or enjoy — but I can will. I can find some real life in the mere respect for other forms of life as they pass, even if I can never embrace them as a whole or incorporate them with myself." He does not specify the "other forms of life," but his feelings are of renunciation, and close to despair. "Nature and life," he went on, "have unfitted me for any affectionate relations with other individuals." Wrapped in this winter garment of despondency, William wrote Harry on December 27 that "stomach, bowels, brain, temper and spirits are all at a pretty low ebb," and two days later he told Henry Bowditch that he had "been prey to such disgust for life during the past 3 months as to make letter writing almost an impossibility."[7]

On the first of January William posted his study plan for the year ahead. He hoped, gamely, to "finish Father's works, Schopenhauer, Maudsley, Boismont, Griesinger, Spencer's Biology, Fechner, and Fichte's Introduction," and he tried to steel himself to be content with those modest goals. Then, abruptly, on January 10 or 12, just before or after his twenty-eighth birthday, William suffered a complete "dorsal collapse . . . carrying with it a moral one."

Three days later Minnie sent him a letter, part of which he kept for the rest of his life, tucked behind a photograph of her at sixteen. The letter is courageous and sad, it breathes intimacy and renunciation, and it must have recorded for William a close, telling moment. Minnie's strength and grace can still be felt across 135 years.

The more I live the more I feel that there must be some comfort somewhere for the mass of people, suffering and sad, outside of that which Stoicism gives — a thousand times when I see a poor person in trouble, it almost breaks my heart that I can't say something to comfort them. It is on the tip of my tongue to say it and I can't — for I have always felt myself the unutterable sadness and mystery that envelop us all — I shall take some of your Chloral tonight, if I don't sleep — Don't let my letter of yesterday make you feel that we are not very near to each other — friends at heart. Altho' practically being much with you or even writing to you would not be good for me — too much strain on one key will make it snap — and there is an attitude of mind, (not a strength of Intellect by any means) in which we are much alike. Goodbye.

Your Aff. Cousin, Mary Temple

Minnie must have tried to distance herself from William in an effort to save herself from the intensity — the strain — of their being together. It was a renunciation William would have approved and honored even as it left him emptier and more self-despising than ever.[8]

When, after William's death, his wife, Alice, read the long, moving section on Minnie Temple that ends Henry James's *Notes of a Son and Brother,* she told Henry: "You may not understand in the least how I feel, but it almost seems as if I had had all that she deserved. Were you ever haunted by a 'vicarious Atonement' feeling? That some one else was going without that you might be blessed?" There are two mysteries about Minnie's relationship with William. One is romantic, the other is religious, and Alice's remark here hints at both.[9]

On January 19, William wrote Harry to say that Father had a couple of articles in the *Atlantic* on marriage, and that he, William, had just read *The House of the Seven Gables,* Hawthorne's romance about a family curse. "I little expected so great a work," said William. He also noted that he was still suffering from a recent overdose — "which I took for the fun of it" — of chloral; that is, chloral hydrate.[10] We have to wonder whether "for the fun of it" covers the case or whether he was edging toward suicide again. Six days after this, Minnie was again writing to John Gray, saying, among other things, "Willy James sometimes tells me to behave like a man and a gentleman, if I wish to outwit fate. What a real person he is. He is to me, in nearly all respects, head and shoulders above other people."[11]

Minnie was now very thin, terribly weak, and no longer able to sleep. Her fate seemed to make nonsense of William's belief that people can control their lives, and he collapsed in on himself in yet another crisis, writing in his diary for February 1, 1870, "Today I about touched bottom, and perceive plainly that I must face the choice with open eyes: shall I frankly throw the moral business overboard . . . or shall I follow it, and it alone, making everything else merely stuff for it?" By "moral business" William meant the view that, after all, we are able to will and to choose our path in life, that we are not powerless pawns in an all-determined universe. It is not what fate does to us that matters; what matters is what we do with what fate does to us.

A good part of William's problem was due, he now saw, to his having accepted the view that we are powerless in the hands of fate. He now vowed, however, to give the moral business — the idea that we can choose — a serious, steady, and unconditional trial, rather than using it piecemeal, "to patch out the gaps which fate left in my other kinds of activity."[12] Perhaps he was moved — who wouldn't have been? — by Minnie's refusal to quit. On February 10 she wrote another extraordinary letter to William. It is twelve pages long, and only parts of it survive. In a tone wholly new and unprecedented in James's correspondence, Minnie gives him a solemn and moving account of her recent struggles with religious belief. The letter is clearly a continuation on paper of an earlier discussion.

She had been, all along, unable to really believe in Christianity — except in the Channing-Unitarian version, which talks about Jesus as an example of human perfectibility. Her uncle Henry had tried to get her to see how there might be real truth in the idea of atonement, "a mysterious intervention of God to save us and make us happy by the vicarious suffering of Christ, once for all." As Minnie told it, she had been so tired physically and mentally, so in need of rest, that she at last accepted this idea. But only briefly. By February 10 she had renounced it, telling Willy, "I am after all, a good deal of a pagan." With her clear-eyed candor, Minnie refused orthodox Christianity and declared instead what she was able to believe: "If I had lived before Christ, Music would have come like a divine voice to tell me to be true to my whole nature — to stick to my key-note, and have faith that my life would . . . in some way or other, if faithfully lived, swell the entire harmony — this is a grander music than the music of the spheres. Of course the question will always remain, what is one's true life, — and we must each try and solve it for ourselves. I confess that I am" — the rest of the letter is missing.[13]

Minnie Temple died twenty-six days after writing this. William recorded the event in a way he recorded no other. On a page of his diary all by itself he drew a crude grave marker with the initials *M.T.* and the date of her death.

Part of William James died with Minnie Temple. The part that remained learned to accept. Thirteen days later, on March 22, William tried to answer Minnie's last question, What is one's true life? "By that big part of me that's in the tomb with you," he wrote, "may I realize and believe in the immediacy of death." He had been sunk in and preoccupied with his own troubles, but Minnie alone of his contemporaries had broken through his self-involvement, and now it was Minnie who was dead. Startled by guilt, but moved too by Minnie's finer spirit, he tried not just to mutter self-indulgently about suicide but to take Minnie's road, as he tried to declare, as fully as he could, what that way really meant. "Minnie, your death makes me feel the nothingness of all our egotistical fury. The inevitable release is sure: wherefore take our turn kindly, whatever it contains. Ascend to some sort of partnership with fate, and since tragedy is at the heart of us, go to meet it, work it to our ends, instead of dodging it all our days, and being run down by it at last. Use your death (or your life, it's all one meaning) *tat tvam asi*."14

That last phrase is from the Chandogya Upanishad. It literally means "that you are," and it comes from a passage in which a father is trying to instruct his son about the nature of the ultimate reality of the universe and his son's inescapable place in it. After showing that everything has its root in Being, the father declares that Being is the soul of the world and that the son, as part of that world, has himself a share in that Being. *Tat tvam asi* asserts that "you are that [ultimate] Being." The principle of God is common to both the universe and the individual. William James's use of this phrase at this time can only mean that he had realized — as by a sudden revelation and not a Christian one — that Minnie's spirit was the same as, and therefore the key to, the spirit of the whole universe.

It would be thirty-two more years before James could return to deal with this central insight, this revelation, in the mysticism chapter of *The Varieties of Religious Experience*. "This overcoming of all the usual barriers between the individual and the Absolute," he wrote in that book, "is the great mystic achievement. In mystic states we both become one with the Absolute and we become aware of our oneness. This is the everlasting and triumphant mystical tradition . . . 'That art Thou!' say the Upanishads, and the Vedantists add: 'Not a part, not a mode of That, but identically That, that Absolute Spirit of the World.'"15

However it was, at last, between them, Minnie's death left William James stunned, as though he had been struck by lightning, or by revelation. Minnie's engagement with religion made religion real for him for the first time. The closing days of Minnie Temple's life mark the first time in James's life that he was able to accept the active religious struggle of another person as a valid religious experience. What Minnie felt and said as her death swung nearer was not theoretical or theological or historical or ecclesiastical; it was not a collapse or a concession. It was not one of Father's "ideas." Minnie's death, as Henry James was to say many years later, marked the end, for him and for William, of youth. But it was the end of more than youth for William. It was the wreck of the romantic intensities and intimacies and soul sharing that early love sometimes comes wrapped in. It was also his first glimpse of something else, a view of life as larger than our individual lives. What he could not have foreseen was that worse trouble was just around the corner.

II. THE ACTION OF CONSCIOUSNESS

17. Hitting Bottom

THE EARLY MONTHS OF 1870 mark the low point of William James's early life. His back gave out in January on his twenty-eighth birthday, bringing with it what he called a "moral collapse." On the first of February he "about touched bottom." On the ninth of March he learned that Minnie had died the day before. On the twenty-second he wrote his moving apostrophe to her. And sometime this spring, most likely between Minnie's death and the end of April, James experienced his worst crisis of all, a terrible moment of unstringing fear that became a defining moment in his life. If he noted it in the diary he kept for recording his troubles, the entry has disappeared (many pages were cut out of this intriguing diary), but he wrote a vivid account of it many years later.[1]

"Whilst in this state of philosophic pessimism and general depression of spirits about my prospects," James wrote,

> I went one evening into a dressing room in the twilight to procure some article that was there: when suddenly there fell upon me without any warning, just as if it came out of the darkness, a horrible fear of my own existence. Simultaneously there arose in my mind the image of an epileptic patient whom I had seen in the asylum, a black-haired youth with greenish skin, entirely idiotic, who used to sit all day on one of the benches, or rather shelves against the wall, with his knees drawn up against his chin, and the coarse gray undershirt, which was his only garment, drawn over them enclosing his entire figure. He sat there like a sort of sculptured Egyptian cat or Peruvian mummy, moving nothing but his black eyes and looking absolutely nonhuman.

As often happens when James recounts a dream or describes an essentially imaginative experience, things merge into one another. "This image and my fear entered into a species of combination with each other," he went on. "That shape am I, I felt, potentially. Nothing that I possess can defend me against that fate, if the hour for it should strike for me as it struck for him." James moved easily toward the Other, toward the troubling, like the children of the Plains Indians who were taught to move toward, not away from, the first sounds of trouble. "There was such a horror of him," James continued, "and such a perception of my own merely momentary discrepancy from him, that it was as if something hitherto solid within my breast gave way entirely, and I became a mass of quivering fear." The experience was eerily similar to his father's vastation, and, also like his father's, this was a life-altering moment. "After this," he said, "the universe was changed for me altogether. I awoke morning after morning with a horrible dread at the pit of my stomach, and with a sense of the insecurity of life that I never knew before, and that I have never felt since."[2]

The experience not only changed James, it changed his view of other people. "It was like a revelation," he said, "and although the immediate feelings passed away, the experience has made me sympathetic with the morbid feelings of others ever since." James added that while the vividness of the experience faded, he was nevertheless "unable to go out into the dark alone" for months, that he dreaded to be left alone, and that he concealed his condition from his mother. Then he struck off in an entirely different direction. "I have always felt that this experience of melancholia of mine had a religious bearing." And he expanded on the point in terms that remind us again of his father but that had their most recent echoes with Minnie: "I mean that the fear was so invasive and powerful that if I had not clung to scripture texts like 'the eternal God is my refuge,' etc., 'Come unto me, all ye that labor and are heavy-laden,' etc., 'I am the resurrection and the life,' etc. I think I should have grown really insane."[3]

We do not know when James first wrote this experience down; it first appears in print in 1902, in his chapter on the sick soul in *The Varieties of Religious Experience*. But what matters as much as the exact sequence of William's troubles this spring is the terrible compounding of them. Between 1868 and 1873, we cannot trace in James's inner life a plain pattern of collapse after which he slowly but surely climbs out of his depression into a steadily more active and happy life. The pattern is rather one of crash, resolution, and only partial recovery, followed by another downward spiral, which is halted painfully by new resolutions followed by uncertain, easily sidetracked recovery, then down again, and so on around the whole discouraging circle.

The central, extended account given above may have been one specific event, but there were others quite like it, though none so vividly and memorably told. When William wrote his description of his own vastation, he footnoted his father's similar experience, which had occurred around the same age. It is interesting — perhaps even suspicious — that James left no record of the experience at the time, unless he wrote it and then cut it out of his diary. He was generally all too ready, as his mother noted, to dwell on every last detail of his troubles, and it is possible that he wrote a diary account that is now missing. Still, in the case of major problems, as with his back trouble in 1866, James had the same impulse to concealment as his brother Henry.

Two more things about this experience stand out. One is the turn to biblical texts as a defense against a feeling of impending madness. James was not at the time much of a churchgoer or Bible reader, though he was becoming more and more interested in religious questions in early 1870. Rereading his father's works, exploring Buddhism and the Upanishads, shaken terribly by Minnie's death and by her urgently religious correspondence, James seems to have recognized genuine religious feeling in himself this spring. The above account, with its headlong, AA-like narrative, may well have been the hour at which religion finally struck for him, just when the clock had pointed to despair.

Notable too in the above account is the clarity, almost the sunshine, of hindsight. James says his own case had "the merit of extreme simplicity." In layman's language, he called it an incident of "sudden fear"; it was probably what would now be called a panic attack. In the medical language of the time, James called it an "acute neurasthenic attack with phobia."[4] Neurasthenia, also called nervous exhaustion or nervous prostration, was a new diagnosis in 1870. It was the specialty of Dr. George Beard, who wrote an article on it, published in the *Boston Medical and Surgical Journal* on April 29, 1869, well before his widely noticed book *American Nervousness* appeared in 1881.

Beard understood neurasthenia to be a "large family of functional nervous disorders that are increasingly frequent among the indoor classes of civilized countries, and that are especially frequent in the northern and eastern parts of the U.S."[5] Beard thought neurasthenia to be most prevalent in "brain-working households," he thought it was transmittable, and he considered it to be an essentially American disease.[6] Since the main symptom was understood to be the depletion of a person's nervous energy, which was then widely assumed to be finite, the generally prescribed treatment was rest and a proper diet. William James suffered from chronic neurasthenia for years — his fear episode was an example of the acute form of the disease — with the added problem that his eyes were affected (as his father's had been after *his* experience), making it impossible for him for years at a time to read for more than three or four hours a day.

Yet he did read — often was read to — and his reading was sometimes quite literally lifesaving. If the sudden spasm of identification with the green-skinned idiot was representative of the worst of William's bad moments, an episode toward the end of April illustrates his peculiar absorptive resiliency, his uncanny ability to pick up redemptive ideas from his reading. Perhaps it was grasping at straws, but it served him, and sometimes the straw turned out to be a solid plank. On the last day of April 1870, six weeks after the death of Minnie Temple, he wrote in his diary: "I think that yesterday was a crisis in my life. I finished the first part of Renouvier's 2nd Essay and saw no reason why his definition of free will — the sustaining of a thought because I choose to when I might have other thoughts — need be the definition of an illusion. At any rate, I will assume for the present — until next year — that it is no illusion. My first act of free will shall be to believe in free will."[7]

William had first read the work of Charles Renouvier (1815–1903) in October 1868, toward the end of his *Wanderjahr*. Renouvier was a neo-Kantian, but it was his "vigor of style and compression, going to the core of half a dozen things in a single sentence," that first drew William's admiring attention. The first work of Renouvier's that William read was a hundred-page summary of nineteenth-century French thought. Renouvier gave a great deal of space to the development of positivism, to Comte and his followers, but he treated it as something already past its prime, on the defensive, and sustaining itself only with difficulty.[8]

Positivism, priding itself on equating knowledge with measurement and on having built itself on what were understood to be physical laws governing everything from matter to human society, was, for Renouvier, a new dress for the old doctrine of determinism. But his great point is just the opposite, that humans are free. Renouvier is elegant and urbane, has a highly developed sense of irony and a wry appreciation of how proponents of one kind of belief can end up adopting the views of opponents — a sort of Stockholm syndrome for intellectuals. "The same persons," he writes, "who valiantly won religious liberty for themselves in the sixteenth century became the ardent proponents of an omnipotent deity and absolute predestination, and those who defended ecclesiastical government and constraint of conscience acknowledged a certain moral freedom for humans in their dealings with God. The Protestants and the Jansenists [predestinarian Roman Catholics] fought against free will, and the Jesuits defended it. In freeing oneself from one authority, it is natural to look, by way of compensation, for support and certitude from another; in putting up with one aspect of authority, it is natural to seek emancipation — even if only the shadow of it — from another." For Renouvier the path to freedom began with Kant's critical philosophy, which, he said, "has its center in morals, and, within morals, its center in freedom . . . It leads and subordinates everything to the recognition of human freedom." Renouvier's clinching argument in the 1867 piece, repeated in the essay on freedom James read in April 1870, is the argument James seized on. "This recognition," writes Renouvier, "is itself a free act, and critical philosophy demands that each of us perform this act."[9]

Somehow James recognized that perception alone was not enough, that perception was not helpful unless it led to action. In the diary entry for April 30, 1870, James goes on in a sort of dialogue with himself:. "For the remainder of this year, I will abstain from the mere speculation and contemplative grubelei [brooding, with overtones of grubbing in a pit, mine, or grave] in which my nature takes most delight, and voluntarily cultivate the feeling of moral freedom, by reading books favorable to it, as well as by acting." He determined to try this course until January, when he thought he might "perhaps return to metaphysic study and skepticism without danger to my powers of action."

In attempting to reroute his energies from speculation to action, James already understood the power and importance of habit, as both inertia and momentum. "Recollect," the new Willy sternly warns the old Willy, "that only when habits of order are formed can we advance to really interesting fields of action — and consequently accumulate grain on grain of wilful choice like a very miser — never forgetting how one link dropped undoes an indefinite number." He felt that he was making a beginning. "Today has furnished the exceptionally passionate initiative which Bain posits as needful for the acquisition of habits," and he repeats the original insight. "Not in maxims, not in *anschauungen* [perceptions, opinions] but in accumulated acts of thought lies salvation."[10]

This is a substantial diary entry, quite enough for a single day, one might think, but James does not stop here. Taking himself at his word, he pushes himself on to further acts of thought, the first a repudiation. "Hitherto," he writes, "when I have felt like taking a free initiative, like daring to act originally, without carefully waiting for contemplation of the external world to determine all for me, suicide seemed the most manly form to put my daring into." In a flash, like a person impulsively jumping a brook, James is on the other side. "Now I will go a step further with my will, not only act with it, but believe as well; believe in my individual reality and creative power." Not only must he act, he must believe in his actions. And in order to believe, he must reformulate the question for himself. Resiliency, the ability, even when down — especially when down — to regroup and move forward, is the central fact of the inner life of William James. "My belief to be sure can't be optimistic," he concludes, "but I will posit it, life (the real, the good) in the self-governing resistance of the ego to the world. Life shall be built [on] doing and creating and suffering."[11]

Optimism is a temperamental possibility as well as an explanatory style, and therefore it is a temptation for many people. James is unusual in trying to find for himself a personal starting point that excludes what Walt Whitman once called "mere optimism." In one way, this is the Stoic turn: do not concern yourself with things that are beyond your control; concentrate on those things that are under your control. But there is more than Stoicism here. (Indeed a Stoic might well include suicide as something under one's control.)

This is one of the first of James's great psychological insights. Almost one hundred years later, in 1968, Erik Erikson said that James's "formulation for a self-governing as well as a resisting aspect of the ego" is "a principle dominant in today's ego psychology." He calls attention to the way James insists on "the inner synthesis which organizes experience and guides action."[12] Erikson goes further than this. He cites Henry Senior's report on another, slightly later moment when William told his father that he had "given up the notion that all mental disorders require to have a physical basis." Taken together, says Erikson, these two insights "are the basis of psychotherapy, which, no matter how it is described and conceptualized, aims at the restoration of the patient's power of choice."[13]

This is a sweeping claim, but there is, to be sure, a not yet exhausted force in James's spare phrasing of "the self-governing resistance of the ego to the world." But even more interesting, and certainly harder to explain, is the fact that James reached and formulated this general, not to say abstract, truth out of private troubles, in a heave of will, a practical effort to change his own life.

18. The Turn to Physiology

FOR ALMOST TWO YEARS after Minnie Temple's death, James seems like a man with his back against a wall. He struggled all during the spring of 1870 to control his despondency and general depression of spirits. It was all very well to talk about the "self-governing resistance of the ego to the world," but the practical consequences of such a belief, by itself, with no supporting enthusiasm, no recent victories, were stark. We hear no more of optimism, nothing further of scriptural texts. His ebullience over Renouvier temporarily evaporated. On May 5 he had a tooth pulled. Two days later, his jaw still aching, he wrote Harry describing Cambridge as cold and rainy, and himself as hunkered down under an "Indian Winter," as "melancholy as a whippoorwill." William came back to the subject of resistance; this time it sounds lonely and grim and far from hopeful. "All a man has to depend on in this world," he told Harry, "is, in the last resort, mere brute power of resistance." William here seems a little like Henry Adams, who would be appointed to teach history at Harvard in September 1870, at the age of thirty-two, and who would write in *The Education of Henry Adams*, "Resistance to something was the law of New England nature."[1]

William did not know it, but Harry was already on his way home from Europe with Aunt Kate. They landed on May 10, after a nine-and-a-half-day voyage without a storm or serious discomfort. The Harry who returned to Cambridge in the spring of 1870 was on the threshold of his first real success as a writer. He had now published fourteen stories, many of them running to around fifty pages; there was enough for a good-sized volume. He had also written forty-two critical articles and reviews. He was about to undertake a commission for a series of travel articles on America, and his first novel, *Watch and Ward*, was going to be serialized in the *Atlantic*. Florence and Italy were on his mind and in his plans. Henry's general position was now in the greatest possible contrast to William's. William was working out a grim doctrine of resistance and endurance. Henry was a rapidly emerging, successful, confident, and calmly focused young writer as he stepped ashore and returned to the family home on Quincy Street.

The James family went to Pomfret, Connecticut, again in the summer of 1870, and William continued to work out his idea of resistance, which now seemed, even to him, more bleak than heroic because it was too passive and too negative. He wrote brother Bob a distilled version of his position. "All thought," he wrote, "all emotion which does not tend to action, is morbid and should be suppressed." By "action" William here means just resistance — that is, our "power to resist pain, to rely on our hearts alone, to do without sympathy."[2]

This is a Stoic line of thought, not a Christian one. As James bore down on it during the summer at Pomfret, it developed into a quasi-existentialist position. He laid out the idea of the human being as "a bundle of desires, more or less numerous. He lives, inasmuch as they are gratified, dies as they are refused."[3] These desires simply exist: there is no transcendental self, let alone a creator behind them. They are backed by exactly nothing except the self. "They exist," wrote James, "by mere self-affirmation; and, appealing for legitimation to no principle back of them, are the lowest terms to which man can be reduced."[4]

In place of an idea of evil, James put instead the idea of limits or abridgment of gratification. He identified two human tendencies, the centrifugal, or "expansive embracing tendency," and the centripetal, inward-moving or "defensive." He noted that these tendencies represented two different modes of self-assertion, the expansive representing the sympathetic mode, the centripetal the self-sufficing mode, and he wondered, inconclusively, if the two together might add up to self-respect.[5]

James now saw that to "accept the universe" and "to protest against it" were voluntary alternatives.[6] He himself wished to accept it, but without illusions; he therefore termed his acceptance "resignation," and thought of it as strictly provisional. To be resigned, he thought, should not be taken to mean "it is good," "a mild yoke," but rather, "I'm willing to stand it for the present." So resistance came to mean not so much rejection as provisional resignation, to be measured by three things James listed as necessary to determine: "1) How much pain I'll stand; 2) how much others' pain I'll inflict (by existing); 3) how much others' pain I'll accept without ceasing to take pleasure in their existence."[7]

One wonders whom he had in mind in points 2 and 3. Perhaps it was his sister Alice. More likely it was Minnie. James wrote his Pomfret philosophy notes that summer of 1870, and the rest of that year and most of 1871 were a curiously empty, flat time for him. The four months from August to November 1870 are a blank. He wrote no letters and diary entries that we know of; he figures only marginally in Harry's letters, in which his health is the only aspect of his life discussed, and that minimally, guardedly, without detail. To Grace Norton, the sister of Charles Eliot Norton and a life-long friend of both Harry and William, Harry wrote in September 1870, "My brother's health has small fluctuations of better and worse, but maintains steadily a rather lowly level."[8]

William's eyes and back were giving him trouble. Amid the silences and muted notices, William made strange minor errors of dating, poked into unlikely subjects, and put things off. He wrote the date June 21, 1870, at the head of the diary he had started in 1868, then made no entry for that June date. He kept a book list headed 1870, but when he continued the list for 1871, he put the new date down as 1870. In December 1870 he wrote Tom Ward that he had resolved to "look into mathematics . . . if I ever get able to study."[9] On December 29, he started a letter to Henry Bowditch, telling about his light reading. Full of self-disgust, he broke off the attempt to write, and picked the letter up again only on January 23, 1871.

Yet if the second half of 1870 and most of 1871 represent a low point in an otherwise active life, they were also a seed time during which James read widely. This was also a period of gathering resolve, for in mid-1871 he made a decisive turn toward physiology.

Simply to list the books he read in 1870 and 1871 gives one the sense that James was, in this downtime, busily filling up the well. He read travel books, favoring those by naturalists. He read Alfred Russel Wallace's *Malay Archipelago*, Raphael Pumpelly's *Across America and Asia*, and the travel writing of Georg Forster, who had been around the world with Captain James Cook. He read Henry Thoreau's *A Week on the Concord and Merrimack Rivers*, Thomas Cubbin's *Wreck of the Serica*, Jane Smith's *Captivity Among Indians*, and Daniel Drake's *Pioneer Life in Kentucky*.[10]

He read very little in the classics, a bit more widely among standard authors. Cicero's *De Amicitia* and *De Senectute* appear on his list, as does Saint Augustine, probably for his *Confessions*. He read, among Shakespeare's history plays, *Henry VI Part 2*, *Richard III*, and *Henry VIII*. He read Carlyle's *Sartor Resartus*, Prescott's *Conquest of Mexico*, Parkman's *Jesuits in North America* and *The Discovery of the West*, and Goethe's *Torquato Tasso*. In July 1871 James acquired two volumes of Emerson's writings.

He read novels, ranging from Dickens's *A Tale of Two Cities*, George Eliot's *Mill on the Floss*, Goethe's *Sorrows of Young Werther* (again), Hawthorne's *Scarlet Letter*, and Turgenev's *Récits d'un Chasseur* (*Huntsman's Sketches*) to the light political-historical novels of Erckmann-Chatrian (*Histoire d'un Sous-Maître*) and the Swiss Victor Cherbuliez (*Prosper Randoce*). James also did quite a bit of family reading, keeping up with Harry's frequent stories, going back for yet another try at *Substance and Shadow*, as part of the systematic read-through of Father's work that William had been engaged in since the fall of 1869.

William kept up a certain amount of reading in religious studies. By the time of Minnie's death, he knew something about the Upanishads. Now, during 1870, he read several books on Buddhism and Hinduism, including Alabaster's *Modern Buddhist*, volume one of Koeppen's *Religion des Buddha*, Hippolyte Taine's *Le Buddhisme*, Bastian's *Weltauffass der Buddhisten*, and Keshab Chunder Sen's *Brahma Somej: Four Lectures*. Still trying in 1871 to take his father's measure, he read Swedenborg's *Divine Love and Wisdom* and his *Divine Providence*. He also read a tight little theological book by his uncle the Reverend William James, called *The Marriage of the King's Son*. This is not a novel; the title refers to a New Testament parable.

His preferred light reading (ignoring the fact that William would have considered everything just listed as light because it wasn't physiology) ran to biography and memoir. As he put it to Henry Bowditch, "I fill my belly with husks — newspapers, novels and biographies." He read Lord Herbert of Cherbury's autobiography, Prince Eugène's memoirs, Channing's memoirs, Margaret Fuller's memoirs, Blanco White's autobiography, Stanley's life of Dr. Arnold, Sir Samuel Romily's autobiography, and that of Benjamin Franklin. He read the better-known and the lesser-known alike: Massimo d'Azeglio's recollections, W. M. Rossetti's memoir of Shelley, Marmontel's memoirs, F. W. Robertson's life and letters, and the life of Sir James McIntosh. James's partiality for biography and memoir — for narratives of personal experience — stayed with him, feeding what, over time, became a central structural principle in some of his best writing.

Somewhere around April 1871, James's reading took a more professional turn, toward books and articles on physiology, psychology, and philosophy. These three fields, which now seem so disparate (perhaps because they belong to different divisions in modern universities), were then more closely associated, and at a certain level of generalization, one sees why. Physiology concerns itself with the physical processes of the body. Psychology, as it was newly being shaped, was concerned with interactions between mind and body, while philosophy, having left behind such subdivisions as natural philosophy (i.e., science), was more and more concerned simply with mind. One book James read was John D. Morell's *Introduction to Mental Philosophy*. He also read Wilhelm Griesinger's *Pathologie und Therapie der Psychische Krankheiten*, Hippolyte Taine's *De l'Intelligence*, Henry Maudsley's *Body and Mind: An Inquiry into Their Connection and Mutual Influence*, Joseph Pierre de Gros Durand's *Essais de Physiologie*

Philosophique, Thomas H. Green's *Facts of Consciousness,* Samuel Bailey's *Letters on the Philosophy of the Human Mind,* and Herbert Spencer's *Principles of Psychology.*[11]

It wasn't just books that impelled William James toward physiology just now; it was also, and perhaps principally, his friend Henry Bowditch. In April 1871 James wrote to Bowditch that he had just bought a ticket for a course of lectures, "Optical Phenomena and the Eye," to be given by B. Joy Jeffries. He told Bowditch it was "the first mingling in the business of life which I have done since my return home."[12] He had been home for two and a half years, and if his statement to Bowditch is not exactly a full account of what he had done, it does show how he felt about this time. His letters to and from Bowditch are a substantial percentage of James's surviving correspondence from these years, and Bowditch seems to have been the only person outside the family and outside Cambridge with whom James kept in close touch.

It is hard to imagine a greater contrast than that between their careers to date. Where James had tacked this way and that, hesitated, and now lay hove to, Bowditch had already steered a brilliant career course, as befitted the grandson of Nathaniel Bowditch, the author of *The American Practical Navigator.* Henry Bowditch was two years older than William James, and had entered Harvard in 1857 while William was attending school in Boulogne and thinking he would be an artist. After college, Bowditch entered the Lawrence Scientific School at the same time as James. He soon left, served as a lieutenant in the 1st Massachusetts Cavalry, then returned to the Lawrence School, where he studied comparative anatomy under Jeffries Wyman and also fulfilled the requirements for a degree from Harvard Medical School. Bowditch took his M.D. in 1868, one year before James did, and went abroad to Paris, where he studied physiology with Claude Bernard and neurology with Jean-Martin Charcot, who was later a teacher of Sigmund Freud's. Bowditch next moved to Leipzig when he had a chance to enter the lab of Carl Ludwig, "the greatest trainer of physiologists who ever lived."[13] Bowditch promptly invented a new method of recording blood pressure changes, discovered by experiment the nature of cardiac muscle contraction, and found that the compound delphinine (found in larkspur and similar to atropine) would make the apex of an isolated heart beat rhythmically.

Bowditch was a "sturdy, gallant, well-set-up figure, of medium height, with aquiline features, pointed beard, and a cavalry mustache." By 1871 he was well on his way to becoming a leading American physiologist. His work on rates of growth in school-age children was the basis for the first school lunch programs. His steady application and his laboratory orientation represented exactly what William James said he wanted for himself. In April 1871, just as James was struggling back to work and writing Bowditch about it, Harvard's President Eliot offered Bowditch an assistant professorship of physiology and invited him to help reform medical education at Harvard. Bowditch wrote James in June to say he was bringing home lots of apparatus and books. He hoped the medical faculty would give him a room and some money so "we can set up a laboratory at once." His use of the "we" was not accidental, as he explained in his letter to James: "I say we for I expect you to join me in working at experimental physiology."[14]

William James in this period of his life was an accomplished complainer. During 1870 and 1871 we hear endlessly about his eyes, his back, his low spirits, his aimless existence. No doubt he felt down much of the time, but his drone of misery conceals something important and different. Beneath all the *Sturm und Drang* he was in fact pursuing, and preparing to further pursue, physiology, not just in an intellectual but also in a practical way. He was already at work, and his letter of April 8, 1871, has at least one line of thought and phrase that would hold good and reappear in *The Principles of Psychology*. "It is a pleasing confidence," he wrote, "that . . . by working our stint day by day on the one line we have chosen, without looking ahead or thinking much of the final result, we are sure of waking some fine morning, experts in our particular branch, with a tact, so to speak for truth therein: a judgment, and ideas and intuitions of our own — all there without our knowing exactly how they came."[15]

This sounds like a person ready to go. James now believed it, and Bowditch did too, for it was after reading this letter that Bowditch wrote to say he expected James to join him when he came home.

19. *The Metaphysical Club and Chauncey Wright*

CHARLES DARWIN IS SAID to have remarked, "There were enough brilliant minds at the American Cambridge in the 1860s to furnish all the universities of England."[1] Darwin would have had in mind his colleague, friend, and defender Asa Gray, and perhaps his stubborn antagonist Louis Agassiz, but he would also have included at the top of the list Chauncey Wright, who was the intellectual-boxing master of Charles Peirce, Wendell Holmes, and William James.

Wright was an antitheological positivist, a philosopher who was at the center of a series of discussion clubs in Cambridge for twenty years, from 1856 until his death in 1875. First with the Septem, then with the Metaphysical Club, Wright gathered around himself a number of extraordinary persons who took over and revolutionized Harvard, defended and advanced the work of Darwin, and founded and spread the as yet unnamed philosophy of pragmatism.

Chauncey Wright was twelve years older than William James. Born in Northampton, Massachusetts, he had graduated from Harvard in 1852 and immediately taken a job as a mathematical calculator for the *American Ephemeris and Nautical Almanac.* He learned to compress the annual work for this inexpressibly dull, Bartleby-like job into three months, leaving the rest of the year free for philosophy and friends. In 1856, when he was twenty-six, Wright and a number of former classmates started a group called the Septem. It included James Thayer (a friend of Emerson's, a law partner of Wendell Holmes's, and later a professor of constitutional law at Harvard Law School), William Ware (later an architect and a founder of American architectural education), Ephraim Gurney (later a professor of history at Harvard and the first dean of the faculty of Harvard College), Charles Dunbar (later the editor of the *Boston Daily Advertiser* and then the first professor of political economy — i.e., economics — at Harvard), George Shattuck (later a law partner of Thayer's), and Darwin Ware (later a minor poet). It was a convivial group and its purpose was philosophical discussion — whiskey punch not to be neglected — and the force that held it together was Chauncey Wright.

Wright stood five feet ten inches and had a massive build, which one cannot detect in early photographs, in which his long face, high forehead, regular features, and inexpressive mouth are set off by thin, long, straight hair that we are told was red. He looked at a person with "strange conflicting, conscious light blue eyes." He smoked a pipe incessantly, whether in his informal gray dressing gown or his public outfit with high collar and bow tie. He was adept at sleight of hand and juggling and was good with children. Chronically depressed — one friend called his depressions "uncontrollable" — he drank heavily when he was feeling down. The daughter of a friend once asked him what were the saddest things in the world. He answered, "Those beginning with 'd' as death, debt, disease, dishonor and all the d — d disses."[2]

Every university has around it somewhere one person who is more loved and listened to than most, who tutors and prepares his friends for their exams but who never takes his own, who is generally acknowledged as the most brilliant and gifted of all, who has every gift except the ability to use his gifts. He is the one who never quite finishes, never quite succeeds, never quite writes the great book — a person like Sherlock Holmes's older brother, Mycroft (who solves Sherlock's thorniest problems by sheer force of mind without stirring from his chair), or like a member of Melville's choice circle of the Divine Inert who stands wholly, tragically superior to the working world and the arts the working world requires for success and fame. In the American Cambridge of the 1860s and 1870s this figure, the village Socrates who lived on in the minds of his great students, was Chauncey Wright.

Wright was in many respects the most important intellectual in Cambridge in the 1860s. He was crucial for Charles Peirce, crucial for pragmatism, and crucial for William James. He was an institution, apart from and in some ways more effective than Harvard itself. He was a great teacher and talker, though only twice did he give a formal course (some lectures in psychology in 1870 and a course in mathematical physics in 1874), and he published very little, though what he did publish mattered.

The Septem was revived in June 1865, when James was in Brazil. Into the circle of old regulars, Shattuck, Thayer, and William Ware, now came Eldridge Cutler and Charles W. Eliot. The latter, as we saw, was James's old chemistry teacher, soon to be president of Harvard. The club fell apart again in 1868. The following year was a bad one for Wright's drinking and depression, but in 1870 he was asked by Eliot to give a series of university lectures in psychology.

Late in 1871 or early in 1872, a group calling itself the Metaphysical Club gathered around Wright, who was then forty-two. It was not a formal group, it was only rarely referred to by name, and it is not clear how it started or how James came to be part of it. The new club included, besides William James, then thirty, Wendell Holmes and Charles Peirce, thirty-one and thirty-two, respectively. Joseph Warner was the youngest at twenty-four, and Nicholas St. John Greene, who was Wright's age, was the oldest. The group met sometimes in James's room, sometimes at Peirce's, and it also occasionally included John Fiske, then thirty, and Francis E. Abbott, thirty-six.[3]

Wright was rigorously antitheological. He calmly dismissed what he called mysticism, which he conceived as the essence of unscientific procedure. He had read Emerson's "Divinity School Address" while at Harvard and liked particularly Emerson's critique of "historical Christianity." James Thayer related how one conservative woman told Wright that "she believed implicitly that the world was made in six days. He looked at her," said Thayer, "as if she were a new order of being, and I shall never forget the tone of his exclamation: 'Is it possible!'"[4] Wright was strongly influenced by John Stuart Mill, from whom he learned that "the determination of the vexed problems of metaphysics was to be sought in a properly scientific and not in an a priori or spiritualist psychology."[5] As an empiricist Wright rejected the idea of necessity, as he rejected all other abstractions and absolutist claims. Wendell Holmes said Wright taught him that "we could not assert necessity of the order of the universe."[6] "'How could you know,' he asked Holmes, his pale blue eyes alight with a cold passion, 'how could you know what the universe considers necessary?'"[7]

Wright believed in positive science. His friend Charles Eliot Norton explained that Wright "used the term positive, as it is now commonly employed, as a general appellation to designate a whole body of thinkers who in the investigation of nature hold to the methods of induction from the facts of observation, as distinguished from the a priori school who seek in the constitution of the mind the key to the interpretation of the external world."[8]

Wright stood, in general, for the universe of physical causation and for a frank, antispiritualist view of nature. James was later to praise Wright's "power of analytic intellect pure and simple," and to call him "the great mind of a village — if Cambridge will pardon the expression." James went on to say that "either in London or Berlin he would, with equal ease, have taken the place of master which he held with us."[9]

James also noted Wright's "shyness, his want of ambition, and to a certain degree his indolence," and he insisted that "his best work has been done in conversation." James accurately caught Wright's particular slant of mind when he wrote, "Whereas most men's interest in a thought is proportioned to its possible relation to human destiny, with him it was almost the reverse. When the mere actuality of phenomena will suffice to describe them, he held it pure excess and superstition to speak of a metaphysical whence or whither, of a substance, a meaning or an end." Wright coined the phrase "cosmical weather," James observed, "to describe the irregular dissipation and aggregation of worlds . . . When it was objected to him that there must be some principle of oneness in the diversity of phenomena — some glue to hold them together and make a universe out of their mutual independence, he would reply that there is no need of a glue to join things unless we apprehend some reason why they should fall asunder. Phenomena are grouped — more we cannot say of them."[10]

Chauncey Wright was in some ways William James's true college, the whaling ship that taught him what he really needed to know. Wright schooled the naive idealism out of James. At some point in the early 1870s James wrote a short essay against Wright's "nihilism," objecting that Wright "denies this to be a universe and makes it out a 'nulliverse.'" Wright penciled lengthy notes on James's manuscript; the notes show the meticulous care Wright lavished on his young men, and they suggest that, after Agassiz, it was Wright more than anyone else who taught James the level of attention to detail at which an argument becomes significant.

To take just one example, James tried to argue for intentionality, saying that "the goodness or rightness of a state or act can be described by saying they are meant to be, that the rationality of a set of thoughts points to something which means them, and that our feelings of preference for certain experiences and claims have a quality . . . a different character over and above their intrinsic character as feeling." Wright's note barred the way with a steely objection: "This quality appears to me to be merely a negative one — simply — and no part of the phenomena of our activity."[11] Wright went on for hundreds of words, refusing to let James get away with smuggled assumptions, hidden agendas, buried premises, or received terminology. It would be impossible for a young man not to feel flattered by this depth of attention, by having his work read and responded to with such exhaustive seriousness.

In 1871, just as the Metaphysical Club was taking shape, Wright published a defense of Darwin, against the ideas of the Jesuit scientist St. George Mivart, in the *North American Review*. Wright's article so impressed Darwin that he had it reprinted as a pamphlet and circulated in England. The following year, Wright traveled to Europe and visited Darwin, who asked Wright "to turn his analytic powers to work on the problem of determining, in connection with the idea of evolution, when a thing can properly be said to be effected by the will of man."[12] The result was "The Evolution of Self-Consciousness," which Wright published in the *North American Review* in April 1873, an article James would first make use of when he came to write his chapter on reason in *The Principles of Psychology*. Wright took it for granted that if Darwin was right, the line separating humans from other mammals would be a very small, almost imperceptible development. Wright undertook "a critical re-examination of the phenomena of self-consciousness in themselves, with reference to their possible evolution from powers obviously common to all animal intelligences."[13]

On the night of September 11, 1875, while he was writing at his desk, Chauncey Wright suffered a stroke. He was found early the following morning; he then suffered a second stroke. Henry James Jr. was the only close friend of Wright's not away on vacation. He rushed through the streets of Cambridge as soon as he got the word, but arrived a few minutes after Wright died. William eulogized Wright as belonging "to the precious band of genuine philosophers." Henry spoke for many when he said Wright was "the most wasted and doomed, the biggest at once and the gentlest of the great intending and unproducing . . . bachelors of philosophy, bachelors of attitude and of life."[14]

20. Charles Peirce

CHARLES SANDERS PEIRCE, credited with founding semiotics and called "the most original and versatile of American philosophers and America's greatest logician," was the gifted and doomed son of the "facile, brilliant, impatient, and error-prone" Benjamin Peirce, professor of mathematics at Harvard College. Benjamin was convinced from the start that Charles was destined for greatness, and he announced the boy's birth by referring to his "coming, almost come celebrity," and adding, "As soon as he publishes his Celestial Mechanics I will send you a copy."[1]

By his own account, written with who knows what inherited or youthful exaggeration when he was a college senior, Charles "fell violently in love with Miss W. and commenced my education" at age five. At seven he "fell violently in love with another Miss W whom . . . I will designate Miss W[1]." At ten he wrote a story called "The Library," which starts, "Charles was one day sitting in his room when suddenly he heard a rustling noise and looking up he saw all the books moving from their places and coming toward him."[2] It might have been true: early and late, Peirce pulled knowledge to himself as though he were a magnet. At eleven he wrote a history of chemistry, at twelve became interested in logic, at fourteen "set up for a fast man and became a bad schoolboy." At sixteen he began to study Kant, whose work he knew almost by heart before he was out of college. Peirce graduated from Harvard in 1859, stayed on in Cambridge, and entered the Lawrence Scientific School one year before William James did.

James's first glimpse of Peirce, in September 1861 — just a month before Peirce married Harriet Melusina Fay, called Zina — was enough to reveal Peirce's brilliance, his energy, and a troubling hint of violence. James told his family about "a son of Prof. Peirce, who I suspect to be a very 'smart' fellow with a great deal of character, pretty independent and violent though."[3] Peirce was, when James first knew him, a stocky man, standing about five feet seven and very handsome. His class picture shows a clean-shaven, dark-haired young man with enormous dark eyes, a heavy nose, and a large mouth with sculptured, sensuous lips. Peirce suffered all his life, as did his father, from severe "facial neuralgia" (what is now known as trigeminal neuralgia), for which he took ether, tincture of opium, and, later, morphine. "When the pain was on him," his biographer writes, "he was, at first, almost stupefied, and then aloof, cold, depressed, extremely suspicious, impatient of the slightest crossing, and subject to violent outbursts of temper."[4]

Peirce was left-handed, and his nephew reported that he had the ability "to write on the blackboard, ambidextrously and simultaneously, a logical problem and its answer."[5] He was an accomplished amateur actor, he loved to declaim, and he knew a great deal of Shakespeare by heart. He lived extravagantly and was always in debt. He was a dandy and an aesthete. He once hired an expensive sommelier and spent two months acquiring a knowledge of Médoc wines.

In the mid-1860s, when James was flailing away at medical school, Peirce worked for the U.S. Coast Survey as a gravimetrician (he made an important contribution to the use of pendulums to measure the earth) and in his off hours pursued an interest in logic. He gave a series of public lectures on the logic of science in the fall of 1866, at least one of which William James went to hear.[6]

Peirce published a series of papers on logic in the *Journal of Speculative Philosophy* in 1868 and 1869, just as Zina, an active feminist, was publishing five articles on "cooperative housekeeping" in the *Atlantic*. In 1867, at twenty-eight, Peirce published a bold and far-reaching piece, "A New List of Categories," in which, implicitly putting himself on a level with Kant, he argued that there are only three major categories, that everything is a quality, a relation, or a representation (that is, a sign).[7] Later he called these three categories — with no improvement in clarity — the monadic, the diadic, and the triadic. Still later he labeled them "firstness," by which he meant something like "feeling"; "secondness," which is to say "reaction";

and "thirdness," or "mediation." This austere system, with its faintly Hegelian implication of progress and its emphasis on mediation, was the beginning of Peirce's lifelong involvement in what would come to be known as semiotics.

The Metaphysical Club, which we know mainly through Peirce's later descriptions of it, was apparently set up after Peirce's return, in March 1871, from an extended stay in Europe. It is hard to measure, but not hard to imagine, the impact of Peirce's strange, brilliant, eccentric, and deeply original mind on the members of the club.

Peirce had the superb scorn of the young for American philosophy; he was primed for new work, convinced that everything was yet to be done. "No American philosophy has as yet been produced," he said in 1866. "Since our country has become independent, Germany has produced the whole development of the Transcendental Philosophy, Scotland the whole philosophy of Common Sense, France the Eclectic Philosophy and Positive Philosophy, England the Association Philosophy. And what has America produced? Hickok has made a not very creditable modification of German Philosophy and Frothingham has supposed two Absolutes, which is a contradiction in terms. That is all."[8]

Peirce possessed a happy gift for phrase and had obvious powers of mind. "Reality," he once said, and James recorded it in a notebook, "is that which finally and universally will be believed."[9] "Thought," he says elsewhere, "is a thread of melody running through the succession of our sensations."[10] In his sixties Peirce would say, "The truth is that the whole fabric of our knowledge is one matted felt of pure hypothesis confirmed and refined by induction."[11] With grand simplicity that still echoes for us, he observed that "chance begets order."[12] He could make direct, winning appeals. "Let us not pretend," he once said, "to doubt in philosophy what we do not doubt in our hearts."[13] Describing what would later be called pragmatism, he said, "The essence of belief is the establishment of a habit."[14] Like the Englishman Alexander Bain and like his friend James, Peirce put considerable emphasis on habit. James once told, in conversation, about a meeting of the Metaphysical Club: "They assembled; Peirce did not come; they waited and waited. Finally a two-horse carriage came along and Peirce got out with a dark cloak on him. He came in and began to read his paper . . . He set forth," James said, "how the different moments of time got into the habit of coming one after another."[15]

Peirce had a rigorous mathematical mind; he was systematic and went into things so deeply as to require new terminology, in which he clearly delighted. For example, he distinguished among three basic kinds of evolution, the tychastic, the anancastic, and the agapastic — that is, evolution by fortuitous variation, by mechanical necessity, and by creative love — and he insisted that "tychasm and anancasm are degenerate forms of agapasm."[16]

Peirce considered himself a scientist first and last. "I am," he wrote, "saturated through and through with the spirit of the physical sciences." He came early to accept Darwin's idea of random, fortuitous variation (what he called tychasm or tychism; James would, on occasion, use the same term), but he never accepted the idea that natural selection is sufficient to account for the evolution of mind. For the latter Peirce would require "the gentle purposive action of love," or what he called agapasm.[17]

Peirce was what philosophers call a realist, someone who believes that general concepts have an existence independent of individual cases. Realists stood in opposition to nominalists — James was a nominalist — who believe that concepts have no real existence at all, being only verbal generalizations of individual cases.

Pragmatism was born and formed in Cambridge in the early 1870s, in the Metaphysical Club, though we must wait until 1878 for Peirce's "pragmatic maxim": "Consider what effects, which might conceivably have practical bearings, we might conceive the object of our conception to have. Then our conception of these effects is the whole of our conception of the object."[18] Peirce firmly believed that "a prerequisite for successful experimentation is an external world resistant to actions arising from misconceptions of it."[19] And indeed Peirce's later life, which more and more resembled a Greek tragedy, may be said to have borne this out with grim regularity.

The young Peirce was breathtakingly ambitious. He intended to "outline a theory so comprehensive that . . . the entire work of human reason . . . shall appear as the filling up of its details."[20] Peirce's father had taught mathematics "as a kind of Pythagorean prayer. He proclaimed the mystical doctrine that, however the supernatural might be, it existed in the natural world and was experienced there."[21] Benjamin Pierce believed, and his son Charles came also to believe, "that nature and the mind have such a community as to impart to guesses a tendency toward the truth, while at the same time they require the confirmation of empirical science."[22]

Peirce's later career was one long series of dreams, controversies, and disasters, the turbulent swings of which make James's life look tranquil by comparison. He made enemies readily. His first wife, Zina, left him after fifteen years. Unable to get an academic position after having served a five-year appointment at Johns Hopkins, and forced to resign his Coast Survey job at the end of 1895, Peirce retired with his second wife, Juliet, to a house in the country, in Milford, Pennsylvania, a town on the Delaware River.

Peirce was broke, his wife's income did not cover their taxes, he had to sell books from his library, but he continued to go to New York City, where he spun great dreams with his friends at the Century Club. His friend the painter Albert Bierstadt invented a railroad car that opened out into a room; Peirce had a scheme to license these. Peirce, Bierstadt, and E. C. Stedman (a poet, banker, and anthologist) decided they could make a fortune producing light from acetylene gas; Peirce invented and patented a key piece for the generator. And then there were the philosophical projects, prospectuses for books, and all the writing by this astonishing genius, thought by many to be the "most original and the most versatile intellect that the Americans have so far produced." Between 1884, when he had left Johns Hopkins, until his death thirty years later, Peirce wrote some eighty thousand unpublished pages. That is sixteen million words, five times the length of Henry Thoreau's fourteen-volume *Journal*.

By the mid-1890s Peirce was sinking. His brother James Peirce told William James, "I fear [Charles's] total breakdown . . . The case is one of real urgency." Peirce was by now essentially destitute. He asked his cousin Henry Cabot Lodge for work at a dollar an hour. He wrote a friend in November 1894, "I don't know where anything to eat is to come from tomorrow. In the last 25 hours, one cracker and a little oatmeal." James met every appeal from Peirce or on behalf of Peirce with solid help. Sometimes he sent money, sometimes he arranged paying lecture engagements.[23]

One morning in late December 1906, just after James had returned to Cambridge from giving a talk in New York, one of his students, Henry Alsberg, who was living in a rooming house called Prescott Hall, at 472 Broadway in Cambridge, near James's home, was called by his landlady "to come into one of the rooms to see an old gentleman, who had been ill and was very likely dying. When he went in he saw a sick, worn body of a man obviously suffering from undernourishment and lack of care; and when he asked his name, he was told 'Charles Peirce.' In a wild confusion of emotion, Alsberg and a friend went to find William James, and caught him coming out of class. James listened to the story. 'Why,' he said, his face changing, 'I owe him everything!' and he swung them into a cab to call for Peirce and take him home."[24]

Peirce had come to Cambridge with Juliet to make a few dollars reporting on a meeting of the American Academy of Sciences for a New York paper. Juliet had returned to their Pennsylvania home, but Peirce had stayed on to write his report, living for a week on a loaf of bread and $1.70 before James and Alsberg rescued him. Peirce's life and career were now an Ozymandian wreck. His biographer writes, "With a distant grief, I muse about his tragic life — about the pain, the folly, the failed great ambitions, the immense and exacting labors; the unrelenting search for truth; the great loyalty of his friends, the blindness of his enemies; the power, the prescience, the care for truth and the startling beauty of his philosophical creations."[25]

Over the next few months James wrote to well-off friends and acquaintances to raise a pension of a thousand dollars a year for Peirce. Whatever Peirce's failings, he had a grateful heart. He renamed himself Charles Santiago (for Saint James) Peirce. The money made a difference to him, to be sure, but it was James's esteem more than his money Peirce valued. Writing about James in 1911, Peirce said, "I really lack the self-command to repress my reflections when I have once set down his name. Who could be of a nature so different from his as I?" While Peirce was one of the world's great logicians, James was a man for whom logic was "an inconvenience." "He so concrete, so living," Peirce went on, "I a mere table of contents, so abstract, a very snarl of twine. Yet in all my life I found scarce any soul that seemed to comprehend, naturally, (not) my concepts, but the mainspring of my life better than he did."[26]

The Metaphysical Club in the early 1870s would have been an extraordinary group in any age, by any standard. Most extraordinary, perhaps, is that its heyday came at the start of the intellectual lives of James, Peirce, and Holmes, among other gifted members. The era and the place were charged to the muzzle with new beginnings. Positive science, laboratory science, the life sciences, the ideas of Comte, Mill, Helmholtz, and Darwin, were bringing a new world into being. Those young Americans, who had enough intellectual energy, singly and together, to "twist the tail of the cosmos," as Holmes put it, give an impression of blithe hubris. They were young, unknown, untested; the yet more powerful sons of already powerful fathers, they talked and thought and wrote a new world of mind into existence. William James bravely copied out for the front of one of his early notebooks the superbly impertinent lines that conclude Emerson's poem "Give All to Love": "Heartily know, when half gods go, the gods arrive."[27]

21. Cambridge and Harvard, 1872

CAMBRIDGE ITSELF WAS fast becoming a new world by the early 1870s. It had been a quiet rural village, so quiet that John Holmes, Oliver Wendell Holmes Sr.'s brother, who lived on Appian Way, could say that when two cats crossed the street, all the neighbors rushed to their windows.[1] Around the college yard and the Cambridge Common ran wooden fences, the split rails let into granite fence posts. In 1856 there were a dozen shops in Harvard Square. By 1863 a hundred horsecars a day traveled between Cambridge and Boston, running on iron rails in the middle of the streets, the rails set flush with the paving. Henry James Sr. walked along the car tracks when the sidewalks were covered with ice. The horsecar trip from Harvard Square to Charles Street, across the Charles River in Boston, took forty minutes.

By 1864 Charles Eliot Norton could say that "old Cambridge grows a little more like a city every day."[2] As soon as Harvard's new young president Charles W. Eliot was installed in May 1869, Harvard became a construction site, with Thayer Hall going up in 1869, Weld Hall in 1870, and Matthews in 1871. Work on Memorial Hall began in the fall of 1870. Socially, there was something paradoxical about the town. Henry James wrote Grace Norton about "our dear, detestable, common Cambridge." Henry Adams, newly appointed to Harvard this fall to teach history, noted wryly how "several score of the best educated, most agreeable and personally the most sociable people in America united in Cambridge to make a social desert that would have starved a polar bear." Cambridge society, said Adams, was a "faculty meeting without business."[3] William James at this same time also felt the "social dreariness," the "selfconsciousness, suspicion, etc," of Cambridge, but he could also ride to the defense of what he prized at other times as our "charmed circle."

The real action at Harvard was not so much the new construction — though Eliot was to put up during his term thirty-five buildings, one more than had been erected in the preceding 233 years — but new appointments and a new liveliness to intellectual life. In 1868 Harvard was still a small, backward country college. It had a library of 168,000 volumes and an endowment of just over two million dollars. Tuition was one hundred dollars a year. There were five resident graduate students.

Eliot was adept at finding bright, mostly young people and persuading them to take academic positions. A number of appointments went to people in William James's immediate circle of friends. Eliot, thinking no doubt of the English model, quickly instituted a series of "University Lectures," intended as graduate-level instruction. Emerson was for the first time invited to teach at Harvard, to give a round of philosophy lectures together with Francis Bowen, John Fiske, Charles Sanders Peirce, James Elliot Cabot, Frederic Henry Hedge, and George Fisher. All accepted, and the University Lectures were duly offered starting in September 1869.

In February 1870 Wendell Holmes began teaching at Harvard Law School. In September of the same year, Henry Adams began teaching history at the college. This was the year Chauncey Wright taught a course in psychology. Among the most important of these innovations, as we have seen, was Eliot's invitation, in April 1871, to Henry Bowditch to come back from Europe and join in the "great work" of reforming the medical school. When Bowditch returned from Germany in September 1871, he immediately set up the first physiology lab in America, in two rooms at the top of the old Grove Street medical building.

Nothing was more central to the revitalization of learning in the late nineteenth century than physiology, which was no longer synonymous with physics. By the early 1870s physiology was more interested in process and function than in descriptive classification and taxonomy. It was seen as "an acquaintance with the phenomena, the aggregate of which constitute life. It is the science of life." Everything that in the twentieth century would be considered part of the life sciences was, in the 1870s, considered physiology.[4] Two historians of Harvard Medical School later wrote that 1869 marked "the dawn of a revolution in medical ideas and medical training, based on the new work of Pasteur and the realization of the marvels revealed by the microscope, and on the physiological methods of study then in their infancy in France and Germany."[5]

New beginnings, new horizons abounded. In April 1871 James Thayer rescued Emerson from his University Lectures, which had been much harder work and more of a strain than Emerson had anticipated. Thayer arranged for a six-week trip to California by private railroad car; Wilky James was one of the party. William spent much of the summer taking "sea baths" at Scarborough, Maine, staying with Mother, Father, Aunt Kate, Alice, and Bob at the Atlantic House, near Prout's Neck. Many friends, among them the Bootts, the Sedgwicks, the Ashburners, and Wendell Holmes, were in the vicinity. William Dean Howells's novel *Their Wedding Journey* and Henry James's first novel, *Watch and Ward*, were both being serialized in the *Atlantic* beginning that summer of 1871. In March 1872 Wendell Holmes became engaged. He had gone to the Boston Athenaeum and borrowed Hobbes's *Leviathan* again. On the way home he ran into Fanny Dixwell, asked her to marry him, and when she said yes, he turned around and took the book back to the Athenaeum. For the second time — fortunately for American law — Holmes's life got in the way of his study of the dour and pessimistic Hobbes.

In the spring of 1872, James's old teacher Jeffries Wyman decided to give up teaching comparative anatomy and physiology at Harvard. President Eliot seems to have approached Henry Bowditch about taking over Wyman's post. But Bowditch, who had his medical school position and laboratory, suggested to James that he take over for Wyman, subject of course to Eliot's approval. At this time James was working almost every day in Bowditch's lab. Eliot quickly approved, and William James was appointed instructor in physiology in the college on August 3, 1872. It was a great opportunity. James's acceptance of this appointment put him, in one small, seemingly irrelevant step, at the forefront of the all-important emerging field of physiology just when physiology and medicine (and even Harvard) were poised for the sudden jump to modernity.

22. *Teaching*

WILLIAM WAS SCHEDULED to begin teaching in the spring semester of 1873. During the previous spring, most of the James family was again on the move. On May 11 Harry departed with Alice and Aunt Kate for England and the Continent, where he noted "Alice's immense improvement." Harry was himself thinking of a permanent move. "I incline more and more to decide to remain abroad," he wrote William.[1] Father and Mother went to Milwaukee by rail, starting out on May 30, to visit Wilky and Bob, both of whom had settled there after the collapse of the Florida schemes.

William's eyes were still giving him trouble, so he hired students to read to him, but he felt well enough otherwise to make a three-day trip to Newport, where he found the family's old stone house "dismally mildewed and dirty inside."[2] It was not like William to dwell on his own past. He was very fond of reading autobiographies, but he never wrote anything approaching one himself. His recollections of the past were apt, like this one, to be sad. "The old wall papers in the 3rd story smote me with their familiarity," he told Harry and Alice and Aunt Kate, "but they were peeling from the walls, and the old views from the little low windows were masked by the upgrowth of the trees." His impression was of a world, and a self, that no longer existed. "The ghost of my dead self with his ignorance and weakness seemed to look out strangely at me from the whole place — it was the same in Pelham Street and wherever I went, and made the total impression of the visit a very sad one."[3]

With his sense of his own ignorance and weakness now in abeyance, and with his health slowly getting better, James plunged, as he usually did, into anything he could regard as a new life. In June he and his father attended the wedding of Wendell Holmes and Fanny Dixwell. In July he left Cambridge for Mount Desert, Maine, just then becoming a popular summering spot for New Englanders. "You steam into a harbor," he wrote Alice, "studded with steep rocky islets feathered with birch and fir, up to a wharf behind which is a settlement of white wooden buildings dumped about miscellaneously . . . Behind the settlement rise two good-sized hills or mountains as they call them here, and over the bay is a long waving blue line of others, more distant and still higher, on the mainland of Maine."[4]

There was already by the summer of 1872 a considerable colony in and around Bar Harbor of sociable, intellectually inclined people from Boston, Cambridge, and New Haven, people who talked, sailed, rowed, botanized, and "commun[ed] with the sea from the cliffs." There were Ashburners, Sedgwicks, Parkmans, Paines, Trowbridges, and Andersons. William was particularly attentive to Sara Sedgwick, then in her early thirties, a year or two older than William. He described her to Alice as "the most lovely of beings"; to Harry he said, "I am absolutely ashamed of not falling in love with Sara Sedgwick." There was also an Elizabeth Greene, "the only woman I have met who can be classified with Minnie Temple for originality and inexhaustible good nature."[5]

James was now thirty, but he neither talked nor wrote about marriage — that we know of — beyond repeated assertions that he was unsuited and unfit for it. This seems to reflect his conviction that he was too sickly and neurasthenic to be a proper husband or father. But it was more than that, and it was more than an unwillingness to follow the model of his own father. Beneath William James's flirtatious and animated exterior was a completely different person, and one he loathed. He said once that he felt "chained to a dead man."

James finished, while at Bar Harbor, a long review of Hippolyte Taine's

On Intelligence. He praised the early chapters as containing "the clearest and best account of the psychology of cognition" he knew, and he predicted the book would "play a vital part in the revival of philosophy on an empirical basis which is about to begin in France."[6] Taine, a well-known French critic, was working, in this book, along the English line of Bain, Spencer, and Mill; he was trying to eliminate transcendentalism from psychology.[7] Taine was opposed to so-called faculty psychology, to Cartesianism, to philosophical realism, and to the concept of universals. In place of all this, he proposed a psychology of naturalism based on the scientific method and on clinical data. He emphasized the connection between psychology and the neural sciences, and was deeply attentive to Darwin. Taine regarded such notions as "faculty," "capacity," and "power" as examples of what Alfred North Whitehead would call misplaced concreteness. Such words, Taine said, "do not indicate a mysterious and profound essence, remaining constant under the flow of transient facts."[8] Transient facts were exactly what he did accept. "In little, well-selected, important, significant facts, stated with full details and minutely noted, we find at present the materials of every science."[9]

Taine wrote provocatively and boldly. "History," he said, "is applied psychology, psychology applied to more complex cases." He began his book with a long discussion of signs. "What we have in our minds when we conceive general qualities and characters of things, are signs, and signs only." All our ideas can be reduced to images, and these images constitute our reality. Taine gives the example of Flaubert. "My imaginary persons affect me," Flaubert wrote, "pursue me, in fact, I live in them. When I was describing the poisoning of Emma Bovary I had so strong a taste of arsenic in my mouth, I was myself so far poisoned, that I had two consecutive fits of indigestion, and real indigestion, for I threw up my dinner."[10]

James pulled up short, for now, of accepting some of Taine's cleverest points, such as the view that "external perception is an internal dream which proves to be in harmony with external things; and instead of calling hallucination a false external perception, we must call external perception a true hallucination."[11] This, says James, is admirable, considered as psychophysiology, but it raises a philosophical problem, which is "how, out of a conspiracy of hallucinations, anything real can be hatched."[12] James was strongly attracted by Taine's liveliness, his vivid style, his passion for detail, his narrative method, his distrust of vague and unsupported generalities, and his bright sympathy with the empirical approach.

On July 27, 1872, William wrote Alice about "Bowditch's offer to let me replace him in teaching the physiology elective next Spring term." When the appointment came through, William wrote Harry that the work was "a perfect godsend to me just now. An external motive to work, which yet does not strain me — a dealing with men instead of my own mind, and a diversion from those introspective studies which had bred a sort of philo-sophical hypochondria in me of late."[13]

William was experiencing a general turn toward the outer world this summer — Goethe's advice was always that turning outward to the world was health, while turning inward was disease — and he reveled in female company and in nature, and sometimes in both together. He went with a local boatman and some friends for a long row to Great Head, four miles south of Bar Harbor. The wind came up on the return trip; he sat beside Sara Sedgwick and steered the boat. "The fresh wind, the interminable spotless twilight, the dark, heaving ocean, the solemn might of the cliffs on our left hand, the incipient northern light which later became one of the finest I have ever seen, all made a first-class night of it."[14] Later, in mid-August, he took the steamer back to Portland, then drove by buggy to the Atlantic House, near Prout's Neck, where he'd been the previous summer with his family. There he saw old friends and people who remembered Al-ice and Wilky and Aunt Kate.

Here too William found himself open to things. He enjoyed "the steady heavy roaring of the surf" coming "through the open window borne by the delicious salt breeze over the great bank of stooping willows, field and fence." He told Harry he had "never so much as this summer felt the soothing and hygienic effects of nature on the human spirit." This new in-terest in nature made him sorry that he had let his drawing die out. He said he regretted not having stuck to painting, and he thought he ought still to learn to sketch in watercolor. He knew, as he now said, that a per-son "needs to keep open all his channels of activity, for the day may al-ways come when the mind needs to change its attitude for the sake of its health."[15]

As his spirits rose, his feistiness returned. He hectored Harry about his writing style: "Your own tendency is more and more to over-refinement, and elaboration. Recollect that for Newspaporial purposes" — William had in mind Harry's recent travel sketches — "a broader treatment hits a broader mark."[16] Here, as so often, William's remarks reflect his own case and his own aspirations as much as or more than Harry's. It was becoming a pattern with him. He would criticize Harry, then read something splen-did by him — he soon was calling Harry's "Madonna of the Future" "a masterpiece" — then apologize for his earlier criticism.

The fall went swiftly. Chauncey Wright was in England, visiting Darwin in September. In early November William wrote a warm letter to Charles Renouvier: "Thanks to you I have for the first time, an intelligible and reasonable conception of freedom." He told Renouvier that because of his, Renouvier's, philosophy, "I am beginning to be reborn to the moral life."[17] The link was clear to him. If we are not free to make choices, we are not responsible for our lives. If we are free, we are responsible.

On November 9 and 10 a huge fire destroyed 775 buildings in downtown Boston. "Rich men suffered," William wrote easily to Harry, "but upon the community at large I should say its effect had been rather exhilarating than otherwise." William seems not to have known that in one of those buildings was the studio of his former painting teacher, William Morris Hunt, who lost all the works stored there. But he undoubtedly knew that heroic volunteers had saved the Old South Church by spreading wet blankets on its wood-shingle roof while fire engines from as far away as New Hampshire sprayed the steeple with water.

On November 18, Bob James, now twenty-six, married a young woman from Milwaukee named Mary Holton. Bob and Mary made a trip east soon after, and William reported that "Mary has won the hearts of all of us by her combination of prettiness, amiability, vivacity, and modesty with a certain dash of pluckiness which is very charming."[18] But by late December William was writing Bob again about depression. Bob had not written for a while; William said he was afraid it was "one of your low-spirited moods again." It was probably at least partly his own condition he had in mind when he told Bob, "When the mind is morbid only the gloomy images have any vividness. We may try to realize the reverse of the picture, but it won't *bite*, and even concentrated reflection will fail often to give it substantiality for us. Then the only thing is to have faith and wait, and resolve whatever happens to be faithful 'in the outward act' (as a philosopher says) that is *do* as if the good were the law of being, even if one can't for the moment really believe it. The belief will come in its time."[19]

"Your If is the only peacemaker," says Touchstone in *As You Like It.* "Much virtue in If."

In January 1873, just after his thirty-first birthday, William James began to teach. His first course was an elective, Natural History 3: Comparative Anatomy and Physiology of Vertebrates. The course came under the Department of Natural History, the examining committee of which had had Henry Thoreau as a member in 1859 and 1860. Thomas Dwight was responsible for the anatomy part, James for the physiology. The course attracted fifty-three students, all upperclassmen, and met at eleven o'clock in the Museum of Comparative Anatomy, which was then located in Boylston Hall. James received three hundred dollars for his work; it was the first substantial money he had earned, even if it amounted to only 10 percent of what Harry would make this year. Neither William nor Henry mentioned the contrast, but in a family where money mattered, it would have been noted by both of them.

The new instructor still parted his hair in the middle, though he kept it shorter than before. In 1869 he had worn a full mustache, and now he added a full beard, trimmed to medium length. Photographs show a serious, unsettled face with a faintly troubled expression around the eyes. One acquaintance of his from around this time said that he looked "foreign": "He was very slender, his clothes were of an entrancing, unfamiliar cut, he had a little pointed beard, he wore a soft flowing blue-and-green-plaid necktie, its bows and ends outside his waistcoat." He had an "air."[20]

He was disappointed in his students at first. His mother spoke in a letter of the "loutish character of the young men generally, so few show intelligence or interest, — still there are a few."[21] "Dealing with students is a queer thing," William wrote a friend. "There is no rebound to them. You say your say and they depart in silence." This suggests that James was not yet the teacher he would become. Still, he enjoyed teaching from the very beginning. He wrote Harry that he found "the work very interesting and stimulating," and he added that it might be "not unpleasant as a permanent thing. The authority is at first rather flattering to one." William's fond father saw it as a wild success. "Willy goes on swimmingly with his teaching," he wrote Harry, adding with his burdensome optimism that the students "are elated with their luck in having such a professor, and next year he will have no doubt a larger class still, attracted by his fame."[22]

As William settled into teaching, his spirits and outlook underwent a marked change for the better. His physical health was slower to mend, but even that seemed to him better. By mid-February he was writing to Harry, "My own spirits are very good as I have got some things rather straightened out in my mind lately, and this external responsibility and college work agree with human nature better than lonely self-culture."[23]

One day in mid-March William came into the living room of the Quincy Street house. As his father recorded the scene, Willy, after walking the floor in an animated way for a moment, exclaimed, "Dear me! What a difference there is between me now and me last spring this time." Last spring, Willy said, he had been a hypochondriac, "and now feeling my mind so cleared up and restored to sanity. It is the difference between death and life." When his father asked "what specially in his opinion had promoted the change," William replied, his father said, "Several things: the reading of Renouvier (specially his vindication of the freedom of the will) and Wordsworth, whom he has been feeding on now for a good while: but specially his having given up the notion that all mental disorder required to have a physical basis . . . He saw that the mind did act irrespective of material coercion, and could be dealt with therefore at first-hand, and this was health to his bones."[24]

We must be careful not to take Henry Senior's words completely at face value. What he reports is what he longed to hear, but the general drift of his account fits well with the rest of William's new outlook. William had already rejected strict psychophysics (the idea that measurements of reaction times and other physiological processes are the sole legitimate basis of psychology) and accepted the notion that, as Milton moved it and Emerson seconded it, the mind is its own place. It is primary and active, not secondary and passive.

William James's decision to teach was a major turning point in his life, marking the beginning of the end of his early troubles. James is famous for his work in psychology, philosophy, and religion, but it is clear that his real vocation was teaching. It gave him a position of authority he had never had before, and it kept him in constant contact with bright young people. At the end of the first week of April, William told Eliot he would take on both parts of the anatomy and physiology course for the next year. This triumphant, if a trifle premature, announcement is the subject of the final entry in the diary of troubles William had been keeping for the past five years, ever since the gloomy days in Germany in April 1868.[25]

James's initial term of teaching, some fifty classroom hours of it, was the first regular work James had done in his life. It taxed his precarious health, and he was glad enough when the term was over, but it had a tonic effect on him. Now that he was a working man, and with the enthusiasm of a convert, James wrote a piece on vacations for the North American Review. He loudly denounced the proverbial New England advice "Better wear out than rust out," and he called for the institution of vacations for all working people. He even proposed the establishment of "vacation trusts": "One million dollars properly invested would set free every year no fewer than fourteen hundred such persons" for a "month of idleness." He does not supply the math behind this; neither does he say where the funds would come from.[26]

23. To Europe and Back

THE ROUTINE OF TEACHING agreed with James, and he began immediately to consider it as a career possibility. There was, however, the annoying question of what to teach. His deepest interest continued to be philosophy, but there was no job teaching philosophy on the horizon. He felt he could wait no longer because he needed to be making a living. He could always apply to Father for money, but taking at least a step toward self-sufficiency was becoming an urgent matter of self-respect. On February 10, 1873, just as he was starting to teach, he wrote in his diary, "I decide today to stick to biology for a profession in case I am not called to a chair of philosophy, rather than to try to make the same amount of money by literary work while carrying on more general or philosophical study. Philosophy I will nevertheless regard as my vocation."[1] Biology was for James a catchall phrase that included, prominently, physiology.

In early April President Eliot inadvertently made James's dilemma a bit worse by offering him the whole course — that is, physiology plus anatomy — for the following year. But William had now changed his mind, and his impulse was to say no. He wrote Harry that he had told Eliot, "I had resolved to fight it out on the line of mental science," even though the job he was being offered "might easily grow into a permanent biological appointment, to succeed Wyman, perhaps."[2] On April 9 William changed his mind again, and told Eliot he would take on the anatomy as well as the physiology. In his diary he tried to persuade himself that "philosophical activity as a business is not natural for most men and not for me." Then, too, there was the problem of concreteness, of James's already strong empirical streak. "The concrete facts in which a biologist's responsibilities lie form a fixed basis from which to aspire as much as he pleases to the mastery of universal questions when the gallant mood is on him." The long diary entry concludes by observing that "the ends of nature are all attained through means; perhaps the soundest way of recovering them is by tracking them through all the means."[3]

Throughout his first term of teaching, James went back and forth about not only what to teach but whether to teach at all the following year. The alternative would be to travel, rest up, and concentrate on improving his health. Teaching had raised his spirits, but not, it was now clear, his physical condition. He wrote Harry in May, "I believe I told you in my last that I had determined to stick to psychology or die. I have changed my mind and for the present give myself to biology." With a little roll of the drums and a cymbal clash of martyrdom he went on: "This is virtually tantamount to my clinging to those subjects [anatomy and physiology] for the next 10 or 12 years if I linger so long."[4]

Harry picked up on Willy's self-pity and wrote back, "There seems something half tragic in the tone with which you speak of having averted yourself from psychology." Stung by this, perhaps, Willy replied with a blaze of assurance that completely concealed the thrashing indecision in which he labored. He told Harry, "The only thing with me now is my health; my ideas, my plan of study are all straightened out." Indeed he was feeling better about teaching, and about working somewhere along the continuum from physiology to psychology to philosophy, but his health was, even by mid-July of 1873, still a major problem. "I alternate," he wrote Harry, "between fits lasting from 4 or 5 days to three weeks of the most extreme languor and depression, weakness of body and head and pain in the back — during which, however I sleep well — and fits of equally uneven duration of great exhilaration of spirits, restlessness, comparative bodily and mental activity — coupled however with wakefulness of the most distressing sort that makes me absolutely sick."[5]

By late May he was as yet uncertain about teaching in the coming year. When his classes and the exam were at last over, he went off to Magnolia, Massachusetts, then to the Isles of Shoals off the New Hampshire coast, and, in August, to the Catskills. On August 25, at the last possible moment, he wrote Eliot to ask if a substitute could be found to teach in his place. Eliot replied affirmatively on September 2, and William made hurried plans to go abroad.

He had a feeling of urgency, almost of desperation about the trip. "I feel," he wrote Harry, "that I must get well now or give up. It seems as if I should too — for nothing remains but this g—d——d weakness of nerve now." "Weakness of nerve" was his medical diagnosis, not a moralizing reproach. He used the same phrase to describe himself in another letter, to brother Bob, also dated September 2, 1873.[6]

He left on October 11 on the Cunard liner *Spain*. The weather during the crossing was mostly dismal. He arrived in London and wrote home, on October 25, that he was feeling "awfully blue and homesick." The weather continued endlessly cold, dark, and rainy. "The awful fullness and solidity of life here in England discourage one."[7] He skipped Boulogne, scene of his boyhood happiness, and sped along to Paris. It rained steadily, day after day. He found Paris, then being reconstructed by Baron Haussmann, "a terribly monotonous looking city." He told his sister that he had had "a pretty melancholy time" in both London and Paris. After a day or so in the latter, he took a train for Turin and then Florence, where Harry was working and living. It poured rain the entire way. Harry — whom William now referred to almost always as "the angel," with exactly what tinctures of irony and affection we can only guess — was, said William, "wholly unchanged." Harry was no balder than when he had left America, and his beard, said William, was very rich and glossy from his using brilliantine on it. "He seems wholly devoted to his literary work and very industrious." Once again "the angel" was showing Willy the way.

In Florence William still complained of "the seedy spell in which I have been plunged for upwards of a fortnight," and of a "heavy lethargy," though he predicted it would soon wear off.[8] His first impressions of Florence and, subsequently, Rome were quite as negative as those of London and Paris. None of these places seemed picturesque. He recoiled from the "slimy streets and caverns in which people live," and he thought the "human race here has a debilitated look, undergrown and malformed." He could hardly believe this was "the great Italian people whom Taine and Stendhal etc. bully us with." He spent November in Florence, December in Rome, and January back in Florence. He was, he said, disgusted with "all this dead civilization crowding in upon one's consciousness." In Rome he saw the Colosseum Byronically, under a "cold sinister half moon," and was repelled by a scene so "inhuman and horrible that it felt like a nightmare." He saw at first in St. Peter's "so perfectly explosive a monument of human pride, insolence, and presumption . . . that for a moment I felt fully like Martin Luther." He explained his strong antipathetic reactions in a letter to Wilky: "One has to grow up to Europe again when he comes, just as if he'd never been here before." And he did grow up, or at least warm up, again, somewhat, to Rome and then to Florence.[9]

But real life for William was in America. Wilky was married in November to Caroline Cary, whom everyone called Carrie, and Bob and Mary had a baby boy, Edward, the elder Jameses' first grandchild. William talked some about working in the Florence lab of a physiologist named Moritz Schiff, but nothing came of it.[10] He did begin a journal in Florence, in which he wrote about the picturesque, about his own diminished interest in art, about Jacob Burckhardt's *Civilization of the Renaissance in Italy* (which he was reading in German), but most interestingly about Emerson.

"I am sure," he wrote, "that an age will come when our present devotion to history, and scrupulous care for what men have done before us . . . will seem incomprehensible; when acquaintance with books will be no duty, but a pleasure for odd individuals; when Emerson's philosophy will be in our bones, not our dramatic imaginations."[11]

While in Rome, William contracted a mild case of malaria and was advised to go back to Florence. As soon as he recovered, Harry came down with a fever (not malaria), and it was William's turn to nurse Harry, and Harry's turn to tell the folks at home that Willy was "a ministering angel, and nursed and tended me throughout with inexpressible devotion."[12] More significant, Harry commented in the same letter on Willy's overall mental condition. For all his groaning about Europe, "Willy is," said Harry, "most vigorous and brilliant. He seems *entirely* the Willy of our younger years again — in looks, spirit, humor and general capacity." Harry liked to report good news, he habitually put a good face on things, and he was capable of prodigious concealment, but this comment has the ring of truth — it's the italicized word "entirely" — that seems finally to spell the end of William's long-troubled twenties and early thirties.

William now described himself as "overflowing with homesickness." He told a friend he had "little heart for this loafing life." He told Bob, "My heart is not in the thing here, for I want to be hard at work in Cambridge." To Alice he wrote, "The weight of the past world here is fatal — one ends by becoming its mere parasite instead of its equivalent." Harry noted that William was "intensely impatient to get home and return to work."[13]

William went to Venice in February, finding the galleries and churches very cold — a situation that has not changed in the 130 years since. He went on to spend ten days in Dresden, then sailed for home from Bremen, reaching New York on March 13, 1874. Back in Cambridge, he was surprised at the "diminished scale of interest" and at how "mean and flimsy" things looked. But he began to feel better physically within a week of his return. He was working regularly in Bowditch's lab.

In a letter to Bob he gave a thumbnail account of his earlier crisis, and it says a good deal about his spiritual condition — if we may use such a phrase — in 1874. "I worked through it [the crisis] into the faith in free-will and into the final reign of the good conditional on the cooperation of each of us in the sphere — small enough often — in which it is allowed him to be operative. Why God waits on our cooperation is not to be fathomed — but as a fact of experience I believe it — and having that belief open to me I have lost much of my former interest in speculative questions — I have taken up Physiology instead of Philosophy and go along on a much calmer sea with a more even keel." While the calm, unprotesting reference to God may surprise us, James's expression of belief is thoughtfully and typically conditional: any triumph of good depends on the cooperation of each of us. The idea that God needs man is not argued for, but simply stated as a fact of personal experience. A specific belief is not a refuge or a rock or a thing to cling to, but a matter of certain possibilities being open to one, and of assent to those possibilities.[14]

His going along on a more even keel as regards the big issues made it possible for him to open himself to other books and ideas. When he had first read George Eliot's *Middlemarch,* he had remarked to Harry, in December 1872, on its "tremenj'us intellectual power" and had called it "the biggest novel ever written." By February 1873 his opinion had changed almost completely. He thought it a "blasted artistic failure." He liked the Lydgate-Rosamund story, calling it a "pure artistic study," but he thought "Ladislaw-Dorothea suggest[ed] too much and solve[d] too little." Now, in March 1874, just home from Europe, William revised his revised opinion, saying the book was "fuller of human stuff than any novel that was ever written." Consistency, for James, was not in itself a virtue. Vacillation was now a fixed habit. He was so open to almost any kind of experience that he was apt to change his mind repeatedly about any single piece of it, from a career plan to a recent book.[15]

He was now, again, interested in "investigating" spiritualism (those are his ironic quotes). He told Catherine Havens, a frequent correspondent, "I went a few days ago to see a medium who was said to raise a piano in broad daylight." James might indeed be open to the possibility, but he was no fool. "She was a deceiver," he went on, "performing the feat by means of her wonderfully strong and skilful knee." He thought he was bound to make an important discovery if he kept on with spiritual investigation. He would find either that "there exists a force of some sort not dreamed of in our philosophy" or that the voluminous testimony thereof really constitutes "a revelation of universal human imbecility." He was open to either conclusion, but it was a principled openness, not gullible, not indifferent, not fuzzy-minded, and certainly not overeager to see mysterious forces lurking under every piano. He might not have it yet, but he was sure there would actually be a conclusion when all the evidence was in.[16]

24. Emerson, Mill, and Blood

A BOUT A MONTH after returning to the United States in April 1874, William James was invited to a dinner party at the Tappans' in Boston. Caroline Sturgis Tappan had been romantically attracted to Ralph Waldo Emerson, and he to her, some thirty-five years before. Emerson, who would be seventy-one in a month, was present at the dinner, as were his daughter Ellen and Dr. Holmes. Holmes did all the talking. Emerson's aphasia was now advanced. "Emerson looks in magnificent health," William wrote Harry, uncomprehendingly, "but the refined idiocy of his manner seems as if it must be affectation."[1]

Emerson was to have a large and in some ways decisive effect on James, but it was a long time coming, and it came despite as well as because of James's exposure to the man. Of course the whole Emerson family was a vivid presence in the James household for years. Emerson was a good friend of Henry Senior's. The guest room in the house was called "Mr. Emerson's room." Edward Emerson, a year younger than Harry, spent a couple of vacations with the Jameses at Newport. Ellen and Edith Emerson visited there too, making a deep impression on Alice. Wilky and Bob attended Frank Sanborn's school in Concord; both Sanborn and his school were very much part of the Emersonian circle.

Harry's account of Emerson in his memoirs is respectful, and his portrait of Emerson's Concord in *The American Scene* is close to worshipful, but even as he assures us in one place that he knew from an early age that Emerson was the greatest person among his father's friends, his description in another place ripples with light, elegiac irony: "Not a russet leaf fell for me . . . but fell with an Emersonian drop."[2] Emerson was inescapably famous and had almost all his best work well behind him when, in 1862, Tom Perry and Willy and Harry James paid a short visit to Concord. Perry recalled how he had "gently giggled over the Sage of Concord" with the James brothers.[3]

William James might giggle, but Emerson had already laid his mind on him — to borrow the wonderful comment of Rufus Jones about the effect of James on *him* — and in a notebook of the year of the Concord visit, 1862, William wrote on the title page the last lines of his favorite poem of Emerson's, "Give All to Love." The poem calls the reader to "leave all for love," but it also urges, when the loved one eventually feels the need of "a joy apart from thee," letting the loved one go free, "though her parting dims the day." In a letter of January 8, 1868, to Tom Ward, James again invokes this poem and its advice to hold nothing back and to not hold on too long.[4]

Emerson was useful to James both materially and intellectually. When William went abroad in 1867 he carried a letter of introduction from Emerson to Herman Grimm. In a letter to a friend in March 1868 James clearly shows what he was getting from Emerson at this time: "Emerson speaks of a plus quantity being essential to every hero — that is a feeling of superiority to all circumstances however solemn, a carelessness, a dash of recklessness, which implies a certain disrespect for every thing but one's own will — (I don't father this amplification on Emerson) and men who have this buoyancy of will may doubtless go far with it."[5]

The Emerson James needed and found in these years is the Emerson of "Self-Reliance" and "The American Scholar." In his copy of the latter James marked the passage that says, "Action is with the scholar subordinate, but it is essential. Without it he is not yet man. Without it thought can never ripen into truth . . . Only so much do I know as I have lived. Instantly we know whose words are loaded with life and whose not."[6] By 1873 James found himself not only accepting Emerson's outlook but, to some extent, living it himself.

Perhaps Emerson was not yet in James's bones, but he was certainly vividly present in his imagination. In June 1874, a couple of months after the dinner at the Tappans', William went to Concord at Edward Emerson's invitation. Edward's sister Ellen had planned a house party, "a carnival of youth and beauty," and William found it extremely pleasant. He wrote Bob a letter while sitting in the Emerson parlor with "a southerly rainstorm washing the grass, the apple, and the chestnut trees outside, a big wood fire in the grate, with Edith Forbes, née Emerson, Ida Higginson, née Agassiz, and Miss Una Hawthorne sitting around me sewing and gossipping with each other. The whole afternoon," William told Bob, "in some respects was better than the pride of Greece and Rome, as I delighted Miss Ellen by remarking." Emerson was "courtesy itself," but he showed "the tooth of age in his almost absolute oblivion of proper names, and his increasingly groping way of talk."[7]

Yet James was filled with a sort of Emersonian pleasure in the moment. Concord seemed magical, filling him, as he said, with "deep admiration." He added, "I suppose there are a good many small German towns where one could get the same combination of primitive simplicity with the highest intelligence, but I don't think there are many American towns." Ellen Emerson's talk, and Edward's too, James thought "fit for royal tables."

James could now separate the mythological Concord, the Concord of an earlier, golden age, as it were, from the present power and incitement to be found in Emerson's writings. He was responding to Emerson the liberator, Emerson the champion of the single self. And in one crucial way, Emerson's great central doctrine was already James's as well. This is the doctrine that, says Van Wyck Brooks — paraphrasing James's "Rationality, Activity, and Faith" — "has marked all the periods of revival, the early Christian age and Luther's age, Rousseau's, Kant's and Goethe's, namely, that the innermost nature of things is congenial to the powers that men possess."[8]

Of the other Emerson, the person who understood from Faraday that the world may not be made of "matter" after all, but may instead consist of fields of energy; the Emerson who knew that life cannot be contained in Aristotle's ten categories of being, and who wrote "Illusion, Temperament, Succession, Surface, Surprise, Reality, Subjectivism, — these are threads on the loom of time, these are the lords of life"; of this Emerson who knew so much about the fringes and edges of the mind, James had as yet only a faint glimpse.[9]

Ten days after the Renoir-like party at the Emersons', James was reading, with high enthusiasm, John Stuart Mill's autobiography. Three quarters of the way through, he exclaimed, in a letter to Catherine Havens, "Autobiographies are the first department of literature for me."[10] A good autobiography can reanimate a person who has been entombed by a good reputation, so while Mill shrank, for James, into a "much less colossal figure," he — by the very process — "helps you to understand his philosophy by telling you of his life."

James had read and reviewed Mill's *On the Subjection of Women* in 1869. He had read Mill's *Auguste Comte and Positivism* before 1870.[11] He knew Mill's *Examination of Sir William Hamilton's Philosophy* before 1872.[12] James also owned a copy of Mill's *System of Logic*, was discussing it by 1875, and using it as a course text a half-dozen years later. Mill's ideas, especially his early attraction to Comtean positivism and his lifelong commitment to utilitarianism, were foundational for James. When, years later, he published *Pragmatism*, the dedication was "To the memory of John Stuart Mill from whom I first learned the pragmatic openness of mind and whom my fancy likes to picture as our leader were he alive to day." By then James did not believe in the existence of ideas apart from the men and women who held them. His interest in autobiography was not casual; it was a crucial aspect of his whole approach to ideas.

Mill's education, the famous concentrated hothouse forcing, was at the opposite pole from James's random, wandering, inconsistent, and fragmented schooling, but in both cases, their education was a major project and preoccupation of their fathers. Mill began Greek at age three, "neglecting" Latin until he was eight. At seven he read the first six dialogues of Plato, at eight he began the *Iliad* in Greek, then read Pope's translation, then composed a one-book continuation of Homer as an exercise in writing English verse. At twelve Mill began logic, starting with the Scholastics. At thirteen he studied the political economy of David Ricardo and Adam Smith. Mill was appreciative — to say the least — of what his father did for him, though he could not help noticing that "for passionate emotion of all sorts, and for everything which has been said or written in exaltation of them, [his father] professed the greatest contempt. He regarded them as a form of madness. The 'intense' was with him a bye-word of scornful disapprobation."[13]

By the age of fifteen Mill had acquired an "object in life: to be a reformer of the world." This may not seem unusual for a fifteen-year-old, but Mill meant to do something about it. At sixteen he began writing extensively for newspapers; at seventeen he was helping his father launch the *Westminster Review*. At eighteen his own work began appearing in that review, and at nineteen he was active in politics, in debating, in writing and publishing. At twenty he fell into a depression.

It was the autumn of 1826. "I was in a dull state of nerves," he wrote, "such as everybody is occasionally liable to: unsusceptible to enjoyment or pleasurable excitement: one of those moods when what is pleasure at other times becomes insipid or indifferent." While in this frame of mind he asked himself: "Suppose that all your objects in life were realized: that all the changes in institutions and opinions which you are looking forward to, could be completely effected at this very instant: would this be a great joy and happiness to you?" Mill recounts that then "an irrepressible self-consciousness distinctly answered 'No!'" "At this," he says, "my heart sank within me: the whole foundation on which my life was constructed fell down. All my happiness was to have been found in the continual pursuit of this end. The end had ceased to charm, and how could there ever again be any interest in the means? I seemed to have nothing left to live for."[14]

James too had been through a long vocational crisis marked by unshakable depression. Mill's situation and his response were different from

James's, but James would not have been indifferent to Mill's plight. Utilitarianism, the greatest good for the greatest number, assumed that men and women were motivated by the desire to increase pleasure and decrease pain. But the utilitarians did not see this as a matter of emotions. Rather, they understood it to involve a rational calculus of happiness by which all pleasures and pains were "measurable in terms of intensity, duration, certainty, rapidity, fecundity, purity, and extensiveness."[15]

After this thunderbolt "no!" Mill felt — though he could not, he said, make his position intelligible to his father and friends — that all feelings, all emotions, were dead within him. Six months later, he tells us, "a small ray of light broke in upon my gloom. I was reading accidentally Marmontel's *Memoirs,* and came to the passage which relates his father's death, the distressed position of the family, and the sudden inspiration by which he, then a mere boy, felt and made them feel that he would be everything to them — would supply the place of all they had lost. A vivid conception of the scene and its feelings came over me, and I was moved to tears. From this moment," says Mill, "my burthen grew lighter. The oppression of the thought that all feeling was dead within me, was gone. I was no longer hopeless: I was not a stock or stone."

From this episode Mill says he learned the importance of cultivating the feelings; this now "became one of the cardinal points in my ethical and philosophical creed." Mill turned to Wordsworth, whose poetry had taught him that "there was real, permanent happiness in tranquil contemplation . . . not only without turning away from, but with a greatly increased interest in the common feelings and common destiny of human beings."[16]

William James had already walked a similar mile himself. Mill next turned in his autobiography to his unrestrained praise of Harriet Taylor and "the most valuable friendship of my life." Harriet — who married Mill only after a twenty-year friendship of exactly the sort of passionate intensity his father despised — was, said Mill, "the most admirable person I had ever known." Her mind Mill considered "a perfect instrument." He learned, he said, "more from her teaching than from all other sources taken together." His friendship with her was "the honor and chief blessing of my existence."[17] This was a road that William James had not yet traveled.

It is no surprise to hear that James was influenced by Emerson. James has the same optative ebullience, the same metaphorical panache, the same bedrock faith in the individual. Nor is it surprising that John Stuart Mill would be a long-standing influence on James. Utilitarianism was stepfather to pragmatism and to its concern with results, with "fruits not roots." No active thinker in the mid- to late nineteenth century could easily escape the shadows cast by Emerson and Mill. But almost everyone except William James escaped the influence of Benjamin Paul Blood, whose pamphlet *The Anaesthetic Revelation* James read and reviewed a few months after the Emerson party in Concord.[18]

Blood was a writer of letters to newspapers. Ten years older than James, he was a nonacademic, a philosopher, a mystic, and, it would turn out, a pluralist to boot. Blood had been born in 1832 in Amsterdam, New York, just west of Schenectady. He went to Union College, then returned home to the "large brick house on the south side of the Mohawk as you enter Amsterdam from the East."[19] Blood had heard or read Henry James Sr., and he credited him as "the first to impress me with the presence of that transcendent [quality] we call genius." Blood was, delightfully, much more than a metaphysician. Interested in machinery, he had patented a "swathing reaper." He had been a gambler, making and losing, he told James, "bar'ls" of money. He had been a "fancy gymnast" and had fought "some heavy fights — notably one of forty minutes with Ed. Mullett, whom I left senseless." "I have worn out many styles," he wrote James years later, "and am cosmopolitan, liberal to others, and contented with myself." If Blood sounded like Whitman, he looked like a cross between Poe and Nietzsche. He sent James a photo of himself at age twenty-eight, taken when he had just "lifted by a chain on my right shoulder and around my right arm 1160 lbs." "I never could value things at others' rates," Blood wrote James, "never was respectable or conforming . . . The chaff blows off, the grain remains and I could borrow the city treasury if I wanted the money."[20]

In 1875 this Paul Bunyan of Amsterdam, New York, sent William James a pamphlet announcing the discovery of "a mystical substitute for the answer which philosophy seeks, [an] ontological intuition, beyond the power of words to tell of, which one experiences while taking nitrous oxide gas and other anaesthetics."[21] Blood located the moment of insight not in the instant of "going under," not in the swirling down the ever-accelerating, ever-darkening red whirlpool one remembers from a childhood tonsillectomy, but in the moment of "recall from anaesthetic stupor to sensible observation, or 'coming-to,' *in which the genius of being is revealed*" (Blood's italics). The awakening moment, with its "primeval prestige" and "all but appalling solemnity," solved the world's mystery. "This world," Blood wrote and James quoted, "is no more that alien terror which was taught me. Spurning the cloud-grimed and still sultry battlements whence so lately Jehovan thunders boomed, my gray gull lifts her wing against the nightfall, and takes the dim leagues with a fearless eye."[22]

Perhaps Blood's prose stirred memories for James of the gulls at the mouth of the Amazon. At any rate, he compared the state Blood described to "Nirwana" and to what was suggested by the old proverb *In vino veritas.* "Ontological emotion, however stumbled on, has something authoritative for the individual who feels it," James wrote, adding, "The duty of the intellect toward it is not suppression but interpretation." James did not think that laughing gas was necessarily the best way of getting at the revelation in question. "What blunts the mind and weakens the will," he wrote, "is no full channel for truth." He preferred, he was careful to say, "the intoxication of moral volition."[23]

The essence of it for Blood was the discovery that "fulness of life . . . forestalls the need of philosophy," that life itself is a "sufficiency, to which . . . a wonder or fear of why it is sufficient cannot pertain, and could be attributed to it only as an impossible disease or lack." This repose in the sufficiency of life, the rejection of the fundamental lack or dearth, is at the opposite pole from the core convictions of William's father, whose best prose is a hectic poetry of dearth.

"The secret of Being," as James summarized Blood, "is not in the dark immensity beyond knowledge, but at home, this side, beneath the feet and overlooked by knowledge."[24] James was attracted to Blood's energy, his forceful reasoning, his idiosyncratic boldness, his unconventional defense of an altered mental state. He also liked Blood's conclusion, and he especially admired his writing. Blood was, said James, "a man with extraordinary power over the English tongue."[25] Blood talked about "pounding and punching the chaos into the logos," and his writing swoops and soars in a sort of blind onward rapture. "And does not pluralism have in it its own negation," Blood wrote James in 1897, "as the many (per se) must afford a specimen of the one. The world has long believed in limited space (subjective), unity of intelligence, community, a home, a heaven, a duty, an order, a chance for fame that is known of all, not a world, but the world, under control — all facts and possibilities known and realized — imperial peace." Who could resist a man who talked like that? "You have the greatest gift of superior gab since Shakespeare," a delighted William James wrote Blood.[26]

James's interest in people like Blood — figures from the intellectual underworld — exasperated his professional colleagues even as it moved them, sometimes, to admiration. James's judgment, said one, was "corrupted by kindness." George Santayana, first a student of James, then a colleague and rival, and finally a eulogist, said James "kept his mind and heart wide open to all that might seem, to polite minds, odd, personal, or visionary in religion and philosophy. He gave a sincerely respectful hearing to sentimentalists, mystics, spiritualists, wizards, cranks, quacks, and imposters . . . He thought, with his usual modesty, that any of these might have something to teach him . . . Thus," Santayana concluded, "William James became the friend and helper of those groping, nervous, half-educated, spiritually disinherited, passionately hungry individuals of which America is full."[27]

Twenty years after James died, a medium named Jane Revere Burke published a book she said had been written, through her, by William James.[28] It was called *Let Us In;* its main idea was that the world, our world, is crowded with the spirits of the dead, the "discarnate," who vastly outnumber the incarnate — the living — and who are always pressing and pleading with us to allow them into our minds. We feel compelled to smile, of course, but there is at least a metaphorical truth here. James's willingness to listen, his risking of ridicule, his spiritually democratic openness, still moves us to let them all in, just as he let into his life a parade — like the finale of a Fellini film — of healers, reformers, and visionaries. He let in Horace Fletcher, the diet guru and messiah of munching; Annie Payson Call, the currently invisible author of still useful books on therapeutic relaxation; Tom Davidson, the ebullient philosophy teacher and apostle to the working man; S. H. Hadley, whose conversion in a New York waterfront mission prefigures Bill Wilson and Alcoholics Anonymous; Clifford Beers, who fashioned his own harrowing story of mental illness into a biting and effective call to reform; Elwood Worcester, the co-founder of the Emmanuel movement and popularizer of Gustav Fechner; Fechner himself, the German psychophysicist who, after a serious illness, woke to see the entire universe as alive; and Bill Bray, the working-class English evangelist whose vision has the reality of a summer morning and whose feet walked the road while his head swam in heaven.

William James let into his life all these and many, many more whose brash originality, looping idiosyncrasies, and private languages effectively shut out most communication with others. They are not mad, but they are not mainstream. They are strong, roiling back-eddies along the edges of the great river of mind, but they are as much a part of the river as the main channel, and William James knew it.

25. *From Physiology to Physiological Psychology*

I N T H E F A L L O F 1874 William James returned to Harvard and again
taught Natural History 3: Comparative Anatomy and Physiology. He
had fewer students this time, thirty-three, compared to fifty-three the
first time, and he was paid six hundred dollars for the yearlong course. His
attitude was changing and he was edging toward stability, both inner and
outer. He behaved more and more like a man with a place and a purpose.
He had for years championed America over Europe as a place to live. Now
he began to talk proudly and a little defensively — but with humor —
about Cambridge. "There are very good elements here," he told Kate Havens (the Catherine Havens whom James met in Dresden in 1868), "but
every one lives in his shell, doesn't care to be spoken to, and evening visits
are only paid by one man who is so profound a philosopher and so late
a visitor as almost to make his friends wish to transport him."[1] He began
to have a little proprietary feeling about Harvard too. In an obituary notice of Jeffries Wyman, the Harvard professor of comparative anatomy
and physiology, James's teacher, and the man whose position James had
filled, James spoke personally about the force of Wyman's "example on us
younger men," and he referred comfortably to "our Cambridge" and "our
University."[2]

James was now the acting head of Wyman's Museum of Comparative
Zoology, and in December 1874 he joined the Harvard Natural History Society.[3] The old order seemed finally to be passing. Agassiz had died in December 1873, Wyman the following April. President Eliot's energy and ambitious building projects were remaking Harvard. By 1874 the large dining
room in Memorial Hall was finished and opened as a commons. Sanders
Theatre was substantially completed by May 1875 and used for commence-
ment the following year.[4]

James's world, both its professional and its social side, revolved around
the rising generation. He went to Edward Emerson's wedding, and was invited to Naushon by Will Forbes, who had married Emerson's daughter
Edith. Of his visit to this most private and storied of the Massachusetts islands, summer redoubt of the Forbeses, James wrote, "They live in great
opulence but not in state for they are the simplest and most genuine and
unpretending of human beings . . . They have a great shabby old house,
two yachts, and no end of horses, and the way we galloped through the

beautiful old beech woods dashing past their trunks and under their level boughs at the risk of smashing knees and heads was enough to make one's hair stand on end."[5]

Back in Cambridge, his life settled quickly into a routine. He taught his class and went to the lab every day except Sunday. He undertook a program to improve his eyes, forcing himself to read for half a minute, then a minute longer each day until he had worked himself up to three hours. He avoided tobacco and coffee (neither Harry nor Alice could drink it either) and read for half an hour every night before bed. On Sundays he paid a morning visit to the Sedgwicks: there seems to have been a little something between him and twenty-three-year-old Theodora Sedgwick. When the Metaphysical Club was reorganized in late 1875 or early 1876, it met on Sunday afternoons for three hours. For relaxation and "wash[ing] out the cobwebs from the mind," James went to the theater, as he had ever since he was a little boy in New York.

Early in the fall of 1874, Henry James came back from Italy, first to Cambridge, then to New York. His writing had been going splendidly. He was now thirty-one. By the end of 1874 he had published eighty-three reviews, twenty-eight travel sketches (one in eight installments), and twenty-four short stories. He would bring out his first three volumes in 1875: *A Passionate Pilgrim and Other Stories* in late January, *Transatlantic Sketches* in April, and *Roderick Hudson* at year's end, following its serial appearance in the *Atlantic Monthly*.

William, for his part, had published twenty reviews, an obituary, the piece on vacations, and a letter to the editor. None of it was substantial, none of it was even signed. Not until 1874 did he make any serious effort to concentrate on one subject, physiology. So compared with Harry, he had achieved almost nothing. His sense of rivalry still expressed itself in frequent advice to his brother about how to write, advice that Harry allowed to pass over him with exemplary patience. When William suggested to Harry that the characters in *Roderick Hudson* reflected too much on themselves, Harry responded with a long and admiring description of Turgenev characters doing just that.

William's reviewing, if it was insignificant when set beside Harry's, was nevertheless bright, informed, and decisive. It was an apprenticeship of sorts, as well as a barometer of his mind. In December 1874 he took time to write the editor of *The Nation* on the subject of science and faith. "Physical science," he wrote, "has well earned the great authority she enjoys." But he was wary that some scientists were becoming so confident that they sometimes allowed their conclusions to run well in advance of proof, yielding occasionally "to the pleasure of taking for true what they happen vividly to conceive as possible."[6] Troubled now by a too easy use of the word "science" as a simple synonym for "truth," and of "scientist" to mean "authority," he said such usage represented "the mood of Faith, not Science." Dubious already about too large claims, he concluded, "In 'science' as a whole, no man is expert, no man an authority; in other words, there is no such thing as an abstract 'Scientist' — fearful word!"[7]

But James's own working life was precisely that of a scientist. He was not an abstract "scientist," however. He had learned thoroughly from Agassiz and loved to repeat that no one "could understand more of a generalization than his knowledge of particulars would cover."[8] James both taught and conducted lab work in anatomy and physiology. He dissected frogs even while on vacation. He wrote a short piece in February 1875 defending vivisection. It was not that he couldn't identify with the lab animals, nor did he sidestep the awfulness. "A dog strapped on a board and howling at his executioners, or still worse, poisoned with curara, which leaves him paralysed but sentient, is, to his own consciousness, literally in a sort of hell," he wrote. He called for compassion among researchers, and he thought the day might be near when all that could be learned from vivisection would have been learned. But he also said that, at present, the entire science of physiology "is based, immediately or remotely, upon vivisectional evidence . . . To taboo vivisection is then the same thing as to give up seeking after knowledge of physiology."[9] He also argued in a way a modern reader finds uncomfortable that if the dog understood what was going on, "and if he were a heroic dog, he would religiously acquiesce in his own sacrifice."

James was, in fact, enormously fond of dogs. In the summer of 1875, on his way home from his Wisconsin trip, he acquired a setter pup named Dido. He adored her, as did Alice, and when Dido began to bark too much and range too far, and couldn't be kept from "swill debauches" in the neighbors' garbage "and consequent nocturnal attacks," James reluctantly sent her off to Bob in Wisconsin and got Alice a Scottish terrier.

James spent a good deal of time during 1874 and 1875 trying to look after Bob. In the summer of 1875 he went west to see him. Bob, though settled in Wisconsin, married, with a son, Edward, born in 1873, and another child on the way (she would be a daughter, Mary), was in profound spiritual trouble and writing harrowing letters to William, who had a special tenderness for Bob. "When the darkness seemed totally cruel and the despair too savage for anyone to bear," Bob wrote, "I have tried prayer and friendship and memory . . . But thro' them all I have always felt the avenue that I am treading growing narrower and less well cheered until finally I have reached that part of it w[h]ere we are alone, quite alone and the power of despair ahead of you."[10] Bob too had some of the family gift for vivid self-expression as well as the family curse of depression. "I cannot understand," he went on in a letter to William, "how even the smallest experience of human insufficiency can fail to make one crave and demand with a loud voice some little or great entrance behind the horrid mask which clothes us."

William's own mood this year ranged from gaiety to melancholy. Apropos the hundredth anniversary celebration of the battles of Lexington and Concord, James wrote Kate Havens, "The beauty of it is that the hatred of tory and rebel was brotherly love compared to the sentiments of Lexington and Concord today toward each other, each wishing to have the sole credit of the first battle." To Annie Ashburner he wrote to say that her photograph (James was an avid exchanger of photographs) brought back the old days, but, he added, "Alas, I fear me those days are past forever." He went on to lament, in reference to which friendship he does not say, "Every year changes our personality, and the splinters of a parted friendship will not keep sharp enough to rejoin exactly as they broke." Perhaps one reason James seldom referred to the past was that thinking about it gave him such an acute sense of loss.

But it was science, especially new science and its procedures and assumptions, that now commanded his deepest, steadiest attention. He maintained his interest in Darwin and Darwinism; in 1875 he was reading in modern physics as well. James Clerk Maxwell had become in 1871 the first professor of experimental physics at Cambridge University in England. In 1873 he brought out his *Treatise on Electricity and Magnetism.* In May 1875 James read and reviewed a book called *The Unseen Universe,* by the physicist and mathematician Peter Guthrie Tait (who helped develop modern mathematical physics) and the physicist and meteorologist Balfour Stewart (whose work on radiant heat helped found modern spectrum analysis). *The Unseen Universe* was written to show that "the presumed incompatibility of Science and Religion does not exist."[11] Tait and Stewart suggested that "the visible system is not the whole universe, but only, it may be, a very small part of it; and that there must be an invisible order of things, which will remain and possess energy when the present system has passed away."[12] The authors clearly regarded this as a live issue. They formulated the thesis in a grotesquely compressed form ("thought conceived to affect the matter of another universe simultaneously with this may explain a future state") and published it — to establish priority — in *Nature* in 1874, in simple cipher. The announcement as printed in *Nature* read, "A8 C3 D E12 F4 G H6 I6 L3 M3 N5 O6 P R4 S5 T14 U6 V2 W X Y2."[13]

"Modern physics," James begins his review, "postulates, in addition to the gross matter which we can weigh and feel, another form of material existence called the ether or medium." Details aside, James goes on, "The upshot of all these speculations is that matter and the medium, or the visible and the invisible, are considered materially and dynamically continuous."[14] It makes all the difference in the world whether we regard this notion of matter and ether as a new outbreak of the visible and invisible worlds of, say, Cotton Mather, or as a forerunner of, say, A. S. Eddington's twofold description of the table — one description emphasizing the commonsense substantiality of the table, the other the scientific description in which "there is nothing substantial . . . it is nearly all empty space — space pervaded, it is true, by fields of force." Maxwell's ether would disappear with later discoveries, but the distinction between the apparent table and the scientific table is still with us. James was interested in how the new physics of his day made it possible to entertain the conception of "a continuity of being, both conscious and material, between the worlds." He was also interested in how Tait and Stewart aimed simply "to explode the notion that science debars the supposition of such a continuity."[15]

Since this continuity was, from now on, an important and recurring possibility for James, it is necessary to understand how nuanced and ambivalent his approach to it really was. He objected, for example, that the invisible world of modern physics was "by no means identical with the world 'behind the veil' of religion," noting that religion spoke not just of "another" but of a "better" world. But then James doubled back on himself and noted that Tait and Stewart believe in the "betterness" of the "other" world, not because they are scientists, but by "the same simple act of teleologic trust, the same faith that the end will crown the work, with which the most narrow-minded old woman so quickly envelops her briefly recited cosmogony." Then, in the most surprising turn of all, James swept on: "We for our part not only hold that such an act of trust is licit, but we think, furthermore, that any one to whom it makes a practical difference (whether of motive to action or of mental peace) is in duty bound to make it."[16]

This is not a modern version of Pascal's wager (it makes sense to bet on the existence of God, because if God exists we will be better off, and if God doesn't we have lost nothing by such a bet). Nor is it a modern version of Kant's categorical imperative (act only on those principles you are willing to have everyone act on). We are obliged to believe, James says here, because such a belief will make a difference in how we live. Whitehead uses a similar line of thought to announce the imperative of education. "Where attainable knowledge could have changed the result," he wrote in "The Aims of Education," "ignorance has the force of vice."

Elsewhere James expressed a more provisional skepticism. In, for example, his June 1875 review of Fernand Papillon's *Nature and Life,* he expresses doubt about "a rewatering of the well-watered thoughts of Janet, Lévèque, and Vacherot," writers who, "adopting recent scientific theories about the conservation of energy and the constitution of matter, spiritualize the latter by identifying its force with the will-force, which is the only [force] of which we have any immediate personal experience. Matter is motion, motion is force, force is will." James met the new physics with only provisional acceptance. It seems to have been enough for him to think of the invisible world of the new physics as a possibility, without for the moment having to press it into probability or fact.

James shook himself free of Cambridge in mid-June 1875, after classes and exams ended. He headed west, mainly to see his brothers. Bob had taken a railroad job in Prairie du Chien, Wisconsin, eight hours by rail west of Milwaukee. But he had recently left this position, and with money from Father he bought a farm in Whitewater, a couple of hours southwest of Milwaukee. The farm was terribly hard work, a second child was due in August, and Bob was depressed and uncertain. He began to drink again, and also to lean heavily on religion.

Wilky was in Milwaukee and also married. He had left his railroad position and gone into the chain and bolt business with a man named Whaling. William visited Milwaukee, where both his sisters-in-law had family. Then he went home the long way, traveling to St. Paul and down the Mississippi to Prairie du Chien, then to Chicago, Niagara, down the St. Lawrence to Montreal, and home by rail through Vermont, where Alice and Aunt Kate were staying at the Bread Loaf Inn in Ripton. His summer reading included Darwin's *Expression of Emotion* and the poetry of Shelley and Whitman. Thinking back to his first enthusiasm for poetry seventeen or eighteen years earlier, he wrote, "No verse has ever renewed that feeling in me as Walt Whitman has succeeded in doing this summer."[17]

Chauncey Wright died in September 1875, before James got back to Cambridge from his summer travels. College started up again, and James taught Natural History 3 for the third time, to yet fewer students. He was also giving a graduate course in the relations between physiology and psychology, and he offered a small, informal course in practical anatomy. "The only way to understand the brain is to dissect it," he wrote later. "The brains of mammals differ only in their proportions, and from the sheep's one can learn all that is essential in man's." He recommended several printed guides, noting that if one couldn't get the books, a few practical notes — subjoined — would suffice. "The instruments needed are a small saw, a chisel with a shoulder, and a hammer with a hook on its handle . . . In addition a scalpel, a pair of scissors, a pair of dissecting forceps and a silver probe are required." James made it all seem easy. "The solitary student can find homemade substitutes for all these things but the forceps, which he ought to buy."[18]

In October Harry returned to Europe, this time with a sense that he was going for good. "I take possession of the old world," he wrote home in a triumphal letter from London on November 1. "I inhale it — I appropriate it!"[19]

Less dramatically, but no less decisively, William reached out this fall in an effort to take hold of his own life. In early December he wrote to President Eliot proposing a new course, in psychology. James began by explaining how the course would fit in with existing offerings. The letter thus shows how James conceived of the entire broad field he now called "mental science" rather than "philosophy." Mental science, he says, is "the study of one thing, the human mind, its laws, its powers, and the authority of its conclusions."[20] He identified four subdivisions: "a) logic, b) History of Philosophy, c) Metaphysics (involving 'erkenntnisslehre' [epistemology] methodology, or all questions as to the reach of man's cognitive faculties), d) psychology." James noted that the four courses already in the Harvard catalogue belonged mainly to the history of philosophy.

James went further and, in the same letter, specified the need for the particular kind of psychology he wanted to teach. "On every side," he noted, "naturalists and physiologists are publishing extremely crude and pretentious psychological speculations under the name of 'science.'" On the other hand, "professors whose education has been exclusively literary or philosophical, are too apt to show a real inaptitude for estimating the force and bearing of physiological arguments when used to help define the nature of man." Now, James wrote, "a real science of man is . . . being built up out of the theory of evolution and the facts of archeology, the nervous system and the senses." Since neither the pure physiologist nor the literary person who lacked firsthand knowledge of "nervous physiology" could really do the job, James proposed "a union of the two disciplines" in one man, a man such as himself. And if Eliot and the college wanted a traditional appointment, James pointed out that Rudolph Hermann Lotze, at Göttingen, and Wilhelm Wundt, first at Heidelberg and then at Zurich, were the kind of person James was proposing. Like James, both Lotze and Wundt had started out as students of medicine, both were interested in physiological psychology, both brought wider philosophical views into consideration. James made it plain to Eliot that he, William James, embodied just such a union of disciplines.

James had an interview with Eliot during December; Eliot spoke of offering James an increase in salary. In February 1876 James was promoted to assistant professor of physiology at an annual salary of $1,650. The new course, Natural History 2: Physiological Psychology, was offered during the next school year.

26. *Days of Rapture and Heartbreak*

ONE DAY EARLY IN 1876, one of William James's new friends, a philosophical Scot named Thomas Davidson, said to James, "Come with me this evening to Mrs. Sargent's, and I'll introduce you to the woman you ought to marry." Mrs. Sargent and her husband, the Reverend John T. Sargent, lived at 77 Chestnut Street in Boston. Their house was the meeting place for the Radical Club, a group, Gay Wilson Allen notes, "of Unitarian ministers and liberal laymen, formed to discuss the abolishing of all vestiges of supernaturalism in the Unitarian religion and finding ways to make the human religious experience more spiritual." Members included T. W. Higginson, Julia Ward Howe, Henry James Sr., John Greenleaf Whittier, Elizabeth Peabody, and Lydia Maria Child. At its meetings one might also hear Emerson or Mark Twain or the geologist Nathaniel Shaler.[1]

The person Davidson wanted James to meet was Alice Gibbens, a young woman of outgoing temperament with a "gift of vivacious and humorous talk." She was twenty-six. She had brown hair and expressive dark eyes. She often sat on a low rocker, "leaning forward a little from the hips conversing eagerly." She possessed a "vigorous affirmative temperament," and she had a way of "drawing forth no end of confidences." Hers was an "experiencing nature" — it was her phrase, soon to be William's, then Cambridge's; one still heard it at Harvard in the 1950s — and she had already gathered a "marvelous collection of her own adventures and other people's personal histories — things strange, poignant, bizarre, laughable, tragic," things that lost nothing in her lively telling. Brought up in Massachusetts, she had lived abroad for some years in Heidelberg, Dresden, and Florence. She was fluent in French and German. She and William were immediately attracted to each other. Alice told her mother the next day that she'd met the man she wanted to marry. William's father, with the sentimental bribery that was second nature to him, told his son, "If you'll marry Alice Gibbens I'll support you."

Alice came from Weymouth. Her father, a handsome, strong-bodied, hard-drinking, outgoing man, was a doctor. Her mother, of an opposite temperament, was quiet and reserved, a "lovely flower of New England conscience and reticence."[2] "The only social gathering she ever went to without scruple," said Alice, "was a funeral." In 1855 Dr. Gibbens took the family to California. They went by ship via Central America, where, in Nicaragua, they ran across the American filibuster William Walker and his guerrillas. The six-year-old Alice watched all day "the bodies of the killed lying deserted in the hot sunshine."[3] Despite the fighting, the heat, and an outbreak of cholera, the Gibbenses made it across the Isthmus of Panama, got on another ship, arrived at San Francisco, sailed into the bay, and soon settled on a small farm or ranch outside Los Altos, in the Santa Clara Valley. The farming was difficult; Dr. Gibbens seems not to have practiced medicine, and his "sprees used to be followed by moods of desperate melancholy." Alice, still a little girl of seven, would be "hurried off to find and hide his pistol and razors."

She grew up outdoors, learned the names of all the flowers and trees and birds. She had an imaginary playmate, Johnny Green. When the Santa Clara venture came to an end in 1857 (a man having shown up with a court-approved Spanish land grant to their property), the eight-year-old Alice felt terrible about going away. The last thing she did before leaving was to hide her favorite plaything, a china dog, in the hollow of a live oak tree.[4]

Back in Massachusetts, the family faced hard times. In Weymouth, the mother of Mrs. Gibbens took in her daughter and the children — Alice had two younger sisters — while the doctor lived in Boston. When the Civil War broke out, the impressionable and sensitive young Alice "couldn't bear to lie in bed and think of the soldiers who were stretched on the bare ground." So "for weeks she slept on the floor." In November 1862 her father went to New Orleans to fill a civil position under the northern military occupation. Due to start for home on Christmas Day 1865, he was found in Mobile, Alabama, shot with his own revolver, an apparent suicide.[5]

Mrs. Gibbens was so devastated by this blow she could not make the funeral arrangements, and Alice, now sixteen, essentially took over the family, which consisted of Mrs. Gibbens and the three daughters. Finding their resources more limited than they had thought, and hearing that it was cheaper to live abroad, Alice read a piece in the *Boston Advertiser,* wrote to the author, and through her wrote to a pastor in the German village of Leihgestern, arranging for the pastor to provide lodging, board, and lessons for the whole Gibbens family.

They sailed for Bremen in July 1868. After disembarking they learned that their host had fallen ill and had, without consulting them, assigned the Gibbenses to another pastor. The family traveled in a "great open hack with our luggage . . . crash[ing] down a noisy little street between the dreary cement stucco houses of Leihgestern." Alice described the wreck of their arrival in later years to her son Henry:[6] "The door of the house opened and out rushed upon us the pastor and his family. We had never seen such a man. His hair hung down to his shoulders where the ends curled up. His front teeth were all gone. But in spite of that it seemed to us that he fell on us like a wolf. His wife was a hard-faced woman who fairly clawed at us to get us into the house. The place from which they issued looked impossibly dreary dirty and squalid. We were horrified and panic stricken." Alice, now nineteen, took charge, kept the family in the carriage, explained as well as she could that they couldn't be bound by an arrangement they had not entered into, and "after difficult and vociferous argument" got the hack turned around and the family taken back to a hotel in nearby Giessen.

They next went to Heidelberg, where they soon settled into a pension in the suburbs. Alice had a fine voice, she studied with Clara Schumann, and in later years she was often called on to sing German lieder. The family stayed abroad for five years, returning not to Weymouth but to Boston, where Alice's grandmother Gibbens now lived and where Alice became a teacher in Miss Sanger's private school for girls. She and her mother were both close friends of the Quaker poet John Greenleaf Whittier, who gave Alice a warmly inscribed copy of his *Prose Works* in 1874.[7] Alice moved in interesting circles. There was the Radical Club; there were dances with the Harvard students. And, early in 1876, there was the young, just-appointed Assistant Professor James.

When he met Alice, William was feeling better physically than he had for some time. He was reading Baudelaire and studying Hume with his friends in the Metaphysical Club.[8] In March 1876 he wrote his first letter to Alice Gibbens. It is very short, starting, "My dear Miss Gibbens, I return your poem, which we all found very amusing." After a couple of polite phrases, it ends "very truly yours, Wm James."[9]

The Centennial Exhibition was opened by President Grant in May in Philadelphia. James went to see it in June, paying attention mostly to the paintings. Sometime this spring Henry Senior became ill; it may have been a stroke of some sort, and he recovered only slowly. During the summer of 1876 James visited Nantucket and Martha's Vineyard and, most notably, he went to Keene, New York, in the Adirondacks, with a large and shifting crowd of mostly male friends: Joseph Warner, Arthur Sedgwick, James Jackson Putnam, Charles P. Putnam, Henry Bowditch, and others. "A most free and jolly time," James wrote in August. "The most salutary thing . . . I ever did." Some of this enthusiasm may stem from the fact that Alice Gibbens also spent a good part of the late summer at Keene.

It was really at Keene that William and Alice found themselves swept up in what William later called their "delirious affair." He could not sleep for thinking about Alice all during August and September, and he finally took himself off a short distance, to Lake Placid, in order to tell her in a letter what he couldn't say to her face. "My dear Miss Gibbens," he began. "It seems almost a crime to startle your unconsciousness in the manner in which I am about to do; but seven weeks of insomnia outweigh many scruples, and reflecting on the matter as conscientiously as I can, it seems as if this premature declaration were fraught with less evil than any of the other courses possible to me now." Then he took the plunge. "To state abruptly the whole matter: I am in love, *und zwar* [it's true] (— forgive me —) with Yourself."[10]

William wrote this from the Brewster Hotel in Lake Placid to Alice at Beede's Hotel in Keene. Right behind, indeed along with, the avowal came an ominous avalanche of self-scraping scruples and backpedaling protestations. "My duty," he wrote, "is to win your hand if I can . . . What I beg of you now is that you should let me know categorically whether any absolute irrevocable obstacle already exist to that consummation." Having made his declaration, he fell at once into an agony of qualification and explanation. "It seems at first sight that my demand is an outrageous one. It seems as if I were in a manner trying to force your hand, and convert an indecision about denying a proposal suddenly made and probably unthought of hitherto by you, into an explicit admission of the possibility of future acquiescence." The letter labors along like a seminar. Doubts accumulate. "I can furnish you with unheard of arguments against accepting any offer I can make." Nevertheless he flung himself at Alice's feet. "I conjure you then, in case you consent to meet me again, to absolutely disregard the thought of what the consequences [of saying no] to me may be, to feel as utterly untrammeled as you were on the eve we first met, and when the day of reckoning arrives to have no tho't but of your own interests, for there your sole duty will lie."

For all the stiff phrasing and rationalizing, for all the effort to make it sound like a diplomatic maneuver, it is perfectly plain that the thirty-four-year-old James was as madly infatuated as any teenage boy. "If your reply addressed Brewster's Hotel, Lake Placid, be given to the stage driver who leaves Beede's house tomorrow with orders that he make it over to the driver of the Saranac coach whom he will meet coming from E-town [Elizabethtown] I shall get it tomorrow afternoon. I need not say how much I wish to get it then."

What Alice responded to this painfully labored proposal we do not know. (Her son burned her side of the correspondence many years later. Only a few scraps and examples of the thousands of letters Alice wrote have survived.[11]) But she cannot have been completely discouraging. She was strongly attracted to him, and as her son and biographer noted, "She had never encountered anything remotely resembling his incandescent, tormented, mercurial excitability."[12]

No sooner had they acknowledged their strong mutual attraction than William began talking about the "morality of marrying," about the "open, healthy, powerful, normal life of the world," and about "crimes" against that life, crimes such as "the marriage of unhealthy persons." In another letter he seems to be bracing for disappointment, speaking of "the thought that if you and I are really in any degree one, in the heart of being that fact is somehow represented whatever becomes of our persons."[13]

As had happened to William once before, with Minnie Temple, his temperament meshed so closely with another's that it raised the possibility of marriage, and with that possibility came a host of problems. Years later, describing how his parents had met, their son Henry James III — who had just reread all the correspondence on both sides — explained what happened:

> Soon [after meeting] they were very much in love, and each was fully informed about the other's feeling. But then my father felt that he must make Mother understand what manner of man he was. If he had to confess nothing more complicated than that he had been a thief, a murderer or an adulterer, it would have been comparatively easy for both. They might soon have decided whether to part and try to forget each other or to dismiss the past

and hope to make each other happy. But my father's case was not so simple. He must make my mother realize him as a soul tormented almost to desperation by questions about the cosmos and his relations with it — a troubled and therefore troublesome spirit encased in a fragile and ineffectual body.

The mere prospect of joining his life to Alice's seems to have undone all of William's recent positive gains and plunged him back as into a cold bath of his former debilitated, neurasthenic state. His eyes still gave him trouble, he had dysentery this fall, his energy flagged to where, he said, he had only a "little spoonful ready for each day, and when that's out as it usually is by 10 o'clock A.M. I'm good for nothing." "As he tried more and more anxiously to appraise his qualifications for the role of husband and father," his son went on, "he conceived a morbid fear that he had no moral right to ask any woman to be his wife or to bear his children."[14]

By mid-November of 1876 his letters to Alice had taken on a dark and troubled tone: "You, sitting self-contained and self-supported at a distance, not needing me will have some day to recognize me, to respect me, to admit — to admit — that whatever our feelings may be, our beings after all have something in common, something to say to each other. That is all I want. Love may be a disease, it may mean nothing — or worse than nothing, but it shall not poison me. It shall save my soul. I will feed on death and the negation of me in one place shall be the affirmation of me in a better. For this your undivided work I eternally thank you, and you ought to feel happy for it. No other experience of my life has ever shadowed forth an idea of it."[15]

The scrupulosity was not one-sided. Alice had a "passion for acknowledging errors or wrongs and making amends." So, her son tells us, "though she hadn't the slightest doubt about her own feelings, she persuaded herself that she would probably be a burden and restraint upon Father if she married him, and that brought her to the conclusion that she could serve him best by sending him away."[16]

It is impossible not to smile at the furious duel of mutual assured self-abnegation that followed, but it was searingly real and dreadfully protracted at the time. In December James wrote Tom Ward that the wonderful affair of the summer "is at an end. She cares no more for me than for a dead leaf, nor ever will."[17] He spoke in a strangely revealing way, telling Tom to "bury the whole matter," and confessing that he felt his "potentialities (of intellectual work etc)" to be beyond his "actualities," and concluding, "Each of us walks round with a dead man chained to him, which the world don't recognize."

But then the dead man was unchained and turned out in the spring of 1877. William and Alice went for a carriage ride on April 21, and everything changed during that ride. "My friend, my sister," James wrote, "I am bowed down with this solemn happiness. What right I have to it I know not, but I will try to be a mate for it and you. But," he went on, "the decision must be postponed . . . If we end by being a law unto ourselves at last" — one wonders if he had proposed something like this to Minnie — "nothing will be lost by not plighting ourselves today. We shall simply have a shorter instead of a longer engagement."[18]

There was to be nothing simple about it. Two days after the ride he was telling Alice she must go to England. Three days after the ride he wrote, "I have come to see that my saying you must go to England is pedantic folly." He talked crazily about "the likeliest plan for generating the much hoped for aversion to me in your mind," and then, recognizing his flip-flops, he concluded, "In short I am an idiot, unfit to advise you."

By June he was writing Alice to rationalize his behavior as that befitting a sound philosophical position, a kind of modern stoic acceptance of the way things must be. "Last fall and last winter what pangs of joy it sometimes gave me to let you go! To feel that in acquiescing in your unstained, unharnessed freedom I was also asserting my deepest self, and cooperating with the whole generous life of things."[19] By July William was frantic; what remains of a letter to Alice is full of wild and whirling words from this Hamlet of Harvard Square:

> I renounce you! Let the eternal tides bear you where they will! In the end they'll bear you round to where I wait for you. I'll feed on death now, but I'll buy the right to eternal life by it . . . (20 hours later) O Friend of my soul how could you write the note which has thrown me into such a frenzy? Which has been like the touch of red hot coal to gunpowder. Here in the dead bowels of the night I consecrate myself afresh. I will not abdicate — [manuscript excised] shall rule whateer be [excised] will condemn me [excised] how great a pr [excised] distress.
>
> Devotedly and [excised]
If so, Amen! Amen my own Alice Gibbens, now
And forever mine. WJ[20]

During this summer of 1877 Alice removed herself to Canada to see if distance might in some way clarify matters or show them which direction to take. But before she went north she made William a little gift to help him orient himself and to point the way to her. The gift was a small compass, a large hint. William never forgot "how, that summer when you were

William James, self-portrait, c. 1866

Mary Walsh James, c. 1865

Henry James Sr. in the 1870s

William James at sixteen, 1858

William in Geneva, around 1860

Henry James Jr., age twenty or
twenty-one, 1863 or 1864

Garth Wilkinson (Wilky) James
in Milwaukee, 1875

Robertson (Bob) James, around 1872

Alice James in 1870

William James in Brazil, 1865

Louis Agassiz, leader of the Thayer
expedition to the Amazon, 1865–66, and
the major American opponent
of Charles Darwin

Charles W. Eliot, c. 1875. Assistant Professor
Eliot was James's chemistry instructor in
1861–62 and served as president of
Harvard from 1869 to 1909.

Chauncey Wright at the time of his gradua-
tion from Harvard in 1852. Wright was
an early Darwinian and the leading spirit
of the Metaphysical Club.

Oliver Wendell Holmes Jr. at about forty.
Holmes was later appointed to the
U.S. Supreme Court.

Charles Sanders Peirce in 1859, when he
graduated from Harvard. A great logician
and semiotician and a longtime friend
of William James's, he was credited
by James with originating
pragmatism.

William James in 1869

Mary (Minnie) Temple

William James in 1868 or 1869

"Here I and Sorrow Sit"

Wilky convalescing
in Newport. He
was badly wounded
in the Civil War.

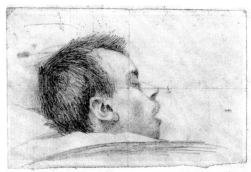

Cowled friar

Alice Gibbens in the mid-1870s.
Alice married William James
on July 10, 1878.

William James
with his daughter,
Margaret Mary
(Peggy), in 1892.
Photo by May
Whitwell.

in Canada, I used to walk for the mail through the sandy gap in the inky darkness [of Keene Valley] and never got a letter!"[21]

Looking back on this time, eleven years later, and rereading his letters, William wrote to Alice, "A stranger reading those letters alone would think of a man utterly morally diseased." He had finally, he said, "got out of that whole frame of mind, not by any acute change or act or discovery, but simply gradually and by living with you." And yet, he insisted, "knowing what I then knew about myself, and revering you as I did, I was right, right, right to feel torn asunder as I was and perplexed in the extreme."[22]

And Alice, answering William from her own perspective eleven years on, leaped to meet him with a warmth we can still feel across more than a hundred years: "Deep down in my heart has lain so long the sad doubt of your well-being, and a thousand times I've trembled before the thought that I had been over sure of your need of me and that you might have been better off if I'd never crossed your path. It's a long, long story, all this morbid pain, but it was in the bond, and not wholly unforeseen by me in those days and weeks of rapture and heartbreak when you were writing me those letters." Two days later, on March 11, 1888, Alice again wrote William about "those sacred burdened letters" and admitted, "Oh I yearned over you then with the same kind of tenderness, only greater, that I have since felt for the children. Had you been a lesser man, I should have had a keener consciousness of my strange attitude but when sometimes I grew miserably mindful of it, the real you, your wraith would turn on me so sad a look that I could only be sure afresh that you were the victim, not I, and chose above all happiness the right to take our life and together learn to bear it. There were great hours then for both of us."[23]

In September 1877 things came close to falling through again. In December James sent off his first important philosophical paper (on Herbert Spencer's definition of mind). In February 1878, while James was giving a series of lectures at Johns Hopkins and angling for a position there, the affair with Alice took a positive turn again. Then, on May 10, while walking together "when the flowering trees and shrubs of the Boston Common perfumed the air," William proposed again, and this time Alice accepted.[24] He later recalled "the spot on the Common where it occurred (and I began really to live) and which I visit [this was 1903] almost weekly for the purpose of recalling the indrawing of breath with which you murmured 'yes.' But oh, the curious inner feeling of miracle of those succeeding days."[25]

In June 1878 Harry's tragic love story "Daisy Miller" was published, making a considerable stir. On July 10 William and Alice were married, making very little stir. The groom was thirty-six, the bride twenty-nine.

The wedding was held at 153 Boylston Street in Boston, the home of Alice's grandmother Mary Howe Gibbens. The minister of the First Church in Boston (Unitarian), the Reverend Rufus Ellis, performed the ceremony. It was a small private wedding. William's parents were there, but none of his brothers. Nor was his sister there, the other Alice.

The whole experience was not so much a courtship as a conversion, and James's strong sense of what had happened during those early months and years, when he and Alice were trying to figure out what to do, found expression again and again in oddly religious terms. "I'm strong and sound," he told Alice in 1888, "and that poor diseased boy whom you raised up from the dust no longer exists." He assured her repeatedly: "Your faith your trust, is fully verified, and I am born again through and through, your child as well as husband. You have been right from first to last!"[26]

27. The Trouble with Herbert Spencer

JAMES'S INFLAMED, HEADLONG, riven pursuit of Alice Gibbens was not so much all-absorbing as all-inspiriting. At the same time he was hoping to win Alice, from early 1876 through 1878, he began seriously to maneuver for a better teaching position, he made a decisive shift from physiology to psychology, he wrote his first important papers, and, in two sets of lectures, one at Johns Hopkins and one in Boston for the Lowell Institute, he edged significantly toward his great subject, the action of consciousness.

In some way the emotional roller coaster of his courtship, together with his habitual feeling of torn-to-pieces-hood, released energies in James that found expression in the striking intellectual advances and the professional claim-staking of these years. It may be impossible to say precisely what here is cause and what effect, but what happened somehow, between January 1876 and October 1878, was that William James was reborn emotionally and set on his feet in the narrow professional sense. During this period, he began to write the work that carries his distinctive contribution to modern thought.

In March 1876, about the time of his first letter to Alice Gibbens and a month after his promotion to assistant professor of physiology, James wrote a review of a new French philosophy journal, *Revue Philosophique de la France et de l'Étranger,* edited by Théodule Ribot. He made a remark in passing about the new German psychophysics that suggests why he was no longer so enthusiastic about it. Though associated with rigorous laboratory work and though created by physicists such as Wundt, Helmholtz, and Fechner, psychophysics in Germany was said, James reported, to be "but a brilliant commentary on the deductive conclusions of the idealistic philosophers of that country."[1]

In June 1876, when he was revisiting Newport ("the same magic mildness and blondeness in the light and color"), attending the Centennial Exhibition in Philadelphia (where, as we saw, he concentrated on the painting gallery and, unlike Henry Adams, ignored the huge four-story Corliss steam engine that powered the entire vast fairground with its ten-foot stroke, its thirty-foot flywheel, its twenty-two miles of shafts and forty miles of belts), and reading George Eliot's *Daniel Deronda,* James published a review of the third edition of Alexander Bain's *Emotions and the Will* and Charles Renouvier's *Essais de Critique Générale.* This review not only clearly records James's impatience with determinism but shows his new agility — which owes much to Renouvier in particular — in turning pejorative terms into positive concepts. "Doubt itself is an active state," says James, and he quotes Renouvier for support: "The radical sign of will, the essential mark of that achieved development which makes man capable of speculating on all things and raises him to his dignity of an independent and autonomous being, is the possibility of doubt." Renouvier goes further yet, claiming, with his Emerson-like flair for phrasing, "Properly speaking there is no certitude; all there is is men who are certain."[2] Rather than see doubt and uncertainty as troublesome or negative, Renouvier, with James right behind, recognizes that what we call freedom in human affairs rests on and grows out of what in physics is called chance — that is, not determinism. Just as the possibility of there being such a thing as a chance occurrence is what we mean by the word "freedom," so doubt, instead of meaning a lamentable loss of certainty, meant, for James, the positive possibility of certainty.

In July James visited Nantucket and Martha's Vineyard and spent a few days vacationing with Holmes and his wife, Fanny, at Mattapoisett, just north of New Bedford on Buzzard's Bay. Holmes still went to meetings of the Metaphysical Club, but there was less personal warmth now between him and James. Holmes was a very different sort of person than James: he was stiff, formal, and fanatical about work. While laboring on his edition of James Kent's *Commentaries on American Law* (which when published had Holmes's name but not Kent's on the title page), Holmes had kept the manuscript by his side at all times in a green book bag. He carried out monthly fire drills "designed to instill in each member [of the household] the duty to rescue the green bag above all."[3]

Henry James thought Holmes's demeanor like "a full glass carried without spilling a drop." Watching Holmes down by the seashore one day in Mattapoisett, James described him with detachment: "He is a powerful battery, formed like a planing machine to gouge a deep self-beneficial groove through life, and his virtues and faults were thrown into singular relief by the lonesomeness of the shore, which as it makes every object rock or shrub, stand out so vividly, seemed also to put him and his wife under a sort of lens for you."[4]

To Charles Renouvier William James wrote in July that he was hoping to be "transferred to the philosophical department" at Harvard for the academic year 1877–78. He complimented Renouvier handsomely, saying that the Frenchman had finished what Hume had begun, then adding, in a burst of youthful optimism, "After your Essays, it seems to me that the only important question left is the deepest one of all, the one between understanding and mysticism, between the principle of contradiction and the Seyn [Sein] UND Nichts" (being and nothingness). James's characteristic reaction, when pressed to take a stand on a familiar abstract dilemma, is to look for a way to keep both alternatives in play a little longer. He told Renouvier he couldn't just now "burn my ships behind me, and proclaim the belief in the One and the Many to be the Original Sin of the Mind."[5]

In the fall of 1876, just as he was working himself up to tell Alice he loved her, he was plunged back into teaching. He had a new course to offer, the one he had proposed to Eliot the previous December, Natural History 2: Physiological Psychology. He had nineteen students, mostly seniors, and he used Herbert Spencer's *Principles of Psychology* as a text. He soon found himself in vehement, almost outraged opposition to Spencer. Spencer was an English philosopher who wrote about evolutionary purpose before Darwin's *Origin of Species* came out. He became a dedicated Darwinist, and was the coiner of the phrase "survival of the fittest." Spencer was, like James, essentially self-taught. His ten-volume *Synthetic Philosophy,* which explained everything in terms of evolutionary progress, was a huge influence on and expression of the great scientific movement of the second half of the nineteenth century.

James had been reading and studying Spencer since the early 1860s, and there were excellent reasons why James used Spencer's book for his new course. Spencer started with the physiology of the nervous system and went on to treat mind as "a function of an evolved organism dealing with a physical environment."[6] Thus, says Ralph Barton Perry, "James's biological approach to psychology, originating in the order of his studies, was confirmed and adopted as the standpoint of his [James's] mature work in this field." As late as 1904, James praised the originality of Spencer's *Principles of Psychology* for "its revolutionary insistence that since mind and its environment have evolved together, they must be studied together."[7]

But in the fall of 1876 James blazed with a beginner's impatience. By December he was, he said, completely disgusted with the eminent philosopher, and he was calling Spencer "absolutely worthless in all fundamental matters of thought." He had serious reservations about important parts of Spencer's work, namely, "the theory that the only meaning of rationality or rightness in mental life is 'correspondence with the environment,' and the theory that an acquired habit in the ancestor may become an innate aptitude in the descendent."[8]

James allowed himself some fun with Spencer's clunky prose. First he told his students to learn Spencer's famous law: "Evolution is an integration of matter and concomitant dissipation of motion; during which the matter passes from an indefinite incoherent homogeneity to a definite coherent heterogeneity; and during which the retained motion undergoes a parallel transformation." Then James restated it: "Evolution is a change from a no-howish untalkaboutable all-alikeness to a some-howish and in general talkaboutable not-all-alikeness by continuous sticktogetherations and somethingelseifications."[9] The seventeenth and last question on James's final exam for the course was "Mention all the inconsistencies you may have noticed in the book."[10]

James was also teaching his other courses, including Natural History 3: Comparative Anatomy and Physiology of Vertebrates (the course he had been hired to teach in the first place) and his graduate course on the relations between physiology and psychology, now generally recognized as the first graduate course in psychology in America. There were other demands on his time as well. In February 1877 he gave a talk at the Harvard Natural History Society on hypnotizing frogs, and on March 1 he spoke on recent investigations of the brain before a thousand people in Sanders Theatre, under the auspices of the same group.

On the following day, Friday, March 2, a special commission awarded twenty disputed electors from Florida, South Carolina, and Louisiana to Rutherford B. Hayes on a party-line vote. Hayes thereby won the Electoral College by one vote, having lost the popular vote for the presidency to Samuel Tilden, who received a quarter million more votes than Hayes. There was no time to spare. The inauguration was to be held on Monday,

March 5, but rumor had it that Tilden meant to declare himself President and have himself sworn in on Sunday, the fourth. President Grant invited Hayes to the White House the night before and arranged for Chief Justice Morrison R. Waite to come over and swear in Hayes on the spot, secretly. Sunday passed without incident, and Hayes was sworn in again, publicly, on Monday. James preferred Hayes to Tilden anyway, Hayes having come out for civil service reform, for currency backed by gold and silver, for public schooling, and for returning full autonomy to the states of the former Confederacy, by, for example, ending the federal military occupation of the South Carolina statehouse.

The politics of his own Harvard appointment were much more on James's mind than were such presidential matters. He had been promoted from instructor to assistant professor of physiology in February 1876, about a month after he'd met Alice Gibbens. The advance in rank was welcome, but James no longer wished to confine his career to physiology. In April 1877 he wrote to the president of the new Johns Hopkins University in Baltimore, indicating his availability for a philosophy position there should one open up.

Getting an appointment in philosophy at Harvard looked unlikely. The mere fact that James was teaching a course using Spencer as a text seems to have created a problem. An old friend, Ephraim Gurney (one of Chauncey Wright's original Septem group, a professor of history and dean of the Harvard faculty from 1870 to 1875), wrote James in July 1877 to say he hoped James could get himself "another elective also in philosophy, that you may not be identified in the minds of that only half-intelligent and semi-clerical body the board of overseers, with Herbert Spencer and what they might fancy scientific materialism." Religious conformity was still an issue, even in Eliot's new Harvard.[11]

Harvard's tiny, two-person philosophy department also posed problems for James's advancement. The senior person in the department was Francis Bowen, who had been born the same year as William James's father. Bowen was sixty-five in 1876, having been appointed in 1853. His approach was firmly theistic; he had Kantian leanings, was vigorously opposed to the theory of evolution, and took pride, as Gurney said confidentially to James, in striking down new champions of Error. The other person in the department was George Herbert Palmer, who was the same age as William James. Palmer had a degree in divinity from Andover Theological Seminary. He had been made an instructor in philosophy in 1872, been promoted to assistant professor the following year, and been appointed department chairman in 1876.

Palmer was a short, forceful, impressive man. His "bushy brows over deep-set eyes lent a suggestion of concentrated will, which seemed perpetually on duty."[12] He was the first to break away from the textbook-and-recitation mode of teaching philosophy at Harvard; he worked out his own ideas in his lectures. His great subject was the theory of ethics — he was partial to Hegel — he wrote widely on literary subjects (Shakespeare, Sophocles, Virgil), and he edited the works of George Herbert in three volumes. It was Palmer who had said that William James's judgment was corrupted by kindness. Maybe so, but where Palmer had ability, James had brilliance. Still, Palmer was a complex, capable, and intriguing man who once wrote a book called *The Glory of the Imperfect.*

Because of Bowen and Palmer, it was by no means clear what future there might be at Harvard for James, even if President Eliot himself kept a good deal of control over new appointments, understanding that if change was ever to come to Harvard, appointments could not safely be left to incumbents.

In June 1877, just when James was writing a particularly revealing letter to Alice Gibbens about "the real me," he was also realizing that his change of specialization from physiology to philosophy (which would of course include psychology, there being no separate psychology department at Harvard until 1934) pretty much obliged him now "to write some things fit to print, in order to advertise myself as a candidate for some vacancy in that line."[13]

It is hard to know what real connections, if any, existed among this cool calculation of professional advancement, his ever-increasing involvement with Alice, and his new sense of his "real" self. He wrote at some length about the last of these to Alice: "I have often thought that the best way to define a man's character would be to seek out the particular mental or moral attitude, in which, when it came upon him, he felt himself most deeply and intensely active and alive. At such moments there is a voice inside which speaks and says 'this is the real me.'" This attitude, James said, involved "trusting outward things to perform their part so as to make it a full harmony," but he was explicit that such a trusting attitude would be immediately spoiled, made "stagnant and stingless," if there was any guarantee that things would so perform their part. He functioned best, that is, without the guarantee, feeling a "sort of deep enthusiastic bliss, of bitter willingness to do and suffer anything, which translates itself physically by a kind of stinging pain inside of my breast-bone (don't smile at this — it is to me an essential element of the whole thing)." The attitude, he wrote, can't be put in words, but it "authenticates itself to me as the deepest principle of all active and theoretic determination which I possess."[14]

This was written in June 1877, at the height of James's fevered pursuit of / flight from Alice, and not long before Alice gave him the compass with its none-too-subtle implication — its "immaterial mandate," James called it. But this time he was really able to trust the compass needle of his own experience, and the immediate sequel to this bit of self-revelation was the writing of a substantial article, "Remarks on Spencer's Definition of Mind as Correspondence." This is James's first important professional piece. It was signed, it was published in W. T. Harris's *Journal of Speculative Philosophy*, and it takes issue, in a major way, with the dominant philosopher of science of the time.[15] It marks James's emergence as a philosopher with his own stance.

James argues that mind is broader, more various, and above all more active than Spencer thinks it is. He starts by citing Spencer's treatment of the entire process of mental evolution as "the adjustment" or "correspondence" of "inner to outer relations." James's first objection is that Spencer includes in the "entire process of mental evolution" only phenomena of cognition. Spencer omits "all sentiments, all aesthetic impulses, all religious emotions and personal affections."[16] James insists on a different view. Mind "as we actually find it," he writes, "contains all sorts of laws — those of fancy, of wit, of taste, decorum, beauty, morals and so forth, as well as perception of fact."[17]

Not only does Spencer limit mind to acts of cognition, he understands mind as "pure product," formed by aligning itself with its outside non-mental environment and acting more or less mechanically to further the survival and physical well-being of the individual. James objects to this and offers counterproposals. "Survival," he says, "is only one out of many interests . . . that makes survival worth securing." He lists "the social affections, all the various forms of play, the thrilling intimations of art, the delights of philosophic contemplation, the rest of religious emotion, the joy of moral self-approbation, the charm of fancy and wit."[18]

It is not enough, for James, to rest everything on the survival of the individual, as Spencer does, since the individuals who supply the above "interests" are protected and helped to survive by their fellows even if, individually, they would not, because "to the individual man, as a social being, the interests of his fellows are a part of his environment." In place of bean-counting acts of cognition and single-minded calculations of benefit, James offers us Emerson's poem "Brahma" as an example of how mind actually works.[19]

> If the red slayer think he slays,
> Or if the slain think he is slain,
> They know not well the subtle ways
> I keep and pass, and turn again.

What exactly would a Spencerian (or a Holmesian) calculation of self-benefit make of such claims? Spencer takes no account of our active interests, those interests which, James says, we bring with us and simply posit or take our stand upon, and which are "the very flour out of which our mental bread is kneaded." "Not a cognition occurs but feeling is there to comment on it, to stamp it as of greater or less worth." Toward the end of the piece, James offers his own definition of mind, or as he now prefers to call it, consciousness, as "not merely intelligent . . . it is intelligent intelligence. It seems both to supply the means and a standard by which they [the means] are measured. It not only serves a final purpose, but brings a final purpose, — posits it, declares it."

James's conclusion, from which he never retreated, is that mind or consciousness is fundamentally active. "The knower is not simply a mirror floating with no foothold anywhere, and passively reflecting an order that he comes upon and finds simply existing. The knower is an actor, and co-efficient of the truth on one side, whilst on the other he registers the truth which he helps to create . . . In other words, there belongs to mind from its birth upward, a spontaneity, a vote. It is in the game, and not a mere looker on."[20]

In his attachment to Alice Gibbens, his commitment to teaching, and now as a philosopher, James himself was at last in the game, no longer a mere looker-on but an active participant.

28. The Action of Consciousness

ABOUT A MONTH AFTER he sent off his "Remarks on Spencer's Definition of Mind as Correspondence," James sent off, in January 1878, an article called "The Sentiment of Rationality." He later described it as "the first chapter of a psychological work on the motives which lead men to philosophize," and he noted ruefully that it might better have been called "The Psychology of Philosophizing."

We may, at this distance, prefer the original title, if only for its fresh and unorthodox, not to say brash, announcement that rationality is at bottom a feeling. Not a matter of logic or math, not reasoning or ratios, not induction, deduction, or syllogism, not something higher than and detached from the senses, not the opposite of a feeling or emotion — rationality is itself a feeling or emotion. He might even have called the essay "The Feeling of Rationality." He begins by asking how we recognize the rationality of a conception, and he answers, "By certain subjective marks, that is, a strong feeling of ease, peace, rest." He amplifies, saying, "This feeling of the sufficiency of the present moment, of its absoluteness — the absence of all need to explain it, account for it or justify it — is what I call the Sentiment of Rationality."[1]

James simply sidesteps the long history of reason, right reason, pure reason, and practical reason, walking right past the conventional notion that rationality means abiding by set rules of reasoning. James is not really interested in the history of philosophy or the taxonomy of logic; he is interested in how particular minds actually work. His starting point is not Greek or medieval philosophy but modern scientific or experimental knowledge of the functions of the brain and the senses. "All logical processes," James says in another piece written at this same time, "are today hypothetically explained as brain processes."[2]

James wants data, facts, and examples. He is suspicious of grand, prematurely unified schemes, and we may suspect that he has Herbert Spencer in mind when he observes that "the craving for monism at any cost is the parent of the entire evolutionist movement of our day."[3] This does not constitute a rejection of Darwin, just a rejection of Spencer's pre-Darwinian, totalizing, monolithic — and in James's view, forced — unification of everything into a grand theory of evolutionary progress. It is Spencer, not Darwin, whom James has in mind when he says, "The ignoring of data is, in fact, the easiest and most popular mode of obtaining unity in one's thought." James is also suspicious of Hegelian moves to unify. "The crowning feat of unification at any cost is seen in the Hegelian denial of the Principle of Contradiction. One who is willing to allow that A and Not-A are one can be checked by few farther difficulties in philosophy." James argues against the passion for unifying and for its opposite, the passion for "distinguishing" — that is, for "the impulse to be acquainted with the parts rather than to comprehend the whole." Now "the greatest living insister on the principle that Unity in our account of things shall not overwhelm clearness is Charles Renouvier."[4]

However much James might wish to explain everything in terms of "molecular movements," he is unwilling at present to accept any explanation as the final explanation. "A single explanation of a fact only explains it from a single point of view," he writes. This is a workable pluralism. He cites a colleague's formulation of the "truth which constitutes the backbone of this article, namely that every manner of conceiving a fact is relative to some interest, and that there are no absolutely essential attributes."[5] In his own rephrasing he says, "No concept can be a valid substitute for a concrete reality except with reference to a particular interest in the conceiver."

"The Sentiment of Rationality" stakes out ideas James will fight to hold for years. Already suspicious of such Hegelians as William T. Harris, who controlled America's only philosophy journal, and G. H. Palmer, who had a main hand in setting the course for the Harvard philosophy department, James was opposed to the Hegelian unifying that tended to reinsinuate God — cloaked now as the Absolute — into modern thought, with arguments based on logic rather than revelation. James's first skirmish with the Absolute, in this piece, is an effort to put it, too, into psychological terms. "The Absolute," he writes, "is what has not yet been transcended, criticized or made relative. So far from being something quintessential and unattainable as is so often pretended, it is practically the most familiar thing in life. Every thought is absolute to us at the moment of conceiving it or acting upon it." James ends this extraordinary essay, which is a call for a whole new philosophy of mind based on what mind actually is and does, by saying, provocatively, "The peace of rationality may be sought through ecstasy when logic fails," and he appeals for an example to Whitman: "Even the least religious of men must have felt with our national ontologic poet, Walt Whitman, when loafing on the grass on some transparent summer morning that 'Swiftly arose and spread around him the peace and knowledge that pass all the argument of the earth' . . . To feel 'I am the truth' is to abolish the opposition between knowing and being."[6]

To James's "Remarks on Spencer," published in January 1878, and "The Sentiment of Rationality" must be added a third essay, "Brute and Human Intellect," also completed and sent off for publication that same month. This piece is James's take on the question Charles Darwin put to Chauncey Wright, namely, At what point does the thing known to us as human consciousness arise? Once more James frames his essay as an attack on Herbert Spencer and then proposes an alternative. "Devoted to his great task of proving that mind from its lowest to its highest forms is a mere product of the environment . . . [Spencer] regards the creature as absolutely passive clay, upon which 'experience' rains down. The clay will be impressed most deeply where the drops fall thickest." James goes after this with gusto and with a mildly zany example. According to Spencer's theory, he says, if there were a "race of dogs bred for generations, say in the Vatican, [they] would have characters of visual shape, sculptured in marble, presented to their eyes, in every variety of form and combination," and the result of this repeated "experience" would be to make them "dissociate and discriminate before long the finest shades of these peculiar characters. In a word, they would infallibly become, if time were given, accomplished connoisseurs of sculpture."[7]

What this leaves out, of course, is the factor of active interest. The mind must have some interest in a given subject before it even bothers to register impressions, let alone form opinions. "My experience is what I agree to attend to" is how James puts it. What the dogs will attend to in the sculpture gallery will be "Who peed on this pedestal?" The dogs can be as smart, lovable, conscious, sensitive, and attentive as you like, but, says James, "the great, the fundamental defect of their minds seems to be the inability of their groups of ideas to break across in unaccustomed places. They are enslaved to routine . . . Sunsets will not suggest heroes' deaths, but only supper-time. This is why man is the only metaphysical animal."[8]

Taken together, these three essays — which James tried to place in the most important journals — suggest a platform for a new kind of philosophical work, a new account of mind, based on the new physiological psychology, the whole enterprise seeking to learn, for the first time, how mind actually works.

In early February 1878, James went to Johns Hopkins to give a series of ten lectures to an audience of about sixty people: "The Brain and the Senses and Their Relation to Intelligence." His opening lecture gives a good indication of the context in which he understood himself to be working. "Geology, zoology, astronomy and human history all seem to be coalescing," he said, "into a vast system called the theory of evolution."[9] The big question, then, is What is the relation of mind or consciousness to evolution?

James's procedure was to start with a barrage of physiological detail, an empiricist survey of the operation of the senses ("the study of sensation . . . is the base of psychology"), focusing particularly on the mechanics of vision. James took issue with the prevailing Spencerian position that consciousness is composed of small units, which, like bricks, are assembled in our minds into larger units. Surviving notes for these lectures are sketchy, but they do show that James approached the subject on a detailed and technical level. He later recalled these lectures as "exclusively experimental," meaning he limited himself to reporting what could be shown experimentally.

His mind was very much on Alice Gibbens even while he was giving the lectures in Baltimore. Alice saved the following passage from James's letter of February 24: "To me such decisions" — probably about whether to marry and have children — "seem acts by which we are voting what sort of a universe this shall intimately be, and by our vote creating or helping to create 'behind the veil' the order we desire."[10] This is a modern, democratic version of Pascal's wager. Since there is no certain way to prove or disprove the existence of God, it makes sense to put one's money on the existence of God and behave accordingly. James drops the principle and the language of gambling in favor of the idea of voting. The decisions we make about how to live are not bets but ballots for a particular kind of world. It is perhaps no accident that this way of viewing the importance of individual decisions comes up in James's thought shortly after the disputed Hayes-Tilden election.

In the spring of 1878, James was voting on several issues that would profoundly affect his life. He and Alice were close to a final vote to trust their love for each other, a vote against the obstacles of infirmity, hereditary instability, and feelings of personal inadequacy and unworthiness. James was also casting a vote of confidence in his Baltimore lectures by negotiating to present them as Lowell Lectures in Boston. He cast a similar vote of confidence in his ability to make sense of his new field when he accepted a proposal from the publisher Henry Holt to write a textbook on psychology for Holt's American Science Series. James warned Holt that the project would probably take two years. Holt replied that he was "a little staggered" by such a length of time, but he agreed nonetheless. One wonders what Holt would have done if he had known it would take James not two years but twelve.

There were also, this spring, a pair of new colleagues who would in different ways be with William James for life. In June, Granville Stanley Hall became the first student to complete the new graduate program in philosophy at Harvard, and at the same time Josiah Royce became one of the first four people to earn a Ph.D. at Johns Hopkins, the new university founded exclusively for graduate study. Hall was well built, athletic, and full of energy. A hiker and climber with a dominating personality, he had deep-set eyes and a broad, high forehead. He was two years younger than James. He came from an impoverished New England family with *Mayflower* ancestors on both sides. Hall had gone to Williams College to become a minister. Next he attended Union Theological Seminary, but after a talk with Henry Ward Beecher he went to Germany, where he studied theology with Isaac August Dorner and philosophy with Friedrich Trendelenburg. In 1874 he read Wilhelm Wundt's *Grundzuge [Characteristics] der Physiologischen Psychologie* and quickly became convinced that the future of psychology lay in physiology. In 1876 he went to Harvard, where he served as an instructor in English while working on a Ph.D. in philosophy. His thesis was "The Muscular Perception of Space," one of the subjects James was most interested in. The thesis was based on work done in Bowditch's lab. Hall quickly set about writing a textbook on the new psychology. He later became a professor at Hopkins, then the president of Clark University. It was Hall who invited Freud to America in 1910 and who presided over the conference at Clark where Freud gave the lectures that were published as *Five Lectures in Psychoanalysis*. The founder of the *American Journal of Psychology* and the first important writer on adolescence — its inventor, one might say — Hall became a dominant figure in American psychology. His early attitude toward James was not only respectful but enthusiastic. As time passed, however, they would pursue quite different paths and Hall would come to feel a sharp rivalry with James.

Josiah Royce was born in California in 1855, in Grass Valley, a mining town in the foothills of the Sierra Nevada. Royce's English parents had set out for California by wagon in the gold rush of 1849. The trip took them six months. They got lost, were rescued, had to abandon their wagon, and just made it over the mountains, on mules, before the winter snows. They did not find gold.

Royce was short, stocky, and unathletic, with an enormous round head set close on his shoulders. He had light, almost invisible eyelashes, intense blue eyes, and full lips that seemed pouty. He talked and smoked incessantly, stayed up late, and took little exercise. As a boy of ten he read astronomy books. At night he would gaze at the stars. "I came to seem so far from home," he would write later, "and the contemplation of the mere magnitude of Being gave me a choking in the throat, and a lonely kind of fear, — a fear which seemed all the more hopeless because nothing that I could conceivably do, or could pray God to do, or could hope for, could be expected to alter in the least the essential situation, or make this cold world of the beautiful stars and the terrible distances comfortably smaller."[11] A yearning for what he called "the beloved community" was one of the permanent themes of his life.

His family moved to San Francisco when he was eleven. At sixteen he entered the brand-new University of California at Berkeley, graduating in 1875. Encouraged by the president of the university, Daniel Coit Gilman, and with letters of introduction from him, Royce set off for Germany. On the way he stopped in Boston, where he was invited to dinner by George Dorr, a Boston socialite who came to have a strong interest in psychic research. At this dinner Royce met William James for the first time, and James later recalled the occasion as notable for "the charm and delight" of Royce's conversation.[12]

Royce spent a year in Germany, at Göttingen and Leipzig, listening to Lotze and Wundt, among others. In 1876 Gilman, who had left the University of California to be the president of Johns Hopkins, offered Royce a fellowship (in literature) there. Gilman was assembling a true community of scholars. The recently opened university was a very modest assembly of "six professors, several associates, occasional lecturers, and twenty-one fellows."[13] Royce loved his time at Hopkins. In addition to studying and writing his Ph.D. dissertation, he gave a course on Schopenhauer and a set of five lectures called "Return to Kant."

James, Hall, and Royce all had unconventional educations. Each worked in a wide variety of academic fields, which in those days had loose, semipermeable boundaries. Each followed paths that branched, backtracked, and crisscrossed in unexpectedly fruitful ways. Hall thought of himself as a scientist, wrote much on education, and in 1917 published *Jesus, the Christ, in the Light of Psychology*. Royce took a job as instructor in English at Berkeley after earning his Ph.D. in philosophy in 1878.

In 1877 Royce visited James in Cambridge, hoping for encouragement in pursuing philosophy as a career. When James gave his lectures on the brain at Hopkins in February 1878, Royce was there. In 1882 James found a way to get Royce to Harvard, where a series of temporary positions finally turned into a permanent one. Royce published early and widely in philosophy. He wrote a book about California and a novel. Eventually a famous philosopher of religion, Royce was thirteen years younger than James but published four books before James had finished a single one.

He and James were close lifelong friends who differed on most important matters. The boy from the California gold camp insisted on the importance of community in all his mature work, while the boy from the East Coast and European communities became a spokesman for the individual. Hall and James became rivals, in part because they were somewhat alike, and their later relations were uneasy at best. Royce and James were warm friends and colleagues who disagreed merrily with each other. James said Harvard would be known in a hundred years as the place where Royce had taught, and he once wrote Royce, with his usual mischief, "I am sorry you say we don't see truth in the same light, for the only thing we see differently is the Absolute, and surely such a trifle as that is not a thing for two gentlemen to be parted by."[14]

After their July wedding in Boston, William and Alice left immediately for a ten-week honeymoon in the Adirondacks, at the Putnam family camp, a primitive shanty — more camping than housekeeping — at the end of the only road into the mountain village of Keene Valley, New York. Both William and Alice had been there before: the town was a tiny level opening deep in the wild High Peaks region, fifty miles from the Canadian border. William long retained the image of Alice, this summer of 1878, in her green plaid dress "as we used to stumble up the hill together and you would stop and laugh with dilating nostrils at me!"[15]

"Matrimony is an easy and natural state," he told Arthur Sedgwick, and to another friend, Francis J. Child, the ballad scholar, he wrote, "We have spent . . . a ballad-like summer in this delicious cot among the hills. We only needed crooks and a flock of sheep. I need not say that our psychic reaction [James is having fun with his professional jargon] has been one of content — perhaps as great as ever enjoyed by man." William was dictating to Alice — his eye trouble again — and Alice here inserted "(and woman! A.H.J.)." They wrote to thank the Putnams effusively for "the privilege of passing a honeymoon in this romantic and irresponsible isolation."[16] Things went swimmingly, apparently, as William sent off on August 10 a longish technical paper about space and how we experience it. By the end of August Alice was pregnant.

III. THE PRINCIPLES
OF PSYCHOLOGY

29. Spaces

IN CAMBRIDGE, HOWEVER, 1878 was a sad summer for William's sister. Alice, who was approaching her thirtieth birthday, suffered a major collapse. Her stomach hurt so horribly she felt she was only "hanging as it were by a cobweb to sanity."[1] She was unable to walk or even get out of bed, as her legs were paralyzed. Depressed and despairing, she thought and talked of suicide. Her biographer argues persuasively that Alice's terrifying breakdown was her response to William's preferring and loving and marrying another Alice. William's relation to his sister included gallantry, chivalry, teasing, and emotional intimacy in the shorthand version that sometimes marks a close-knit family. There is no record that he recognized any link between his flirtatious attentions to his sister or his marriage to another Alice and his sister's collapse.[2]

Early in March 1878 Alice had returned from a trip to New York with a cold. By April 15 Mary James was writing Harry, who was in England, that Alice had been "a good deal enfeebled" for some time. When William and Alice Gibbens announced their engagement, Mary James wrote that Alice was not only too ill to visit, but was too ill for her, Mary, to leave. By late May Mary was writing Bob that Alice had had a "nervous breakdown of a very serious character."[3]

In June Alice was slightly better, her "periods of depression and feeling of inability to meet life are less frequent," Mary told Bob. Alice was too ill to attend William's wedding on July 10. In mid-September Henry Senior was writing Bob, "We are so wholly immersed in Alice's malady, that we are apt to think no one else sick and suffering in the world, unless we are distinctly told of it." Alice was "half the time, indeed more than half, on the verge of insanity and suicide." Alice told her father that she "felt very strongly tempted" to kill herself and asked him if he thought suicide a sin.

Alice's father may not have had much insight into the causes of Alice's trouble (though he tried, in his way, to tell her it was not her fault, but rather "a diabolical influx into the human mind from the spiritual world"), and he may have been self-serving, as he often was, but he now took a brave, risky step, an astonishing thing for any father to do. He so completely acknowledged Alice's pain as to say that so far as he was concerned, "she had my full permission to end her life whenever she pleased" — this is all in a letter to the none-too-stable Bob — "only I hoped that if ever she felt like doing that sort of justice to her circumstances, she would do it in a perfectly gentle way in order not to distress her friends."[4]

As soon as her father conceded suicide to be her right, Alice immediately felt less inclined to "break bonds or assert her freedom" in just that way. She told her father that she "never could do it," though she continued to tell him — and often — that she was "strongly tempted still."

That was how her father told it. Alice's own comment is far more devastating, and all the more powerful for being written in her diary fourteen long, flat years later. "I have been dead so long," she wrote, "since that hideous summer of '78, when I went down to the deep sea, its dark waters closed over me and I knew neither hope nor peace."[5]

William and his Alice returned to Cambridge in late September. They took rooms, bought furniture, and boarded at 347 Harvard Street, a block and a half from William's parents and sister. William was happy in his marriage but not in his position at Harvard. Within hours of getting back, he was writing to President Gilman about giving lectures at Johns Hopkins, and Gilman responded at once with an exploratory mention of a possible permanent position for James there. Before classes had well begun at Harvard in the fall of 1878, James was saying he would probably not decline an offer from Hopkins.

In the second half of October, James gave a series of six lectures, called "The Brain and the Mind," at the Lowell Institute in Boston. The institute had been founded in 1835 and endowed by John Lowell, son of a wealthy cotton manufacturer. Recognizing that New England was a "sterile and unproductive land," he realized its prosperity would be contingent on education and information. His institute accordingly offered free or nearly free lectures of the highest quality on many subjects.

James may have used material from his February Hopkins lectures, but surviving outlines and partial drafts suggest a marked shift in emphasis.

The Lowell Lectures were for a more general audience, but even so, James reached for a more complex, more carefully shaded view of his subject, which, he said, was to see "exactly how much recent investigations have explained its [the brain's] action, and in particular how much they might be said to have cleared up or made less mysterious the action of consciousness."[6] He rejected pure psychophysics, "the assertion . . . that the only sound psychological science is that founded in physiology," and he was inclined much more than in February to recognize the claims of introspective psychology, or what was then called the "subjective method." ("When a man tells you he is cold, cold he is, however little cause you might see for it.") The subjective method, he now said, "has not only given us almost all of our permanently secure psychological knowledge but has also suggested all our interpretations of the facts of brain psychology."

The crude positions James wants to leave behind are "the old views of mental action all based on a priori speculations and metaphysics" and, on the opposite side, "the most brutal materialism." The rather dry tone and the steady experimental detail of the Hopkins lectures give way in the Lowell Lectures to a certain urgency, as though human lives, not just laboratory data, were at stake. "Every act," says James in the second lecture, "leaves a trace in the individual," and this fact is important for moral education. "The great thing is to form habits which then leave [the] hemis[pheres] free for higher flights and, in forming habits, to keep them unbroken."

But if James insists on the power of consciousness to choose to form habits, he is not thereby inclined to undervalue physical, bodily events. "It is a fact," he says, "that no conscious event can occur without some parallel event occurring in the nervous system on which the conscious event depends. In this couple the bodily event is the condition, the mental event the consequence. What we esteem the highest is at the mercy of what we esteem the lowest, and must ask its permission to exist."[7]

The freshness of James's views in these lectures comes partly from his tenacious returning again and again to the question of what it is about consciousness that makes it a trait favored by evolution. The value — the evolutionary or survival value — is the issue. "If consciousness can load the dice, can exert a constant pressure in the right direction, can feel what nerve processes are leading to the goal, can reinforce and strengthen these and at the same time inhibit those which threaten to lead us astray, why, consciousness will be of invaluable service."[8]

In a purely physical world, ideas about the good or the desirable don't exist. "Matter has no ideals," says James. It is "entirely indifferent" to carbon, nitrogen, oxygen, and hydrogen "whether they combine in a live or a dead organism." We need consciousness, and if we survey it, James insists, "we shall find that it always seems to be comparing and selecting." Historically, he notes, consciousness seems least developed in the "lowest animals, whose least instable brain least needs a rudder." Consciousness thus "appears step by step as brain defect grows more prominent." The inference is that consciousness develops or evolves "to remedy defect of brain."[9]

Most important, the advent of consciousness (James is still thinking in evolutionary terms) means the end of the reign of chance and the beginning of the reign of intelligence.[10] Accepting consciousness as an active, choosing, comparing process also means abandoning pure materialism and pure determinism. "I for one," James concluded his sixth and last lecture, "as a scientific man and practical man alike, deny utterly that Science compels me to believe that my conscience is an *ignis fatuus* or outcast, and I trust that you too after the evidence of this evening will go away strengthened in the natural faith that your delights and sorrows, your loves and hates, your aspirations and efforts are real combatants in life's arena, and not impotent, paralytic spectators of the game."[11]

The new tone of these Lowell Lectures, with their urgency, their insistence on what the individual consciousness can do, their practical, almost therapeutic concern, may owe much to Alice James. It is hard to know just how Alice's collapse affected William; his letters to Harry from 1876 to 1882 are missing. But it is impossible to think that her condition left him unaffected. Certainly that last sentence of his last lecture seems like an effort to speak directly to her condition, a life preserver tossed out by a person who knew how it felt to be drowning.

Between the happiness of his new life with his wife Alice and the heaviness of the condition of his sister Alice, between his new worries about his aging parents and the demands and awkwardnesses of his academic position, William kept working. He even seems to have thrived on all the confusion and complexity. In addition to his regular teaching load and the Lowell Lectures for their broader audience, he wrote articles and books that ranged from narrowly professional "contributions" to wider, more popularly aimed pieces.

The article he sent off a month into the honeymoon was called "The Spatial Quale." It was a technical, professional effort to clarify the important but difficult question "How do we understand and experience what Aristotle called 'extension,' and what modern thought called 'space'?" *Quale* is the Latin root of the word "quality," and James could have called the piece "The Quality of Space." But he was replying to a piece by James Elliot Cabot in Harris's *Journal of Speculative Philosophy* which argued that we do not experience space directly, that space is "a system of relations, it cannot be given in any one sensation." Cabot concluded that space "is a symbol of the general relatedness of objects constructed by thought from data which lie below consciousness." According to Cabot, the position of something in space is not felt at all; it is deduced from perceived relations.[12]

James vigorously disagrees, arguing that the quality of extension, the quality of space, is a unitary, primary form of sensibility that we feel or experience directly before we become aware of any order in the various bits. From deep in the Adirondacks, in the middle of his honeymoon, he writes, "The sound of the brook near which I write, the odor of the cedars, the feeling of satisfaction with which my breakfast has filled me, and my interest in writing this article, all simultaneously coexist in my consciousness without falling [at least in the beginning] into any sort of spatial order." Space for James is no abstraction, not a symbol; it is a "simple, specific quality of retinal or cutaneous sensation."

The article, despite its eye-glazing title, is a good example of how James approaches philosophical problems as psychological ones. For James it is physiology, not logic, that provides us with the laws governing thought. He does not look to syllogism but to the laboratory for examples and proofs. His is neither a materialist nor an idealist approach, but experimental, or as it will come to be called, phenomenological, or functional. James adduces a host of experiments (for example, holding successively a board, a lattice, and a sieve up to the ear of a blind person and asking the person what differences he feels) and concludes that "the psychologic problem which the study of space perception suggests is not what has been generally assumed . . . Our real problem is: How come we to notice the simultaneous differences at all? How can we ever evolve parts from a confused unity, if the latter did not yield them at first? How, in a word, does a vague muchness ever become a sum of discrete constituents? This is the problem of Discrimination and he who will have thoroughly answered it will have laid the keel of psychology." James himself was now convinced that "emotional interests are the great guides to selective attention." He knew the problem was important, and he was not satisfied with his essay, which appeared in Harris's journal in January 1879. His discussion of the perception of space would eventually make up 150 pages of his *Principles of Psychology*.[13]

All through 1878 and early 1879, James was working more productively, on more different fronts at once, than ever before. Also in January 1879, his essay "Are We Automata?" appeared, which was a revision and restatement of the last of his Lowell Lectures, delivered on November 1, 1878. Less than three weeks later, the finished essay was in the hands of George Croom Robertson, editor of the new English journal *Mind,* which James came to prefer to the Hegelian Harris's *Journal of Speculative Philosophy.*

"Are We Automata?" is an oppositional piece. James was once again stirred to work out his own ideas as a response to the well-put or well-received position of someone else. Just as his "Remarks on Spencer" was intended to correct Herbert Spencer's idea that the mind is basically something passive on which experience is sprayed, and just as "The Sentiment of Rationality" was a protest against the overvaluing of logic as a guide to how mind works, and just as "The Spatial Quale" was written to refute Cabot's view that we can't directly experience space, so "Are We Automata?" is a head-on challenge to the then popular view that human beings are really just machines.

The chief spokesman for this view was Thomas Huxley, whose "On the Hypothesis That Animals Are Automata" put the case with his customary polemical vigor and gimlet-eyed clarity. The lower animals, says Huxley, are guided by instinct rather than reason. This means that "they are machines, one part of which (the nervous system) not only sets the rest in motion, and co-ordinates its movements in relation with changes in surrounding bodies, but is provided with special apparatus, the function of which is the calling into existence of those states of consciousness which are termed sensations, emotions, and ideas . . . It may be assumed, then, that molecular changes in the brain are the causes of all the states of consciousness of brutes." Huxley thought the same thing to be true of humans, that "all states of consciousness in us, as in them, are immediately caused by molecular changes in the brain substance . . . In men as in brutes," he goes on, "there is no proof that any state of consciousness is the cause of change in the motion of the matter of the organism." The conclusion, presented without qualification so as to lose none of its traction, is that "we are conscious automata."[14]

James's initial objection to this idea that "we are pure material machines" is that it ignores or sidelines the entire realm of feelings. Feeling, in Huxley's theory, "is a mere collateral product of our nervous processes, unable to react upon them any more than a shadow reacts on the steps of the traveler whom it accompanies. Inert, uninfluential, a simple passenger in the voyage of life, it is allowed to remain on board, but not to touch the helm or handle the rigging."[15]

James's reply begins mildly, by wondering how someone like Huxley, who professed to believe Hume's demonstration that we cannot really determine cause and effect but can only observe sequence, that we can only say that one event follows another — how someone who believes that can use the word "cause" as easily as Huxley does. But the real force of James's reply is in his adroit use of a Darwinian example to counter this particular conclusion by the greatest of the Victorian publicists of evolution. Let us inquire, says James, what possible use or survival advantage would make consciousness something to be kept and valued by natural selection. "Consciousness," he writes, "has been slowly evolved in the animal series, and resembles in this all organs that have a use. Since the mere supernumerary depicted by the Conscious-Automaton-theory would be useless, it follows that if we can discover the utility of consciousness we shall overthrow that theory."[16]

Noting that "consciousness is presumably at its minimum in creatures whose nervous system is simple," James suggests that consciousness "is most needed where the nervous system is highly evolved," and he asks what defects exist in highly evolved nervous systems for which consciousness might be the remedy. "Whoever studies consciousness, from any point of view whatever, is ultimately brought up against the mystery of interest and selective attention." James concludes that the function of consciousness is to enable us to select, to give us the ability "always to choose out of the manifold experiences present to it [consciousness] at a given time some one for particular accentuation, and to ignore the rest." The passenger may, if it interests him, and if he selects it for attention, take hold of the helm and raise, lower, or reef the sail, and so, in small but meaningful ways, direct the voyage. Such a person, taking such actions, cannot fairly be called an automaton.[17]

30. The Heart Wants Its Chance

JANUARY 1879 SAW William James with more confidence than he had ever felt before. In midmonth he had an "explicit conversation" with President Eliot and came away convinced that he had the inside track for Francis Bowen's position in philosophy, if and when Bowen retired. Vague as this prospect might seem, and despite the risks of delay,

James decided to stay at Harvard and take his chances, so he scrupulously wrote Gilman to say he wouldn't be available for a job at Hopkins. "The Spatial Quale" came out in the January issue of the *Journal of Speculative Philosophy*, and "Are We Automata?" appeared in the January issue of *Mind*. In February James agreed to teach women for the Harvard Annex (which would become Radcliffe), and despite an already overfull schedule he proposed yet another series of Lowell Lectures, "Evolution and Mind."

His eyes still gave him trouble, but his sister was better now, and he found time in early April for a quick visit to Milwaukee to see his brothers. In Cambridge, the old Metaphysical Club, which after the death of Chauncey Wright had been held together by Davidson, Howison, and Cabot — all of them friends of James's — came to an effective end in the latter part of April. James remarked that the group seemed about talked out. But his attention was elsewhere. On May 8 Alice gave birth to a son, named, inevitably, Henry.

Alice and the baby stayed with her mother and her two as yet unmarried sisters in the mother's Boston house at 29 West Cedar Street. The four Gibbenses, together with an ever-changing roster of cooks and housemaids and an "encompassing ring" of aunts and cousins, constituted a large, formidable realm made up almost entirely of women. Alice, her sisters, and their mother did everything together. They mended and sewed and talked together, or one of them read to the others. They "were welded together in the closest affection and community of experience. Their memories were a common storehouse." William had a special place in this circle, of course, but it was and it remained a world of women.[1]

William was permitted to visit, but not to live, with his wife and new baby. He was archly proud of his eight-and-a-half-pound "domestic catastrophe," with his orange complexion, black head of hair, "musical but not too musical disposition," and a "lovely and benignant little expression on his face." They swaddled him with nicknames: Embry, Goblin, Goblington, Fatling. Staying at her mother's place gave Alice a comfortable setting and abundant female support, and it left William more or less free to hover about, travel, and work. He was neither expected nor allowed to take on a share of the load of raising the child. Not surprisingly, therefore, he kept working, and just about the time Henry III was born, William wrote a piece he called "Rationality, Activity, and Faith."

It was the capstone of almost two years of high emotional excitement, rapid maturation, and feverish activity. It was in August 1877 that Alice had given him the little compass as a present and a broad hint. That fall, while teaching a full load, he wrote his first signed piece (on Spencer), arguing that the central fact of mind is not the passive recording of, or reacting to, outside stimuli, but the active quality of preference or interest. In retrospect, this is clearly the central and never-to-be-relinquished perception of James's life and work. Alice's compass seems to have done the trick on more than one front.

James conceived "Rationality, Activity, and Faith" as a continuation of "The Sentiment of Rationality."[2] The point of the earlier essay, he now insisted, was "the exhibition of the failure of the purely logical function in philosophizing." The essay starts from "the assumption that if thought is not to stand forever pointing at the universe in a maze of helpless wonder, its movement must be diverted from the useless channel of purely theoretic contemplation." James then undertook to redeem thought from what he understood as unmoored theory. He aimed, he said, to determine "what that definition of the universe must be which shall awaken active impulses capable of effecting this diversion." He was looking, not for some definition of the universe that would prove "true" in some absolute or abstract way, but for a definition that would call upon our best energies. "A conception of the world which will give back to the mind the free motion which has been checked, blocked, and inhibited in the purely contemplative path will . . . make the world seem rational again."[3]

The boldness and novelty of this approach can hardly be overstated. James seemed and can still seem to have abandoned the centuries-old notion that philosophy is the search for the truth. He already doubted that either "the search" or "the truth" existed or could exist. He was trying to turn the river of thought into a new channel. To be successful, to be generally accepted, a philosophy must be able, he felt, "to define the future congruously with our spontaneous powers." No philosophy that "baffles and disappoints our dearest desires and most cherished powers can succeed."

James here singles out for disapproval "a pessimistic principle like Schopenhauer's incurably vicious Will-substance, or Hartmann's wicked jack-of-all-trades, the Unconscious." The trouble with determinism, fatalism, pessimism, the unconscious, and materialism is that in our better hours we feel such limited and limiting forces to be "so incommensurate with our most intimate powers as to deny them all relevancy in human affairs." Each explains away the objects of our thought or translates them "into terms of no emotional pertinency, [leaving] the mind with little to care or act for."[4] James pins his argument to daily life. "It is far too little recognized how entirely the intellect is built up of practical interests," he writes. "Cognition is incomplete until discharged in act."[5]

Having set out the checkers on the board, James steps back for a wider view of the game. "If we survey the field of history and ask what features all great periods of revival, of expansion of the human mind, display in common, we shall find, I think, simply this; that each and all of them have said to the human being, 'the inmost nature of the reality is congenial to powers which you possess.'"

This is William James, not yet forty, at the top of his form. This is the "philosophical assemblage" for which Whitehead would single him out. James here aligns himself with what we may call the liberal Platonic tradition, a Platonism not of the *Republic* but of the *Timaeus*. James instances "the emancipating message of primitive Christianity," the "Platonizing renaissance," Luther and Wesley, the "wildfire influence of Rousseau," Kant, Fichte, Goethe and Schiller, Carlyle, and, above all for James, Emerson. "Emerson's creed," writes James, "that everything that ever was or will be is here in the enveloping now; that man has but to obey himself — He who will rest in what he is, is a part of Destiny," and this thought, says James, is "an exorcism of all scepticism as to the pertinency of one's natural faculties."[6]

This is the central, sustaining — or, as we would now say, empowering — conviction. The most successful, because most widely adopted, philosophy will contain an "assurance that my powers, such as they are, are not irrelevant to [the Universal Essence] but pertinent, that it speaks to them and will in some way recognize their reply, that I can be a match for it if I will, and not a footless waif."[7]

James is quick to insist that we are all, nevertheless, different, that although "all men will insist on being 'spoken to' by the universe in some way, few will insist on being spoken to in just the same way."

James moves on to the third term of his title, to the "one element of our active nature which the Christian religion has emphatically recognized," and which philosophers have "tried to huddle out of sight in their pretension to found systems of absolute certainty." That is "the element of Faith," which he adroitly defines as "belief in something concerning which doubt is still theoretically possible: and as the test of belief is willingness to act, one may say that faith is the readiness to act in a cause the prosperous issue of which is not certified to us in advance." Faith, says James, is an essential function; it is "the power to trust, to risk a little beyond the literal evidence . . . Any mode of conceiving the universe which makes an appeal to this generous power, and makes the man seem as if he were individually helping to create the actuality of the truth whose metaphysical reality he is willing to assume, will be sure to be responded to by large numbers."[8]

In fact, he maintains, "we cannot live or think at all without some degree of faith. Faith is synonymous with working hypothesis." He moves now to examine "a certain class of truths" that "cannot become true till our faith has made them so." He asks us to consider a climber in the Alps who has worked himself "into a position from which the only escape is by a terrible leap." With hope and confidence, he feels he can make the leap. But if "fear and mistrust preponderate," he may hesitate until "at last, exhausted and trembling," he launches out in a moment of despair, misses his footing, and falls into the abyss. "In this case," which, James insists, "is one of an immense class, the part of wisdom is clearly to believe what one desires, for the belief is one of the indispensable conditions for the realization of its object." Faith here "creates its own verification." "Believe, and you shall be right, for you shall save yourself. Doubt, and you shall again be right, for you shall perish. The only difference is that to believe is greatly to your advantage."[9] This is not a leap to faith but a leap resulting from faith.

So the individual matters, or at least may matter. "That the course of destiny may be altered by individuals no wise evolutionist ought to doubt," he writes, and he explains why. "Whenever we espouse a cause we contribute to the determination of the evolutionary standard of right . . . Again and again," he urges, "success depends on energy of act, energy again depends on faith that we shall not fail, and that faith in turn on the faith that we are right — which faith thus verifies itself."[10]

It is hardly too much to see the germs of his later books, *The Will to Believe, The Varieties of Religious Experience,* and even *Pragmatism,* in this stirring essay, the arguments of which were now active in James's own life. In choosing, in acting, in "voting" to marry Alice, to have children, to stick it out in Cambridge, to address the wider audience and the professional one, indeed to get out of bed in the morning and go to work, James was acting on faith, risking his happiness, taking his chances, rather than waiting and planning for certainty. But then, as he said, "all that the human heart wants is its chance."[11]

31. *The Feeling of Effort*

JAMES TRIED HARD to find someone to publish "Rationality, Activity, and Faith," but it proved difficult. He asked his brother Harry to submit it to various English periodicals; Harry tried three, including the *Fortnightly Review* and the *Contemporary Review,* but none of them wanted it, and Harry was obliged to send it back to William with "much sorrow and shame at British unappreciativeness." The piece was personal, urgent, well written, and accessible; it was also sketchy, with the argument not fully developed and with many details and processes remaining to be worked out. Then too, the author of the piece was, in the general public's mind, nobody in particular. He was still Dr. William James, assistant professor of physiology. The essay was not published until three years later, in the *Princeton Review,* and it had no real impact until it was retitled (and slightly revised) as "The Sentiment of Rationality," and then it was not published until 1897 — eighteen years later — as one of the essays in *The Will to Believe.* In one sense, James was, in 1879, well ahead of the arc of his recognition.[1]

Living space continued to be a problem. The baby made the boarding arrangement at Harvard Street untenable, and there were problems, particularly for William, with having Alice and the baby at her mother's place in Boston. In June 1879 William began to think about building a house on the lot owned by his father on Quincy Street, though the most elementary accounting would have shown that he could afford no such thing. In July he went to the Adirondacks and the White Mountains, trying, especially in Franconia, New Hampshire, to find summer quarters suitable for his new family. In August, while working on the chapter on space perception for his *Principles of Psychology* he rushed back to Cambridge and rented a small house (no longer standing) at 4 Arrow Street, which he described to a friend as a "box 20 feet by 50."

We catch a glimpse of James's life this fall from his friend Jim Putnam, who came and had tea with William and Alice in their "cozy house." Tom Davidson dropped in while Putnam was there; Putnam noted it was "quite a treat" to hear the two of them. Davidson, said Putnam, was "as learned, dogmatic and hard-headed as any North German." Davidson assailed a new book by John Fiske, insisting there were "some contradictory statements made at the very start." James said, "Yes, it was perfectly true, but did not interfere with the argument at all, but they could only be noticed by little critics who could jab at them and only end in showing how insignificant they themselves were." Davidson's reply is not recorded.[2]

At Harvard James was freer to concentrate on psychology. He no longer had to teach the big comparative anatomy and physiology course. He gave a course in the philosophy of evolution, another on Renouvier, and his graduate course on the relations between physiology and psychology.

When he could, he worked on his book. His eyes, he told G. Stanley Hall in January 1880, were "damnable." He proceeded by fits and starts, laboring in late August over the problem of how humans perceive space, for what would become the 150-page chapter 20, deep in book two. In the winter of 1879–80 he worked on "association," which would become chapter 14.

Associationism was a crucial problem for James because his idea of consciousness being a stream depended on his being able to discredit the standard idea of the association of ideas, which had held the field since the publication of David Hartley's *Observations on Man, His Frame, His Duty, and His Expectations* in 1749. Newton had suggested that "vibrations of corpuscles of light might cause vibrations in the retina of the eye and the brain and produce the sensation of sight." Hartley followed up on this, arguing that "physical vibrations in the brain, spinal cord and nerves are the basis of all sensations, all ideas, and all motions of men and animals, and that all learning is the consequence of repetitive juxtapositions of corpuscular vibrations and mental associations in space and time, producing habits according to the pleasure-pain principle." Herbert Spencer extended the idea, welded it to Lamarck's notion of how socially useful adaptations are passed on, and argued that "the evolution of species, and even the origin of forms of thought, could be accounted for by an extension of the association of ideas."

The mechanism by which association was thought to proceed was atomistic; that is, it was assumed that the mind takes in simple impressions or sensations a bit at a time and then assembles the bits by the process of association into complex impressions or ideas. But James was now convinced that this was too neat, too simple, too orderly a description of how the mind works, and he announced that "the whole historic doctrine of psychological association is tainted with one huge error — that of the construction of our thoughts out of the compounding of themselves together of immutable and incessantly recurring simple ideas." James had concluded the "doctrine of simple ideas or psychic atoms" to be simply "mythological."[3]

It is not ideas at all that we associate together, James thought. Ideas constitute a huge jungle of possible connections: "existence, succession, resemblance, contrast, contradiction, cause and effect, means and end, genus and species, part and whole, substance and property, early and late, large and small, landlord and tenant, master and servant." It is *things* that we associate together, not ideas about things. The basic laws of association are "laws of motor habit in the lower centers of the nervous system. A series of movements repeated in a certain order tend to unroll themselves with peculiar ease in that order ever afterward." He gave as an example children's counting rhymes, such as:

> Ana mana mona mike
> Barcelona bona strike.

The second time one says it is easier than the first, and after many repetitions the second line will rise unbidden in the mind when the first line is recited.

In March 1880, just as his piece on association was published, James went into what he described to his brother Bob as his annual "collapse," which, he said, "lasts till I get to the country." His house plans were his great interest of the moment, even though it was still unlikely he could afford to build. He had approached H. H. Richardson, one of the best-known architects of the time, to design a small house — Harry referred to it as a cottage — on the Quincy Street lot. A surviving sketch shows the "cottage" with a ground-floor study twenty by thirty feet and a dining room eighteen by seventeen, with four bedrooms on the second floor. James was both attracted and repelled by the project, however, and by April he was planning a summer vacation alone in Europe, "out of reach of the house building and domestic cares."[4]

Amid it all, he kept at the psychology book, another piece of which, "The Feeling of Effort," was published as an article in June 1880. No one in modern times has written more movingly about the "amount of effort we are able to put forth"; no one has seen more clearly how closely our understanding of what constitutes will is tied to what we call effort. James tried to start from the beginning and ask what effort is and what is the source and path of the feeling of effort. How do we experience effort?

James is here, as so often, disconcertingly literal and physical; he wants not high moral urgency or lofty formulations, such as freedom of the will, but "the physiology and psychology of volition." Starting from the fact that "we have a feeling of effort," James marches out the standard explanation, that of Bain, that "the sensibility accompanying muscular movement coincides with the outgoing stream of nervous energy, and does not, as in the case of pure sensation, result from any influence passing inwards, by incarrying of sensitive nerves." James, who was usually at his best when he was combative, objected. "In opposition to this popular view," he writes, "I maintain that the feeling of muscular energy put forth is a complex afferent [incoming] sensation coming from the tense muscles, the strained ligaments, squeezed joints, fixed chest, closed glottis, contracted brow, clenched jaws etc."

This is a foretaste of the later James-Lange theory of emotion, which holds that we do not cry because we are sad, or run because we are frightened, but that we are sad because we cry, and afraid because we run. What James argues is that volition is not a simple matter of the brain issuing an order, a fiat, via the appropriate nerves to the appropriate muscles. "What makes it easy to raise the finger, hard to get out of bed on a cold morning, harder to keep our attention on the insipid image of a procession of sheep when troubled with insomnia, and hardest of all to say No to the temptation of any form of instinctive pleasure which has grown inveterate and habitual?" It is a question of what we call will, but it is more complicated and elusive than that. It is a question of getting to the point where we want to will something or other. "In our bed we think of the cold, and we feel the warmth and lie still, but we all the time feel that we can get up with no trouble if we will. The difficulty is to will. We say to our intemperate acquaintance 'you can be a new man, if you will.' But he finds the willing impossible."[5]

Most of the time, says James, we find that the looked-for result just suddenly happens, without any specific output of will. "I am lying in my warm bed, engrossed in some revery or other, when the notion suddenly strikes me 'it is getting late,' and before I know it, I am up in the cold, having executed without the smallest effort of resolve, an action which, half an hour previous, with full consciousness of the pros and the cons, the warm rest and the chill, the sluggishness and the manliness, time lost and the morning's duties, I was utterly unable to decide upon."[6]

James's search for the precise mechanism of volition leads him through many pages of physiological experiments to suggest, finally, that we are able to take an action only when the reasons for not taking it disappear. The more we struggle and debate, the more we reconsider and delay, the less likely we are to act. Don't wait until you feel better to go the gym; go to the gym and you will feel better. The physiology lab provided fresh, detailed scientific backing for what Goethe's Faust had found earlier. To begin anything, it is not word or thought or power that matters; it is the act that matters.

In a further effort to describe the all-important moment of decision, the fiat, the "let's do it," James says, "It is literally a fiat, a state of mind which consents, agrees, or is willing, that certain represented experiences shall continue to be, or should now for the first time become part of Reality." The "action of the will," he concludes, "is the reality of consent to a fact of any sort whatever, a fact in which we ourselves may play either an active or a suffering part. The fact always appears to us in an idea: and it is willed by its idea becoming victorious over inhibiting [and competing] ideas, banishing negations, and remaining affirmed." In a terse ten-point summary, James throws out this astonishing line: "Attention, belief, affirmation and motor volition are thus four names for an identical process, incidental to the conflict of ideas alone, the survival of one in spite of the opposition of others. The surviving idea is invested with a sense of reality which cannot at present be further analysed."[7]

His own life was, at the moment, full of problems and conflicts that seemed always to scuttle the full focus of attention. His eyes continued to limit both his reading and his writing. His back gave him trouble; he had severe stomachaches. He engaged in a prickly and strained tug of war with Frank Abbot, who was trying, so far without success, to get a Ph.D. in philosophy at Harvard.

Francis Ellingwood Abbot, six years older than James, was self-pitying, emotionally inauthentic, ambitious, and narrow, determined equally to lose and to make an immense tragic fuss about losing. He was tetchy, courted martyrdom with gloomy self-satisfaction, and had what would now be called a passive-aggressive character. He had, say his biographers, the "unique gift for being able to derail or ruin almost every organization or cause to which he belonged." Abbot wanted to take his examination on such and such a day. James replied that he would be out of the country. Abbot wrote a long, snide critique of James's "Sentiment of Rationality," which he assured James he had written "after I had recovered from the delight caused by its unsurpassed literary charms." Abbot could not fathom why he could not persuade James that he, Abbot, had taken "up [James's] view and Mill's too, and perfectly reconcil[ed] the truths which you and he alike have grasped."[8] We will see more of Abbot later.

James wrote Renouvier that he was "more unsettled than I have been for years." He was also being a difficult husband, not easy to live with, though it is often hard to be sure when he is serious and when he is clowning and when he is both at once. "How can you be so cruelly careless," he wrote Henry Bowditch, the colleague who had steered him into physiology at Harvard and a close friend with whom James kept up a ping-pong match of mock-hostile banter, beginning one letter to Bowditch with "Schurk, Lump, Unverschampter [shameless] Mensch, Halb-physiologue . . . You showed my note to your wife, or left it, as she says, lying about and the consequence is she has sent it to my wife." James is dictating this to Alice, who is the one actually penning the letter, and we have to imagine the two of them together here. "I have had a scene with her and my mother-in-law which I shudder to recall," James said and Alice wrote. "They have gone off together, I hope for good, and I am to sail on Wednesday for Berlin where I hope Helmholtz's lectures, Munck's vivisections in the veterinary school and a year of laboratory work under Hall will bring peace to my distracted soul." In fact, James no longer trusted Helmholtz, had mixed feelings about vivisection, and could imagine nothing more awful than spending a year in anybody's laboratory, Hall's least of all. The whole letter is a joke, but hardly the joke of a placid and contented soul.[9]

On June 5, 1880, he sailed for England alone. He needed to get away from school, from home and baby, from house plans, from Abbot. And as soon as a little physical distance opened up between him and home, James sent back a steady stream of mushy, loudly intimate, yearning letters and postcards. He was full of affection and of promises to do better. "I have but one business in life now, to be your husband well — better than I have been it."[10]

In England he stayed with Harry, whose sixth novel, *Washington Square*, was just beginning to appear serially. William was introduced at a reception to Robert Browning, who, however, "would not speak to me." He also met Alexander Bain, "a little hickory nut of a scotch man" with "no atmosphere to his mind." Bain, he wrote Alice, "does not read German, and altogether makes me glad to have seen him once but never more." Shadworth Hodgson was another matter entirely. He was, said James, "shy and silent on general subjects, wears spectacles and blushes when spoken to, is about my own figure." And James was elated to find that Hodgson, whose work he much admired, considered Renouvier "the most important living Philosopher."[11]

James had a brief, polite, but inconsequential lunch with the great Herbert Spencer. He saw Henry and Clover Adams, visited the Isle of Wight ("never saw such an absurdly picturesque spot in my life"), then rushed on to Heidelberg, where Alice had once lived, and where he and G. S. Hall talked psychology for twelve or more hours a day for three days running. Then it was on to the heart of Switzerland and the Bernese Alps. He went by wagon to Grindelwald, under the Eiger, then on foot four hours farther to a little chalet, the Rhône Glacier Hotel. "As I write in my little wooden bedroom," he told Alice, "an avalanche thunders on the Wetterhorn opposite." The next night, irritable and full of rage at himself for what he called his "unmanliness" (by which he must have meant his impetuous escape to Europe), he underwent what he described to Alice as "a great crisis."

James, in his published writings, always disclaimed having had mystical experiences, taking pains, we may guess, not to seem to distance himself from ordinary life and daylight reasonableness. But as the following necessarily lengthy extract from his letter to Alice shows, he did have experiences that, if not mystical, are well down the road toward mystical.

> A sort of moral revolution poured through me. I seemed to have been rolling down hill and now to be beginning to mount again, and this dear sacred Switzerland, whose mountains, trees and grass and waters are so pure, so good, and as it seemed to me so honest, so absolutely honest, all got mixed up in my mood, and in one torrent of adoration for them, for you, and for virtue, I rose toward the window to look out at the scene. Over the right hand near mountain the Milky Way rose, sloping slightly toward the left, with big stars burning in it and the smaller ones scattered all about, and with my first glance at it I actually wept aloud, for I thought it was you, so like was it unto the expression of your face — your starry eyes and the soft shading of your mouth. Dearest, I'm afraid you'll think I've gone crazy and I certainly hope you won't read this aloud at the Petersham dinner table, for they will be sure of it. [Alice was spending much of the summer with her mother and small son in this Massachusetts town.] I am not crazy dear at all, only I had one of those moral thunderstorms that go all through you and give you such relief . . . I felt ten years younger the next morning although I'd slept so little and Nature, God and Man all seemed fused together in one life as they used to 15 or 20 years ago.[12]

Beneath the ragged and frantic scurrying, the *Zerrissenheit,* the avalanche of everyday living, the pieces of James's inner life were coalescing, fusing together. At least he hoped they were.

A few weeks later, toward the end of August, he sailed from England back to Boston, arriving a little ahead of the publication of another essay, this one called "Great Men, Great Thoughts, and the Environment." It was a defense of the idea that great persons influence the course of history; its argument had a neat Darwinian twist. "The relation of the visible environment to the great man," said James, "is in the main exactly what it is to the 'variation' in the Darwinian philosophy. It chiefly adopts or rejects, preserves or destroys, in short selects him." Potentially great individuals arise at uncertain intervals in the natural course of events. But only those who are selected by their social environment come to have an effect on society. Both the individual and the "social environment with its power of adopting or rejecting both him and his gifts" were needed for social change. This piece was also aimed explicitly at Spencer, but James's mood, in the fall of 1880 and in general now, was not skeptical or contradictory. "I am tired," he wrote to Davidson, "of the position of a dried-up critic and doubter. The believer is the true full man."[13]

32. Hegel in Cambridge

R ETURNING TO CAMBRIDGE in the fall of 1880, James took up teaching his usual courses, but he and Tom Davidson also attended Assistant Professor Palmer's new seminar on Hegel's logic, where, as Palmer later recalled, James "gave free expression to his dissatisfaction with both the author and the teacher." Just when the old Metaphysical Club was winding down, a new enthusiasm for Hegel was blowing into Cambridge from several directions at once.

Palmer had been summering for several years with the Scottish Hegelian Edward Caird (and Caird's wife and their dog, named Ding-an-Sich). An active Congregationalist and alert to possible connections between modern Christianity and Hegelian thought, Palmer was energetic and effective and he had help. Two of the students in his six-student seminar were Samuel Emery and Edward McClure, from Quincy, Illinois; they were older students, successful businessmen, enrolled in Harvard Law School, but with a real passion for speculative philosophy. Emery came to Cambridge with a three-volume manuscript copy of the translation — never published — of Hegel's "Larger Logic," made by the leader of the St. Louis Hegelians, Henry Brokmeyer. Hegel had also made a local appearance at the lectures of W. T. Harris and others at the Concord School of Philosophy, in its first two sessions, the summers of 1879 and 1880. James's friend George Holmes Howison, though he was abroad in 1880, was strongly influenced by Hegel, had been part of the St. Louis group of philosophers, and was in regular correspondence with James about Hegel.[1]

Henry Brokmeyer, whose originating energy among the St. Louis Hegelians was now being felt everywhere in Cambridge, had his first exposure to Hegel around 1848, when Brokmeyer was a student at Brown University and Frederic Hedge was the Unitarian minister in Providence. Hedge had printed short but well-chosen bits from Hegel in his 1847 *Prose Writers of Germany;* Brokmeyer would have seen there Hegel's electrifying claim, a claim that also caught Walt Whitman's eye, that "the history of the world is the progress in the consciousness of freedom . . . The scheme is this: the oriental world only knew that one is free [that is, the ruler]; the Greek and Roman world knew that some are free [the ruling classes]; but we know that all men, in their true nature, are free, — that man, as man, is free."[2]

In 1858 at a small philosophical discussion group in St. Louis the thirty-year-old Brokmeyer met twenty-three-year-old William Torrey Harris, a sharp-featured, spare, muscular young man who had just arrived in the city. Harris had been a student at Yale, where he'd been warned against the "new philosophical infidelity." Attracted, naturally, he went straight to Concord, Massachusetts, where he attended Bronson Alcott's 1857 "conversations." The experience was crucial. Harris dropped his "phrenological theories, mesmerism, spiritualism, the water-cure, vegetarianism, socialism, and all manner of reforms" and devoted himself to philosophical idealism. In St. Louis he found work in the public schools. Howison later told how Brokmeyer had collared Harris one night, preached Hegel at him till dawn, and converted him. Brokmeyer was the master, Harris the disciple. Harris later gave Brokmeyer the highest possible compliment, saying that his mind was on a level with that of Hegel himself.[3]

The St. Louis Hegelians were substantial men. Brokmeyer would serve as a colonel in the Civil War, write the Missouri state constitution, run successfully for lieutenant governor, and serve as acting governor. Harris, in addition to running his *Journal of Speculative Philosophy* and lecturing at the Concord School of Philosophy, would become assistant superintendent of schools in St. Louis. He was the first to make kindergarten, for which Elizabeth Peabody had campaigned so ardently, part of a public school system. He was appointed superintendent of schools in Concord before serving as U.S. commissioner of education from 1889 to 1906. This was a heady period for public education in America. During those seventeen years a new high school was opened somewhere in the country every day.[4]

In 1859 Harris invited Bronson Alcott to St. Louis. If it is fair to say that there was a tug of war between Plato and Hegel for the philosophical soul of that midwestern city, it would be necessary to add that Brokmeyer and Hegel won. In 1859 and 1860, Brokmeyer was at work on the grand project of translating the "Larger Logic," the three-volume *Wissenschaft der Logik,* into English. The Civil War intervened. By the end of the war, Tom Davidson had found his way to St Louis, as had George Holmes Howison. The Hegelians there were now a serious movement. Alcott visited them again in 1866, when the St. Louis Philosophical Society was founded. The next year Emerson came to visit — more, he noted with chagrin, because the Hegelians wanted him to listen to them, rather than the other way around. It was in 1867 that Harris started his *Journal of Speculative Philosophy.*

The philosophical program then emerging in St. Louis was a serious, extended, civic-minded effort to address the problems growing out of the Civil War and Reconstruction, and the destiny of America and the place of St. Louis in it, by applying Hegelian thought — specifically Hegelian dialectic — to them all. Faced with materialism, agnosticism, and pessimism, Brokmeyer prescribed "Hegel's doctrine that for a man to understand anything he must see it in its relations . . . All that is finite is provisional, no antagonisms are final, and all objects and all institutions are but phases of a process referable to a dialectic of thesis, antithesis, and synthesis." Brokmeyer identified the position of the American South as that of "abstract right"; the North's position he considered "abstract morality." The synthesis would be a new "ethical state," a new union emerging from the tragic conflict. Clearly it was part of Hegel's attractiveness for Brokmeyer and the others that using the dialectic presented a way to rationalize and redeem conflict.[5]

Beginning in the early 1870s St. Louis Hegelianism began a drawn-out but steady move to Cambridge and Concord, which was to have a major impact on William James. In 1871 Howison left Washington University in St. Louis, and by 1872 was teaching philosophy at MIT. The next year, James Elliot Cabot was elected an overseer of Harvard; he visited Howison's classes at MIT to give himself a standard by which to appraise Harvard's offerings in philosophy. Cabot was an independent philosopher, four years younger than Thoreau and attracted to Emerson and transcendentalism. Eventually he would become Emerson's editor, literary executor, and biographer. Now, in 1873, aged fifty-two, he was so impressed with Howison that he proposed him (successfully) as an overseer of Harvard in 1874. The next year Cabot got Tom Davidson, who had just come to Boston from St. Louis, onto the Board of Overseers as well.[6] Palmer's seminar in Hegel started in September 1880. By December of 1881 Harris had organized a Hegel Club in Cambridge; it was devoted to Hegel's *Logic.* The Harvard Board of Overseers, which still exercised some influence over the curriculum, was packed with Hegelians and with those generally sympathetic to German idealism.

William James's acquaintance with Hegel's thought went back to 1867, when he'd read Hegel's *Aesthetik* in Dresden. He knew the "Smaller Logic" in William Wallace's English translation, a book he acquired in 1876.[7] James began to get exercised about Hegelianism in the fall of 1879. He was invited to lecture alongside Harris and the others at the Concord School of Philosophy. He wrote G. S. Hall that Palmer had returned from abroad all swept up "into the great arcanum of the identity of contradictories."[8] James abused Hegel merrily. "Of all mental turpitudes and rottennesses," he thought, Hegelianism took the cake. "The worst of it is," he told Hall, "it makes an absolute sterility where it comes." James wrote Royce in February 1880, groaning that "my ignorant prejudice against all Hegelians except Hegel himself grows wusser and wusser. Their Sacerdotal airs! And their sterility!"

After his bracing summer in Switzerland and his equally bracing meeting with Shadworth Hodgson, who shared James's high opinion of Renouvier, James returned to the United States to find Hegelianism spreading. He told Xenos Clark in December 1880, "The Hegelian wave which seems to me only another desperate attempt to make a short cut to paradise, is deluging the College this year and will, if I am not mistaken, completely sterilize its votaries." He wrote Royce on Christmas Day that Palmer and Emery were making "a very able and active propaganda here; and part of my fun this winter is trying to scotch it." To Renouvier James sent this assessment: "I think his [Hegel's] philosophy will probably have an important influence on the development of our liberal form of Christianity. It gives a quasi metaphysic back-bone which this theology has always been in need of." He added his by now reflexive reaction to Hegel ("fundamentally rotten and charlatanish"), but went on to concede that "as a reaction against materialistic evolutionism it has a use, only this evolutionism is fertile while Hegelism is absolutely sterile."[9]

James's friend Howison heard from Tom Davidson in May 1881 that James and Davidson were having "rare fun in making mincemeat of Hegel for the amusement of the boys at Harvard." Then Howison lit into James himself: "I feel quite sad at your outcome with Hegel . . . I was in hopes that your gifts would be enlisted in behalf of what seems to me the real interests of reason and depth and clearness . . . I am confident that the so-called Hegelian view is substantially rational, and the most rational, and is capable of a perfectly lucid and non-fallacious statement."[10]

But James was not listening. He wrote and gave a paper to Palmer's group, and then, as though to celebrate his new appointment, effective in April 1881, as assistant professor of philosophy, he sent off a piece for publication called "On Some Hegelisms." It is a short, all-out, quintessentially Jamesian attack on Hegelian logic. "We cannot eat our cake and have it," James wrote; "the only real contradictions there can be between thoughts is where one is true, the other false. When this happens, one must go on forever; nor is there any 'higher synthesis' in which both can wholly revive." James disliked the way Hegel dissolved conflicts and contradictions, making them, with the famous triadic logic, into a paradigm of progress: thesis, antithesis, synthesis. James ended his paper by saying, "That there are real conflicts, irreducible to any intelligence . . . is an hypothesis, but a credible one."[11]

James had no Emerson to tell him that when you strike at a king you must kill him. James's friends were dismayed by the piece, which James called his "skirmisher's shot," but what the sober Hegelians found unforgivable was not so much James's argument — thin as it was — as his tone, which they took to be facetious. In a long note to the printed version of the essay James explained that he had finally, if inadvertently, come to understand "both the strength and the weakness" of Hegel's thought when he had experimented with taking nitrous oxide. Inhaling the gas gave him, he said, "the tremendously exciting sense of an intense metaphysical illumination. Truth lies open to the view in depth beneath depth of almost blinding evidence." He further noted the relation between "the immense emotional sense of reconciliation which characterizes the 'maudlin' stage of alcoholic drunkenness" and the sense, produced by the nitrous oxide, "that all contradictions, so-called, are but differences; that all differences are of degree; that all degrees are of a common kind; that unbroken continuity is of the essence of being."[12]

James appended a list of thoughts that came to him while he was intoxicated and that seemed at the time "fused in the fire of infinite rationality." The best, he thought, was "There are no differences but differences of degree between degrees of difference and no difference." No doubt many philosophers found it outrageous that James should treat as serious philosophical matters experiences that had come to him while he was intoxicated. But for James any experience had a validity of its own, and in showing how the nitrous oxide had affected him, he was just repeating what he had been saying for some time, that our emotions, our temperaments, and our current states of mind do affect what we are pleased to call our ideas. We cannot finally separate the thinker from the thought.[13]

The upshot of the Hegelian revelation was, for James, "a pessimistic fatalism, depth within depth of impotence and indifference, reason and silliness united, not in a higher synthesis, but in the fact that whichever you choose, it is all one." For James, Hegel's logic was the reverse of what it claimed to be. "The identification of contradictories, so far from being the self-developing process which Hegel supposes, is really a self-consuming process." The final effect of Hegelian thought was, James felt, pernicious. It encouraged us "to see the world good rather than to make it good."[14]

"Rotten" was James's way of expressing mild distaste. "Charlatanish," another often-repeated adjective, meant for James "pretentious." Calling Hegel's thought sterile was at once sillier and more serious, because Hegelian thought, especially with regard to Marx, has been anything but sterile. James's problems with Hegel ran deep in his own life. As R. B. Perry has noted, "'Hegel,' 'Hegelian,' and 'the Hegelians' became to James symbols of the great rival way of philosophizing — of determinism, intellectualism, absolutism — in short, of that 'monistic superstition' under which he had 'grown up' and from which he had been delivered by the true gospel of pluralism."[15] In other words, "Hegelian" came to stand for everything James most distrusted and recoiled from in his father's way of looking at things.[16]

Yet in later years James would concede that there was something important in Hegel. And there is a strain — a submerged one — in James's own thought that may be called Hegelian. An example of this is a piece he tried out on his friends at Beede's, in the Adirondacks, the same month, September 1881, he sent off the Hegel essay for publication. This new piece is called "Reflex Action and Theism." James's idea was to approach theism from "the strictly natural history point of view."[17]

He begins with the definition of what he calls the doctrine of reflex action: "The acts we perform are always the result of outward discharges from the nervous centres, and that these outward discharges are themselves the result of impressions from the external world, carried in along one or another of our sensory nerves." James's argument is logically structured; it fairly squirms with just the kind of abstraction and technicality James so abhorred in Hegel. He intends, he says, to show "that a God, whether existent or not, is at all events the kind of being, which, if he did exist, would form the most adequate possible object for minds formed like our own to conceive as lying at the root of the universe." The William James of this piece is a logic-chopper, going on to argue, "Anything short of God is not rational, anything more than God is not possible." The piece was aimed at and delivered to Unitarian clergymen; James's argument against Calvinism was now physiologically grounded. "A God who gives so little scope to love, a predestination which takes from endeavor all its zest with all its fruit, are irrational conceptions, because they say to our most cherished powers, there is no object for you."[18]

As with Calvinism, so with materialism and agnosticism: they leave the "practical third of our nature" out of account, whereas theism, says James, "always stands ready with the most practically radical solution it is possible to conceive. Not an energy of our active nature to which it does not authoritatively appeal . . . at a single stroke, it changes the dead blank it of the world into a living thou, with whom the whole man may have dealings."[19]

James seals this transit from "it" to "thou" and from the biblical "I am that I am" with a long quotation from Tennyson's "The Two Greetings," entrusting his conclusion, as he often did, to literary expression.

> Live thou, and of the grain and husk, the grape
> And ivyberry, choose; and still depart
> From death to death through life and life, and find
> Nearer and ever nearer Him who wrought
> Not matter, nor the finite-infinite,
> But this main miracle, that thou art thou,
> With power on thine own act and on the world.

We may remember here James's earlier interest in the Chandogya Upanishad. To the revelation "that art thou" is now added a duty, or at least a sequel — that power is not power until it is expressed in action.

33. Death of a Mother

RETURNING TO CAMBRIDGE in the fall of 1881 from their second summer at Keene Valley, William and Alice moved houses yet again, this time from the box on Arrow Street to a rented house on Quincy Street, just across from William's aging parents, who were undergoing one of the periodic visits of the youngest and least stable of their sons, Bob. At the end of September William's sister Alice returned to America from a European jaunt. In October William delivered his "Reflex Action and Theism" piece to the Unitarian Ministers Institute in Princeton. In early November brother Harry returned from England for a visit. George Howison was scolding William for his views on Hegel, and Tom Davidson and Henry Holt were scolding him about theism. In December Wilky traveled from Milwaukee to see his parents.

In January 1882, as Harris's Hegel club ground logically on, meeting every Saturday at 3:15 in Tremont Temple in Boston, William James turned forty. On the twenty-third his friend Wendell Holmes was appointed professor of law at Harvard, and on the twenty-eighth James attended a Harvard Club banquet in Chicago, where he gave a short speech. It was "splendid as I composed it in my head," he wrote his wife, "but unfortunately I left out all the transitions and one half of the substance," thanks to the champagne. As William was returning on the train to Cambridge on the twenty-ninth, his seventy-one-year-old mother, who was thought to be recovering from a bout of bronchial asthma, took a sudden turn for the worse, and before William got home, she died.

We know less about Mary Walsh James than about any other member of the family. She looks out from the few photographs of her that remain with a pleasant round face, her mouth set, neither smiling nor frowning. Her hands are clasped and her entire figure is enveloped in black taffeta, with an unconvincing bit of white material at the throat. Her hair is parted in the middle and is pulled back severely over her head and behind her ears. Her eyes are anxious and weary. Harry was her favorite son, the one who gave her the least trouble. William's illnesses, ditherings, and sensitivities irked her. Bob was increasingly hostile and troublesome. Wilky stayed away from Cambridge. With Alice she had an especially close bond. Some pictures of Alice make her look a little like her mother. But these differences and preferences, real as they are, do not tell the whole story, for in practice Mary James treated all her children with fond endearments, steady concern, tactful (mostly) advice, and fundamental respect. Harry said she was the "sweetest, gentlest, most natural embodiment of maternity — and our protecting spirit, our household genius."[1] In his journal he wrote, "She was our life, she was the house, she was the keystone of the arch. She held us all together and without her we are scattered reeds."[2]

Harry could exaggerate, he could conceal, and he could be sentimental, but there is an important core of truth to this description of his mother. The Jameses were almost always scattered around the country and the world — Mary's funeral marked the first time since the Civil War that all five children were together under one roof — and what held them together, more than anything else, was writing. For years it was Mary James who managed and directed the family correspondence, the network of letters that was the institutional expression, so to speak, of a family that was so strong it could seem like a nation unto itself.

She kept track of who had heard from whom: "Elly Van Buren writes Wilky," she told Alice, "that she saw you in New York looking as fat as butter." She was the arranger: "I wrote cousin Helen on Sunday that we would be with her on Tuesday 22nd at 5 o-clock, so be sure to be on the spot," she wrote Alice. She retailed gossip about who liked whom. Again to Alice: "Minny I think is quite disenchanted and evidently looks at Holmes with very different eyes from what she did." She gave detailed instructions to her grown children on how to deal with each other. When William abruptly decided to go to Europe and was obliged to curtail a much-anticipated visit with his nineteen-year-old sister, Mary wrote Alice that Willy "feels very badly to go off in this way just before you get back, . . . so make light of it to him." She most always tried to control, but sometimes she made a real effort not to. "Such a burden has been taken off my heart by Harry's decision to come home," she wrote Alice, going on to say that Father felt the same way, but he said nothing, "not wishing to add to my anxiety and wishing to leave Harry free." When Alice went to Paris, Mary wrote in make-believe shock, "My daughter a child of France!"

Mary herself never left Cambridge, not wishing to leave her husband's side. She had her own rules, both for life and for correspondence. Letters should be regular. "Don't let more than a fortnight pass without writing," she warned Willy. "It is necessary to our happiness to know how you are getting along." If a letter wasn't in time, she would write, "We are longing and looking every day for some news of you." She expected replies to correspond to written inquiries. When they didn't, or when a correspondent fell down on the job, she was quick and tart. "Wilk writes that he did get a letter from you about six weeks ago and means to write soon," she told Willy. "Don't be surprised if you don't get a letter for six months." Both her own preferences and certain broad hints, as well as her good-intentioned evenhandedness, shine out in a letter replying to Willy, who had written from Florence about how sick he and Harry had been. "Of course his [Harry's] 'angelic patience' shows forth, as you say," Mary writes, "but happily that side of his character is always in relief and does not need great occasions (as it does with some of us) to bring it to view. My heart yearns over both of you my precious children" — they were thirty-two and thirty — "to think of you both being ill and I so far away!"[3]

Mary was sitting in the closing dusk on Sunday evening, January 29, with her sister Kate, apparently recovering from her illness, when she unexpectedly collapsed and died of an "affection of the heart." Harry was in Washington, D.C., with Henry and Clover Adams when he was called home. He found Father and Aunt Kate at the house. Bob was already in town. William arrived shortly from Chicago, Wilky from Milwaukee. On the day of the funeral, February 1, the four boys carried their mother's coffin to a temporary vault in the part of the Cambridge Cemetery — not the Mount Auburn Cemetery, but the plainer one next to it — that lies near the Charles River. Harry recorded that it was a "splendid winter's day — the snow lay deep and high."[4]

Harry, the angel, was now thirty-eight; he had become a "large, stout, vigorous looking man" (Aunt Kate's description) with a receding hairline and a full beard, trimmed close. He looked strong, almost hard, and his eyes were penetrating. He was, by any measure, the most successful of Mary's children. He was a working journalist and novelist of phenomenal productivity and substantial reputation. He lived like a gentleman on money he made from his writing. He had published some sixteen books, including *Roderick Hudson, The American, Washington Square,* and *The Europeans. Daisy Miller* had been a huge success, and *The Portrait of a Lady,* just out, was also much admired. A fourteen-volume "Collective Edition" was only about a year ahead. He was permanently settled in London. Indeed, during the current trip back to America he wrote, sitting in a room in Boston, "My choice is the old world — my choice, my need, my life . . . My work lies there — and with this vast new world, *je n'ai que faire* [I haven't to do at all]. One can't do both, one must choose."

Harry was a social success too. Welcome everywhere, he was a gifted talker who took pains to make himself interesting to others. In Boston he saw much of Isabella Stewart Gardner. "Mrs. Jack," the most brilliant, unconventional, amusing, and ambitious woman in town, had a serious, sustained interest in the arts. Harry read her his new dramatic version of *Daisy Miller,* with its happy ending. In New York he stayed with E. L. Godkin, longtime family friend and editor of *The Nation,* which James Bryce thought the best weekly not only in the United States but in the world.

In Washington Harry's social center was the home of Henry and Clover Adams. He met everyone, dined with diplomats, senators and congressmen, the President, even Oscar Wilde. In the middle of this whirl, which impressed Harry not at all (he thought there wasn't in Washington "enough history recorded or current, to go round"), a telegram came from William's wife Alice: "Your mother exceedingly ill. Come at once." He had just written her a letter: "Beloved mother, I must write to you and embrace you, though I am afraid it will be some time before you can return these attentions. I heard from Bob of your illness, two days ago and immediately begged him to give me more news." Mary died the day the letter was written and mailed.[5]

Wilky, Mary's "Darling Wilkums," who had arrived in Cambridge from Milwaukee just a couple of hours before the funeral, was genial, gentle, kind, affable, much loved, and had by now a son, Joseph, who was seven, and a daughter, Alice, who was six. But his life was a sad mess. He was ru-inously optimistic, never good at handling money, and his chain and bolt business had failed. In 1877 he had declared bankruptcy, his debts amount-ing to twenty thousand dollars more than his assets. Bob and his father held Wilky's notes and lost by his failure. His health had started to deterio-rate even before 1877. The rheumatism in his wounded foot got so severe at times that it put him on crutches. He was also developing kidney and heart problems. He was thirty-six the year his mother died; the grand epoch of his life was long behind him. In the spring of 1880 he and Bob attended a reunion of seven thousand Union army veterans in Milwaukee. In Novem-ber that same year he wrote and delivered a speech about his war experi-ences. Thanks to a gift of $250 from Harry, Wilky traveled to Cambridge, which he was still calling home, to see his mother and father in December 1881. He was grateful for Harry's openhandedness, thanking him warmly with "a fraternal blessing for your princely gift." No one knew that Wilky had less than two years to live.[6]

The youngest brother, the handsome "Hoppergrass Bob" of earlier years, was, at thirty-five, the most troubled. Pinched by poverty, going from rail-road jobs to farm work for his father-in-law, married to a woman who wouldn't leave Milwaukee and her family, Bob spent much of 1881 es-tranged from his wife and living in Cambridge, where his alcoholism, phi-landering, and moody behavior dismayed and burdened his parents and his sister. He had a bad temper and was often belligerent and full of maud-lin self-pity. He showed up in Cambridge drunk and abusive; his mother thought him "apoplectic."

In the summer of 1881 Bob checked himself into an asylum. He stares out from photographs of 1882 with knit brows and troubled eyes, carelessly dressed, with a full beard, and looking a lot like William. Bob's afflictions seemed endless: he suffered from headaches, vertigo, rheumatism, lack of appetite, and sleeplessness. He was, said his father, "grim, self-inverted, thoughtful, speculative, religious, manly." Father also thought him "the most subjective and self-conscious of creatures, sensitive, shy, suspicious, moody, cloudy, raining, freezing if need be." Alice, Mother, and Father all dreaded his visits. But Harry remembered Bob's "aptitude for admirable talk . . . charged with natural life, perception, humor and color." Bob's talk, said Harry, sometimes "struck me as the equivalent, for fine animation, of William's epistolary [talk]."[7] Bob got on especially well with William's wife, and he loved going to their house and chatting with their friends. William stuck by Bob through everything, writing him warm and encouraging let-ters with a boundless fondness and, one suspects, strong fellow feeling.

Bob always found everything around him unsatisfactory. One has a persistent feeling that something crucial was missing in his makeup. Bob made repeated, futile attempts to study Swedenborg and his own father's writings. He explained darkly and at some length that the latter "has not been fruitful of good . . . I have put my most earnest desire into understanding him and the fruit of it all has been nothing but sorrow to myself and my dear wife."[8] Bob found Father's moralism and Christianity particularly objectionable. "In that book the family . . . is treated of at great length as a thing very little short of hellish." William noted with a clinical eye that Bob had "no affection . . . yet in his crises he goes through the emotional expressions of an angel." Bob's life lurched from trouble to trouble.

Alice was now thirty-three and had made remarkable gains since her terrible collapse of 1878. With her companion, Katharine P. Loring, Alice made a number of excursions during 1879 and 1880. Katharine, a year younger than Alice, was from an old Massachusetts family; she was the eldest of four children. Her sight was so weak she learned Braille early on. She was a strong person, clearly capable of looking after both herself and Alice. She was active in public health and women's educational organizations; her brothers — one a Massachusetts supreme court justice — deferred to her opinions. Katharine traveled and hiked extensively. When she and Alice went by themselves to the Putnam Camp in July 1879, where William and Alice Gibbens had spent their honeymoon the year before, Katharine kept a revolver handy. She and Alice also traveled to the White Mountains, to Lake Winnipesaukee, to Maine, Newport, and Cape Cod.

Alice's life at this time was not at all that of a neurasthenic invalid. In 1881 Alice borrowed $2,500 from Father, bought some oceanfront land in Manchester, Massachusetts, and started building a three-story "cottage," which was soon complete with horse, carriage, pier, rowboat, and boatman. Also in 1881 Alice and Katharine traveled to England, where her brother Henry thought Alice "rather weaker in body than I expected, but stronger in spirits, cheerfulness etc." He remarked on her "animation, vivacity, gladness to see me, wit, grace, gayety etc." This was for the benefit of Quincy Street. In private he was puzzled and a little miffed by Alice's exclusive devotion to Katharine, finding himself "a fifth wheel to their coach."

Katharine was now Alice's companion for life. The two women had the kind of intense and exclusive relationship that has been called a Boston marriage. William's wife suspected that Alice and Katharine were actually lovers, but said so only to William.

In the fall of 1881 Alice and Katharine returned to the United States; the family pronounced Alice "vastly improved."[9] Alice's inner desire to "succeed" as a person, "to find something whole and authentic in her experience," was of course the real struggle of her life, and far more important than outward successes, as Father tirelessly taught. But outward things must count for something too, and Alice now found herself, all told, more fully a match for life than ever before. Her mother even left Alice what property she possessed, which was mostly railroad stock that had lost value in the panic of 1879.

We do not know how Mary's death affected her eldest son. William had always been Father's favorite, just as Harry was Mother's. It has been supposed that William felt the loss of his mother very little, since he left no rich outpouring like Harry's tribute in his journal. But for an overcompensating, self-castigating person like William, the lack of warmth or appreciation between mother and son would have made her death harder, not easier, for him.

And there is the letter William wrote his parents in July 1880, just after leaving England, in which he said, "I found myself thinking in a manner unexampled in my previous life, of Father and Mother in their youth coming to live there as a blushing bridal pair, with most of us children still unborn, and all the works unwritten; and my heart flowed over with a new kind of sympathy, especially for the beautiful, sylph-like and inexperienced mother . . . Better late than never! But I wish that this new feeling might enable me to be more of a comfort to you in your old age than I have been of late years."[10] At least William had not saved all his flowers for the funeral.

34. Goodbye, My Sacred Old Father

EIGHTEEN EIGHTY-TWO was a difficult, unproductive year — a year of losses — for William James. Early in the spring, following his mother's death, his sister Alice and Father moved from Quincy Street in Cambridge to a small house at 131 Mount Vernon Street in Boston, at the foot of Beacon Hill. In March Bob decamped impulsively for Faial in the Azores. In the middle of April Charles Darwin died. At the end of April Emerson died. William and Harry were part of the group that went by special train from Cambridge to Concord for the funeral. People came "in waggons, on foot, in multitudes," wrote Harry five years later. "It was a popular manifestation, the most striking I have ever seen produced by a man of letters."[1]

Harry returned to England in early May. William was planning to take his upcoming sabbatical abroad. During the spring, therefore, he wrote Royce in California and worked in Cambridge to get Royce appointed to fill in for him at Harvard. On June 17 his wife Alice gave birth to their second son, named, to no one's surprise, William. It was soon spelled Willyam to distinguish him from the professor, who went to New York six days later. Alice had moved in with her mother and her two unmarried sisters, the "essential household," as William's oldest son later recalled it. "During my waking hours they seemed to share all Mother's activities, including the care of us children," Henry III wrote, "for although Father clearly bore an important relationship to the matriarchy and especially to my mother, he was out of the house during a great part of the day."[2] With a new baby, there was also a nurse, Mlle. Lespierre, who seems to have had firm ideas. Father William was not to sleep in the same room as his wife and baby.

William's health during the spring had taken a downturn; he was sleeping badly, his eyes were giving him trouble again, and he was, as usual, exhausted by the end of the school year. Domestically, he was just in the way, and so he traveled about after Willyam's birth, going from New York to Newport to Magnolia to Albany, sending back a stream of letters that were irked, lonely, adoring, complaining, guilty, concerned, fervent, and longing by turns, and often pretty rapid turns. He fretted about his "exile," remarked grimly on a highly unsatisfactory short "visit" home. He wrote, with unconcealed annoyance, "My dear — no, I cannot say 'wife' — for they hedge you in and compass you about so that I am the person in all the world least able to get near you. What a horrid mockery was my visit home yesterday! I'm inclined to think I'd better cut you altogether until Miss Lespierre clears out."[3]

With only so-so health, with getting no work done, and with a trying domestic situation, it is not surprising that James set off by himself for his sabbatical in Europe, on September 2, 1882. The ostensible idea was to meet and talk with other psychologists and, above all, to work on his book.

The ship, the *Parisien*, went from Quebec to Liverpool by the short but sharply more northern route, passing through the Strait of Belle Isle between Newfoundland and Labrador. On reaching the other side, James went at once to Germany and spent the next two months rattling around

Europe at a furious pace, visiting in succession Nuremberg, Salzburg, Vienna, Venice, Prague, Dresden, Berlin, Leipzig, Cologne, Liège, Paris, and London.

The world was changing. Transatlantic telegraph service was available, electricity lit up theaters, and typewriters — to which James was an early convert — were coming into use. He wrote long, fond letters to Alice and made, at first, strenuous efforts to relax, reading Ingraham's *Beautiful Cigar Girl,* Carlyle's *Reminiscences of My Irish Journey,* Erckmann-Chatrian's *Les Deux Frères,* and Howells's *A Modern Instance* instead of working on the psychological perception of space. In October his reading took a more serious turn: G. O. Trevelyan's *Cawnpore,* Plato's *Theaetetus,* Ruskin, and Tom Davidson's translation of Antonio Rosmini Serbati's philosophy.

By mid-December 1882 he had written just six pages of the book he had gone to Europe to write. He had, to be sure, met people, and he had attended some lectures. In Prague he heard Ewald Hering, a physiologist and psychologist who worked on space perception, give "a very poor physiology lecture." He was escorted all over Prague by Carl Stumpf, a psychologist whose work on the conception of space James already knew, and whose book on the psychology of music would come out in 1883. Stumpf believed that our perception of, for example, musical tone is immediate, not a logical inference built up from other isolated facts. Some years later, knowing Stumpf would agree with him, James wrote Stumpf to say, "The feeling of distance is a feeling or nothing is a feeling." Now, in Prague in 1882, James found Stumpf "clear-headed and just-minded." He and James were to become very good friends.[4]

Also in Prague James met and spent an unforgettable four hours in conversation with the physicist Ernst Mach, with whom James also felt an instant intellectual rapport. "I don't think anyone ever gave me so strong an impression of pure intellectual genius," he wrote Alice. "He apparently has read everything and thought about everything, and has an absolute simplicity of manner and winningness of smile when his face lights up that are charming."[5] Mach, born in Austria and forty-four years old in 1882, was a physicist, a physiologist, a psychologist, and a philosopher. His great work, *The Science of Mechanics,* would come out the following year.[6] Einstein credited this book and the same writer's *Theory of Heat* as the works that most influenced him in his youth. Mach was looking for a principle, "a point of view to which he could cling in any research, one which he would not have to change when going from the field of physics to that of physiology or psychology."[7]

Mach adopted a strong empirical point of view. No statement, he held, can be admissible in natural science unless it can be empirically verified, and his standards for verification were high. He believed that any physical theory that refers to objects not reducible to sensory experience must be rejected as metaphysical. Accordingly, he dismissed as metaphysical what he understood as the Kantian ideas of absolute space and time. Absolute space, he said, "is a conceptual monstrosity, purely a thought-thing which cannot be pointed to in experience."[8] All statements, including those that occur in scientific theories, are in the end reducible to statements about sensations. Further, since all our testimony concerning the so-called external world relies only on sensation, Mach held that we can and must take these sensations and complexes of sensations to be the sole content of those testimonies, and therefore that there is no need to assume in addition an unknown reality hidden behind the sensations. Mach is anti-Plato and anti-Kant, but very close to William James. James heard Mach lecture on gravity in Prague in early November 1882.

James moved on to Berlin, where he heard Helmholtz "give the most idiotic lecture I ever listened to," also on gravity. He also heard the classical scholar Eduard Zeller on Pythagoras. While in Berlin James stopped at the veterinary school in which the great brain vivisector Hermann Munck taught, and spoke with him. In Leipzig he went to see Wundt lecture — "a more refined elocution than anyone I've yet heard in Germany."[9] Wundt was cordial, "dimly trying to remember my writings," but James was not overwhelmed by him, or indeed by Germany. To both Alice and Harry he wrote that as a teaching university Harvard was "on the whole superior to anything I have seen."[10] Measuring himself personally against the Germans, he concluded that his own "information in regard to modern philosophic matters" was broader than that of anyone he had met. He also considered "our Harvard post of observation . . . more cosmopolitan." That is to say, he had heard of them, but they hadn't heard of him.[11]

In Cologne it was the interior space of the cathedral that finally provoked James's wholehearted admiration and wonder. "It is a pleasure," he wrote Alice, "to find one thing in the world that completely satiates the expectation it arouses. Your eye travels round it and finds everywhere a crescendo, the later impression going you one stronger on the preceding like rhymes on rhymes and rhymes without end." Here was a real space, and a real experience of space, beside which the Kantian abstraction seemed empty and unreal, a mere verbal thing.

James made a quick trip to Lièges, in Belgium, where he met Joseph-Rémi-Léopold Delboeuf, a psychologist and philosopher interested in logic and hypnotism. Watching Delboeuf teach a class, James admired "his powerful good spirits and vivacity coupled with his extraordinary clearness and power of questioning."[12]

James was still, in late November, getting almost nothing written. He had, however, met "all the men I cared to see," and that was a gain. He told his brother, "I feel remarkably tough now and fairly ravenous for my psychologic work." But the news from home was not good. A letter arrived from Father saying that Wilky, who had grown very thin, had been diagnosed as having a "valvularly enlarged" heart. But far from suggesting that William return to Cambridge, Henry Senior's letter urged him to stay abroad: "There is absolutely nothing that I see in the circumstances of your own family to require your presence, and I am sure that there is nothing in ours to do so."

This was written on November 7, 1882. Three weeks later a letter from his wife gave James his first full sense of what was really wrong at home. Father was significantly weaker. He had attacks of nausea and faintness, and while Dr. Ahlborn said it was indigestion and he would rally if he got through the night, Henry Senior was convinced that he was dying. "He does not speak, nor seem, like a very sick person, but he insists that he is dying," Alice wrote. Her letter, which shows how sensitive and levelheaded a manager she could be, explains without alarming. "He has distinctly made up his mind not to live," she wrote. The burden of Father's decline fell mainly on Alice James, who now "wanted some one to share the responsibility with her," preferably Harry.

The atmosphere in the Mount Vernon Street house must have been unbearable. Henry Senior had "grown indifferent to things and people," and his attitude toward his daughter had entirely changed. "She seems off his mind," William's Alice reported. Alice James was herself far from well now, and she withdrew as much as she could, spending most of her time in her room with Katharine Loring. Aunt Kate was staying with them, and it was she who sat up with the old man. She and William's wife saw things the same way: they agreed that "when he wants to go, he will not linger."

Everyone agreed that William should not rush home. His wife wrote, "It is not hard to tell you that you could not be much comfort to that household now." Furthermore, Alice told him, "remember that the conditions you faced when you went away are not changed, only intensified." By "conditions" Alice meant that they still had no settled home, that she and the two children were at her mother's house with sisters and servants, and that they could not even be sure there was a room available for William if he came back now. William's dissatisfaction with the domestic arrangements would only make him chafe. There was nothing, Alice assured him, he could do for his father that wasn't already being done, and if he returned without having made any headway on the book, his mood would only worsen. Alice was filled with affection and tenderness for her husband, but she saw the situation clearly and she kept gently urging him to stay abroad. "Dear William how I love you, and want to comfort you!" she wrote.[13]

From Alice's letter, and another from Aunt Kate, William pieced together the situation. Sister Alice finally decided to telegraph Harry to come home. William's Alice was afraid it was too late.[14] Harry, it was understood, was coming more for his sister's sake than his father's, but he was also to be the executor of Father's will. Harry sailed for America on December 12. Two days later William accepted the fact that he would not return, and he sat down and wrote his father a farewell letter.

In the Mount Vernon Street house, Henry Senior stopped eating. When Dr. Ahlborn told him on December 6 that he was dying, "it seemed to fill him with contentment." On the ninth he told Aunt Kate "he had already begun the immortal life." William's Alice added, "To me he seems already gone." It was a death in life, like that of Prince Andrey in *War and Peace,* and as also with Prince Andrey, a world was dying with the old man. He complained that "his pulse would keep going in spite of his great weakness," and now his daughter Alice gave him her permission to die. "Never mind, father," she said, "the old pulse will stop soon."[15]

On December 18, when she entered the room, he greeted her with "Well, darling," but he was laboring for breath. The doctor gave him morphine. Once he awoke to say, "I am going with great joy." Another time he said, "Oh I have such good boys — such good boys." At the end only Aunt Kate was with him; he cried out, "There is my Mary!" He died at two-thirty in the afternoon.[16]

Father's funeral was at eleven A.M. on December 21. The same day, at noon, Harry arrived in New York. Pushing on, he got to Boston by eleven at night. When William's last letter to Father arrived, Harry went out to the cemetery and, he wrote William, "stood beside his grave a long time and read him your letter of farewell — which I am sure he heard somewhere out of the depths of the still, bright winter air."[17]

"Darling old Father," William began:

. . . We have been so long accustomed to the hypothesis of your being taken away from us, especially during the past ten months, that the thought that this may be your last illness conveys no very sudden shock. You are old enough, you've given your message to the world in many ways and will not be forgotten, you are here left alone, and on the other side, let us hope and pray, dear, dear old Mother is waiting for you to join her. If you go, it will not be an inharmonious thing. Only if you are still in possession of your normal consciousness, I would like to see you once again before we part. I stayed here only in obedience to the last telegram, and am waiting now for Harry who knows the exact state of my mind, and who will know yours, to telegraph again what I shall do. Meanwhile, my blessed old father, I scribble this line (which may reach you though I should come too late) just to tell you how full of the tenderest memories and feelings about you my heart has for the last few days been filled. In that mysterious gulf of the past, into which the present soon will fall and go back and back, yours is still for me the central figure. All my intellectual life I derive from you, and though we have often seemed at odds in the expression thereof I'm sure there's a harmony somewhere, and that our strivings will combine. What my debt is to you goes beyond all my power of estimating, — so early, so penetrating and so constant has been the influence. You need have no anxiety about your literary remains — I will see them well taken care of . . .

As for us, . . . we will stand by each other and by Alice, try to transmit the torch in our offspring as you did in us, and when the time comes for being gathered in I pray we may, if not all, some at least, be as ripe as you. As for myself I know what trouble I've given you at various times through my peculiarities; and as my own boys grow up, I shall learn more and more of the kind of trial you had to overcome in superintending the development of a creature different from yourself for whom you felt responsible. I say this merely to show how my sympathy with you is likely to grow much livelier, rather than to fade, — and not for the sake of regrets. — As for the other side, and Mother, and our all possibly meeting, I can't say anything. More than ever at this moment do I feel that if that were true, all would be solved and justified. And it comes strangely over me in bidding you goodbye how a life is but a day and expresses mainly but a single note, it is so much like the act of bidding an ordinary goodnight. Good night my sacred old Father. If I don't see you again — Farewell! A blessed Farewell!

Your William

Henry, whose last letter never reached his mother, stood by his parents' graves and read out into the cold winter air William's letter which never reached their father. Letters, even undelivered, outlast life. It was a scene a novelist would be hard-pressed to improve.

35. *The Wonderful Stream of Our Consciousness*

THE ELDER HENRY JAMES left an estate worth about $95,000 (about $1.5 million today). It was more than William thought it would be, which was good news, because William, with his growing family, felt pressed for money. The troubling part was that Wilky had been excluded from Father's will. It is not clear whether the exclusion was Aunt Kate's doing, as Wilky believed, or whether, as William believed — on information provided by his wife — Father was expressing his sense of "what he considered justice to his children."

A great deal of the family money had already gone to Wilky, and had disappeared. Wilky had bought $40,000 worth of land in Florida between 1866 and 1869. Much of the money came from Henry Senior; it was a substantial fraction of his assets, and he was left holding the deeds when the venture collapsed.[1] William's impulse was to let the will stand, in deference to Father's wishes, but for each of the other siblings to contribute a portion to Wilky so that he would end up with the equivalent of about three fourths of a full share.

Harry, who had been named executor by his father, had better instincts.[2] He traveled to Milwaukee and saw how sick Wilky was. On January 23, 1883, he judged him "pretty well finished."[3] Harry proposed to ignore the will and make an even distribution of the money. Strict justice might argue for a reduction in Wilky's portion, but Harry saw the blow to Wilky's pride and saw nothing to be gained in letting his father's hurtful will stand.

The long family irony here is that Henry Senior had been treated unfairly in *his* father's will, and had come into the fortune that floated his own life only by contesting and breaking that will. William had no animus toward Wilky; he deplored the exclusion and worked out ways to make most of it up to him. But William was motivated by other considerations as well. He was aware that Wilky's wife had a good deal of money, that Wilky's children were therefore provided for, and he may have had a lingering memory of Wilky's wife flaunting her diamonds in Cambridge. All these things blinded William to what the exclusion would really mean to Wilky, that his father loved him less than the others. Harry's better sense prevailed; William agreed to an even redistribution, though not without much discussion. William couldn't quite let it go. It seems uncharacteristic of him to contend for principle over particular human experience, and it cost him something. William may have been correct, but Harry was right. A balance shifted, and now it was Harry who was functioning as the moral center of what remained of the old James family.

Harry's new position of authority led to another curious episode in early 1883. William, though comfortable enough in Harry's rooms in London, was not writing, was much occupied with events at home, and was teetering on the edge of returning home. Harry now undertook to tell William that he was not needed in Cambridge and that he should not go home early. Henry put the message strongly; he wrote William, telling him flatly not to return, because "your idea of going to live in some other house [than that occupied by his wife and children] would give a dreary and tragic completeness to such a collapse [of European plans] and would have the air of your having committed yourselves to inconsistent and accidental (not to say shiftless) ways." Harry was incensed at William's domestic chaos. Expressing yet again his "sense of the (as it were) painful want of form there would be in your coming back — a few weeks after Father's death — after having been away at that time, and through all his illness — to live in a homeless and nondescript way in Cambridge, where you have ceded your place — and where, for the time, you would be neither in the college nor out of it."[4]

William bridled at "being treated like a small child who didn't know what his own motives or interests were," and he fired back a smoking letter defending himself, his domestic arrangements, his position in the college, and the reasonableness of an early return. He thanked Harry for his solicitude, but informed him starchily that he, Harry, had "a great misconception of all the premises that are operative in the case." He explained to Harry that he had decided to take his sabbatical only for the sake of his psychology project. "Then," he wrote, "I long doubted whether the better way would not be to finish that in Cambridge, and not come away; and finally decided that the chance of hygienic benefit and refreshment for me, and undisturbed possession of its mother by the baby, spoke in favor of departure." William bristled at Harry's horror of Cambridge ("poor nudified and staring Cambridge," Harry called it) and insisted that "there is not a man in the college who knows me, to whom my return now would not seem the most natural and proper of acts." What is unusual about this letter is that William should take such pains to explain himself to Harry. He seems to have recognized that his behavior needed explaining.[5]

Neither brother had any intention of letting a rift grow between them, so they hashed it out by letter. But William was not being entirely candid with Harry. William's going abroad when he did had to do with more than "the psychology," the housing dilemma, and the new baby. "You know darling," he wrote Alice, "how much of humbug there was in my coming abroad 'to see the other psychologists,' and how it was really done for that other reason."

That other reason seems to have been a marital crisis, a suspicion, perhaps a mutual one, that he and Alice could no longer live together and would be better off living apart. Trouble stood waiting at the front door of this marriage. William and Alice had married comparatively late, when each had long been accustomed to the self-determination of single life. And now with the arrival of the second child — a rough spot in many marriages — their doubts, especially William's, came knocking. But by early January 1883 the forty-one-year-old William was able to see through his recent behavior. He regretted it and determined to do better. He wrote to his wife that he had learned "the same thing I learned three summers ago, and that is that the mere absence from you is not what I want: and I think after this experience of its inefficacy that we may in future set our minds at rest and enjoy each other's company as long as we are on the earth together without the hateful suspicion that we might be doing better apart."[6]

Alice's response to this was to smooth the way for William's return. "No body can judge but yourself about your health and work," she wrote. "If the two are furthered by returning — Come!" Later letters assured him, "I shall respect you in returning, for I know you will do it, if you come, for most serious reasons." She went to some lengths to let him know that he would have, at her mother's and if he wished, "a good room, quiet, sunny, large, well-heated, with a comfortable bed and dark shades to the windows," so he could sleep. Above all, she assured him that she loved him. "I sometimes wonder," she wrote, "if I really loved you in the old engagement days, the torrent of my affection has grown so mighty. Some days I am half benumbed, the time is so long without you."[7]

At the same time that he was working through the doubts and irritations that had driven him abroad, and was reaffirming his bond with Alice, William was coming to a moment of clarity about his real, long-term relationship with his father. As had happened before, troubles seemed to stir in him impulses toward determined action. To Harry he wrote, in early January 1883, "I must now make amends for my rather hard non-receptivity of his [Father's] doctrines . . . As life closes, all a man has done seems like one cry or sentence. Father's cry was the single one that religion is real." Reconciliation with Alice and with Father went hand in hand. "Dear," he wrote Alice, "you have one new function hereafter . . . You must not leave me till I understand a little more of the value and meaning of religion in Father's sense, in the mental life and destiny of man. It is not the one thing needful, as he said. But it is needful with the rest. My friends," he added, "leave it altogether out."[8]

William was now comfortably settled in Harry's rooms in London, though he was not above abusing London to needle Harry. "After Paris," he wrote, "London seems like a medieval village, with nothing but its blanket of golden dirt to take the place of style, beauty and rationality." But if he suffered, he was suffering in good company. He went to a meeting of the Royal Society and to a dinner with its associated Philosophical Club. He had the use of Harry's club, the Athenaeum. He dined with the Rabelaisian Club, attended the Aristotle Club, went to galleries, exhibitions, and dog shows.[9]

The most congenial and challenging group of acquaintances was the collection of psychologists and philosophers who called themselves the Scratch Eight. There was Edmund Gurney, very tall, very handsome, a founder the year before of the Society for Psychical Research. There was George Croom Robertson, a professor of philosophy at Cambridge and the editor of *Mind*. There was Leslie Stephen, the editor of *Cornhill Magazine* and, just recently, of the *Dictionary of National Biography,* the author of *The History of English Thought in the Eighteenth Century,* and the father of a one-year-old girl named Adeline Virginia, who would later marry Leonard Woolf. There was Shadworth Hodgson, whose philosophical writings James ranked with Renouvier's as the best of modern work. James found this group stimulating in most matters, though he complained to Alice that "the men of the Stephen and Robertson lot here are atheistical, and shut out even from any play of the imagination on the religious side."[10]

Comfortable he might be, but he was still writing nothing. "Day after day I hope to begin: day after day my whole eye-time goes to the writing of letters and notes and when it does not it is taken up in trying to read the books of the men I am seeing." But in late January, whether because he had mended matters with Alice, or because he was beginning to face up to the meaning of his father's life, or from the stimulation of London intellectual life, or because he had essentially decided to call it quits abroad and return home — whatever the reason, the logjam gave way and James began to write his psychology book.

"The Psychology moves at last," he told Alice on January 25, and it was still moving four days later, though he now saw, he said, "in spite of all the books I brought, how impossible it is to work really comfortably at it without being in the middle of my own and of the Harvard libraries at home."

He was invited to give a talk to the Scratch Eight on February 10. Under the pressure of last-minute preparation, he got into "one of my fevered states . . . when ideas are shooting together and I can think of no finite things." He "wrote a lot at headlong speed and in the evening, having been appointed, gave an account of it."[11]

What James presented to the Scratch Eight that night was his first pass at what became "On Some Omissions of Introspective Psychology." It is one of James's worst titles, conveying nothing whatever of the exciting and novel idea at its heart, that consciousness is not a state or a sum of impressions, not a pool or a reservoir, but a stream. The title does, however, remind us that once again James moved toward a major idea by starting out in opposition or resistance to received ideas. He sweepingly notes, "What immense tracts of our inner life are habitually overlooked and falsified by our most approved psychological authorities."

Trying to understand what consciousness is, physiologically speaking, trying to describe what really happens in the process we so easily label consciousness, James gives as his subject "the wonderful stream of our consciousness." He is quick to vary the description — and the image — lest he find himself substituting a new verbal formula for an old one, or a new static abstraction in place of a previous one. As for the actual quality of mental life, he wrote that it, "like a bird's life, seems to be made of an alternation of flights and perchings." The resting places are the substantive parts, the flights are the transitive parts. The difficulty here is "seeing the transitive parts for what they really are. If they are but flights to a conclusion, stopping them to look at them before the conclusion is reached is really annihilating them." On the other hand, "if we wait till the conclusion be reached, it [the conclusion] so exceeds them [the flights] in vigor and stability that it quite eclipses and swallows them up in its glare."[12]

Defending what he understands as a "stream of sentiency," James sets out his position squarely against "the Platonizing schools" and their concept of a "supersensible Reason." He lobbies in the direction of greater complexity. Talking about a "feeling of relation," he notes that Herbert Spencer tried to reduce the number of possible relations to four, then asserts that our feelings of relation are in reality "numberless, and no existing language is capable of doing justice to all their shades." Arguing, for example, for the existence of "a feeling of if," James says, "Language almost refuses to lend itself to any other use." Our common use of language imposes a mythological, nonlegitimate uniformity on shifting fields and running streams of impressions (how many separate personal variations are hidden from sight under a blanket term like "depression"?). "We are so befogged by the suggestions of speech that we think a constant thing, known under a constant name, ought to be known by means of a constant mental affection."[13]

This essay is James's fight not only with the Platonists and transcendentalists but with the Cartesians who wish to concentrate mainly on "clear and distinct" ideas. His challenge is to say that, on empirical grounds, our mental life is not clear and distinct at all; it is elusive and disorderly. William James reports the wavering and uncertain moves of consciousness with a skill and tenacity Henry will show in his late novels. We are reminded why George Santayana preferred William's *Principles of Psychology* to his other works because in it James showed the actual life of the mind. "Suppose we try to recall a forgotten name," he proposes. "The state of our consciousness is peculiar. There is a gap therein; but no mere gap. It is a gap that is intensely active. A sort of wraith of the name is in it, beckoning us in a given direction, making us at moments tingle with the sense of our closeness, and then letting us sink back without the longed-for term."[14]

If we look at and report faithfully on what passes through our minds, we find there is much more than the "clear and distinct ideas" of Descartes and others. "Once admit that the passing and evanescent are as real parts of the stream as the distinct and comparatively abiding; once allow that fringes and haloes, inarticulate perceptions, whereof the objects are as yet unnamed, mere nascencies of cognition, premonitions, awarenesses of direction, are thoughts sui generis, as much as articulate imaginings and propositions are; once restore, I say, the vague to its psychological rights," and a true psychology becomes possible.

The great artist, Henry James would say, is one "on whom nothing is lost." The same may be said of the great psychologist. William was announcing himself, so to speak, serving notice in "Some Omissions" of the inadequacy of the standard-model English psychology that had held the field since the seventeenth century. James's proposals were new in that they were post-Enlightenment. In another sense, he was going all the way back to Heraclitus in his argument that consciousness consists at bottom of nothing more fixed than a stream, a flow of impressions. We should have our eye on the process as well as — perhaps more than — the product, on the path as well as the goal. This is a view of mental life Emerson had grasped (in such sentences as "Art is the path of the creator to his work"), though by means of quite different tools and training.

James's psychology book was launched at last. It was fairly out into the stream, and perhaps James can be forgiven for a little crowing, a momentary outbreak of satisfaction that February, as he wrote Alice, "I've got some really big and simple views in psychology, which will make the book, if it ever du get written, I really believe, a new starting point in the science."[15]

36. Not a Simple Temperament

JAMES HIMSELF, as he appears before us in 1883, is as hard to pin down, isolate, or explain as the stream of mental events he describes. John Jay Chapman, who first knew him about this time, says, "There was, in spite of his playfulness, a deep sadness about James. You felt that he had just stepped out of this sadness in order to meet you and was to go back into it the moment you left him."

The many photographs of James bear this out. He is almost never smiling, almost always serious, with traces of care about the eyes. At five feet eight, he was now a prosperous 157 pounds, heavier, he wrote Alice, than he had ever been before. To Santayana, who was an undergraduate at Harvard from 1882 to 1886, James seemed "short rather than tall, erect, brisk, bearded, intensely masculine." He had lively blue eyes and wore his full beard trimmed short. He still dressed colorfully, coming to class one winter morning wearing "a pair of tan shoes, a silk hat, cane, frock coat and red-checkered trousers." He was intensely active, taking stairs two or three at a time. He craved exercise and thought nothing of walking to Boston from Cambridge. Out hiking in the country he was often "among the foremost," Jim Putnam recalled. "He had a peculiarity in climbing, of raising himself largely with the foot that was lowermost, instead of planting the other and drawing himself up by it, as is so common." He drank moderately and would have a cocktail before dinner at the Parker House. He liked sweets, especially banana fritters. He could make a dinner of soup, six baked potatoes, and absinthe. He had stopped smoking and drinking coffee in the mid-1870s, when he was in his early thirties, though he sometimes lapsed in the matter of cigars.[1]

He was a poor sleeper. In Paris in 1882, he would sleep "for three quarters of an hour coiled up on the sofa before the fire . . . every afternoon as soon as it becomes too dark to read." At home the college bell killed his sleep. When he considered building a house out near Mount Auburn

Cemetery, he arranged to sleep experimentally at a friend's house there to see if he could stand the chapel bell. If not, he predicted darkly, "the house will be a regular murder-trap and buying the land will be the worst act of my life." He frequently suffered from insomnia, which became worse whenever he got really involved in his writing. In the late 1880s he began using chloroform to put himself to sleep. When his eyes could stand it, he would sit up alone and read until eleven or twelve at night; he found it "very much enlarges the day."[2]

William Sansom has characterized the modern mind as oscillating between jumpiness and coma. That describes James perfectly. "I have got quite out of the state of torpor into that of jiggle," he wrote Alice, "and am lying awake." He loved whatever was exuberant, spontaneous, alive. One summer night in Cambridge, around midnight, he ran out naked under the apple tree while Royce and another friend turned the garden hoses on him.[3]

He was nervous, mercurial, taut, and edgy; his indecisiveness drove friends and relations to distraction. He decided at a meeting one morning in Paris that Alice should hop over from Cambridge for three weeks. He sent a telegram at two P.M. to say so. At five P.M. he discovered the telegram hadn't been sent because he owed the telegraph company another twelve and a half francs, whereupon he dropped the whole idea. He changed the name of his youngest child when the child was three. One friend, James Ward, got a blank postcard from him one day; James had addressed it but forgot to turn it over and write a message. He loved gadgets. In the 1870s he tried copying ink, which allowed the writer to make a copy by pressing a blank sheet of paper over the written sheet with a small press. He took up typewriting enthusiastically before there was a machine with lowercase letters.[4]

James in the mid-1880s was in many ways a quite different person than he had been earlier. His son noted that "during most of the twelve previous years [before his marriage] there had been too little plan and continuity about his existence, and his nervous system had rattled and frayed itself almost to pieces." The "stabilizing and consolidating processes . . . proceeded gradually," Henry III noted. "After some years Father himself felt and knew that he was a man renewed. He had sloughed off the morbid personality of the latter sixties and early seventies." This does not mean he became a calm person or anything remotely resembling a calm person. His son saw him as clearly as anyone. "The mood and habit of his parents' household," the son went on, "which had hitherto supported him and been his only home, had encouraged rather than corrected his uneasy mobility and his nervousness. For several years the practical decisions which can be simplified or dismissed if the months and years are planned and ordered — such as whether and how far to go with medicine, what to do for his health, whether to go to Europe, when to come home, whether to commit himself to a teaching engagement — such questions and decisions had cost him recurrent harassment and perplexity and too often he had dealt with them impulsively and not very successfully."[5]

James never really outgrew this impatient, high-strung flailing about, this genial cyclonic tumult of induced restlessness and acquired disorder. He seemed to himself always on the verge of collapse, never quite recovered from the last trial, never quite prepared for the next one, but staggering on, bearing up as best he could.

Not only his home but his education fed his restlessness. "He never acquired," wrote Santayana, "that reposeful mastery of particular authors and those safe ways of feeling and judging which are fostered in great schools and universities." Van Wyck Brooks observed that the generation of writers responsible for what he called the flowering of New England — Emerson, Thoreau, Whittier, and the rest — had three things in common: family roots in the American Revolution, a classical education, and a connection with the land. William James lacked all three. He had roots in commerce, a hit-or-miss early education followed by a narrowly scientific later one, and a city boy's connection with only those aspects of nature that possessed spectacular scenery and provided tonic vacations.[6]

James was a rebel, an outsider. He combined a strong intellectual claim for order with a social taste for chaos. Ralph Barton Perry noted how James could not resist taking potshots at leading authorities such as Herbert Spencer. Perry said James was "a natural poacher, with the poacher's characteristic dislike of the gamekeeper." Somehow he had the trick of embracing his disorderliness and rebelliousness and turning it to account. His class Philosophy 2: Logic and Psychology usually met at noon. In one of his lectures he gave this description of preparing for class: "I know a person who will poke the fire, set chairs straight, pick dust specks from the floor, arrange his table, snatch up a newspaper, take down any book which catches his eye, trim his nails, waste the morning anyhow, in short, and all without premeditation — simply because the only thing he ought to attend to is the preparation of a noonday lesson in formal logic which he detests." Like as not, the lecture, when finally prepared, would be somehow interrupted. (Life, said James, consists of a series of interruptions.) He would slap his forehead, said Santayana, "and ask the man in the front row 'what was I talking about?'" His mind, said Chapman, "was never quite in focus, and there was always something left over after each discharge of the battery." But what he may have lacked in steady focus he made up for in portable intensity and pandemic enthusiasm. Here is Chapman again: "He seemed to me to have too high an opinion of everything. The last book he had read was always a 'great book'; the last person he had talked with, a wonderful being."[7]

If he seemed to overflow his role as professor, it was not with self-satisfaction. His friend Tom Davidson liked to berate James for the miserable academic quality of his thinking, and James himself told Grace Norton, a Cambridge neighbor and old friend, "The professor is an oppressor to the artist I fear . . . What an awful trade that of professor is — paid to talk, talk, talk. I have seen artists growing pale and sick whilst I talked to them without being able to stop. And I loved them for not being able to love me any better."[8]

"If art is an image of the world seen through a temperament," says George Simmel, "then philosophy may be called a temperament seen through its image of the world."[9] James's temperament was not the roast-beef-and-beer-for-breakfast sort; it was ruled neither by sturdy cause and effect nor by the familiar old material versus spiritual. Empirical by choice, artistic by inclination, believing that experience always trumps theory, James was characterized by what Emerson calls, in his essay on experience, the "lords of life," namely, "Illusion, Temperament, Succession, Surface, Surprise, Reality, Subjectiveness."[10]

James's temperament shines through all his works and days. It is not a simple temperament — nothing so manageable as mere optimism, nothing so steady as to count for even a closeted determinism, but always there, like the fifth string on a banjo. James's temperament is a nuancing one, always fine-tuning, always shifting, often elusive. And in that always present temperament is the general note of sadness, sometimes a "minor key of sadness" such as Charles Eliot Norton found in the *Rubáiyát*, sometimes the "epic wind of sadness" James himself found in the poetry of his friend Nathaniel Shaler.

James's astonishing openness to experience in all its shifting, momentary, inconstant shadings meant openness to trouble, both his own and other people's — and also, we must keep in mind, openness to healings and recoveries of all kinds. Aldous Huxley, who knew D. H. Lawrence well, said Lawrence's "great responsiveness to the world came from the circumstance that his existence was one long convalescence, it was as though he were newly reborn from a mortal illness every day of his life." James was like Lawrence in that regard, and he was like Coleridge, in that he could take "failure itself as his most liberating and radical subject."[11]

Spending his life caught inside this gorgeous, always shifting labyrinth of ever-flowing perceptions, ever-shifting mental states, and ever-fluid temperament, James seized on habit formation as the thread to guide him. James on habit, then, is not the smug advice of some martinet, but the too-late-learned, too-little-self-knowing, pathetically earnest, hard-won crumbs of practical advice offered by a man who really had no habits — or who lacked the habits he most needed, having only the habit of having no habits — and whose life was itself a "buzzing blooming confusion" that was never really under control.

37. What Is an Emotion?

THE SCRATCH EIGHT TALK got James back to writing, but he immediately sabotaged himself by going off to Paris for a month, looking up the apartment his parents had rented in 1856 and 1857, and going to the theater most evenings. Soon he was complaining to Alice, "I seem to be having the usual annual collapse which overtakes me about February." Crossing the English Channel had revived his interest in sea-sickness, and he reported to his mother-in-law his new remedy, which was to chafe the skin behind his ears. One of James's long-standing experimental interests was determining the function of the semicircular canals of the inner ear. He had already published a study citing results from hundreds of experiments he — with Bob sometimes as helper — had performed on deaf-mutes (plus two hundred Harvard students and instructors as controls), placing each subject in a swing, twisting it up, then letting it spin and checking to see if the subject could walk straight afterward.[1]

Convinced now that he needed to return home to really get to work, he arrived in New York in late March and proceeded straight to his mother-in-law's house in Cambridge. The plan worked, and James later said he got more writing done in April 1883 than in the previous six months. He stayed in good working trim during May, June, and July, even as a tide of cares and duties began to rise around his ankles. "The gap left by father is even greater than I supposed it would be," he wrote Bob. "Life can never again seem solid to me as it did a year and a half ago." His sister Alice was in bed much of the time at Mount Vernon Street, where she and Henry were keeping house together this year. Her outlook seemed to William a grim one. Wilky's suffering from his "valvular heart disease" had increased seriously by early May, and the rheumatism in his old war wound was worse. The miserable truth was that Wilky was now broken in both body and spirit. Henry, who was no pessimist, thought he did not have long to live.[2]

William agreed to give a series of lectures at the Concord School of Philosophy. He was also trying, as a son and as literary executor, to assemble for publication an appropriate volume of Father's best work. Even though he was not teaching at Harvard — Royce was filling in for him — he fretted about resuming his place on "the old collegiate treadmill." He was reading the *Letters and Memorials of Jane Welsh Carlyle* and *The Correspondence of Thomas Carlyle and Ralph Waldo Emerson*. He found himself admiring Jane Carlyle but not Thomas, who, James said, seemed "hardly anything but a phrase-monger."[3]

In July he heard George Howison give what he thought was the best philosophy lecture, "in point of form and impressiveness," he ever heard, on Hume. James delivered his own lectures in Concord to a good audience of about forty persons. Stirred to industry by the occasion, James wrote up the lectures — which were an expanded version of what he had given the Scratch Eight in February — immediately afterward as "On Some Omissions of Introspective Psychology." He told Renouvier it was "the most rapid piece of literary work I ever did." He completed both the Concord lectures and the write-up in six days.[4]

In August at Keene Valley, he met and was "extremely pleased" with Felix Adler, who had, as a young man of twenty-five, founded the Society for Ethical Culture in New York City in 1876. What he admired in Adler was the rare "union of intellectual fineness with practical will." Later in August Harry returned to London, glad to put some distance between himself and the long-drawn-out family to-do about wills and property and money. "I sail tomorrow," he wrote a friend, "for the ancient world." In September William and his family moved from Alice's mother's house, where they had been living for the past year, into a house they had bought at 15 Appian Way in Cambridge. William's interest in psychic research continued; he made a trip to western Massachusetts to see Caroline Tappan — with whom, as we saw, Emerson had flirted long years before — who performed a sort of parlor game in which she would write out her impressions of a person gathered simply by holding in her hand a piece of writing by that person. His English friend Edmund Gurney wrote a long letter to James discussing the great desirability of pressing forward with psychic research and talking about his forthcoming book, *Phantasms of the Living*.[5]

The news from Milwaukee was very bad. Wilky had been diagnosed with Bright's disease, so he had severe kidney trouble on top of all else. He was utterly demoralized, had no appetite, and had barely the strength to write William, on September 25, "It looks as if it would not be long before I shall peg out." William, alarmed, rushed to Milwaukee. Wilky was indeed sinking. William's presence only excited him, and William judged it best not to stay, since, as he wrote home to Alice, "every thing that interests him brings on an attack of hard breathing . . . All he wants is complete quiet and mental repose."

Wilky, the affectionate, genial, darling Wilkums, hopeless with money but loved by everyone, died on November 15. His wife and children were with him. Brother Bob remarked on their tenderness and, as Bob himself was enjoying a calm interval in his own stricken life, he provided William with an account of Wilky's end: "Two days before he died he spoke to me a jumble of words all of which were lost owing to the difficulty of articulation — save the one word 'dying.' I kissed him and I think he felt no fear because he pressed my hand and there was an inclination of the head as if he would have said, 'it's all right.'" Wilky had been thirty-eight. Three of the seven members of the family had died in just under two years.[6]

William's feelings about Wilky's death were complicated, and his hard side, a heavy-handed, almost grasping concern with money, became uppermost again, directed not at Wilky exactly, but at his widow, Carrie. It was as if there were an inherited James family curse affecting matters of inheritance. William wanted Carrie to sign papers guaranteeing that if Wilky's children should not survive their mother, Wilky's share of the James money would revert to other James heirs and would not go to Carrie and her family.

This may look as though James were acting out of bad feeling, but he would claim it was quite a different matter. In December 1883 he sent off to *Mind* for publication a short but revolutionary piece called "What Is an Emotion?" Citing the bodily changes that are often considered to be produced by emotion, James argues that such changes *are* the emotion. He challenges the usual way of thinking about the standard emotions — surprise, curiosity, rapture, fear, anger, lust, greed, etc. — which is that "the mental perception of some fact excites the mental affection called the emotion, and that this latter state of mind gives rise to the bodily expression." James says it is the other way around: "My thesis on the contrary is that the bodily changes follow directly the PERCEPTION of the exciting fact, and that our feeling of the same changes as they occur IS the emotion." We are accustomed, he says, to think that "we lose our fortune, are sorry and weep; we meet a bear, are frightened and run; we are insulted by a rival, are angry and strike. The hypothesis here to be defended says that this order of sequence is incorrect . . . We feel sorry because we cry, angry because we strike, afraid because we tremble, and not that we cry, strike or tremble because we are sorry, angry or fearful."[7]

This is a physical — a physiological — understanding of emotion; it is revolutionary because it was generally assumed before James that an emotion — say fear — was a cognitive response to a situation, and that the brain or higher nerve centers then sent messages out to the body to bristle, tremble, and run. James's reversal of this has been questioned. Some modern psychologists argue for at least a cognitive component in the process, but as late as 1984 James's theory (which was independently brought forward by the Danish psychologist Carl Lange the following year and which has since been known as the James-Lange theory) was regarded as "the starting point for most contemporary theories of emotion."[8]

James was the first to propose that the physical expression of emotion is the emotion, but this insight owed something to the earlier interests of others. Charles Bell's *Essays on the Anatomy of Expression in Painting,* first published in 1806, had called vivid attention to bodily changes accompanying emotions: to how, when horrified, the eyes widen, the nostrils flare, the mouth opens, the fingers spread, the head comes up, and the back straightens. Bell was interested in how painters portrayed emotion through what is now called body language. Charles Darwin wrote a book called *The Expression of Emotion in Man and Animals.* By illustrating the many parallels between human and animal expressions of feeling — Darwin is especially good on dogs and on an orangutan named Jenny — he intended to show how much people and animals have in common, to break down the stubborn prejudice that humans were fundamentally different from and superior to animals, and thus to encourage acceptance of his view that human beings descended from animals, so humans are themselves animals.

James was attentive to Bell's and Darwin's points, but his own aim was psychological, and he wanted to learn what constitutes emotion, what causes it, and what control or direction, if any, we can exercise over it. His earlier experiences as a painter and as a student of chemistry and comparative anatomy (James was the only major psychologist of his era trained in comparative anatomy) and physiology may have disposed him to seek knowledge in physical rather than metaphysical ways. But whether or not we can satisfactorily identify a sequential chain of causes, it remains a fact that James's characteristic approach to knowledge lies through experience. He could write about emotion as he did because he was not asking what causes an emotion or what emotion means, but what is the actual experience to which we give the name of this or that emotion.

In "What Is an Emotion?" James has also taken another step toward the testimonial method that marks his most original and most convincing work. A substantial part of the essay consists of examples given in narrative form, which a hostile critic would call anecdotal evidence and what an admirer might call documentary evidence, a method analogous to the medical history every good doctor learns to work up on each new patient. At one point, for example, James gives the following as evidence for the claim that "particular perceptions do produce wide-spread bodily effects by a sort of immediate physical influence":

> The writer well remembers his astonishment, when a boy of seven or eight, at fainting when he saw a horse bled. The blood was in a bucket, with a stick in it, and, if memory does not deceive him, he stirred it round and saw it drip from the stick with no feeling save that of childish curiosity. Suddenly the world grew black before his eyes, his ears began to buzz, and he knew no more. He had never heard of the sight of blood producing faintness or sickness, and he had so little repugnance to it, and so little apprehension of any other sort of danger from it, that even at that tender age, as he well remembers, he could not help wondering how the mere physical presence of a pailful of crimson fluid could occasion in him such formidable bodily effects.[9]

If the theory of the physical nature of emotion is true, James cautiously and conditionally observed, then "a necessary corollary of it ought to be that any voluntary arousal of the so-called manifestations of a special emotion ought to give us the emotion itself . . . Smooth the brow," he suggests, "brighten the eye, contract the dorsal rather than the ventral aspect of the frame, and speak in a major key, pass the genial compliment, and your heart must be frigid indeed if it do not gradually thaw!"[10]

Samuel Johnson once noted that he could be sunk in a mire of lethargy and immobility so deep he could stare for hours at the village clock and not know the time of day. He was unable to think his way out of this condition, but sometimes if he just heaved himself out of his chair, the mere physical movement was enough to get him started. Act first; the emotion will follow. In the beginning was the deed.

38. The Literary Remains of Henry James Sr.

A S JANUARY 1884 came around, and with it William's forty-second birthday, he was complaining to Carl Stumpf that his work "has hardly advanced at all in the last six months." This was only partly true, but it expresses James's impatience and the fact that his energies, as so often, were scattered in many directions, over many projects, with competing claims pulling at his attention. The big psychology book was progressing very slowly, though he did manage to finish the 137-page chapter on space perception in February. His articles were attracting attention and being taken seriously not only at home but also abroad. Ernst Mach wrote him in January from Germany to say that he had taken James's experiments in dizziness into account in his new book. Théodule Ribot wrote from France to say that an analysis of "On Some Omissions of Introspective Psychology" had appeared in the *Revue Philosophique* and to ask for a chapter of James's psychology book to translate. In England James was now a regular and prominently featured contributor to *Mind*, whose editor was as heartily anti-Hegelian as James.[1]

College life had its demands too. James was angling for teaching appointments for Davidson (unsuccessfully) and Royce (successfully). He was teaching again. The Harvard faculty was debating whether to drop Greek and Latin requirements and whether to shorten the undergraduate course of study to three years. William and Alice and the two boys were living in the rather small house on Appian Way, where, on the last day of January, Alice gave birth to their third son, who had dark hair and who looked, William thought, distinctly Jewish. From London, Harry implored William to give the baby a name of his own, not a family name, and to give him one name, not two. William and Alice took half of Henry's advice and named him, no one seems sure why, Herman Hagen James, after a faculty friend, a German-born entomologist Louis Agassiz had brought to Harvard.[2]

As the months passed, Alice and the baby flourished, though Alice's life was necessarily centered on her three boys. Sister Alice, by contrast, was not well, and went off in April to New York for treatment. Harry was hard at work on two big projects for which he had great hopes, *The Bostonians* and *The Princess Casamassima*.

William's family spent a disjointed summer. First they all went to

Otsego Lake (the Glimmerglass of *The Deerslayer*, near Cooperstown, about halfway between Albany and Syracuse). Then William went back to Cambridge alone, to work in the Appian Way house, which was fast becoming too small. Later he went to Keene Valley with his son Henry, who was now five. In October Alice James set out for England with Katharine Loring, where she would remain for the rest of her life. It was only one more Jamesian move, but it underscored and deepened the shift or divide in the family. Father, Mother, and Wilky were dead; Harry and Alice were living in England. In America there was William and his family, and Bob and his.

William had for some time regarded Bob as his special responsibility, just as Harry had taken pains with Wilky and was now doing the same for Alice. Bob made frequent trips east; sometimes he worked as William's research assistant, sometimes as a secretary and letter writer, and sometimes he roomed nearby and took meals with William's family. It was, then, an added heaviness when, in the fall of 1884 — still unsuccessfully fighting alcoholism — Bob left his wife and children and his Milwaukee home for a fling with a Miss B. William did what he could with Bob, who felt terrible after the very brief affair was over. William offered advice, money, friendship, and general support, and he wrote gentle, solicitous, but frank letters to Bob's wife, Mary, trying not to smooth things over but to hold things together.[3]

With this string of cares and changes, it is unsurprising that William made little headway on his psychology book. It was not that he stopped working, however; he kept busy enough, giving a talk called "The Dilemma of Determinism" at the Harvard Divinity School in March 1884. Free will versus determinism is of course a very old problem, appearing frequently as a sort of game of capture the flag, with freedom flying over one goal and determinism over the other, despite the fact that chance and habit seem to occupy most of the ground between. James starts out with an adroit, happy protest that he has no wish to erect a coercive argument for the existence of freedom. This is in the same spirit in which Isaac Bashevis Singer once answered the question "Do you believe in free will?" "Of course I believe in free will," Singer is supposed to have replied. "Do I have a choice?"[4]

James repeats his old personal turning point, the insight he had gotten from Renouvier: "Our first act of freedom, if we are free, ought in all inward propriety to be to affirm that we are free." The dilemma, as James sees it, in the argument for a completely determined world, is both a moral problem and a mathematical, statistical problem. In one way, James's piece is an updated version of William Ellery Channing's "Moral Argument Against Calvinism." (Channing, as we saw, was one of the thinkers most admired by William's Alice.) James is determined that the argument should take place in an arena of particulars, and so he cites "the confession of the murderer at Brockton the other day; how, to get rid of the wife whose continued existence bored him, he inveigled her into a desert spot, shot her four times, and then, as she lay on the ground and said to him, 'You didn't do it on purpose, did you dear?' he replied, 'No I didn't do it on purpose,' as he raised a rock and smashed her skull." James says with lethal mildness, "We feel that although a perfect mechanical fit to the rest of the universe, [this incident] is a bad moral fit, and that something else would really have been better in its place." James drives home his point, saying, "For the deterministic philosophy, the murder, the sentence, and the prisoner's optimism were all necessary from eternity and nothing else for a moment had a chance of being put in their place."[5]

Seen another way, in terms of chance and probability, the problem with determinism is that it leaves no room for the operation of chance, which the nineteenth century was coming to recognize more and more as a major factor in everything. James's striking move here is to point out that chance is really the same thing as freedom. "Chance," he says, "is at bottom exactly the same thing as . . . gift, the one simply having a disparaging, and the other, a eulogistic, name for anything on which we have no effective claim." With a shrewd sense of where his opposition lay, James observes, "The stronghold of the determinist sentiment is the antipathy to the idea of chance."[6]

Chance, of course, is crucial to Darwin's argument about how species originate (in natural, as opposed to artificial, selection the all-important variations are random, completely a matter of chance), and James, in "The Dilemma of Determinism," moves from the world of Jonathan Edwards and William Ellery Channing to the world of Charles Darwin. James is relentlessly plain in his defense of chance, or as he also calls it, indeterminism. He points out that he is, for example, free to walk home after the lecture via Divinity Avenue or Oxford Street. For all practical purposes, we are, in such matters, quite free to choose. The result is "a pluralistic, restless universe, in which no single point of view can ever take in the whole scene; and to a mind possessed of the love of unity at any cost, it will no doubt remain for ever inacceptable."[7]

James was now pretty well committed to his "pluralistic restless universe," and he rushed into battle whenever he saw it challenged. In the January 1884 issue of *Mind,* the piece printed right after James's "On Some

Omissions of Introspective Psychology" was an effort by the young J. S. Haldane to give a modern, physiologically phrased defense of the old idea of design. Noting how some creatures can regrow lost limbs and how cut nerves can regenerate, Haldane argued that we should regard the body not as separate parts with separate functions but as a whole, and that this wholeness operates "through and through" an organism, affecting and directing every part of it.

James could spot contraband rationalism when it washed up in front of him. He was fond of controversy (out of liveliness more than belligerence), he was increasingly sure of his own positions, and he charged in at once to attack Haldane. The editor of *Mind* made room for James's response in the next issue. James called his short piece "Absolutism and Empiricism," and in it he flatly admitted to having "a strong bias toward irrationalism." Far from thinking of it as a pejorative term, James considers irrationalism just another way to describe empiricism, or respect for fact before system, just another way to register his opposition to what he saw as neoscholastic rationalism. "Fact," he says, "sets a limit to the 'through and through' character of the world's rationality." Once again James quotes with approval Faust's decisive rejection of "In the beginning was the word" and his replacing it with "In the beginning was the deed." He ends by articulating a problem that concerned him all his professional life. "The one fundamental quarrel Empiricism has with Absolutism," he writes, "is over the repudiation by Absolutism of the personal and aesthetic factor" — temperament, he would call it elsewhere — "in the construction of philosophy."[8]

James's main work during the summer and early fall of 1884 was the preparation of *The Literary Remains of Henry James*, in the course of which, as he told his cousin Kitty Prince, "I seemed to sink into an intimacy with Father which I had never before enjoyed." He gave up his original idea of selecting all the best passages from the elder James's writings and settled instead for a volume that contained the book Father had been working on when he died, plus a lightly disguised autobiographical fragment and essays on Carlyle and Emerson. The volume began with a 119-page introduction in which William exerted himself to restate and summarize his father's work. The introduction is a filial and personal coming to terms with his father; it is also James's most serious and extended consideration of religious matters so far.

Early in the introduction, William takes on the problem of style, that quality Alfred North Whitehead called "the ultimate morality of mind," which is, paradoxically, both the weakness and the strength of Henry James Sr.'s work. Indeed his style, said William, "to its great dignity of cadence and full and homely vocabulary, united a sort of inward palpitating human quality, gracious and tender, precise, fierce, scornful, humorous by turns, recalling the rich vascular temperament of the old English masters, rather than that of an American today."

The problem with Henry Senior's style — besides its Carlylean tilt toward incendiary rant — is his Alice-in-Wonderland use of terms to suit himself. What most people call "theism" he calls "deism." "Moralism" is for him a pejorative term meaning the opposite of religion. "Conscience" is, however, a positive term, often used by Henry Senior to mean "religion." And so on. Instead of throwing up his hands, William cut through all this, seeing in his father's style not only high originality but an intensely personal, indeed a raging articulation — an essentially prophet-like utterance and repetition of a few central ideas. "With all the richness of style," William wrote, "the ideas are singularly unvaried and few . . . saying again and again the same thing: telling us what the true relation is between mankind and its Creator."[9]

Henry Senior's central ideas were bonded to his temperament, and were difficult — perhaps impossible — to express satisfactorily. "The core and center of the thing in him was always instinct and attitude," William wrote, "something realized at a stroke, and felt like a fire in his breast: and all attempts at articulate verbal formulation of it were makeshifts of a more or less desperately impotent kind. This is why he despised every formulation he made as soon as it was uttered, and set himself to the Sisyphus-like labor of producing a new one that should be less irrelevant."[10]

"His truths were his life," said William; "they were the companion of his death-bed: and when all else had ebbed away, his grasp of them was still vigorous and sure." He was now, for his eldest son, an old-fashioned truth teller, "a religious prophet and genius [who] published an intensely positive, radical, and fresh conception of God, and an intensely vital view of our connection with him." Henry Senior's work "all flowed from two perceptions, insights, convictions, whatever one pleases to call them . . . In the first place he felt that the individual man, as such, is nothing, but owes all he is to the race-nature [i.e., human nature] he inherits, and the society in which he is born. And secondly, he scorned to admit, even as a possibility, that the great and loving Creator who has all the being and all the power and has brought us as far as this, should not bring us through and out, into the most triumphant harmony." This is a first formulation of what William would later say were the two fundamental teachings of all religions: first, that something is wrong, and second, that it can be set right.[11]

Some of the elder James's best writing occurs in his repeated efforts to shadow forth the appalling extent of what it is that is all wrong. William quotes the following, from *Substance and Shadow:* "Every man who has reached even his intellectual teens begins to suspect this: begins to suspect that life is no farce; that it is not genteel comedy even: that it flowers and fructifies on the contrary out of the profoundest tragic depths, — the depths of the essential dearth in which its subjects' roots are plunged . . . The natural inheritance of everyone who is capable of spiritual life, is an unsubdued forest where the wolf howls and every obscene bird of night chatters."[12]

This dearth or lack or emptiness or nothingness is the central fact of our individual lives or selves. The unaided individual is nothing, is destitute, is helpless. "So too our ennui, and prevalent disgust of life," wrote the elder James, "which lead so many suffering souls every year to suicide, which claim so many tender and yearning and angel-freighted natures to drink, to gambling, to fierce and ruinous excesses of all sorts, — what are these things but the tacit avowal . . . that we are nothing at all and vanity, that we are absolutely without help in ourselves."[13]

Standing over against this scorched and raging cry, this voicing — half Ecclesiastes and half a premonition of Allen Ginsberg — of the emptiness within, is Henry James Sr.'s other main point, that there exists a "Divine-Natural Humanity"; that "the creator gives invisible [but real] spiritual being to the creature, the creature in his turn gives natural form — gives visible existence to the creator"; and finally that "society is the movement of redemption, or the finished spiritual work of God." As individuals we are exactly nothing; it is only as we associate, only as we are present and useful to others, that we are saved.[14]

William's account of his father's vision is more lucid than his father's own account. Indeed, for the modern reader who has tried again and again, without success, to grasp the elder James's ideas, William's version is the most helpful one there is.[15] William is also quite aware that he has injected clarity into what was for his father a most intense but not at all clear urgency. In referring to his father's "scheme" he wrote: "I fancy that his belief in the truth was strongest when the dumb sense of human life, sickened and baffled as it is forever by the strange unnatural fever in its heart of unreality and dearth struggling with infinite fullness and possession, became a sort of voice within him, and cried out 'this must stop!'"[16]

It was only after his father died that William recognized him as one of that small group of people who are perhaps too quickly labeled prophets and thus are elevated from ordinary life by verbal promotion, but who, by their witness, make religion real. "Mr. James was one member of that band of saints and mystics," William wrote, "whose rare privilege it has been, by the mere example and recital of their bosom experiences, to prevent religion from becoming a fossil conventionalism — and to keep it forever alive."[17]

With this generous summary, as indeed with the whole introduction, William comes to the end of his long resistance to his father and gives him his due. And in the very statement just quoted, in which he sums up his father's work and life, he sets out, so to speak, on his own religious search. The testamentary method of the later *Varieties of Religious Experience* is here hinted at. Religion must be the firsthand experience of particular persons or it is nothing but shells and formulas, costumes, magic, and books. But it was his father's example, much more than his ideas, that propelled William now. William disagreed profoundly with his parent's conception of the self as nothing, and he disagreed equally profoundly with the idea that "being" is what matters, not "action."

In a coda to his introduction to his father's memorial volume, William sketches out some of the great questions he will take up later. He notes the difference between the pluralism — indeed the polytheism — of popular religion (commonsense theism, he calls it, and he points to the multiple gods, saints, and devils of popular Christianity) and what he sees as the much rarer "ultra phenomenal unity" of true monotheism. William also contrasts what he was now calling the "healthy-minded" as opposed to the "morbid" view of life. "The feeling of action . . . makes us turn a deaf ear to the thought of being; and the deafness and insensibility may be said to form an integral part of what in popular phrase is known as healthy-mindedness." But thinking perhaps of poor Bob, or of his own earlier self, William acknowledges the power of the other, the morbid, way of living. "To suggest personal will and effort to one "all sicklied o'er" with the sense of weakness, of helpless failure, and of fear, is to suggest the most horrible of things to him . . . Well, we are all potentially such sick men."[18]

Throughout this long piece William carefully refers to his subject as "Mr. James." Only in the last sentence, the sendoff, does he drop the formality and refer simply to "my father" and to the "life-long devotion of his faithful heart."[19] As he was finishing the introduction in Cambridge, William wrote to his wife, who was with the children at Otsego Lake, "I feel as if I had stated the gist of him in a way he would be glad of and glad that I should do. How petty were all my criticisms of inessential details, like 'Pantheism,' 'Idealism,' 'self-consciousness,' etc. even when I was right!

Why couldn't I more heartily acquiesce in the big heart of the whole, the scorn of a salvation not universal, and the scorn of any creative love not able to quicken our very nature in the end!"[20]

The book came out in December 1884, just after James finished work on another, much shorter piece called "The Function of Cognition," a dry, semitechnical bit of epistemology prepared for delivery to the Aristotelian Club. It was duly published in *Mind* in January 1885 but not put in book form until 1909, in *The Meaning of Truth*, in which it forms the lead essay and where, in a footnote, James cites this essay as the starting point of the pragmatic conception of truth.[21]

"The Function of Cognition," which might more helpfully have been called "What Cognition Is," claims only to be "a chapter in descriptive psychology . . . not an inquiry into the 'how it comes,' but merely into the 'what it is' of cognition." It is, says James, "a function of consciousness," which "at least implies the existence of a feeling." He explains that he is using the word "feeling" to "designate generically all states of consciousness," including those sometimes called "ideas" or "thoughts." "Feeling" remains for James the most general, most inclusive term for "state of consciousness." If it leaves him open to charges or irrationalism and subjectivity, he welcomes them, believing, as he now does, that no adequate account of mind can exist that does not take full cognizance of subjective and nonrational states of mind and feeling.

In this short essay James makes a clear distinction between a perception and a thing perceived, and he works to avert solipsism by saying, "Let us . . . reserve the name knowledge for the cognition of 'realities,' meaning by realities things that exist independently of the feeling through which the cognition occurs." The nature and limits of cognition become clearer when James illustrates — in an example Ezra Pound would imitate many years later in his "Canto 2" — how "everyone knows Ivanhoe . . . [but] few would hesitate to admit that there are as many different Ivanhoes as there are different minds cognizant of the story." Here, as later, the test question for James is, can two minds know the same thing? An affirmative answer, at least now, requires him to take a step toward belief. "In the last analysis then, we believe that we all know and think about and talk about the same world, because we believe our PERCEPTS are possessed by us in common."[22]

Three of the pieces William James wrote in 1884 were published only much later in book form, though they were all quickly printed as articles when first written. "The Dilemma of Determinism" initially appeared in a book thirteen years later, in *The Will to Believe*. "Absolutism and Empiricism" appeared twenty-eight years later, after James's death, in 1912 in *Es-*

says in Radical Empiricism, and, as already noted, "The Function of Cognition" appeared twenty-five years later as the opening essay in the 1909 *Meaning of Truth.* If one looks just at the sequence and chronology of James's books, it can easily seem that his "later" work followed his interest in psychology. But what we think of as his later interests actually arose at the same time that he was working on his *Principles of Psychology,* and it is almost as though that book couldn't itself go forward until certain religious and philosophical problems had been faced and resolved in a preliminary but important way.

39. *The Death of Herman*

THE LITERARY REMAINS OF HENRY JAMES was William James's first book as well as his father's last. William was now a respected academic whose articles were appreciated by small circles of significant psychologists and philosophers, but his achievement still paled beside that of his brother Harry. Harry had, by the end of 1884, become quite famous. He had published twenty-two volumes, Macmillan had issued its Collective Edition in 1883 of fourteen volumes, and his work was on the list of standard topics for Harvard student themes in freshman English. Henry James was a great and public success on both sides of the Atlantic, and he was making an impressive amount of money. The Boston publishing firm of James R. Osgood, for example, offered him five thousand dollars for *The Bostonians.*

At the same time that Harry was being swept along on a wave of good fortune, his relations with William were somewhat strained. Harry considered William to have essentially abandoned his wife and children when he went abroad right after the birth of his second son, William.[1] Harry was further irked by William's staying abroad all through their father's last illness, and he found William's stiff attitude toward Father's will and Wilky a tiresome additional burden. Harry did not like Wilky's wife (he found her scheming, ostentatious, lacking manners and conversation), but he sent her money anyway, and he urged that she be left Wilky's money without strings attached. Harry had lectured William on the naming of his children, and he all but sneered at William's having mistaken a parody of Matthew Arnold for the real thing. "It seems to me poor as a parody,"

Henry wrote William, "and it marks the (geographical) gulf that separates Appian Way from Bolton St! [Harry's street in London]." Nor did Harry have much good to say about the seminal papers William was publishing. "I have attacked your two *Mind* articles, with admiration," he told William, "but been defeated."[2]

With the publication of *The Literary Remains of Henry James*, Harry's attitude toward William softened. William of course sent copies to Harry, who admired the introduction, saying, "It must have been very difficult to do and you couldn't have done it better." Harry also admired the "beautiful and extraordinarily individual (some of them magnificent)" extracts William had assembled, even as he, Harry, admitted that he couldn't "enter into it (much) myself — I can't be so theological nor grant his extraordinary premises." Harry also reported that while sister Alice had been very bad for some months, William's memorial volume "evidently gives her great pleasure. She burst into tears when I gave it to her, exclaiming 'how beautiful it is that William should have done it! Isn't it, isn't it beautiful? And how good William is, how good, how good!'" One wonders if Alice ever allowed herself to think about such a volume being done for her.

In any case, *The Literary Remains of Henry James* sank with scarcely a ripple. A dismissive notice appeared in, of all places, Godkin's *Nation;* a few friends wrote brief, labored acknowledgments. The publisher sold five copies in six months.

Back in Cambridge, William learned that he was to be promoted to full professor with a five-hundred-dollar-a-year increase in salary. He immediately began thinking again of building a house out near Mount Auburn Cemetery, to escape the neighborhood of the college bell that wrecked his sleep. William vacillated about the new house. One day he thought he could afford it, the next day not. When his salary increase was announced, he again thought he could; the next day he was sure he couldn't.

In late January 1885 James received a copy of Josiah Royce's first real book, *The Religious Aspect of Philosophy*, in which Royce took a long step toward what was to be his lifelong defense of the Absolute. James wrote a warm, friendly review of the urbane and clever book, which presented him with a major difficulty. Royce argued that common sense will show "that our thought and the reality [of the thing thought about] are two wholly disconnected things."[3] James's summary of Royce's argument continues: "If thought be one thing and reality another, by what pincers, from out of all the realities, does the thought pick out the special one it intends to know? And if the thought knows the reality falsely, the difficulty of answering the question becomes indeed extreme."

Royce's bold stroke is to assume that there really is such a thing as error, and for that to be so, "an 'Over-Soul' of whose enveloping thought our thought and the thing we think of are alike fractions — such is the only hypothesis that can form a basis for the reality of truth and of error in the world."[4] Error and doubt are not, for Royce, to be evaded or "answered." The existence of error and doubt — and the existence therefore of truth — requires the existence of an Absolute mind to know and distinguish them. Royce's proof of the Absolute (here called the Over-Soul) depends on the reality of error. James thought this quite brilliant of Royce and did not as yet see his way around it. "And here again," James wrote, "from the very depths of the desert of skepticism, the flower of moral faith is found to bloom. Everything in Dr. Royce is radical." James was delighted for his protégé turned friend.[5]

At the beginning of March 1885, Alice, who had been "busyissimus" with house and family, came down with scarlet fever. Since the fever was at the time suspected of being highly contagious, and since it affected mainly children, the James children were sent over to their grandmother's house and Alice was isolated and quarantined in her room. (Scarlet fever, or scarlatina, is a virulent form of strep throat; today it is rare and easily treated with antibiotics.) Food, coal, and water were placed outside her door. "She stealthily takes them in, like an antique leperess," William wrote Kitty Prince. William left books and papers outside her door; she burned them after reading them. Alice found her situation more than tolerable. "She is all alone there — and happy," wrote William. She "rightly considers that a life of such independence, without husband, babies, callers, witnesses, notes to write or duties to perform, is an opportunity for enjoyment and self-culture which comes but once in a life-time and must be made the most of when it does."[6]

Alice stayed isolated for six weeks. William read *Crime and Punishment* (in French). He reported in mid-April that Alice was now out and rejuvenated and that his psychology book was at last, he hoped, under way.[7] In May James R. Osgood declared bankruptcy and was unable to pay Harry the five thousand dollars he owed him. This was a very substantial sum, even for the well-off and ever-generous Harry. It was twice William's annual salary, and it left Harry scrambling to meet current expenses. William rose to the occasion and sent Harry a check for a thousand dollars.[8] Money was a problem for William too at this time, and in June he and Alice decided to rent out once again their small Appian Way house and move back in with Alice's mother.

Sometime early in June, Herman, whom William called Humster, came down with a bad case of whooping cough.[9] By mid-June Alice had it as well. It was not clear whether Humster would be well enough for the family to get him out of Cambridge and up to Jaffrey, New Hampshire, for the month of July. On the twenty-fifth William wrote from the country, where he was hunting for a place to bring the family, that he had dreamed "that poor little Humster had a hooked nose and was moribund!" On June 28 the baby's condition was "precarious," and the doctor said he couldn't be moved. William told Aunt Kate that Humster had "constant bronchitis which is apt to be fatal if it gets headway in babies." The next day, fearing the worst for the little one he was now calling "the flower of the flock," William returned to Cambridge. "Our poor little baby is in a very critical condition," he wrote Kitty Prince. On July 9, after a protracted and desperate struggle with convulsions and with pneumonia brought on by the whooping cough, Herman died. He was just eighteen months old.

They buried him at noon on July 11. William described it to Aunt Kate: "Between six and seven this A.M. Alice and I started in a buggy at Waverly and gathered pine, oak, and young birch leaves, wild flowers, ferns, and grasses to deck his little coffin withal. We had got a wicker basket, made for a cradle, which was just the right size and shape. We draped white canton flannel around it, laid him in with the tree sprigs round his head, the flowers in the middle, the ferns and grasses at his feet, and it was as lovely and touching a little sight as you ever looked on." He added that he had always "looked down on these dressings," but he understood that "there is usually a human need embodied in any old human custom." It was a need he and Alice both felt now.

Alice's inner strength and her devotion to Herman showed William new things too about the wife he thought he knew so well. "Six weeks with no regular sleep, 9 days with never more than 3 hours in the 24, and yet bright and fresh and ready for anything as much on the last day as on the first," he told Kitty Prince. And to his sister William said that his wife's "conduct during [Herman's] illness made me for the first time fully understand what the word 'mother' means." He added ruefully, "We get these retrospective illuminations pretty late."[10]

It cannot have made it easier for William that he felt, looking back, that he "had hardly known [Herman] or seen him at all." As he told Harry, "I left him so to his mother, thinking he would keep."[11] Some time later he would observe that "every individual existence goes out in a lonely spasm of helpless agony."[12]

It is hard to survive the death of one's child. Some aspects of it do not fade. But there was for William, in the end, a kind of consolation, an almost physical consolation, contingent, it seems, on not rushing into a belief in personal immortality. "To anyone who has ever looked on the face of a dead child or parent," he wrote in 1907, "the mere fact that matter could have taken for a time that precious form, ought to make matter sacred for ever after. It makes no difference what the principle of life may be, material or immaterial, matter at any rate co-operates, lends itself to all life's purposes. That beloved incarnation was among matter's possibilities."[13]

40. Mrs. Piper

THE SUMMER OF 1885 was unusually hot. Along with the heat, a marked sadness hung over the Jameses. At night William walked over to Appian Way, and he wrote to his wife, who was away in New Hampshire, how he "looked at our old empty house under the clouded moon." He picked out "the closed shutters of the little room in which our little one began his career." The experience made him feel close again to Alice. He further reported to her that he was back at work and getting on wonderfully with Mrs. Gibbens. "We understand each other better than any other members of the family."[1]

Sometime around the middle of September 1885, a couple of months after Herman's death, Mrs. Gibbens paid a visit to a twenty-six-year-old woman named Leonora Piper, who lived on Beacon Hill with her in-laws. Eliza Gibbens had heard about Mrs. Piper's psychic powers during the summer, probably through the gossip of servants.[2] Eliza returned from her visit to say that "Mrs. P. had given her a long string of names of members of the family, mostly Christian names, together with facts about the persons mentioned and their relations to each other, the knowledge of which, on her part, was incomprehensible without supernormal powers." One of Eliza's unmarried daughters went to see Mrs. Piper the next day, "with still better results, as she related them." Mrs. Piper appeared to have "a most startling intimacy with this family's affairs, and to know things which gossip could not possibly have conveyed to her ears." Among other things, Mrs. Piper "accurately described the circumstances of the writer of a letter which she held against her forehead, after Miss G had given it to

THE PRINCIPLES OF PSYCHOLOGY

her. The letter was in Italian, and its writer known to but two persons in this country."[3]

Hearing these things from his sister-in-law and his mother-in-law, James's response was skeptical. "I remember playing the *esprit fort* on that occasion before my feminine relatives and seeking to explain by simple considerations the marvelous character of the facts which they brought back." Though skeptical, James was sufficiently intrigued to go, together with Alice, a few days later to see Mrs. Piper for himself. They concealed their names and their connection to the Gibbenses. Mrs. Piper went into a trance, repeated names she had given the Gibbenses, and added others. "My wife's father's name of Gibbens was announced first as Niblin, then as Giblin. A child Herman (whom we had lost the previous year)" — James was writing this five years later, and his chronology is flawed — "had his name spelt out as Herrin."

James returned, he said, "a dozen times that winter," sometimes with Alice, sometimes alone. He sent twenty other people to see Mrs. Piper. He studied her, with her consent of course; he hypnotized her to see whether her trances had anything in common with ordinary hypnotic trance. They didn't. His conclusion, after five years, gives one pause. It needs to be quoted in full: "My impression after [the] first visit was, that Mrs. P was either possessed of supernormal powers or knew the members of my wife's family by sight and had by some lucky coincidence become acquainted with such a multitude of their domestic circumstances as to produce the startling impression which she did. My later knowledge of her sittings and personal acquaintance with her has led me absolutely to reject the latter explanation and to believe that she has supernormal powers."[4]

The present-day reader understandably shrinks from the mere mention of parapsychology and the paranormal. Serious interest in spiritualism, in the "discarnate," and in mediums is harder to maintain now than it was a hundred years ago. The odds against spirit communication and thought transference have lengthened. Much research has been done, there is very little to show for results, and it can no longer be said that spiritualism — the idea that the principle of life is immaterial, that it takes on bodily form for a while, then continues in immaterial form — has not been given a hearing. When William James took up the subject, he did so as part of the overall field of psychology. He wanted to investigate so-called spirit phenomena by the same strictly empirical methods one would use for any other phenomena. James struggled against isolating and discrediting anything in advance. To label something as paranormal or parapsychological was to exclude or marginalize it at the start. James was not interested in parapsychology but in an inclusive psychology, in a science that would impartially investigate everything from reaction time in individuals to haunted houses.

If James went at this with more enthusiasm and openness than we can muster today, it should be kept in mind that spiritualism was, in the 1880s, comparatively new. The entire modern movement of spiritualism fell within James's lifetime. It began (there is wide consensus on this) with the Fox sisters, who were Canadian born and who moved to Hydesville, New York, in 1847, where mysterious rappings first occurred in 1848. They went to live in Manhattan in 1850 and were taken up by Horace Greeley; interest in séances grew rapidly and soon spread to England. In 1864 the first national convention of what would become the American Association of Spiritualists was held. Five years later William James reviewed, skeptically, a book about mediums and séances called *Planchette.* During the 1870s Sir William Barrett began experiments in thought transference that brought the subject under the gaze of science. In 1875 came the end of the American Association of Spiritualists, in part because many spiritualists were not comfortable in institutional settings, in part because new organizations were rising. Within the next five years Helena Blavatsky founded the Theosophical Society; Mary Baker Eddy wrote *Science and Health;* Alfred Russel Wallace, co-discoverer of evolution and a convinced spiritualist, wrote *Miracles and Modern Spiritualism;* Blavatsky published *Isis Unveiled;* and Eddy founded the Church of Christ, Scientist.

In 1882, the year of Darwin's death, a group of Englishmen, including F.W.H. Myers, the philosopher Henry Sidgwick, and Edmund Gurney, founded the Society for Psychical Research in London. James met Gurney in December of 1882 and soon became involved with the society's work, which was to bring modern scientific methods to the study of psychic phenomena. In 1884 the society sent Richard Hodgson to India, where Madame Blavatsky was currently practicing; Hodgson produced a scathingly negative report on her activities. The same year saw the launching of the American Society for Psychical Research, in which James was a leading figure, being appointed at the start, with his friend Henry Bowditch, to draw up the society's research plan.

By June 1885, a month before Herman died, William James was busy attending séances and reporting on mediums, which he said he found a "loathsome occupation."[5] The mediums James thought so distasteful, not to say fraudulent, were so-called materializing mediums, who worked in darkened rooms and produced "phenomena" such as scarves and letters fluttering down from the ceiling and "spirits" moving about and touching sitters. Leonora Piper, by contrast, was not a materializing medium but a trance medium. She would put herself into a trance and then spirits would take control of her and speak to her or through her.

Leonora Piper was born in 1859 in New England, into a Congregationalist family. One day when she was eight she was playing in the garden when "suddenly she felt a sharp blow on her right ear accompanied by a long sibilant sound. This gradually resolved itself into the letter s, which was followed by the words "Aunt Sara, not dead, but with you still." It was not until several days later that "word was received from a distant part of the country that at the very hour and the very day" of the little girl's experience, her mother's sister Sara had suddenly and unexpectedly died.[6]

Some weeks later, Leonora called out for her mother one night. She couldn't sleep, she said, because of the "bright light in the room and all the faces in it," as well as because "my bed," a big old-fashioned four-poster, "won't stop rocking."[7] In 1881 she married William Piper of Boston. In late June 1884 she visited one J. R. Cocke, a professional Boston medium who made a specialty of "developing latent mediumship."[8] The next day Leonora was part of a circle meeting; when her turn came, she saw in front of her "a flood of light in which many strange faces appeared." She rose, walked in an unconscious and trance-like state to a table, wrote a message, then handed it to a member of the circle, a person unknown to her, and returned to her seat. When she awoke, it transpired that she had given a Judge Frost of Cambridge a note from a son he had lost thirty years before. When word of this experience got around, Mrs. Piper found herself besieged with requests for sittings. Her daughter, in the biographical account she wrote about her mother, says that Mrs. Piper was averse to publicity, reluctant to become a known medium practitioner, and was drawn in only by the interest of Professor James. Drawn in she was, however, and James would be associated with her off and on for the rest of his life. Mrs. Piper herself lived until 1950.

Actual stenographic transcripts of sessions at which James was present are rare and not very satisfying. There are exceptions, however. William and his wife were present at one sitting during which Mrs. Piper said that Aunt Kate had died just the night before. When William and Alice returned home, they found a telegram to that effect. Alice recorded part of the session with Mrs. Piper: "It may be worth while to add that early at this sitting I inquired 'How is Aunt Kate?' The reply was, 'she is poorly.' This reply disappointed me," Alice went on, "from its baldness. Nothing more was said about Aunt Kate till towards the close of the sitting, when I again said, 'Can you tell me nothing more about Aunt Kate?' The medium suddenly threw back her head and said in a startled way, 'Why, Aunt Kate's here. All around me I hear voices saying "Aunt Kate has come."' Then followed the announcement that she had died very early that morning, and on being pressed to give the time, shortly after two was named."[9]

In 1887 Richard Hodgson, a member of the London Society for Psychical Research and the person sent by the society to investigate Madame Blavatsky, traveled to the United States to investigate Mrs. Piper. Hodgson was flatly skeptical; he came to expose and explain, to repeat his triumph in the Blavatsky business. He spent a good part of the rest of his life, some eighteen years, working with Mrs. Piper. He even brought her to England, isolated her from friends, family, familiar surroundings, and newspapers in order to eliminate possible sources of inside information. Hodgson said he reluctantly came to accept the spiritualist explanation of her performances. Mrs. Piper is one of the few mediums ever to cooperate extensively with skeptical-minded investigators who identified themselves with modern scientific methods. She remains one of the few mediums who was never unmasked or exposed or otherwise shown up. She might not convince us today; she certainly convinced William James.

"If you will let me use the language of the professional logic-shop," James said in his presidential address to the Society for Psychical Research in 1896, "a universal proposition can be made untrue by a particular instance. If you wish to upset the law that all crows are black, you mustn't seek to show that no crows are; it is enough if you prove one single crow to be white. My own white crow is Mrs. Piper. In the trances of this medium, I cannot resist the conviction that knowledge appears which she has never gained by the ordinary waking use of her eyes and ears and wits."[10]

James was not, generally speaking, a credulous person. His refusal to rule out anything on principle did not mean he ruled nothing out. He applauded Richard Hodgson's "demolition of that jade Blavatsky," and he found the autobiography of Andrew Jackson Davis "an *ergotzliches* [delightful] work for sanctimonious and slimy hypocrisy."[11] Davis, known then as the Poughkeepsie Seer and now as the philosopher of spiritualism, was the uneducated son of a shoemaker, who was blindfolded and put into a clairvoyant state by a "magnetic operator" in 1843, when Davis was seventeen. Between November 1845 and January 1847 Davis delivered in New York City 157 lectures in a trance state. These were written down, by a Reverend Fishbaugh, and published as *The Principles of Nature, Her Divine Revelation, and a Voice to Mankind*. Davis cobbled together Swedenborgian and Fourierist ideas; he was hailed as prophesying the Fox sisters' revelations. Henry James the elder defended him at first, though he dismissed him ten years later as a "mere sentimental sot." Davis's full-blown visionary complacency clearly repelled William James. Of a vision of the human brain Davis wrote: "The superior organs of the cerebrum pulsated with a soft, radiant fire, but it did not look like any fire or flame that I had seen on earth. In truth, the brain seemed like a crown of spiritual brightness, decorated with shining crescents and flaming jewels."[12]

Although he seems almost rashly open to a Benjamin Paul Blood and his Anaesthetic Revelation, or a Leonora Piper, James was actually threading a middle way, rejecting the slipslop visions and bland assurances of a Blavatsky or a Davis on one side, and the rigid rationalism of an equally self-confident Francis Ellingwood Abbot on the other. Abbot's *Scientific Theism* reached James in December 1885. Its author, who, as we saw earlier, was a difficult former student of James's, had objected when the National Unitarian Conference of 1865 referred to its members as "disciples of the Lord Jesus Christ." Abbot became a leader of the Free Religious Association, founded in 1867. Emerson addressed the Free Religionists twice. Free Religion, Abbot thought, must replace "God in Christ" with "God in Humanity."[13] In 1872 Abbot organized opposition to a proposed amendment to the U.S. Constitution that would have declared Christ the ruler and the Bible the control of national life.

Abbot advocated an avowedly non-Christian religion of science, as his book's title indicates. It essentially presents Thomas Paine's position, but without Paine's lucid and memorable language. Paine had said, in *The Age of Reason,* that nature, not the Bible, is the true revelation, and "science is the true theology."[14] Whereas Emerson had said he did not "see how the great God prepares to satisfy the heart in the new order of things," Abbot had no trouble seeing it: "For the idea of God which science is slowly, nay, unconsciously, creating is . . . that of the immanent, organific, and supremely spiritual Infinite Life, revealing itself visibly in Nature, and, above all, invisibly in Nature's sublimest product — human nature and the human soul. Scientific Theism utters in intelligible speech the very heart, the Infinite Heart of the Universe itself."[15]

James was irked by Abbot's neoscholastic tone and his confidence that logical reasoning about airy abstractions would deliver reality. He thought Abbot used terms carelessly, self-servingly, and without reference to received meanings. Abbot indeed does not sound like a scientist; he sounds more like William's father. James wrote Abbot a friendly but blunt letter saying he was disappointed in the book and its "rankly idealistic conclusions."[16]

Though he felt that he should be spending more time on his psychology book, James was, in late 1885 and early 1886, drawn further and further into psychical research. In March 1886 he was experimentally hypnotizing — James uses "mesmerizing" as a synonym — Harvard students, including the two sons of H. H. Furness, a Shakespeare scholar who was himself interested in mediums. In April James visited various "materializing mediums," as he wrote Kitty Prince. As with his exposure to Andrew Jackson Davis, he found it "a strange and in many ways disgusting experience, which I have conscientiously undertaken to sit out."[17] In June he investigated stories of haunted houses on Beacon Hill, wrote a report on his twelve visits to a pair of sisters named Berry for the Society for Psychical Research, and, as part of the same report, gave a brief account of his experiences with Mrs. Piper.[18]

James's involvement with the society, the death of baby Herman, and his sittings with Mrs. Piper not only quickened old interests in troublesome and disputed areas of psychological investigation, they also seem to have changed the way he thought about such things. "I have hitherto felt," he wrote his father's old friend Dr. J. J. Garth Wilkinson, "as if the wonder-mongers and magnetic physicians and seventh sons of seventh daughters and those who gravitated towards them by mental affinity were a sort of intellectual vermin. I now begin to believe that that type of mind takes hold of a range of truths to which the other kind is stone blind. The consequence is that I am all at sea, with my old compass lost, and no new one, and the stars invisible through the fog."[19]

James's middle ground was neither large nor easy to defend. The spiritualist community (as represented, for example, by the Boston-based periodical *The Banner of Light*) looked upon him and the Society for Psychical Research as skeptical debunkers and enemies who unreasonably demanded concrete evidence for everything, while many scientists looked upon him as a gullible spiritualist because he took up such matters at all, legitimizing spiritualism by giving it the status of a scientific project. James found many of the mediums and other spiritualists trying; he was also indignant at the hard-shell positivist prejudice calling itself science. "I don't know whether you have heard of the London 'Society for Psychical Research,'" he wrote Carl Stumpf in Germany in January 1886, "which is seriously and laboriously investigating all sorts of 'supernatural' matters, clairvoyance, apparitions etc. I don't know what you think of such work, but I think that the present condition of opinion regarding it is scandalous, there being a mass of testimony or apparent testimony about such things, at which the only men capable of a critical judgment — men of scientific education — will not even look . . . It is a field in which the sources of deception are extremely numerous. But I believe there is no source of deception in the investigation of nature which can compare with a fixed belief that certain kinds of phenomenon are impossible."[20]

William's sister Alice was better during early 1886. She had four times as many visitors as before; her conversation sparkled. Harry saw her having a bit of a social triumph and predicted that if she stayed in London and continued to improve she would end up "a great success and queen of society." William read Harry's *Bostonians* in book form and wrote Harry a graceful letter praising it, apologizing for his earlier accusations about Miss Birdseye and Miss Peabody, and promising not to judge a book in future by an early magazine installment. William also sent a large package to Harry by steamer. It contained a new set of weights, ropes, pulleys, and handles that one could set up at home as in a gym. William had been converted to weight training, and Harry had expressed interest. William recommended that "a quarter of an hour practicing from 10 to 20 movements of each kind through a series of from 10 to 20 different motions will wake one up all through one's cubic contents." If the psychical side of life demanded attention, so did the physical.[21]

41. My Only Absolutely Satisfying Companion

IN MARCH 1886 William's wife Alice made an effort to "develop" latent qualities that might help her become a medium. Reaction in the family was mixed. Alice's mother and one sister were sympathetic. Sister Alice was skeptical about Mrs. Piper and, presumably, about the whole business. Aunt Kate urged William's wife not to do it. Harry wrote William to say he felt sorry for Alice's "trying to 'develop' for your use, qualities she may not have."[1] This is a curious comment coming from Henry James, who was, with William's wife, somewhat more open to communications from "the other side" than William.

Alice's son Henry would write years later that his mother carried on a flirtation with the supernatural and that she never stopped hoping for a message from William after his death. Like her husband, she considered a communication from the other side possible; like him, she was never satisfied that it had happened. Alice's sister Mary became, in 1889, something of a medium, and Alice herself had one terrifying experience in England, "an adventure with an invisible felt presence in an English country house which haunted her and Peggy [her daughter Margaret, born in 1887] for two exhausting nights." "Until then," she said, "I had always believed that there could be nothing malign in the spirit world. But that thing was malignant and evil. It shook my confidence."[2]

Despite this experience, Alice, like her husband, maintained her balance and even had a sense of humor about such matters. She went once, her son would write, "to a theosophical medium who told her she had thrice been burned to death as a heretic, once in Egypt, once during the Roman Empire, once by the Spanish Inquisition. The news of these appalling experiences . . . kept her in good spirits for a week."[3] There is a two-page manuscript in the James archive that throws an interesting light on Alice's view of her husband's work with mediums, trances, and hypnosis. It is a list in Alice's handwriting, headed "Valuable and much prized by W.J.," and it includes twelve items, among them "The Welsh Fasting Girl and her Father," a manuscript by W. M. Wilkinson and Dr. J. J. Garth Wilkinson, Henry Senior's old friend; a letter from Dr. Wilkinson to William; a book by S. Weir Mitchell, *Mary Reynolds: A State of Double Consciousness;* a book by Albert Barnes Dorman, *The Book of Mystery: Life of Mary Whitley, the Catholic Medium;* and *The Revelator,* "An Account of 21 Days Entrancement at Belfast Maine by Abraham Pierce, a Spirit Medium."[4]

If Alice had the same sort of active but not indiscriminate curiosity about spiritualist matters as her husband, it was only one of many interests they had in common. And despite the large family and household she oversaw and the constant moving around, they were always intellectually close. Indeed Alice seems to have had a considerable intellectual influence on William. She was as comfortable with French and German as he; she read to him when his eyes were bad; she wrote letters for him and went with him to the theater. He wrote her once to say how he missed her "soft chuckling beside me."[5]

She was not merely a secretary; she had a keen intelligence of her own, with strong views and her own books, her own favorite quotations, her own intellectual style. Before she met William she was friendly with the Quaker poet Whittier, who was old enough to be her father, and who seems to have given her inscribed copies of at least five of his books.[6] Alice liked to say, "Qui n'accept pas le regret, n'accept pas la vie" ("If you cannot accept regret, you cannot accept life"). She also liked "Si jeunesse savait; si age pouvait" ("If youth only knew; if age only could"). William read his drafts to her: "When some passage pleased her particularly, her exclamatory enthusiasm was immediate, and then her imagination would some-times seem to take fire and flame up with a suggestion. 'Oh William, that's splendid. Do keep it. Can't you go on and add what you were saying to me the other day? You remember, about — Don't you recall what Carlyle said . . . ?'"[7] Once when he was dictating a letter to Tom Davidson about the only kind of theism he, James, defended being that of "simple un-philosophical mankind," Alice chipped in on her own account, "If there be a God, how the devil can we know what difficulties he may have had to contend with?"[8] They discussed books, by letter, when apart. In one, he thanks her for her "dear letter this a.m.," adding, "I am curious to know what you mean about the wife of Tolstoi's hero."[9]

Alice enjoyed biographies and essays. She took a special interest in "mind cure," the popular new form of healing based on the belief that our troubles are all in our heads, but leaning more toward faith healing than psychoanalysis, and in a contemporary campaign to simplify English spelling. She also read widely. Her son noted that books were a constant resource for her. She read J. A. Froude's *Caesar: A Sketch,* Frederick Locker-Lampson's *My Confidences,* Jane Austen's *Mansfield Park* (twice), and Cowper's letters and poems. She read Emerson as well as Tolstoy and all of George Eliot's novels. She recommended George Meredith's *Rhoda Fleming* to William. Once, speaking about John Ruskin's soundness of mind, she said sanity was the lowest virtue, adding, no doubt with a chuckle, "You must use people who have it and thank heaven it is no worse." She was accustomed to reading what William wrote; once in a while she ran into difficulties. About radical empiricism she wrote him that "it is an aw-ful thought that I cannot understand it, but just that is the truth." William replied that his friend the psychologist Theodore Flournoy couldn't un-derstand it either.[10]

Once, when William couldn't figure out how to end a speech he had to make, it was Alice who gave him the biblical reference that inspired his final sentence. When Harvard's President Eliot asked James for a text for the frieze of Emerson Hall, the new philosophy building, it was Alice's suggestion (Psalms 8:4) that was adopted: "What is man that thou art mindful of him?" She was quite capable of taking her own line. William re-marked on her "siding with a certain opinion of Renouvier against me."[11] After reading and admiring Harry's piece on George Eliot in the *Atlantic Monthly,* she thought, "If he had only said a word more about generosity of character being the main pre-occupation of G.E. in all her novels, it would have been absolutely perfect."[12]

While it might seem to a modern reader that William was always dashing off somewhere without his family, it should be remembered that we know about many of these trips only because he wrote frequent, sometimes daily, letters to Alice. Their oldest son maintained that his mother was his father's "almost inseparable companion." It is often hard to understand the real dynamics of the marriages of one's own family or intimates, let alone those of strangers a hundred years ago. Families faced with the choice of saving or destroying letters need not accept Hawthorne's injunction to reveal, if not the worst, then at least some trait by which the worst may be inferred. William James must have been very difficult to live with. He was continually confessing his shortcomings or apologizing for some outburst of temper. "Dear child!" he wrote her once, from Maine. "I hope you are not having a headache. And I seem to myself to have been so peevish on departing. Shall I ever learn to take things genially, and not to sting back, like a wasp? But you know me, and that it is over in a moment, and means nothing."[13] Another time, when Alice was off in South Carolina and reporting that she felt lighthearted, William replied that it was "due to the fact that I the millstone, I the marplot, the complainer, the maker of impossibilities, the worrier, the contradicter, denyer and forbidder, am no longer there."[14]

Alice clearly felt very protective toward her husband. "I feel like guarding your present immunity from [distractions]," she would write. "I say to myself 'one week nearer, one week more of rest secured to him.'" Another time she wrote that "Aunt Kate talked to me of how you ought to be shielded from all appeals to your sympathy."[15] If a dominant note of William's letters to Alice was apology, a dominant note of hers was tender and sympathetic concern. "I am filled with sorrow and sympathy for you, so far away," she wrote William as his father lay gravely ill, "trying to wrest the whole truth from the bare words that have just gone over the wires. I can think of you away from me when you are prospering, but to know you alone and in trouble is almost more than I can bear. The dear, dear old man lies there, filled with the desire to die. O, William dear, your father and mother have been so dear to me, so endlessly kind to me and mine. I am losing a part of my own life in this dear old home of yours."[16]

Alice herself was a complex person. Her colorful derogatory descriptions of people she disliked were remembered. She disliked Jews, Catholics, and customs officers. She disliked Royce's wife. She sat over old correspondence in the attic, digging up evidence against a student of William's she considered a bigamist. Not all her grandchildren remember her fondly.

She kept tight reins on people, including herself. William told Alice's mother that Alice "won't wear her good things — new bag, ruby ring . . . She seems to think she is not good enough for anything good."[17]

But however we may find ourselves struck by one hint or another of trouble, there is no question but that William and Alice regarded the marriage as mostly a great success. William called her "my only absolutely satisfying companion."[18] And Alice, toward the end of her life, wrote to her oldest son, "I have had a beautiful day quite to myself — thinking of all that has been given — of the miracle of this day forty-four years ago when your Father and I were engaged, having so pathetically considered all our disqualifications and resolved to trust the future. The apple blossoms were out and all the spring seemed blessing us. I ought to go on my way gratefully, for I have had my turn."[19]

William trusted her and relied on her, in intellectual as in all other matters. Once, in 1888, he sent her a book by Prentiss Mulford, which, he explained, "I have not time to read. Pray read it if you can and tell me what is in it when we meet. Mark any good passages and note the pages of 'em in the fly-leaf."[20] Some years later William took up the work of Mulford, a mind-cure enthusiast, in his discussion of healthy-mindedness in *The Varieties of Religious Experience*.

Through good times and bad, whether apart or together, Alice Gibbens James was a steady and important influence on William James's intellectual life, just as she was central and indispensable to every other aspect of his life. With William, she passionately held to the idea that it was legitimate and crucial for people to believe. After going to hear William Salter give a sermon on William Ellery Channing, she reported to William that "in his discourse on Channing, Salter said that 'of all skepticism, the saddest is the refusal to believe in the possible.'"[21] It was one sadness neither Alice nor William had to face.

42. Hypnotism and Summers at Chocorua

THE MID-1880S WERE an expansive time in America. In 1885 the U.S. postal rate doubled, to two cents. The firm of Johnson & Johnson was founded; so were Stanford University and Bryn Mawr. The Boston Fruit Company, which would become United Fruit, opened for business. George S. Parker thought up a game called Banking and started Parker Brothers. With newly invented machines, American tobacco companies produced a billion cigarettes a year. In 1886 the first trainload of California oranges made its way to the East Coast. Coca-Cola went on sale in Atlanta in May, the same month the Haymarket riots occurred in Chicago. The Knights of Labor and others were agitating for an eight-hour workday. William James deplored the riots, but defended the new labor organization.[1] Strikes were rampant in the United States and England, where Henry James was working on his most political novel, *The Princess Casamassima*. Marx's *Capital* appeared in English. The Statue of Liberty was dedicated in New York Harbor.

James was making real progress with his psychology book, though the huge scope of the project — nothing less than how, physiologically, the human mind works — kept pushing him outward, centrifugally, even as his effort to clarify, illustrate, and set it all down provided a counterimpulse, a centripetal force. It was exasperating that every time he got down to writing, he became unable to sleep.

One of his tangential interests, hypnosis, was to prove not really tangential after all. Today hypnosis enjoys some mainstream acceptance in America, used as an anesthetic (mostly in dentistry), as a treatment for eating disorders and smoking cessation, and as relaxation therapy, but the road to acceptance has been a rocky one. Originally called mesmerism, after the eighteenth-century Viennese doctor Franz Mesmer, hypnosis was discredited by Mesmer's extravagant showmanship and his claims for the wonders of "animal magnetism," which, he said, worked by means of a "magnetic fluid" that supposedly passed from an operator to a subject. A royal commission, which included Benjamin Franklin and Antoine Lavoisier, the founder of modern chemistry, examined the subject and reported in 1784 that it could not accept the evidence for magnetic fluid.

In the 1840s Dr. James Braid of Manchester, England, reinvestigated the somnambulistic trance, which was the most obvious aspect of mesmerism, and found it to be not at all the terrifying mechanism for controlling others that Mesmer had made it seem. In Braid's view, the hypnotic trance could be induced only in a willing subject, and it consisted of an altered psychic state, the leading feature of which seemed to be anesthesia, which could occur in any part of the body and which was initiated by a suggestion made while the subject was in the trance state.[2] Braid renamed the somnambulistic trance "hypnosis." But this sober and promising line of investigation met two serious setbacks in the late 1840s: the Fox sisters' carryings-on again cast the shadow of charlatanry over any kind of trance state, and the discovery of the anesthetic properties of inhaling ether meant that the chief usable effect of the hypnotic trance was no longer needed.

To make matters worse, the famous neurologist Jean-Martin Charcot, Freud's teacher, who began working at the Salpêtrière Hospital in Paris in 1862, was soon teaching that hypnosis was a symptom of hysteria or of hystero-epilepsy, a view that was generally rejected by the late 1880s. Ambroise-August Liébeault, at Nancy, had much success with less sensational views; he saw how important expectation was to inducing a trance, and he understood that increased suggestibility is the main feature of a trance. James had been familiar with Liébeault's work for many years, having written a long, thoughtful, and sympathetic review of Liébeault's *Du Sommeil et des États Analogues* back in 1868.

In his review, James had noted especially how attention is focused, diverted, intensified, or redirected in the hypnotic state, and he strongly approved of Liébeault's suggestion that the therapeutic possibilities of hypnotism should be pursued. "As the mind calls forth disease in hypochondriacs and hysterics, so it should be employed to banish it." He had ended the review by saying it was "high time that a realm of phenomena which had played a prominent part in human history from time immemorial should be rescued from the hands of uncritical enthusiasm and charlatanry and conquered for science."[3]

Now, eighteen years later, James picked up the subject again. As a member of the Committee on Hypnosis of the Society for Psychical Research, he hypnotized a recent Harvard student, Gouverneur Carnochan, at a meeting of the society in January 1886, and he wrote up the experiment in a report delivered in June of that year. He further reported hypnotizing fifty or sixty others, mostly Harvard students, with the aim of trying to learn more about the physiology underlying the hypnotic trance. His (tentative) finding was that its main feature was not "sensorial anaesthesia," not a simple "failure to notice," but a much more complex thing, an "active counting out and positive exclusion of certain objects."[4] The idea that hypnotism is not a passive state but an active, if very narrow, one was something he had glimpsed and even commented on eighteen years earlier. ("Sleep, in other words, is an active function set up by a state of extreme concentration of the attention."[5]) It occurred to him that hypnosis might be something for his sister Alice to try. He wrote Harry to say so.[6]

During the summer of 1886, James wandered about New England, looking for a summer place he might buy. "The earth hunger grows on us," he wrote his sister. "The more we live the more attached we grow to the country," he told Harry. He visited Portsmouth, New Hampshire, then Jaffrey. He climbed Mount Monadnock, circled back through Cambridge, then went to Bar Harbor, where he was down with a fever for eight days. But for all the traveling, he was working well, which meant he wasn't sleeping. He read *Tristram Shandy* and Robert Louis Stevenson's new book. Stevenson was already, for William, the "most delightful of living writers, except Harry." He wrote his sister that his wife "began to read aloud Stevenson's *Kidnapped* yestreen, and I ache for the hour to go at it again. That man is a magician!" He wrote her again, a little later, to add that "there is something about the story that sings, from beginning to end," and he thought it had a good chance of lasting.[7]

On a different scale, he began this summer to read F. H. Bradley, the English idealist and neo-Hegelian philosopher. Attracted perhaps in part by the vigorous clarity of Bradley's bright prose, in his article in *Mind* called "Is There Any Special Activity of Attention?" (Bradley thought no, James thought yes), James picked up and read Bradley's *Principles of Logic* while traveling through the White Mountains. "What a fresh book," he wrote George Croom Robertson. "How he plows up the black mould in every direction! I don't know when I have read a more stimulating and exciting book. And in the style there is a man, tho' whether his sarcasms flow from an acidulous and unsocial, or from a genuinely humorous temper, I can't well make out. At any rate, it will be long ere I 'get over' the effects of reading this book and digest its results."[8]

It was a good summer for James. He resolved to give up psychical research for a year to concentrate on finishing the psychology book. His health improved and his spirits rose, so he could say he had never felt more in the mood for the start of the college year. Central to the new mood was the decision, formed by mid-September, to buy, for $750, a seventy-five-acre farm known as the Savage, or Salvage, Farm, with two houses — one a farmhouse — and a barn overlooking Mount Chocorua, on the southeastern edge of the White Mountains.

James loved these mountains as he loved the Adirondacks. He was an avid hiker, and he said over and over how he felt a real craving, a hunger for nature, a physical need to spend several months a year in the country. The farmhouse required work, of course, but James was delighted by its fourteen outside doors. James was drawn to the freedom of open spaces; his son would say of him that he "would have been happy sleeping and working in rooms as big as the nave of a cathedral." This was in sharp contrast with Alice, who did not like a house to be wide-open and whose idea of comfort was snugness. She yearned for "a sound little old New England farmhouse with the typical central chimney of brick ovens and its intricate economy." What they got was a "sprawling and poorly built" place it took her years to make into "something very personal and homelike."[9]

The town, then called Tamworth Iron Works and now called Chocorua (local legend has it that James and his friend John Runnels got their neighbor Grover Cleveland to use his Washington influence to change the name of the post office), was and is little more than a tiny village crossroads in the middle of New Hampshire. But three trains a day ran up from Boston on the Boston & Maine, and there was a stop in nearby West Ossipee. Getting to the farm from Boston took four hours on the train and an hour's buggy ride. The farm sits two and a half miles north of the village center, on the right-hand side of the road, now Route 16, overlooking Lake Chocorua and the 3,500-foot Mount Chocorua. The Hammond Trail up the mountain, the trail on which the visiting Henry James once got lost, takes off just three tenths of a mile north of the James place, opposite a big boulder by the roadside. It is still easy to get lost on this trail as it winds through the mixed New England forest of beech, birch, scarlet oak, hemlock, and maple.

Chocorua was just beginning to become a summer colony. Marshall Scudder, whose brother Horace was an editor at the Riverside Press and later the editor of the *Atlantic Monthly,* bought the Emery house in 1874. James's friend Charles Pickering Bowditch bought the Cone Farm on the lake. The farm had been sold at auction because the previous owner, Sylvester Cone, was in debt and in prison for killing one of a group of local boys who swam naked in the lake after Cone had warned them not to.

The summer people, known to at least one local as the "summer complaints," also included John Runnels, president of the Pullman Palace Car Company, whose daughter Alice married William James's son William; the Lorings, the family of Alice James's companion, Katharine Loring; George Baker, of Harvard's "47 Workshop" for aspiring playwrights; Sophie Hunt, a Browning scholar and head of the English department at Wellesley; and various Cummingses, Wards, and Peabodys. Fathers would arrive from the city on Friday and leave on Sunday.

There were many summer parties, there was much gaiety, and the young people trooped from house to house and fell in love over the long warm days. They swam in the lake from a raft. They took hikes and had picnics. They swung the young birch trees (the gray ones, not the white ones); they played Scouts, which was like Prisoner's Base, except you catch people by saying their names. They played charades, and in the evening, when it was really dark, they would take a pack of Necco Wafers and show each other how the candy disks gave off a spark when they were broken.

Chocorua was a marvelous place. The whole family loved it, but nobody loved it more than William James. As the Jameses worked on the house, the surrounding area became ever more developed and visited. The very old Liberty Trail up Mount Chocorua was improved in 1887, made into a toll bridle path in 1892, and in 1894 more than a thousand visitors registered at the Peak House, halfway up the trail.

The school year began at Harvard on October 1, 1886, and James plunged in with enthusiasm. His psychology book was well under way, seeming more and more substantial, as can be glimpsed from James's excited publishing plans. He corresponded with Robertson, the editor of *Mind,* about printing either the 140-page chapter on the perception of space (eventually chapter 20 in *The Principles of Psychology*) or the almost equally long chapter on the self.[10] James also toyed with publishing the short chapter on instinct (later chapter 24), but decided not to. All this material was ready to go, more or less, but the only piece that was actually published this fall was "The Perception of Time" (chapter 15), in the October number of Harris's *Journal of Speculative Philosophy.*

As he does with all his subjects, James asks in this piece, How, physiologically, do we experience (in this case) time? He provides what would come to be called a phenomenology of time, just as his treatment of space provides a phenomenology of space. Both pieces clearly anticipate phenomenology, though he does not use that modern-sounding word. Abstractly speaking (his argument goes), we say time consists of the past, the present, and the future. But the real present is so short, so like a knife edge, that as soon as we say "now," the uttered word becomes a part of the recent past.

Practically speaking, then — and James here draws heavily on Shadworth Hodgson and E. R. Clay — our apprehension of time consists of four parts: the obvious past, the specious present (which I just called the recent past), the real present, and the future. Strictly speaking, three of these four are "nonentities," which in turn means that our sense of time is almost completely a sense of Clay's "specious present" — that is, of things recently passed, passing as we speak, or expected soon. "The unit of composition of our perception of time is a duration," James writes, "with a bow and stern, as it were — a forward and a rearward-looking end." The rest of the chapter discusses experimental efforts to determine the actual length, in seconds, of the durations of which we are in fact aware. "The specious present," James concludes, "varying in length from a few seconds to probably not more than a minute, . . . is the original intuition of time."[11]

James found time this fall to read Benjamin Paul Blood's *Lion of the Nile* and George Eliot's *Spanish Gypsy*. He took time to write a short preface for a book on ethics by a Harvard graduate of 1881, a Unitarian minister who had died young (J. E. Maude, *The Foundations of Ethics*), and he gave time to the huge two-volume *Phantasms of the Living*, just published by Edmund Gurney, F.W.H. Myers, and Frank Podmore. James considered the book to have "at least forced a new present branch of study on the unwilling scientific world."[12] Much of the evidence concerned thought transference, which was something James considered possible. "The moment a context is found to make it continuous with other phenomena, I shall be much surprised if it does not become an orthodox scientific fact."[13] Inclined to believe, James still held out for proof with an eloquent hedge: "The next twenty-five years will then probably decide the question. Either a flood of confirmatory phenomena, caught in the act, will pour in . . . or it will not pour in . . . In one case Messrs Gurney and Myers will have made an epoch in science, and will take rank among the immortals as the first effective prophets of a doctrine whose ineffectual prophets have been many. In the other case they will have made as great a wreck and misuse of noble faculties as the sun is often called to look down upon."[14]

In late December he began reading John Dewey's *Psychology*, with which he was disappointed, as he had been "hoping for something really fresh" from the twenty-seven-year-old Dewey, who had just published a couple of lively articles on psychology and philosophy in *Mind*.

Dewey was seventeen years younger than James. He came from Vermont, studied under George Sylvester Morris at the University of Vermont, then took a Ph.D. in 1884 at Johns Hopkins. *Psychology* was his first book, and while it has been described as an effort to mesh neoidealist Germanic thought with laboratory psychology, the book is heavily and rather obviously written in the language of idealism. "All products of the creative imagination," Dewey writes, "are unconscious testimonies to the unity of spirit which binds man to man and man to nature in one organic whole . . . Every concrete act of knowledge involves an intuition of God; for it involves a unity of the real and the ideal, of the objective and the subjective."[15]

James did not have much to learn from Dewey just yet. But when Dewey read James's *Principles of Psychology* in the early 1890s, and as a result changed his whole view of psychology to a wholehearted endorsement of what Dewey then called the biological approach, the two men became colleagues and allies in the shaping of the new American psychology and philosophy.

43. Instinct and Will

FOR THOSE WHO WERE not mired in want in the late 1880s, good times and a celebratory mood prevailed. In November 1886 Harvard celebrated its 250th year with brightly uniformed cavalry, banners, and a speech by Grover Cleveland. In 1887 came Queen Victoria's Jubilee, celebrating her fifty years on the throne. Visiting New York, William James found it wonderfully lively and entertaining. His own mood was up as well. His health had never been better, and despite persistent insomnia he felt himself in excellent working trim. He was busier than ever, with more irons in more fires. He had new friends and colleagues, new experiments, and new college duties. All this new activity seemed to grow from or call out James's increasingly fruitful constructive energies, which were focused on two main projects: finishing the psychology book, of which he began to see the end, and renovating the Chocorua place. The physical and the intellectual constructions went hand in hand.

In January 1887 his "Perception of Space" chapter appeared in *Mind*. Much noticed and praised, it ran in four successive numbers of the journal. James now undertook to raise money for a salary for Richard Hodgson, who was to be the paid secretary of the American Society for Psychical Research. In an effort to cure his intractable insomnia he tried a mind-cure doctor named Annetta Dresser. Dresser, together with her husband, Julius, and Mary Baker Eddy, was among the first disciples of Phineas Quimby, the father of the mental-healing movement called New Thought. (Annetta's son Horatio became a prominent New Thought writer, whose works James would treat with respect in *The Varieties of Religious Experience*.) James was dubious about Mrs. Dresser at first, unsure whether the mind cure was doing him any good, but he determined to give it a full fair trial of a dozen sessions. "I sit down beside her," he wrote his sister in February 1887, "and presently drop asleep whilst she disentangles the snarls out of my mind. She says she never saw a mind with so many, so agitated, so rootless etc." It had been sister Alice's view of William all along, as he laughingly reminded her.[1]

James seized a moment in February to run up to Chocorua to talk with a carpenter about the changes he had in mind. He wrote Harry predicting confidently that his psychology book would be finished in a year, bragging that he was more than two thirds done. Neither of these proved exactly accurate, but the important thing was that James now felt he was on the final downhill stretch, and the feeling gave him energy and new resolve. He told his German friend Stumpf that he now had "few days without a line at least."[2]

Perhaps, too, he was beginning to feel some urgency, because other psychology books were coming out right and left. Besides Dewey's, there was James McCosh's *Psychology,* Borden P. Bowne's *Introduction to Psychological Theory,* and George T. Ladd's *Elements of Physiological Psychology.* In one sense, however, James may have welcomed the appearance of these books, because all four of them — some more receptive to new work than others — were in the end restatements of the idealist position. In his gentlemanly, generous, but firm review of Ladd, James had only to quote Ladd's conclusion: "The assumption that the mind is a real being, which can be acted on by the brain, and which can act on the body through the brain, is the only one compatible with all the facts of experience." Once you have come to think of mind as a process, it can only confuse or obscure matters to refer to mind as "a real being." The language suggested a transphysical or metaphysical entity. James no longer had much patience with such verbal juggling. "The chief stumbling-block there," James remarked, "is the utter barrenness, for scientific purposes, of your real spiritual being, or principle of unity, when you have got him."[3]

The great event of March 1887 was the birth, on the twenty-fourth, of a daughter, who, after three weeks or so, was named Margaret Mary. Alice had the last word on her name, just as William had had on Herman, whose death was not quite two years in the past.[4] Within two days William was reporting to his mother-in-law, who was off in Aiken, South Carolina, that "the infanta is the most modest and unselfish little thing, quite different from the coarse boy-babies, — tactful, not excessive or extreme in anything, sedentary and gifted with a beautiful voice."[5] Harry was now seven and Bill four; children were much on William's mind as he worked on his chapter on instinct, which he published this year in two parts in general-interest magazines, *Scribner's* and *Popular Science Monthly.*

Instincts "exist on an enormous scale in the animal kingdom," he begins. They are the "functional correlatives of structure." With any given organ or attribute there goes, "almost always, a native aptitude for its use." James gives the example of a bird's gland for the secretion of oil: "She knows instinctively how to press the oil from the gland, and apply it to the feather." If we ask for a definition, James has this: "The actions we call instinctive all conform to the general reflex type." Instincts are reflexes. They are impulses; they are very numerous. They are often transitory. They seem to exist to encourage the formation of habit, but they can often be blocked or negated by other impulses. James cites the example of a gosling that was reared indoors, in a kitchen, away from all water. "When the bird was some months old, and was taken to a pond, it not only refused to go into the water, but when thrown in scrambled out again, as a hen would have done." Born with an instinct to swim, but habituated early not to swim, the original impulse soon faded out.[6]

Instinct, James says, is the "faculty of acting in such a way as to produce certain ends, without foresight of the ends, and without previous education in the performance." He is at some pains to refute the old idea that humans differ from animals "by the almost total absence of instincts" and the related idea that humans operate instead by reason. James claims that, on the contrary, humans have "a far greater variety of impulses" than any animal, and that people, like animals, are driven more by instinct and habit than by reason. James tries to indicate the range of human instincts, starting with those of infants: "crying on contact with the air, sneezing, snuffling, snoring, coughing, sighing, sobbing, gagging, vomiting, hiccupping, starting, moving the limbs when tickled, touched or blown upon."

Almost all of James's treatment of instinct is focused on children. He takes up sucking, biting, chewing, grinding the teeth, licking, grimacing, spitting out, clasping, grasping, pointing at, "sounds expressive of desire," "carrying to the mouth of the object when grasped," crying, smiling, "protrusion of the lips," "turning the head aside as a gesture of rejection," holding the head erect, sitting up, standing, and locomotion. He quotes a variety of authors and experimenters, but the reader feels the continual presence of real children behind every page: "Yesterday the baby sat quite contentedly wherever he was put; today it has become impossible to keep him sitting at all, so irresistible is the impulse, aroused by the sight of the floor, to throw himself forward upon his hands . . . My own child, when creeping, was often observed to pick up objects from the floor with his mouth."

James considers vocalization, imitation, emulation or rivalry, pugnacity, anger, resentment, sympathy, the hunting instinct, and fear. Apropos the fear of strange animals, James writes that the idea that "the fear of 'vermin' ripens gradually, seemed to me to be proved in a child of my own to whom I gave a live frog once, at the age of six to eight months, and again when he was a year and a half old. The first time he seized it promptly, and holding it, in spite of its struggling, at last got its head into his mouth. He then let it crawl up his breast, and get upon his face, without showing alarm. But the second time, although he had seen no frog and heard no story about a frog between while, it was almost impossible to induce him to touch it."[7]

Treating the instinct for appropriation or acquisitiveness, James gives this account: "I lately saw a boy of five (who had been told the story of Hector and Achilles) teaching his younger brother, aged three, how to play Hector, while he himself should play Achilles, and chase him round the walls of Troy. Having armed themselves, Achilles advanced, shouting 'Where's my Patroklos?' Whereupon the would-be Hector piped up, quite distracted from his *rôle,* 'Where's *my* Patroklos, I want a Patroklos! I want a Patroklos!' — and broke up the game. Of what kind of a thing a Patroklos might be he had, of course, no notion — enough that his brother had one, for him to claim one too."[8]

James also discusses instincts for kleptomania, constructiveness, play, curiosity, sociability and shyness, secretiveness, cleanliness, modesty, shame, love, and jealousy. He ends with the instinct for parental love. To his customary learned sources he adds that "the passionate devotion of a mother — ill herself perhaps — to a sick or dying child is perhaps the most simply beautiful moral spectacle that human life affords. Contemning every danger, triumphing over every difficulty, outlasting all fatigue, woman's love is here invincibly superior to anything that man can show."[9]

In the instinct chapter James is making the point that a great deal of childhood is instinctual and reflexive, not volitional, but it is also in this chapter, more clearly than in any other, that we see and feel the immediate and pervasive presence of Alice, Herman, Margaret Mary, Billy, and Harry all around William James.

By the end of April 1887 James's health was still excellent, which was unusual for him around this time of year, as he tended to sink and become frazzled as the academic year accelerated to its exhausting close. While William reveled in good health, though, brother Bob was in dreadful shape. "His case is incurable because the drinking comes from his pathological mental condition which is part of his very nature," William wrote Harry.[10] Harry was himself down with terrible headaches and jaundice; it was his longest sick spell since boyhood. The baby Margaret Mary, called

Peggy, was also having a rough time, with ear abscesses and punctured eardrums. William and Alice fretted about possible hearing loss.

Finally the term ended, and James too went into a brief slump. He apologized to his wife for his "dullness of tone," which, he said, was caused by "the depression which always seizes me the first week [of vacation]." He felt like one stunned; he slept all the time and reported "it does great good."[11] He accomplished little this summer on his book and was instead heavily involved with the remodeling work on the Chocorua place, which he rashly intended to maintain as a working farm. He plunged into country life, spent time with his boys — Peggy's ear problems persisted — and eventually returned to Cambridge in good health and spirits and ready to face 123 chicks (undergrads in Philosophy 2: Logic and Psychology) and "one advanced chicken" (the lone grad student in Philosophy 9: Questions in Philosophy).

In October 1887 it was Alice's turn to be in Chocorua, overseeing their ambitious plans. Three or four carpenters had worked all summer. New rooms had been added. Instead of fourteen outside doors, there were now eleven. There was a "Gibbens wing" and a "James wing." William had bought a horse and wagon and had enjoyed talking with the locals about possible horse trades. He'd spent all of one summer day putting Paris green on the potato plants. Another day he planted tomatoes. When Alice was superintending, he sent up a dozen currant bushes, two dozen raspberry bushes, some gooseberries, climbing roses, hollyhocks, and Virginia creeper. He and Alice corresponded about seeding the lawn, running a drainage ditch, fencing, plowing, and woodcutting. William already hankered for more land to "protect" themselves. Alice had ambitious plans to bank up the ground back of the house and to reroute the road out front. The water supply was a problem. The house still needed painting, staining, and papering. Though James sometimes felt oppressed by the endless demands of the place, he loved it and exulted in it. Once when he was up there he wrote Alice to say that he pitied the poor city fellows who, unlike "we farmers," didn't know what life is.[12]

While Alice was effecting major changes at Chocorua, William was working in Cambridge on a piece called "What the Will Effects," given as a paper before the New England Normal School Teachers Association on October 28, 1887, and published the following year in *Scribner's Magazine*. James's long technical pieces in *Mind* were intended for academic or professional colleagues; they were the printed versions of his talks to philosophy clubs, to the Harvard Natural History Society, to Harvard Divinity

School, and to the gathering of Unitarian ministers. He published regularly in professional journals of philosophy and physiology and psychology. He had also for some time had a second audience: his pieces in *Scribner's* and *Popular Science Monthly* were for the educated general reader, whom James knew how to address without condescension. He began to have a third audience in mind, teachers — an audience that became increasingly important to him over the next decade. One reason for James's remarkable influence was this triple focus. When *The Principles of Psychology* finally appeared, it would be intended for and read by all three audiences.

James now thought he might finish the book by Christmas — would certainly finish during the winter (of 1887–88) — and one can see in "What the Will Effects" some of the grand themes of the book rising at last to full sight above the thickets of detail. The essential point of the "New Psychology" James proposes is the notion that "all our activity belongs at bottom to the type of reflex action, and that all our consciousness accompanies a chain of events of which the first was an incoming current in some sensory nerve, and of which the last will be a discharge into some muscle, blood vessel, or gland." The normal end of the process "is always some activity." From this point of view, then, "the thinking and feeling portions of our life seem little more than halfway houses towards behaviour . . . Some reactions are involuntary and others are voluntary," James asserts, "and the first point which the New Psychology scores, is that the voluntary reactions are all derived from the involuntary."[13]

From this spirited opening, James moves on to the voluntary actions, just as his chapter on instincts had emphasized the involuntary reactions. With voluntary actions, "the act is foreseen from the very first. The idea of it always precedes its execution." Unsurprisingly, James maintains that "before the will can get to work it needs a store of recollections of how various movements may feel." Then, surprisingly, he adds, "It needs nothing else." He illustrates this with an adroit description of a person trying to get out of bed on a cold morning, a description we have glanced at before, but it must be quoted in full because the episode contains, in miniature, James says, "the data for an entire psychology of volition."[14]

> We all know what it is to get out of bed on a freezing morning in a room without a fire, and how the very vital principle within us protests against the ordeal. Probably most of us have lain on certain mornings for an hour at a time unable to brace ourselves to the resolve. We think how late we shall be, how the duties of the day will suffer; we say "I must get up, this is ignominious," etc; but still the warm couch feels too delicious, the cold outside too

cruel and resolution faints away and postpones itself again and again just as it seemed on the verge of bursting the resistance and passing over into the decisive act. Now how do we ever get up under such circumstances? If I may generalize from my own experience, we more often than not get up without any struggle or decision at all. We suddenly find that we have got up.

Most of what we call will is really just consent, James says. In this case, the contrasting, inhibiting, blocking impulses simply disappear for a moment and bingo, we have acted on the original impulse to get up because suddenly nothing impeded that impulse.[15]

There are, of course, other cases, cases of volition that involve real determination, when we must make a distinct effort — a "slow dead heave of the will," James calls it elsewhere — to hold on to an idea, to "fill our mind with an idea which, but for our effort, would slip away." Here, suddenly, the physiological view opens into a wide moral view. Conceived this way, "the will has as much to do with our beliefs and faiths as with our movements. It is, in fact, only in consequence of a faith that our movements themselves ensue. We think of a movement and say 'let it ensue! So far as we are concerned let it be part of reality!'"[16]

Just how one becomes a person capable of such will is not clear, but it does happen. Some people "choose their attitude and know that the facing of its difficulties shall remain a permanent portion of their task . . . They find a zest in this difficult clinging to truth, or a lonely sort of joy in pressing on the thorn and going without it, which no passively warranted possession of it can ever confer. And thereby they become the masters and the lords of life. They must be counted with henceforth; they form a part of human destiny." It is not just the Napoleons of the world James has in mind here; it is people like his sister.[17]

The fall semester rolled along. Benjamin Rand, who would later do notable work on Stoicism, was James's assistant and exam grader. Early in November G. S. Hall brought out the first number of his new *American Journal of Psychology*. Hall was now a bristling, hard-edged man, soon to be president of Clark University and focused, in his psychological work, entirely on laboratory experiments and German-style research. He not only refrained from asking James to contribute, he wrote him a haughty, insulting letter to say that the worst thing that could be done for the new journal would be the "brief and generally complimentary note" James had been asked to write for *The Nation*. Hall seems to have been enraged that his journal was to receive a mere note when he hungered for sustained critical attention.[18]

James was so flustered by the conflicting requirements of Hall, of *The*

Nation, and of his own conscience that he ended by writing nothing at all. His own work was taking almost all his energy. He labored over his chapter on reasoning (chapter 22), in which he reached all the way back to Chauncey Wright's work on the origin of human consciousness and Wright's Darwinian sense — with which James now agreed — of the substantial common ground between humans and animals. Much of what we call reasoning is "immediate inference," a capacity we share with, for example, our dogs. James quotes Darwin: "When I say to my terrier in an eager voice (and I have made the trial many times) 'Hi! Hi! Where is it?' she at once takes it as a sign that something is to be hunted, and generally first looks quickly all around, and then rushes into the nearest thicket, to scout for any game, but finding nothing she looks up into any neighboring tree for a squirrel. Now do not these actions clearly show that she had in her mind a general idea or concept, that some animal is to be discovered and hunted?" Darwin's dogs, like James's children, led interesting lives.

In January 1888 Alice took the children to spend the rest of the winter in Aiken. Little Peggy's health was still not very good, and the town of Aiken, near the Georgia border, with its generous, broad shaded boulevards, was (as it is still) calming, restorative, and warm. In Cambridge James read *Paradise Lost* and set himself to committing long stretches of it to memory, as an experiment. He timed how long it took him to memorize a line, then worked on memorizing something completely different, then went back to Milton. The idea he was testing was the assumption that tackling something else between doses of *Paradise Lost* would exercise memory itself and make memorizing Milton go faster when he returned to it. It didn't.

In February he went to see John Singer Sargent's bold portrait of Isabella Stewart Gardner, Mrs. Jack, which was on display at the St. Botolph Club, a gathering place for Boston's nonstarving artists and writers. He found the portrait "damnation clever, but not great."[19] He read a report from the Perkins Institute for the Blind about an eight-year-old child named Helen Keller. He finished the chapter on perception for his book and somewhat unperceptively told Alice that he would have a strong impulse to kiss their amiable housemaid, Lizzie, who was leaving them, when she came to say goodbye. Alice did not let this pass, and it was some time before William heard the end of it. He believed in his impulses, defended this one, and despite Alice's protests, he did kiss Lizzie goodbye.

The fuss over the kiss shows how comparatively light James's problems had become, especially when they are contrasted with his earlier life or with the problems of those around him. His close friend and neighbor Royce suffered a major nervous collapse in 1888. It was "depression, apparently aggravated by insomnia," says his biographer. Royce compared his state of mind to a line in Coleridge's "Dejection": it was, he said, "a grief without a pang, void, dark, and drear." Royce could not carry on teaching, a leave was arranged, and he set off on a long voyage to Australia by way of a cure. James's brother Bob was lodged for a time in an institution this same year.[20]

James spent some time with a young woman named Annie Payson Call, soon to be a leader of the New Thought or mind-cure movement, which was rising as fast as revivalism in America. Call's popular self-help books would be based on James's views about the power of habit. James, in turn, learned much about the importance of relaxation — muscular relaxation — from Call's work.[21] In March a huge blizzard paralyzed most of the East Coast. As April approached, James felt in exuberant health for the second year in a row. He missed Alice more and more, wrote constantly, sometimes several times a day, and yearned to be off alone with her. He read in *Scribner's* the personal essay by Robert Louis Stevenson called "The Lantern Bearers." He thought its description of how to spot the joy in a person's life the "best thing in all Stevenson." Life for James had never been better.[22]

44. Santayana at Harvard

T HOUGH HE FELT himself on the home stretch with the psychology book, countless other matters pressed for William James's time and attention. Alice was due to return to Cambridge from South Carolina in May, but was delayed because the baby, Margaret Mary, was again sick. Alice began the move north by shipping a horse. James went down to the docks in Boston, saw to the unloading and then the reloading of the animal on a train for Chocorua. He also thought about buying a cow. He couldn't find shoes that fit him properly. He wrote his cousin Ellie, "Yesterday driving a cow home and drilling a hole in a rock to blast, today staining a floor, and so forth to the end of time."[1]

He was trying galvanization and, sometimes, chloroform to get to sleep. He went to New York to investigate a medium, Madame Dess de Bar, whom he described as "obese, wicked, jolly, intellectual, with no end of go and animal spirits." He corresponded with Christine Ladd Franklin, a fellow psychologist and philosopher, and he patched up relations with G. S. Hall. He missed Alice dreadfully, writing in every letter and lamenting, "Why can't we ever be alone together such a night as this?" We do not know whether Alice found this endearing or just tiresome.[2]

There were hard losses too. Lizzie Boott, with whom William had talked and lounged on the lawn at Pomfret, Connecticut, way back in the late 1860s, and who had married the painter Frank Duvenek, died in Paris in March 1888. Then in June Edmund Gurney, whom James regarded as the great hope for psychical research, died of an overdose of chloroform. He was found "dead in bed holding an impregnated sponge to his mouth," Harry reported, adding, "Suicide is suspected — I gather — from the strangeness of the form of his death." "These deaths," William wrote back, "make what remains here seem strangely insignificant and ephemeral, as if the weight of things as well as the numbers, was all on the other side."[3]

During the summer he went back and forth between Chocorua and Cambridge. Early in August he reported to Alice from Cambridge that he had ordered a plow, harness, and whiffletree, canvas for the piazza cover, and lag screws for the "piece against the house." He was reading an autobiographical novel of Restif de La Bretonne, *Monsieur Nicolas,* a racy and extended account of Restif's sentimental and sexual adventures. Alice seems not to have approved, but James was interested enough to keep reading, explaining to her, "It is not for the dirt but for the whole sense of reality of which the dirt is part that I find these books so renovating." He also read the Danish psychologist Carl Lange's book *On the Emotions,* a "brilliant little work I learned to know some months ago," he wrote a friend in July 1888. He read Tolstoy's *Confession* in a French translation, which had been written in the early 1880s, after, and in many ways about, Tolstoy's conversion. James found the book "coldly and ironically analytical both of himself and everyone else," and marked by "artistic malice."[4]

Harvard made calls on James's time and energy too, calls that were welcome, that were more or less manageable for a man of forty-six, but that were still taxing. He had eighty-seven students in Philosophy 2: Logic and Psychology, thirty in Philosophy 4: Ethics (Recent English Contributions to Theistic Ethics), and five advanced chickens in Philosophy 20a: Questions in Psychology. Royce was back from his long recuperative trip to Australia. His depression had lifted, and he was in good health. The Philosophy Club — mainly grad students — flourished and was something James enjoyed. There were more graduate students in philosophy now, and many of them would have lives of accomplishment. Benjamin Rand, who later did work on Shaftesbury (Anthony Ashley Cooper, third Earl of

Shaftesbury, author of *Characteristicks of Men, Manners, Opinions, Times,* was the great champion before Rousseau of the idea that people are basically good), was James's reader for Philosophy 2. George Herbert Mead (of the Harvard class of 1888 and later a well-known professor of philosophy at Chicago) was the tutor for the James boys. There were five prospective students in the wings. One, Charles Augustus Strong, who had graduated from Harvard in 1886 and was later a colleague of James's and the author of a remarkable book, *Why the Mind Has a Body,* was writing James for career advice. And Strong's close friend and classmate George Santayana returned this fall to Harvard to complete his Ph.D.

First as a student of James's and then as a colleague, Santayana was to be closely associated with James for many years. He was different not just from James but from the world in which he found himself. Elizabeth Flower and Murray Murphey point out that Santayana was "a Catholic in a Protestant country, a humanist in an age of science, a pessimist in a nation in which optimism was a national religion, a fatalist in a culture which preached the ability of creative intelligence to master the world, a man who advocated resignation as a cardinal virtue in a land wedded to activism."[5]

Interested more in aesthetics than in practical matters, a Platonist rather than an Aristotelian, a homosexual in a society in which his sexual life had to be hidden, Santayana would seem to have had little in common with James. It is often said that they didn't like or understand each other, but Santayana's writings suggest otherwise. By being so different, they were perfect foils for each other. Underlying good will counted for something. Each made room for the other in his intellectual universe, both wrote better prose than anyone in the Harvard English department of the time, and Santayana wrote some of the best and most generous descriptions we have of William James.[6]

Santayana was now twenty-five. Born in Spain in 1863, he was twenty-one years younger than James. He had been sent to Boston for an education; he was taken in by the family of his mother's first husband, and he spent eight years at Boston Latin School. He entered Harvard in 1882, writing poetry, studying philosophy, helping start a new magazine, excelling in everything. He felt himself an outsider at Harvard, as nearly everyone there does. Santayana was drawn to things bohemian and was fond of the company of brilliant, good-looking young men. Between Boston Latin and Harvard College, Santayana acquired the rounded classical education James had missed out on. "William James enjoyed in his youth what are called advantages," Santayana began a much later piece on James. Advantages for Santayana meant money; for all his superb education, he had expensive tastes and limited means and was self-conscious about it all.

Santayana's college class photograph shows a broad-faced, strong, handsome young man with short, somewhat curly hair, a mustache that concealed nothing, and large, deep-set, striking eyes that revealed everything. Margaret Münsterberg, the daughter of a colleague of Santayana's, also noticed his "dark Spanish eyes," in which "there was a sudden illumination, an extraordinary focusing of light rays having the effect of a blaze of pure spirit . . . and then his laugh! He laughed not with his lips only, but with his whole face. His was a laugh to delight a child's heart, the laugh of Peter Pan, brimming over with pure merriment."[7]

Santayana had won a fellowship to travel and study abroad, had been reading and going to lectures in Germany in pursuit of a Ph.D., which he now returned to Harvard to finish. He wanted to write a dissertation on Schopenhauer, but his adviser, Royce, "shook his head," saying Schopenhauer might do for a master's thesis but not for a doctorate. Santayana should write on Rudolph Hermann Lotze, a key figure in physiological psychology and founder of a philosophy called theistic idealism. This Santayana did, though his later opinion was that Lotze was only "a higher form of George Herbert Palmer."[8]

Santayana passed his Ph.D. exam in late May 1889 and was appointed instructor in philosophy at Harvard, where he started teaching the following fall. James praised his thesis as "simply an exquisite production," and told a prospective employer that Santayana was "the best intellect we have turned out here in many a year." Santayana later said he was told by his teachers that he was "the most normal doctor of philosophy they had ever created."

It is doubtful that Harvard was fully responsible for either claim; Santayana was self-possessed to an unusual degree, and even as an undergraduate there was a whiff of presumptive equality in his relations with his teachers, or at least in the account he gave of them. He admired Josiah Royce's "powerful and learned mind," and found that Royce's "comfortless dissatisfaction with every possible idea opened vistas" for him. He studied Locke, Berkeley, and Hume with James. During 1889 Santayana was part of a small class with which James read and discussed chapters from his manuscript of *The Principles of Psychology*. Later Santayana considered the *Principles* to be James's best achievement. "What distinguishes it is the author's gift for evoking vividly the very life of the mind."[9]

Santayana observed how James, in these years, gave a medical turn to everything, and he referred to the importance, for his own thought, of "the early medical psychology of James."[10] And he recognized, in James's teaching, the ultimate common ground for such different personalities: "Here there was as much honest humanity in the teacher as in the texts."

45. *The Psychology of Belief*

JAMES'S PUSH TO FINISH *The Principles of Psychology* was balanced by the philosophy course he was teaching during the fall of 1888 on recent English contributions to theistic ethics. As part of the preparation for this he read, not for the first time but with new interest, Plato's *Republic* and works of Aristotle, Adam Smith, Bishop Butler, William Paley, and Baruch Spinoza. The news from London was all about the mutilation and murder of seven women between August and November. The crimes were called the Whitechapel murders; the unknown assailant came to be known as Jack the Ripper. Harry's short novel *The Reverberator* (about a naive and unscrupulous newspaper reporter) and his great short story "The Aspern Papers" appeared. William spent weekends, when he could, with Alice at Chocorua, where she kept between six and ten men working at what had become an enormous undertaking of painting, plastering, and papering, a colossal amount of regrading the land, moving the barn, moving the road, moving even the old stone walls.

In November James sent off to *Mind* a piece called "The Psychology of Belief." Perhaps it was one of the chapters James read to his small graduate seminar. As was his habit, he began by squarely facing the question: What exactly is going on in the process we call believing? James starts boldly: "Everyone knows the difference between imagining a thing and believing in its existence, between supposing a proposition and acquiescing in its truth. In the case of acquiescence or belief, the object is not only apprehended by the mind, but is held to have reality. Belief is thus the mental state or function of cognizing reality."[1]

If we ask what kind of mental state, James's reply is: "In its inner nature belief, or the sense of reality, is a sort of feeling, more allied to the emotions than to anything else." What Walter Bagehot called the "emotion" of conviction, James calls the emotion of acquiescence or consent. Consent is not passive; it is "recognized by all to be a manifestation of our active nature." Both consent and belief are, James argues, "inwardly stable." Disbelief is just as stable as belief, so the "true opposites of belief, psychologically considered, are doubt and inquiry, not disbelief." Belief and disbelief, he insists, "are but two aspects of one psychic state."[2]

James draws on Franz Brentano and Spinoza as he describes the actual mental processes involved here. "Any object which remains uncontradicted is ipso facto believed and posited as absolute reality." (By "object" he means mental as well as physical objects. This is a strong and precise foreshadowing of what would later be called phenomenology.) Each person, each thinker, has habits of attention, and these habits "practically elect from among the various worlds some one to be for him the world of ultimate realities." Reality, James says, "means simply relation to our emotional and active life . . . Whatever excites and stimulates our interest is real." The wellspring and origin "of all reality . . . is thus subjective, is ourselves." We give reality to whatever objects we think of, for they are really phenomena, or objects of our passing thought, if nothing more."[3]

Ever alert to the practical implications of the new physiological psychology for teaching, James pulls the argument down to earth. "Whatever things have intimate and continuous connection with my life are things of whose reality I cannot doubt. Whatever things fail to establish this connection are things which are practically no better for me than if they existed not at all." What are the minimal conditions for belief? James answers, "Any relation to our mind at all, in the absence of a stronger contradictory relation, suffices to make an object real." He reaches back to his trip up the Amazon for an example. "The most useful doll I ever saw was a large cucumber in the hands of a little Amazonian Indian girl; she nursed it and washed it and rocked it to sleep in a hammock, and talked to it all day long — there was no part in life which the cucumber did not play."[4]

James moves on to connect the psychology of belief with his ideas about emotion. "The more a conceived object excites us, the more reality it has," and he gives the following example: "The thought of falling when we walk along a curbstone awakens no emotion of dread; so no sense of reality attaches to it [the thought of falling] and we are sure we shall not fall. On a precipice's edge, however, the sickening emotion which the notion of a possible fall engenders makes us believe in the latter's imminent reality, and quite unfits us to proceed." James rakes in examples from many fields. "The whole history of witchcraft and early medicine is a commentary on the facility with which anything which chances to be conceived is believed the moment belief chimes in with an emotional mood."[5]

After asking what objects we most believe in, James asks what theories we most believe in. "That theory will be most generally believed," he says, "which besides offering us objects able to account satisfactorily for our sensible experience, also offers those which are most interesting, those which appeal most urgently to our aesthetic, emotional and active needs." And here James reaches backward and inserts five pages from his 1882 piece "Rationality, Activity, and Faith." What we will not in the long run believe is any "philosophy whose principle is so incommensurate with our most intimate powers as to deny them all relevancy." James is thinking of fatalism and determinism. What, on the other hand, we will believe, as all great periods of revival and expansion of the human mind show (I am paraphrasing James here), is any philosophy that teaches that "the inmost nature of . . . reality is congenial to powers which you possess."

This idea cannot be too often repeated; it is the secret of James's continuing appeal — as well as Emerson's, and James now adds his friend Royce to this select group. He quotes Royce as saying, "Our own activity of attention will thus determine what we are to know and what we are to believe." James pays Royce a handsome compliment, noting that chapters 9 and 10 of his friend's *Religious Aspect of Philosophy* "are on the whole the clearest account of the psychology of belief with which I am acquainted."[6]

The close of this keystone chapter of James's consolidates his ideas about will and emotion with his ideas about belief and attention, and with his overarching concept of the primacy of action. "If belief consists in an emotional reaction of the entire man on an object, how can we believe at will? We cannot control our emotions." But there is a method. "We need only in cold blood ACT as if the thing in question were real, and keep acting as if it were real, and it will infallibly end by growing into such a connection with our life that it will become real."[7]

Real force of mind is the ability to join familiar things together in unfamiliar ways. This remarkable chapter in a remarkable book, looking backward to sweep up work done in the early 1880s and forward to prefigure work that would be done around the turn of the century, for *The Varieties of Religious Experience* — work that joins James's theory of emotion with his ideas about the reasonableness of believing — this chapter ends with two strong, fresh combinations. The first is that "will and belief, in short, meaning a certain relation between objects and the self, are two names for one and the same PSYCHOLOGICAL phenomenon." The second is "Our belief and attention are the same fact."[8]

As if to underline the importance of this chapter, James proceeded to act on his belief, retitling the piece from "The Psychology of Belief" to "The Perception of Reality." With this change and this title, we reach very close to the center of William James, to that hot spot in his consciousness, the habitual core of his best energies. The titles mean the same thing, to be sure, but the earlier is objective, detached, and scientific, a philosopher's title; the later one accepts, affirms, and endorses, like an artist. The philosopher, at the end of his furrow, has only reasons to believe, but the artist — and James was always half an artist, as his son has reminded us — the artist believes.

As the new year of 1889 opened, Harry wrote William to ask why they had heard nothing about Bob for months, and to lament over how the seventy-seven-year-old Aunt Kate's letters from New York seemed to show her failing rapidly. Neither was the news from London good. Sister Alice had suffered what Henry called "a very bad attack of the heart." It was apparently not what would today be called a heart attack, but rather something like palpitations, brought on by "nervous agitation (it is always dread and fear)," serious enough for Alice to telegraph Harry, who was on the Continent, to rush back. This episode aside, however, Alice was, in general, "certainly greatly better," at least according to Harry's assurances. Perhaps so, but we seem to catch Harry's real feelings as he closes the letter by saying how, as he returned to his much-loved London, the city "seemed *all* foul fog, sordid mud, vile low black brick, impenetrable English density and irrecoverably brutal and miserable lower classes."[9]

By contrast, things were very well with William's immediate family, and as often happens, the more he and Alice undertook, the more they accomplished. William was teaching a full load, working toward completion of his book, spinning off pieces that didn't quite fit the book. Alice was running the large household and looking after three young children. There was their joint project, the massive redesign and renovation of their Chocorua farm. With all this going on, William bought a Cambridge lot, a portion of the Norton estate, and began at long last to design and build what he hoped would be a permanent family home, at what would be 95 Irving Street. He met with the architect and the contractor. It was going to be a big place in the modish shingle style, with three full floors and a large loft or attic on the fourth. The ground-floor library, the second-floor master bedroom, and the third-floor in-law apartment each measured 23 by 28 feet. It was all going to cost $15,000, which is roughly $300,000 in today's money. Alice was fretful, even "desperate," about the money. They talked about renting the whole thing or renting the library part of it as a way to recoup some of the outlay.

Once they had decided to build, James plunged in. One day he waited around for the furnace people to show up. There was a question of whether to have an elevator. Closet placement was important, as was the design of the library. William began losing sleep over it all, a common enough problem with him, but now made worse, no doubt, by the substantial sums of money he needed to borrow.

Poor old Aunt Kate slid into aphasia; William rushed to New York to see for himself how she was. She spoke, but the words made no sense. She died in March, leaving to William's sister Alice only the lifetime use of a shawl and some silver and the right to make a permanent disposition of these trifles to a male heir. Alice was dumbfounded and hurt by the bequest, but Aunt Kate may have simply remembered that Alice's mother had left her entire estate to Alice, and that William with his large family needed money. At any rate, Aunt Kate left $9,000 to William. This, of course, made the new house much easier. His salary had been increased to $3,500 a year, but he had borrowed more than two and a half times that amount to pay for the lot and the first payment to the contractor.

His wife Alice continued to fret about their finances. William sought to assure her that he was being financially responsible, that the large sums borrowed and spent for the house were an investment, that they were not really living beyond their means.[10] Actively involved with both family and students, redesigning and rebuilding one home and designing and building another from scratch — all while finishing a book almost three thousand pages long in manuscript — William James was constructing his life with all the energy he had.

46. Reunion with Alice: The Hidden Self

THESE BIG PROJECTS — the two houses and the book — to say nothing of teaching and a crowded family life, took a predictable toll. By May 1889, as the end of the academic year approached and with Alice up at Chocorua, James became very restless, telling Alice, "I must break away from all customary sights and responsibilities . . . I feel now like going to Europe or anywhere, just for any entirely new attitude of mind."

He had been invited to an International Congress of Physiological Psychology, to be held in Paris in early August, and he wanted to see his brother and, especially, his sister. After some backing and filling he set off from Boston, unaccompanied, on the *Cephalonia* on June 22, getting off at Queenstown, now Cobh, in southern Ireland. He complained mightily about the "loathsome voyage" and felt unsettled and depressed, despite having had the company of Wendell Holmes on the ship and despite having read Harry's *London Life* ("extremely good"), Alphonse Daudet's *L'Immortel* ("diabolically good"), and Edward Emerson's memoir of his father ("on the whole chilling").

Once onshore, he headed for Dublin by way of the Lakes of Killarney. His American eye was agreeably overwhelmed by the Irish countryside, and while he seems not to have felt moved by it as his ancestral homeland, he did describe what he saw in stirring detail for his wife. The Glengarriff scenery "is wild and desolate, mountains comparable in height to the Adirondacks, but the roadside and foreground luxuriantly clad in vegetation, matted and thick with wild flowers, in a way of which we have no example." He found Dublin magnificent. But the undertone, the refrain or drone note in all of James's letters home, is anger. He repeats the word three times in each letter. He felt, he said, "anger, anger, anger, all the time, at my wanton leaving of you at home." He vowed not to do it again, that he would be a better man in the future. James urgently needed to get away from both the college and his family from time to time, and, typically, as soon as he was well away, he despised himself for needing to go.[1]

James was conscious of his Irish background, and his sympathies were with the Irish in their struggle with England, though he was not the fiery Irish patriot his sister was. But he could say, to his wife, "What revolutionists we should all be if we had to live in the midst of this pot-bellied, stall-fed densely steeped protestant Establishment."[2]

From Ireland he went to Scotland, writing home, "I don't think I ever saw a place that suited me like Edinburgh." In mid-July he headed for London, where he found Harry in his "delightful" apartment at 34 De Vere Gardens. It was, he said, "4 stories high, floods of light, and beautifully shaped and furnished rooms, just charming and cheerful to live in and no more." Harry himself he found "serene and harmonious — much freer than of yore, rides on top of busses, travels 3rd class, frequents a cheap tailor and buys ready-made shoes."[3]

James intended to go up to Leamington Spa, two hours by rail north of London, near Warwick and Stratford-on-Avon, to meet sister Alice in her rooms there. William had deliberately not written her that he was coming, nor had Harry told her. They both knew that Alice became "perturbed at expecting things," as William put it, and as Harry agreed, saying, "You are quite right in supposing that every form of expectation, surprise, waiting etc. is a bad element for her." The plan was for William to visit Warwick Castle and give Harry two hours (his usual visit was six) with Alice. If Harry thought Alice was up to it, he was to go out on the balcony and wave a white handkerchief, which would be William's signal to advance.

Harry's visit went well; he and Alice had lunch. Alice's account takes up the story: "We had just finished luncheon and were talking of something or other when H[arry] suddenly said, with a queer look upon his face, 'I must tell you something!' 'You're not going to be married!' shrieked I. 'No, but William is here, he has been lunching upon Warwick castle and is waiting now in the Holly Walk for the news to be broken to you and if you survive, I'm to tie my handkerch[ief] to the balcony.'" William, meanwhile, had "paced the street ¾ of an hour beyond the expected time (2 o'clock) and begun to give up all hope." Then — as William told the story to his wife — "suddenly Harry's portly form appeared on the balcony furiously cheering me on. I rushed up — Alice on her bed, in a fainting panting condition, white as a sheet, with outstretched arms into which I threw myself, and all was over."[4]

It had been five years since they had seen each other. Alice thought, as she said when she collected her thoughts two weeks later, that William didn't look much older and was "simply himself, a creature who speaks in another language as H says from the rest of mankind and who would lend life and charm to a treadmill." The shared, mutually recorded, real-life Proustian moment stirred Alice and elicited some of her finest writing: "What a strange experience it was, to have what had seemed so dead and gone all these years suddenly bloom before one, a flowing oasis in the alien desert, redolent with the exquisite family perfume of the days gone by, made of the illusions, the memories and the point of view in common, so that my floating-particle sense was lost for an hour or so in the illusion that what is forever shattered had sprung up anew, and existed outside our memories — where it is forever green."[5]

The meeting meant a lot to William as well. "She was excessively agitated," he wrote, "and kept gasping out, 'You understand, don't you, it's all my body, it's all physical. I can't help it.' Etc etc over and over again." She seemed to William, as he to her, little changed in five years. Living in England had evidently been good for her. "She was exceedingly elegant and graceful both of gesture and of voice, more so than of yore, and talked and laughed in a perfectly charming way making me feel ashamed of my dull and ponderous moral way of taking her these last years. She was witty and animated and curious about everything." William's account of the meeting ends, "Suffice it for now that the electric current is closed between myself and sister, and that the non-conducting obstruction is wholly melted away. It is a great relief." There was even, for Alice, a touch of romance to this highly charged meeting. "Enter Wm not a la Romeo, via the balcony," Alice told her diary. She needn't have explained, but she did: "The prose of our century to say nothing of that of our consanguinity making it super-erogatory."[6]

Harry presided and facilitated; he was, William observed to his sister, "beneath all the accretions of years and the world . . . still the same dear, innocent old Harry of our youth." He might be the author, most recently, of *A London Life* and *The Tragic Muse,* yet he had looked, Alice said, "white as a ghost" as he and William left her after the visit. But he was still and al-ways "a native of the James family and has no other country," as William said, in a phrase that has become famous. William and Alice were citizens of that same country, and this grand scene gives us more of the actual psy-chology of that remarkable family than any other single episode we know anything about.[7]

If the personal meeting with Alice was a great success, so was the pro-fessional meeting — the first International Congress of Physiological Psy-chology — William attended in Paris in early August. A hundred and twenty people took part, discussing the "muscular sense," heredity, hypno-tism, hallucinations (a particular interest of the English Society for Psychi-cal Research, which was well represented at the congress), and "abnor-mal associations of sensations." James was made much of; "The Feeling of Effort" had been translated into French and was widely admired. There were old friends from England — Sidgwick and Myers. There was a Hugo Münsterberg from Germany, later a close associate of James's. James said the persons who impressed him most were Charles-Robert Richet, a physiologist, the general secretary of the congress, who would discover anaphylaxis and win a Nobel Prize in 1913, and Pierre Janet, a psychologist and neurologist, recently appointed director of the psychology lab at the Salpêtrière Hospital. Janet was interested in hypnotism and in disorga-nized or multiple personalities; he anticipated Freud's exploration of the unconscious. James wrote to his wife that the congress was "one of the pleasantest ten-day periods of my life." The concluding banquet was held on a platform of the Eiffel Tower, where the assembled psychologists drank a toast to "anti-chauvinism in science" as they gazed down on "the won-derfully illuminated landscape of exhibition grounds, palaces and foun-tains spread out below, with all the lights and shadows of nocturnal Paris framing it in."[8]

Eager to get home and finish his book, feeling professionally "much less lonely in the world," and appointed to the permanent committee of the International Congress of Experimental Psychology he had just helped found, James cut short his stay abroad and sailed for Boston on August 15.

But there were many obstacles to getting down to work. He longed for Alice, who was up at Chocorua, and he proposed various schemes for getting a day or two alone with her. "How would it do to meet in West Ossipee in the pm and we two run off to the mountains for a couple of days together before I go home?" He had 128 students in Philosophy 2 to look after as the fall semester opened in Cambridge. Eliot wanted to appoint James to Bowen's position as the Alford Professor of Moral Philosophy, but James, with his newly stoked enthusiasm for psychology, countered with a plea that Eliot catch up with the times and appoint a professor of psychology, conceivably himself, but in any case somebody, so that Harvard not get too far behind Clark and Johns Hopkins and Wisconsin. Eliot, only a few weeks later, offered just such a professorship to James.[9]

Finishing the house at 95 Irving Street became William's responsibility, what with Alice in New Hampshire and pregnant again. James camped out, first in Grace Norton's place next door, then in the unfinished house itself. The painters came; wallpaper samples were stuck all over, there was floor finishing to think about. Boxes of all kinds were moved into the cellar. Other houses were going up on Irving Street, one being built two doors away, at 103 Irving, by the Royces. It was a cross-gabled colonial revival with five rooms, one of which was Royce's study. When the rest of the house was dark, James would throw stones against Royce's lighted study window when he wanted to see him.[10]

Alice miscarried toward the end of October. She was with her mother and the children at Chocorua. William was his usual solicitous self. "The shock of what you have been through is always very great," he wrote, urging her to "take things gently, until it is over." He went to hear Edwin Arnold lecture on the *Mahabarata* ("splendid") and read Janet's *L'Automatisme Psychologique*, a demonstration, with numerous clinical examples, of how certain experiences can exist in the mind at a subconscious level. James then wrote a piece for *Scribner's* called "The Hidden Self."

Vivid, pointed, written on the spur of the moment, "The Hidden Self" has not been widely read.[11] It begins with an extended plea to pay attention to "wild facts," irregular phenomena, strange experiences, facts that fit no stall or pigeonhole, events often labeled mystical. The opening demonstrates James's acute awareness of just whom he is writing for — in this case the educated layperson. "The great field for new discoveries," he begins, "is always the Unclassified Residuum."

The essay is largely a presentation of Janet's ideas about "unconscious mental life," ideas Janet derived from the close clinical observation of a group of disturbed patients then classified as hysterics. Janet found that in one important respect, a waking hysteric was just like a well person in a hypnotic trance; both showed a marked contraction of the field of consciousness. Janet found that by hypnotizing a hysterical patient named Lucie, he could relieve her of her waking problem, which was an overall anesthesia coupled with near-total deafness and a greatly reduced field of vision. When hypnotized, Lucie lost most of her symptoms. One day Janet made further hypnotic passes over the already hypnotized Lucie; she then entered a third state, in which no trace of her anesthesia remained. In the third state Lucie had different sensibilities, different memories than before. She was "a different person in short."

Janet began to think of his patient in her different states as Lucie 1, Lucie 2, and Lucie 3. What he had come upon was later called multiple personality disorder, which is now known as dissociative personality disorder.[12] Janet found that he could gain access to the different personalities by means of hypnosis and, sometimes, by automatic writing. When Lucie 1 was talking and answering questions, Lucie 2 (if she had been so instructed when "awake" as Lucie 2) could bring out her answers by automatic writing. "This simultaneous co-existence of the different personages into which one human being may be split is the great thesis of M. Janet's book," James wrote. And the "proof by automatic writing of the secondary consciousness's existence is the most cogent and striking one." The automatic writing revealed that it was not automatic at all: "a self presided . . . a split-off, limited, and buried, but yet a fully conscious self."[13]

Janet speculated that "the anaesthesias, paralyses, contractions [reduced vision], and other irregularities from which hysterics suffer seem, then, to be due to the fact that their secondary personage has enriched itself by robbing the primary one of a function which the latter ought to have retained." He concluded that "an hysteric woman abandons part of her consciousness because she is too weak nervously to hold it all together. The abandoned part, meanwhile, may solidify into a secondary or sub-conscious self." A modern analysis reads: "Children are not born with a sense of a unified identity — it develops from many sources and experiences. In overwhelmed children, its development is obstructed, and many parts of what should have been blended into a relatively unified identity remain separate."[14]

"The Hidden Self" came out in March 1890. Alice James read it and it struck a deep chord, especially the part about abandoning parts of oneself, and in a long, thoughtful diary entry she described her own life as one lived on just that brink of abandonment. "Conceive," she wrote, "of never being without the sense that if you let yourself go for a moment your mechanism will fall into pie and that at some given moment you must abandon it all, let the dykes break and the flood sweep in." Harry too was affected by "The Hidden Self"; in 1906 he wrote a story called "The Jolly Corner" in which his narrator encounters his own hidden self.[15]

In November 1889, the long-suffering Henry Holt, who had commissioned *The Principles of Psychology* back in 1878, wrote James to inquire about "your confounded health," about the "new house, and the shingles and the range," and to say that he had "a vague though possibly mistaken impression that you had some idea of sending me the manuscript of a Psychology to publish. If you remember anything of the kind," Holt archly concluded, "please let me know how the matter stands."[16]

The new house was finally completed in December, and the family moved in. William exulted in his grand first-floor library. "I am in Elysium," he wrote Harry. "I didn't know that material comfort could do a man such inward good." The house was finished and so — almost — was the book. On his forty-eighth birthday, he wrote Holt suggesting that he send him part of the manuscript so he could begin setting type. Holt replied that he would wait till the whole manuscript was sent. James toiled away on it, "working for dear life" to get it done. He wrote Holt again in March, saying that he had 1,700 pages of manuscript ready for the printer, that he was eager not to lose a day, and that he didn't understand why Holt couldn't set the first part in type while he finished the rest. Holt, amused and exasperated, replied, "Of course you don't understand why I need the whole of [the manuscript] before printing begins — it's not in your line to know." Holt explained how many times in the past he had set printers to work on part of a manuscript that then had to be shelved and delayed endlessly because the promised remainder did not arrive from the writer in time.[17]

James had one chapter left to write and five or six to revise. He envied Henry's flow of words — some thirty books now, many in two or three volumes. "How you produce volume after volume the way you do is more than I can conceive," he had written his brother. "But you haven't to forge every sentence in the teeth of irreducible and stubborn facts as I do. It is like walking through the densest brush wood." Writing had never come easily to William. He once told Renouvier that, when working on the theory of cognition, "[I] tore up almost every day what I had written the day before." There were times when he got up at two-thirty in the morning and worked until five in the afternoon, but this always had a high cost. "As soon as I get warmed up and interested in any chapter," he told his sister, "I have to stop, for bang goes my sleep." The sheer size of the project forced him to change his approach. "As the writing proceeded I found that I could not weave in quotations from other authors in anything like the abundance which I originally had in mind." Even so, he cut pages and parts of pages out of some of the books he cited (and which he owned) to paste into the manuscript, to save retyping. He did the same with his own published articles.[18]

Hard as it was for James to write in the first place, he also did a good deal of rewriting. "If there is aught of good in the style of it," he wrote Sarah Whitman, a Boston artist, hostess, and good friend, "it is the result of ceaseless toil in rewriting. Everything comes out wrong with me at first; but when once objectified in a crude shape, I can torture and poke and scrape and pat at it till it offends me no more."[19]

At last the manuscript — 2,970 pages long — was done. He put the finishing touches on it at two A.M. on May 22, then went to bed. When he got up, about ten in the morning, he felt, he said, a "great feeling of weariness" come over him. He took down a volume of Tennyson; it was a habit to reach for poetry at low moments. He wrote his wife; he would order the lawn mower tomorrow. Insuring the manuscript for a thousand dollars, James flung it into the mail to Holt with this spasm of self-excoriation: "No one could be more disgusted than I at the sight of the book. No subject is worth being treated of in 1000 pages! Had I ten years more, I could rewrite it in 500, but as it stands it is this or nothing — a loathsome, distended, tumefied, bloated, dropsical mass, testifying to but two facts; 1st that there is no such thing as a science of psychology, and 2nd that WJ is an incapable." Then he recovered himself enough to close, "Yours provided you hurry things up, Wm James."[20]

IV. THE VARIETIES OF RELIGIOUS EXPERIENCE

47. *Response to* Principles *and the Moral Philosopher*

TEN DAYS AFTER SENDING off the manuscript, a testy and impatient William James wrote Holt to say that he had heard nothing from him and therefore felt "no farther responsibility whatever about having the thing published by October." He announced with aggrieved vehemence — sometimes these things burst out of him — that he intended to take a vacation and wouldn't promise even to look at proofs until the following summer.

In fact Holt was moving at what today would be editorially reckless speed. Twenty-seven days after James had mailed off the manuscript, Holt mailed back the first batch of proofs. Soon James was getting twenty pages of proofs by every mail. Cambridge had four mail deliveries a day. He hated the work; it kept him in town, slaving away daily until nine at night. By August 12 he was finished. On August 21 he mailed off the index and turned at once to preparing his fall classes.

Alice, pregnant again after her miscarriage, was at Chocorua with Harry, eleven; Billy, eight; and Peggy, three. Brother Harry's *Tragic Muse* — first of the splendid novels of his middle period — had been published in June. William was full of enthusiasm: "At last you've done it and no mistake . . . It is a most original, wonderful, delightful and admirable production." But sister Alice had a serious breakdown this summer, and by early September Harry was expressing his deepening concern to William. "She has been growing weaker, and weaker, more and more emaciated, etc., and is unable to do things or bear things (exertions, fatigues etc.) that she could a year ago. I know not what the end will be — sometimes I think it won't be very distant."[1]

There was no question about Alice's physical decline, but her mind was stirring with other things as well. Her invalidism was never simple. Earlier in the summer, before the collapse, Alice had sent out a letter for publication, signed "Invalid," to *The Nation*. It was a wry anecdote about an American woman in England wanting to rent a room from the invalid's landlady. So William responded to the news of Alice's collapse with sympathy, of course, but also with a reference to this, Alice's debut in print, with words that were meant to be encouraging: "I am entirely certain that you've got a book inside of you about England." William had books very much on his mind at this moment. He wrote Howells to praise the just published *A Hazard of New Fortunes*. His own book, the first he could really call his own, was published on September 22, 1890, four short months after James had packed off the manuscript to Holt. William was forty-eight.[2]

For some readers — and not just those interested in psychology — *The Principles of Psychology* is William James's great book. For Jacques Barzun, who has written the finest general assessment to date of the *Principles*, the book is "an American masterpiece which, quite like *Moby Dick*, ought to be read from beginning to end at least once by every person professing to be educated. It is a masterpiece in the classic and total sense — no need of a descriptive or limiting word before or after."[3] George Santayana, writing in 1920 and taking the largest possible view, said that *Principles* was James's best book because of its author's "gift for evoking vividly the very life of the mind."[4] Even for those who have concluded that *The Varieties of Religious Experience* or *A Pluralistic Universe* or *Radical Empiricism* is a greater individual achievement, *The Principles of Psychology* remains the acknowledged ramp from which all the later achievements took off.

When the book first appeared, it was not, for academic philosophers and psychologists, altogether unexpected. Ralph Barton Perry notes that "most of its doctrines had already been presented in articles" — though they were, to be sure, his own articles — "and had received their baptism of critical fire." But it was a striking synthesis of recent work, and it was attractively written, personally urgent, and accessible to a general reader.[5]

By the end of 1891, fifteen months after publication, the book was in its third printing and a total of 1,800 copies had been distributed.[6] James's friends had of course sent enthusiastic congratulatory notes, though some also had serious reservations. Tom Davidson wished that James had turned his attention more to Aristotle, as he himself had been doing. Shadworth Hodgson, who considered himself to be in James's camp — the "experiential as distinguished from the empiricist" — was fretful that James's book had put a spoke into the chariot wheel of Hodgson's own work.

Charles Peirce wrote a review for *The Nation* (infuriating William's brother Henry) in which he called James "materialist to the core," and accused him of "tricks of language," of "uncritical acceptance of data," and of making "a complete rupture with accepted methods of psychology and of science in general." One really expects better of a man who had himself such a gift for rupture, innovation, and linguistic razzle-dazzle. The anonymous reviewer for *Science* — possibly James M. Baldwin, who spent many years assembling the received opinion of the era into his *Dictionary of Philosophy and Science* — found James's book "too personal, unsystematic, etc.," too "unlike the ordinary textbook to be valuable for students."

G. Stanley Hall, speaking for hard-line experimental psychology, for the Wundtian, positivistic laboratory psychology, committed to psychophysics, brass instruments, and precise measurements, said James lacked the experimental spirit, yearned for the old-fashioned idea of soul, and had written an impressionistic book. Hall was flatly unable to see that for modern psychology, as for French painting, impressionism was a breakthrough. "The author," Hall wrote, "is a veritable storm-bird, fascinated by problems most impossible of solution, and surest where specialists and experts in his field are most in doubt, and finding it very hard to get up interest in the most important matters, if settled and agreed to, even to state them well."

James Sully, reviewing *Principles* for *Mind,* conceded that James had done "the big thing," but had so many reservations that John Dewey could satirically sum up Sully's verdict on *Principles* as "a good book, but too lively to make a good corpse, and every scientific book ought to be a corpse." James's work was received fairly well in Germany. His friends Stumpf, Mach, and Paulsen admired it, but Paulsen wrote to complain that he had seen articles making fun of the book. Even so, there were soon four separate requests to translate it into German.[7]

The Principles of Psychology has endured, and even gained ground, as a classic in its field. Writing in 1969, a group of distinguished psychologists, including E. G. Boring, author of the most influential history of experimental psychology, collectively claimed that "James's *Principles* is without question the most literate, most provocative, and at the same time the most intelligent book on psychology that has ever appeared in English or in any other language."[8] A hundred years after the book was published,

Barbara Ross listed the following nine points as James's fundamental contributions to psychology:

[1] his account of space perception: [2] with Lange, his revolutionary views of emotion: [3] the inclusion of the investigation of instinct as an essential part of the study of the human mind: [4] his conception of habit as the basic principle of mental organization: [5] his use of materials drawn from the pathological side of mental life to illuminate the normal: [6] his psychology of self, which included a version of what later becomes Maslow's concept of self-actualization: [7] his treatment of memory in terms of stages that anticipated the currently popular information-processing model: [8] his appreciation of the universal importance of inhibition in the organization of behaviors: [9] his conscious and systematic struggle for the recognition of the vague, the transitory and the mystical.[9]

Principles also had an impact, right from the start, on philosophy and was also recognized as a specifically literary achievement. James's friend Josiah Royce saw clearly that James did not belong to the metaphysical, the associationist, or the neurological school; Royce called him a "naturalist" who adopts moments of consciousness as the fundamental units of psychological description. Royce also noted the considerable implications for ethics of James's "analysis of volition as an act of attention."[10] James's *Principles* jolted John Dewey out of his neo-Kantian slumber; it is reported that Dewey regarded the book — especially the chapters on conception, discrimination and comparison, and reasoning — and not James's later *Pragmatism*, as the best introduction to the pragmatic theory of knowledge.[11]

Edmund Husserl, usually regarded as the originator of modern phenomenology, began an intensive reading of *Principles* soon after it was published. The existential philosopher John Wild has noted this and has also noted that Gordon Allport (the modern psychologist best known for his work on personality) thought that *Principles*, "if properly understood, might have inaugurated a native phenomenological movement in the U.S." Wild's 1969 book, *The Radical Empiricism of William James*, does for James what Stanley Cavell has done for Emerson and Thoreau and what George Kateb has done for Whitman. Wild holds up James as a founder (in this case, of phenomenology), a figure at the center — perhaps one should say at several centers — of modern thought. Wild and Allport here remind us why Alfred North Whitehead considered James one of "the four great thinkers whose services to civilized thought rest largely upon their achievements in philosophical assemblage."[12]

Santayana put his finger on what has so irritated some of James's readers and so pleased others. Whatever G. Stanley Hall and others like him wished to believe, James's book showed, said Santayana, that "there is no body of doctrines, held by all competent men, that can be set down in a book and called Psychology." Santayana described *Principles* as a "work of imagination" and pointed specifically to James's "lively style."[13]

This claim has been made repeatedly, if a little hesitantly, as if we are afraid that calling it literary will detract from its standing as science or knowledge or thought. But James's work is literary in the broad, eighteenth-century meaning of the word, which included, along with poems, plays, and novels, Johnson's journalism, Burke's political speeches, and Gibbon's history of Rome. James himself said that anything considered historically should be considered part of the humanities. It was Rebecca West who first observed, in 1916, that one of the James brothers grew up to write fiction as though it were philosophy, and the other to write philosophy as though it were fiction.[14]

But the idea that James's work has a real, substantial literary claim goes back further. Writing in 1907, William Allen Nielson, of the Harvard English department, called William James's literary style better than Stevenson's, and he added, as a sort of note of local interest, "It has been one of the glories of the Harvard Department of Philosophy that it contained more men who write with distinction than any other department of the University."[15]

Recognition that James had written something that might last ("Literature," Ezra Pound reminds us, "is news that stays news") came, in fact, almost at once. William Dean Howells's review of *Principles* in *Harper's Magazine* in July 1891 focused on its literary qualities. James was delighted; he had harbored some such hope from the start. He had written his brother on August 22, 1890, the day after he mailed off the index to Holt, that what with Howells's *Hazard of New Fortunes*, "your *Tragic Muse*, and, last, but by no means least, my psychology, all appearing in it, the year 1890 will be known as the great epochal year in American Literature." He was funning, of course, but not entirely. He noted with satisfaction to Holt a year later that the book seemed "a decided success — especially from the literary point of view." And when he surveyed his competition he was quick to observe that all the other books — except Taine's *De l'Intelligence* — were "so uninterestingly written."[16]

The Principles of Psychology comes complete with huge hundred-page chapters on such topics as the neurological details of space perception. It lacks a formal organization, seeming to be more a collection of monographs, as Santayana called it, on subjects that happened to interest James.

It is equipped with diagrams and algebraic notation to help us follow nerve currents from N1 to N2. The book is a partly unweeded garden, but it is a garden, and James's style is everywhere at work. He writes concretely, with attention to physical detail. His fondness for poetry shows up frequently. Whenever there is to be a test of memory or of attention, the content of the experiment is often lines of verse. He coined words and gave new life to old ones. He was the first to use "hegelism," "time-line," and "pluralism." He had a gift for phrases that stick in the mind: "the bitch-goddess success," "stream of consciousness," "one great blooming, buzzing confusion," "the moral equivalent of war," "healthy-minded," and "live option." He used examples, anecdotes, jokes, anything to impart narrative dash and energy to the page. And there are many places where, standing on the arid plain of experimental data, James turns to face the reader, reaching outward through his own experience to us, in prose that can stand comparison to anyone's.

"We measure ourselves by many standards," he writes toward the end of the ninety-five-page chapter on will. "Our strength and our intelligence, our wealth and even our good luck, are things which warm our heart and make us feel ourselves a match for life. But deeper than all such things, and able to suffice unto itself without them, is the sense of the amount of effort which we can put forth . . . He who can make none is but a shadow; he who can make much is a hero."

Lest we think this is easy uplift, James circles back to consider just how hard and how dark the challenge often is. Effort, for James, is linked to acceptance now, not to resistance or denial, but acceptance even of calamity and disaster. "The deepest question that is ever asked admits of no reply but the dumb turning of the will and the tightening of our heart-strings as we say, '*Yes, I will even have it so!*' When a dreadful object is presented, or when life as a whole turns up its dark abysses to our view," this is when effort becomes so difficult and so necessary. Even for the heroic mind, James says, "the objects are sinister and dreadful, unwelcome, incompatible with wished-for things." But the heroic mind, he insists, "can stand this universe . . . He can still find a zest in it, not by 'ostrich-like forgetfulness,' but by a pure inward willingness to take the world with those deterrent objects there."

James leans his whole weight on the argument; by consenting to take the world as it is, by accepting the risks and running them, a person becomes, he says, "one of the masters and the lords of life." It is a phrase from Emerson. Such a person, James writes, "must be counted with henceforth; he forms part of human destiny. Neither in the theoretic nor in the practical sphere do we care for, or go for help to, those who have no head for risks, or sense for living on the perilous edge."[17]

This is where *Principles* peaks (though there are two more chapters to follow), as James connects attention to will, will to effort, and effort to our basic, irreducible consent or nonconsent to the world we confront. Nowhere is the full literary-humanistic aspect of James's work clearer than in his final paragraph on this personally urgent issue. "Thus not only our morality, but our religion, so far as the latter is deliberate, depend on the effort which we can make. '*Will you or won't you have it so?*' is the most probing question we are ever asked; we are asked it every hour of the day, and about the largest as well as the smallest, the most theoretical as well as the most practical, things . . . We answer," James goes on, "by consents or non-consents and not by words. What wonder that these dumb responses should seem our deepest organs of communication with the nature of things! What wonder if the effort demanded by them be the measure of our worth as men! What wonder if the amount which we accord of it be the one strictly underived and original contribution which we make to the world!"[18]

It took some effort to return to teaching at the end of September 1890. As always, James found getting started was "disconsolate work." He had a full load of courses, including the new Philosophy 2, a psychology course with twenty-four undergrads and four graduate students. James assigned his brand-new book and set the students to doing laboratory exercises on attention and imagination. The assignment for the lab on attention was for each student to try to recite one line of poetry out loud while writing down a different line, timing one's efforts, and noting how one's attention veered (or not) back and forth. For imagination James asked his students to sit down an hour after breakfast and recall the breakfast table, with special attention to matters of illumination, definition, and coloring.[19]

If he had not seen it before, his students made James see that his *Principles* could do with some revision, so he had his personal copy of the two-volume work removed from its binding, interleaved with blank pages, and rebound in four volumes, to make it easy for him to rewrite.[20]

On October 3, James had the pleasant job of writing to Mary Calkins to welcome her to his Thursday evening psychology seminar. Calkins taught psychology at Wellesley, had a year off for advanced study, and had been trying to get permission from the Harvard authorities to attend graduate classes. Eliot had not been eager to see this happen; he felt that Radcliffe (in those days the Annex) was the place for women's education. A few

Harvard professors taught there, for extra pay, but Harvard classes were for men only. James had written Eliot, pleading Calkins's case. He wrote to Calkins, "It is flagitious that you should be kept out. — Enough to make dynamiters of you and all women. I hope and trust that your application will break the barrier. I will do what I can." On this occasion, Harvard relented. On October 1 Mary Calkins received permission to attend upper-level Harvard courses for graduate students taught by Royce and James.[21]

William's eldest son, Harry, now eleven, started attending the Brown and Nichols School in Cambridge this fall; the boy felt at once "quite over-burdened" by homework. Alice and the other children stayed at Chocorua as long as they could, going back to Cambridge in mid-October. Financial problems loomed, not disastrous ones, but worrisome nonetheless. On October 1 William and Alice had a bank balance of $55, with $522 in unpaid bills, no money due in from the Syracuse properties until November 8, and nothing from the college until December 1. He tried to reassure Alice, pointing out that they had gotten behind by spending on the house, which William again insisted was an investment, not money lost.

Alice had other things to worry about too. She was in the last months of her pregnancy this fall, and three days before Christmas she gave birth to a boy. The birth "went off most beautifully," William wrote Harry. The baby's name was a bit of a problem. He was first called Francis Tweedy; William called him Tweedy, Alice called him Francis. For a while he was called John. William addressed him on postcards as Mr. Cherubini James. When the boy was three his parents renamed him Alexander Robertson James. If his name was unsure, his welcome was not. When she saw the new baby, three-year-old Peggy asked, "Whose baby is it?" William told her, "It's your baby." Whereupon Peggy went downstairs and screamed out to her grandmother, "I've got a baby, a real live baby!"[22]

One of the main subjects of *The Principles of Psychology* was volition, or will. Late in the fall of 1890, James wrote a piece further working out the ethical implications of his ideas about will. He tried the piece out on some of his advanced students, and one of them reported that it "was very much enjoyed and appreciated."[23] James then took the piece to New Haven and presented it before the Yale Philosophical Club. Not one word about the talk was spoken, either at the lecture or at the dinner that followed, at the home of Professor (and Reverend) George T. Ladd. James's chance for a receptive hearing was no doubt cooked by his first two sentences: "There is no such thing possible as an ethical philosophy dogmatically made up in advance . . . There can be no final truth in ethics any more than in physics, until the last man has had his experience and said his say."[24] Ladd was a firm teleologist, believing that all mental activity serves a plan, whether we grasp the plan or not. James refused to begin by positing any plan at all. And while he was pointedly opposed to what he called "ethical scepticism," he could not start with an abstraction; he could start only with the concrete world — a rich, inclusive world (he insists on the word "inclusive") — of the actual desires of real people.

James's rejection of a plan (and a Planner) is like Ivan Karamazov's. James declares it impossible to accept "a world in which Messrs Fourier's and Bellamy's and Morris' utopias should all be outdone and millions kept permanently happy on the one simple condition that a certain lost soul on the far-off edge of things should lead a life of lonely torture."[25] One of the Harvard students heard the talk and remembered how James had pursued this point beyond his text, saying, "Gentlemen, as long as one poor cockroach feels the pangs of unrequited love, this world is not a moral world."[26]

Bypassing (not rejecting) the theological model, James lays it down that "we see not only that without a claim actually made by some concrete person there can be no obligation, but that there is some obligation wherever there is a claim." The only possible basis for morality, for ethics, for the existence of right and wrong, is the actual existence of desires. "Take any demand, however slight, which any creature, however weak, may make. Ought it not, for its own sole sake, to be satisfied? If not, prove why not. The only possible kind of proof you could adduce would be the exhibition of another creature who should make a demand that ran the other way." He says a bit later, "The essence of good is simply to satisfy demand." He then works this out for practical ethics: "The guiding principle for ethical philosophy . . . [is] simply to satisfy at all times as many demands as we can . . . That act must be the best act . . . which makes for the best whole, in the sense of awakening the least sum of dissatisfactions." It is always the larger, richer, "more inclusive" world that James has in view. Work toward such a world requires of us what James calls the strenuous rather than the easygoing mood.[27]

Perhaps Professor Ladd was still listening, even if Reverend Ladd had given up, when toward the end of his talk James seems not only to leave a back door open but to slip in through it: "Every sort of energy and endurance, of courage and capacity for handling life's evils, is set free in those who have religious faith." This leads directly to what he calls his "final conclusion," that "the stable systematic and moral universe for which the ethical philosopher asks is fully possible only in a world where there is a divine thinker with all-enveloping demands." Not that we can rely on the divine thinker to do all the work. "The solving word," and this is where James leaves it, "for the learned and the unlearned man alike, lies in the last resort in the dumb willingnesses and unwillingnesses of their interior characters, and nowhere else."[28]

48. *Flooded by the Deep Life*

IN MARCH 1890 James had voted with a majority of the Harvard faculty to trim the requirements for a bachelor's degree from eighteen and a fraction to sixteen courses. The vote capped years of meetings and studies. James had been on most of the committees, so in January 1891, just when brother Harry's play *The American* was opening in the provinces in England, William was asked to write an article for the *Harvard Monthly* explaining the majority decision on the curriculum. James's protracted, invisible labors, and even his bemused impatience with the process, show how deeply his life was now entwined with institutional Harvard. "Members of our dear Faculty," he wrote, "have a way of discovering reasons fitted exclusively for their idiosyncratic use, and though voting with their neighbors, will often do so on incommunicable grounds."[1] James was explaining why neither he nor anyone else could speak for the whole majority. He himself favored change almost as such; he instinctively sided with reformers, but underneath, and animating his entire involvement with the curriculum committees, was his growing commitment to teaching as such.

Confronting what he considered reactionary arguments that shortening the college's course would "lower the standard of its degree" and lead to "a general degradation of the higher education in America," James argued the opposite case, that speeding up college was a way to combat the "listlessness, apathy, dawdling, sauntering, the smoking of cigarettes and living on small sarcasms, the 'Harvard indifference,' in short, of which outsiders have so frequently complained." James thought this apathetic attitude was "the direct fruit of keeping these men too long from contact with the world of affairs." All James's personal experience told him that it was not the students but the system that was at fault. Noting that he had been teaching at Harvard for nineteen years, he said he had "become sensible of a curious improvement in the tone of the students. They are maturer; you meet them more as equals, you expect more and you get more from them."[2]

He might reasonably have expected more from the administration, but he didn't get it. Five years of committee work went for nothing, the university rejected the faculty vote, and things went on as before. Institutions have their ways. While Martin Luther was nailing his ninety-five theses to the door of Wittenberg's cathedral, the faculty of his university was debating its curriculum.

In March 1891 James wrote a glowing review of a short book on popular psychology written by an acquaintance, Annie Payson Call's *Power Through Repose*. Since his own two-volume opus was being widely praised — or at least taken seriously — he was thinking about preparing a condensed version for Holt, and amid all this flattering attention he was open to the merits of a simple self-help book that most scholars found, and still find, beneath notice.

Call identified a common condition that she said a European doctor had called "Americanitis," which was not the American Nervousness or neurasthenia of Charles Beard. Call's Americanitis was the perceived American habit of living on the edge, on the stretch, clenched and tense. James summed up the symptoms: "The brow and eyes are contracted, the mouth screwed up or down or to one side; an expression of subdued agony or anxiety, or else a smile so intense as to squeeze all further possibilities out of the countenance." The condition Call described, a "constant tension of so many muscles not in use" and "the habitual over-contraction" of most of our muscles most of the time, seems to have struck James with special force. Whether it applied to all Americans or not, it certainly applied to William James, as any group of photographs of him will testify.

What Call taught and what James was ready to hear was a gospel of relaxation, and he would eventually write a piece with that title, a piece strongly indebted to Call's book. Call was not, strictly speaking, one of the mind-cure people, nor was she a Christian Scientist. She took a direct and very physical approach. Her idea is that if we carefully and deliberately relax the muscles not in active use, we will relax in general, and as a result, we will have more energy for things we want to do.

Physical unclenching is the key. "A perfectly calm and placid tone of mind is out of the question with a system that is never completely relaxed, but always quivering with residual and incipient contractions. Such a person never rests with his whole weight on his chair. His feet still press the ground, half-ready to rise, his fingers convulsively clutch the chair's arms or work at each other. On the pillow the neck muscles still are rigid." Call recommends for everyone "systematic training in relaxation," one muscle at a time, deliberately. The result, she says, and James endorses it, "will regenerate their nervous strength, their temper, their ability to attend, their speech, their powers of effective work in every direction, and of course their cheerfulness, their gait, and grace of presence."[3]

James could hardly praise the book too highly. His review was unreservedly enthusiastic, and Annie Call wrote to thank him. It is sometimes suggested that James was a great psychologist despite his lapses into enthusiasm and credulousness, but his unsnobbish ability to spot — and what is more, to accept — real therapeutic possibilities even in the plainest popular form was in fact a great strength. His taking up Annie Payson Call was not a lapse to be deplored but a lively example of James's peculiar ability to find value and strength in overlooked places. He found the value because, like any good teacher, he expected to find it.

If he couldn't shorten the college course, he could shorten his own book. Publishing *The Principles of Psychology* had been for James the moral equivalent of a Ph.D. thesis. He had worked out the subject in unsparing detail, adopting the professional standards of his intended audience of peers. Publication and the reviews constituted a public vetting. James had given little thought to the book's usefulness as a text; teaching from it had now shown him that much could be done to make it a more useful book. In February 1891 he began corresponding with Holt about a one-volume revision. He planned to spend the summer working on it, and indeed he did get down to work on it around the first of July.

But before he was well started there had come, in June, a letter from Katharine Loring: Dr. Clarke had discovered a "heart defect" in sister Alice. Heart trouble, specifically with the valves, was fairly common in the James family; it had shown up in Henry Senior and in Wilky. William himself had reported in May of this year a "heavy fullness of heart and throat," which in retrospect seems worth noting. William was not surprised by this report of Alice, but he was naturally sympathetic. Then, on July 6, just as he was settling into the condensation of the book, came news from Katharine about another visit by Dr. Clarke and the discovery of a tumor in Alice's breast. If, as seemed likely, it was cancer, it was a death sentence, as Alice and her brother were both aware.

William walked right up to the fact, as he knew Alice would expect him to, and he wrote her a letter in language as carefully qualified and nuanced as anything his brother might write. "I didn't myself see very well how a heart-defect as you could now be having could account for anything like the 'heft' of your symptoms and condition," he wrote her, "and so far from being shocked, I am, although made more compassionate, yet (strange to say) rather relieved than shocked by this more tangible and immediately-menacing source of woe." Respect for Alice made evasion impossible. "Of course if the tumor should turn out to be cancerous, that means, as all men know, a finite length of days: and then good bye to neurasthenia and neuralgia and headache, and weariness and palpitation and disgust all at one stroke."[4]

To Annie Payson Call's diagnosis of too much muscular tension and her proposed cure of systematic relaxation, James had responded with hope and enthusiasm. To this vastly more serious — this essentially hopeless — diagnosis, James could respond with only a dead heave of grim acceptance and words that suggest how well he really knew his sister. "I should think," he said, "that you would be reconciled to the prospect with all its pluses and minuses! I know you've never cared for life, and to me now, at the age of nearly fifty, life and death seem singularly close together in all of us — and life a mere farce of frustration in all, so far as realization of the innermost ideals go."

William recognized and saluted his sister's strength of spirit, the fact of her illness, and her utter rejection of self-pity. Her willingness to "have it so," to embrace her lot, is precisely the heroic spirit William had written about. "Your fortitude, good spirits and unsentimentality," he now told her, "have been simply unexampled in the midst of your physical woes, and when you're relieved from your post, just that bright note will remain behind, together with the inscrutable and mysterious character of the doom of nervous weakness which has chained you down for all these years."[5]

As the letter makes clear, James's empathy with his sister's seemingly impossible life situation helps explain several of the directions James's work took. "These inhibitions, these split-up selves," he told Alice, "all these new facts that are gradually coming to light about our organization, these enlargements of the self in trance etc. are bringing me to turn for light in the direction of all sorts of despised spiritualistic and unscientific ideas. Father would find in me today a much more receptive listener." He even considers the possibility of immortality.

We should bear in mind that this is a letter to a dying sister, not a paper for a medical journal or testimony in a court of law. Whether James believed in immortality, or believed only in one's right to believe in it, or in one's right to act as though one believed in it, cannot now be known. But what was to be gained by stamping out possibilities? "What a queer contradiction," William wrote Alice, "comes to the ordinary scientific argument against immortality (based on body being mind's condition and mind going out when body is gone) when one must believe (as now, in these neurotic cases), that some infernality in the body prevents really existing parts of the mind from coming to their effective rights at all, suppresses them and blots them out from participation in this world's experiences, although they are there all the time."

William writes tenderly to "my dear little sister," but he never forgets that she has as full a citizenship in the James nation as he has. "It may seem odd for me to talk to you in this cool way about your end; but . . . if one has things present to one's mind, and I know they are present enough to your mind, why not speak them out?" He closes with brotherly, doctorly advice, to save herself from bodily pain if she can, to take as much morphine as she wants and not be "afraid of becoming an opium-drunkard. What was opium created for except for such times as this?"

The Jameses understood each other at least as well as their biographers have, and Alice leaped to embrace and answer her brother's letter. Her reply, with its sisterly note of triumph, is one of her best.

> My dearest William,
>   A thousand thanks for your beautiful and fraternal letter, which came, I know not when, owing to Katharine's iron despotism. Of course I could have wanted nothing else, and should have felt, notwithstanding my "unsentimentality" very much wounded and incomprise, had you walked round and not up to my demise.
>   It is the most supremely interesting moment in life, the only one in fact, when living seems life . . . I have a delicious consciousness, ever present, of wide spaces close at hand, and whisperings of release in the air.
>   Your philosophy of the transition is entirely mine and at this remoteness I will venture upon the impertinence of congratulating you upon having arrived "at nearly fifty" at the point at which I started at fifteen! — 'Twas always thus of old, but in time, you usually, as now, caught up . . .[6]

These last letters of William's (and Alice's replies, and Henry's reporting) show, as well as anything that survives, the scorching directness, the emotional candor, the acceptance and validation of the worst as well as the best of life, the sheer intensity toward life in all its forms, the avidity for experience, the honesty of mind and perfect pitch of heart that has become, in this case more than most, transpersonal but family-fixed. This is the Jamesian take on life.

Perhaps the extremity of Alice's situation helped William settle down to the task of shortening *Principles*. Whatever the explanation, what had taken twelve years to write took six weeks to rewrite. He was finished by mid-August. He cut the book by more than two thirds, reducing 1,280 pages to 400. But it was not just cutting. He reshaped the book, adding chapters on the senses at the beginning and ending more emphatically with the will. Some things had to be expanded. His airy footnote at the end of chapter 1 says, "Nothing is easier than to familiarize oneself with the mammalian brain. Get a sheep's head, a small saw, chisel, scalpel and forceps and unravel its parts either with the aid of a human dissecting book such as Holden's *Manual of Anatomy* or Morrell's *Comparative Anatomy and Dissection of Mammalia.*" Dashing recklessly through preliminaries was James's own style, but for *Psychology: Briefer Course* he slowed down long enough to provide nine pages of practical notes on how to dissect the sheep's brain.

His attitude toward the work of revision was one of fidgety impatience and distaste, conveyed to Holt by James in his best rhetorical blather. He sounds as jumpy as a man with Saint Vitus's dance: "By adding some twaddle about the senses, by leaving out all polemics and history, all bibliography and experimental details, all humor and pathos, all interest in short, and by blackening the tops of all paragraphs [boldface headings] I think I have produced a tome of pedagogic classic which will enrich both you and me, if not the student's mind."[7]

James's work on *Psychology: Briefer Course* sharpened and deepened his views on habit. When the book was published, James was still not done with the subject, and he wrote in his copy by hand at the head of chapter 10, "Habit," "Sow an action, and you reap a habit; sow a habit and you reap a character; sow a character and reap a destiny."[8] The preface of the new book emphasizes teaching. The book soon became "the most widely used English text in the subject."[9]

James's widening commitment to teaching is visible not only in the *Briefer Course* volume but in the fact that in the spring of 1891, as he was still just thinking about condensing his big book, he became involved in an undertaking that would lead, years later, to the third and shortest of his psychology books. He agreed in early April to give a series of lectures on psychological topics of interest to teachers — on the psychology of education, really — in conjunction with Paul H. Hanus, the newly appointed professor of pedagogy at Harvard.

James was himself a remarkable teacher who changed lives. His lectures were engaging and unconventional, and his courses at Harvard routinely drew hundreds of students. He talked from carefully prepared notes, not from a written-out text. He sometimes lost his train of thought and asked a student what he had just said. He could be sufficiently entertaining that a student once broke in to say, "But professor, to be serious for a moment . . ." But James's interest in teaching went far beyond the classroom. He invited students to meals at his home, and not only students he knew well. Once when he was in Cambridge without his family, he fell into conversation with a student in front of a bookstore window. Agreeing that the new O. Henry should be bought, James invited the student back to his house for dinner. They talked for hours before the new freshman discovered who his host was.[10]

James was quick of sympathy, gregarious, a brilliant talker but a listener as well, always ready with advice, but ready also to get involved in people's lives. Mary Calkins, the gifted psychologist and philosopher who went on to be the first woman president of the American Psychological Association and the first woman president of the American Philosophical Association, started study with James in the fall of 1890. "My absorbed study of those brilliant, erudite and provocative volumes [*Principles*] was my introduction to psychology," she recalled.[11] When Walter Cannon, later a well-known professor of physiology at Harvard Medical School, was an undergraduate, he told James he was inclining toward philosophy. "He turned on me seriously," Cannon remembered, "and remarked, 'Don't do it. You will be filling your belly with east wind.'"[12]

W.E.B. Du Bois came to Harvard from Fisk, in Nashville, in the fall of 1888 and signed up for James's Philosophy 4: Theistic Ethics. Du Bois wrote how his philosophy work at Fisk had eventually "landed me squarely in the arms of William James of Harvard for which God be praised." Du Bois remembered that he had been "repeatedly a guest in the house of William James, he was my friend and guide to clear thinking."[13] In one account Du Bois said it was James who "guided me out of the sterilities of scholastic philosophy to realist pragmatism." But whether or not James decisively influenced Du Bois's thought, he took an active interest in his life. Du Bois earned excellent grades, James encouraged him, but when Du Bois told his professor his ambition was to teach philosophy, James gave him the same advice he gave Cannon: "If you must study philosophy you will, but if you can turn aside into something else, do so. It is hard to earn a living with philosophy."[14]

James was not much interested in collecting and training disciples. He was amused when he found someone, such as his friend Howison, "applying the last coat of varnish to his pupil."[15] He was interested in other people, and willing, indeed eager, to take them on their own terms. He was open to others on principle as well as by temperament. Hutchins Hapgood, the reformer who wrote *The Spirit of the Ghetto, The Spirit of*

Labor, and *An Anarchist Woman,* was at Harvard from 1889 to 1893; he went one day to call on Professor James. He entered the room, saw that James was busy writing, and started to withdraw. But James turned toward Hapgood and asked him to sit down, explaining, in Hapgood's oddly stiff transcription, "I never allow myself to be too busy to make room for any demand upon me. If I did not accept all challenges, it would mean that the reservoirs of my nature, which are unplumbed and unfathomable, would tend to dry up. We are all of us capable of far more than we think and if we keep our minds and hearts open to every new appeal and influence we grow constantly in power and consciousness. At any moment you or another sophomore might contribute something of great importance to me."[16] The phrasing doesn't sound quite like James, but the sentiments do. James struck people as generous, and he was, but his generosity and openness served him well. He was convinced that others had things to teach him and that the way to increase one's resources is to spend them down all the way, again and again. The well that is used most refills quickest.

Gertrude Stein, who entered Radcliffe — the Annex — in 1893, studied with Hugo Münsterberg in 1894 and took James's seminar the following year. She got advice similar to Hapgood's from James, but her ear for speech was excellent and her account brings James the teacher sharply to life. Speaking about the creative life a few months before her death, Stein said, "Everything must come into your scheme, otherwise you cannot achieve real simplicity. A great deal of this I owe to a great teacher, William James. He said 'never reject anything. Nothing has been proved. If you reject anything, that is the beginning of the end as an intellectual.' He was my big influence," Stein went on, "when I was at college. He was a man who always said, 'complicate your life as much as you please, it has got to simplify.'"[17]

James gave his students advice, warnings, encouragement, and dinner; he gave it all with disarming earnestness and utter conviction. Sometimes, as when he lectures his brother on how to write novels, he can seem insensitive, officious, even bullying. But often, in the ample anecdotal reminiscences about James that have survived, he has something of the healer — the wounded healer — about him. He was a doctor, after all, and it is not quite true that he never practiced medicine. He never took money for it, but he prescribed pills and procedures to friends and family. He hypnotized students with therapeutic intentions. He looked for ways to help people cope with trouble; he believed in the elasticity and regenerative power of individuals. When Hapgood's sister died, James, who was a friend of the family, told Hapgood that his mother "would recover from her loss, the silent forces of nature growing new moral and spiritual fibers, and that which was burst or destroyed in her would give place to the vicarious functions of her larger personality."[18] Whether or not it worked for others, some such process seems to have worked in James himself, and he felt impelled to apply it to others.

At his best, James opened doors. When Mary Austin (later the well-known author of *The Land of Little Rain*) went to hear him lecture on relaxation in Oakland in 1898, she found a way to talk to him at some length afterward. "What he recommended to all intellectuals was the relaxation of the rather strained surface tensions which was the preferred intellectual mode of the time," she recalled. One should relax "in order that the whole personality might be flooded by the deep life that welled up from below the threshold of selfness."

Austin was already interested in the kind of "spontaneously produced art — similar to that created by Indians after powerful dreams [that] could be facilitated by exploring one's own consciousness." She told this to James, and she says he "validated my own experience of the swinging door, the door that opens out of consciousness with the same effect of . . . an icy shiver as when an actual door behind you shudders on the latch and lets in a draught of coolness. When you are sitting with the elders of the tribe, when the sayings of the Ancient Men are passing, and suddenly at a word dropped, an incident related, whole areas of human evolution let blow upon you a wind out of your own past."

It was just this sort of inner exploration James loved to egg on. "What I got out of William James and the Medicine Man," Austin says, "was a continuing experience of wholeness, a power to expand the least premonitory shiver along the edge of primitive apprehension to the full diapason of spiritual sophistication which I have never lost."[19] If half the stories told about him are true, William James was one of America's great teachers.

49. The Death of Alice James

THE FINAL BIT of work on the manuscript for *Psychology: Briefer Course* was the section on how to dissect a sheep's brain. James finished it on August 12, 1891, then sent it to the publisher and took off by himself for a two-week trip in the mountains of North Carolina. He had been working almost steadily for two years, including substantial parts of two consecutive summers, and he felt he needed a complete break in a wholly new place. The trip stirred him to superlatives. Climbing Mount Mitchell, the highest point east of the Rockies, he called it "the most beautiful forest walk (only five hours) I ever made." He also climbed Roan Mountain and Grandfather Mountain.[1] The Johnson City & Cranberry Railroad was "perhaps the wildest and most romantic little narrow-gauge concern that the world contains." Linville was "simply the most high-toned and gentlemanly 'land enterprise' to be found on the continent," and its roads "the only roads I have seen in America which resemble the great Swiss roads."[2] James especially recommended that New Englanders should get out and see more of a country that contained such wonders.

This trip had another side, involving different scenery, which gave James a moment of insight that he would later write up in "On a Certain Blindness in Human Beings." The blindness is that "with which we all are afflicted in regard to the feelings of creatures and people different from ourselves."[3] "Some years ago," he wrote,

> whilst journeying in the mountains of North Carolina, I passed by a large number of "coves" as they call them there, or heads of small valleys between the hills, which had been newly cleared and planted. The impression on my mind was one of unmitigated squalor. The settler had in every case cut down the more manageable trees, and left their charred stumps standing. The larger trees he had girdled and killed, in order that their foliage should not cast a shade. He had then built a log cabin, plastering its chinks with clay, and had set up a tall zig-zag rail fence around the scene of his havoc to keep the pigs and cattle out . . . The forest had been destroyed, and what had "improved" it out of existence was hideous, a sort of ulcer, without a single element of artificial grace to make up for the loss of nature's beauty.

After more similarly gloomy meditation, James writes, "I said to the mountaineer who was driving me: 'What sort of people are they who have to make these new clearings?' 'All of us,' he replied: 'Why we ain't happy here unless we are getting one of these coves under cultivation.' I instantly felt," James's account goes on, "that I had been losing the whole inward significance of the situation. Because to me the clearings spoke of naught but denudation, I thought that to those whose sturdy arms and obedient axes had made them they could tell no other story. But when they looked on the hideous stumps, what they thought of was personal victory." It was not just other people who were blind; it was not only students to whom James was open.

The willingness to meet any new demand, which James had talked about to Hapgood, and the deliberate and restless openness — suggesting, too, how easily James became bored with work and the obligations at hand — means that much of James's life, much of the direction of his attention, was not really under his control, and suggests that he preferred it that way. The calm life, the minutely controlled vector of ambition, the life devoted to one end only that we associate with his brother Henry, was never a possibility for William. At fifty he was still essentially at the mercy of any well-aimed claim upon him.

In September 1891, just back from North Carolina, he heard from Henry that Alice was "in a very alarming condition."[4] William felt that he had to see her, even though classes were about to start. Rushing to London by steamer and train, he found Alice very weak, able to lie only "in one position on the bed" and "in a profoundly miserable condition." Yet she did her best to conceal it, talking about the coming London opening of Henry's play *The American* and her own approaching end. Alice sternly refused to pity herself — it was always one of her strengths — and it was not vanity that made her unwilling to admit her misery to her visitor. She held firmly that it was William's sensibilities that had to be protected. She was thus still stage-managing the grand domestic theatrical.

William was allowed only short visits of half an hour or so, which, he reported to his wife, were "very successful," as he learned through Katharine, who said that his sister was "highly pleased" at his coming. William suggested hypnotism as an anodyne, in addition to the morphine she was already taking. Alice had every medical attention possible; she had been seen by the best physician in England. "It is hard to believe, from her animation," William wrote home, "that she will not last long . . . She talks death incessantly, it seems to fill her with positive glee."[5]

Because he had rushed over to say goodbye to Alice, William happened to be in London on September 20, 1891, for the opening of *The American*. The first-night audience was full of writers, painters, millionaires, and ministers of state. Henry's close friend and companion, Constance Fenimore Woolson, described the scene: "Pink satin, blue satin, jewels of all sorts, splendour on all sides of us. The house was packed to the top, and the applause was great. When the performance was ended, and the actors had been called out, there arose loud cries of 'Author, author!' After some delays, Henry James appeared before the curtain and acknowledged the applause. He looked very well, quiet and dignified, yet pleasant: he only stayed a moment."[6] Afterward there were supper parties, reviews, a tremendous to-do.

The contrast with Alice's private drama at 41 Argyll Road in Kensington could not have been greater. After ten days, which had afforded him only a few short visits with Alice, William headed home, writing to his sister from the steamer some of the things he had left unsaid. Part of what he had to say was that Alice herself should not be left unexpressed; her voice was not to be lost. He foresaw how Harry would miss her conversation, and he added, "Between us we promise you to try to work some of it into Philosophy and the Drama so that it shall become a part of the world's inheritance."

The trip left him feeling a bit diminished himself. "I go back," he told his sister, "to a life of which the main interest now is that of seeing that the children turn out well — insidious change in one's ambitions brought about by life's changing course. Your name will be a mere legend amongst them — until we are all legends."[7]

Back home in early October, James found many interests plucking at his sleeves. He had, as usual, a full teaching load, though his share of the 176-student introduction to philosophy course he taught with Palmer and Royce would not begin until January. But his psychology course had 65 students (up from 25 the year before), including 9 grad students, and he taught a graduate seminar on aesthetics. He was one of the college advisers for freshmen, one of whom, this year, was his brother Bob's son, Ned. There were also field trips, such as the one James took in May 1892 with sixteen grad students to interview the twelve-year-old Helen Keller. Keller later recalled that James "brought me a beautiful ostrich feather. 'I thought,' he said, 'you would like the feather, it is soft, light, and caressing.'"[8]

All fall he read the proofs of *Psychology: Briefer Course,* and on top of everything else he gave ten special lectures on topics of interest to teachers, such as "inhibition, association of ideas, attention, imagination, apperception, and will." These lectures were the result of boiling down the already drastically shortened *Psychology: Briefer Course* by another 75 percent. They were the basis of similar lectures James was to give throughout the 1890s, published at last in 1899, in 110 pages, as *Talks to Teachers.*

But this book and its enormous popular success were far in the future. In November 1891 James was caught up in an unpleasant row between Frank Abbot and Josiah Royce. Abbot had temporarily taught in Royce's place in 1888. His lectures were published as "The Way Out of Agnosticism," which took an unnecessary slap at the Harvard philosophy department. Royce reviewed Abbot's book, issuing from on high, as it were, a "professional warning to the liberal-minded public concerning Dr. Abbot's philosophical pretensions."[9] Abbot replied with a fiery personal attack on

Royce and an equally highhanded demand that Harvard discipline Royce for daring to speak as if he were the voice of Harvard.

Protracted and bitter negotiations over how to publish the volleys of replies and ripostes got out of hand. Royce was pompous, spoke ex cathedra; Abbot was troubled and troublesome. Royce brought in a lawyer. Charles Peirce weighed in with a letter in *The Nation* defending Abbot; James replied with a detailed defense of Royce. There was no light to be had, it was all personal, and James ended up defending harsh and intemperate reviewing when he intended only to defend his close friend and neighbor.

A part of James doubtless enjoyed the fray. Alfred North Whitehead once called William James "that adorable genius"; the phrase has stuck, and with it the suggestion that James was gentle and sweet. This misapprehension can obscure the feisty, combative, confrontational side of the man. One day in 1885, when he had three children under the age of six at home, he was riding a Cambridge horsecar into Boston, meditating on the idea his wife had picked up from Kipling that our whole social order and civil life "had for their ultimate sanction nothing but force," however we might disguise it, and mediating too on his brother Henry's indignant protests about the "outrageous pertness of the American child." He became aware of a little five-year-old singing aloud "in such a hoarse, nasal voice that I was on the point of getting out of the car twice." He summoned, as he told Logan Pearsall Smith, "all sorts of ethical religious and sociological principles to the aid of my trembling courage," and spoke up politely: "I think, madam, you can hardly be aware that your child's song is a cause of annoyance to the rest of us in the car." The mother answered that she couldn't stop the child. Whereupon a "gallant American" who had been following the exchange broke in indignantly, "How dare you sir, address a lady in this ungentlemanly fashion!" James, stirred up by Kipling's idea about naked force, fired back, "Sir, if you repeat that remark I shall slap your face." The man repeated it, James slapped him, and the man "collected the cards of the rest of the passengers, all eager to serve as witnesses in my trial for assault and battery." There are several versions of this story; Smith says James then told him that the passengers next "all sat down; and as the car clattered along through the dust towards Boston, with the child still shrilly singing, the grave burden of the public disapproval which William James had encountered became almost more, he said, than he could bear.

"He looked from hostile face to hostile face, longing for some sign of sympathy and comprehension, and fixed at last all his hopes on a lady who had taken no part in the uproar, and whose appearance suggested foreign travel perhaps, or at any rate a wider point of view." When the car reached Boston and they all got out, James addressed this lady. "'You, madam,' he said, addressing her, 'you, I feel sure, will understand.' . . . Thereupon the lady drew back from him and exclaimed 'You brute!'"[10] Smith prefaces this account by calling James the most charming man he ever met. James could also be reckless, even cruel. Still, his willingness to tell this story on himself shows that he was at least aware that he could be blind and thus insensitive to the feelings of those around him.

Another of the things demanding James's time and energy in the fall of 1891 was the psychology laboratory. James had been working in and teaching from laboratories since medical school. It is generally conceded that Wundt set up the first psychology lab in Germany and James the first one in America, though G. S. Hall once disputed this. In 1892 James had gotten $4,300 for his psychology lab at Harvard. His lab course now had eighty students, and he found himself spending four hours a day in the lab. James did a fair amount of laboratory work, for which he has gotten scant credit, largely because he himself frequently complained about the work, groaned over it, and professed himself unfit for it. He once declared, apropos German laboratory investigation, that it couldn't flourish among a people capable of boredom. Although James had started a lab for psychophysics in 1885, laboratory psychology, as the chemist-president Eliot would have understood it, was not a high priority for James. Indeed, Eliot wrote James in December 1891, "I think your *Psychology* atones for the absence of laboratory instruction during the past ten years."[11]

With his laboratory duties weighing him down, with no major commitment to experimental psychology, and with Eliot's attitude, James found the psychology lab situation at Harvard untenable, and he soon got Eliot's permission to sound out a possible replacement, twenty-eight-year-old Hugo Münsterberg of Freiburg. Münsterberg had studied with Wundt, but had come to disagree with him about the will, taking a position closer to James's own. Münsterberg had published what James called "a little masterpiece" on the subject. As we saw, James had met him at the Paris Congress of Physiological Psychology.

Münsterberg was a tall, solidly built man. A colleague recalled him as looking "trimmed for action. The roving observant blue eye, the springy step, the slight bend in the body in a kind of formal lunge, all suggested alertness."[12] Charles A. Strong knew him in Germany and reported to James, "He lectures and experiments all day, talks brilliantly in the evening, and then works at his desk till three or four in the morning, writing from fourteen to sixteen printed pages at a sitting." Münsterberg was still a young man when James described him as "a great force in psychology, a wonderfully active thinker . . . a teacher whom it is impossible to surpass."[13]

Would Münsterberg accept a three-year probationary appointment at Harvard? James threw himself into persuading him. He wrote him that Harvard "must lead in Psychology," that it wanted a first-rate lab director, "a man of genius." After some negotiations Münsterberg accepted, in early May 1892. James wrote at once: "A telegram arrives from you 'joyfully accepting the call.' Gottlob! I believe this has been the best stroke I ever did for our university!" It was a good stroke for himself as well. "It is an enormous relief to me," he confessed to Münsterberg, "to see the responsibility for experimental Psychology in Harvard transferred from my feeble and unworthy shoulders to those of a man as competent as you."[14]

One thing James could not transfer from his shoulders was his position in the Society for Psychical Research. In February 1892 he had chaired a meeting of the society in New York City and addressed four hundred people on "What Psychical Research Has Accomplished."[15] He admitted to Henry that he loathed the position but that the speech went off well enough. It was a spirited defense of the society as the only place where a "systematic attempt to weigh the evidence for the supernatural" existed. The spiritualists and the theosophists were, he said, "sickened by the methods" of the society, while the scientists, on the other hand, were "sickened by the facts," leaving the society "in a rather forsaken position."[16]

What most interested James was Frederick Myers's work on the "subliminal self," and he approvingly quoted the conclusion that Myers's studies of "hypnotism, hallucinations, automatic writing, mediumship, and the whole series of allied phenomena" had led him to: "Each of us is in reality an abiding psychical entity far more extensive than he knows — an individuality which can never express itself completely through any corporeal manifestation. The Self manifests itself through the organism; but there is always some part of the Self unmanifested; and always, as it seems, some power of organic expression in abeyance or in reserve."[17]

The family news from London was grim. Henry wrote on February 6, 1892, that Alice's "weakness increases — her bad times are very very bad and it is weeks and weeks since she has left her bed, which she will evidently never leave again." Henry wrote long, painful, detailed letters filled with what would have been for anyone but Henry James inexpressible sadness. William, who could only read the letters from afar, no doubt felt helpless. "Her condition is one of great suffering," Henry wrote on March 2; "that is [the] sad part of it, and she is really a tragic vessel or receptacle, of recurrent, re-newable, inexhaustible forms of disease." On March 5 Alice was unable to talk without bringing on spasms of coughing. She whispered a message for Henry to cable to William: "Tenderest love to all. Farewell. Am going soon." The next day, in the evening, another telegram came, this time from Henry: "Alice just passed away painless. Wire Bob."

William immediately telegraphed Henry to make sure the death was re-ally a death and not some sort of "trance trick" of her own susceptible na-ture. But the next morning reality set in, and William let out his feelings in a letter to Henry, even as Cambridge waited for the London letter that would have all the details. "What a relief!" William wrote. "And yet long as we had thought of it and wished it, it seems too strangely sudden to have it dispatched in the twinkling of a telegram . . . Poor little Alice! What a life! I can't believe that that imperious will and piercing judgment are snuffed out with the breath."

There were many things about Alice and about his own relationship to her that James did not fully understand, but he understood quite a bit about her illness, especially about how she carried it. "Now that her out-wardly so frustrated life is over," he wrote Henry, "one sees that in the deepest sense it was a triumph. In her relation to her disease, her mind did not succumb. She never whined or complained or did anything but spurn it. She thus kept it from invading the tone of her soul . . . Her life was any-thing but a failure."[18]

Alice's body was cremated. Katharine Loring carried the ashes back across the Atlantic, where they were placed in the Cambridge Cemetery lot with her father and mother, in order, as Henry said, that she not become a myth. In the year ahead, William would design a monument for her grave. On it he had inscribed two lines from Dante's apostrophe to Boethius, the Roman philosopher and author of *The Consolation of Philosophy*, lines that we may take as a counter to the famous inscription over the entrance to Hades. The lines for Alice read:

> Ed essa da martire
> E da essilio venne a questa pace.
>
> (She came from martyrdom and exile to this peace.)[19]

On the side of the monument were to be the emblems from Henry Senior's family seal, on one side a serpent with its tail in its mouth, on another a jar with a butterfly escaping.[20]

50. European Sabbatical

T HERE WAS, OF COURSE, much more to James's life now than seeing the children through, but the children were a major, indeed an overriding, concern as William and Alice and the entire family set off for Europe in late May 1892. Just moving from place to place with so large a group — it was seven on the way over (six Jameses and a maid) and nine on the way back (two more maids Alice picked up in Switzerland), with twenty-eight pieces of luggage — was a full-time task. Alice wrote to her mother that William "gives his whole mind to transporting the family and he does it beautifully."[1]

On the voyage over, half the children were seasick; in addition, Billy had facial neuralgia and Peggy a headache. "They lie one on either side of me, two patient wilted hopeless little creatures," Alice wrote her mother. William looked after the baby, who was now one and a half, while the nursemaid went to breakfast. To a bystander watching his efforts William said, "When I get to Europe I shall look out for a place as a nursemaid." The man answered in his imperfect English, "I thought you was always so!" Harry, just turned thirteen, was his usual quiet self. Billy, who was almost ten, was miserable, "in the deeps," Alice told her mother, "loathing the ship and Europe. The first night of his sickness he lay motionless, looking, as William said, like a dead crusader. The big tears rolled down his cheeks for the next two days and he would cry out, 'if only I were at home with grandmamma!'"[2]

The idea of the trip was to give William a good long sabbatical vacation, to give Alice a much-needed break from housekeeping, and to give the children a chance to learn European languages and get a taste of European schooling. Incredibly, they planned nothing in advance. Arriving in Freiburg, William installed the family in temporary digs, then went ahead by himself to Switzerland to scout out a place to live, schools for the boys, and boarding arrangements. After months of "anguish, perplexity, and shilly-shallying" they more or less settled in Lausanne. It was not until late July that Harry and Billy went off to their respective schools, each of them boarding with a nearby pastor.

Almost at once the question arose of where to spend the winter. Alice's letter to her mother shows how decisions were made. "You will not be surprised to hear," she wrote, "that our plans are entirely changed. William could not stomach a whole winter in Lausanne nor did the prospect appeal to me. No society, no pictures, no music, no theatre, nothing but climate, schools, cheapness." The entire European venture was ruinously expensive, and saving money was a constant theme for Alice and William. "Well," Alice went on, "William proposed Stuttgart and I did not know what to say or do because I felt sure S[tuttgart] would bore us both. I went to bed profoundly discouraged and feeling so utterly helpless and inadequate to my problem that I 'give it up,' and with all that is within me called for help and to sleep I went with a placid mind." Sometimes, as now, things just came to Alice. "When I awoke in the morning, I found that we were going to Florence." She then proposed Florence as her choice to William and found "he was delighted." So they spent six months there. As his father had done with him and his siblings, William moved restlessly from place to place without seeming to notice the similarity or to remember how he had once felt about such a life.[3]

Some of the children were old enough to have their own views of things and were no longer mere passive appendages. Harry, the oldest, was temperamentally more like his uncle Henry than his father. When William showed him the cathedral in Cologne and tried to "make [him] dilate with emotion," Harry said, "Are we never going to get out of this?" Though he was so quiet he worried his father, Harry was bright, verbal, and witty. His school in Florence was putting on a play, based on a dramatic adaptation of a novel made by Pasquale Villari, a historian and friend of the family. Harry calmly sat down and rewrote the ending, saying that after a certain speech, Villari's play "sort of trembled out into nothing, just waggled away." When Harry was off at school, William wrote him — as he wrote all his children — with news and advice. "Live energetically; and whatever you have to do, do it with your might." A few days later it was "Do your darnedest in every respect. Live hard!"

Harry got the message. Years later, when he had become a successful lawyer, the trustee of an annuity, and a writer (he won the Pulitzer Prize for a biography of Charles W. Eliot), Harry prepared an anthology (never published) of his father's writings, to be called *Counsels of Courage*. His preface spoke of the urgent need to act, and he quoted his father's favorite lines from Tennyson: ". . . thou art thou, / With power on thine own act and on the world." "If proof be wholly lacking," Harry wrote, "one must hazard all on a belief. For act one must. From that ultimate duty he [William James] saw and sought no escape."[4]

Billy was almost ten when the family left for Europe in May 1892. He had been reluctant to go, and was no more docile a sightseer than his older brother. When his father tried to interest him in the castles along the Rhine, Billy counted the cars of the passing freight trains. He sketched much of the time; "he is frantic to be taught drawing," his mother told Henry. Schools were a problem for both boys. Harry's Latin was not good enough to qualify him for the school that otherwise best suited his needs. Billy complained, after studying French all winter in Florence, that "all that he has learned has been a few tenses of the verb *aimer*." Both boys idolized their uncle. "I heard Harry and Billy talking about you," William wrote his brother, "and resolve to read one of your stories this Easter" — then Billy said, reflectively, "I suppose there is nothing Uncle Harry can't spell!"[5]

Peggy was five. She was sick a lot of the time, but she learned to speak French and, all things considered, improved, her father observed, "more than any of us." She, too, idolized her uncle. Taking a cold bath one morning, she cried out, "Wouldn't Uncle Harry call me a good girl if he could see me now!" During the first summer abroad, William took Peggy to a sixth-century church one morning "and told her that it was a place to worship God in." Alice related the story to her mother. "At last in a gloomy part . . . she piped up: 'Why have they 'shupen God into this dark place, because he was naughty?'"[6]

The baby, Tweedy to William, Francis to Alice, Aleck in later years, was a year and a half old. He learned to talk this year, and what he learned was French, which was kept up after the return to Cambridge by means of the two Swiss bonnes who came home with the family. When Alice and William got away in 1893 for a month together in England, Aleck, then two, was unhappy when Alice returned, and he would not at first come to her, saying, "Peur de Maman" ("Scared of Mama"). He was excitable and could be stormy; he was dyslexic, but no one knew this at the time. Rowing on Lake Lucerne with his father one day, "he wanted constantly to get out of the boat, and was only pacified at last by pouring water over his hands. When we landed he rolled on the ground and roared to go back again."[7]

Alice loved being in Europe and seems to have been hoping from the start to stay for two years. She wrote her mother from Lucerne, "Life from here looks so hard so expensive and even bare in America." She told her mother, "In another year [you] must consider the question of renting your house and coming on." Domestic help was available and inexpensive. She wanted her children to learn German and French. She stayed abroad as long as she could, arguing that it was "her and the children's duty to drink the last possible drop of Europe." But William wrote his mother-in-law, "I think what weighs most on Alice is a real dread (I am sorry to say) of Cambridge housekeeping and no feeling of satisfaction in our house, and she hates to face what to her is an evil day." Travel arrangements might be complicated and living space cramped at times, but life abroad was for Alice vastly freer than the work of maintaining not one but two large establishments at home.[8]

William, however, yearned for home, or said he did, though one suspects he enjoyed describing his European chaos even if he didn't enjoy the chaos. "Here in this precipitous Alpine village," he wrote Grace Ashburner from Gryon-sur-Bex in July 1892, "we occupy rooms in an empty house with a yellow plastered front and an iron balcony above the street. Up and down that street the cows, the goats, the natives and the tourists pass . . . On that iron balcony all the innermost mysteries of the James family are blazoned and bruited to the entire village. Things are dried there, quarrels, screams and squeals rise incessantly to Heaven, dressing and undressing are performed, punishments take place, recriminations, arguments, execrations, with a publicity after which, if there were reporters, we should never be able to show our faces again."

In Florence they had larger quarters, but when it got cold and when the boys were home from school, things got crowded: "Reading with Alice, the two boys, Peggy, Tweedy, and the nurse all carrying on their various avocations and vociferations by the same one lamp, round the same small table, in one narrow (if high) room around a dreadful little sheet iron stove." In January 1893 William found himself longing for his spacious library at home, with its walls of familiar books and its four sofas. Florence, he wrote Henry, was "considerably below freezing, no hot water in the house for a good part of the day, and almost no possibility of hot water at any time, one servant in bed with suppurative tonsillitis, Billy ditto with bronchitis, [Dr.] Baldwin out of town, one room, 15 x 12 in which all the 'sitting' of the family, all my study and that of the boys, are done."[9]

Inevitably, he and Alice got on each other's nerves from time to time. In the middle of the Florentine winter, William returned to their rooms one day with a couple of paintings for which he had paid quite a bit. Alice became upset: "Oh William how could you!" William picked up a pair of scissors and cut the paintings to pieces. Maybe Alice pushed him, maybe she grabbed for the scissors. In a letter written a little later, she apologizes for her "'deed of violence' for which I can only atone by future temperateness and gentleness."[10]

But these were isolated difficulties in what was, generally speaking, a good year for William. Free of college duties and with no big book under way, he could relax, see old friends, read undisturbed every evening after dinner, and write an occasional review. His health was, for him, very good. He came to accept the fact that he was predisposed to nervous problems ("neurasthenic diathesis," he rather formidably called it). When he climbed the Righi in May 1893 with a friend, he noticed that he sweated copiously while the friend was "comparatively dry." In the absence of other symptoms, no one seems to have thought this might be an indication of a heart problem.

James took advantage of his sabbatical to read and write outside the professional grooves he was making for himself. He had admired Rudyard Kipling enormously, telling one friend in early 1891 that Kipling "has all the major effects at his disposition." But he was dismayed now by the anti-American, antidemocratic excesses of Kipling's *American Notes.* "They are autobiographic," he wrote Henry, "and reveal such a little blackguard soul" that he found it hard to believe in Kipling's future as a writer. He reveled, however, in George du Maurier's *Peter Ibbetson,* which he thought destined to be "one of the classics of the English tongue. He also read and luxuriated in George Meredith's *Beauchamp's Career,* a novel that combines radical politics with interests in Darwin and in the position of women in the Victorian world. "G. M. is great," he wrote Henry. "You can breathe deep in his air . . . He can make manly men and womanly women."[11]

He luxuriated too in random reading. He asked Harry's advice on histories of Florence, he met Mark Twain and Charles Godfrey Leland, he read Yriarte on César Borgia and Oliver Lodge on electricity. In November he read Henry's "Lesson of the Master," which had been published in February, and he wrote Henry, "I think it exquisite all through — the most finished and mature execution of anything yet." He was at first enthusiastic about a book called *Euphorion: Being Studies of the Antique and Medieval,* by "Vernon Lee," whose real name was Violet Paget. He went to see her, but when he learned from Henry that she had taken advantage of him, and had maliciously satirized him in a story ("Lady Tal") in a book called *Vanitas: Polite Stories,* William wrote her, "You will not be surprised to learn that seeing the book has quite quenched my desire to pay you another visit." Even if loyalty to his brother had not been involved, a writer willing to publish a transparent satirical portrait of a person who had befriended her and was trying to help her was hardly the kind of acquaintance William needed.[12]

In January in Florence, Alice read Arthur Conan Doyle's fourteenth-century romance *The White Company* with the children, and William tried to find a copy of David Brewster's well-known *Life of Newton.* In February he went to visit his eldest son, who was in school in Munich, and took him to see a dramatic adaptation of *L'Assommoir*, Zola's gritty, realistic story about the appalling effects of alcohol on the working people of Paris.[13]

If one of the goals of a sabbatical is to work on one's big project, another is salutary disengagement from one's main pursuits. The success of James's year off can be gauged by the fact that among the slender sheaf of his writings for the year is a letter to a newspaper, in French, protesting the miserable, tomb-like conditions of French pigs, and a spirited letter to the editor attacking the new practice of binding periodicals with steel staples instead of the traditional stitching. He was not working on a book, and he turned out roughly a review a month, most of them quite short.

The last significant piece of work he had done was a seven-page piece called "A Plea for Psychology as a Natural Science," published back in March 1892, as Alice was dying. In the piece, he observed that psychology was "hardly more than what physics was before Galileo, what chemistry was before Lavoisier," and insisting that while psychology could not yet claim to be a natural science, he had "wished by treating [it] like a natural science to help her become one." Besides this ostentatious modesty, he wrote that the psychology he is interested in is not a pure science, not a body of knowledge studied for its own sake, but an applied science, a search for ways to control states of mind by controlling the physical events from which mental states arise. "All natural sciences," he asserted, "aim at practical prediction and control, and in none of them is this more the case than in psychology today . . . We live surrounded by an enormous body of persons who are most definitely interested in the control of states of mind," craving, indeed, "a sort of psychological science which will teach them how to act . . . What every educator, every jail-warden, every doctor, every clergyman, every asylum superintendent, asks of psychology is practical rules."[14]

Nowhere is James clearer than when he stated that the psychology he is interested in is not a metaphysical, theoretical inquiry into the ultimate nature of mind. If forced to choose between psychology as a science and psychology as the metaphysics of mind, James said he would take the former, because "almost all the fresh life that has come into psychology of recent years has come from the biologists, doctors, and psychical researchers." Idealist, Germanic metaphysics is not helpful. "We need," he wrote, "a fair and square and explicit abandonment of such questions as that of the soul, the transcendental ego, the fusion of ideas or particles of mind-stuff etc by the practical man; and a fair and square determination on the part of philosophers to keep such questions out of psychology."[15]

If we sometimes think of James as narrowing the gap between psychology and philosophy, we must realize that at this point in his life, he was doing his best to hold them apart, trying to separate and distinguish psychology from philosophy, or from the then dominant neo-Hegelian and neo-Kantian idealism that pervaded professional philosophy. Not only is James now interested in psychology as a practical, indeed therapeutic, tool for controlling mental states, he is at pains to dissociate it from psychophysics on one side and abstruse metaphysical inquiry on the other. Whether his sister's decline and death helped James to clarify this position or not, the short essay shows that James was more, not less, involved with psychology as a field that offered potential "control over certain states of mind." And he was becoming increasingly interested in some of the more extreme states of mind that cried out for such control.[16]

51. *Abnormal Psych 1*

THE COUNTRY TO WHICH William James returned in September 1893 was far from placid. The Pennsylvania militia had been called out to put down the 1892 strike at the Carnegie steel plant in Homestead. Federal troops had been called into Idaho to protect silver mines, the mine owners, and their strikebreakers from angry miners. In March 1893 Grover Cleveland was sworn in as president. By fall there was spreading financial panic.

The Sherman Silver Purchase Act of 1890 mandated that the national government buy four and a half million ounces of silver a month and turn it into money. A gold reserve of a hundred million dollars was supposed to back this open-ended, essentially unlimited coining of silver. Business interests, the sound-money people, the people who always opposed the printing of money as a solution, feared a devalued currency and worked to protect the dollar by stopping the buying and coining of silver. While Congress debated, the gold reserve fell to eighty-one million dollars; confidence fell with it, and the result was "the worst financial depression [the country] has ever known," James told his friend Carl Stumpf with some exaggeration. But the Gibbenses' finances crumbled; Alice's legacy lost two thirds of its value.

Along with the depression and the labor troubles went other changes.

The four hundredth anniversary of Columbus's voyage to Hispaniola was celebrated at the Columbian Exposition in Chicago, the "White City" on the lakefront, made mostly of wood and plaster done up to look like marble. The previous year, 1892, had witnessed the Portland Deliverance, in which the annual General Assembly of the Presbyterians declared the Bible to be "without error." This was a major step toward, if not the actual start of, the modern fundamentalist movement in America.[1] Now, just a year later, in September, one of the most visible of the events under the aegis of the Columbian Exposition was the convening along the lakefront of the World's Parliament of Religions. This harbinger of a new religious pluralism drew "together the widest spectrum of speakers and participants ever assembled from the religious traditions of the world."[2]

The rising national pride so evident at the Chicago exposition induced imperial stirrings. Americans in Hawaii overthrew the monarchy there and clamored for annexation. President Cleveland alienated a portion of his own party by refusing to go along with annexation. The Chinese Exclusion Act was found to be constitutional and was extended for ten years. A large tract of land between Kansas and Oklahoma was bought from the Cherokees by the federal government and opened to homesteading. Patriotism and jingoism became hard to tell apart. Katharine Lee Bates wrote "America the Beautiful," and Francis Bellamy, who had left the Baptist ministry for a career in advertising, thought up the Pledge of Allegiance and published it on September 8, 1892, in *The Youth's Companion.*

Upon his return, James was immediately caught up "in the gigantic wheels of the [Harvard] machine," and, as he wrote his brother in London, it was at first "quite a pleasant sensation" after the *dolce far niente* of the fifteen-month sabbatical. But his good mood quickly faded as he fell into what he called a "really awful melancholy." He complained of "a curious sense of incapacity, a sere-and-yellow-leafiness." James felt that he had forgotten everything he knew about psychology; each lecture seemed "a ghastly farce." Again and again he referred to his condition as "melancholy."

By December it lifted. He had undergone eighteen treatments with a Miss Clarke, who apparently practiced a kind of mind cure that involved massage. James now considered that he had suffered "a new kind of melancholy," the proof of which was that he was now, in his recovered state, experiencing a refreshing kind of sleep he had not known for many years.[3]

His ailments were a trial not only to him but to those around him. His friend Myers, who was trying to persuade James to shoulder the presidency of the Society for Psychical Research, began a letter to him, "I am very sorry that you are feeling ill: but a touch of something is mixed with my sympathy that I may as well have out — It seems to me that your mental and physical disorganisation and decay is never by any chance perceptible to anyone but yourself," with much more in the same vein.[4] Myers's fatherly hectoring worked: James took the job.

He was also closely involved in the planning of a new journal, to be called the *Psychological Review,* which was to make up for Hall's journal, which James now thought a "little inadequate back-shop sectarian affair."[5] He was extremely busy teaching, with three courses, one a general psychology course, another a course in cosmology, and the third a brand-new offering in "mental pathology," in which he took up "general psycho-pathy, cranks and geniuses, morbid impulses . . . systematized delusions . . . hysteria . . . double personality and other trance states . . . the history of witchcraft . . . classic types of insanity . . . [and] criminological literature."[6] This interest in what would today be called abnormal psychology would be an important part of James's teaching, reviewing, and public lecturing over the next three years.

James's long-standing but newly focused curiosity about sleep and hypnotic states gains a sharp interest for us when we recall that the standard history of "dynamic psychology," with its central emphasis on psychoanalysis, describes its subject as an arc of development from mesmerism to hypnosis to psychoanalysis.[7] Rapport in mesmerism and in hypnosis is the same thing as transference in psychoanalysis. All three phenomena depend on the existence of subliminal or subconscious or split or dissociated selves, and James's new interest in abnormal psychology, or "exceptional mental states," was concentrated on his intense attraction to dissociated personality. With his two big psychology books behind him, James was becoming less and less interested in laboratory psychology and increasingly drawn to clinical, therapeutic psychology.

James's life and that of his friends and family tossed up new conundrums, strange evidences of buried selves. In January 1894 came the news, devastating for Henry, hard to believe for William, of the apparent suicide of Constance Woolson in Venice. Woolson, a successful American novelist and short story writer, had long enjoyed an intimate, and for the most part concealed, friendship with Henry. "For my part," William wrote, "however gloomy to think of are the sufferings which must precede suicide, I think such an act as hers must have had an element of triumphant feeling about it. It is strange to me to hear you and KPL [Katharine Loring] write of her morbidness, when what struck me most about her during the short time I saw her was her gaiety." Harry replied that William's impression was natu-

Josiah Royce (right) visited James in Chocorua, New Hampshire, in September 1903. One morning, as he and William were deep in conversation, Peggy took two snapshots, one after the other. When James heard the first camera-click, he cried, "Royce, you're being photographed! Look out! I say *Damn the Absolute!*"

The Cambridge home of William and Alice James, 95 Irving Street, in the early 1890s

William James's library at 95 Irving Street

Leonora Piper in 1890. James spent a great deal of time exploring psychic phenomena with Mrs. Piper, a Boston medium. Photo by Eveleen Tennant Myers.

William James and a Mrs. Walden at a séance

Henry and William in 1900 at Henry's home, Lamb House, in Rye

Alice and William James in 1904 or 1905. Photo by Theodate Pope Riddle.

Eliza Putnam Gibbens, William James's mother-in-law, to whom he dedicated the *Varieties,* in her garden at 107 Irving Street, Cambridge, around 1912

William James in 1907. Photo by Alice Boughton.

ral enough and shared by many, but that there was another Constance Woolson under the cheerful one, that her gaiety was "a purely superficial and social, a purely exterior manifestation . . . a cheerfulness which was really intensely mechanical and which left her whole general feeling about life, her intimate melancholy, utterly unexpressed — any more than the flower pot in the window of a room expresses the figure lying on the bed."[8]

In January 1894 James read and reviewed with great admiration Pierre Janet's *État Mentale des Hystériques*. Janet's work, James told a friend, "seems to outweigh in importance all the 'exact' laboratory measurements put together," and had "opened an entirely new chapter in human nature," leading "to a new method of relieving human suffering."[9] As we saw, James and Janet had met in 1889, when they attended the First International Congress of Physiological Psychology and the overlapping First International Congress of Experimental and Therapeutic Hypnotism, both in early August. Janet had presented his thesis work — essentially his book *L'Automatisme Psychologique* — at the latter convention. James was much struck with Janet's description of "hidden selves" and discussed it in *The Principles of Psychology*, published the following year.

Pierre Janet, whose uncle Paul was a well-known philosopher, came from a well-off aristocratic Parisian family. At fifteen he had suffered a depression and a religious crisis. He attended the École Normale Supérieure at the same time as Émile Durkheim, and in 1882 heard the famous lecture by Charcot that rehabilitated hypnosis. Janet was, like James, a professor of philosophy with a major interest in psychology. When the two met, Janet was thirty and just beginning his medical studies. He was slender, stood five feet five inches, wore pince-nez and a beard, and lived in a splendid apartment at 54 Rue de Varenne. His consulting room was small and held an antique desk and satin-covered chairs and a divan. A Boston visitor observed that he had a "staccato personality . . . He tended to make short sharp chopping gestures with his extended hands in order to emphasize his point."[10]

James was very enthusiastic about the new book, saying it "set the seal on the revolution which during the last decade has been going on in our conceptions of hysterical disease." Pointing out that "hysteria is now allowed to be a male complaint" as well as a female one, James gave this summary of Janet's work: "In the constitution called hysterical the threshold of the principal consciousness is not fixed but moveable. It can be shifted by physical and moral shocks and strains so that sensations and ideas of which the patient ought to be fully aware become 'subliminal' or buried and forgotten . . . The nucleus of these subconscious fixed ideas usually consists of reminiscences of the shock by which the mind was originally shattered." These suppressed — Freud would say repressed — shocks become associated with suppressed strata of personality, sometimes appearing as multiple personalities or split consciousness or dissociated personalities (all these terms occur in James's writing between 1893 and 1895).

Where earlier investigators often wished to prove the existence of such personalities or states of personality by means of automatic writing or hypnosis, Janet sought to cure the affliction. Building on the by now well-established fact that people under hypnosis tend to be suggestible, Janet went after the subconscious "fixed ideas" of a patient one by one. His patient "Marcella" had hallucinations that reproduced earlier painful experiences. "As each one was removed by suggestion, a deeper and older one came to the surface and worked itself off until with a final outbreak of suicidal frenzy, the girl got entirely well." Mesmeric healing had given way here to hypnotic healing. With Janet we are on the threshold — as Henri Ellenberger remarks — "of all modern dynamic psychology."[11]

The same issue of the *Psychological Review* that contained James's review of Janet also had a brief review by James of the short paper by Josef Breuer and Sigmund Freud that is usually identified as the starting point of the psychoanalytic movement.[12] James was probably led to Breuer and Freud by Janet, who concluded his *État Mentale des Hystériques* with a long, laudatory account of this paper, published in 1893 as "On the Psychical Mechanism of Hysterical Phenomena."[13]

James was acutely aware that a word such as "hysteria" was an easy label to slap on any conduct one might consider pathological. "The name hysteria, it must be remembered," he wrote at about this time, "is not an explanation of anything, but merely the title of a new set of problems."[14] What had cheered James about Janet, and now about Breuer and Freud, was the emphasis on a possible cure, a novel method of treatment. "Hysteria for [Breuer and Freud] starts always from a shock and is a 'disease of the memory,'" James reported. This brief review is the first known mention of Freud by an American, and while Breuer and Freud's paper probably meant less to James than Janet's work or Myers's, he understood what was happening and gave a capsule description of what would soon become known as the psychoanalytic treatment. "Certain reminiscences of the [initial traumatizing] shock fall into the subliminal consciousness, where they can only be discovered in 'hypnoid' states. If left there, they act as permanent 'psychic traumata,' thorns in the spirit, so to speak. The cure is to draw them out in hypnotism, let them produce all their emotional effects, however violent, and work themselves off." This was the famous cathartic treatment, the "talking cure." The phrase was first used by Bertha Pappenheim, the "Anna O" who was Breuer's patient, whose case had aroused the curiosity of Breuer's young colleague Freud, and whose story was a major source for the paper James was reviewing.

James turned fifty-two in January 1894 and shortly thereafter suffered his first (recorded) attack of angina pectoris, the severe chest pains usually caused by an insufficient flow of blood to the heart.[15] Having complained of reactivated neurasthenia for the past couple of years, James now experienced compounded symptoms. He came down with influenza around Christmas 1893, and by March 1894 was so fatigued that he tried a course of eight injections of Brown-Sequard's testicular elixir, a "glycerine extract prepared from bull's testicles, used hypodermically every other day."[16] Many patients reported a stimulating effect "not unlike that of strong coffee . . . The sexual appetite if present is increased, if absent it is often renewed, sometimes in elderly men to an inconvenient extent."[17] But the main result of James's taking these shots was a painful abscess that kept him in bed for five weeks. In May he had a persistent headache; for treatment he went to Miss Clarke, the mind-cure healer to whom he had gone the previous December and whose ministrations seemed to help, though James did express reservations.[18]

In March, before the abscess laid him up, James publicly opposed a bill then pending in the Massachusetts legislature that would have outlawed all healing except by licensed physicians. This would have made mind-cure methods illegal, except when practiced by an M.D., and it would have wiped out the therapeutic massage that James was trying. "I regard therapeutics as in too undeveloped a state for us to be able to afford to stamp out the contributions of all fanatics and one-sided geniuses," he explained to a friend. He wrote a long letter to the *Boston Transcript* explaining his position. In a second letter to the editor he said that he was altogether in favor of another bill in the legislature that would make it illegal to call oneself Doctor or describe oneself as a physician unless one had an M.D. In other words, he was all for protecting people from fraud but against the outlawing of what we now call alternative medicine.[19]

Also in March 1894 — a busy month — another hidden life that had found expression, though sadly no cure or rescue, popped to the surface like Queequeg's coffin. It was the diary of Alice James, privately printed by Katharine Loring in an edition of four copies, one for herself and one for each of Alice's surviving brothers. William wrote at once to Henry to say the diary had produced "a unique and tragic impression of personal power venting itself on no opportunity," and he added that "it ought some day to be published. I am proud of it as a leaf in the family laurel crown."

Harry agreed. He thought it "magnificent" and "wonderful," spoke of his "immense impressedness by it." He wrote of the "extraordinary intensity of her will and personality [which] really would have made the equal, the reciprocal life of a 'well' person — in the usual world — almost impossible to her — so that her disastrous, her tragic health was in a manner the only solution for her of the practical problem of life."[20] But for Harry there was a problem. A fair amount of Alice's diary recorded gossip that he had retailed to her, complete with names and his often biting comments left in. Harry was all for publishing it, yes, but only in an edited form, with some things left out and some names changed. It would be 1934 before the diary was made public and Alice's voice began to be brought back.[21]

"I make it a rule," Alice wrote, "always to believe the compliments implicitly for five minutes and to simmer gently for twenty more." She may have had a narrow field, but she had a good eye and a lively wit. She wrote how at fifteen she had read a description of the body of a murdered man given by a witness: "He looked pleasant-like and foaming at the mouth." She could laugh at her sickbed misery and the times "when my shawls were falling off to the left, my cushions falling out to the right, and the duvet off my knees," but she could also face things straight on. "Pain was as the essence of the Universe to my consciousness," she wrote. "One must know how to suffer and the science of pain is the unique science of life."[22]

William's reading that March included a book he despised; it was by Max Nordau and was called *Degeneration* (*Entartung*). Applying "Nordau's method to the description of his own person," James said, revealed the author as "a megalomaniac of the arrogant and insulting type, and . . . a victim of insane delusions about a conspiracy of hysterics and degenerates menacing the moral world with destruction unless the sound-minded speedily arm and organize in its defense."[23] Nordau, who had changed his name from Sudfeld, saw degeneration everywhere: in Wagner, Tolstoy, Ruskin, Burne-Jones, Rosetti, Zola, Ibsen, and Nietzsche. "The trouble," wrote James, "is that such writers as Nordau use the descriptive names of symptoms merely as an artifice for giving objective authority to their personal dislikes. The medical terms become mere 'appreciative' clubs to knock men down with."

One place that had clearly not degenerated, in James's view, was Harvard, which celebrated Charles W. Eliot's twenty-fifth year as president in June 1894. Beginning in 1869, Eliot had doubled Harvard's endowment every seven years, reaching $6.7 million in 1889. Faculty salaries had increased faster than that. The number of professors had doubled, from 45 to 90, between 1869 and 1889, and the number of undergraduates had grown from 529 to 1,180 in the same time. Incoming tides of books overflowed the libraries and overwhelmed successive classification schemes. By 1890 there were 272,000 books and 150,000 pamphlets in the college library alone. Despite all the buildings put up under Eliot, Harvard was unable to provide living space for all its students. On Mount Auburn Street, Claverly Hall was one of the first of many grand apartment buildings built with private capital and operated by independent owners, who rented rooms at exorbitant rates to the better-off students. If Harvard was transformed from a country college to an internationally respected university between 1869 and 1894, it was due more to Eliot than to anyone or anything else. He quoted approvingly (and approximately) Ezra Cornell's saying, "I would found an institution in which anyone may study anything."[24]

James sent Eliot a letter congratulating him on his years as president, praising, among other things, his "devotion to ideals." Eliot replied warmly: "I have privately supposed myself to have been pursuing certain educational ideals; but so many excellent persons have described the fruits of the past twenty-five years as lands, buildings, collections, money and thousands of students, that I have sometimes feared that to the next generation I should appear as nothing but a successful philistine." No single thing Eliot did for Harvard was more important than his encouragement of William James. "You carry me back farther than anybody else — to 1861," Eliot wrote, and he closed his letter, "Your coming to the university and your career as a teacher and writer have been among my most solid grounds of satisfaction." James was not moved by the inevitable testimonial dinner. "Choate's address to Eliot very common and poor," he told Alice. "Eliot's reply too cold." But James valued Eliot's letter all the same, and he sent copies to his wife and to Harry in London.[25]

52. Talks to Teachers

IN JUNE 1894 James made a second excursion to the North Carolina mountains before heading for Chocorua again. He worked this summer on a couple of short pieces for which he professed contempt, but each was a real step toward clarity. In an article he wrote for *Johnson's Uni-*

versal Cyclopaedia, "Person and Personality," which he disparaged as "the only genuine rubbish that I ever wrote," James sharply specified personality as personhood, as designating individuality or what is called "personal identity." It is neither a principle nor a constant entity, but is "something which is made from moment to moment." The article goes on to comment on multiple personality, to raise the question of what unifies the personality, and to state that "the margins and outskirts of what we take to be our personality extend into unknown regions."[1]

The other piece he worked on was a talk he had to give in December at the annual meeting of the American Psychological Association, on "what it is the fashion nowadays to call 'epistemology.'" It would be titled "The Knowing of Things Together," and James worried while writing it that it would end up as mere "shapeless debris." In his *Principles of Psychology* James had said that if psychology wanted to be a natural science it would have to abandon to metaphysics "the whole business of ascertaining how we come to know things together or to know them at all." Now he changed his mind, not in the direction of calling for physiological experiments, but by trying to draw a clear distinction between representative knowledge — for example, never having been to India, I nevertheless know that there are tigers in India — and experiential, firsthand knowledge of those animals in that place. This was not an academic issue. Eventually James's preference for direct knowledge (knowledge by personal acquaintance) rather than knowledge about something (secondhand knowledge) would lead him to reject all forms of representative knowledge — including, at times, even logic — in his endorsement of pure experience directly apprehended.[2]

The fall of 1894 brought his usual seasonal slump. He called it a "depression" and was sure it would lift. "How many I've been through before." Alice called him "sad-hearted," and empathized with him and his "lonesome days" in Cambridge. James wrote almost nothing about the past; he had less interest in it even than Emerson, but the past laid its hand on him anyway, often through feelings of nostalgia, which raked him from time to time with strange force. "The crickets sound sadly," he wrote Alice this fall, "taking one back to things that are past, past, past — and altogether the world seems in the sere and yellow leaf with the wan dull day and the dusty and desiccated vegetation." It was not just September in Cambridge. From Chocorua he wrote to a friend, "This little place of ours, which we rather stumbled into at first and kept stumbling deeper into as time went on, always seems so unutterably sad, reeking with sadness and dead things, when we first arrive. But later it cheers up."

James was a man who had willed himself into being a positive, upbeat, forward-looking person. But the persistent note of dejection, and the brilliance with which it was expressed, remained as warning flags that something else, perhaps an underlying feeling of loss, was also going on. There is a Proustian quality to his comments to his brother about "the sadness of things — things every one of which was done either by our hands or by our planning, old furniture renovated, there isn't an object in the house that isn't associated with past life, old summers, dead people, people who will never come again, and the way it catches you round the heart when you first come and open the house from its long winter sleep is most extraordinary."[3]

He tried electrical treatments again. Then he sprained an ankle. It was turning into a difficult autumn. Dr. Holmes died. James went to visit Wendell, his old friend, and found him alone and playing solitaire in a remote den at the top of his house. James was then reading Dwight's life of Jonathan Edwards and Stevenson's *The Wrecker*.[4]

In November and December 1894, James gave a number of talks to teachers in Boston. These talks, which he presented over and over to audiences mostly of teachers, were shaking down to a set of seven or eight, starting with "Man as a Reacting Organism" and going on to "Impulses and Instincts," then to "Habits," then "Association," then "Memory," then "Attention," then "Conception and Reasoning" — or sometimes "Perception" — and invariably ending with "Will." The printed collection of these, *Talks to Teachers* (1899), begins with "Consciousness," perhaps reflecting James's adjustment to audience expectations. James almost never speaks about the content of education. He has nothing to say about the value of the classics or the need for more science or languages, no expressed opinion on the value of any one subject over another. His emphasis is on how most effectively to teach whatever it is you wish to teach. What he has to say about education in *Talks to Teachers* could also be described as "Practical Hints on Teaching and Learning, Suggested by Modern Physiology and Physiological Psychology."

He begins by endorsing coeducation, "in whose benefits so many of us heartily believe," and by deprecating the craving for novelty. "There is no 'new psychology,'" he says; "there is nothing but the old psychology which began in Locke's time, plus a little physiology of the brain and senses and theory of evolution." The crucial founding idea for education is that "in each of us, when awake (and often when asleep) some kind of consciousness is always going on . . . The existence of this stream is the primal fact, the nature and origin of it form the essential problem, of our science." James's overriding interest is not, of course, in consciousness as such, but in consciousness as it practically, tangibly affects our conduct and lives. This emphasis he modestly ascribes to Darwin's discovery: "Consciousness would thus seem in the first instance to be nothing but a sort of super-added biological perfection — useless unless it prompted to useful conduct, and inexplicable apart from that consideration." The function of the teacher is to enable the student to take advantage of what evolution has dropped in his lap, "training the pupil to behaviour."[5]

With the stage thus set — or perhaps cleared — James argues that human beings are, most simply, organisms "for reacting on impressions." What is true at the physiological level has major implications for the teaching process. "No reception without reaction, no impression without correlative expression." We cannot be said truly to receive something unless we actively react to it; we do not really have a solid impression of anything until we express it. Everything begins with our basic or native reactions. "The first thing, then, for the teacher to understand is the native reactive tendencies — the impulses and instincts of childhood — so as to be able to substitute one for another and turn them on to artificial objects."

James then lists these native impulses and instincts. Fear, love, and curiosity are followed by five "ambitious" impulses — namely, imitation, emulation, ambition, pugnacity, and pride. These are followed by instincts for ownership, constructiveness, love of approbation, shyness, and secretiveness. The first time we react to a given stimulus is an act. The second and all subsequent times are habit. "We are subject to the laws of habit in consequence of the fact that we have bodies." James is always superb on habit; it is one of his great subjects. He likens habit to a sheet of paper that has been folded. "Habit is thus a second nature, or rather, as the Duke of Wellington said it is 'ten times nature' . . . The great thing in all education," James insists, "is to make our nervous system our ally instead of our enemy." The force of this is only increased when we remember that James was always fighting with his own nervous system.[6]

James next explains "association." Within the stream of consciousness, that "ever-flowing stream of objects, feelings, and impulsive tendencies," we are able to think and feel by associating things with one another. "Your pupils, whatever else they are, are at any rate little pieces of associating machinery," he says. "The 'nature,' the 'character' of an individual means really nothing but the habitual form of his associations." A good teacher will find ways to direct the associating process. "An object not interesting in itself may become interesting through becoming associated with an object in which an interest already exists." If a child is interested in coins, teach her history, economics, and *Moby Dick* with coins. James has disarming, simple, above all useful advice. "The child will always attend more to what a teacher does than to what the same teacher says . . . I have seen a roomful of college students suddenly become perfectly still to look at their professor of physics tie a piece of string around a stick . . . but immediately grow restless when he began to explain the experiment."[7]

From "interest" James moves on to "attention." "Whoever treats of interest inevitably treats of attention, for to say that an object is interesting is only another way of saying that it excites attention." The freshness of James's observations, even at this distance, is at least partly due to the fact that he views almost everything as a physiological issue rather than a moral one. Elsewhere in James, attention has the same force as belief; here he only wants to argue that to sustain the student's attention, "the subject must be made to show new aspects of itself . . . in a word, to change." You cannot, for example, focus on a dot for long unless you "ask yourself successive questions about it."[8]

The mind, James keeps asserting, "is essentially an associating machine." The secret of a good memory thus lies in "forming diverse and multiple associations with every fact we care to retain." *Thirty days hath September . . .*

Sympathetic always to the unconventional, James recommends patience with the kind of mind that does poorly on examinations. Such a mind "may, in the long examination which life sets us, come out in the end in better shape than the glib and ready reproducer, its passion being deeper, its purposes more worthy, its combining power less commonplace, and its total mental output consequently more important."[9]

The talks always ended with a consideration of will, because, James insists, "Mentality terminates naturally in outward conduct." Physiologically speaking, "there is no sort of consciousness whatever, be it sensation, feeling or idea, which does not directly and of itself tend to discharge into some motor effect." This situation is complicated by the great variety of inhibitions that in human beings are needed to keep us from acting on every little impulse. Most of us, then, act when inhibitions are, for the moment, removed. We finally get out of bed on a cold morning when the inhibition ("It's really cold out there") vanishes for a second ("Yikes, I'm late!") and we find that we have acted without conscious volition; we are out of the bed and standing up. There are, James goes on, two types of will, the precipitate and the obstructed. The precipitate will acts on impulse; the obstructed will is shackled with inhibitions.[10]

Just as there are two kinds of will, there are two kinds of inhibition: inhibition by repression or negation, and inhibition by substitution. Inhibition by repression leads to the kinds of problems reported by Janet, Breuer, and Freud. What a teacher needs to know is how to use inhibition by substitution. In the brilliant and moving coda of the final talk, and indeed of the whole series of talks, James invokes this inhibition by substitution, which he says he learned from Spinoza, but which also has a marked resemblance to Emerson's doctrine of compensation. "Spinoza long ago wrote in his *Ethics* that anything that a man can avoid under the notion that it is bad he may also avoid under the notion that something else is good. He who habitually acts *sub specie mali,* under the negative notion, the notion of the bad, is called a slave by Spinoza" (for example, "I have to go to school today"). "To him who acts habitually under the notion of good he gives the name of freeman" ("I get to go to school today").

We can see James leaning over the lectern and hear his voice rise as he warms to the point: "See to it now, I beg you, that you make freemen of your pupils by habituating them to act, whenever possible, under the notion of a good."[11]

53. *Abnormal Psych 2*

L ATE IN DECEMBER 1894 came the miserable news of the end of "the painful and hurrying pilgrimage" of Robert Louis Stevenson. He had died on December 3, at the age of forty-four, of a cerebral hemorrhage in far-off Samoa. His "splendid life," which Henry James described as "converted into a fable as strange and romantic as one of his own," had ended with his taking up the cause of the native Samoans in their struggles against domination from outside. The day after he died at his home, Vailima, Stevenson, who was called locally Tusitala, was carried by sixty Samoans, who considered him their chief, to the summit of Mount Vaea and buried there.

Everything about Stevenson is interesting. He used four different styles of handwriting. He had married — to the horror of his English friends — an American woman from Virginia City, Nevada, had crossed America traveling as an immigrant, and had sailed from San Francisco for the South Seas. Never in good health, always a brilliant talker, "there was something about Louis Stevenson's appearance that immediately aroused the hostility of customs officers, bank managers, hoteliers and the police."[1]

Henry James was his closest and best friend, and the most accepting of his nomadic life and of his vivid wife, Fanny Osbourne. "He lighted up a whole side of the Globe and was himself a whole province of one's imagination," Henry wrote. William never knew Stevenson personally, but he read his books, followed his movements, and already, as we have seen, considered "The Lantern Bearers" one of his permanent literary beacons.

In January came the opening night in London of Henry James's *Guy Domville*. Apprehensive to a painful degree ("lonely and terrified" was his self-description), Henry could not bear to sit through his own play, going instead to see Oscar Wilde's *Ideal Husband* and returning to his own theater at 10:45, in time to be treacherously lured onstage and greeted with "hoots and jeers and catcalls" from the cheap seats, which for a quarter of an hour contested the "gallant prolonged and sustained applause" of the other half of the audience. The ordeal, probably the worst moment of his life, left Henry "weary, bruised, sickened, disgusted," and it drove him away from writing for the theater and back to fiction. The incident also revealed, at least to William, how invincibly Henry believed in himself. "Don't worry about me," Harry wrote after the debacle. "I'm a rock. If the play has no life on the stage I shall publish it: it's altogether the best thing I've done." We may smile and call this protesting too much, but that would miss the point. Henry simply refused to allow doubt about his abilities to enter his mind.[2]

In February 1895 William was in touch again with Charley Peirce, who was now destitute. James could be counted on to respond to any appeal from Peirce or on his behalf. He wrote letters to drum up paying work — anything — for this old and troubled friend.[3]

In late January 1895 James gave a lecture on the effects of alcohol to the Harvard Total Abstinence League. He had lectured to the league some years earlier, when it was founded. Now he reviewed for his hearers the physiology of drinking and drew some blunt conclusions. Though he himself took an occasional drink, he insisted that "to work on alcohol is a most treacherous business, even where it does stimulate, if it does. In most cases it merely masks the fatigue and makes the work worse . . . The whole bill against alcohol is its treachery. Its happiness is an illusion and seven other devils return." Willing as he was to experiment and experience everything, he was also willing to judge. "Say what you will about the quality of existence . . . the gas lit spurious hilarity with sickness afterwards is not the real quality," and he applied the Spinozist substitution he talked about to the teachers: "The best way to wean people from intemperance is to fill them with a love of temperance for its own sake," to replace the ideal of drinking with "the ideal of having a constitution in perfect health."[4]

In February he delivered a set of three lectures in Boston, "Recent Investigations into Abnormal States or Types of Character." This was an outgrowth of his new college course and a preliminary to the longer series of talks on the subject he would give, twice, in 1896. His general position, as Santayana understood it, was that "the best way to understand the normal is to study the abnormal."[5] Another of his students recalled that James was "ready to do sympathetic justice to the most unaccredited, audacious or despised hypothesis. His thought was that there was no sharp line to be drawn between 'healthy' and 'unhealthy' minds, that all have something of both." This same student, Herbert B. Adams, also remembered "once when we were returning from two insane asylums, . . . his saying, 'President Eliot might not like to admit that there is no sharp line between himself and the men we have just seen, but it is true.'"[6]

In one of the lectures on abnormal states, James listed some of "the so-called manias, Dipsomania, Kleptomania, Pyromania, Suicidal and homicidal mania, all sorts of impulses belonging to the sexual sphere," and concluded, "These show graver trouble [that is, graver than general anxious melancholy] though they exist in germ in the healthy." Elsewhere he said, "A life healthy on the whole, must have some morbid elements."[7] In the course and in the talks James explored and reported on several different though related subjects. He was, for one thing, laying out and elaborating nothing less than what one modern commentator calls a "dynamic psychology of the subconscious."[8]

He accomplished this mainly through an extensive consideration of the concept of dissociated personality. When James gave these talks as Lowell Lectures in the fall of 1896, the first four covered dreams and hypnotism, automatism, hysteria, and multiple personality. Ranging widely over material he knew from Janet, Breuer, Freud, and his own observations, he ended lecture four with a retrospective summary: "I myself have no question that the formula of dissociated personality will account for the phenomena I have brought before you. Hypnotism is sleep. Hysteria is obsession not by demons, but by a fixed idea . . . that has dropt down" from the conscious to the unconscious mind.[9]

In lecture five James passed to the question of demoniacal possession, which he considers to be one more type of alternate personality, a type he rather startlingly identifies as mediumship. "History shows that mediumship is identical with demon-possession," he said. "When the pagan gods became demons all possession was deemed diabolic, and we have the medieval condition." Seeking an explanation, not a dismissal, James pursued the symptoms shared by demoniacal possession and modern mediumship. "Convulsions, altered character, new name, 3rd person, supernormal powers, amnesia. Well between intervals." Unwilling to invoke the usual enlightened diagnosis of fraud, James could only conclude, "If there are devils — if there are supernormal powers it is through the cracked self that they enter!"[10]

Lecture six took up what was for James the darkest of these subjects, witchcraft. He had read up on it, had studied the 1486 *Malleus Maleficarum* (*Hammer of Witches*), concentrating on sixteenth-century European witchcraft, though he gave some consideration to late-seventeenth-century Salem, Massachusetts.[11] He offered case histories, emphasizing the cruel and ingenious tortures described in the *Malleus,* an infamous book that, James claimed — mistakenly — had been "confirmed by successive popes as a manual of canon law." Incapable of simply saying "lunacy," as so many others had, James struggled to grasp the mentality of witch-hunters. He imagined a small mind "guiding a will that stuck at nothing in the way of cruelty, and a conscience raised to fever heat by the idea that the battle was directly waged with God's enemy Satan, there in the very room." The torture sessions in the *Malleus* gave him, James said, "the most curious gruesome rathole feeling."

There followed a lecture on degeneration and one on genius, in which James tried to convert the lurid pessimistic social theories of Max Nordau and Cesare Lombroso into overstated accounts of mere "neurotic constitution." And he opened his lecture on genius by saying, "The prevailing opinion of our times supposes that a psychopathic constitution is the foundation for genius."[12] Nordau might point to Wagner, Ruskin, Ibsen, Tolstoy, and Zola, but James noted that geniuses who didn't fit the psychopathic pattern were just left out by Nordau. "What shall we say to Walter Scott, Goethe, Browning, George Sand . . . Emerson, Longfellow, Lowell, Oliver Wendell Holmes, Whittier?" Genius had, James insisted, "no necessary connection with morbidness."[13]

Summing up, James said, "We have taken up many lurid things and made them tamer." Hypnosis is sleep, hysteria is a kind of hypnotism, demon possession is a form of mediumship, hysteria and hypnotism go a long way toward explaining witchcraft. The idea of genius as insane, while romantic, doesn't hold widely enough. The result of all this, he thought, is to make disease less remote from health. "Who shall absolutely say that the morbid has no revelations about the meaning of life? That the healthy-minded view, so called, is all?"[14]

James's interest in abnormal psychology dominated a good part of at least four years of his life, roughly from 1893 to 1897. He taught it as a course four times, he presented three public talks on it in February 1895, and he twice gave a series of eight lectures on it in 1896. But he then pulled back, never published the lectures, and never tried to write a book on the subject. Perhaps it was because the therapeutic picture was unclear. Although more and more descriptions of abnormal behaviors poured in, there was no consensus about treatment, and James was much more interested in treatment than in taxonomy. In addition, abnormal mental states, especially witchcraft, involved mobilizing one's empathy to understand people who habitually looked at the world *sub specie mali*, as though evil and enemies were everywhere.

James seems to have been shaken by the witchcraft material in particular, and he was gloomily eloquent about it. The "friars of the Inquisition and other judges were the most conscientious of men, the puritans of their day," he wrote. But their good intentions went for nothing. "To diminish the power of the Prince of hell, a hell wantonly and of whole cloth was manufactured upon earth. There is no worse enemy of God and Man than zeal armed with power and guided by a feeble intellect . . . The great lesson of history," he concluded somberly, "is to keep power of life and death away from that kind of mind, the mind that sees things in the light of evil and dread and mistrust rather than in that of hope."[15]

Another problem with pursuing abnormal psychology was that there was, for James, another way of regarding the subconscious, a way not covered by Janet, Breuer, and Freud, a way suggested by James's friend F.W.H. Myers. For Janet, Breuer, and Freud, the subconscious was a pathological formation, a repressed or otherwise distorted realm made up of decayed or dislodged and distorted bits of our normal consciousness. Myers and, increasingly, James tended to look on the subconscious as something not pathological but normal, though different from our daylight consciousness. Myers proposed that the subconscious might be the place in each of us where the normal daylight personality can make contact with something larger than our daylight self. In his lecture on multiple personality James pointed to this alternative view: "Whether supernormal powers of cognition in certain persons may occur, is a matter to be decided by evidence . . . The hypnotic condition is not in itself clairvoyant, but is more favorable to the cause of clairvoyance or thought transference than the waking state. So alternate personality, the tendency of the Self to break up, may, if there be spirit influences, yield them their opportunity."

For all these reasons, then, William James turned his attention away from what he called "the varieties of witchcraft" and toward a much larger interest, which would bring him, some eight years later, to the second of his great achievements — for people interested in religion, perhaps the greatest of all — *The Varieties of Religious Experience*. In leaving behind witchcraft and demonology, James was not trying to shield a cloistered or dainty optimism. He had, and always would have, a robust appreciation of evil and its role in human affairs. It is one of his strengths. But he was taking his own advice, and Spinoza's: "Anything that a man can avoid under the notion that it is bad, he may also avoid under the notion that something else is good." If attention, in the end, is the same as belief, then attention to the larger world of religious experience would go hand in hand with a broad embrace of religious belief in all its thousand-faced manifestations. James's move away from witchcraft was thus a crucial, if not *the* crucial, step on the path to the Gifford Lectures, which were later published as *The Varieties of Religious Experience*.

54. *Sarah, Rosina, and Pauline*

AS WILLIAM JAMES turned fifty-three, in January 1895, his life was rich and full. He was a good father and a committed, if impatient, teacher with an inveterate habit of helpfulness. He had a host of colleagues whom he treated as equals, and a host of friends whom he treated as intimates. He was happily, solidly, married — though he contracted a mad crush on every other woman he met.

There was, for example, Sarah Wyman Whitman. She was exactly James's age, an artist who won major commissions for her work in stained glass, a book designer for Houghton Mifflin, and a lively, beautiful, generous, and wealthy married woman whose home and studio were focal points for art and artists in Boston. Her circle took in Royce, Santayana, Holmes, James, John Jay Chapman, Sarah Orne Jewett, Willa Cather, and many others. She and James met sometime in the 1880s and struck up a warm friendship. The "high pressure at which she lived" and the fact that "she never stopped long in the outer courts of friendship" endeared her at once to William James, who lived the same way.[1] She warmed especially to the artist in James, telling another friend, Minna Timmons, that he had said, "Looked at from one point of view, the artist was like any other man, except for the greater rapidity of his intuitions; what he saw at once others saw more slowly."[2]

Sarah Whitman helped him read the proofs of *The Principles of Psychology*. He took to going to her studio at 184 Boylston Street on the last Saturday of every month, just after his noon lecture (Harvard then had Saturday classes) and before the two-thirty dinner of the Saturday Club. There was a strong social intimacy, a bond of confidence, a guaranteed sympathy between them. When sister Alice's diary arrived in its tiny edition of four copies — complicated as its birth was by Henry's worries about gossip disclosures — William loaned his copy to Mrs. Whitman.

He called her "beloved madame" and many other endearments, delivered with gallant mushiness, irony damascened with sentiment. Merely affectionate banter, one concludes, but that seems not quite to cover it. He recommended she read Bettina von Arnim's *Goethe's Correspondence with a Child,* a still vivid masterpiece of the intimacy possible in correspondence. He liked Bettina's side of it more than Goethe's. Bettina led, challenged, held nothing back; Goethe responded with warm avuncular aplomb. James would tell Sarah Whitman about the sadness of the country place in Chocorua. He would invite her to the Adirondacks and ask her to imagine him "with thou beside me singing in the wilderness." When he brought out "Is Life Worth Living?" in late 1895, she promised her friends copies and praised it in advance as "an eager and noble cry from such a brave and tender heart."[3]

Then there was Rosina Emmet. She was a cousin, the daughter of Ellie Temple and a niece of Minnie Temple. Rosina came in the fall of 1894 to live with the James family and attend Radcliffe for a year. Rosina was twenty-one, a bright, outgoing person who wanted to write novels. Other young people clustered around her. When she first arrived at the Jameses', her sister Bay (who would later paint an excellent portrait of William James) came for a while. Kitty Emmet's daughter Elizabeth, and her sons Willy and Grenville, visited. Other young people from Cambridge and Boston were in and out. Suddenly the James house was "full of laughing, piano-playing etc young people, acting and making personal comments just like those we used to make together in the old days of innocence with 'the Temples,'" William wrote Harry. "They [Rosina and Bay] are the most wholesome, innocent, free-hearted and generous girls, and it has done me real good."[4]

Rosina brought back the past, the old gaiety of Newport and New York, the long-gone days of youth, the summer girls at summer hotels. Most of all, she reminded William James of Minnie Temple. "She is so much the type of Minny," he wrote Harry, that if Harry were to meet her, "it would call up all sorts of dead and buried things." She had, for James, "an extraordinary perceptive-personal intellect." She wrote "finely in a slap-dash way," and was capable of "that direct swoop at the vital facts of human character." One evening as William was writing letters, Rosina entertained two of her "'gentleman friends' by telling their character by their handwriting." James overheard her saying to one, "You enjoy sombre, wolfish, gloomy things."[5]

James was immediately taken with Rosina. Less than a month after she arrived, he was writing to Harry that she was "a regular trump," and adding, "In fact were I a youngster I should aim right at her 'hand.'" Alice was bruised and hurt by William's all too evident crush on Rosina, who was, after all, thirty years younger than he. Alice was unable to recover for herself the youthful, high-spirited tone that now prevailed around the house. She went to visit a sister. William typically did not draw back, even though he knew Alice was upset. He believed in acting on impulse, and he had his way. Eventually Alice came around, with what inner reluctance or misgivings we can well imagine.

In time William began to voice reservations about Rosina; he complained to Harry that she was a little selfish, a little egotistical, and "destitute of tenderness." "She doesn't give one any sentimental returns for her board." But he retained a soft spot for the sprightly Rosina. When she went to Paris in late 1896, William sent her a hundred dollars spending money via Henry, with instructions to Henry not to acknowledge the money in his next letter.[6]

When James was writing with teasing gallantry to Sarah Whitman, and was attracted and haunted by the ghost of Minnie Temple in Rosina Emmet, he met another young woman with whom he was quickly — and lastingly — smitten. He first met Pauline Goldmark in September 1895, after presenting his teacher talks in Colorado Springs. When he returned to his beloved Adirondacks, he felt, he told his wife, more alive than he'd felt in years. Then, in this fine positive mood, he met Pauline and his letters to Alice suddenly soar: "I have been happy, happy HAPPY! With the exquisite imperishable beauty of this place, the place I know so well. Nature has made it for falling in love in, passing honeymoons and the like. There is a perfect little serious rosebud of a Miss Goldmark whom Miller [Dickinson Miller, a student of James's who later became a well-known teacher] seems very sweet upon." She was a Bryn Mawr graduate, a biologist, one of the children of the remarkable Goldmark family. Her father, a doctor and revolutionary in 1848, had fled to America from Austria and had gone into munitions manufacture. One of Pauline's brothers was a chief engineer on the Panama Canal project. A sister, Alice, married Louis Brandeis, the U.S. Supreme Court justice; another sister, Helen, married Felix Adler, the founder of the Ethical Culture movement and school.

Pauline loved the Keene Valley life; she was for James "such an up-at-sunrise, out-of-doors, and mountain-top kind of girl." To another friend he described Pauline as a "tramper and camper and lover of nature such as one rarely meets, and withal a perfectly simple, good girl, with a beautiful face — and I fairly dote upon her and were I younger" — James was fifty-seven when he wrote this — "and 'unattached' should probably be deep in love." Pauline *was* beautiful. Her face was shaped much like Alice's, though she did not have Alice's dark-eyed intensity. Pauline had regular yet mobile features; she looked composed, happy, self-confident, and unselfconscious.[7]

Perhaps because James had met Pauline in the Adirondacks, he always considered her part of the glorious outdoor life there. Indeed, as her sister Josephine perceived, Pauline was for James a "symbol of a mood, a region, a way of life." Much later, Josephine wrote about Pauline and William James that "the primeval forest, uncut, uncleared; its primitive freedom; delight in these wild aspects of nature as compared with the trimmer and mellower European landscapes of other summers — all this was implied in their friendship."[8]

James wrote Pauline Goldmark many letters, more than to almost anyone except his immediate family. He openly yearned for her company. "Two words from you have made me king of the world," he wrote her, in French. At the very least he was king of the sweet-talkers, though it is clear that Pauline meant a great deal to James. Years later, he wrote her from Europe, "The sight of you, sporting in nature's bosom once lifted me into a sympathetic region, and made a better boy of me in ways which it would probably amuse and surprise you to learn of, so strongly are characters useful to each other, and so subtly are destinies intertwined."[9]

William James had always been attracted to interesting women. His mother had noticed it warily. Women found him attractive too. There has never been so much as a breath of scandal about these friendships. Of course one or more of them may have taken a physical turn, of course revealing letters may have been destroyed, and certainly the Jameses as a family could keep a secret. But even if James never ran off for a fling — as his brother Bob did once, as we saw — James's women friends were an important part of his life and a source of dismay and sorrow for Alice.

Of course Alice held a steady place in James's heart; there is the unending stream of warm and intimate letters to her to prove it. And of course she was the mother of his children and the idea of separating, which, as noted earlier, Alice and William had briefly considered early on, never arose again in their later life together. All this may be true, but it leaves something unsaid. James's spontaneity was crucial to him, to his idea of himself, and it made him reckless, self-indulgent, and sometimes cruel when it came to friendships with attractive, vital women. He lived off their vitality, just as his brother Henry lived off that of Minnie Temple and Constance Woolson.[10] If James was a natural poacher, with the poacher's dislike of the gamekeeper, he was also a natural philanderer, with the philanderer's lack of interest in settled arrangements. The cost of these happy, rejuvenating attachments never worried James. It was Alice who paid.

Alice knew all about all these crushes and pashes — and there were more. There was nothing clandestine about any of James's enthusiasms, and Alice was always politely included in the correspondence. Sarah Whitman once wrote William to say she was relieved to hear that his health was better, but she would not positively believe it until "a certain person who cannot lie" confirms it. After the year of Rosina's living with them, Alice became melancholy, and sometime around August 1895 she must have asked William whether he was now sorry he had married her.

His reply was that of a man who knows what is good for him. It was not a romantic reply, not gallant or flirtatious. He must have known it was a serious question. "When I look back over the years that we have passed together and see into what an entirely new man I have grown, all my normality and efficiency dating from my marriage, I cannot imagine anything different or what sort of a thing an alternative could be. That's why I haven't answered your question — it is asking whether I am sorry or not that this planet is the earth." He signed himself "your own everlasting husband."[11] He was also everlastingly himself. Exactly seven days after writing this, he met, and was gushing to Alice about, Pauline Goldmark. William James must have been quite a handful.

55. Is Life Worth Living?

ROSINA EMMET'S UNSETTLING SIMILARITY to Minnie Temple revived aspects of William's uncertain, yearning, tumultuous past, and it may have been these associations that led him to put together and deliver, in April 1895, a talk for the Harvard YMCA called "Is Life Worth Living?" He took up the old question that had weighed heavily on him and his sister in his twenties and thirties, the question of taking one's own life, of "ending it when you will." James's essay on suicide is no Sunday morning objection, no debater's problem formulated in advance to lead to an already established conclusion. It is, like John Donne's *Biathanatos*, a hard-eyed look at an act the awful attractiveness of which the author recognizes, darkly welcomes, but finally honors more by his serious and sustained attention than by actual approval.

Many of James's strengths coalesce in this one piece and around this one issue. His basic position and conclusion are religious; his working procedure is psychological. The overall structure of the argument is philosophical; its power to connect — its accessibility — comes from his immersion in teaching and public lecturing. It is pitched to bright and troubled young people, to the spirit, perhaps, of Minnie Temple. It depends heavily on literary examples, and it rises stylistically to the kind of urgent eloquence that marks great writing. It is a liberating achievement that is too preoccupied with its practical effect to care how it is to be catalogued and shelved.

James begins with a quick glance at "temperamental optimism," the great example of which is Walt Whitman, for whom "the mere joy of living is so immense . . . that it abolishes the possibility of any other kind of feeling." "I do not see one imperfection in the universe," James quotes Whitman, "and I do not see one cause or result lamentable at last."[1] Opposed to this is "temperamental pessimism," the "standing refutation," an answer, and a convincing one, to Whitman. James's example here — he quotes two full pages of it — is James Thomson's "City of Dreadful Night":

> My wine of life is poison mixed with gall,
> My noonday passes in a nightmare dream,
> I worse than lose the years which are my all:
> What can console me for the loss supreme?

"Lo, you are free to end it when you will" is all Thomson has to offer. James quotes Thomson and then says, plainly enough, "These verses are in truth a consolation for all to whom, as to him, the world is far more like a steady den of fear than a continual fountain of delight." He goes on to face up to reality, to the facts. "That life is not worth living the whole army of suicides declare."[2]

James is quick to concede that he can do nothing about the likely majority of suicides, those resulting from insanity or "sudden frenzied impulse," and, like a good Stoic, he narrows his task practically: "My words are to deal only with that metaphysical *tedium vitae* which is peculiar to reflecting men."[3]

After making it unmistakably clear that he means to confront the darkness and take it at its full fighting weight, he moves, without spiritual slither, to frame it as a religious problem. "Pessimism is essentially a religious disease," he declares. It is not physiological, not psychological, not philosophical. "The nightmare view of life has plenty of organic sources but its great reflective source has at all times been the contradiction between the phenomena of nature and the craving of the heart to believe that behind nature there is a spirit whose expression nature is."

By religion James does not mean simply "Christian." Quoting a passage of Carlyle's on "the everlasting no," which so deeply impressed Melville, James suggests that "the initial step towards getting into healthy ultimate relations with the universe is the act of rebellion against the idea that such a god" — a "moral and Intelligent Contriver of the World" — "exists." He quotes Carlyle's rebellion with approval: "Wherefore, like a coward, dost thou forever pip and whimper, and go cowering and trembling? Despicable biped! . . . Hast thou not a heart; canst thou not suffer whatsoever it be; and as a Child of Freedom, though outcast, trample Tophet itself under thy feet, while it consumes thee? Let it come then; I will meet it and defy it!"[4]

James's argument comes down, as he said it would at the beginning, to a question of religious faith. "I use the word [religion] in the supernaturalist sense, as declaring that the so-called order of nature, which constitutes this world's experience, is only one portion of the total universe, and that there stretches beyond this visible world an unseen world of which we now know nothing positive . . . A man's religious faith . . . means for me essentially his faith in the existence of an unseen order of some kind in which the riddle of the natural order may be found explained." Science cannot really help here, because our science is only "the minutest glimpse of what the universe will really prove to be when adequately understood."

James proposes that we put scientific skepticism aside for a time and learn to trust our religious demands, which "means first of all to live in the light of them, and to act as if the invisible world which they suggest were real." That is to say, maybe they are true, and just as Shakespeare's Touchstone declares there to be "much virtue in 'if,'" James now proposes that, whatever science may counsel, we embrace the idea of "maybe." "Not a victory is gained, not a deed of faithfulness or courage is done, except upon a maybe; not a service, not a sally of generosity, not a scientific exploration or experiment or textbook, that may not be a mistake." It is only, he concludes, "by risking our persons from one hour to another that we live at all. It is all a question of 'maybe.'" James brings up Meister Eckhart's saying, which has flowered in modern theology, that God needs man as much as man needs God. "I confess," James writes, "that I do not see why the very existence of an invisible world may not in part depend on the personal response which any one of us may make to the religious appeal. God himself, in short, may draw vital strength and increase of very being from our fidelity."[5]

At the close of the essay, James swings the argument back to his own testimony, his own experience, to the only possible authentication within our reach: "If this life be not a real fight, in which something is eternally gained for the universe by success, it is no better than a game of private theatricals from which one may withdraw at will." That is, you can end it when you will. "But it feels like a real fight — as if there were something really wild in the universe which we, with all our idealities and faithfulnesses, are needed to redeem; and first of all to redeem our own hearts from atheisms and fears. For such a half-wild, half-saved universe our nature is adapted."

And then he adds a passage, a grand passage like Melville's description of the ancient god throned on yet older gods, which one discovers winding one's way down to the lowest levels of the Hôtel de Cluny in Paris; it is a passage that shows how the new interest in abnormal psychology — in Janet, Breuer, and Freud — and the revelation of the hidden self feed into James's religious search. From the lines just quoted he races on to: "The deepest thing in our nature is this *Binnenleben* [hidden life, hidden self] . . . this dumb region of the heart in which we dwell alone with our willingnesses and unwillingnesses, our faiths and fears. As through the cracks and crannies of caverns those waters exude from the earth's bosom which then form the fountain-heads of springs, so in these crepuscular depths of personality the sources of all our outer deeds and decisions take their rise. Here is our deepest organ of communication with the nature of things."[6]

56. The Gospel of Relaxation

JAMES'S OLDEST SON, Henry James III, turned sixteen in May 1895, took the entrance exam for Harvard in June, and was admitted as a freshman in July. James was proud of the boy and told him so. In August James gave his talks to teachers in Colorado Springs. He had a good audience, but he felt that the edges of his talks were "all getting worn off . . . by repetition."

The scenery was fresh and exciting; his painter's eye responded enthusiastically to the Rockies. "They stand here against the western sky, as if breathed on a canvas in their pink delicacy of tint[;] they form the most exquisite foil to the great plain broken by low bluffs that stretch to the illimitable eastern horizon." He saw Denver, and got as far west as Grand Junction; his entire trip was dominated by the mountains, "which every afternoon fill themselves with the most glorious rain and cloud and lightning effects." He particularly loved the high country and the gold camps, and he wrote his brother about driving to Cripple Creek, "3 miles in the starlight on top of a 6-horse-stage of which one couldn't see the leaders for the darkness, and a very uneven road." He had supper in a tarpaper shack, slept in a bed that smelled of the previous occupant's tobacco, and marveled over the "tremendous scenery . . . gorges and torrents, high passes, beautiful valleys and plateaus, and extraordinary Doré-esque bluff formations and deserts." It was just after this glorious western trip that he went to Keene Valley in September and met the perfect little rosebud Pauline Goldmark.[1]

In October G. Stanley Hall's eagerness to advance his own school, Clark University, led him to claim, in print, that experimental psychology had come to Harvard from Clark. One might easily claim just the opposite. Hall had studied experimental psychology at Harvard as a student of William James. James flared up like a man challenged to a duel, called the assertion "ridiculous," cited his own work, and stiffly demanded a printed retraction. "You will of course rectify the error in your next number" (Hall's *American Journal of Psychology*). James readily conceded his own "great inferiority as a laboratory teacher and investigator," but he was angered that Hall had ignored "the good will with which I have tried to force my nature, and . . . the actual things I have done." James was also offended because "the misstatement concerns the credit of my university." Hall explained that Herbert Nichols, the Clark man recently hired by Harvard, had supposed himself the first who was chiefly a laboratory man and first to offer a purely experimental course. Hall's reply made it clear that it was James's anger, not his argument, that moved him. "If you wish me to make any statement in the *Journal* tell me just what will satisfy you."[2]

If James could get testy over matters of professional and institutional pride, he showed that he could also leave his professional world to take a political stand on one of the great issues of the day. Venezuela had requested U.S. help in a border dispute with England over the boundary between Venezuela and British Guyana. On December 17, 1895, the issue burst into wide public notice. President Cleveland sent a message to Congress, asserting that only the United States had the right to settle the dispute (it being about land in the Western Hemisphere) and threatening to go to war if England insisted on having any say in the matter.

Cleveland's belligerent invocation of the Monroe Doctrine was received with wild approval by Congress and by most of the newspapers. James was appalled by the sudden threat of war and by the swift upwelling of jingoistic nationalism and Anglophobia. He fired off an open letter to his congressman — printing it in the *Harvard Crimson* — denouncing the "calamity which President Cleveland and Congress together have sprung upon the country." James felt embarrassed for his nation. "We have written ourselves squarely down as a people dangerous to the peace of the world," he told Representative Samuel W. McCall. He also wrote the old family friend E. L. Godkin, editor of *The Nation* and the *New York Evening Post,* to complain that "three days of fighting mob-hysteria at Washington at any time can undo the peace-habits of a hundred years." Godkin, whose paper and magazine were among the few voices raised against Cleveland's move, wrote back: "The newspapers stand between this generation and the light . . . The press is now the great enemy of good government and of rational views of human affairs."[3]

James could be quickly stirred; usually he calmed down just as quickly, but not this time. His opposition to the Venezuela affair ran deep. He wrote to another friend, "Cleveland in my opinion by his explicit allusion to war has committed the biggest political crime I have ever seen here." On January 2, 1896, Theodore Roosevelt, then president of the Board of Police Commissioners in New York City, sent a long letter to the *Crimson* opposing James's views and supporting Cleveland. Roosevelt, an alumnus, wrote about "the honor and dignity of the United States," the "honor of the American flag," about dissenters betraying the American cause, and he ended, "If Harvard men wish peace with honor they will heartily support the national executive and national legislature in the Venezuela matter; will demand that our representatives insist upon the strictest interpretation of the Monroe Doctrine; and will farther demand that immediate preparations be made to build a really first-class navy."[4]

Roosevelt's accusation that anyone opposing Cleveland was betraying the nation infuriated James, who replied to Roosevelt, once more via the *Harvard Crimson:* "May I express a hope that in this university, if no where else on the continent, we shall be patriotic enough not to remain passive whilst the destinies of our country are being settled by surprise."[5]

At the end of January James delivered a talk, "Psychology and Relaxation," to students at Wellesley College. He repeated it at Bryn Mawr, and later at Vassar. All three were women's colleges. The talk was not only to women, it was for women, though the subject was, in his view, a concern for both men and women. The problem, as James put it, was reminiscent of that described in Charles Beard's *American Nervousness.* Americans are too excited, too worked up, too much on edge, on the clench, overloaded, and overwhelmed. "For by the sensations that so incessantly pour in from the overtense excited body the overtense and excited habit of mind is kept up; and the sultry, threatening, exhausting, thunderous inner atmosphere never quite clears away." Though this sounds like a description of his own mind (or of the Rocky Mountains in late summer), James explicitly calls this a social phenomenon. "The American overtension and jerkiness and breathlessness and intensity and agony of expression are primarily social, and only secondarily physiological, phenomena."[6]

Even so, he thought the solution, the cure, to be within the reach of the individual. He cited with solid approval Annie Payson Call's *Power Through Repose* and claimed, "If you should individually achieve calmness and harmony in your own person, you may depend upon it that a wave of imitation will spread from you." The point is not where the advice comes from; it is the good advice that matters. "Unclamp, in a word, your intellectual and practical machinery, and let it run free." To teachers he said, "Prepare yourself in the subject so well that it shall be always on tap; then in the classroom trust your spontaneity and fling away all farther care." He gives examples of people who have learned how to unclamp, and then concludes: "The need of feeling responsible all the livelong day has been preached long enough in our New England. Long enough exclusively, at any rate — and long enough to the female sex. What our girl-students and woman-teachers most need nowadays is not the exacerbation, but rather the toning down of their moral tensions." The young women received this talk with "resounding, and as it were oceanic applause," as the delighted speaker reported to his colleague Hugo Münsterberg, who was off in Germany.[7]

The talk was not just vague uplift or well-intentioned generalities. It was a careful application of the James-Lange theory of emotion, recommending that the individual "pay primary attention to what we do and express, and not to care too much for what we feel." "To wrestle with a bad feeling only pins our attention on it, and keeps it still fastened in the mind; whereas if we act as if from some better feeling, the old bad feeling soon folds its tent like an Arab and silently steals away."[8] "Act as if"; this is the essence of James's advice.

The talk is a short one, written in what we may call William James's third style. His first style is the labored technical writing of his early papers and parts of *The Principles of Psychology;* his second style, the middle style, he used when addressing college philosophy clubs. *The Will to Believe* is almost entirely made up of pieces written in the second style. The third style is his plainest, clearest, most public style. It is at once vivid, personal, comprehensible, and without a shred of condescension. It is best exemplified in *Talks to Teachers.* The longer James worked over a subject, the simpler and shorter and more direct he made it. He did not usually rewrite. He tended to throw out the earlier try and start all over.

The secret of the self-help movement, whether it is exemplified by Ralph Waldo Emerson or Ralph Waldo Trine, Annie Payson Call or Alcoholics Anonymous, is that effective self-help can be entered into only through the door of a kind of belief that we might as well admit is religious, though not necessarily orthodox, in nature. When AA invokes a "higher power," it does not mean Jehovah; it means a power higher than oneself. A small community of two or three will do nicely. Successful reliance on an even slightly higher power requires a religious act of belief. Toward the end of "Psychology and Relaxation" James drops this comment: "Of course the sovereign cure for worry is religious faith."

What drives and validates self-help is a belief, a religious conviction, that our energies and abilities are finally congruent with the universe; that our minds — as Francis Bacon had proposed and hoped back in the Renaissance — are at bottom a match for the nature of things; that we are not fallen, incapable, helpless, doomed, or damned. James's main examples in "Psychology and Relaxation" are from Hannah Whitall Smith's *The Christian's Secret of a Happy Life* ("It is your purpose God looks at . . . not your feelings about that purpose") and from Brother Lawrence, who, in *The Practice of the Presence of God,* learned to trust himself and his situation without anxiety and thereby was able to live his "life in perfect liberty and continual joy," a condition that followed "the relaxation of all unnecessary solicitudes and anxieties in him." James would underline the fundamentally religious nature of his piece when he came to put it in a book, where he retitled it "The Gospel of Relaxation."[9]

57. The Right to Believe

IN APRIL 1896 James gave another talk to the Yale Philosophical Club. It was, James told Sarah Whitman, a "most remote and listless audience, my host Ladd, as on a former occasion, uttering no syllable of comment on the words to which his ears had been exposed." The lecture was called "The Will to Believe," and while James was ready to concede that it might more properly have been titled "The Right to Believe," it was an important talk for him. Even before he delivered it, he began planning a book around it.[1]

The essay, closely argued in ten parts, begins by saying it will be about "justification of faith," not "justification by faith." That is, it will be "a defence of our right to adopt a believing attitude in religious matters." The essay asks the reader to choose among competing hypotheses. Choosing one hypothesis over another is not, for James, a mere matter of logic. If we pay attention to how choices are actually made, he says, we will see that some hypotheses are live, others are dead. "A live hypothesis [or a live option] is one which appeals as a real possibility to him to whom it is proposed." The deadness or liveness of an option is measured by a person's willingness to act on the option. The final point of the piece is prefigured when James says, "He who refuses to embrace a unique opportunity loses the prize as surely as if he tried and failed."[2]

The essay unfolds a choice between a religious hypothesis and a scientific — that is, a positivist — hypothesis. James begins with Pascal's wager. Either there is a God or there isn't. If there is, you'd best believe. If there isn't, you lose nothing by believing that you wouldn't have lost anyway. On the whole, then, you'd best believe. It's gambling, and the smart thing is to figure the odds. James dislikes both the gambling aspect and the coercive logic, which he calls "a last desperate snatch at a weapon against the hardness of the unbelieving heart." It is, for him, unconvincing, not possible, a dead option.

Next — and this takes up most of the text — comes the opposite, and for James the even less possible, option, that of W. K. Clifford, who says, "It is wrong always, everywhere, and for anyone to believe anything upon insufficient evidence." This is the statement that evidently set James off, and he offers a detailed critique of the problems inherent in this view.[3]

Science was central for James. All his formal education, his interest in the natural world, in Darwin, in chemistry, in comparative anatomy, and in physiology gave him a permanent connection to science that he never abandoned. He writes here with a cool, wistful elegance about "the magnificent edifice of the physical sciences" and calls attention — as to the Great Wall of China — to the "thousands of disinterested moral lives of men [that] lie buried in its mere foundation; what patience and postponement, what choking down of preference, what submission to the icy laws of outer fact are wrought into its very stones and mortar." Now comes Clifford, exhorting us, in the name of science, to "believe nothing, [to] keep your mind in suspense forever, rather than by closing it on insufficient evidence incur the awful risk of believing lies." James quotes Clifford again: "Better go without belief forever than believe a lie."[4]

James is not content simply to say, "I myself find it impossible to go with Clifford," though he does begin with that. He pursues the issue, locating and exploiting the flaw in the logic of scientific verification. "The most useful investigator, because the most sensitive observer, is always he whose eager interest in one side of the question is balanced by an equally keen nervousness lest he become deceived." James does not use the word "nervousness" lightly or unintentionally. He goes on, "Science has organized this nervousness into a regular technique, her so-called method of verification; and she has fallen so deeply in love with the method that one may even say she has ceased to care for truth by itself at all. It is only truth as technically verified that interests her." Science is not interested in one-time-only events — in, for example, miracles. "The truth of truths," James says, "might come in merely affirmative form, and she would decline to touch it."[5]

Now James sets up the logical conditions for the hypothesis he is climbing toward. "Wherever a desired result is achieved by the cooperation of many independent persons, its existence as a fact is a pure consequence of the precursive faith in one another of those immediately concerned . . . A whole train of passengers (individually brave enough) will be looted by a few highwaymen, simply because the latter can count on one another, while each passenger fears that if he makes a movement of resistance, he will be shot before anyone else backs him up. If we believed that the whole car-full would rise at once with us, we should each severally rise, and train robbing would never even be attempted . . . There are, then, cases where a fact cannot come at all unless a preliminary faith exists in its coming."⁶

Nine of the ten sections of "The Will to Believe" exist solely to ground — to make live — the option or hypothesis offered in section ten. "What then do we now mean by the religious hypothesis?" James asks. "Science says things are; morality says some things are better than other things." Religion says, first, that "the best things are the more eternal things, the overlapping things, the things in the universe that throw the last stone . . . and say the final word." Second, and crucially, religion says, "We are better off even now if we believe her first affirmation to be true." It is true, you may be duped, but "dupery for dupery, what proof is there that dupery through hope is so much worse than dupery through fear?"⁷

Granting all this, the conclusion, for James, is inescapable: "This feeling, forced on us we know not whence, that by obstinately believing that there are gods (although not to do so would be so easy both for our logic and our life) we are doing the universe the deepest service we can, seems part of the living essence of the religious hypothesis."⁸

In June 1896, after classes were over, James pulled together a collection of his essays for possible publication as a book; his title from the start was *The Will to Believe and Other Essays in Popular Philosophy*. Thinking to stir up a little rivalry between publishers so as to profit from the competition, James sent the manuscript off to editors at Scribner with a letter asking them to make an offer, then sent the manuscript to Holt so he could make an offer too. Holt heard from James about this scheme and contacted Scribner, which then declined to join in competitive bidding. James got his Irish up over what he saw as Holt's undermining, and he fired off a stiff letter: "Your veto on the auction business has roused in me all the freeman-blood of my ancestors, and makes it now quite impossible to publish the book with you, when before it was not only possible but probable."⁹

The Will to Believe was published by Longmans, Green in early 1897; it was dedicated to "my old friend, Charles Sanders Peirce," acknowledging a debt to Peirce for "more incitement and help than I can express or repay." The ten essays in the volume had been written over a span of seventeen years. Four of them, "The Sentiment of Rationality," "Reflex Action and Theism," "Great Men and Their Environment," and "On Some Hegelisms," had been written before the fall of 1881. "The Dilemma of Determinism" was written in 1884, "The Importance of Individuals" in 1890, "The Moral Philosopher and the Moral Life" in 1891, and "What Psychical Research Has Accomplished" in 1892. The only recent works were the first two pieces in the book, "Is Life Worth Living?" and the title piece, which had grown out of "Is Life Worth Living?" and the not yet published "Gospel of Relaxation."

Any unity the book has is thus a result of consistencies in James's thinking over the years and the fact that nearly all the essays were written as talks for the same audience, college philosophy clubs. Parts of *The Will to Believe* look backward, then, to James's early work; its first four pieces focus on his present concerns (especially "defending the legitimacy of religious faith"); and the preface James wrote for the book, in December 1896, looks forward to radical empiricism and pluralism. Seen another way, this volume is our best warrant for saying that James was always interested in psychology, religion, and philosophy, and that what we are sometimes tempted to regard as a progression is simply the continual turning this way and that of a grand central concern that had all three facets for James.[10]

The preface makes clear that by late 1896 James regarded himself as having a "tolerably definite philosophic attitude," that of a radical empiricist committed to a pluralistic view of things. "I say 'empiricism' because it is contented to regard its most assured conclusions concerning matters of fact as hypotheses liable to modification in the course of future experience; and I say 'radical' because it treats the doctrine of monism itself as an hypothesis." James now believed that "the difference between monism and pluralism is perhaps the most pregnant of all the differences in philosophy," and he asserts that the world is, on the face of it, plural. Monism is, for James, the conviction — which he does not share — that the universe is at some level unified. Pluralism for him meant the possibility that the universe may be a pluriverse. It may be that we each apprehend a different aspect of the one true universe; it may also be that the universe itself is not a single system but a loose collection of many separate systems. He quotes his friend Benjamin Paul Blood, the homegrown philosopher-rhapsodist, for the clincher: "Not unfortunately the universe is wild — game flavored as a hawk's wing. Nature is miracle all; the same returns not, save to bring the different."[11]

Religious questions and interests moved more and more to the center for James in 1896 and 1897. A new correspondent, Henry Rankin — a librarian at the Mount Hermon School in western Massachusetts — sent James books and lists of books, and elicited from James some of his least coy and most direct descriptions of his own beliefs and intentions. "I am more interested in religion than in anything else," he wrote Rankin in January 1896, "but with a strange shyness of closing my hand on any definite symbols that might be too restrictive. So I cannot call myself a Christian, and indeed [I] go with my father in not being able to tolerate the notion of a selective personal relation between God's creatures and God himself as anything ultimate."[12]

In June 1896, just as he was sending off the manuscript of *The Will to Believe,* James wrote Rankin, "I envy you the completeness of your Christian faith, and the concreteness of association between your abstract theism and the Christian symbols." James reiterated his own problem, sounding a bit like his father and a bit like the Emerson of the "Divinity School Address." "Historic Christianity, with its ecclesiasticism and whatnot, stands between me and the imperishable strength and freshness of the original books." Then James revealed his hand: "I shall work out my destiny; and possibly as a mediator between scientific agnosticism and the religious view of the world (Christian or not) I may be more useful than if I were myself a positive Christian."[13]

Something about Rankin drew James out; many of James's best letters about religion went to Rankin. James's newness and freshness — in religion as in psychology and philosophy — comes from his steady prizing of religious experience itself, the actual experiences of real people, not from the housings and casings, not from the histories and habits and received formulas, of religious observances. It is entirely characteristic that some of his most brilliant and far-reaching ideas about religion should appear first not in essays and books but in letters to friends. His bold rethinking of conversion, for example, first shows up in a letter to Rankin early in 1897, just as *The Will to Believe* was being published. "In the matter of conversion," James wrote, "I am quite willing to believe that a new truth may be supernaturally revealed to a subject when he really asks. But I am sure that in many cases of conversion it is less a new truth than a new power gained over life by a truth always known."[14]

It was just like James to call attention to what conversion enables one to do, not to what conversion does to one.

58. High Tide

WILLIAM JAMES at fifty-five seemed a man of unlimited energy. He carried a full teaching load every year. He did an extra course at Radcliffe and lectured in the Harvard summer school and around the country. In 1897 he had one book coming out and two more in the works. His oldest son was at Harvard, on the staff of the *Crimson*. Billy, who turned fifteen this year, was as tall as his father. Peggy was ten, Tweedy (Aleck) seven. Alice was so busy with home and family she rarely traveled.

William was heavily involved in departmental politics and in great demand as a speaker and reviewer. He was hospitable, restless, a good friend, a good citizen, and more or less incapable of refusing any demand made on him. His life was a still accelerating whirl and blur, one long wild ride atop a stagecoach plunging blindly down a mountain road at midnight. His brother Harry marveled from afar at "the human deluge which seems to roll over you . . . so many nets out and raking the waters . . . Every glimpse you give me of your domestic life is a picture of heroic sacrifice, romantic charities, and acceptances of every one else's burdens. It is magnificent," he added, "if it doesn't kill you."[1]

William was already living at the high-tide mark, yet every day the water rose a little higher than the day before. Every time he settled down, a new wave would lift him and float him off. His life was exhausting; just tracing it is exhausting. In June 1896, as he was writing Henry Rankin about the mediating role he saw for himself, he was reading *War and Peace* with vast admiration, going briefly to Chatham on Cape Cod, trying out the mescal S. Weir Mitchell gave him. Mitchell, an acquaintance who was a novelist as well as a neurologist, promised "fairyland" and glorious visions of colors. James got only stomach pains and a hangover, and said, "I will take the visions on trust."[2]

In late June he wrote President Eliot to remind him that he'd promised to have electricity run to the psychology labs on the upper floors of Dane Hall. In early July he gave his teachers' talks for a Harvard summer school audience, then traveled west, staying six and a half days at Chautauqua, where he delivered an afternoon lecture to 1,200 people. He also heard John Dewey lecture on the imagination in education. Dewey was just hitting his stride at the new University of Chicago; James liked his talk very much and wished for more. But the uniform good will, undiluted uplift, and bread-baking sobersidedness of the irony-free Chautauquans annoyed James. "I've been meeting minds so earnest and helpless that it takes them ½ an hour to get from one idea to its immediately adjacent next neighbor . . . And when they've got to the next idea, they lie down on it with their whole weight and can get no farther, like a cow on a door mat, so that you can get neither in nor out with them." He yearned (playfully — need it be said?) for a little nutmeg of wickedness, "the flash of a pistol, a dagger, or a devilish eye, anything to break the unlovely level of 10,000 good people."[3]

After *War and Peace* he read *Anna Karenina,* which he thought "perfection in the representation of human life."[4] He went back to New England in early August, canceled a proposed trip to Nova Scotia, and spent ten days with Alice up at Intervale, near North Conway, New Hampshire (they had rented out the Chocorua place). In late August William returned to Cambridge, then snatched ten days in the Adirondacks, then went on to Chicago. "There is a great fermentation in 'paedagogy' at present in the U.S.," he wrote a friend. W. T. Harris, the old St. Louis Hegelian, was the U.S. commissioner of education; every year saw 350 new high schools in America. Dewey would publish his revolutionary credo, "My Pedagogic Creed," in 1897; James's talks to teachers were right in tune with the times.

In September he returned to Keene Valley for a blessed three weeks in the woods. His old friend Francis J. Child died. James had known Child, the great scholar of English and Scottish popular ballads and the founder of the modern Harvard English department, from his earliest days in Cambridge, when they had taken meals at the same boarding house. "I loved Child more than any man I know," he said. He read a book called *Riddles of the Sphinx* by F.C.S. Schiller and wrote the author an appreciative note. Schiller, an Englishman who was studying at Cornell, replied in late September. He was eager to sign up with James: "Need I say that you may count on me in every way in your prospective campaign against the Absolute." Schiller would soon become a valued friend and ally and the chief promoter of pragmatism in England.[5]

The fall term began. James taught two courses at Harvard: one on Kant, the other on abnormal psychology. The Kant course was Royce's; James and Royce had traded classes, and Royce taught psychology this year. James taught a third course, on the philosophy of nature, at Radcliffe. Twelve days into the term, James also began giving a series of Lowell Lectures in Boston on abnormal psychology that extended through the middle of November. In late October he had to beg President Eliot for two hundred dollars more for electrical work in the department. In November he gave a public lecture at Harvard on immortality. In December he was trying to mollify Holt by promising him the *Talks to Teachers* volume, waiting around for a visit from a young mathematician named Bertrand Russell, attending the annual meeting of the American Psychological Association in Boston to discuss the inheritance of acquired characteristics, and writing and delivering a long, generous portrait of Louis Agassiz for the American Society of Naturalists.

In 1897 Henry James brought out *The Spoils of Poynton* and *What Maisie Knew*, two of his liveliest, wittiest, and shortest novels. The younger generation of Jameses now began to appear in print. Ned James, Bob's son, published stories in the *Harvard Monthly;* Rosina Emmet had a story, "Alternating Currents," in *Harper's Weekly;* and William's son Henry James III had his first story, "Above the Trail," published in the *Harvard Advocate.*[6] William was swamped in desk work, trying to extract money from Eliot (this time for lab assistants), arrange summer teaching for himself at Berkeley, and lure Münsterberg back to Harvard from Germany. James did not want to have to reassume the burdens of practical — meaning laboratory — psychology. Boston dinner parties "kill regularly one or two evenings a week," he wrote Rosina.

Into this roiling pool of wildly diverse activities there now fell a clarifying drop. A letter arrived from the University of Aberdeen inquiring whether James would be interested in giving the Gifford Lectures there in 1898–1899 and 1899–1900. This put James in a ticklish situation. Lord Gifford had handsomely endowed two-year lectureships (ten lectures per year, usually given in January and February) at Edinburgh and at Aberdeen. The topic was always to be a "serious treatment of some aspect of Natural Religion."[7] James really wanted the Edinburgh Giffords; he had friends there, and Edinburgh carried more prestige. But he couldn't accept Edinburgh if he took Aberdeen, and he might lose both if he turned Aberdeen down. James had already been voted an honorary degree at Edinburgh, and he seems to have felt fairly sure of a Gifford invitation there; so he said no to Aberdeen, despite a wail of protest from Alice.

In February he gave a lecture to the New York Academy of Medicine, another at Vassar College, stopped over three nights at Newport, and went out to Concord to talk with Mary, Bob's wife. Bob was drinking again; apparently there was another woman. Bob's son, Ned, still at Harvard, had "cut" Alice in the street a couple of times, and he had quarreled with his father. James did what he could, reporting to Harry on all that and on the Syracuse property he still oversaw for the family.

Much of this he took in stride. At one point he even said this year was easier because he no longer had to worry about "practical psychology." When Münsterberg finally decided to return to Harvard — for good — James saw to it that he was named professor of psychology, and James was retitled professor of philosophy. This no doubt reflected James's desire to have Münsterberg feel that psychology at Harvard was his domain, rather than indicating any sudden shift in James's own concerns.

One new commitment that caused him a lot of work and worry was his agreeing to give a major address at the unveiling of Augustus Saint-Gaudens's Shaw Memorial in Boston. The monument, which stands opposite the statehouse on Beacon Street, is a large bronze frieze showing the black soldiers of the Massachusetts 54th and their colonel marching off to the Civil War. Booker T. Washington was also going to speak. James agonized over the address, which brought back all his old uncertainties about himself during the war. He delivered it on May 31, 1897, at the Boston Music Hall before a huge audience. The speech was "a great success," but he told his brother Harry it was a "schoolboy composition, in good taste enough, but academic and conventional." The whole event was "the last wave of the war breaking over Boston." He told Harry, "I will never accept such a job again."[8]

The mail brought letters from Charley Peirce, thanking James for the dedication of *The Will to Believe,* quarreling with most of the ideas, complaining about not having eaten "for very near three days," and proposing to write a physiology of misery. James's response was to stir himself to make arrangements and raise money for Peirce to give a private set of lectures in Cambridge. The mail also brought a letter from Jack Chapman, who complained about Royce: "I never heard a man talk so much nonsense in one evening . . . In art you 'imitate the ideal.' This ought to be stopped. He is misleading the youth. I see why they killed Socrates."[9]

Chapman was irascible, but at least he was amusing; he next wrote to shower abuse on *The Will to Believe.* "The faith you begin to talk about has been so justified and bolstered and drugged up and down and ironed and wired — Damme if I call that faith." James was delighted, and he roared right back: "Damme if I call that faith either . . . All this rubbish is for public purposes. In my individual heart I fully believe my faith is as robust as yours. The trouble about your robust and full-bodied faiths, however, is, that they begin to cut each other's throats too soon."[10] Less combative but even more helpful was Henry Rankin, who poured out names for James's reading, names that would figure prominently in *The Varieties of Religious Experience:* Charles Grandison Finney, Catherine Adorna, Catherine of

Siena, Saint Teresa of Ávila, John Bunyan, Mark Rutherford (William Hale White), David Brainerd, James Hudson Taylor, Sarah Pierrepont Edwards, John Wesley, George Whitfield.[11]

Other correspondence was less entertaining. One Charles Henry Fitler stretched James's by now legendary tolerance when he wrote in 1897 to send James the first of the 105 volumes, of 191 pages each, that he had written in the past few years. James briefly referred to "the idiotic Fitler" in a letter to Alice. Nothing further ensued.

When classes ended, James made a quick trip to Nova Scotia, then returned to Cambridge, while Alice settled in Chocorua. He rode his bicycle, shopped, went to receptions; he rushed up to Beverly, Massachusetts, for a weekend house party at Sarah Whitman's, where a steady stream of people poured in and out. James summarized it pithily for Alice: "Many callers called." This was the summer when, arriving at last at Chocorua himself, he wrote an old friend, "The constitutional disease from which I suffer is what the Germans call *Zerrissenheit* or *torntopieceshood*. The days are broken into pure zigzag and interruption."[12] They had guests to entertain. "Billy in bed with pleurisy and intercostal rheumatism caught by a drenching day on the Mountain. Tweedy entering into a similar spell, Alice with sick headache, visits from doctors, neighbors, haymakers, work to do on place and a lecture to write etc. etc." Nothing except 95 Irving Street seemed settled. William and Alice now seriously considered whether to buy a place in Keene Valley or hang on to Chocorua. Alice was for holding on; William had the land hunger again and wanted a place in the Adirondacks.

The children got better; James climbed Chocorua with all four in late August. In September he went to Keene Valley and walked over possible land with John Dewey, who had been attracted to the area by Tom Davidson's summer institute at Glenmore. He climbed Giant and Noonmark mountains. He wrote Sarah Orne Jewett to say how much he liked *The Country of the Pointed Firs*. Classes began again. His salary was now $5,000 a year; this year he made $1,158 in royalties from his psychology books, and for the first time he thought about cutting back his academic commitments. He wanted to teach two instead of three classes, and he wanted to do fewer public talks.

He was getting an invitation to speak in almost every mail; in one two-day period he got five requests. He was forced to decline most of them. At age fifty-five, James, like most people, had enough energy for the things he really wanted to do, but he no longer had unlimited energy. Even though he felt on principle that he had to respond to every demand on him or his springs would dry up, he began to look for areas in which to pull back a lit-tle. His life was a kind of existential pluralism: he didn't write and think as he did because he lived this way, he lived this way because he thought as he did. It would be impossible to change the life without changing the ideas.

One new idea he took up, in a lecture in November 1897, was that of "A Future Life," later retitled "Human Immortality." "How can we believe in life hereafter," he begins, "when Science has once for all attained to proving, beyond possibility of escape, that our inner life is a function of that famous material, the so-called 'gray matter' of our cerebral convolu-tions? How can the function possibly persist after its organ has undergone decay?"[13] James proposes, on what he modestly insists are mere logical grounds, that it is possible that the brain is more than the producer of thought. What if the brain is also the transmitter of some larger thought or life or mind that exists out there in the world? Transcendentalism, New Thought, mind cure, and Jungian thought all confidently embrace the no-tion that there is a "world soul," a "mother sea," a "greater consciousness" that includes but exceeds our normal consciousness. James will go no fur-ther than his cautious suggestion that such a larger life is possible, that it cannot be rejected out of hand.

Life kept throwing him challenges large and small. He was still trying to arrange for Peirce to lecture in Cambridge and begging him to talk on something besides logic, which James thought would interest few. Peirce replied in a balked rage of gratitude: he was stewing in misery, and writing, he said, in a room that was 34 degrees Fahrenheit — and insisting on logic as his subject. James had too much to read, writing to a friend, "One lives on an inclined plane of hopes as regards reading, on which like the snail of mental arithmetic one slips back more in 24 hours than one gains."[14] There was a new puppy; should they keep it or give it away? Zola's "J'accuse" roused the consciences of intellectuals everywhere. The Arctic explorer Fridtjof Nansen, who got closer to the north pole than anyone before him, lectured at Carnegie Hall; *there* was real courage and real discovery.

Santayana was up for promotion; James wrote an enthusiastic endorse-ment. "We shall always have 'hustlers' enough — but we shall not often have a chance at a Santayana, with his style, his subtlety of perception, and his cool-blooded truthfulness."[15] Santayana was duly promoted, becoming one of the quintet of philosophers that historians have in mind when they talk about the golden age of philosophy at Harvard. The students thought of them as characters in *The Three Musketeers*: "Royce, the all-knowing Athos; Münsterberg, the enthusiastic Porthos; Palmer, the subtle and diplomatic Aramis, always with some scheme in the making. James was the dashing, adventuresome D'Artagnan, while Santayana, who never quite belonged, was the remote and elegant Duke of Buckingham."[16]

Late in January 1898, the University of Edinburgh's senate voted to make James its Gifford Lecturer for 1899–1900 and 1900–1901. His friend at Edinburgh, Andrew Seth Pringle-Pattison, cabled him the news. The university would pay James £700 pounds, or $3,500, per set of ten lectures, usually given over a six-week stretch. There were no other duties. Alice wrote to tell Henry: "William takes this with his usual incredible modesty, but he knows in his heart that it really is a great honor."[17] James said little about the Giffords at first, but the prospect of having to prepare them began, right away, to figure importantly in his plans.

59. Walpurgisnacht

SOON AFTER THE "great honor" of the Gifford Lectures, classes began again at Harvard, on February 14. The following day the battleship *Maine* blew up and sank in Havana Harbor while moored to a buoy assigned it by the Havana port authorities. The American papers and the public leaped to the view that the explosion was external. James followed events closely, noting that the evidence for a hostile attack was "of the very slimmest."[1] On April 19 the U.S. Congress passed a resolution calling for the liberation of Cuba from Spain and pledging American withdrawal once Cuba was free. Two days later President McKinley sent an ultimatum to Spain, which replied by declaring war. James was at first not really opposed. He even thought intervention might be a good thing. America *should* help Cuba throw off colonial rule.

As William's spring term ended in Cambridge, his brother Harry was considering purchasing a house in the seaside village of Rye, southeast of London on the English Channel, with Hastings on one side and Romney Marsh on the other. William's son Henry was headed abroad, in part to visit his uncle. Billy had broken his wrist in a bicycle accident and was taking his entrance exam for Harvard. Peggy had plans to travel by herself to Chocorua and stay with her aunt and uncle. William sometimes ended letters home with an epistolary flourish; it might be a note for Aleck-Tweedy with his "ransy tansy tissimitee."[2]

After William finished reading final exams, he attended an anti-imperialist rally at Faneuil Hall in Boston on June 15. By then he had become thoroughly disillusioned about what John Hay called the "splendid little war," especially about the part of it that took place in the Philippines. "We had supposed ourselves," he wrote his friend the philosopher François Pillon, "a better nation morally than the rest . . . Dreams! . . . At the least temptation all the old military passions rise, and sweep everything before them." After the meeting James headed for the Adirondacks and a much-needed vacation.[3]

When he arrived in Lake Placid, he had a virulent cold with a fever and a runny nose — catarrh, as it was called. He wondered if it was something worse than a cold, and he told Alice he felt more depleted than in all but a very few Junes past. Alice replied tenderly to her "Dear Wandering William," offering to come and see him through the illness. But the cold passed, and he moved on June 25 to the next town south, on what is now Route 73, to the Adirondack Lodge in North Elba, close to John Brown's old farm. He began to take two-hour walks to the Ausable River and back, and quickly — almost miraculously — felt much better. "This place is an absolute sanctuary; never was such a feeling of peace and security known. The pure heavy redolent air seems loaded with repose, and the old and rather worn down but thoroughly comfortable house, all running now apparently just for me" — he was the only guest at the time — "seems like some magical providential provision. I sleep all right, read a great deal, and feel just as I ought to feel, neither depressed nor extra-hearty."[4]

He was reading with, he said, "great satisfaction" the *Journal* of George Fox, the seventeenth-century English founder of the Society of Friends. From an early age, Fox, who began as an apprentice to a shoemaker and wool dealer, experienced what he called "openings." At twenty-two he was "walking in a field on a first-day morning" when, he wrote, "the Lord opened to me that being bred at Oxford or Cambridge was not enough to fit and qualify men to be ministers of Christ." Instead of listening to the minister of his church, Fox went "into the orchards or the fields, with my Bible, by myself." He replied to those who questioned his approach, "Did not the apostle say to believers, that they needed no man to teach them, but as the anointing teacheth them?" Another opening provided Fox with another fundamental point: "It was opened in me that God, who made the world, did not dwell in temples made with hands . . . but that His people were his temple, and He dwelt in them." Christianity, for Fox, was not a matter of outward observance but of an inner light. James recommended the book to Alice, with the qualification that she read "skippingly."[5]

James took longer and longer hikes. He addressed a letter "to any member of the Goldmark Family," suggesting that whoever was around might organize a party and meet him on Mount Marcy. On June 30 he climbed Mount MacIntyre; it was three hours up and two down. Next day he climbed Mount Jo. Four days later it was a fourteen-mile walk south to Lake Colden and back. On July 7, with arrangements made by telegraph to meet Pauline Goldmark and some friends, James set out for Marcy.

Mount Marcy, due west of Keene Valley, rises 5,344 feet and is the highest point in New York State. It is in the middle of a great, wild region. Most of the area is now included in Adirondack State Park, which is the largest park in the United States, larger than Grand Canyon, Yellowstone, and Glacier national parks combined. James's extensive hiking — this July 7 trip in particular — was a wilderness trek comparable in some ways to Thoreau's adventures on and behind Katahdin a half century earlier. Mountain climbing was now, William told his brother, his "main hold on primeval sanity and health of soul."[6]

James left the Adirondack Lodge at seven A.M. with a guide and carrying an eighteen-pound pack. By noon he was on top of Mount Marcy, where he lingered. Around four in the afternoon, hearing the sound of an ax below, he went down the west side of Marcy to Panther Gorge Camp, where he found Pauline Goldmark, her brother Charles, Waldo Adler (the fifteen-year-old son of Felix Adler), another schoolboy, and two other Bryn Mawr girls. The six of them had just come from camping out at Loon Lake to the north.

That night in the camp, James had an extraordinary experience. "Quite unexpectedly to me," he wrote Alice, "the night turned out to be one of the most memorable of all my memorable experiences." He was wide awake; his companions (except for Adler) were asleep and motionless. "The guide had got a magnificent provision of firewood, the sky swept itself clear of every trace of cloud or vapor, the wind entirely ceased so that the fire smoke rose straight up to heaven. The temperature was perfect either inside or outside the cabin, the moon rose and hung above the scene before midnight, leaving only a few of the larger stars visible, and I got into a state of spiritual alertness of the most vital description."[7]

James had a hard time being very specific about the experience. "The influences of Nature, the wholesomeness of the people round me, especially the good Pauline, the thought of you" — he is writing Alice — "and the children, dear Harry on the wave, the problem of the Edinburgh lectures, all fermented within me till it became a regular *Walpurgis nacht*." Unable to sleep, he left the cabin and walked out into the night woods, "where the streaming moonlight lit up things in a magical checkered play, and it seemed as if the gods of all the nature-mythologies were holding an indescribable meeting in my breast with the moral gods of the inner life." James simply could not describe the significance of it all, only that it *was* extremely significant somehow. "The intense inhuman remoteness of its inner life, and yet the intense *appeal* of it; its everlasting freshness and its immemorial antiquity and decay . . . all whirled inexplicably together . . . It was one of the happiest lonesome nights of my existence and I understand now what a poet is. He is a person who can feel the immense complexity of influences that I felt and make some partial tracks in them for verbal statement."[8]

Describable or not, several things stand out. Whatever happened was in strong contrast to the cool logic and skillful argumentation of "Human Immortality." He had been reading George Fox; openings, or sudden illuminations, were on his mind. The experience was fundamentally inexpressible, yet it seemed to James that it involved real knowledge. James was always firm in insisting that he had not himself had mystical experiences; he was scrupulous to claim that he was just a seeker, never that he had found or seen the truth. Unlike Fox, he would not talk about things being opened to him. It is also notable that as he tries to tell his experience to Alice, he reverts to the upcoming lectures three separate times. "The Edinburgh lectures made quite a hitch ahead," he says of this night. Finally, he could say only that he was unable to "find a single word for all that significance, and don't know what it was significant of, so there it remains, a mere boulder of impression." But still he thinks of the lectures: "Doubtless in more ways than one though, things in the Edinburgh lectures will be traceable to it."[9]

Perhaps it wasn't a real mystical moment, but whatever it was, it seems to have been a triggering, originating, or catalyzing moment for *The Varieties of Religious Experience,* a moment of certain but inarticulable knowledge that real religion is religious feeling, and that it can be experienced by anyone, even a sleepless wanderer in the gorgeous Adirondack night.

The next day brought another life-changing experience, but this time it was a powerfully sobering one. The entire party set out on a tough bushwhacking and pathfinding hike cross-country to Keene Valley, a trek that William's son Henry identified as the "adventure that first strained WJ's heart." Henry later described "this arduous second day" in a note on his father's correspondence: "WJ let his guide carry things for the girls and added to his own pack what he had originally engaged his guide to carry for him. So he was heavily loaded. The girls probably had no understanding of the unwisdom of this for a man of WJ's age. My mother, who was unable to find Pauline Goldmark sympathetic, could never forgive her for thus absorbing WJ's guide."

The valleys run north and south in this part of the Adirondacks; the party's route lay due east. They climbed Mount Marcy — again — then went down its east side, up Bason Mountain, down the other side, then up and down the Gothics before reaching Putnam Camp. For William James it had been ten and a half hours of "the solidest walking I ever made, and I, I think, more fatigued than I have been after any walk."[10]

He was never quite the same physically after this mountain adventure, but he was, at least at the moment, exalted by the experience. He went to see Tom Davidson and his throng of adoring students at Glenmore, walked over some land he intended to buy north of Keene Valley near Elizabethtown, and wrote Pauline suggesting another trip soon. Then it was back to Cambridge to prepare for the trip to California, where he had been invited by his old friend Howison to deliver a lecture at Berkeley.

60. *California*

HE SET OUT FOR the West by rail, going first to Montreal and then to Banff. He was reading Melville's *Typee*. The Canadian Rockies, after the Adirondacks, appeared as "great palisades and fortifications thrown up against the sky, forming terrific precipices," but the whole scene seemed "so inhuman and hostile to life, that it is at first more terrible than engaging." Then it was on to Seattle, a scene of dust, heat, and black stumps, "rawness unspeakable." "It has all got to be ploughed under, like all the works of man and the men themselves of this generation, in the new west." In Washington and Oregon he saw evidence of fire everywhere. "The magnificent coniferous forests burnt and burning, as they have been for years and years back." By August 10 he was in San Francisco, his headquarters for the stay in California. He set out at once for the Mariposa Grove of giant trees and the nearby Yosemite Valley. He took a pack trip, slept out, saw coyotes; the trip was marred only by the heart palpitations he felt at 8,300 feet, which discouraged him from further climbing.[1]

Late in August he went to work, giving the talks he had come to give, which were to pay for the splendid trip. He began with "Philosophical Conceptions and Practical Results," presented to George Holmes Howison's Philosophical Union at Berkeley. Howison had designed the whole year's program around James's talk, which had been much discussed through the mails. Howison made it a great occasion; James gave the talk before eight hundred people in Berkeley's octagonal gym. The talk is famous as "the beginning of the pragmatist movement."[2]

Pragmatism is the philosophical notion, which quickly spread from its academic birthplace to the wider American culture, that the meaning of anything is to be found in its fruits, not its roots. It is results, not origins, that matter. James began with an image right out of his recent adventure: "No one like the pathfinder himself feels the immensity of the forest [of truth] or knows the accidentality of his own trails." For his own choice of trail, James went to Charles S. Peirce, whom he now called "one of the most original of contemporary thinkers," and the one who first enunciated "the principle of practicalism or pragmatism as he called it, . . . at Cambridge in the early 70s."

James proceeded to explain that principle in several different forms. "To develop a thought's meaning, we need only determine what conduct it is fitted to produce; that conduct is for us its sole significance." Then James expands it, trying for maximum clarity. "To attain perfect clearness in our thoughts of an object, then, we need only consider what effects of a conceivably practical kind the object may involve — what sensations we are to expect from it, and what reactions we must prepare. Our conception of these effects, then, is for us the whole of our conception of the object." Hoping perhaps that triangulation would offer precision, James restates it a third time: "The effective meaning of any philosophical proposition can always be brought down to some particular consequence, in our future practical experience, whether active or passive." This, for James, is a self-illuminating, self-demonstrating principle. In order to grasp its importance, he says, we "must get accustomed to applying it to concrete cases." If there is a dispute about, say, how many angels can dance on the head of a pin, and no possible answer can make any imaginable difference in any of our lives, then the dispute and the question are without meaning. "There can *be* no difference which doesn't *make* a difference," James says grandly, "no difference in abstract truth which does not express itself in a difference of concrete fact, and of conduct consequent upon the fact, imposed on somebody, somehow, somewhere, and somewhen."[3]

This, then, is James's first full statement of the pragmatic test, but he inserts it here only to suggest a method for approaching the main topic. The

377

rest of James's talk turns the light of this pragmatic principle on a religious problem — namely, whether theism or materialism gives the better explanation of our world. "Now the principle of practicalism says that the very meaning of the conception of God lies in those differences which must be made in our experience if the conception be true."[4]

James's little talk on pragmatism here takes a somewhat surprising turn as he examines the idea of the perfections of God as presented by orthodox textbooks. For theologians, God is a "being existing not only *per se*, or by himself, as created beings exist, but *a se*, or from himself; and out of the 'aseity' flow most of his perfections. He is, for example, necessary; absolute; infinite in all respects; and single. He is simple, not compounded of essence and existence, substance and accident, actuality and potentiality, or subject and attribute, as are other things. He belongs to no genus; he is inwardly and outwardly unalterable; he knows and wills all things, and first of all his own infinite self, in one indivisible eternal act. And he is absolutely self-sufficing and infinitely happy." With unusual pointedness, James turns on this kind of talk: "Now in which one of us practical Americans here assembled does this conglomeration of attributes awaken any sense of reality? And if in no one, then why not?"

This is the exasperated tone of a person for whom religion is real, and James moves out briskly, burning his theological bridges. Just as he was opposed to theories without facts in psychology, and opposed to metaphysical system-building and definitional branding in philosophy, so he was opposed to dogmatic theology in religion. In each case he wanted something closer to our actual experience. The "orthodox deduction of God's attributes is nothing but a shuffling and matching of pedantic dictionary-adjectives, aloof from morals, aloof from human needs, something that might be worked out from the mere word 'God' by a logical machine of wood and brass as well as by a man of flesh and blood . . . The attributes which I have quoted," he explains, "have absolutely nothing to do with religion, for religion is a living practical affair."[5]

James is not so rash as to dismiss all descriptions of God, noting, for example, that God's omniscience and justice do indeed have a practical application to life itself. "With the one he sees us in the dark, with the other he rewards and punishes what he sees." But James is relentless in his attack on abstract dogmatic theology. "What keeps religion going," he asserts, "is something else than abstract definitions and systems of logically concatenated adjectives, and something different from faculties of theology and their professors." This is his father's impatience with false religion, perhaps, but what William James now offers as real religion is his own idea.

"All these [abstract] things are after-effects, secondary accretions upon a mass of concrete religious experiences, connecting themselves with feeling and conduct that renew themselves [forever and ever] in the lives of humble private men." These experiences include "conversations with the unseen, voices and visions, responses to prayer, changes of heart, deliverances from fear, inflowings of help, assurances of support."

"Philosophical Conceptions and Practical Results" is an introduction before the fact to *The Varieties of Religious Experience*. "These direct experiences of a wider spiritual life with which our superficial consciousness is continuous, and with which it keeps up an intense commerce, form the primary mass of direct religious experience on which all hearsay religion rests, and which furnishes that notion of an ever-present God, out of which systematic theology thereupon proceeds to make capital in its own unreal pedantic way."[6]

James's lecture was popular, emotional, and, as he recognized, it was "a rehearsal for Edinburgh." He deprecated the talk, saying it represented only the mere margins of an idea, but his central concern was clear enough. Wendell Holmes had said that the life of the law had not been logic, it had been experience. James now said, similarly, that the life of religion is not theology, it is experience.

James had two more weeks to spend in California before heading home in mid-September. He saw the brand-new Stanford University and admired its campus, its tall, earnest farmer-president David Starr Jordan, and its coeducational commitment. He thought it would be good place for Billy and Peggy.

He also saw a good deal of Edwin Starbuck, who was an assistant professor of education at Stanford. Starbuck came from an old Nantucket Quaker whaling family. He had taken an M.A. in divinity at Harvard in 1895 and become keenly interested in the empirical study of religion, which he regarded as a new inductive science. "The psychology of religion," he wrote, "is a purely inductive study into the phenomenon of religion as shown in individual experience . . . The end in view is not to clarify and define the phenomena of religion, but to see into the laws and processes at work in the spiritual life."[7] Starbuck had painstakingly amassed a collection of statements about personal religious development. He would publish the first *Psychology of Religion* in 1899, and he generously gave James "a lot of his religious-experience material to use for my lectures, and will send me more later."[8]

In September James gave his teachers' talks in Berkeley. One of the people attending the evening lecture on psychology and relaxation, on the twelfth, was the western writer Mary Austin, who met and spoke with James. After the concentrated spurt of lecturing — eight lectures in four days — he was more than ready to go back home. "Do be alone in the house," he wrote Alice, "if *you can.*"

The trip to California, the impressive "Philosophical Conceptions and Practical Results," the Stanford visit, the teachers' talks, everything went well. It was, in its way, triumphant. He was famous, well received, and well paid. But the western trip had a curious effect, calling James's attention not to himself but to something else, something quite different and outside himself. To his brother Henry, off in London (Henry who had no concept of the Adirondacks, of Chautauqua, let alone of California), William wrote, "When one sees the great West one also feels how insignificant in the great mass of manually working humanity the handful of people are who live for the refinements." A month later he wrote Henry again: "These magnificent railroads and new settlements bring home to one the fact that all life rests so on the physical courage of the common man."[9]

61. *A Certain Blindness*

ON THE LAST DAY of September 1898, James wrote Henry Rankin to thank him for the shower of books, letters, and clippings. He was not, he told Rankin, "a Christian in the sense in which you are one, and yet in some way or other I shall probably come out not incongruously with your specifications." He had written nothing toward his Gifford Lectures, which were a little more than a year away, but he had thought about them constantly and did have a subject and an approach. "I mean them to be on the psychology of the religious consciousness, in its developed state, and not anthropological. I want to quote as many first-hand documents as I can of the different elements and factors that enter into man's religious needs." With his customary self-deprecation he added that his "serious education in the subject has all to be made in the next fourteen months."[1]

He was plunged back into full-time teaching, into Cambridge social life, and into the ever-expanding circle of admirers and their requests. No, he wouldn't come to nearby Brookline to lecture. But yes, he would write a preface for the English translation of his new friend Wincenty Lutoslawski's *Seelenmacht* (*A World of Souls*).

In late October he presented "On a Certain Blindness in Human Beings."[2] This talk, with its strong central image from Stevenson's "The Lantern Bearers," became for James a central statement. The blindness he means is "the truth . . . that we are doomed, by the fact that we are practical beings with very limited tasks to attend to, and special ideas to look after, to be absolutely blind and insensible to the inner feelings, and the whole inner significance of lives that are different from our own. Our opinion of the worth of such lives is absolutely wide of the mark, and unfit to be counted at all."[3]

When the book containing "On a Certain Blindness" was published, James sent a copy to Pauline Goldmark, saying he wanted her to read it, "because I care very much indeed for the truth it so inadequately tries by dint of innumerable quotations to express, and I like to imagine that you care for it, or will care for it too. What most horrifies me in life is our brutal ignorance of one another." To Elizabeth Glendower Evans he wrote even more plainly, calling "On a Certain Blindness" "the perception on which my whole individualistic philosophy is based."[4]

When the essay came out in book form — it was included in *Talks to Teachers* — James tried again in the preface to explain why its message meant so much to him. "The truth is too great for any one actual mind, even though that mind be dubbed 'the Absolute,' to know the whole of it. The facts and worths of life need many cognizers to take them in. There is no point of view absolutely public and universal." Again he drew out the political significance: "The practical consequence of such a philosophy is the well-known democratic respect for the sacredness of individuality — is, at any rate, the outward tolerance of whatever is not itself intolerant."[5]

During the first week of November 1898, James sent Henry Holt a letter and, the next day, the manuscript of *Talks to Teachers*. James was in a hurry. The *Atlantic* was going to publish many of the talks; *Scribner's Magazine* would print at least one. James wanted to know at once what Holt planned to do. Holt replied to the letter before even seeing the manuscript: he would publish it. He offered James 10 percent of the list price until he recovered his costs, and 20 percent thereafter. James responded as many an author has yearned to do but has lacked the nerve. He proposed to publish the book himself (edit, design, print, and bind it), then let Holt advertise and distribute the book and take 10 percent of the list price for his pains.

Publishers do not like this kind of talk. But Holt wanted the book.

James's royalties from Holt for 1898 for *The Principles of Psychology* and *Psychology: Briefer Course* came to $1,281.03. This was a substantial fraction of James's income, and it meant that his work had been very profitable for Holt. Besides, Holt liked James, so he wrote back that James could have it his way, only he would have to understand that teachers got a 20 percent discount and dealers got another 20 percent. James would manufacture the book and would receive either 50 percent of the retail price (the book was to sell for a dollar) or 60 percent of the net (defined as the teachers' price of 80 cents).

This arrangement cost James a huge amount of work and correspondence, as he worried about paper, design, type, binding, production schedules, bills, delivery and pickup, and coordination with Holt, who gleefully hounded James with details. Holt obviously wanted to make the whole process as difficult as possible so that James's cheekiness didn't spread to other authors. But the book appeared in April 1899, and in January 1900 James got word that the Indiana Teachers' Reading Circle had adopted it. This meant sales of between ten and fourteen thousand copies; James stood to make a minimum of $4,500 from this one adoption, and there were others to come. This was a great deal of money, more than the Giffords paid for a year and nearly the same as a year's salary at Harvard. *Talks to Teachers* freed James of money worries. His feisty, provocative, and unconventional publishing gamble had paid off, even though it was a nuisance to bring off. James had learned something, and when the *Varieties* was ready for publication, he made a similar deal with Longmans, Green.[6]

Ever since his *Walpurgisnacht* and the next day's overexertion, James had been experiencing "queer cardiac symptoms." He had first had heart palpitations while camping out in California. In November he reported to Howison, "My heart has been kicking about terribly of late, stopping and hurrying, and aching." He went to see a doctor, probably Jim Putnam, who picked up a murmur indicating a "slight valvular lesion." The same thing had been diagnosed in Wilky years before. James also described his present condition as "valvular insufficiency." He was shocked at the finding, he said, but he professed to be encouraged that he had no symptoms of impaired circulation.[7]

As the new year, 1899, turned, James was teaching, trying to look after his heart, and hoping to find time to work on his Giffords. In spite of the splendid large library on the ground floor of his home, James now preferred to write in the attic, which was a bare room fifty-two feet long with nothing in it but a chair, a table, and the work he brought up with him.

Royce was in Aberdeen giving *his* Giffords, which were published about a year later under the ambitious title *The World and the Individual*. In 1898 other ambitious Americans had charged up San Juan Hill in Cuba. The firing line was three miles long; Teddy Roosevelt and his much-heralded Rough Riders were there — on foot — and so were elements of the unheralded 10th U.S. Cavalry (the black "buffalo soldiers"). American ships sank the Spanish fleet off Santiago Harbor on the southern coast of the island, while Admiral Dewey defeated another Spanish fleet in Manila Bay in the Philippines. An American fleet on its way to the Philippines casually annexed Guam. The U.S. Army doubled in size overnight. Hawaii was annexed. Great Britain pressured China to open all its inland waterways to foreign commerce, signed a ninety-nine-year lease for the Kowloon Peninsula opposite Hong Kong, and sent Kitchener to Sudan to defeat Khalifa Abdullah and reconquer Khartoum. Russia was demanding Port Arthur and Dalian, the dominant ports of the Liaotung Peninsula, between northern China and Korea. Imperial expansion was everywhere; James found himself more and more opposed and drawn further and further into the fray. He attended mass meetings for anti-imperialist demonstrations, and over the next eighteen months he wrote and published six pieces against American policy in the Philippines.

The first salvo he fired off was the angriest article he had ever written. Called "The Philippine Tangle," it appeared in the *Boston Transcript* on February 26, 1899. After U.S. troops defeated and evicted the Spanish from the Philippines, James expected the Americans to recognize the local independence movement, made up largely of Tagalog people under Emilio Aguinaldo. But to the dismay of James and others, President McKinley refused to deal with Aguinaldo, kept him out of Manila, and bottled up his forces while installing an American protectorate to rule until the Filipinos proved "worthy of self-rule."

The battle against Aguinaldo would take three years and cost hundreds of thousands of Filipino lives. James was incensed at the American war spirit; he also felt, as did many, that American business interests were dictating foreign policy. Albert Beveridge, then running for the U.S. Senate from Indiana, talked about "the beginning of the commercial empire of the republic," and maintained that "the commercial supremacy of the republic means that this nation is to be the sovereign factor in the peace of the world."[8]

James's attack on American policy in the Philippines radiates outrage. "I have been cheered and encouraged at the almost unanimous dismay and horror I find individuals express in private conversation over the turn which things are taking," he wrote, adding that the most frequent comment he heard was "a national infamy." He noted what "an absolute savage and pirate the passion of military conquest always is," and he called the American treatment of Aguinaldo's movement "piracy positive and absolute," with the American people appearing as "pirates pure and simple."[9] He warmed to his subject: "We are now openly engaged in crushing out the sacredest thing in this great human world — the attempt of a people long enslaved to attain to the possession of itself, to organize its laws and government, to be free to follow its internal destinies according to its own ideals." He denounced what he called "war fever," "the pride which always refuses to back down when under fire," and the "belief . . . in a national destiny which must be 'big' at any cost." Responding to the popular notion that Americans should "take up the white man's burden," James erupts with rage and scorn: "Civilization is, then, the big, hollow, resounding, corrupting, sophisticating, confusing torrent of mere brutal momentum and irrationality that brings forth fruits like this! . . . The issue is perfectly plain at last. We are cold-bloodedly, wantonly and abominably destroying the soul of a people who never did us an atom of harm in their lives."[10]

All during the spring of 1899, his letters rumbled with impotent, inarticulate outbursts of fury and despair. "I am too heart-sick over the infamy of our Philippine conduct to care for much else," he wrote one friend. "The stars and stripes . . . are now a lying rag, pure and simple."[11] And it was now, while he was contemplating empire and expansion, that he came to detest what he called "mere bigness." He wrote about it to Sarah Whitman: "I am against bigness and greatness in all their forms; and with the invisible molecular moral forces that work from individual to individual, stealing in through the crannies of this world like so many soft rootlets or like the capillary oozing of water and yet rending the hardest monuments of man's pride, if you give them time."

James's vascular imagery, his "heart-sick" response, was deeply felt, deeply rooted in the family habit of strong language and perhaps even in his own physical condition. James trained his prose on imperial expansionism, but his own experience was with the ever-growing institution of Harvard, and while he does not say so here, Harvard's expansion would have given him no great satisfaction. "The bigger the unit you deal with, the hollower, the more brutal, the more mendacious is the life displayed. So I am against all big organizations as such, national ones first and foremost, and in favor of the eternal forces of truth which always work in the individual and immediately unsuccessful way, underdogs always, till history comes after they are long dead, and puts them on the top."[12]

James's anti-imperial activism was not incidental; it grew naturally from his advocacy of pluralism and individual self-determination and from his conviction that we are mostly blind to the vital centers of the lives of others — to the lives of, for example, Filipinos.

62. *The Logic of the Absolute*

ANOTHER FORM OF BIGNESS that James was still fighting against was what Josiah Royce and all the neo-Hegelians called the Absolute, a word by which they meant "that which is not relative . . . the ultimate principle of explanation of the universe."[1] Royce, who deeply believed in the existence of this abstraction, was delivering his Gifford Lectures at Aberdeen in January 1899, and well before they came out in book form, James sent him, in March of that year, a closely argued critique of the logic supporting the Absolute.

Royce and James were by now old friends. Royce, thirteen years younger, continued in his role as James's genial antagonist, the person who, more than any other, forced James to sharpen his arguments, focus his intellectual energies, and express his convictions. He and James were in daily contact, as Harvard faculty colleagues and Irving Street neighbors. For Royce, as he once told James, "Harvard originally meant to me *you*, and the old association remains still the deepest." For James, as he told his wife, Royce was "by far the biggest mind I have ever known." Royce attracted students; he was a nonstop talker, and he made abstract ideas seem alive and urgent. He had wit: John Charles Frémont, he said, "possessed all the qualities of genius except ability." He was available and engaged: Mary Calkins felt free to send him a list of problems she had with a recent talk of his. Another student recalled how Royce had told the students in his Hegel seminar that "to read Hegel you had to acquire his vocabulary, but you could do this only by reading him." The student added, "It was like going to a concert and being told that admission tickets would be given to you as you passed out."[2]

Royce's thought had, from start to finish, a strong community focus. In an early work, *California: A Study of American Character*, he wrote, "It is the State, the Social Order, that is divine. We are all dust, save as the social order gives us life."[3] At a gala dinner in his honor in 1915, Royce said, "I strongly feel that my deepest motives and problems have centered about the idea of the Community." He went further, maintaining that "we are saved through the community."⁴ He believed we ought not to seek to be happy as individuals, that individualism is "the sin against the holy ghost," that "nothing practical can be final."⁵ There is the spirit of William James's father in these statements; James's own views were a world apart from Royce's, yet for something like thirty years he read Royce, praised him, confronted him, disagreed with him, but always took him seriously over the course of their long, drawn-out "battle of the Absolute."

Royce, like F. H. Bradley, was a late-blooming Hegelian, though he disliked the label, which, as John Clendenning remarks, had become "another name for saintly pedantry." Royce preferred to describe his thought as "post-Kantian, empirically modified idealism, somewhat influenced by Hegelian, but also not uninfluenced by Schopenhauerian motives, with a dash of Fichte added."⁶ But Royce's thought was and is called absolute idealism, as is Hegel's. The most Hegelian period of Royce's life was the stretch of nine years from 1889 to 1898; during this time he taught an ongoing seminar in metaphysics on "the development of the Hegelian system with particular emphasis on the *Phänomenologie des Geistes*" (*Phenomenology of Spirit*). For Hegel, the Absolute is "the self-developing process of man's collective cultural and historical endeavors. As cultural beings, we all participate in the Absolute and share a part of it; conversely, the Absolute lives in and through our own cultural and historical actions."⁷

In *The Religious Aspect of Philosophy*, written in 1885, Royce advanced the argument that "to admit finite error implies absolute truth"; that "infinite error and evil are actual and are eternally so judged by an inclusive infinite thought." This inclusive infinite thought is the Absolute. Ten years later, in *The Conception of God*, Royce had reworked the idea to include the "experience" on which James always insisted. "There is an Absolute Experience," Royce wrote, "for which the conception of an absolute reality is fulfilled by the very contents that get presented to this experience. This Absolute Experience is related to our experience as an organic whole to its fragments." Student gossip at Harvard had it that Royce wrote his books in German, and then his wife translated them into English.⁸

Royce's Aberdeen lectures contained a further modification or expansion of the Absolute. "In my first book," Royce said, "the conception of the Absolute was defined in such wise as led me then to prefer, quite deliberately, the use of the term Thought as the best name for the final unity of the Absolute. While this term was there so defined as to make Thought inclusive of Will and of Experience, these latter terms were not emphasized prominently enough, and the aspects of the Absolute Life which they denote have since become more central in my own interests."[9]

James had not seen the printed version when, in March 1899, he sent Royce a detailed critique of the idealist logic he said Royce employed. Where once James had been content merely to poke fun at Hegelian thought, he seems to have realized that Hegelianism would have to be dealt with, and, if possible, on its own terms. It would no longer be enough to say simply that no such thing as the Absolute is needed to account for the world we experience — though that is James's real answer. The logic used by the proponents of the Absolute would have to be shown to be faulty. Hence the long letter or memorandum he sent to Royce. "Royce starts with fact *assumed* unknown," James wrote. "He ignores his idealistic principle ["where there is no knowing there is no fact"] by saying that there are no facts even though unknown." Echoing Royce's early argument that the existence of error implies there must be a truth to be wrong about, James accuses Royce of similar (Hegelian) logic: "To posit nothing is to posit being, and so on through the rigmarole . . . A thing completely is, only in so far forth as it has been mediated by the negation of its own negation."[10]

Royce waved all this aside in a detailed rebuttal he sent to James this same month of March 1899. "Well, these assumptions are yours not mine," Royce wrote, then moved to the attack. According to Royce, James was stuck with the argument that nothing true could be said about anything in the future because a fact had to exist before it could be true. "Do you mean," asked Royce, "to assert any of the following propositions? An astronomer's present assertion about the eclipses of the year 2000 is neither true nor false until these eclipses occur? . . . It is neither true nor false that you are to be absent from Harvard during the next year? What then were we talking about lately? Neither truth nor falsity? Nothing real?" And so on through "President Eliot will write Shakespeare's plays tomorrow."

James fought back in comments written on Royce's manuscript: "Neither true nor false, in the strict sense! For the facts that could make these hypotheses either true or false are non-existent as yet . . . Of course we practically treat them as true or false for ourselves." But Royce was not to be easily answered, and James knew it. As he planned out the Gifford Lectures, he tentatively called one of them "Demolish Royce."

Talks to Teachers came out in April 1899. Billy and Harry headed west for summer Forest Service jobs; William took off, as he had the previous year, to the Adirondack Lodge, in North Elba, New York. Although Alice was urging him by letter, for the sake of his health, not to argue and not to climb, he could not resist hiking. He climbed Mount Jo on June 17. The next day he took the Indian Pass Trail "very slowly." It was an eight-and-a-half-hour walk, after which he reported feeling his "good old solid elastic internal tone."[11] Two days later it was a seven-hour walk to Lake Colden and back via Avalanche Pass. Then on June 22 he set out to climb Mount Marcy, as he had the year before. Going down, he missed the trail back to North Elba and the lodge and found himself unexpectedly in the Johns Brook Valley. What should have been an easy three-hour downward saunter turned into an exhausting seven-hour up-and-down scramble. When he finally emerged at Keene Valley it was ten-fifteen at night, he had been out for thirteen hours, and he was feeling severe chest pains.[12]

At first he fudged the incident to Alice, writing her that he was "none the worse" for his outing, but in early July he told his sons that he had done himself "no good." Returning to Cambridge, he and Alice and Peggy departed almost at once (July 15) for Bad Nauheim, a spa in Germany that specialized in heart trouble. Bit by bit the truth leaked out in letters to friends. James had many connections at Harvard Medical School, and it is clear that he received the best available diagnosis and treatment. He had a mitral valve "insufficiency," detectable by a murmur. But now the heart was seriously enlarged (a "bad dilatation"), and he had "abominable subjective symptoms after even slight exertion." The conclusion was inescapable: James's heart was seriously damaged.

The treatment prescribed for James was complete rest for six to eight weeks. He was to make no rapid movements, he was not to get excited about anything. Certainly he was not to "ascend anything." He hated the regimen, calling it a "vile, inert, cowardly, professional-invalid life." All he did was "eat, sleep, bathe, read, and *crawl* around the Park," he wrote his youngest son, who had been left in Cambridge with his grandmother. Two days out of three, James took a *Sprudelstrom* bath. "It consists of a rush of water through your bath tub, escaping at the top, intensely salt, and fizzling as it touches you much like Apollinaris water, through the escape of the CO_2 gas."[13]

At the end of the third week of September, James seemed marginally better; he and Alice left Nauheim for Switzerland. Then, in early October, they went on to England, staying first at Harry's new house in Rye. By October 11, the day the Boer War broke out, they were in London at Harry's apartment, 34 De Vere Gardens. Two days later William wrote to Harry, who was still at Rye, "Gifford work actually begun, hurrah!"

But the cheering didn't last long. No sooner had he fairly begun — he had done essentially nothing except a little reading since the previous December — than he experienced a "regular thoracic collapse with the formidable chest pain which I had before I left America." The collapse was sudden, devastating, not easily explained. His heart, the doctors said, was no longer enlarged. There were new diagnoses of "lithaemia," "arterial degeneration," "undue dullness and pulsation under the clavicles," "aortic dullness."[14] Dr. Bezley Thorne thought James had "an exceedingly bad case of atheroma" (atherosclerosis). By December he was no better. Just reading a newspaper or dictating a note brought on "acute thoracic distress." But on reexamination, Dr. Thorne found James's "heart and aorta absolutely normal now in size," and suggested that the trouble was "a neurosis [that is, something neurological] more than a structural alteration."

Whatever it was exactly, it stopped James's work on the Gifford Lectures. He had, as of December 3, six pages written. Giving the lectures in January was obviously out of the question, and Edinburgh agreed to postpone both sets. James's letter to the Harvard authorities sums up his situation: "I regret to inform you that since last June I have been affected with a serious infirmity of the heart which has so increased as to unfit me for any work at present." The letter was dated two weeks before his fifty-eighth birthday.

63. Religion Is Real

I N   M I D - D E C E M B E R   1899, as the year, and in some minds the century, drained away, William James went to visit Henry in his rented place in Rye on the English Channel. William found it "a most exquisite collection of quaint little stage properties, three quarters of an acre of brick-walled English garden, little brick courts and outhouses, old-time kitchen and offices, panelled chambers and tiled fire places but all very simple and on a small scale." On December 23 he wrote Fanny Morse, the social worker friend of both William and Alice, that he and Alice had "lived down the solstice after which the year always seems a brighter, hopefuller thing."

His heart was, he thought, a little better, but only so long as he didn't try to walk. Nevertheless, at the end of December he seems to have put in an appearance at a party at Stephen Crane's tumbledown house, Brede Manor, some six miles from Rye. With abrupt telegraphic approval, James noted the party, which lasted for three days, was "entirely unenglish, unconventional, good missionary work." To a crowd of sixty, including Joseph Conrad and his wife, H. G. Wells and his wife, and lots of beautiful American girls all dancing away the night until two or three A.M., the Cranes served a midday breakfast of bacon, American sweet potatoes, and beer. Crane tried to teach Wells to play poker. Wells wouldn't concentrate and told stories during the game. "In any decent saloon in America, you'd be shot for talking like that at poker," said Crane.[1]

If James couldn't walk, he could at least read and write. Trying to keep up with the work of friends and students, he read Théodore Flournoy's *Des Indes à la Planète Mars* (*From India to the Planet Mars*) and Royce's *The World and the Individual,* and he wrote to President Eliot recommending Dickinson Miller and Ralph Barton Perry, a new Ph.D., for possible positions at Harvard.[2]

The Boer War was not going well for the English. An interdenominational church group declared January 7, 1900, a "Day of Humiliation and Prayer," presumably to ask the god of battles to intercede for the English. James wrote a letter to the London *Times* to suggest that "both sides to the controversy might be satisfied by a service arranged on principles suggested by the anecdote of the Montana settler who met a grizzly so formidable that he fell on his knees, saying, 'Oh Lord, I haint never yet asked ye for help, and aint agoing to ask ye for none now. But for pity's sake O Lord, don't help the Bear.'" The *Times* declined to print it.[3]

Things did seem to change after the winter solstice; good news tumbled in from all sides. James's Gifford invitation was reissued, with the dates pushed forward. This gave him a year — actually a year and a half, if needed — to get the first set of ten lectures ready. His friend Carl Stumpf told him he'd been proposed as a corresponding member of the German Akademie der Wissenschaft. Harvard granted him a second year off, with the unlooked-for additional offer of half pay. Holt wrote to tell him of the Indiana teachers' adopting *Talks to Teachers*. Best of all, James's health improved just as he passed his fifty-eighth birthday. He and Alice left London in mid-January for Hyères, a town in the south of France just west of St. Tropez. Robert Louis Stevenson had spent time at Hyères trying to mend his health. Now William and Alice moved in with F.W.H. Myers and his wife, Eveleen, and a Mrs. Rosalie Thompson, a charming medium Myers was interested in. By early February 1900 James was settled and, finally, back to work.

His overall plan, set out in a letter to Fanny Morse in December 1899, was a double-barreled project, a "perfectly bully pair of volumes." The first was to be "an Objective study of 'the Varieties of Religious Experience,'" and the second "my own last will and testament, setting forth the philoso-phy best adapted to normal religious needs." He thought of the second vol-ume as "The Tasks of Religious Philosophy."[4]

As he set to work in earnest on the Edinburgh lectures he was still think-ing of the project as a whole, writing Eliot about how he intended, in part two, to "destroy both [Royce] and the Absolute, at any rate give them an uncomfortable quarter of an hour." To Stumpf he wrote that he planned, in volume two, to defend radical pluralism and "tychism" (Peirce's snappy term for chance or freedom). But as the spring wore on, the subject of reli-gious experience gripped him more and more. By April he had written the first three lectures and was telling Fanny Morse:

> The problem I have set myself is a hard one; 1st to defend (against all the prejudices of my "class" [professional philosophers]), "experience" against "philosophy" as being the real backbone of the world's religious life — I mean prayer, guidance and all that sort of thing immediately and privately felt, as against high and noble general views of our destiny and the world's meaning; and second, to make the hearer or reader believe what I myself in-vincibly do believe, that although all the special manifestations of religion may have been absurd (I mean its creeds and theories) yet the life of it as a whole is mankind's most important function.[5]

He began by depreciating philosophers and lamenting the inability of philosophy and even of language to capture experience whole. The present moment, he said, "stands and contains and sums up all things: and all change is within it, much as the developing landscape with all its growth falls forever within the rear window-pane of the last car of a train that is speeding on its headlong way. This self-sustaining in the midst of self-removal which characterizes all reality and fact, is something absolutely foreign to the nature of language."

Despite this and other adroit turns of phrase ("Religion is the very inner citadel of human life"), James wisely abandoned this opening — why run down your tools and your trade as you set out to build your house? — and began again, not with the weakness of philosophy and the insufficiency of language but with the matter at hand. His subject, he said, was "not reli-gious institutions but rather religious feelings and religious impulses." It was not church history, not dogmatic theology, and not the anthropology of religion. "Interesting as the origins and early stages of a subject always are, yet when one seeks earnestly for its full significance, one must always look to its more completely evolved and perfect forms." James is intrigued, as always, with religious experience itself, religion as people feel it to exist, and he insists that he is after "existential facts" and "the purely existential point of view."[6]

We think of William James as an affirmer, like Emerson or Whitman, so it is sobering to note just how much of what one usually thinks of as religion James rejects at the start. He has no interest, he claims, in "your ordinary religious believer, who follows the conventional observances of his country, whether it be Buddhist, Christian, or Mohammedan. His religion has been made for him by others, communicated to him by tradition, determined to fixed forms by imitation and retained by habit." James was drawn to original or personal religious — or what is now called spiritual — feeling, not to the sociology of religious groups or institutions. "It would profit us little," he says, "to study this second-hand religious life. We must make search rather for the original experiences which were the pattern-setters to all this mass of suggested feeling and imitated conduct."[7]

This is not an elitist approach, merely a wish to apprehend primary and original religious feeling, whether of famous founders such as George Fox and John Wesley or of obscure workers in city missions. He wants the pattern setter, not the pattern. Fighting against what he saw as mere intellectual routines, James notes how "the first thing the intellect does with an object is to class it along with something else." Then, in a bright sally, he adds, "Probably a crab would be filled with a sense of personal outrage if it could hear us class it without ado or apology as a crustacean and thus dispose of it. 'I am no such thing,' it would say; 'I am MYSELF, MYSELF alone.'"[8]

James further refuses what he bluntly calls "medical materialism," the view that the spiritual authority of a Saint Teresa can be undermined by classing her as a hysteric, that of a Saint Francis by calling him a hereditary degenerate, that of a George Fox by pointing to his disordered colon. "In the natural sciences and industrial arts it never occurs to anyone to try to refute opinions by showing up their author's neurotic constitution . . . It should be no otherwise with religious opinions."[9]

None of the reductive explanations of medical materialism can stand up to actual experience on its own ground. James moves on briskly to say, "*Immediate luminousness . . . philosophical reasonableness* and *moral helpfulness* [his italics] are the only available criteria" for judging religious experience. The continuing authority of James's own work comes in large part from his steady insistence on asking what the effect is of this or that religious belief on our own lives. His mantra is "By their fruits ye shall know them, not by their roots."

Religion, like medicine or chemistry or anything else, must be evaluated by its results or outcomes, its effect on people's lives. James shrewdly points out that this may be pragmatism, but it is not just modern psychological sleight of mind; it is the preferred yardstick of no less a figure than Jonathan Edwards, whom James now quotes. "There is not one grace of the Spirit of God," Edwards wrote, "of the existence of which, in any [believer], Christian practice is not the most decisive evidence." James has not yet made his argument, only announced what it is to be, but he was never above having a little fun with his audience. So it is comically premature but still disarming when he says, "You must all be ready now to judge the religious life by its results exclusively, and I shall assume that the bugaboo of morbid origins will scandalize your piety no more."[10]

He was, at long last, working well. By the end of March he had finished the second lecture. In this one, too, he continued rather sharply with his philosophical *via negativa*, his clear statement of what he was *not* doing. He dismisses premature efforts to delineate the essence of religion. "The theorizing mind," he says mildly, "tends always towards the oversimplification of its materials." He rejects as well the notion that there is such a thing as *the* religious sentiment. "There is," he says, "no ground for assuming a simple abstract religious emotion to exist . . . by itself, present in every religious experience without exception." James's refusal to privilege (as we say today) one religious emotion over others seems straightforward enough, but it has long consequences. "As there thus seems to be no one elementary religious emotion, but only a common storehouse of emotions upon which religious objects may draw, so there might conceivably also prove to be no one specific and essential kind of religious object, and no one specific and essential kind of religious act."[11]

James repeats his intention to distinguish between institutional and personal religion. "Churches," he says, "live at second-hand upon tradition; but the founders of every church owed their power originally to the fact of their direct personal communion with the divine. Now in these lectures I propose to ignore the institutional branch entirely, to say nothing of the ecclesiastical organization, to consider as little as possible the systematic theology and the ideas about the gods themselves, and to confine myself as far as I can to personal religion pure and simple." It is perhaps needless to say that James continues to be attacked by church leaders and systematic theologians for his failure to start where they start. James is making a radical departure, more radical even than that of Friedrich Schleiermacher, who sought to show that religion resided in human feelings, but who insisted that no religious experience was complete until it was communicated to another person.[12]

Lecture two swerves from what James will not do to what he will do. He explains what he means by divine ("not a deity *in concreto,* not a superhuman person, but the immanent divinity in things, the essentially spiritual structure of the universe"), and he points to Emersonian and American transcendentalism for a working example. James is careful — as his father was — to separate religious feeling from matters of morality.[13] He takes pains to distinguish between the essentially moral teachings of classical Stoicism — compatible as it may be with Christianity, and with which he had long had some sympathy — and something different that the religious person alone possesses. "There is a state of mind," says James, "known to religious men, but to no others, in which the will to assert ourselves and hold our own has been displaced by a willingness to close our mouths and be as nothing in the floods and waterspouts of God."[14]

This is decidedly not Stoicism.

64. *The Religion of Healthy-Mindedness*

LIFE IN HYÈRES with the Myerses had its distractions. Mrs. Thompson, the medium, gave sittings. Eveleen Myers cold-shouldered Mrs. Thompson. Fred Myers tried to make peace. Eveleen turned to Alice James for support, but Alice despised Eveleen's highhandedness. William wrote home with items from the sittings for his eldest son to verify for him: "what Mrs. Dunbar's full name was; whether D walked latterly with a stick."[1] In England, Peggy, now fourteen, was staying with a family and finding it very difficult. She was sometimes subject to low spirits — depression, we would call it. The word and the condition existed then, but William did not use it in this instance. He wrote Peggy long, encouraging, loving letters full of well-intended advice. He also wrote letters home, dictating often to Alice.

Mainly, however, he kept at his task. By mid-April he had completed lecture three, "The Reality of the Unseen," which is essentially a defense of intuition as coming from a deeper place in us than pure reason does. For James, the era of dogmatic theology is over; he boldly and perhaps mischievously announces the closing of the era of natural theology, "that vast literature of proofs of God's existence drawn from the order of nature," which relied on reason for its persuasiveness. "The truth is," James says, "that in the metaphysical and religious sphere, articulate reasons are cogent for us only when our inarticulate feelings of reality have already been impressed in favor of the same conclusion."[2]

People able to register and respect these inner loomings report strong impressions of the active presence of invisible powers, often called God. Never willing to trust his argument to mere abstract statement, James confronts the reader with fifteen examples, in quotations — often at length — of firsthand accounts of such experiences. Many of these illustrative narratives came from friends and colleagues. The effect of this lavish use of case histories, carefully chosen and edited for their detail and vividness — a method James uses throughout the lectures — is to offer a collection of stories rather than a logical argument. Much of the interest and the conviction called out by the *Varieties* comes from this steady stream of skillfully edited firsthand accounts.

One has to go back to Fox's *Book of Martyrs* to find a comparable example of religious writing that rests its entire enterprise on narrative testimony. Here is part of just one example, from lecture three: "I had a revelation last Friday evening. I was at Mary's, and happening to say something of the presence of spirits (of whom, I said, I was often dimly aware), Mr. Putnam entered into an argument with me on spiritual matters. As I was speaking the whole system rose up before me like a vague Destiny looming from the abyss. I never before so clearly felt the Spirit of God in me and around me. The whole room seemed to me full of God. The air seemed to waver to and fro with the presence of Something I knew not what."[3]

That these feelings — intuitions — come from something other than daylight reason does not disqualify them as valid experiences. James is at some pains to show that these "unreasoned and immediate assurance[s]" are "the deep thing in us, the [reasoned] argument is but a surface exhibition." He shares with Melville a sense that the world revealed by these intuitive glimpses is not always a carefree and happy one, but a world of unplumbed depths and powers. "It were sparrowlike and childish after our deliverance to explode into twittering laughter and caper-cutting, and utterly to forget the immanent hawk on the bough."[4]

In mid-April, with three lectures out of ten written, James's fragile health collapsed again; he decided to take ten weeks off from work to seek help. He and Alice traveled restlessly from city to city, consulting many doctors and other healers. The consensus was that his heart was no longer enlarged. His condition was diagnosed as "aortic-sclerosis." He went to Geneva, then back to Nauheim for more baths, but the first few treatments made him so much worse that he fled.

Peggy was still having trouble at school in England. James wrote her long letters, noting that, since she was developing an inner life, "there will be waves of terrible sadness, which last sometimes for days; and dissatisfaction with oneself, and irritation at others, and anger at circumstances and stony insensibility, etc. etc., which taken together form a melancholy." It must have seemed at times like the old James family curse. It appeared that William's chief problem once again was "nervous prostration." Even brother Henry, who had boundless sympathy for William's physical miseries, became convinced that "your nervous conditions are your worst ones." Hardly knowing where to turn or what to do, William and Alice went to Lucerne in mid-July, where William finally got back to work on lecture four, "The Religion of Healthy-Mindedness."[5]

His approach, his strategy for presenting the material, was now firmly established. For each major point he provided a series of examples; each example was a quotation, often lengthy, from a personal account. The effect on a hearer or reader is of an ever-swelling crowd of witnesses, a growing accumulation of firsthand testimony, all with the authority of personal conviction. The lectures, as given and as printed, are, as a whole, a large, democratic assembly of voices, some very well known and some very obscure.

Tolstoy and Bunyan and Saint Augustine take their places alongside Henry Alline and Billy Bray. Emerson, Alphonse Daudet, and Annie Besant rub shoulders with Lutfullah (a "Mohammedan Gentleman"), Henry James Sr., and Mary Moody Emerson. James quotes from the Greek Anthology (a collection of Greek epigrams ranging from the seventh century B.C.E. to the tenth century C.E.), Robert Louis Stevenson, Luther, Sophocles, Goethe, Miguel de Molinos, and Spinoza. Horatio Dresser, Ralph Waldo Trine, and Annie Payson Call are represented, as are Jonathan Edwards, Sarah Pierrepont Edwards, David Brainerd, Jakob Böehme, and Mary Baker Eddy. Walt Whitman, Richard Maurice Bucke, Marie Bashkirtseff, Bernardin de Saint-Pierre, Saint Teresa, Mme. Ackerman, and Marie Hare are all brought before the reader or hearer, most in their own voices, a few by report. James summons up Plato, Havelock Ellis, Kant, Margaret Fuller, Marcus Aurelius, Henry Thoreau, Thomas Lake Harris, and George Fox.

The approach is anything but elite, unless James's rejection of secondhand experience is so considered. His book gives a courteous hearing to great saints, famous poets, itinerant preachers, illiterate converts, streetmission workers, anonymous responders to questionnaires, and Victorian gentlemen with three names. If someone were to object that James has left out or scanted certain religions or persons, he would, on his own principles, be the first to agree to add their testimony. If his conclusions seem founded on too narrow a base, his own method would urge us to extend the base. There cannot be too much diversity for one whose main point is the diversity of possible experiences.

James could speak slightingly of his own scissors-and-paste technique, but the practical result of presenting a wide sampling of voices is to give these lectures an authority no logical argument could match for immediacy, conviction, personal intensity, and sheer range of articulated experience. Fifty-five different sources are cited or quoted in the mysticism lecture alone, for instance, and forty-seven in the two lectures on the religion of healthy-mindedness. Such a mass of testimony is not easily talked down by general propositions.

James begins his survey of healthy-mindedness with a distinction borrowed from Francis W. Newman, brother of Cardinal John Henry Newman. "God has two families of children on this earth, *the once born* and *the twice born*." The once-born are happy souls from their earliest years, people who, "when unhappiness is offered or proposed to them, positively refuse to feel it"; they are the people "who seem to have started in life with a bottle or two of champagne inscribed to them," those who "see God, not as a strict judge, not as a glorious potentate, but as the animating Spirit of a beautiful harmonious world."[6]

James offers as examples of the once-born Rousseau and Diderot and other "leaders of the eighteenth century anti-Christian movement," but he gives a special place to Emerson, Theodore Parker, and, above all, Walt Whitman. Whitman he calls "the supreme contemporary example of such an inability to feel evil." James distinguished involuntary healthy-mindedness — "a way of feeling happy about things immediately" — from systematic healthy-mindedness, which is "an abstract way of conceiving things as good." He credits "the advance of liberalism, so-called, in Christianity of the past fifty years" as a victory for healthy-mindedness, then moves to an emphatic and extended defense of the "mind-cure movement" as another example. He cites his own "Gospel of Relaxation" and books by Annie Payson Call, Horatio Dresser, Horace Fletcher, and Ralph Waldo Trine. He includes the "Don't Worry Movement," "Divine Healing," and Christian Science. For a man who thought less of roots than of fruits, James takes unusual care to list the doctrinal sources of mind cure, almost as if that would legitimize it. The sources are the four Gospels, plus Emersonianism, Berkeleyan idealism, "Spiritism," the "optimistic popular science evolutionism," and Hinduism. He insists that it is impossible "not to class mind-cure as primarily a religious movement."[7]

It is one of James's greatest gifts that he can recognize the authentic spiritual strengths in popular manifestations such as mind cure, manifestations that are so easily dismissed or condescended to. Perhaps one aspect of being healthy-minded is the belief that anything really popular must have *something* to it. Even that grouchy naysayer Thomas Carlyle once conceded as much.[8] At any rate, James's positive treatment of mind cure helps to redeem for us the idea of suggestion (often used in a dismissive way, as in "mere power of suggestion"); James insists that "suggestion is only another name for the power of ideas, so far as they prove efficacious over belief and conduct."

For James it was another point in favor of mind cure that it "has made . . . an unprecedentedly great use of the subconscious life," and he argued that whatever one thought of mind cure, its results were incontrovertible. "It makes no difference," he says provocatively, "whether you consider the patients to be deluded victims of their imaginations or not. That they seemed to *themselves* to have been cured by the experiments tried was enough to make them converts to the system."[9] When a person feels better because he thinks he has been given a cure, we call it, with complacent condescension, the placebo effect. For James, however, that same effect is simply a cure. You may still have a fatal disease, but if you feel better, you are better, if only by that feeling. It helps no one to underestimate the power of such feelings.

65. *The Sick Soul: Slouching Toward Edinburgh*

NOTHING IN WILLIAM JAMES'S writings is more effective, more disarming, more surprising than the turn he gave to the next lecture. Having convinced the reader that he is firmly of the party of the healthy-minded, James doubles back to make the case for the twice-born, the sick souls, those who have "a way of maximizing evil, if you please so to call it." It is the outlook "based on the persuasion that the evil aspects of our life are of its very essence."

If it is true that "the sanguine and healthy-minded live habitually on the sunny side of their misery-line" ("misery-threshold" he also calls it), it is also true that the sick souls, "the depressed and melancholy" souls, live beyond it in the other direction, "in darkness and apprehension." And here, James suggests, may lie the deeper truth, the truer account of how things are. "Unsuspectedly from the bottom of every fountain of pleasure, as the old poet said, something bitter rises up, a touch of nausea, a falling dead of the delight, a whiff of melancholy, things that sound a knell; for, fugitive as they may be, they bring a feeling of coming from a deeper region and often have an appalling convincingness." Robert Louis Stevenson knew the same thing: "There is indeed one element in human destiny that not blindness itself can controvert; whatever else we are intended to do, we are not intended to succeed; failure is the fate allotted."

That being the case, it is little wonder, says James, that theologians dwell so on failure, lack, dearth, and sin. There is a certain sadness that "lies at the heart of every merely positivistic, agnostic, or naturalistic scheme of philosophy." Seen from the point of view of naturalism, says James, "mankind is . . . a set of people living on a frozen lake surrounded by cliffs over which there is no escape, yet knowing that little by little the ice is melting."[1] Jonathan Edwards himself could not have put the predicament of natural man more vividly.

One curious thing about the sick soul is that it is possible for it to convert its outlook to the opposite one, though the process is generally harrowing. "The securest way to the rapturous sorts of happiness of which the twice-born make report has as an historic matter of fact been through a more radical pessimism than anything that we have yet considered." James quotes extensively from the experiences of Tolstoy, Bunyan, and Henry Alline, then moves to take up what he considers the "worst kind of melancholy . . . that which takes the form of panic fear." He quotes his own experience of years earlier when he "went one evening into a dressing room in the twilight to procure some article that was there, when suddenly there fell upon me without any warning, just as if it came out of the darkness, a horrible fear of my own existence."[2]

This devastating incident from his own life serves as James's ultimate example of the extreme state of the sick soul, presenting us squarely with "not the conception or intellectual perception of evil, but the grisly blood-freezing heart-palsying sensation of it close upon one, and no other conception or sensation able to live for a moment in its presence." We can get no further down. This is the bottom. "Here," says James, "is the real core of the religious problem. Help! Help! No prophet can claim to bring a final message unless he says things that will have a sound of reality in the ears of victims such as these."[3]

This, then, is the profounder view, ranging over and acknowledging a wider, deeper, grimmer, and more generally shared experience than healthy-mindedness. And perhaps the worst thing about the sickness is how it embeds itself in the commonest parts of life. "The normal process of life," says James, "contains moments as bad as any of those which insane melancholy is filled with, moments in which radical evil gets its innings and takes its solid turn. The lunatic's visions of horror are all drawn from the material of daily fact. Our civilization is founded on the shambles, and every individual existence goes out in a lonely spasm of helpless agony. If you protest, my friend, wait till you arrive there yourself! To believe in the carnivorous reptiles of geologic time is hard for our imagination — they seem too much like mere museum specimens. Yet there is no tooth in any one of those museum-skulls that did not daily through long years of the foretime hold fast to the body struggling in despair of some fated living victim."[4]

With "The Sick Soul" James's Gifford Lectures reached their full power and conviction, and his work here joins that of Bunyan and Tolstoy — on whom he leans so heavily — as a major testimonial to the darkness of mind that precedes, complicates, and ultimately leads — sometimes — to the change commonly called conversion.

James had written his lecture on healthy-mindedness back in July 1900. He was unable to complete this next one, on the sick soul, until mid-November. The intervening months were trying ones. In August his doctor peremptorily ordered James back to Bad Nauheim for treatment; James fell into his "Nauheim depression." His blood pressure rose, and he had, he said, "*no strength at all.*" He told Alice, "I have rarely felt more weak and depressed." His friend Henry Sidgwick died at the end of August; two weeks later his dearer and older friend Tom Davidson died. These losses didn't help matters, but they came *after* James's mental and physical collapse and thus had no part in its onset. We cannot "explain" the darkness of James's writing on the sick soul by pointing to current events in his life. It seems more likely that the reexamination of his long-held ideas about evil or the revived memory of the green-skinned idiot in the asylum cast its old pall over his present life. It is not so much that the life influences the work, as that, in James's case anyway, the work is always influencing the life.[5]

The gaseous baths seemed to do no good. He was pushed about in a wheelchair. Dr. Baldwin showed up in Nauheim and treated James with Roberts-Hawley injections, which were to be kept secret from the other doctors. The injections contained "goat's lymph from thoracic duct, the juice of lymphatic glands and brain substance, and testicles — not a glycerine or other solution as in Brown-Sequard's extract, but the straight material sterilized by a process which is the inventor's secret." William told

Henry about the new treatment. Henry exuded sympathy: "Oh your poor distracted doctor-ridden carcase." In a state of advanced and chronic exasperation, William wrote Jim Putnam, "Although I have no confidence in three-quarters of what the doctors tell me, I have so little independent hold on the situation that I am hypnotized by the remaining quarter, and by the prestige of their authority and obey their orders."[6]

By contrast, Henry's life was stabilizing nicely. In early October 1900 he signed papers to buy Lamb House in Rye, and he signed a contract for a novel to be called *The Wings of the Dove*. Also in October William committed himself to begin lecturing at Edinburgh in mid-May 1901; at the same time he told Henry, "I have resigned irrevocably from the second course [of lectures], which under no circumstances, however favorable, could I in the time now left hope to get ready by the . . . date appointed."

Told by his doctors not to return to England with winter coming, James went to Rome, where he had "three acute knock-downs of catarrhal and intestinal disturbance with fever," each one lasting a week, but he kept grimly at work, finishing the lecture on the sick soul in mid-November, and the next one, on the divided self, by December 10. But the end of December brought yet another crash. "My nerves have all gone to pot, and I really feel 'kind o' OLD' as the Adirondack guides say when they wake up in the morning after a night of tending the campfire. My intellectual vitality seems for the first time to have given out . . . The fact is that my nervous system is utter trash, and always was so." As of January 1, the first day of the new century, James calculated that he had four lectures left to write. But by January 9 he had finished the one on conversion.[7]

James's friend F.W.H. Myers — a year younger than James and already very sick with a bad heart and arteries and an associated respiratory problem called Cheyne-Stokes breathing — contracted double pneumonia and died in Rome on January 17. James wrote Eleanor Sidgwick (the widow of his friend Henry Sidgwick and a close friend of the Myerses) that, instead of the usual sickroom atmosphere of "physical misery and moral suffering," Myers's eagerness to go, and his mental clarity up to the time the death agony began, had been a "superb" thing to see, "a demonstration *ad oculos* of the practical influence of a living belief in future existence."

James was, in part, putting on a good front. Another glimpse of the effect of Myers's death on James is provided by a young doctor, Axel Munthe, who, along with Baldwin, attended Myers. Munthe says, in *The Story of San Michele*, that he saw James sitting with notebook and pencil outside the room in which Myers was dying, waiting for some communication from the other side. "When I went away William James was still sitting leaning back in his chair, his hands over his face, his open notebook on his knees. The page was blank."[8]

By the end of January, as he turned to think about the actual giving of the Edinburgh lectures, James realized that while he hadn't completed his outline, he already had enough written to fill ten lectures. The material on healthy-mindedness had grown by the addition of examples to fill two lectures; the same thing happened with the sick-soul material. The contents of the conversion lecture — if we include the consideration of "the Divided Self, and the process of its unification" as an introduction to the subject — would require three lectures and would complete the first series of talks. Apparently James could now see that his ideas about saintliness, mysticism, the philosophy of religion, and some conclusions might easily grow into a further ten lectures. As significant as the expansion of the early part of the subject is the corresponding shrinkage — or perhaps it was just a postponement — of the later part. The philosophy of religion, which James had once envisioned as the subject of the entire second set of talks — half the whole enterprise — would now contract to one tenth of the second series, or one twentieth of the whole.

Spring of 1901 brought another stretch of poor health for James. He told Eveleen Myers he was very short of breath and feeling as if his breast were "shot in two." He complained of continued neuralgia. He dreaded the social side of the coming Edinburgh visit; he wrote ahead to his hosts that dinners and afternoon receptions were out of the question. He looked forward to regaining his equilibrium "after the Edinburgh nightmare is over." He felt more and more like an exile; he and Alice had been abroad for almost two years straight.[9]

He touched up lecture two at Henry's house in Rye, where Henry's new secretary set to work typing William's lectures. In early May his son Harry arrived from the United States. On May 14 William and Alice and young Harry went to Edinburgh.

66. *The Twice-Born*

E DINBURGH IS SURELY the noblest city ever built by man." James saw it with his artist's eye. "The full bodied air, half misty and half smoky holds the sunshine in that way which one sees only in these islands, making the shadowy side of everything quite black. So that all perspectives and vistas appear with objects cut blackly against each other according to their nearness, and plane rising behind plane of flat dark relieved against flat light in ever receding gradation. It is magnificent."[1]

That is not a bad description of his lectures, with their strong contrasts and hard dark edges, with plane rising behind plane. The audience for his first lecture, 250 people, was larger than expected and "exceedingly sympathetic, laughing at everything — even whenever I used a polysyllabic word." The ten lectures were spaced over a month; his health held, more or less. By the fourth lecture (first of the two on healthy-mindedness) his audience was increasing, and he was taking digitalis, going for open drives every afternoon, and resting in bed between lectures. The final three were on conversion.[2]

James's consideration of conversion rises naturally out of his account of the sick soul. Perhaps the chief thing about a sick soul is its divided quality. Conversion is the process by which the sick, divided, or scattered soul, "consciously wrong, inferior and unhappy, becomes unified and consciously right, superior, and happy" — integrated, as we would say — "in consequence of its firmer hold upon religious realities."

This is conversion in its narrow sense; it is preceded and importantly qualified by James's insistence that "to find religion is only one out of many ways of reaching unity; and the process of remedying inner incompleteness and reducing inner discord is a general psychological process." Indeed, he wrote, becoming religious is only one of the types of regeneration; "the new birth may be away from religion," toward unbelief. He even quotes an account of a man who becomes "converted" to avarice. It is also important to note that the sick soul is not, in many cases, changed by conversion into happy healthy-mindedness. "Neither Bunyan nor Tolstoy," James reminds us, "could become what we have called healthy-minded. They had drunk too deeply of the cup of bitterness ever to forget its taste, and their redemption is into a universe two stories deep. Each of them realized a good which broke the effective edge of his sadness, yet the sadness was preserved as a minor ingredient in the heart of the faith by which it was overcome." If there was one thing James understood all the way down, it was the persistence of sadness — it shows in every photograph taken of him — even in all the worlds of joy.[3]

James's most telling example is Tolstoy; conversion does not make him a simple happy creature. Tolstoy comes to be convinced, after his conversion, that "his trouble had not been with life in general . . . but with the life of the upper, intellectual, artistic classes . . . the life of conventionality, artificiality, and personal ambition. To work for animal needs, to abjure lies and vanities, to relieve common wants, to be simple, to believe in God, therein lay happiness again." To this James adds, "And though not many of us can imitate Tolstoy, not having enough, perhaps, of the aboriginal human marrow in our bones, most of us may at least feel as if it might be better for us if we could."

Still, for all the change that came to him, "Tolstoy's perceptions of evil appear within their sphere to have remained unmodified. His later works show him implacable to the whole system of official values: the ignobility of fashionable life; the infamies of empire; the spuriousness of the church; the vain conceit of the professions; the meannesses and cruelties that go with great success; and every other pompous crime and lying institution of this world." James's anger, echoing Tolstoy's, here rises to an almost prophetic scream. "To all patience with such things his experience has been for him a permanent ministry of death."[4]

With the towering figure of Tolstoy before us, James only now moves — in the next, the ninth, lecture — to consider the *process* he calls conversion. He gives a psychological, not an Ovidian, account of how our characters can change. "Whenever one aim grows so stable as to expel definitively its previous rivals from the individual's life," we call it a transformation. Such changes, says James, occur in the "hot place in a man's consciousness, the group of ideas to which he devotes himself, and from which he works." James identifies this place as "*the habitual center of his personal energy.*"[5]

William James psychologizes religion. But what does this vaguely pejorative phrase, so often repeated, amount to? His treatment of conversion is not reductive; it respects, indeed welcomes, complexity, and it glories in personal idiosyncrasy. If there is such a thing as the mind common to the universe — as Emerson thought there was, and as James was willing to consider — then even this universal mind could be revealed to each person only through his or her own mind. And if psychology is the study of mind, how else could conversion, or any other religious phenomenon, come to us? As objective fact? As revelation? Both these things may exist, but we know them, as we know everything, only through our minds — that is to say, psychologically. To psychologize a subject is not to dismiss it or undermine it or unmask it; it is to inquire into the actual process by which that subject comes to us.

What we know, says James, "is that there are dead feelings, dead ideas and cold beliefs, and there are hot and live ones, and when one grows hot and alive within us, everything has to re-crystallize about it." In studying particular cases of conversion, James notes how "the particular form which they affect is the result of suggestion and imitation." He gives two examples of people who understand the mechanism of conversion even as they experience it. The first is Jonathan Edwards, on whom James relies so much throughout these lectures; the second cites urban mission work with alcoholics. James quotes at length from Samuel H. Hadley's account of how he cured himself of drinking and refers the reader to *Hadley's Rescue Mission Work*. James endorses "the absolute need of a higher helper" in the process. He also cites General William Booth of the Salvation Army as believing that the "first vital step in saving outcasts consists in making them feel that some decent human being cares enough for them to take an interest in the question whether they are to rise or sink." It should come as no surprise, then, that Bill Wilson, the founder of Alcoholics Anonymous, which is often cited as the most successful alcohol treatment program ever designed, once wrote a letter to Carl Jung explaining his indebtedness to James's *Varieties of Religious Experience* and saying that in founding AA he had done little more than make "conversion experiences — nearly every variety reported by James — available on an almost wholesale basis."[6]

James cites other conversions, including that of Charles Grandison Finney, the great revivalist, to show "why self-surrender has been and always must be regarded as the vital turning-point of the religious life." For a twice-born person, "there are two lives, the natural and the spiritual, and we must lose the one before we can participate in the other."[7]

As he considers how one idea replaces another as the focal point of our minds, James makes room for a long discussion of the importance of the *margins* of our consciousness. "As our mental fields succeed one another, each has its center of interest, around which the objects of which we are less and less attentively conscious fade to a margin so faint that its limits are unassignable." At some point we cross over into what is *sub*liminal, *sub*conscious, and here James seems to concede that marginal consciousness and even the unconscious have roles to play in many conversions.

But he still opposes the idea that the worth of a thing can be described by its origin, and he ends his account of conversion with an appeal: "If the *fruits for life* of the state of conversion are good, we ought to idealize and venerate it." He cites many examples of the actual changes wrought by conversion. Just as the adequacy of Luther's version of Christianity is attested by "its wildfire contagiousness when it was a new and quickening thing," so James reports Jonathan Edwards's feeling after his conversion, how "scarce any thing among all the works of nature was so sweet to me as thunder and lightning; formerly nothing had been so terrible to me."

Finally there is Billy Bray, who felt, after conversion, "I can't help praising the Lord. As I go along the street, I lift up one foot, and it seems to say 'Glory'; and I lift up the other, and it seems to say 'Amen': and so they keep on like that all the time I am walking."[8]

On June 16, the day before the last lecture, James sat down in Edinburgh with the whole scheme of his project in his head and wrote a long letter to Henry Rankin, his Christian correspondent, who had been an important interlocutor — and representative of at least half of his ideal audience — all along. He acknowledged Rankin's Christian beliefs, but went on to say, "I believe myself to be (probably) permanently incapable of believing the Christian system of vicarious salvation, and wedded to a more continuously evolutionary mode of thought." The parenthetical "probably" is deeply characteristic. James had a genius for isolating himself in a middle position. He could explain the appeal of religion to people who thought of themselves as unbelievers, and he could explain to the religious how the entire subject could be grasped and accepted as processes that took place in the human mind, broadly conceived — yet he is too religious for the unbelievers and not religious enough for the believers.

But as he explained to Rankin, the real heart of the matter was still to come. "The mother sea and fountain-head of all religion lies in the mystical experiences of the individual, taking the word mystical in a very wide sense. All theologies, and all ecclesiasticisms are secondary growths superimposed." The mystical experiences, he now felt sure, "have no proper *intellectual* deliverance of their own, but belong to a region deeper, and more vital and practical than that which the intellect inhabits." He went on, putting the whole argument in one short rush: "I attach the mystical or religious consciousness to the possession of an extended subliminal self with a thin partition through which messages make irruption. We are thus made convincingly aware of the presence of a sphere of life larger and more powerful than our usual consciousness, with which the latter is nevertheless continuous . . . Religion," he concludes, "in this way is absolutely indestructible."[9]

The tone of conviction is unmistakable, and we may imagine it to have marked the last lecture, which was given the next day. It was, James said, "a great success judging by the audience, unparalleled in numbers in Gifford history (about 300) and undiminished to the end." He felt triumphant, relieved, delivered. "Veni, vidi, vici!" he wrote several friends back home. "The awful lectures are over." Most heartfelt, one likes to think, was his outcry to Katharine Rodgers, a distant relation who was living in Europe, and, in another letter, to Royce: "The bloody dog is dead!"[10]

67. Voluntary Poverty

WITH THE FIRST SET of lectures behind him and the second set still a year off, James's spirits and his overall condition improved. He felt stronger and tougher. He wrote to Godkin, "I have got a new tone." He longed for home, for the American scene, but he stayed abroad, partly to take one more "cure" at Nauheim but mostly because he and Alice had rented out both the Cambridge house and the Chocorua summer place through August. Certainly money was not a problem. He had made $10,000 on his books in the past two years. That is the equivalent of two years' full salary, or about $200,000 in today's dollars, so he could, at least for the present, teach or not teach, as he wished.[1]

He was so eager to be home that he began counting the days and hours. On the last day of August 1901 he wrote a friend that in forty-five minutes the family would be rolling toward Euston Station for a noon train and by five they would be at sea. He arrived in Boston with Alice, son Harry, and Peggy three days after McKinley was shot by Leon Czolgosz.

He was sharply conscious of having stayed abroad too long; it had been two years and two months, and now America seemed "half-foreign" to him. The New Hampshire countryside looked pathetic and poverty-stricken after the glories of England and Europe. A veil of strangeness hung over everything, a feeling, he told Pauline Goldmark, he had dreaded from previous experience of it.[2]

But this return was not a repeat of earlier returns in all respects. There is a different cast to James's letters, a pulling away, a sort of disengagement — though with mixed feelings. Brother Bob, who had discovered Catholicism, wrote this fall about "the mixture of active despair and a frivolous spirit" with which he faced his troubles. William experienced a different mix, but the strange, sapping contradictoriness of Bob's outlook was something William shared. Though he felt able again to look to the future with "hopeful eyes and aggressive aims," he was also writing to Pauline Goldmark with the floppy wistfulness of an old man. "What have you read? What have you cared for? Be indulgent to me, and write to me here [Silver Lake, New Hampshire] . . . I find letters a great thing to keep me from slipping out of life."[3]

But he was not slipping away; if anything, he was slipping back into American life. He resumed a light, nominally half-time teaching load at

Harvard, giving just one lecture a week, on Tuesdays, in a course called The Psychological Elements of Religious Life, until he was sure of his health. Even his feelings about Harvard were mixed. He had written Münsterberg, who was busy getting a whole building built just for philosophy, "I am not sure that I shouldn't be personally a little ashamed of a philosophy Hall," but he promised not to say so in public. Then, when Münsterberg wrote happily that Harvard had given him an A.M. degree (Harvard's M.A.), James wrote back genially that Münsterberg was now Harvard "family," but added, in his new, slightly querulous tone, "*I* am still an outsider, having no Harvard degree except an M.D., and I have always felt the exclusion." There is a little self-pity here, no doubt, but also a light wind of disengagement. It appeared in other professional matters. Asked to join the new American Philosophical Society, James responded that he could foresee little good from such a thing. "Count me *out!*"[4]

Whatever his feelings about Harvard, philosophy, and America, James's attachment to family and work saw him through the rough return. What he called "the house of James" seemed mostly to be flourishing. Young Henry was entering law school; he had greatly impressed his father on the recent trip to England. "He has the most beautiful poise and balance of character, and is withal so shrewd and humorous, and getting to be a talker, and stored with facts." Billy was starting his second year at Harvard; he was taller and heavier than his father, rowed against Yale, and took courses from men who remembered his father's student days. Nathaniel Shaler wrote James, "I see your boy William in my newly started class in Geology 14. Curiously enough there is your look of near forty years ago in his eyes." Peggy — Margaret Mary — who had become quite a favorite with Uncle Henry during her two years in England, seemed to have bloomed on her return. James wrote with evident pleasure about her to Katharine Rodgers, "Peggy has improved amazingly since her return; — blossomed into a lively hard-working, self-reliant character." Francis, now called Aleck, was at Brown and Nichols School in Cambridge; he managed the baseball team, and a friend of Aleck's remembered seeing William James sitting by himself in the stands in raw weather, watching his son's team and taking a lively interest in the new idea of sliding into base headfirst. Eddie Grant, later of the New York Giants, was teaching the boys the latest moves in baseball.

There was some trouble in the family. Alice suffered from frequent, severe, and protracted migraines at this time. They seemed to intensify just as she was leaving Europe to return home. "Alice is tired with many adjustments, and looks older," William wrote his brother Henry. Bob's troubles continued; he was in and out of sanatoriums. Old Edmund Tweedy died; another link with the past was gone. The time abroad had dishabituated James to America, but it also had brought a warmer and more dependable closeness between William and Henry.

Henry's hospitality had been unstinting — extravagant, really. He had taken to Henry III (who was temperamentally much like his uncle) as well as to Margaret Mary, and he and Alice seemed to understand each other effortlessly. With unfailing and elaborate sympathy Henry stood behind William and wrote soothing and supportive letters. If there was rivalry still, it was over who could be more solicitous. "I thoroughly believe, dear William, that you *will* work in, work back, work up, if you make it a life-and-death question to give up everything but your own needs *for* it." Henry's steadiness seems to have helped stabilize William, who wrote his brother this autumn to say that the American landscape had reemerged for him, and the "old sense of immediate contact with it has come back. The woods are re-asserting their empire everywhere. Old stone walls in the midst of them marking the boundaries of ancient fields, and old cellars surprising you, showing where ancient farm houses and their barns once stood." There was a little more nostalgia, a little more looking backward in William's new tone.[5]

As he started the fall semester in 1901, his nerves went, as he told Mary Calkins, "to *smash*" (it had been sister Alice's term), "*absolute* nerve prostration!" But he kept working, and his condition, always too closely watched by himself, soon improved. By the end of December William had completed two thirds of the lectures he was to give during his second Gifford stretch. The first five were on saintliness and the value of saintliness. "Saintliness" is an ill-chosen, off-putting word for many people, and the position of these lectures deep in the *Varieties,* which is already filled with attractive (and now of course famous) subjects — the religion of healthy-mindedness, the sick soul, conversion, and mysticism — means that the chapters on saintliness are apt to get less attention than the others. But it should be remembered that the five saintliness lectures constitute a full quarter of the entire two-year project, and that what James means by saintliness is how religious experience affects practical everyday life.

From the point of view of James the pragmatist, then, these chapters are the clincher; the whole venture stands or falls here, where James proposes that we judge religious experiences by their fruits, by their value for living. This is, in the old language of Calvinism, the question of sanctification, saintliness, the idea that if you were indeed saved, you would thereby be enabled to lead a good life here and now. It is one more idea James found he shared with Jonathan Edwards. "Old fashioned hell-fire Christianity well knew how to extract from fear its full equivalent in the way of fruits for repentance, and its full conversion value."[6]

James dives in by declaring simply that "the best fruits of religious experience are the best things that history has to show." Put in personal, psychological terms, "the man who lives in his religious center of personal energy, and is actuated by spiritual enthusiasm differs from his previous carnal self in perfectly definite ways." The saintly character, then, is "the character for which spiritual emotions are the habitual center of the personal energy," and such a person seems to James to possess, on the whole, four fundamental inner conditions. First is "a feeling of being in a wider life than this world's selfish little interests." Second is "a sense of the friendly continuity of the ideal power with our own life, and a willing self-surrender to its control." Third is "an immense elation and freedom, as the outlines of the confining self-hood melt down." Fourth is "a shifting of the emotional center towards loving and harmonious affections," a shifting toward the yes! yes! of emotional impulses and away from the no! no! of our inhibitions.[7]

These inner conditions, taken together, have, says James, "characteristic practical consequences," which are asceticism, strength of soul, purity, and charity. With this rough scheme — just an armature, really, not an argument but something to hold up an argument — James proceeds to flesh it out with examples. His first example of the practical effect of a feeling of the presence of a higher and friendly power is from Henry Thoreau, who recorded the following experience in *Walden:*

> Once, a few weeks after I came to the woods, for an hour, I doubted if the near neighborhood of man was not essential to a serene and healthy life. To be alone was something unpleasant. But in the midst of a gentle rain while these thoughts prevailed, I was suddenly sensible of such sweet and beneficent society in Nature, in the very pattering of the drops, and in every sound and sight around my house, an infinite and unaccountable friendliness all at once like an atmosphere sustaining me, as made the fancied advantages of human neighborhood insignificant, and I have never thought of them since. Every little pine needle expanded and swelled with sympathy and befriended me. I was so distinctly made aware of the presence of something kindred to me, that I thought no place could ever be strange to me again.[8]

James's final example of the practical effects of strong religious feeling is voluntary poverty, a subject that strongly interested him and to which he would return. Voluntary poverty is for James the subject of subjects, the final proof, capping five lectures of proofs, of the reality of religious feeling. "Felt at all times and under all creeds as one adornment of a saintly life," voluntary poverty marks the age-old difference between those who *have* and those who *are*. In one of his few references to Marxism, James observes "the loathing of 'capital' with which our laboring classes today are growing more and more infected seems largely composed of this sound sentiment of antipathy for lives based on mere having." James lingers over the idea and over its details. "Lives based on having are less free than lives based either on doing or on being," he writes, and he quotes with approval — and with the possession-burdened man's envy — the Jesuit father (later canonized as Saint Alphonsus) Rodriguez saying, "In our rooms there must be no other furniture than a bed, a table, a bench, and a candlestick, things purely necessary and nothing more."

We can think of James himself, retreating from his lavish book-lined four-couch downstairs study to his bare fifty-foot-long empty attic to write this. Voluntary poverty is one of the central hot spots in William James. Nowhere else in all his writing does he permit himself to speak, in his own voice and repeatedly, about the mysteries at the heart of religious life. "Over and above the mystery of self-surrender, there are in the cult of poverty other religious mysteries," he writes. "There is the mystery of veracity: 'naked came I into the world,' etc. — whoever first said that, possessed this mystery. My own bare entity must fight the battle — shams cannot save me. There is also the mystery of democracy, or sentiment of the equality before God of all his creatures." Noting that this last notion has been more widespread in Muslim countries than in Christian lands, he enlarges on its importance: "Those who have it spurn dignities and honors, privileges and advantages, preferring . . . to grovel on the common level before the face of God. It is not exactly the sentiment of humility, though it comes so close to it in practice. It is *humanity*, rather, refusing to enjoy anything that others do not share."[9]

Nothing in William James's life that we know about prepares us for this emphasis on voluntary poverty. Yet his language, his insistence on that word "mystery," convinces us that we are seeing as far into the real man as we ever can. His undisguisable admiration for the inner strength and self-command of the person who voluntarily accepts poverty brings him back to the subject again at the very end of the five-lecture unit on the value of saintliness, where he makes a startling proposal: "What we now need to discover in the social realm is the moral equivalent of war; something heroic that will speak to men as universally as war does, and yet will be as compatible with their spiritual selves as war has proved itself to be incompatible . . . May not voluntarily accepted poverty be 'the strenuous life,' without the need of crushing weaker peoples?"[10]

James is not optimistic. "We have lost the power even of imagining what the ancient idealization of poverty could have meant," he says. This loss has not served us well. "It is certain that the prevalent fear of poverty among the educated classes is the worst moral disease from which our civilization suffers." James is equally clear about the benefits of voluntary poverty, and this is another place where he has more in common with Thoreau than at first appears. "There are thousands of conjunctures," says James, "in which a wealth-bound man must be a slave, whilst a man for whom poverty has no terrors becomes a freeman."[11]

Perhaps we should have seen this coming, especially if we look back and recall James's enthusiasm for the blessed austerities of the rustic Putnam Camp and his passion for the outdoor life of the Adirondack high country. He writes of those experiences over and over. And his life in the woods, if we may so call it, seems also to lie behind and lend a sort of veiled personal witness to the next two lectures, those on mysticism, which was even more important to James than voluntary poverty.

68. The Mystical Center

M YSTICISM IS, for many readers and for James himself, the core of *The Varieties of Religious Experience*. Real religious experience is personal experience, and "personal religious experience has its root and center in mystical states of consciousness." He is quick to add — and it is a shrewd, calculated move — that he himself is shut out from such states "almost entirely." The word "almost" leaves a certain amount of ground open, ground such as the *Walpurgisnacht* experience on Mount Marcy.

James lists the four marks that, "when an experience has them, may justify us in calling it mystical for the purposes of the present lectures." (The sober, careful qualifications only increase the reader's confidence. Henry was not the only master at telling a story in the James family.) These marks are, first, *ineffability*. A mystical experience defies expression; "no adequate report of its contents can be given in words . . . [It] must be directly experienced." Second, such states are *noetic;* they "seem to those who experience them to be also states of knowledge." These two characteristics "entitle any state to be called mystical," though there are two further qualities, which James says are "less sharply marked." They are, third, *transiency* — they usually last only half an hour or at most an hour or two — and fourth, *passivity*. A person in such a state feels "as if he were grasped and held by a superior power."[1]

Next James turns to examples. His intent, of course, is to understand mystical experience; his method is entirely literary. He assembles his examples — all, or almost all, in their own voices — into a continuum, starting with common and easily experienced states and progressing smoothly, without a break, by small increments, to more complex states. "The simplest rudiment of mystical experience," he begins, "would seem to be that deepened sense of the significance of a maxim or formula which occasionally sweeps over one. 'I've heard that said all my life,' we exclaim, 'but I never realized its full meaning until now.'" He moves on to lyric poetry and music. "Most of us can remember the strangely moving power of passages in certain poems read when we were young, irrational doorways as they were through which the mystery of fact, the wildness and the pang of life, stole into our hearts and thrilled them." Indeed, he says, "lyric poetry and music are alive and significant only in proportion as they fetch these vague vistas of a life continuous with our own, beckoning and inviting, yet ever eluding our pursuit." He cites Tennyson and Charles Kingsley, then considers "consciousness produced by intoxicants and anaesthetics." Here he cites with apparently complete seriousness the Hegelian feeling of reconciliation, "as if the opposites of the world . . . were melted into unity." He cites his old friend Benjamin Paul Blood, the annunciator of the Anaesthetic Revelation, then pauses, as if we'd reached a landing on a long set of stairs, to quote a conclusion from Blood: "The lesson [of all these examples] is one of central safety: the Kingdom is within. All days are judgment days."

Now the connected, continuous procession of examples climbs step by step to mind cure — citing R. W. Trine, then Walt Whitman, then R. M. Bucke, and then the Hindu Vedantist Vivekananda, the Buddhists, and the Sufi al-Ghazali. Only after that does James take up the Christian mystical tradition, specifically Saint John of the Cross, Saint Teresa, Ignatius Loyola, Böehme, Fox, and others. Glancing back, he picks up "the fountainhead of Christian mysticism [in] Dionysius the Areopagite" and his *via negativa*, then announces, "This overcoming of all the usual barriers between the individual and the Absolute is the great mystic achievement." At this point, at the summit of the book, James turns to Sanskrit and to the ghost of

Minnie Temple to express the possibility — a bare possibility, but still a real one — of individual identification with the divine. *Tat tvam asi.* "That art thou," he quotes, as he had thirty years earlier in his effort to come to terms with Minnie's death, trying to reach beyond conceptual speech to speech as music, or to some other "element through which we are best spoken to by mystical truth."[2]

But as much as the mystical vision of merging, it is the parade of examples — the Homeric or Whitmanesque catalogues, the Chaucerian procession — that makes these lectures live. Such a cloud of witnesses and such a crowd of narratives are not easily brushed aside, silenced, or answered, as James must have realized. So in the end, when he turns at the top of the stairs, as it were, to face the reader and ask, "Can we invoke the mystic range of consciousness as authoritative?" the answer, for many readers, is no longer really in doubt. James quotes Tolstoy again: "Faith, says Tolstoy, is that by which men live. And faith-state and mystic state are practically convertible terms." Mystical states, says James, in fact hold authority over those who have them, and while those who do not have them are under no obligation to accept them, still, James insists, "the existence of mystical states absolutely overthrows the pretension of non-mystical states to be the sole and ultimate dictators of what we may believe."[3]

With the new year, 1902, came James's sixtieth birthday. Freed from teaching, and with the end of his Gifford labors in sight, he redoubled his efforts to complete the lectures. By the end of January he had finished the chapter on philosophy. It was essentially a revision of his Berkeley talk on philosophical conceptions, but with a sharpened and serious attack on Kantianism and Hegelianism, a defense of feelings over logical reasoning (he was of course aware that the present lectures were an attempt to make rational sense of the subject), and a new proposal that his hearers and readers consider the just-emerging science of religions in its effort to account for religious experience. James also renewed his attack on intellectualism, whether called dogmatic theology or the philosophy of the Absolute. James lays it down that the proofs of God's moral and metaphysical attributes "never have converted anyone who has found in the moral complexion of the world, as he experienced it, reasons for doubting that a good God can have framed it . . . We must therefore, I think, bid a definitive goodbye to dogmatic theology . . . We must conclude that the attempt to demonstrate by purely intellectual processes the truth of the deliverances of direct religious experience is absolutely hopeless."[4]

He was reading proofs of all the earlier Gifford Lectures as he drove himself through composing the last two. The goal was to have the book containing the talks published and available just as he finished delivering them. During February he completed lecture nineteen, called — uselessly — "Other Characteristics," as though to conceal the one thing James himself considered original in the whole enterprise. This, "the suggestion (very brief) that our official self is continuous with more of us than appears (subliminal s[elf]) which accounts for the 'striking' experiences of religious persons and that this 'more' on the farther side lies open to transempirical realities and this might allow for the sense of 'union' and other mystical experiences being true." In the lecture James's phrasing includes comments on how manifestations of religious life "so frequently connect themselves with the subconscious part of our existence," and he speaks of how "incursions from beyond the transmarginal region have a peculiar power to increase conviction."[5]

By March 3 he had finished the last lecture, "Conclusions." There was still proofreading to do and an index to prepare, but he felt the job was done. "I finished the Giffords at 5:45 [on March 3]," he wrote Fanny Morse. On April 1 he and Alice sailed for Liverpool. He felt, he told his eldest son, "as well as I ever did in my life." He landed on April 10, rushing to Edinburgh to get his honorary degree the next day. The weather was dreadful. He slept under seven blankets at night; the sun came out for two hours every six or seven days. On May 13 he began the second series of lectures, with a "rather smaller audience," and feeling that "after the great excitement and surprise of success last year," it all seemed "a little flat."

Down at Rye, Henry James finished *The Wings of the Dove* and prepared to join his brother in Edinburgh for the conclusion of the lectures. William got an advance copy of his own book on June 2. On the ninth he gave the last lecture, listing the characteristics of the religious life and affirming that "religious feeling is thus an absolute addition to the subject's range of life. It gives him a new sphere of power. When the outward battle is lost and the outer world disowns him, it redeems and vivifies an interior world which otherwise would be an empty waste."[6] He argues that religion, like individuality itself, is founded in feeling. Summarizing his vast survey of examples, he declares, "There is a certain uniform deliverance in which religions all appear to meet," and it consists of two parts: an uneasiness and its solution. "1. The uneasiness . . . is a sense that there is *something wrong about us* as we naturally stand. 2. The solution is a sense that *we are saved from the wrongness* by making proper connection with the higher powers." It is all, of course, a chance. It may or it may not be so. Nothing, as James liked to say, had been proved. "No fact in human nature is more characteristic than its willingness to live on a chance." The last sentence of the final lecture goes, "Who knows whether the faithfulness of individuals here below to their own poor over-beliefs may not actually help God in turn to be more effectively faithful to his own greater tasks?"[7]

He was done. The audience, which included his brother Henry and which had sat very silent and attentive, apparently did not find James's lectures "flat." It erupted in applause. The room shook with enthusiasm. The students broke into cheers, then sang "For He's a Jolly Good Fellow." James acknowledged the "cordial" reception, but the inevitable letdown had already set in. To Flournoy he wrote, "I am *deadly* tired." Disinclined to linger, turning down invitations from all sides, James fled back to Liverpool with Alice, boarding the *Ivernia* for home the day after the last lecture. Eight days later, at eight in the evening, the ship passed Cape Cod Light, and early the next morning William James was home.

V. THE PHILOSOPHER

69. William James at Sixty

J AMES RETAINED IN 1902 much of the appearance Santayana had noted ten years earlier: he was still "erect, brisk, . . . intensely masculine." But now his light beard was mostly gray; his age was beginning to show. His face was, in some lights, deeply lined. His hands, however, were expressive, brown, and strong.[1] The sadness his friend John Jay Chapman had noted was still there; so was the playfulness of the James who might run out naked under the garden hose at midnight on a hot July night in Cambridge. When another friend called him "the greatest philosopher of our country," James replied, "God help the country." When an enthusiastic clergyman wrote James that he was of the company of Isaiah and Saint Paul, James replied, "Why drag in Saint Paul and Isaiah?"[2]

As his son reminds us, William James was always "one half an artist. His imagination played over and around everything that held his attention. [A] penumbra of feeling always enveloped his thought. An idea might give him a pain in the thorax."[3] His life, even in his later years, was never more than semisettled. Still, he had evolved some routines and habits. He took a nap every afternoon from two to three. He made it a rule to write a note after every social visit, whether he was guest or host. He tried to live up to his conviction that every claim on him imposed an obligation, feeling, as he told one student, that if he failed to meet such claims his inner resources would dry up. He still traveled alone for several weeks in June after classes were over, and he almost always got away by himself to Keene Valley in September before school started up again.

The rest of the time — most of the time — he lived with Alice and his children in Cambridge. His neurasthenia came and went, but his heart was now a constant source of worry; after any physical exertion he could expect an attack of angina. He slept badly, as he always had. His preferred cures were, for neurasthenia, mind cure (a Boston practitioner, Mrs. A. B. Newman, seemed particularly effective); for his heart, a trip to Bad Nauheim; for feeling rundown or seedy, he preferred self-administered galvanism (that is, electrotherapy) or the Roberts-Hawley lymph-compound injections; for sleeplessness, he took chloroform or chloral hydrate or Veronal.[4]

Through all this, the core of James's temperament stayed the same in one vital respect: he had a permanent and insatiable craving for change. "Change," he told Pauline Goldmark, "is . . . perhaps the most imperative of human needs." A complex changeableness marks every aspect of his life and work. It did not produce peace of mind. Writing to his wife about his restless sociability, he said, "Strange that when I enjoy society so much *an und fur sich* [for its own sake] it should have the power of making me ill and poisoning me physically as nothing else does."[5]

Most photographs of James are of a stern, composed, unsmiling man; invariably he looks older than the date of the picture. But something is missing. The photographs do not square with descriptions of him by family and friends, which almost always describe him as active, vivacious, humorous, playful, energetic, and, said Royce, "eternally young."[6] There is one exception, a pair of photos taken of James and Royce sitting on a stone wall at Chocorua in 1903. In the first, Royce is talking; his brow is furrowed, his gaze lowered. His hands lie folded and composed on his right leg, which is crossed over the left. James sits next to him, listening, his face the usual mask, his feet dangling, his powerful knotted hands bunched loosely in his lap. The next instant — in the other photo — James has a broad smile on his face, has turned toward Royce, and has snapped his right hand up to point a finger at Royce, who has pulled back his shoulders, broken into a smile, and looked up at James. The two photos, like a miniature film clip, give an unmistakable impression of James's liveliness.

The Varieties of Religious Experience sold phenomenally well from the start, although the reviews were mixed. James noted wryly that the book "seems to add fuel to the fire that burns in the hearts of God's enemies as well as to that which burns in those of his friends."[7] The book was and is a standing affront to people committed to defending the particulars of their own religion as the best, if not the only, variety, but it cheered many, on the other hand, who had become disillusioned with institutional religion. James said he got more letters about the *Varieties* than about all his other writings put together.[8]

One journalist told James he had saved her life; she wrote him a letter that began, "O King! Live Forever!" Of course his friends admired the book; some even agreed with parts of it. The physicist and philosopher Ernst Mach wrote that it "has gripped me powerfully. Religious inspiration is certainly very similar to the scientific inspiration which one feels when new problems first present themselves."[9] Arrangements were soon made for translations into French, Dutch, and German. In Spain, the philosopher Miguel de Unamuno's early reading of the book marked a turning point in his thought.[10] Harvard's President Eliot had his doubts about the veracity of some of James's informants. Starbuck, from whom James took a great deal of material, was admiring and grateful: "It is something to live for to be noticed in such [a] book."[11] The popularity of the *Varieties* helped considerably to establish the prestige of the Gifford Lectures and set the standard by which they are still judged.[12]

Another mark of the book's success is how well it did with readers. It sold 11,500 copies the first year. It was an expensive book; at $3.20 a copy it cost more than three times what *Pragmatism* would sell for three years later. As with *Talks to Teachers,* James himself paid for the production of the book; he took the manuscript to Houghton Mifflin's Riverside Press in Cambridge to be printed. Longmans, Green, the ostensible publisher, sold it on consignment. James's contract seems not to have survived. If James got half the list price, which seems a reasonable figure, he would have cleared $10,000 after expenses for just the first year's sales. *Varieties* made James a rich man, as he admitted to a correspondent.[13]

An important part of the cultural setting for his new book was revivalism. James met professors in Edinburgh who "assumed that a Gifford lecturer must be one of Moody's partners."[14] Dwight Moody was a farm boy from Northampton, Massachusetts, who had run a rescue mission in Chicago among the very poor in the Sands district, north of the Chicago River. He had enjoyed his first big success in Great Britain, where, in 1873 and 1874, he had drawn to his revival meetings between three and four million people. His message then — and later in America, where extra trolley tracks were laid to accommodate his crowds — was simple: "Holding aloft his Bible, he assured his hearers that eternal life was theirs for the asking, that they only had to come forward and t-a-k-e, TAKE."[15] The road was wide, the gate stood open, the burden was light.

Moody retired in 1892, but his place was soon filled by Billy Sunday. Sunday, another farm boy, this time from Iowa, had been, among other things, an outfielder for the Chicago White Stockings before his conversion. He began holding revival meetings in Garner, Iowa, in 1895 or 1896. He reached ever larger crowds until, in 1917 in New York, he notched more than 1.4 million attendees and presided over 98,000 conversions. Sunday put on a grand show. "Accompanying his contortions, furniture smashing and partial undressing was an unbroken torrent of words. What the church needed," he shouted, was fighting men of God, not "hog-jowled, weasel-eyed, sponge-columned, mushy-fisted, jelly-spined, pussy-footing, four-flushing Charlotte-russe Christians."[16]

The first audience of the *Varieties* was probably not among the revival seekers but among reading people during the time of revivals, the time we now recognize as the modern era — our era.[17] In 1902 Joseph Conrad's *Heart of Darkness* and John Masefield's "Sea-Fever" first saw print. Helen Keller's *Story of My Life* appeared, as did Edwin Arlington Robinson's *Captain Craig.* In that year Dewey's *The Educational Situation,* Gide's *Immoralist,* and Gorky's *The Lower Depths* were published. Yeats's *Cathleen ni Houlihan* premiered in Dublin. Thomas Mann's *Tonio Kröger* came out the following year. In 1903 W.E.B. Du Bois published *The Souls of Black Folk,* and Mary Austin brought out *The Land of Little Rain.* Gertrude Stein had just settled in Paris and was beginning to buy the paintings of Paul Cézanne. Bertrand Russell published *Principles of Mathematics.* James read Robinson, knew Dewey and Keller, and would meet Gorky; Du Bois and Stein (and Theodore Roosevelt) had been his students; he had encouraged Austin and knew Russell.

The world at the turn of the century was becoming mechanized. A Packard accomplished the first automobile trip across the United States, going from San Francisco to New York in fifty-two days. Electric trolleys began running on city streets, Henry Ford organized the Ford Motor Company, and Roosevelt intervened in a coal strike on behalf of the miners. Motor taxis appeared in London, and in North Carolina the Wright brothers made the first manned flight at Kitty Hawk. As if in protest, the first Tour de France bicycle race was held.

American music was changing. In 1903, when Picasso was in his blue period, a band leader named W. C. Handy heard a man at a train station in Mississippi playing slide guitar with a knife and singing what Handy called "the weirdest music I ever heard," soon to be called the blues. The dramatic contrast between the onrushing present and the fast-vanishing past struck Henry Adams, who polarized it as a contrast between thirteenth-century worship of the Virgin and modern worship of the dynamo or generator. In 1902 the first Nobel Prizes were awarded. Marie and Pierre Curie discovered radium that year, and the next year won the Nobel. Around that time Freud's *Psychopathology of Everyday Life* and Lenin's *What Is to*

Be Done? were published. The Bolsheviks appeared in 1903, and the Russian Revolution began in 1905. Sun Yat-sen was stirring in China and organizing to expel the Manchus.

"Where are the snows of yesteryear?" asked the fifteenth-century poet François Villon. Modernity's cold response, it could be said, was formulated in 1905 by Einstein: $E = mc^2$. Einstein's equation for the equivalence of mass and energy, and James's assertion of the equivalence of thought and thinker, forged, together with modern art and modern music, a new world, a world James both lived in and helped bring about.

In mid-June 1902 he returned to Cambridge. In mid-July he gave a series of lectures at the Harvard Summer School of Theology. Called, stiffly, "Intellect and Feeling in Religion," they were a sort of plain man's Gifford Lectures, endorsing what Carlyle had called "natural supernaturalism" as the rescuer of religion. James aligned himself with "spontaneous thought, with metaphysicians and scientists both against me." He quoted Kipling's "Gods of the Copybook Headings": ". . . the dog returns to his vomit, and the sow returns to her mire / And the burnt fool's bandaged finger goes wabbling back to the fire." He ended with a sort of reckless lightheartedness, encouraging his audience to think "that by following up the clues set by all this private regenerative methodistical experience we may gain insight into the meaning of the Universe . . . One may be a Methodist," he concluded, "without even being a Christian."[18]

Though he later repudiated these lectures (writing on the folder that contains them "Trash. Never to be printed"), the notes for them — and they are only notes, they were never written out — still convey James's liveliness as a lecturer. Arguing that "the way an individual's life comes home to *him*" is what matters, that not the church but God is the individual's "only adequate understander and companion," James goes on, "Don't you agree? — Can there be doubt? — Isn't this religion?"[19]

In August came word that Holmes had been appointed to the U.S. Supreme Court. Although the two men were no longer close, moving now in different circles and in different directions, James sent congratulations, saying the new position was Holmes's "natural place"; he also sent a copy of his new book. Holmes's reply was brief but warm, referring as he did to a time and relationship that were lost. His remark had a touch of the blues. "Some day," he wrote, "we shall talk together again with that intimacy of understanding and mutual stimulus which we have known and which I never forget."[20]

70. Bergson

A S SEPTEMBER TURNED into October, James took up teaching again, although he felt, he said, "outside the game." It took him most of the fall to reacclimate. He told one old friend that "absence and half time work alienate one from one's environment in a way that is especially appalling." To do anything, he concluded, "one must have too much to do."[1]

After his return from England, he hungered for a particular kind of work. He wanted to do something "serious, systematic, and syllogistic." He gave a new course this fall, Philosophy 3: The Philosophy of Nature, in which, as he told Schiller, "I am for the first time in my teaching life, trying to construct a universe before the eyes of my students in systematic lectures with no text."[2] The syllabus shows a new scope and reach, a move away from the popular lectures at which he was becoming so adept, an ambition to write something systematic, rigorous, and comprehensive for professionals.

He begins by asking how we may account for such order and harmony as we see in nature. He considers theism ("God's design") and transcendentalism ("Eternal Reason evolving"), then turns to tychism — that is, to "Peirce's suggestion [that] order results from chance-coming, and survival of the more coherent."[3] The syllabus proposes "Pragmatism as our method" and spends much time on a "description of the world as a multitude of moments of experience," and on the idea of "pure experience," before coming to rest in the claim that "tychism is essentially pluralistic, goes with empiricism, personalism, democracy, and freedom. It believes that unity is in process of being genuinely won." The syllabus ends by urging panpsychic idealism as the "most satisfactory theory." Panpsychism is "the theory that all matter, or all nature is itself psychical or has a psychical aspect; that atoms and molecules, as well as plants and animals, have a rudimentary life of sensation, feeling and impulse."[4]

This fall, 1902, James read Pierre Janet's *Les Obsessions et la Psychasthénie,* which he described as "a wonderful mass of observation." The book described many of his own symptoms, but without, alas, any "radical explanation" of them.[5] In October he read his brother's *Wings of the Dove,* about which he wrote Henry with his usual mixture of baffled admiration and disapproval ("very *distingué* in its way . . . in its way the book is most beautiful"), but also bluntly objecting to his increasingly clotted prose. "What shall I say of a book constructed on a method which so belies everything that I acknowledge as law?" William wrote. It is highhanded, it did not help Henry, but it speaks for a number of readers, then and now. "You've reversed every traditional canon of story-telling (especially the fundamental one of *telling* the story, which you carefully avoid) and have created a new *genre littéraire* which I can't help thinking perverse, but in which you nevertheless *succeed,* for I read with interest to the end (many pages and innumerable sentences twice over to see what the dickens they could possibly mean) and all with unflagging curiosity to know what the upshot might become."[6]

James was beginning to angle toward retiring from teaching. "What my wife said about resignation at the end of academic year '04 is probable," he wrote Eliot, "but not certain." He felt, quite reasonably, that he could "produce more by a given effort in writing than in lecturing."[7] His books were selling well; just how well was revealed by a flare-up in James's relations this fall with Henry Holt. Noting a discrepancy in Holt's accounts for *Talks to Teachers,* James discovered that his publisher owed him two thousand dollars. James unaccountably took the discrepancy as evidence of systematic cheating. (This was absurd. No more honorable publisher existed than Henry Holt, who had gone into the trade because he had heard Daniel Coit Gilman — then librarian at Yale, but soon to be president of Johns Hopkins — say that if a book bore the imprint of Ticknor and Fields, you could be pretty sure it was a good book. Holt, a writer of books himself, thought such a reputation a fine thing.)

Holt replied to James, apologizing for the error but pointing out that James's unconventional arrangement with the house made bookkeeping hard, and he explained how the bookkeeping worked. The explanation must have caught James at a bad moment. Instead of being mollified, he exploded. "Am I a baby six years old that you should write me such rubbish?" Holt persevered; eventually James calmed down and even apologized — abjectly — when he came to understand how the error had occurred. But the accusation of bad faith clouded what had been, for James and for Holt, a very satisfactory working relationship. *Talks to Teachers* made James a lot of money. *The Principles of Psychology* and the *Briefer Course,* which were also published by Holt and were widely known by students as "James" and "Jimmy," had also made a lot of money for Holt, having sold, by 1902, 8,144 copies and 51,658 copies, respectively.[8]

Overshadowing everything at this time was James's excited rereading of Henri Bergson's *Matière et Mémoire,* which he had looked at without much attention when it first came out in 1896. When James, who had been reading the work of some of Bergson's students, went back for a second look, he was bowled over, writing Bergson to congratulate him on having produced "a work of exquisite genius. It makes," he said, "a sort of Copernican revolution . . . and will probably . . . open a new era of philosophical discussion."[9]

James had not yet met Bergson, but Bergson's name was now well known. He was a hugely popular lecturer; photographs show people craning their necks, standing on tiptoe, and using scaling ladders to climb to the window ledges where they stood to listen outside his lecture hall at the Collège de France.[10] Bergson was seventeen years younger than James. He would win the Nobel Prize for literature in 1929 and live to see Vichy France, where, shortly before his death in 1941, he stood in line to register as a Jew, having refused the exemption offered him by the authorities.

Bergson's life-changing moment of insight came in 1884. While he was taking a walk one day at Clermont-Ferrand, it came to him that the Platonic assumption that the immutable is higher than the mutable or temporal was wrong. "The whole of the philosophy which begins with Plato and culminates in Plotinus is the development of a principle which may be formulated thus: 'There is more in the immutable than in the moving, and we pass from the stable to the unstable by mere diminution.' Now it is the contrary which is true."[11]

Valuing the moving over the immovable, the actual stream over the idea of a stream, led Bergson to his notion of the importance of time as duration, not as stackable chips of a specific size. As he explained in a letter to James, "It was the analysis of the notion of time, as that enters into mechanics and physics, which overturned all my ideas. I saw, to my great astonishment, that scientific time does not endure . . . that positive science consists essentially in the elimination of duration." This concept James had already met, under the name "the specious present." "This was the point of departure," Bergson went on, "of a series of reflections which brought me by painful steps to reject almost all of what I had hitherto accepted and to change my point of view completely."[12]

Central to everything in Bergson's thought was this idea of duration. James's excited notes and underlinings in his copies of Bergson's books showed how he grasped the idea of duration as life, process, change, and growth, as opposed to stasis, forms, and measurements. "*Durer = changer, croître, devenir*" (To endure means to change, to grow, to become), he wrote on the endpaper of his copy of *Essai sur les Données Immédiates de la Conscience*. In *Matière et Mémoire* Bergson expands the idea of duration into that of memory: "Memory in action is not a dead deposit, it is a living and functional focusing of energies. It is life at the acme of attention, creation, and decision. Memory is life cumulated and brought to bear on alternatives of action . . . Matter is the deposit of life, the static residues of actions done, choices made in the past. Living memory is the past felt in the actualities of realities, of change."[13] One is not entirely surprised to learn that in 1889 Bergson married Louise Neuberger, a cousin of Marcel Proust, who was then eighteen and an attendant at the wedding. Proust's conception of memory has more than a passing resemblance to Bergson's.

Bergson has been called the first "process philosopher," preceding Whitehead in this still vibrant line of thought. Bergson's thought reminded Claude Lévi-Strauss "irresistibly" of "that of the Sioux Indians."[14] Writing a few years after this initial encounter, James recorded the effect Bergson had on him:

> For me, a magician. Whereas, when I open most philosophical books, I get nothing but a sort of marking time, champing of the jaws, pawing the ground, and resettling into the same attitude like a weary horse in his stall, turning over the same few threadbare categories, applying the same solutions and the same objections, here on every page new horizons open. It is like the breath of the morning and the song of birds. And to me it tells of reality itself and not merely of what previous dusty-minded professors have written about what other still more previous professors have thought about reality. Nothing in Bergson is shop-worn or second-hand.[15]

In February 1903 James read Bergson's just published *Introduction to Metaphysics*. Here Bergson denounces concepts themselves — that is, he rejects conceptual thinking as such, with a boldness and panache comparable to James's rejection of consciousness as an entity. All that concepts can do, Bergson argues, is imprison "the whole of reality in a network prepared in advance." What is really needed is what Bergson variously calls "metaphysical intuition," "that intellectual sympathy which we call intuition," or "a kind of intellectual auscultation."[16] It is a direct way of knowing, which works by "placing oneself within the object itself by an effort of intuition," which avoids symbols and is an alternative to conceptual thought. It is a mode of knowing that would soon be called *Einfühlung*, or empathy, a process for which words were first found in the opening decade of the twentieth century.[17]

Bergson went further, claiming that "what is relative is the symbolic knowledge of pre-existing concepts . . . and not the intuitive knowledge which installs itself in that which is moving and adopts the very life of things. This intuition," he concludes grandly, "attains the absolute."[18] What James had seen in Bergson's work in December 1902 was "a conclusive demolition of the dualism of object and subject in perception." What he recognized in Bergson's *Introduction to Metaphysics* in February 1903 was "a philosophy of pure experience," which strongly resembled what he himself was just then struggling to think through.

71. The Ph.D. Octopus and Dewey's New School

I AM NOW VASTLY BETTER than I was last year, and almost infinitely better than I was two years ago." This James wrote to an Italian friend in February 1903. By early April he was able to make a "half-hour's scramble up a very steep and slippery mountain brook" with, he said, "no bad effects whatever." He no longer complained about feeling outside the game; on the contrary, he seemed to have a hand — or at least a finger — on every wheel that was turning in Cambridge.

On top of his usual duties, he provided a testimonial for Edwin Arlington Robinson's new book of poems, and he was instrumental in establishing the Godkin Lectures at Harvard, in honor of his old political mentor. He wrote to the Carnegie Foundation to recommend a grant to Charles Peirce, he worked to arrange a lecture engagement for Peirce, and he inspected and approved a scale model of Frank Duvenek's proposed figure of a seated Emerson for Harvard's new philosophy building. Though he said he dreaded the social scene in Cambridge, he was impulsive, outgoing, keen-eyed, and warm-hearted; social situations waited around outside his study door.[1]

While visiting a former student, now a colleague teaching psychology at Columbia, Charles A. Strong, in Lakewood, New Jersey, James met Strong's father-in-law, John D. Rockefeller. James found him "the most powerfully suggestive personality I have ever seen," and he labored to offer specifics. To his son Bill he wrote that the sixty-three-year-old Rockefeller was "a robust thickset animal, without a spear of hair upon his head or face (a recent affliction), flexible, dramatic, genial, anecdotical, a chiselled face (a regular *Pierrot* physiognomy) sharp, sly, a tremendously passionate nature . . . a most complex old scoundrel." James caught the contradictions in the man. "He plays beautifully with his grandchild, carrying her on his back on his hands and knees, he wrecks businesses, ruins widows and orphans, is a devout Baptist, and, though bred on a farm is probably now the richest man in the world." The great man of business fascinated James but did not really interest him; he wrote Alice that while Rockefeller was to be at Strong's all through the week of James's visit, "I wish he were not."[2]

There were contradictions in James's own life. To Alice he was writing apologetically about the "demon of contradiction" in him, praising her understanding and tact, and promising, as always, to improve. "We shall work out splendidly if I can only find it possible to live more free from social complications." There was of course also something contradictory — or at least confusing — about his continuing friendship with Pauline Goldmark. On his way back from New Jersey, he stopped off to see her and a painter friend of hers, Alexander Schilling, in New York for lunch before catching the train for home.

There may or may not have been anything sexual between James and Goldmark — no evidence, not even a rumor of such a thing, seems to have survived — but James had been a little in love with her since they had met. Perhaps he just enjoyed the impossible romance of it, the flirtation that never gets beyond flirtation, a warmth of attraction that refuses to die. In marked contrast to his letters to Alice, which were now full of domestic cares and apologies and arrangements, his letters to Pauline have an assured intimacy, a feeling of being perfectly understood even when full of compunctions. Right after this visit he wrote Pauline, "I seem to myself to have talked too much — I always do — especially when your friend Schilling was there, I might have listened a little more. Miller said the other day of Royce that he finds lecturing the easiest form of breathing, and we all get more or less like that. But" — and here is the special tone James kept for Goldmark — "as far as lecturing to you goes, my dear, I make it up by long enough silent intervals." What he meant, as his closing shows, is that he saw her only at long intervals, but his phrasing has — is meant to have — a little forlorn, smitten sound.[3]

There were contradictions and crosscurrents in other, more public sides of his life. Early in 1903 he wrote a piece for the *Harvard Monthly* called "The Ph.D. Octopus." James, who had no Ph.D., was alert to what he saw as America's increasingly mandarin society, and was sensitive to the growing reliance on the "three magical letters" as a guarantee of intellectual ability and professional competence to teach. James thought the Ph.D.-producing schools wrong to take pride in making their degrees as difficult and therefore as rare and valuable as they could. He chastised Harvard for being "proud of the number of candidates whom we reject." He thought colleges wrong to insist that all their instructors have Ph.D.s, because he felt that the mere possession of the magic letters relieved hiring committees of the burden of serious assessment of the actual quality of an applicant.

But James worried most about the young people who were attracted by the Ph.D. programs. He was quick to concede that there are "individuals so well endowed by nature that they pass with ease all the ordeals with which life confronts them," and that there are also people for whom the doctoral programs offered a useful stimulus. But there was, he thought, "a third class of persons who are genuinely and in the most pathetic sense the institution's victims." These are students "without marked originality or native force," people inclined toward books and study, "ambitious of reward and recognition, poor often, and needing a degree to get a teaching position, weak in the eyes of their examiners." These, said James, are the real cannon fodder of the wars of learning, "the unfit in the academic struggle for existence."

James's recommendations, while sensible, are beside the point here. He believed that every person "of native power who might take a higher degree and refuses to do so, because examinations interfere with the free following out of his more immediate intellectual aims, deserves well of his country" and should somehow be rewarded. The key point is the indictment of a system that was fast "creating this new class of American social failures," the students who undertake a Ph.D. only to fall by the wayside. Parts of this essay still make for uncomfortable reading.[4]

The real excitement in the first half of 1903 was for James in philosophy itself. What he was getting, from Bergson and others, was corroboration, agreement, support for his own most important views, a feeling that a new consensus was forming. The consensus included Bergson, Schiller, Peirce, and Dewey. Bergson replied to James's enthusiastic fan letter with an equally warm response: "The more I think about the question, the more I am convinced that life is from one end to the other a phenomenon of attention."[5] Schiller wrote from England to say he was thinking of republishing all his papers as a volume of essays. (This would be his 1904 *Humanism: Philosophical Essays,* dedicated to James.) He also asked, "By the way ought we not to join forces with the Chicagoans?" James had finally succeeded in getting Harvard to invite Peirce to give a series of lectures. Peirce and James wrote back and forth, settling on pragmatism as the subject. At Chicago, the rising force was John Dewey and his colleagues.[6]

After reading a piece by Addison Webster Moore in one of the big set of imposing volumes issued by the University of Chicago in celebration of its first ten years, James wrote Dewey, "I see an entirely new 'school of thought' forming, and as I believe, a true one." Dewey replied at once, sending James printer's proof of a volume already in press and asking him if he could "stand for a dedication to yourself." Dewey flatly declared, "So far as I am concerned your Psychology is the spiritual progenitor of the whole industry." The volume was *Studies in Logical Theory*, and the dedication to James expressed thanks "for both inspiration and the forging of the tools."

Whatever the shortcomings of Dewey's style — James found it lacking in "terseness, crispness, raciness, and other newspaporial virtues" — Dewey had mastered the art of laying out his position clearly at the beginning. The eight writers who contributed to the volume agreed, wrote Dewey, "that judgment is the central function of knowing, and hence affords the central problem of logic." Dewey and company were interested in how judgment actually works; they saw it as a problem grounded in functional psychology, which in turn rested on physiology. "Knowledge appears as a function within experience." Dewey and his colleagues were embarked on nothing less than a modern empirical overhaul of the problem Kant had written about in his *Critique of Judgment*.

James wrote a notice — "The Chicago School" — of Dewey's volume, praising it as "a new system of philosophy."[7] "Dewey is a pure empiricist," James said. "There is nothing real which is not direct matter of experience. There is no Unknowable or Absolute behind or around the finite world. No Absolute either, in the sense of anything eternally constant; no term is static, but everything is process and change." "Dewey makes biology and psychology continuous," said James, and he could have added that psychology and logic were, for Dewey and for himself, continuous as well. James observed that "Dewey's favorite word is 'situation,'" and that every situation has two factors, an environment and an organism. Each action of the environment calls forth a reaction from the organism, each reaction by the organism changes the environment. Reality is thus a process of continual reconstruction, another of Dewey's favorite words. Thought itself, James explained, "is thus incidental to change in experience, to conflict between the old and new." In a perfectly adapted situation "where adjustments are fluent and stereotyped, it [consciousness] exists in minimal degree. Only when there is hesitation, only where past habit will not run, do we find that the situation awakens explicit thought." Thought must reconfigure or reconstruct the situation if activity is to be resumed, and the rejudgment of the situation is the final stage of the reconstruction.[8]

Equally fluid, radical, and exciting to James was Dewey's treatment of fact and theory. They are not really different, he thought; "they are both made of the same . . . experience-material. The same material is 'fact' when it functions steadily; it is 'theory' when we hesitate . . . Truth," James concludes with a rush, "is thus in process of formation like all other things . . . There is no eternally standing system of extra-subjective verity to which our judgments, ideally and in advance of the facts, are obliged to conform."[9]

James repeated his praise of the Chicago school over and over through 1903, observing that other American universities had thought but no school (Harvard), or a school but no thought (Yale). Chicago had both. It had "real, true thought," he wrote his brother-in-law. "It's great!"[10]

72. Emerson

N O CONTRADICTION LOOMED larger in James's life just now than the one created by his desire to produce a magnum opus — the audience for which would be other professional philosophers — and at the same time to lecture and write for a more general audience. His *Principles of Psychology* was proof that he could write for the learned, for professionals and peers. *The Will to Believe, Talks to Teachers,* and *The Varieties of Religious Experience* are all examples of James's ability to reach an ever larger general audience without having to sacrifice the respect of the academy. James was becoming very good at reaching this audience, yet in early 1903 he again and again recorded his wish to produce a great work of rigorous and technical philosophy, to reassert his professional legitimacy, so to speak. But month after month passed and he wrote nothing toward that project except notes.

Just how completely these two quite different impulses existed side by side in James can be seen in his comments to friends. To one he writes, "What I want to get at, and let no interruptions interfere, is (at last) my 'system of tychistic and pluralistic philosophy of pure experience.'" Five days later, responding to Schiller's tentative offer of lectures at Oxford, James said no, but immediately added that "the Gifford Lectureship is another matter altogether, and were I re-invited by any of the Scottish Universities I should (I think) gladly accept." James thought of Oxford as a stronghold of idealism, while Edinburgh seemed more receptive to his ideas. Edinburgh may also have seemed a better, because broader, audience. "I am going to concentrate myself on that book [pure experience] anyhow," he told Schiller. "I believe popular statement to be the highest form of art."[1]

Some invitations were hard for him to turn down. The centennial of Emerson's birth was approaching; James was asked to take part in the festivities at Concord. At first he said no. But then, to please Alice — he said — he agreed to do a twenty-minute talk.[2]

Once committed, he went at it with gusto, rereading volume after volume of Emerson. His feeling for Emerson was complicated. There was the old family connection: the Emerson children were among William's friends. He had a long-standing admiration for some of Emerson's poems. As we have seen, "Give All to Love" was a favorite poem and a key to James's headlong, all-or-nothing approach to relationships. "Threnody," Emerson's long effort to come to terms with the death of his five-year-old boy Waldo, came to be another of James's core texts. Reading Tolstoy, as James was now doing, at the same time as he was reading Emerson, made the latter seem thin by comparison, but the cumulative effect of rereading Emerson was profoundly positive. "Reading the whole of him over again continuously," he told Fanny Morse, "has made me feel his real greatness as I never did before."[3]

Always the active reader, James underlined sentences, sometimes with a wavy line for added emphasis. He marked passages with vertical lines in the margin, inserted page numbers for cross-references, made notes and indexed what he wanted to refer to later on the back flyleaf. For some essays, such as "The Method of Nature," which is Emerson's central writing on ecstasy, James marked almost every page and sometimes three or four passages on a page. He marked some bits we might expect him to have noticed. In "Self-Reliance" he underscored "Life only avails, not the having lived. Power ceases in the instant of repose: it resides in the moment of transition from a past to a new state, in the shooting of the gulf."[4] In Emerson's "Spiritual Laws" James marked and carefully indexed under "man a selective principle" the sentences that begin, "A man is a method, a progressive arrangement: a selecting principle." In the margin James referred the passage to another one ninety pages earlier, the passage in "Self-Reliance" where Emerson says, "Not for nothing one face, one character, one fact makes most impression on him, and another none."[5] Some sentences struck James as essential Emerson; these he marked or indexed simply "RWE." In The Natural History of Intellect he so cited Emerson's saying, "Thought exists to be expressed. That which cannot externize itself is not

thought." He also highlighted the lines "Do not trifle with your perceptions. They are your door to the seven heavens and if you pass it by you
will miss your way."[6]

As he reread Emerson now, looking for material for the talk he must
write, some sections reminded him of other writers with whose work he
was currently involved. In "Compensation" he underlined this passage:
"The absolute balance of Give and Take, the doctrine that every thing has
its price — and if that price is not paid, not that but something else is obtained, and that it is impossible to get anything without its price." Here he
wrote in the margin, "Mach." In the margin of the following passage from
"Nominalist and Realist" he wrote "Bergson": "It is the secret of the world
that all things subsist and do not die, but only retire a little from sight and
afterwards return again. Whatever does not concern us is concealed from
us. As soon as a person is no longer related to our present well-being, he is
concealed, or dies, as we say. Really, all things and persons are related to us,
but according to our nature, they act on us not at once but in succession,
and we are made aware of their presence one at a time. All persons, all
things which we have known, are here present and many more than we see:
the world is full."

Clearly James was reading Emerson for what he had to say and not
merely as a historical or canonical figure. James noted places where he
couldn't agree with Emerson, lines such as "I yielded myself to the perfect
whole," because he didn't believe there was such a thing as the perfect
whole. But he found more points of agreement than disagreement. Opposite Emerson's characterizing "the highest truth," the "far-off remembering of the intuition," as a feeling that "you shall not discern the footprint
of any other: you shall not see the face of man, you shall not hear any
name," James wrote, "Anaesthetic Revelation."

Emerson touched James deeply enough for him to index under "motto
for my book" Emerson's phrase "advancing on chaos and the dark." Even
closer to home was his indexing as "motto for my philosophy" this
Emersonian apothegm: "We are born believing. A man bears beliefs as a
tree bears apples."

James had promised to give the talk on May 25, Emerson's birthday. But
on May 13 he hadn't yet started to write it. His first draft focused on Emerson's interest in nature, then moved on to a consideration of the opposed
tendencies in Emerson's thought, one line running to "absolute monism,"
the other toward "radical individualism." After a few pages, James abandoned the draft. As was his habit, he did not rewrite what he had; he simply started over. This time the emphasis was firmly on Emerson's individu-

ality and his teaching of individualism. The opening is subdued, reflective, uncharacteristically backward-looking, but fitting for what was in some ways a gathering of Emerson intimates whose dominant feeling was still one of personal loss.

The 1903 celebration in Concord had the flavor of a family reunion as much as a public event. James began with a quiet observation, that "the pathos of death is this, that when the days of one's life are ended . . . what remains of one in memory should usually be so slight a thing." But the twenty-minute talk rose dramatically in tone as it went. "The matchless eloquence with which Emerson proclaimed the sovereignty of the living individual electrified and emancipated his generation, and this bugle blast will doubtless be regarded by future critics as the soul of his message." He ended with a sentence that can still create a shiver as it turns to direct address. "Beloved master," James called out, "as long as our English language exists, men's hearts will be cheered and their souls strengthened and liberated by the noble and musical pages with which you have enriched it."[7]

James was now a great speaker, but the Emerson eulogy was more than a great speech. Emerson had a practical and urgent message for James. He spoke to James's condition. William wrote Henry that his rereading of Emerson had "thrown a strong practical light on my own path . . . I see now with absolute clearness, that greatly as I have been helped by my University business hitherto, the time has come when the remnant of my life must be passed in a different manner, contemplatively namely, and with leisure and simplification for the one remaining thing, which is to report in one book, at least, such impressions as my own intellect has received from the universe."[8]

What James most admired in Emerson was "the incorruptible way in which he followed his own vocation," and he vowed to do the same himself.

73. The True Harvard

DESPITE EMERSON'S ROUSING CALL to stick fast to his own work, James went on much as he always had, scattering his energy and attention this way and that. The scattershot variety of his undertaking *was* his own real work. He was a pluralist to the bone. It is the monist — self-confessed or not — who can organize a life around one central project, saying no to all offers and openings that may distract from the singular objective. F. Scott Fitzgerald said life is, after all, more successfully looked at from a single window. It is a truth — if it *is* a truth — for which James might have had some sympathy but no lasting patience. His ideal house contained not one window but many doors, all leading outside — like Chocorua when he first saw it.

Yet in mid-August of 1903 he was once again caught up in the desire to wrap up his life work in a grand synthesis, a system, his own philosophical system. "I actually dread to die," he wrote a friend, "until I have settled the Universe's hash in one more book, which shall be *epochmachend* at last, and a title of honor to my children!" James could never quite shake the yearning for permanence and completion; he had himself the quality he had recently observed in the buildings going up in New York City, with their "transient intention of duration." Henry Thoreau never finished the vast "Concord Calendar" he spent his later years on, and Emerson never got his natural history of intellect into a shape that satisfied him. But Thoreau's *Journal is* the grand calendar of Concord, and Emerson's complete works could as well be called the Natural History of Intellect.[1] There are other kinds of completion besides the formally rounded structure of a culminating book.

Back in June, Harvard conferred an honorary degree on James. He attended a long dinner at Memorial Hall, where he made a short speech he had written and memorized for the occasion. He called it "The True Harvard." The visible Harvard of 1903 was a fast-growing, ever more imposing place. The number of students had risen from 1,200 in 1890 to 1,800 by the end of the century. The faculty had grown from 90 to 134. New buildings were springing up: Stillman Infirmary in 1900, the Harvard Union (an effort to democratize the school by providing club-like facilities for the unclubbed) and Lowell Lecture Hall in 1901.

But what fixed the architectural tone of the new era as "imperial Harvard" was the large Greco-Roman coliseum that went up across the Charles River in 1902 and 1903 and the erection of the Memorial Fence around Harvard Yard beginning in 1901. The fence was a huge wrought-iron enclosure of elaborate design, hung on large brick pillars. The fence decisively separated the college from the town, especially from Harvard Square, much to the delight of Henry James, who, when he saw it, rejoiced that America had at last produced something fine enough to want to keep it separate. Not everyone felt that way.

Old departments grew and new ones came into existence. The English department, with George Lyman Kittredge, Barrett Wendell, and Charles T. Copeland, was beginning to attract attention. Sociology started out, as had psychology, in association with philosophy, in the new Emerson Hall. The philosophy department itself included Santayana, Royce, Münsterberg, Palmer, and James. It was, says a modern historian of philosophy in America, "the most famous department of philosophy of which any American University has been able to boast."[2]

Student life was dominated not by study but by social life, by the clubs, and by sports. There was a new spirit of freedom. Students were free to take any course they wanted, were free from compulsory chapel, and free to attend classes or not after 1886. One student went to Havana, leaving a stack of predated letters for his roommate to mail home at suitable intervals. Somehow a maid put the whole lot in the mail at once. When the surprised father showed up in Cambridge, no one in authority had the slightest idea where the student in question was. Taking attendance was reinstated — though attendance at classes was still not required.

The old Lawrence Scientific School in which James had studied was quietly folded into Harvard College between 1889 and 1891; Radcliffe College for women was chartered in 1894. Private entrepreneurs built ever more expensive and luxurious apartment buildings for wealthier students along Mount Auburn Street, which became known as the Gold Coast. Less affluent students lived in college dorms, which looked like the old brick mill buildings of New England.

Social class divisions were widening. Logan Pearsall Smith wrote that in the 1880s "the atmosphere of Harvard was . . . richly colored by the sense of social differences. The prestige possessed by members of the most exclusive clubs, the delight of being seen in their company, and the hope of being admitted into their select circles — these were the animating motives of life at Harvard as I knew it." Santayana, in the early 1890s, noted that the "divisions of wealth and breeding are not made conspicuous at Yale as at Harvard by the neighborhood of a city with well-marked social sets, the most fashionable of which sends all its boys to the college." Samuel Eliot Morison, the historian of Harvard who graduated in 1908, observed, "Since 1890 it has been almost necessary for a Harvard student with social ambitions to enter from the 'right' sort of school and be popular there, to room on the 'Gold Coast' and be accepted by Boston society his freshman year, in order to be on the right side of the social chasm."

One of the few things other than preestablished social status that could help the process of acceptance was earning a place on the freshman crew, which James's second son, Bill, did in 1900. Two years later, Bill was coming under increasing, and increasingly unwelcome, social pressure. At twenty he was "undergoing the curious experience of a real nausea at too much success in social lines," William wrote Henry in July 1902. "He has been elected captain of the University Crew for next year, an exceedingly laborious, responsible and publicly prominent position and is fairly sick at heart at the prospect of another year of politics and publicity and extermi- nating physical training, with no opportunity for inner leisure or advance in study, and all for the sake of an end so essentially childish as spending 20 minutes a year hence rowing a few seconds faster than a crew from Yale." Bill's response to the situation was, after some inner turmoil, to resign as captain of the crew, go to Europe, and spend most of the academic year 1902–03 in premedical studies in Germany.[3]

William James had Bill as well as himself in mind when he made his little dinner speech on receiving the honorary degree. In the talk he did not go after the big new imperial Harvard, or even athletics, the new emphasis on which he more or less approved, within limits. But he did go after the club life and the social system, on behalf of the loners, the "undisciplinables," the outsiders "with whom I belong." He began by in- sisting, "I am not an alumnus of the college. I have not even a degree from the scientific school, in which I did some study forty years ago. I have no right to vote for Overseers and I have never felt until today as if I were a child of the house of Harvard in the fullest sense."

After the personal part of the talk, he turned a cold eye on the larger world, the Harvard of the Gilded Age he saw all around him. "If we were asked that disagreeable question 'what are the bosom vices of the level of culture which our land and day have reached?' we should be forced, I think, to give the still more disagreeable answer that they are swindling and adroitness, and the indulgence of swindling and adroitness, and cant, and sympathy with cant — natural fruits of that extraordinary idealization of 'success' in the mere outward sense of 'getting-there,' and getting-there on as big a scale as we can, which characterizes our present generation." Then James drew a straight line between worldly success and social success in college. "In the successful sense, then, in the worldly sense, in the club sense, to be a college man, even a Harvard Man, affords no sure guarantee for anything but a more educated cleverness in the service of popular idols and vulgar ends." (Emerson had spoken of how colleges could produce a "more instructed fool"; from this point on in James's life there are frequent Emersonian echoes in some of his best phrases.)

At the climax of the speech, James asked, with rhetorical despair, "Is there no inner Harvard" within this outer and empty social shell? Is there not something "for which the outside men, who come here in such numbers, come?" Those who "come from the remotest outskirts . . . without introductions, without school-affiliations, special students, scientific students, graduate students, poor students . . . who make their living as they go"? Yes, said James, "there is such an inner spiritual Harvard, and the men I speak of, and for whom I speak today, are its true missionaries and carry its gospel into infidel parts." These students do not come to Harvard for the club life, but "because they have heard of her persistently atomistic constitution, of her tolerance of exceptionality and eccentricity, of her devotion to the principles of individual vocation and choice." Nothing but religious language will do for James here. "The true church was always the invisible church. The true Harvard is the invisible Harvard in the souls of her more truth-seeking and independent and often very solitary sons."[4]

James loved these outsiders, the "undisciplinables" who he said were "our finest product." He identified with them, considered himself one of them, and was pleased with his son Bill's revolt. But in one crucial way James was no longer an outsider at Harvard. His outsider's independence was, in many eyes, the essence of the place, and he himself, without intending any such thing, had become the visible embodiment of the best of Harvard. President Eliot was well aware of this, and when, in December 1903, James sent in his letter of resignation, Eliot flatly refused to consider it, explaining that he did not want Harvard's name separated from James's in the public mind.

74. A Life of Interruptions

THE JAMES FAMILY was now, for better or worse, a Harvard family. Bill, now twenty-one, had completed the requirements for his undergraduate degree there in three years; after spending a year abroad he returned to graduate with his class and go on to Harvard Medical School in the fall of 1903. He also wrote an article that appeared in the *Harvard Graduates' Magazine* that December, called "Sport or Business?," in which he criticized the increasing professionalization of college sports, the increasing need to beat Yale at any cost that dominated Harvard athletics, and the "New Harvard Spirit," which he said "consists mostly in rehearsing our applause." Bill Junior's writing is forceful and vivid. "There is something ridiculous," he wrote, "in a whole college being hectored and drilled into an applauding machine as an incident in the organization of victory." William was pleased and proud.[1]

Bill's brother Harry was twenty-four in 1903. He had been managing editor of the college newspaper, the *Harvard Crimson,* had gone on to Harvard Law School, and would take his law degree in 1904. Quiet, deliberate, and solid, Harry had puzzled his father, who early on thought him "not a James so far as I can see," but later came to think him similar to his uncle Henry. Harry had been taking over more and more of the responsibilities at Chocorua. "With his mighty chest and shoulders, shirt open at the neck, visible at all times in the fields, with spade, scythe, cultivator or axe, he reminds me," William wrote, "physically and in his moral significance of nothing so much as Millet's 'Semeur'" (*The Sower*).[2]

Peggy was sixteen in 1903. She had had a difficult time in school in England from the fall of 1889 to the spring of 1901 — she had bouts of low spirits that sound like depression — but she had become a favorite of Uncle Henry's and had subsequently bloomed at home. She went to football games, and wrote her uncle, "Billy shouted and I shouted and everybody shouted all the way through." There were dancing lessons, sledding parties, boys. Peggy was pretty and looked a bit like her mother; she was very social. Three years hence she would have a coming-out party. At the same time she was writing poetry.[3]

Aleck, the youngest, was thirteen this year. He had been a stormy child. He was a poor student, averse as Wilky had been to reading. He was probably dyslexic. He failed the entrance exams for Harvard five times. He was manager of the Brown and Nichols School's baseball team. He had stayed in America with his grandmother Gibbens while William, Alice, and Peggy were abroad during the Gifford years, and Aleck later told his own children that he had felt abandoned. James's letters to and about Aleck show the same solicitude he showed for his other children, perhaps a bit more. James always seemed eager to be able to report that Aleck had had a "tip-top" summer or trip or experience. "Aleck is doing splendidly, handsome, healthy, happy and good tempered as the day is long," James wrote Bill. Eventually Aleck, like Bill, became a painter.

James's plan for the summer of 1903 was, predictably, to focus his energies on his new book, his "System der Philosophie." He vowed to his son Bill, "No day without a line." To a friend he wrote about beginning "the writing of a somewhat systematic book on philosophy — my humble view of the world — pluralistic, tychistic, empiricist, pragmatic, and ultra gothic, i.e. non-classic in form." The examples of Bergson and Dewey no doubt spurred him on. He agreed to do a series of five lectures on radical empiricism at Tom Davidson's old summer institute at Glenmore, in the Adirondacks. James was so intent on the new project that he uncharacteristically forgot whom he was lecturing to, and was chagrined to be told that three quarters of his hearers had no idea what he was talking about when he expounded on the Absolute. There is no question that James was itching to get at his new book, but it is no less certain that a host of other claims now descended on him, with each claim imposing an inescapable obligation. To Henry in England, James wrote, in January 1904, "I have been leading a life almost entirely constituted of interruptions, reading manuscripts, making speeches, interviewing students." Each one small, some trifling, the interruptions were unwelcome but peremptory, even necessary, and at least one interruption a month required a piece of writing from James.[4]

There was, for example, his friend Myers's big book, the two-volume *Human Personality and Its Survival of Bodily Death.* James had been present at Myers's death. Now his widow had written James a pathetic, pleading letter: "It seems as if there were no one — no one . . . to care — for his book — and no one to help me."[5] So James wrote a thoughtful review. He told Schiller that Myers's book raised his opinion of the man, but not of "the solidity of the system." Nevertheless, James made the case, forcefully, that Myers had a claim to be considered "the founder of a new science" because of his "conception of the Subliminal Self," that is, "a subliminal life belonging to human nature in general." Myers's book remains impressive today, in both scope and detail. It contains a long second chapter on the disintegration of personality, with excellent summaries of case studies by Freud, Breuer, Janet, and Morton Prince. James labored to be fair to the book and to Myers, and in listing the things he thought had worked against Myers's recognition as a scientist, we see a foreshadowing of what James himself would face. James specified, "first, the nature of the material he worked in; second, his literary fluency; and third, his emotional interest in immortality." One of the differences between Myers and James is that James was acutely aware of precisely these problems.[6]

In May there was the Emerson talk, in June the "True Harvard" speech. Also in June he read W.E.B. Du Bois's *The Souls of Black Folk* and wrote his former student an appreciative letter. With his attention thus drawn to the situation of black people, James wrote in July a letter to the editor of a Springfield, Massachusetts, paper which ran as "A Strong Note of Warning Regarding the Lynching Epidemic from Prof. James of Harvard."[7] Not only was James outraged by lynching, he was outraged by the mildness of the public response, by deprecatory clucking comments about the "deplorably mistaken sense of justice," by newspapers seeming to condone lynching by referring to mobs as composed of "leading citizens," and by other newspapers — he cited a Boston headline, "Charred in Chains, Lynching Well Done" — doing "all they can to convert the custom into an established institution." Published figures suggest that the number of individual lynchings was beginning to decline in the first decade of the twentieth century, but the mass atrocities and the killings of the East St. Louis Massacre of 1917, the Tulsa Riot of 1921, and the destruction of Rosewood, Florida, in 1923 were all ahead.

It seems clear that it was James's personal association with Du Bois that brought the subject home to him. James saw real danger, and not only to the obvious victims. "The average church-going Civilizee realizes . . . absolutely nothing of the deeper currents of human nature, or of the aboriginal capacity for murderous excitement which lies sleeping in his own bosom." The problem, James says squarely, is in us: "Where the impulse is collective, and the murder is regarded as a punitive or protective duty . . . the peril to civilization is greatest." He thought the newspapers and the general public simply did not realize the monster they were unleashing. "Then," James continues, "as in the hereditary vendetta, in dueling, in religious massacre, history shows how difficult it is to exterminate a homicidal custom which is once established." James's comments were picked up and reprinted in New York and Boston. He was famous now and his opinion mattered, even to the newspapers.

In August there were lectures to be given at Tom Davidson's Glenmore. These were the only interruption clearly in the line he wished now to pursue — namely, radical empiricism. In late September classes started again at Harvard, with James giving Philosophy 20c, a seminar on metaphysics, "a pluralistic description of the world." In October he was asked for a contribution to a memorial volume on the life of Tom Davidson. James could not turn this down, of course, so he wrote the piece, often reprinted as "Thomas Davidson: A Knight Errant of the Intellectual Life," praising the booming vitality, the genius for friendship, and the "extreme individualism which he taught by word and deed."

In November he was called on for a talk at the opening of Harvard's new Germanic Museum; in the talk he praised the Germanic or Gothic spirit (as against the classical) and its fondness for strangeness. Later in November he gave a speech at an Anti-Imperialist League meeting in Boston, comparing the United States to a python in its "prehension, deglutition, digestion and assimilation" of the Philippines. He conceded that the anti-imperialists had lost the day: "To the ordinary citizen the word anti-imperialist suggests a thin-haired being just waked up from the day before yesterday, brandishing the Declaration of Independence excitedly, and shouting after a railroad train thundering towards its destination to turn upon its tracks and come back." James thought all that could now be done was face the fact that "in every national soul there lie potentialities of the most barefaced piracy and our own American soul is no exception . . . It is good to rid ourselves of cant and humbug, and to know the truth about ourselves."[8] In December Herbert Spencer died, and James — in luck for once — furnished the *New York Post* with a long piece on Spencer he had written nine or ten years earlier, when Spencer was thought to be dying.

But the real task, which James was so eager to tackle all year long, was the great work that was always disappearing like the railroad train into the distance. The closest he got to it was the set of lectures on radical empiricism at Glenmore and parts of the fall seminar on the metaphysics of pluralism. As his lectures drew near, in August 1903 James wrote his young friend Dickinson Miller, "I have got my mind working on the infernal old problem of mind and brain, and how to construct the world out of pure experiences, and feel foiled again, and inwardly sick with the fever." Hegel once spoke of "seeking the rose of reason in the cross of the present." James was now doing something similar. He continued, to Dickinson, "But I verily believe that it is only work that makes one sick in that way that has any chance of breaking old shells and getting a step ahead. It is a sort of madness however when it is on you."

James was developing an Ahab-like obsession with the project, as he himself recognized. In a notebook, James proposed as "motto for my book" Melville's grand finger-shaking at his monomaniacal hero: "God help thee, old man, thy thoughts have created a creature in thee; and he whose intense thinking thus made him a Prometheus, a vulture feeds upon that heart forever; that vulture the very creature he creates."[9]

James's own mind was never better than when his brain was giving him trouble and when he was under pressure from all sides. He had a strange and ultimately unfathomable ability to bring bits and pieces of order and achievement — trophies dripping from the deep — out of disorder and chaos, perhaps, in part, because he expected to. When the subject of chance came up in his seminar this year, he wrote in his notes the following account of how he understood Peirce's comment about chance begetting order: "In books on probability chance is regarded as revealer of a regular order, if such exist. Perturbations neutralize each other; frequencies come to light. My theory goes farther. Chance *production* occasions effective increase in certain regularities, because other chances are eliminated and these remain and accumulate. If [a number of] men toss pennies, there will be accumulation of wealth in a few hands, by the elimination of those whose stock gives out."[10]

Chance does not simply reveal an underlying order that was there all along; chance actually creates order. Or, we could say, thinking of James's own life, that chance creates and habit retains many of those elements of our life that, as time passes, we are pleased to think of as orderly and meaningful.

75. The Many and the One

THE NEW YEAR BEGAN badly, though perhaps not quite as badly as it appears from the letters between William and Henry. Over the first three months of 1904, William was down with gout, influenza, erysipelas, a "poisonous catarrh," vertigo, and vomiting, with discouragingly short intervals between. He made a quick trip to Florida, traveling with Edward Emerson and family, with whom he stayed in a disappointing Tallahassee hotel. We catch James's mood from a postcard to Alice: "Extremely dreary hotel, to be sold at auction next Monday, us included."[1]

In February the Russo-Japanese War broke out. James took the Japanese side, telling one friend, "The insolence of the white race in Asia ought to receive a check."[2] Closer to home, James gave in to President Eliot's entreaties, withdrawing his resignation and agreeing to stay on at Harvard for the coming year. To Henry, William sent a copy of the ebullient Horace Fletcher's new book, *The New Glutton or Epicure,* which contained a fulsome acknowledgment to William. Fletcher's way to health was to chew each bite of food until it liquefied and a swallowing reflex set in. Henry, who had a long history of digestive woes, found the book entirely to his taste, was so excited by his first reading that he couldn't sleep, and was determined at once to try it.[3] Subsequent letters to William show that Henry was soon hooked on Fletcherizing, even as he poked inevitable fun at Fletcher's "precious definite little munching message" and at "salvation through salivation." Fletcher was cheerful, upbeat, and had a nice sense of humor. He noted how "munching lunches" had become popular in London. Henry merrily told William that he was inclined to swallow Fletcher, at least, whole.

William meanwhile was chewing away at his own book, for which he had made, by October 1903, some two hundred pages of notes and jottings. His working title was *The Many and the One*. By late May 1904 he had written, he said, exactly thirty-two pages. James's expectations for this book were high. He seems to have approached it not as a continuation of his earlier work but in an almost boyish spirit of making a brand-new start at the big questions. "I prefer," he wrote, "to start upon this work romantically, as it were, and without justification."[4] He made huge and impossible claims — "For *myself* the result I shall try to set forth will be true" — even as he recognized the problem with what he was saying. "I am convinced," he had written Sarah Whitman in August 1903, "that the desire to formulate truths is a virulent disease. It has contracted an alliance lately in me with a feverish personal ambition, which I never had before, and which I recognize as an unholy thing."[5]

Beliefs looking very much like conclusions tumbled out in advance of evidence. "I do not believe . . . that even if a supreme soul exists, it embraces all the details of the universe in a single absolute act either of thought or of will." James seems to have settled beforehand the big question, whether the world is at bottom one great fact or many little facts. What, he asked, can "One" "*mean* when applied to such an object as the universe?" The drafts and scraps of drafts James wrote on this project do not make any sort of whole, though some of the parts are excellent. Deprecating the "mere dry chrysalis or cicada skin" of intellect-generated abstractions, James bursts out in protest: "Immediate life holds all the blood." A few sentences later, he wrote, "There must be an intellect that is reconstructive, not destructive."[6]

The best parts of James's scattered assault on the problem are his statements of the problem the book posed for him. James is most articulate and persuasive when describing difficulties, not when prescribing solutions. There is no escaping the influences that have shaped one, he says. "Whatever principles he may reason from, and whatever logic he may follow, he [the philosopher] is at bottom an advocate pleading to a brief handed over to his intellect by the peculiarities of his nature and the influences in his history that have molded his imagination." James was unable or unwilling to understate the complexity of any part of the human condition. "Mental and social life are at all times a strange blending of purpose, accident, and passive drift," he wrote. "Both in biography and history, designs are modified to suit events which interfere with the original plan . . . No man, no nation ever carried out a plan foretold in all its detail. No consciousness ever embraced in a single act of thought the whole of either an individual or a national life."

But while one may suspect that the trouble lay with James's preconceptions — he was inclined to believe in the many and not to believe in the one — the problem at hand became insurmountable when he tried to focus the question. In one draft he wrote, "How, on the supposition that the manyness of things precedes their unity, does any unity come into being at all?" In the margin opposite this paragraph, James wrote, "Stop!"[7]

He tried again, and after several pages reached the position that "substances whether material or spiritual are unrepresentable; and the inherence in them or adherence to them of properties seems a mere verbal figure. The notions of cause, power, possibility are equally unintelligible. Knowledge of one thing by another is a mystery. If things be individual (as common sense affirms) how can they interact at all, for how can what is separate communicate?" Then, opposite this paragraph too, he wrote, "Stop."

76. The Modern Moment: Radical Empiricism

THE MANY AND THE ONE was indeed a doomed project, but something else was already rising out of the depths. Even as he was complaining to his friend the Polish philosopher Lutoslawski, in late May 1904, about having written only thirty-two pages of *The One and the Many*, James had come to the leading edge of a period of astonishing creativity, what John McDermott calls an "explosion" in his thought. Between the end of May 1904 and February 1905 James wrote the eight pieces that form the core of his project on radical empiricism.[1]

One cannot say with certainty what it was exactly that sparked the explosion, but a number of favorable conditions came together just as the school year drew to a close. James's health improved dramatically; he started taking the Roberts-Hawley lymph injections again after an eighteen-month hiatus. He found he could walk for as much as four hours at a stretch. The end of classes brought a sense of relief; he shook off Cambridge, going first to Chocorua, then to western Massachusetts to see friends.

On June 21, 1904, he wrote a short introduction to Gustav Fechner's *Little Book of Life After Death*, praising what he called Fechner's "daylight view — the view that the entire material universe, instead of being dead, is inwardly alive and consciously animated . . . in divers spans and wavelengths, inclusions and envelopments."[2] Fechner was an intellectual wild man; his work clearly excited James, whose introduction is a liberating, radical, imaginative flight. "Once we grasp the idealistic notion that inner experience is the reality," James wrote, "and that matter is but a form in which inner experiences may appear to one another when they affect each other from outside, it is easy to believe that consciousness or inner experience never originated, or developed, out of the unconscious, but that it and the physical universe are co-eternal aspects of one self-same reality, much as concave and convex are aspects of one curve." This is, incidentally, as good a statement of the one and the many as James ever achieved.[3]

On June 24 his close friend Sarah Whitman, the Boston artist, died; James's last letter to her arrived too late and was returned to him. He went to the funeral. Whitman had been just his own age, and her death italicized his own mortality. "I wish George Dorr to be one of my pallbearers," he wrote Alice. Compunctions welled up, as always. "I think I have been a little hard on Mrs W," he told her, explaining in another letter, "I sometimes resented the way in which her individual friendships seemed mere elements in the great social 'business' which she kept going so extraordinarily." But his last comment on Sarah Whitman, to John Jay Chapman, has a gallant, and one feels appropriate, salute. "Dear Mrs. Whitman's death will make Boston seem a different city. It was like her life, spirited and triumphant. Out she went, gracefully and rapidly, on deck to the last, and taking all her secrets with her."[4]

A fierce drought this year left New Hampshire roads six inches deep in dust by late June. Another arid event of the summer was the huge and complicated International Congress of Arts and Science being organized by Hugo Münsterberg, the "results" of which were to be issued in twenty-four volumes and in three languages. James begged off, telling Münsterberg he had nothing appropriate for the congress. This was no doubt true, but the casual disclaimer only masks what was really going on with James, which was a tumultuous confluence of philosophic streams of energy. His seminars, all on metaphysics since his return from Edinburgh, were being devoted to broad philosophical questions, and his notes show him contending in these seminars with Royce, Lotze, Bradley, Leibniz, Berkeley, Hume, Kant, the Cairds, Mach, LeRoy, Peirce, Renouvier, Zeno, Hegel, and, occasionally, Aristotle. Playing over this large field of ideas was

James's current focus on Bergson, Dewey, Emerson, and Schiller, whose work he was defending in spirited letters to F. H. Bradley: "I believe that humanism, whether with or without the Absolute container, is a 'true' account of our finite knowing and I suspect that methodically and morally it will prove full of regenerating power."[5]

He was also reading John Ruskin's letters to Charles Eliot Norton as they came out in the *Atlantic Monthly* this year. Ruskin had died in 1900; the best of the letters were from the early 1860s, when Ruskin was wrestling with a Tolstoy-like turn to social and moral issues. Ruskin's corrosive self-doubt, articulated with titanic self-assurance, and his unconcealed yearning for radical change, made him a deeply sympathetic figure for James. James may also have shared Ruskin's feeling that the late nineteenth century had let him down in large ways. "I looked for another world," Ruskin wrote Norton, "and find there is only this, and that is past for me; what message I have given is all wrong; has to be all re-said, in another way, and is, so said, almost too terrible to be serviceable."[6]

James himself was filled with regenerative energy, caught up in what was more like a maelstrom than a stately confluence. Out of all these tendencies and influences came, in June and July, an epoch-making pair of essays, the twin anchor points of James's philosophy of radical empiricism, "Does Consciousness Exist?" and "A World of Pure Experience."

In "Does Consciousness Exist?," which Bertrand Russell claimed "startled the world," James says the answer is no. "Consciousness is the name of a non-entity." As we generally conceive of it, consciousness is the "faint rumor left behind by the disappearing 'soul' upon the air of philosophy." If we were to speak precisely, James says, consciousness is "only a name for the fact that the 'content' of experiences *is known*." The reason James makes this explicit break is because he has in his sights the old and comfortable dualisms of subject and object, spirit and nature, mind and matter. James argues that instead of dueling entities there is only process. "I mean only to deny that the word [consciousness] stands for an entity, but to insist most emphatically that it does stand for a function."[7]

This was not a wholly new idea for James. Indeed, he specifically refers back to his *Principles of Psychology*, published fourteen years earlier, in which, he reminds his readers, "I have tried to show that we need no knower other than the 'passing thought.'" His thesis now is that "if we start with the supposition that there is only one primal stuff or material in the world, a stuff of which everything is composed, and if we call that stuff 'pure experience' then knowing can be explained as a particular sort of relation toward one another which portions of pure experience may enter."

As Russell would later summarize it, James held that "there are 'thoughts' which perform the function of 'knowing,' but these thoughts are not made of any different 'stuff' from that of which material objects are made." James's own conclusion is that "'consciousness' is fictitious while thoughts in the concrete are fully real. But thoughts in the concrete are made of the same stuff as things are."[8]

"Does Consciousness Exist?" was ready by late July. James followed it at once with "A World of Pure Experience," in which he tried to specify (the title giving the provisional answer) what that one stuff of which things and thoughts are both made might be. What is required, James argues, is an approach he calls radical empiricism. Empiricism, he insists, is the opposite of rationalism. Rationalism tends to emphasize universals and to make wholes prior to parts. "Empiricism on the contrary lays the explanatory stress upon the part, the element, the individual, and treats the whole as a collection, and the universal as an abstraction. To be radical, an empiricism must neither admit into its constructions any element that is not directly experienced nor exclude from them any element that is directly experienced."[9]

This sounds like a description of Henry James's later novels, perhaps because the level of significant detail (to exactly what level of detail must you ascend in order to grasp or render something as significant?) was the same for both brothers. William, like Henry, thought of "the organization of the Self as a system of memories, purposes, strivings, fulfillments and disappointments." And philosophy for William, like fiction for Henry, "has always turned on grammatical particles. 'With, near, next, like, from, towards, against, because, for, through, my,' — these words designate types of conjunctive relations arranged in a roughly ascending order of intimacy and inclusiveness."

It is the relations that matter, not the objects. Indeed, objects are bundles of relations. "In this continuing and corroborating, taken in no transcendental sense, but denoting definitely felt transitions, *lies all that the knowing of a percept by an idea can possibly contain or signify.* Wherever such transitions are felt, the first experience knows the last one . . . Knowledge of sensible realities thus comes to life inside the tissue of experience."[10]

To the question What exactly is experience? James gives what would now be called a phenomenological reply. "Is it not time to repeat what Lotze said of substances, that to *act like* one is to *be* one?" Life is in the living, not the having lived. Like surfboard riders, "we live as it were upon the front edge of an advancing wave-crest, and our sense of determinate direction in falling forward is all we cover of the future of our path." We cannot speak of mind or personal consciousness except as process, as "the name for a series of experiences run together by certain definite transitions, and an objective reality is a series of similar experiences knit by different transitions."[11]

The conclusion has overtones of both Emerson and Bergson. "Life," says James, "is in the transitions as much as in the terms connected; often indeed it seems to be there more emphatically, as if our spurts and sallies forward were the real firing-line of the battle, were like the thin line of flame advancing across the dry autumnal field." It is as though our old language, with its structure of subject, verb, and object, were to be thrown out for a language of all verbs.[12] "Use" and "surprise," "surface" and "dream" can be nouns, or we can live them as verbs.

This is not easy stuff. James recognized as much when he described his two radical-empiricism essays to his friend Giovanni Papini as "highly technical, polemical, abstract and unnatural for the most part." For James, the resort to technical language was an admission of failure, but even if flawed or partly failed in the expression, James's radical empiricism is important.[13] Bertrand Russell thought James "was right on this matter, and would on this ground alone, deserve a high place among philosophers."[14] Alfred North Whitehead attributed to James "the inauguration of a new stage in philosophy," and he explicitly contrasted "Does Consciousness Exist?" to Descartes' *Discourse on Method:* "James clears the stage of the old paraphernalia; or rather he entirely alters its lighting."[15]

James's radical empiricism was an integral part of the early-twentieth-century revolution that swept through politics, thought, and sensibility. Technical and abstract though the two essays may be, they mark the modern abandonment of certain aspects of classical Western philosophy. James transfers our attention from substance to process, from a concept of self to the process of *selving,* from the concept of truth to the process of *truing* (as a carpenter with a plane "trues" or "trues up" a board), from a trust in concepts to an interest in percepts or perceptions.[16] James is arguing that it is relations between things that matter, not objects or subjects as such. If by relativism we mean evaluating things by their relations to other things, then this is relativism, though the better term is relationism.

The result of James's radical empiricism is to move the modern mind away from seventeenth-century Cartesian dualism and toward what we can call process philosophy; to wean us away from falling back on conceptions and to encourage us to trust our perceptions; to admit feelings to full standing, along with ideas, as aspects of rationality. It does not seem too much to call this a revolution — not a Copernican kind of revolution, but a modernist revolution. And if the exact steps by which radical empiricism emerged for James are not fully clear, it is clear that it happened during the first half of 1904. Sometime after the first of December 1903, James wrote in his notes for his seminar: "All 'classic,' 'clean,' cut and dried, 'noble,' 'fixed,' 'eternal' *Weltanshauungen* [worldviews] seem to me to violate the character with which life concretely comes and the expression which it bears, of being, or at least of involving a muddle and a struggle, with an 'ever not quite' to all our formulas, and novelty and possibility forever leaking in."[17]

What James did in early 1904 was to convert the problem, as here stated, into the answer. The classicists, the formalists, the monists, the Hegelians, and the Royceans were finding more order and unity than the world we experience can warrant. Where Bishop Berkeley had claimed matter to be a fiction and David Hume had shown mind to be a fiction, William James now claimed that both matter and mind were aspects of experience — not fictions but realities, not fundamentally opposed but fundamentally linked.

"In the order of existence, behind the facts, for us there is nothing," James wrote. It is his mature, considered challenge to Plato. "When you strike at a king you must kill him," Emerson had told the young Wendell Holmes. Now James was striking to kill. What radical empiricism says is, there is no eternal order of ideas.

77. Schiller versus Bradley versus James

A T THE END OF AUGUST 1904, Henry James arrived in America after a twenty-three-year absence. He had left when he was thirty-eight; now he was sixty-one, a celebrity followed by newspaper reporters. He was well into the period of his late novels — *The Ambassadors* had appeared in 1903, *The Golden Bowl* was just out. His ship landed at Hoboken. When he crossed to New York City, he eagerly noted the "brave sense of the big bright breezy bay, of light and space and multitudinous movement; of the serried, bristling city, held in the easy embrace of its great good-natured rivers."

The trip started so well that after only a few weeks his brother William was already declaring it "a great success." William clearly enjoyed Henry's company. Henry seemed "to be delighted with everything he sees, especially with the prettiness of Chocorua," William wrote Katharine Rodgers. To Pauline Goldmark he wrote about Henry's "delightful fortnight" at Chocorua, adding, "It is a pleasure to be with anyone who takes in things through the eyes." Henry's trip bore its planned fruit as a series of travel pieces, gathered together in book form in 1907.[1]

William's own spirits were high. He felt better than he had in five years, and he too was taking in things through his eyes. Describing Chocorua for Pauline in late September, he burst out, "Such a green and gold and scarlet morn as this would raise the dead." He thought things were really moving his way in the world of philosophy. "It seems to me that the movement [radical empiricism] has all the characters of the birth of a big scientific revolutionary conception." It was, he observed elsewhere, "great fun to be a philosopher after they have once begun to take notice of what you say."[2]

There was, for example, Schiller, whom James had known for some time but who was now becoming important to James. Ferdinand Canning Scott Schiller took two firsts at Oxford (classical moderations and *litterae humaniores*), came to the United States to take a doctor's degree at Cornell, left without the degree, and went back to England, where he settled in as a tutor at Corpus Christi College, Oxford. He was twenty-two years younger than James, high-spirited, brash to the point of recklessness, outspoken, and full of jokes.

He was undeniably brilliant, but his schoolboyish humor, his abusive personal attacks on philosophical opponents, and his eagerness to turn philosophical debate into a blood sport made him enemies. In 1901 he put out a parody issue of *Mind,* the main English journal for philosophy and psychology. Schiller called his parody *Mind!* Among the spoofs were "The Place of Humour in the Absolute" by F. H. Badly and "The Critique of Pure Rot" by I. Cant.[3] Schiller called anyone who disagreed with him "the enemy." He wrote constantly of the need for "a decisive defeat of B[radley]," of "our aggressive campaign against Jericho," of the "big guns" and our "ammunition." He once likened the dispute between the pragmatists and F. H. Bradley to a bullfight. The bull was Bradley, the picadors were Dewey and company, the first banderillero was Schiller. After the bull had been stuck with banderillas named after Schiller's writings — including, of course, *Mind!* — it was time for the "MATADOR: WJ."

Schiller wrote a clear and graceful prose, and his fundamental position was deeply congenial to James. For Plato, Schiller once wrote, "the Idea remains the only true reality and the Idea as such is unchanging Being, out of space and time . . . To Aristotle, the real world, i.e. the world whereof we desire an explanation, is after all the world of change in which we move and live." James was enthusiastic about Schiller's first book, *Riddles of the Sphinx,* which tried to combine Darwinian evolution with philosophic idealism; James called it a "pluralistic, theistic book, of great vigor and constructive originality . . . and quite in the lines in which I incline to tread."[4]

Shortly after moving to Oxford, in the closing years of the nineteenth century, Schiller began to attract attention as a proponent of what James called pragmatism and Schiller himself called humanism. In 1904 Schiller published a book called *Humanism: Philosophical Essays,* dedicated to "my dear friend, the humanest of philosophers, William James, without whose example and unfailing encouragement, this book would never have been written." In it he talked a good deal about James and pragmatism, proposed the name "humanism" for it, and set out to rescue philosophy from "the hands of recluses who have lost all interest in the practical concerns of humanity, and have rendered philosophy like unto themselves, abstruse, arid, abstract and abhorrent."[5]

James reviewed the book favorably, as did Dewey and Flournoy. Many others were offended. Bradley wrote James to explain why a piece he, Bradley, had written contained "strictures on Schiller and incidentally on yourself." In Bradley's view, Schiller had been "advertising himself and his wares for some years incessantly," and had been spreading the idea that he, Schiller, "had behind him a large and important following in Oxford." Münsterberg refused to invite Schiller to his Congress of Arts and Science because he considered "the level of the Congress too much lowered if a personality of his type [should be] in it." Münsterberg openly sneered that "the Congress was not made for men who are unable to pass a Doctor's examination in Cornell."[6]

The stately G. H. Palmer found Schiller "insufferable." Santayana said he "hated Schiller and his thought." James stuck up for him through it all, explaining at length to Bradley why he should take Schiller seriously, and even rebuking J. M. Baldwin for calling Schiller "vulgar" in print. He also wrote Schiller long letters trying to persuade him to calm down. In August 1904 he told Schiller, "It is astonishing how many persons resent in your past writings what seems to them 'bad taste,' in the way of polemical jeers and general horseplay." James explained in detail, with appropriate disclaimers and qualifications. "I think your whole mental tone against our critics is overstrained . . . Nothing is gained by calling them names . . . What I *earnestly beseech you to do therefore is* (no matter at what *literary* cost) to suppress those [first seven] pages." (Schiller had sent James a draft of a new blast against Bradley.) Schiller replied, lighthearted as ever, "Will you pardon me if I'm neither willing nor able to take your advice?" James's tone with Schiller remained friendly and admiring, if at times that of an exasperated parent. "To me," James wrote him, "it is unspeakably sad that when a man reasons and writes as you do, more clean and clear in style than anyone, full of new insights and new handlings of the old on every page, people should consider themselves free to ignore your philosophy because forsooth their taste doesn't quite relish your jokes, and some of your other ways. One of them is mentioning *my* name too often — cut that out!"[7]

If James was pleased, and a little flattered, by Schiller's adherence and was dedicated to working with him, he was also deeply and fruitfully engaged with F. H. Bradley himself, once Bradley began to take notice of James's writings. In 1904 Bradley and James had not yet met.[8] Bradley was four years younger than James. A severe kidney ailment obliged him to lead a quiet, reclusive life. As an undergraduate he read the same subjects Schiller would read later, and though his showing at Oxford was not as good as Schiller's, Bradley received a fellowship at Merton College in 1870. The fellowship was for life, involved no teaching, and would be terminated if he ever married. In 1895 Bradley wrote James a letter about the latter's "The Knowing of Things Together," starting a correspondence that continued off and on until James's death. James was much impressed by Bradley's *Appearance and Reality,* so there was a substantial foreground to the renewed correspondence of 1904 and 1905.

A friend of Bradley's, A. E. Taylor, summed up Bradley's writings by saying they "probably did more than those of any other man to effect the naturalization of Hegelian thought in England which was so marked a feature of the close of the nineteenth century." Bradley believed in "the thoroughgoing super-rational unity of all reality." T. S. Eliot wrote his doctoral dissertation on Bradley, and there are places in Bradley's work where one glimpses foreshadowings of *Four Quartets.* Bradley wrote: "'For love and beauty and delight,' it is no matter where they have shown themselves, 'there is no death nor change'; and this conclusion is true. There things do not die, since the Paradise in which they bloom is immortal. That Paradise is no special region nor any given particular spot in time or space. It is here, it is everywhere where any finite being is lifted into that higher life which alone is waking reality."[9]

Bradley was Platonistic, monistic, and a neo-Hegelian. He was much like Royce, and James's relation to Bradley was much like his relation to

Royce, only Royce was his neighbor and colleague and could talk things out directly with James, whereas Bradley's relationship with James was always through the written word. At first glance, Bradley and James seem poles apart. "Bradley's main affirmation," Timothy Sprigge writes in a recent book, "is the existence of the Absolute, a single infinite experience of which everything finite is an agent, and much of James's thought is devoted to the critique of such a claim."

But James and Bradley — and James and Royce — had, and realized they had, a lot in common. Though James was a pluralist and Bradley a monist, both believed in "panexperientialism," a term of art for the belief that "concrete reality is composed of innumerable pulses of experience." Bradley's monistic world was somehow composed of the same experience as James's pluralist world. Bradley's world incorporates James's, saying the pluralism is only apparent, not real. James, on his side, had a covert monistic impulse, in that he "came to believe in a single mother-sea of consciousness which all finite consciousnesses emerge from, and return to, with enrichments won when separate." Timothy Sprigge compares James and Bradley at length and finds them locked in a symbiotic embrace. Sprigge concludes, "While I think Bradley right upon the whole about the whole, I think James right in very large part about the parts." It is a line Schiller would have liked.[10]

Bradley and James took on the big questions in their correspondence. James had written in 1898 to Bradley, "The *deep* questions which the moral life suggests are metaphysical. 1) Is evil real? 2) Is it essential to the universe? If these questions are to be answered with a yes I cannot see who is responsible, or may be called so." Bradley thought James had failed to account for the "moral and intellectual repugnance" to chance felt by ordinary people. "It is, I presume, certain that the tidings that the best things in the world go, or may go, by chance, would be received by 'the plain man' with horror." Now, in 1904 and 1905, the correspondence flared up again, with Bradley apologizing for having to remonstrate with Schiller, and with James urging Bradley to overlook Schiller's immaturities and recognize the solid substrate of thought.

Most notable in the letters between Bradley and James is the invincible civility of their forthright disagreements. "Naturally I am far from suggesting that there is nothing in 'pragmatism,'" Bradley wrote James in July 1904. "I think there is a good deal, though not as a theory of first principles." James replied to what he called Bradley's "exceedingly courteous letter," defending Schiller's writing as "absolutely *objective*" and insisting that "you, in your article, seem to me to have sought for whatever interpretation of Schiller would allow you to reject the most of him." James could also fault his own *Will to Believe* as a "luckless title, which should have been 'The *Right* to Believe,'" and he took care to sign himself "always truly and amicably yours, Wm James." Where Schiller could be an embarrassing ally, Bradley's unflinching decency, which was reciprocated by James, made him a constructive and welcome opponent.[11]

78. *Royce: Pragmatic Stirrings*

WILLIAM JAMES'S LIFE reached another high tide during the academic year 1904–05. His health remained excellent, his philosophical work was being taken seriously, and his teaching and writing were going well enough to satisfy even him.

Throughout the fall of 1904 until the end of January 1905 he taught the first half of Philosophy 9. It was a "general introduction to philosophy on . . . 'radically empirical' principles," he told one correspondent. "The course as given this year, is more successful in awakening serious interest than any course I have ever given." It was a yearlong course; Royce taught the second half. James explained how it worked in a letter to Bradley: "We have the same students — I give them pluralism the 1st half year, he monism the second half — no one can take a single half of the course, and R and I love each other like Siamese Twins." As the metaphor suggests, James saw it as more than a simple matter of opposition. "I think I understand his absolute pretty well, and it is essentially a vehicle of conjunction, and of making things monistic. He is a first-rate empirical mind, and to a great extent gives away in detail the monism which in general he affirms." Bradley replied good-naturedly that he had "smiled at the idea of the bane and the antidote being put before students in due order."[1]

James's outline for the course has survived, and even in its naked form it makes engaging reading. "Out of chance can come order" is followed at once by "Out of order no chance." There is also a wonderfully succinct restatement of Royce's argument that the existence of error proves that there is such a thing as truth. "If you say there is nothing but opinion, neither truth nor error, that opinion at least claims truth; the opinion that there *is* truth is at least an error." And James gave his students another of the startling images with which his work swarms. If the universe of absolute idealism was like "an aquarium, a crystal globe in which goldfish are swimming," the empiricist universe was "more like one of those dried human heads with which the Dyaks of Borneo deck their lodges. The skull forms a solid nucleus; but innumerable feathers, leaves, strings, beads and loose appendages of every description float and dangle from it, and save that they terminate in it, seem to have nothing to do with one another. Even so my experiences and yours float and dangle."[2]

Both James and Royce brought a saving sense of humor to the undertaking. James took potshots at the Absolute. Royce gave as good as he got. Once he imagined a pragmatist taking his oath on the witness stand: "I promise to tell whatever is expedient and nothing but what is expedient, so help me future experience." The vivid photographs of James and Royce on the stone wall at Chocorua were snapped just as James was saying "Damn the Absolute!"[3]

The crowning achievement — felt as such by James — of this academic year was the series of pieces James produced with uncharacteristic dispatch. In February 1905 he wrote Santayana that he had finished teaching his part of Philosophy 9 and "shall have published 9 articles since September 1." One of these was essentially a reprint of his California talk on pragmatism, another was his piece on Tom Davidson, but the other seven were all professional, technical, or polemical aspects of the radical empiricism that was now firmly at the center of James's energies and interests.[4] To his friend Giulio Cesare Ferrari James wrote in late February that he was more interested in radical empiricism "than I have ever been in anything else." And in March he wrote to the editor of the *Journal of Philosophy, Psychology, and Scientific Methods,* in which most of his work was now appearing, "Every step I make confirms me in the view that radical empiricism is *It.*"[5]

James's active, restless life reached a kind of crescendo during this winter. He completed negotiations to spend half a year teaching at Stanford University. He was writing and reading proofs of half a dozen papers on radical empiricism. He was finishing his lectures in Philosophy 9 and frantically arranging for reprints of his current articles to be run off in time to get them to his students before Royce could lay his monist hands on them. The outside world had claims on him as well. He watched the early days of the Russian Revolution with interest, and accepted the vice presidency of the Filipino Progress Association, one of the anti-imperialist efforts he worked for. He followed the Russo-Japanese War abroad, and he kept an eye on his brother's travels at home. Henry stayed in Washington, D.C., with Henry Adams and dined with President Roosevelt. The novelist ran into an ice storm at Biltmore in North Carolina, visited Charleston, South

Carolina, and lectured on Balzac in Philadelphia and again at Bryn Mawr to crowds of six or seven hundred.

William's reading this winter — one wonders where he found time for it — included Ruskin's *Praeterita,* his autobiographical remembrance of things past, a three-volume work of a nostalgic sort that James had a weakness for. The last paragraph of the book, and the last thing Ruskin wrote, was a memory of a moment shared with James's neighbor Charles Eliot Norton in Siena, when they went together to the Branda Fountain: "I last saw [it] with Charles Norton, under the same arches where Dante saw it. We drank of it together, and walked together that evening on the hills above, where the fireflies among the scented thickets shone fitfully in the still undarkened air. *How* they shone! Moving like fine-broken starlight through the purple leaves."[6]

James also read this winter a social novel called *The Common Lot,* about the life of a corrupt architect who sees the light. The novelist was a former student, Robert Herrick; James wrote an appreciative letter. He now read, apparently for the first time, Gustav Fechner's amazing *Zend-Avesta,* and another book by the English Whitman enthusiast Edward Carpenter, *The Art of Creation.* He had recently read and extravagantly admired William Dean Howells's epistolary novel, *Letters Home.* Hamlin Garland wrote James for help with material for his spiritualist novel, *The Tyranny of the Dark.* If there was always something of the artist about James, there was always something literary too.

As if all this were not enough, James agreed to give, between February 28 and March 10, a series of five lectures at Wellesley College, "Characteristics of an Individualistic Philosophy." He did not write out these talks, but his outlines survive, showing that he was aiming at a more general, less professional audience than his just ended Harvard course on radical empiricism. The five lectures are usually seen as a first draft for *Pragmatism,* but they also embody, at this stage, ideas from what was eventually published as *Essays in Radical Empiricism* and ideas from what would become *A Pluralistic Universe.* From the late winter of 1905 onward, James was working toward all three books at more or less the same time. Inevitably his projects overlapped. The technical work fed the general lectures, beefing up their serious philosophical content, while the requirements of a general audience leavened the technical work, making it accessible to more people.

James devoted the first of the Wellesley talks to individualism, the second to pragmatism. The third talk was on varieties of unity, and the fourth defended the "pluralistic scheme." The fifth argued for empiricism against absolutism. This final lecture also advanced a summary. His outline shows how he ended his last talk; the telegraphic form only amplifies the tone of urgency.

> This then is the individualistic view . . .
> It means many good things: e.g.
> Genuine novelty
> order being *won,* paid for.
> the smaller systems the truer
> man [is greater than] home [is greater than] state or church.
> anti-slavery in all ways
> toleration — respect of others
> democracy — good systems can always be described in individualistic terms.
> hero-worship and leadership.
> the vital and the growing as against the fossilized and fixed in science, art, religion, government and custom.
> faith and help
> in morals, obligation respondent to demand.
> Finally it avoids the *smug*ness which Swift found a reproach.

Then he concluded with a quotation from his old correspondent Benjamin Paul Blood: "What is concluded that we should conclude etc."[7]

He gave the last talk on March 10. Moving at his customary breakneck speed, James boarded a ship the very next day and sailed for Europe and a change of scene.

79. William and Henry

THE SAME TREMENDOUS surge of energy, optimism, and good health that had carried James along since the previous summer now swept him off to the Mediterranean. He arrived in Naples on March 25, 1905, after touching at Gibraltar and Genoa. He saw old friends, met new people; he was never long in one place and always eager to see everything. From Naples he went to Capri, which he thought "glorious," then to the peninsula south of Naples.[1]

He traveled from Sorrento to Positano to Amalfi, and he wrote home describing the road, "a cornice affair, cut for the most part on the face of cliffs, and crossing little ravines (with beaches) on the sides of which nestle hamlets," as being "positively ferocious in its grandeur, and on the side of it the azure sea, dreaming and blooming like a bed of violets." His painter's eye revived, not just in a taste for scenery but also in an interest in the human landscape. One afternoon he "walked alone through the *old* Naples, hilly streets, paved from house to house and swarming with the very poor, vocal with them too, their voices carry so that every child seems to be calling to the whole street . . . the street floor composed of cave-like shops, the people doing their work on chairs in the streets for the sake of light and in the black insides beds and a stove visible among the implements of trade. Such light and shade, and grease and grime, and swarm, and apparent amiability would be hard to match." The "black old Naples streets" seemed to him "not suggestions, they are the reality itself — full orchestra." His description is mixed with a curious sense of regret. "I have come here too late in life," he wrote home, "when the picturesque has lost its serious reality. Time was when hunger for it haunted me like a passion."[2]

He enjoyed the trip hugely. Crossing from Italy to Athens, he wrote his daughter that the whole trip was "almost absurdly ideal." In Athens he saw the usual sights with the usual reactions. "There is a mystery of *rightness* about that Parthenon that I cannot understand." In Athens, at the Hotel Minerva, he ran into George Santayana, the first two volumes of whose just published *Life of Reason* James had read, twice, on the Atlantic trip over.[3]

James had some reservations about the book ("wonderful, though I fear not quite true," he wrote Alice) and about the man: "that gifted fish," he called him. "He's the oddest *spectator* of life — seems as if he took *no* active interest in anything." The book was, however, appealing in some ways. Santayana's very definition of reason, as "a name for all practical thought and all action justified by its fruits in consciousness," would have seemed friendly to James's own enterprise. Santayana wrote beautifully too. "Fanaticism," he remarks, "consists in redoubling your effort when you have forgotten your aim." It was, Santayana says, "visionary insolence in the Germans to make the constructive process anything more than common sense." A few weeks later, back in Italy, writing from Orvieto and thinking about the "baldheaded and bald-hearted young men" of Cambridge, James was moved to say to Santayana, "Can't you and I, who in spite of such divergence have yet so much in common in our *weltanschauung* start a systematic movement at Harvard against the desiccating and pedantifying process?"[4]

James went on to Rome, where he showed up at the Fifth International Congress of Psychology. He had not planned to take an active part in the proceedings, but when he went to register and gave his name, "the lady who was taking them almost fainted, saying that all Italy loved me . . . and finally [she] got me to consent to make an address at one of the general meetings." The talk, written on the run at the last minute, and in French, was called "La Notion de Conscience." It is a thoughtful summary of "Does Consciousness Exist?" and "A World of Pure Experience," and James liked it well enough to include it when he came later to plan a book on radical empiricism.

He used the occasion both to sharpen his attack and to consolidate his new position. Since French lacks a separate word for consciousness, James starts by pointing out that consciousness "is always considered as possessing an essence absolutely distinct from the essence of material objects, which, by a mysterious gift, it can represent and know."[5] This always leads, James says, to a dualistic outlook: there is consciousness and there is the world. James is out to challenge dualism. "The world may well exist by itself, but we know nothing of this because for us it is exclusively an object of experience." In the end, then, both thinker and thought "are made of one and the same stuff, which as such cannot be defined but only experienced; and which, if one wishes, one can call the stuff of experience in general."[6]

James's appearance at the congress was a triumph. The Florentine pragmatists, headed by Papini, formed an admiring circle around him. He found himself referred to as "il più grande psicologo del mondo." His friend Janet declared himself "stupéfait" at James's performance in French. Just as America was welcoming Henry James back and crowding to his lectures in Chicago, Philadelphia, Bryn Mawr, and Boston, so Europe was welcoming and celebrating William.

Pisa was next, where he had lunch with the art critic Bernard Berenson. At Cannes he talked philosophy "hot and heavy" with Charles A. Strong. In Marseille he met Frank Abauzit, the French translator of *The Varieties of Religious Experience*. Then it was on to Geneva and lunch with his old friend Flournoy, then to Paris, where he finally met "the Beautiful Bergson." After this, James made a quick stop at Oxford, where he had lunch with Schiller and three of Schiller's friends. On top of everything, Bradley, whom he did not meet on this trip, sent him a long letter that said, among much else, "I am beginning to wonder whether I have not always myself been a Pragmatist." Over and over, Bradley urged James to put his case at length, in a book; nothing but a whole volume "can possibly do the job." The day after the Oxford lunch James hurried to Liverpool and, on June 2, boarded the ship for home. It had been a triumphal whirlwind tour, but his "damnable spring neurasthenic fag" was upon him as he returned to America and to Cambridge.[7]

The second half of 1905 went badly. Trouble began shortly after his arrival at home late in the day on June 11. On the thirteenth he started his lymph injections again; on the sixteenth Henry James arrived from California and New York, talking about the ghost experiences told him by a man named Bruce Porter in San Francisco.[8] The next day William fired off a letter rejecting an invitation to membership in the American Academy of Arts and Letters in New York City. His letter to Robert Johnson, the editor and poet who was the secretary of the academy, cited his "life-long practice of not letting my name figure where there is not some definite work doing in which I am willing to bear a share." He derided the academy as "an organization for the mere purpose of distinguishing certain individuals (with their own connivance) and enabling them to say to the world at large 'we are in and you are out.'" Heated up now with his drumbeat of opposition, James pushed satirically on: "And I am the more encouraged to this course by the fact that my younger and shallower and vainer brother is already in the Academy, and that if I were there too, the other families represented might think the James influence too rank and strong."[9]

James's feelings about the academy are understandable, though he was already a member of other academies that had no better reason for existence than this one, and he had accepted honorary degrees from Padua, Princeton, Edinburgh, and Harvard. He would eventually be a member of the national academies of France, Italy, Prussia, and Denmark, and would accept further honorary degrees from Durham, Geneva, and Oxford. He was indeed already a member of the parent organization of the academy, the American Institute of Arts and Letters. The academy was to be a very select thirty-member circle enclosing only the inmost of insiders.

One can imagine all this setting William off. Johnson was an officious man who valued good form above all else, and who had requested an "imperial sized" photograph of William. Knowing all this, William would have enjoyed irritating Johnson. But what explains William's gratuitous remarks about Henry? Perhaps it was just another bit of James's habitual irreverence, the epistolary horseplay he so enjoyed. But this is a letter he drafted and then rewrote; his first draft referred only to "my younger and vainer brother." Revision did not soften the edge; it sharpened it. Perhaps William was miffed at being voted in on the fourth and last ballot, whereas Henry had been voted in on the second. Henry had also gotten into *Who's Who* before William did.[10] William can't have thought his unkind crack wouldn't get back to Henry; Johnson knew Henry and had been his editor at *Century Magazine.*

The recently dormant rivalry between William and Henry seemed to have come alive. Despite or perhaps because of their long-standing closeness, there were things each disapproved of in the other. Henry had recently been in Chicago, where he told his hostess he considered William's wife "the finest woman living, only criminally sacrificed." This was passed on to William. A little later, in the fall of 1905, we find Henry writing to William, "I am much puzzled by a mystery and ambiguity in all your sequences — Peg's admission to Bryn Mawr, mixed up with her simultaneous social debut and your California absence etc. When do you go there, anyhow, and when does she go to B.M. and does she go to California with you, and if she doesn't who takes her out, at home, and with whom does she abide?" Henry obviously thought William was neglecting Peggy. Where the unmarried Henry felt free to criticize William's performance as a family man, William showed an equally unearned relish for telling Henry how to write novels.[11]

It is easy to make too much of William's lashing out at Henry in the letter to Robert Johnson. Neither brother was particularly thin-skinned, and we have to remember that in their lifelong relationship there was never anything even remotely approaching a break between them. Jacques Barzun has remarked that William and Henry understood each other better than their biographers have. The longer William and Henry lived, the closer the bond became.

About the only thing that went right for William this summer was his lecture engagement at the University of Chicago at the end of June. Expecting an audience of perhaps fifty, James found himself moved to a larger auditorium and lecturing to seven hundred and fifty people. He gave five lectures under the title "Characteristics of Individual Philosophy." They were a reworking of his Wellesley lectures, and the emphasis was on both the pragmatic method and radical empiricism. The audience never fell below five hundred, and James was euphoric when, at the last lecture, he felt he had the audience so completely won over that they were "pulling on my line like one fish."[12]

Henry returned to England in early July 1905 to begin work on the New York Edition of his writings, an edition planned to appear in twenty-three volumes, just as Balzac's work had. William was sick for six weeks with the flu. Alice's headaches were worse; she tried new doctors, new regimens, morphine. At the end of September classes began again. James gave his seminar in metaphysics as well as the opening part of Philosophy 1a, a general introduction he gave together with Royce and Münsterberg to 226 students. The courses went well enough, and James was confident he was lecturing well, but he sensed he was coming to the end of his teaching career. By the last days of October he was done with his part of Philosophy 1a.[13] Routine and a certain distance had settled over his long association with Royce. James complained to his young friend Dickinson Miller that "Royce has never made a syllable of reference to all the stuff I wrote last year — to me, I mean. He may have spoken of it to others, if he has read it, which I doubt. So we live in parallel trenches and hardly show our heads."[14]

Then he entered a particularly bad patch. From the last week of October through the first week of December James was in utter turmoil, caused either by the actual prospect of resigning or by other anxieties and dissatisfactions brought to the surface by that prospect. James's diary for these weeks records an agony of indecision that seems comic in retrospect but can't have been much fun at the time. Nov 3: "Resign!" Nov 4: "Resign?" Nov 6: "Doubtful about resigning." Nov. 7: "Resign!" Nov. 8: "Don't resign!" Nov. 9: "Resign!" And so on, for six long weeks.[15]

Two days after the last lecture in the big undergraduate course, William wrote Henry about *The Golden Bowl*. It is perhaps the most censorious letter he ever wrote to his brother. The novel puzzled him, William wrote, "and the method of narration by interminable elaboration of suggestive reference (I don't know what to call it, but you know what I mean) goes agin the grain of all my own impulses in writing." William did concede that Henry had achieved "a brilliancy and cleanness of effect, and . . . a high-toned social atmosphere" that was "unique and extraordinary," and he seemed to set a seal of brotherly approval when he acknowledged "your extreme success in this book." But then, falling into the old, loaded James family banter, William ground remorselessly on: "But why won't you, just to please Brother, sit down and write a new book, with no twilight or mustiness in the plot, with great vigor and decisiveness in the action, no fencing in the dialogue, no psychological commentaries, and absolute straightness in the style? Publish it in my name, I will acknowledge it, and give you half the proceeds . . . Seriously," he added, "I wish you *would*, for you *can*, and I should think it would tempt you, to embark on a 'fourth manner.'"[16]

Henry's reply to this was a long letter — the same one in which he voiced his disapproval of William's treatment of Peggy — in which he said he would indeed try to "produce some uncanny form of thing, in fiction, that will gratify you, as Brother." Then Henry turned to attack William's taste: "But let me say, dear William, that I shall greatly be humiliated if you *do* like it, and thereby lump it, in your affection, with things, of the current age, that I have heard you express admiration for and that I would sooner descend to a dishonored grave than have written."[17]

Then Henry moderated his mood ("but it's seriously too late at night . . .") to a more sober awareness of the large differences between them. "I'm always sorry when I hear of your reading anything of mine and always hope you won't — you seem to me so constitutionally unable to 'enjoy' it, and so condemned to look at it from a point of view remotely alien to mine in writing it." Henry wrote more to this effect, concluding with a sigh of regret, "It shows how far apart and to what different ends we have had to work out (very naturally and properly) our respective intellectual lives." Then, in a generous move, an unexpected turn worthy of the master that he was, Henry proffered an olive branch. "And yet I can read *you* with rapture — having three weeks ago spent three or four days with Manton Marble at Brighton and found in his hands ever so many of your recent papers and discourses . . . Philosophically, in short, I am 'with' you, almost completely, and you ought to take account of this and get me over altogether."[18]

What held these two brothers together would always outweigh what drew them apart. In the best-known photograph of the two of them, taken around 1900, Henry stands straight, but his head inclines sharply toward William. William holds his head perfectly erect, but his whole upper body inclines toward, even leans on, Henry.

Besides his complicated and, at the moment, vexed relationship with his brother, William confronted a philosophical problem this fall. Just as the golden bowl in Henry's most recent novel — and the last he would complete — has a flaw, an all but indiscernible crack, and is not quite what it seems to be (it is not gold but gilded crystal), so William came to feel there was a major, indeed a fatal, flaw in his understanding and explanation of experience. As he faced up to the criticism of two philosophical colleagues, Boyd H. Bode and Dickinson Miller (Miller had once been a tutor for William's children), and to perceived inconsistencies between his own work and that of Lotze, Royce, Fechner, Woodbridge, Dewey, and Bergson, James began, in late November and early December of 1905, to fill a pair of notebooks with his thoughts on the problem.[19]

The dilemma involved a serious discrepancy between his account of experience in *The Principles of Psychology* and his current understanding of experience, his new doctrine of "pure experience." In the *Principles* James had argued that every part of our experience is a unique and unrepeatable bit of the ceaseless flow of the river of consciousness. He could say this because he then believed that there was an objective world "out there" that we as individuals could never know. Now, however, James had dropped the old dualism of subject and object and was arguing that experience is all there is.

The problem arose when one set out to show that two minds can know a single thing. If they can, doesn't the agreement show that there is indeed an objective world out there for the two minds to agree on? By early December 1905 he was coming to think there was no satisfactory way to resolve the difference. If reality consisted entirely of a stream of experiences, each experience complete and separate from the one before and the one after, how could one ever maintain that there existed a world beyond our experiences? It was far too late in the day to resort to laboratory work; the subjective experiences James intended to make sense of went beyond what could be measured or weighed. His ongoing effort to defend the notion of pure experience also carried him to places where neither logic nor language was well adapted to help. James's new idea was that the usual dualism of subject and object, of knower and known, is false. On the contrary, there is only experience, and somehow one experience carries or floats the next, and that relationship is what we call knowledge.[20]

James wrestled with this and related problems for the next couple of years. The doctrine of pure experience *is* hard to defend, just as Whitehead remarked that no one can live by pure empiricism (according to which it does not matter how many times a ball drops when you let go of it; you are never entitled to conclude it will drop the next time). Philosophers are still divided as to whether James was here making a misstep or whether he had momentarily lost his way or just lost his nerve. In any case, he felt, especially during the last months of 1905, that he faced a problem. On an early page of what has come to be called "The Miller-Bode Objections" James wrote opposite a summary of an argument by Dickinson Miller, "Methinks that pure experience breaks down here definitively." But toward the end of the notebook, James seems to have concluded against his earlier position and in favor of pure experience: "Thus, to sum up, mental facts *can* ... compound themselves, if you take them concretely and livingly, as possessed of various functions. They can count variously, figure in different constellations, without ceasing to be 'themselves.'"[21]

Following his prickly response to the American Academy of Arts and Letters, the sniping at Henry and the attack on his third manner, the heated vacillation over whether and when to resign, and the growing controversy over pure experience, one final quarrel erupted in this unusually contentious stretch of James's life. After he decided in early December to put off resigning for one more year, after writing a letter proposing himself for a series of Lowell Lectures the next year, after Peggy's first ball, and after the unexpected death of Richard Hodgson — the remaining mainstay, in James's view, of serious psychical research — there came, two days after Christmas, the dedication of Emerson Hall, the new home of the Harvard philosophy department.

Hugo Münsterberg was the chairman of the department, and after working out the details of the Emerson Hall ceremony at a meeting James missed, Münsterberg officiated and, in James's opinion, disastrously dominated the proceedings. James, who could be tact itself in dealing with, say, F. H. Bradley, uncorked a tactless, indeed an offensive, letter to Münsterberg, saying, "I think you committed a fault of taste this afternoon in making such long speeches," and adding, "A young man and a German ought not to have played the chief part in so peculiarly yankee-sentiment-arousing a ceremony."

Münsterberg immediately sent in his resignation to the president of the university, along with an explanation of how the Emerson Hall program had evolved. Notes and letters sped back and forth. Eliot conceded that Münsterberg perhaps thought too much of himself, but he also felt obliged to tell James, "When you recommended Münsterberg for an appointment here you must have expected that he would be different from us, and doubtless reckoned on those very differences as part of the profit to the University."

Doubtless. Still, it must have been with a sense of relief that James boarded the noon train on December 29 and set out for California and a semester at Stanford University.[22]

80. California Dreaming

JAMES HEADED WEST during the final days of 1905 with something less than his usual ebullient anticipation. He took the southern route, stopping to see the Grand Canyon, which he found "solemn, solemn!" with "a unity of design that makes it seem like an individual, an animated being." He also passed through Los Angeles and Santa Barbara before going up the coast to Palo Alto and Stanford. Writing Alice from his hotel in Santa Barbara, James found himself looking back wistfully on his California visit of eight years earlier, and on his earlier self, "so youthful and romantic. It really was the high tide of my life."[1]

He reached Palo Alto on January 8, checked in with President David Starr Jordan, and noted in his diary that he felt "lonely and scared." He betrayed no such feeling in his letters, remarking to his wife, who was to join him as soon as she could, only that he was "pretty tired" and hadn't been sleeping well. Two days later he began teaching.

He had a large (four-hundred-student) general introduction to philosophy. In some ways it was similar to his recent course at Harvard, but in others it was something he said he had never done before. He was, for one thing, the sole instructor. His position at Stanford was that of acting chairman of philosophy, and he understood his job to be "to create an atmosphere." He enjoyed the challenge and what he called the "artistic problem" of designing an appropriate course, though it meant doing no serious writing this semester. He even seems to have left the Miller-Bode notebooks and the radical-empiricism problem behind.

James found his overall situation quite uncomplicated compared with life in Cambridge, where he often spent "the whole of each day in clearing away the stuff that the day itself brings forth." Palo Alto nights were cold, the mornings foggy; the air smelled of smoke and eucalyptus. Stanford, a recently founded university with an already splendid campus, was, James wrote Schiller, "absolutely utopian. It realizes all those simplifications and freedoms from corruption, of which seers have dreamed, classic landscape, climate perfect, no one rich, sexes equal, manual labor practiced to some degree by all, especially by students, noble harmonious architecture, fine laboratories and collections, admirable music." Underlying and surrounding all this, however, James always heard "the great silence of the historic vacuum." He would come to feel differently about some aspects of Stanford, but for the present he responded enthusiastically to its ideal side.[2]

Yet he continued to sleep badly; his diary reveals what his letters do not. Jan. 26: "Bad sleep — it doesn't stop!" Jan. 27: "Bad sleep. In bed 8:40 tonight."[3] He was also asked to give talks. On February 5, for instance, he addressed the Pacific Coast Unitarian Club on reason and faith, which he approached as two different paths by which we reach conclusions. "Faith," he said, "uses a logic altogether different from Reason's logic." His version of faith's logic, so different from the technical syllogisms of classical logic, he called the "faith ladder." This was a series of faith feelings, states of mind expressed as a sequence of ever-stronger, more imperative verbs. It was a postlogical riff, a bit of razzle-dazzle with which James often ended his courses. "Faith's form of argument is something like this: Considering a vision of the world: 'it is *fit* to be true,' she feels; 'it would be well if it *were* true; it *might* be true; it *may* be true; it *ought* to be true,' she says; 'it *must* be true,' she continues; 'it *shall* be true,' she concludes, '*for me;* that is, I will treat it as if it *were* true so far as my advocacy and actions are concerned.'"[4]

James gave every speaking engagement all he had. In the short talk "Reason and Faith" he gave the Unitarians not one but two of his best moments and finest convictions. Like Emerson before him, James brooded on the figure of Luther, declaring that "religious experience of the Lutheran type brings all our naturalistic standards [the world of classical reason] to bankruptcy." What Luther illuminated for James was the psychology of conversion. "You are strong only by being weak," James says. "To give up one's concept of being good, is the only door to the Universe's deeper reaches." And, as he had in the *Varieties,* he turns from Luther to the present, to mind cure and New Thought as well as to evangelical Christianity. What they all reveal is "new ranges of life succeeding on our most despairing moments." James brings his audience to the edge of a cliff, then, rather than climb hand over hand down the ladder, whether of faith or of reason, he simply launches out. There are, in us, "possibilities that take our breath away, and show a world wider than either physics or philistine ethics can imagine. Here is a world in which all is well, *in spite* of certain forms of death, indeed because of certain forms of death, death of hope, death of strength, death of responsibility, of fear and wrong, death of everything that paganism, naturalism and legalism pin their trust on."[5]

A few days after this bright sallying forth, James underwent what he later identified as "the most intensely peculiar experience of my whole life." The experience was of a strange and frightening series of interwoven dreams that began during the night of February 11. James was in his room at Stanford. Alice was on her way west to join him, coming by train from Cambridge. The day after his "Reason and Faith" talk James had come down with gout. "Unitarian gout — was ever such a thing heard of?" he wailed to Tom Perry. It outraged him; it put him on crutches. The compensation, if it can be called that, was that he "slept splendidly" through the gout. But then, six days after the talk, he woke up on February 12 "from a quiet dream of some sort, and whilst gathering my waking wits seemed suddenly to get mixed up with reminiscences of a dream of an entirely different sort, which seemed to telescope, as it were, into the first one, a dream very elaborate, of lions, and tragic. I concluded this to have been a previous dream of the same sleep; but the apparent mingling of two dreams was something very queer, which I had never before experienced."[6]

It was not the content of the dream or dreams that was so strange; it was their interwoven quality, the confusion and the sense of disconnectedness between different dream experiences. James was neither credulous nor superstitious about dreams. He knew about, even if he had not read, Freud's recent *Interpretation of Dreams,* and he himself had no theory of dreams, reductive or complex. Still, the very definition of radical empiricism — nothing that is experienced can be excluded from consideration — meant that dreams had for James full standing as experiences.[7]

James's dreams of February 11 were unsettling, but the dreams of the following night were positively frightening. This time there were not two but three. Here is the full account:

On the following night (Feb. 12–13) I awoke suddenly from my first sleep, which appeared to have been very heavy, in the middle of a dream, in thinking of which I became suddenly confused by the contents of two other dreams that shuffled themselves abruptly in between the parts of the first dream, and of which I couldn't grasp the origin. Whence come *these* dreams? I asked. They were close to *me,* and fresh, as if I had just dreamed them; and yet they were far away *from the first dream.* The contents of the three had absolutely no connection. One had a Cockney atmosphere, it had happened to someone in London. The other two were American. One involved the trying on of a coat (was this the dream I seemed to wake from?) the other was a sort of nightmare and had to do with soldiers. Each had a wholly distinct emotional atmosphere that made its individuality discontinuous with that of the others. And yet, in a moment, as these three dreams alternately telescoped into and out of each other, and I seemed to myself to have been their common dreamer, they seemed quite as distinctly *not* to have been dreamed in succession, in that one sleep. *When,* then? Not on a previous night, either. *When,* then? and *which* was the one out of which I had just awakened? *I could no longer tell:* one was as close to me as the others, and yet they entirely repelled each other, and I seemed thus to belong to three different dream-systems at once, no one of which would connect itself either with the others or with my waking life. I began to feel curiously confused and *scared,* and tried to wake myself up wider, but I seemed already wide-awake.[8]

Over and over James emphasizes, in the memorandum of the experience he made at the time, how thunderstruck he was at the outbreak of "a state of consciousness unique and unparalleled in my 64 years of the world's experience." What the modern reader notices is James's ability to catch the disappearing dream experience by the coattails, to recall and write it down before it slipped through the door into daylight. To record such an experience, however frightening, is a first step toward making sense of it. James's own account continues: "Presently cold shivers of dread ran over me: *am I getting into other people's dreams?* Is this a 'telepathic' experience? Or an invasion of double (or treble) personality? Or is it a thrombus in a cortical artery? and the beginning of a general mental 'confusion' and disorientation which is going on to develop who knows how far?"[9]

But just as James was beginning to exert a sort of professional understanding and control over the experience (something Erik Erikson would note in commenting on this experience of James's), the experience was revealing itself to be, at least potentially, disastrous. "Decidedly," James goes on, "I was losing hold of my 'self' and making acquaintance with a quality of mental distress that I had never before known, its nearest analogue being the sinking, giddying anxiety that one may have when, in the woods, one discovers that one is really 'lost.'"

That the present experience should recall for James his getting lost in the Adirondacks some years earlier was, perhaps, more hopeful than otherwise, for had he not found his way out of that experience, if at some cost to his health? James makes it clear that this shivering, sliding dream kaleidoscope was deeply unnerving. It filled him with dread; his teeth chattered. It gave him, he said, the creeps.

But the experience, while it shook him, was not, as Erikson would come to believe, the beginning of the end.[10] The fractured dream sequence may indeed have been a sign of the "acute identity confusion" Erikson thought it was, but it was definitely not the start of any noticeable or immediate downward spiral into decay, degeneration, confusion, and dissolution.

As he had before, James fought back, trying to make sense of the experience. In later years he returned to the subject with other interpretations, but one of his resources for making sense of it at the time was his recent reading of Morton Prince's *Dissociation of a Personality,* just published, a copy of which Prince had sent James seven weeks earlier. Prince was a prominent Boston physician from an old family. He was ebullient and athletic, an enthralling public speaker, twelve years younger than James, who was a good friend. Strongly influenced by Charcot, Prince became interested in psychopathology, taught at Harvard Medical School and Tufts Medical School, and eventually established abnormal psychology as an important subject of study at Harvard College. Prince founded the *Journal of Abnormal Psychology* in 1906.

The book Prince had sent James was subtitled *A Biographical Study in Abnormal Psychology.* It "created a sensation," said the psychologist Henry Murray in his obituary of Prince, "wherever English was read."[11] The book is a 575-page study of the multiple personalities of one patient, Clara Fowler of Fall River, Massachusetts, to whom Prince gave the name Miss Beauchamp (pronounced Beecham). The careful detail, the lively interchanges between doctor and patient(s), the vivid personality of "Sally Beauchamp" — the third of four distinct personalities — and Prince's overriding therapeutic interest in helping to bring about a reintegration of his patient's personality made this book an instant classic. It was adapted as a Broadway play and a silent film; it still makes impressive reading. The book, says a later commentator, "was a tour de force thrown into the teeth of the rival psychoanalytic school of Freud which championed unconscious psychodynamics."[12]

Prince's book — about "that lady with a whole boarding house of characters in search of a creative author" — had a great deal for James to chew on.[13] Dreams, Prince believed, are "dissociated conscious states." They are related to what he called co-conscious as well as unconscious states. Miss Beauchamp was a neurasthenic, and Prince considered neurasthenic symptoms an "expression of dissociation."[14] Miss Beauchamp's different personalities even had different dreams. The dissociated state of the patient, "an example in actual life of the imaginative creation of Stevenson" — the Jekyll and Hyde story — was a "functional dissociation of that complex organization which constitutes a normal self." Far from being an indicator of insanity, dissolution, decay, ruin, degeneration, or collapse, the separate personalities represented for Prince "elementary psychical processes"; they were "in themselves normal" and, furthermore, were "capable of being re-associated into a normal whole."[15]

A sympathetic reading of Prince's book would have tuned James's quicksilver mind to the hypothesis of multiple selves as a functional and reparable split, not a catastrophic, irremediable break. James's dream experiences of February 11 and 12, 1906, *were* frightening, but Prince's argument might give one hope. Just as, in the book, the real Miss Beauchamp finally emerges — through the disappearance, the "death," of Sally, the mischievous, devilish personality — so James could face the possibility that his own personality was splintering into different dreamers with hope that the process could be reversed.

Notwithstanding Erikson's interpretation, William James's personality was not now coming apart, not really dissociating, though it certainly always possessed a wild centrifugal energy. It is equally certain that various William Jameses existed within the man. He was himself fond of pointing out that a person has as many social selves as he or she has friends and relations. And sometimes we seem to see quite different personalities in one person's varying moods: there is, for example, William the Metaphysician, trying to work out the technical details of an idea, and there is Plain James, the prophet of self-help through conversion.

In some intricate way, James appears to have been, at bottom, both healthy-minded and a sick soul, both tender and tough-minded. Ralph Barton Perry, James's student and biographer, closes his splendid account by identifying four William Jameses. There was first of all "the neurasthenic James." Then there was "the radiant James, vivid, gay, loving, companionable, and sensitive." To this Perry adds a third James, for whom he has no easy label but who might be considered as the conditional James or the ever-not-quite James, whose important qualities of life are "active tension, uncertainty, unpredictability, extemporized adaptation, risk, change, anarchy, unpretentiousness, and naturalness." The fourth James, Perry says, was "the James of experience and discipline . . . the man of the world." Cosmopolitan James, perhaps.[16]

Multiple social selves are not, of course, the same thing as a dissociating or disintegrating sense of identity, though one is sometimes hard put to tell where the line is drawn with William James. Maybe we never know precisely how a life is layered. The day after his second set of dreams, James wrote Pauline Goldmark a chatty and affectionate letter with not a trace of the panicky loss of self he felt on waking up that morning. But James had already written down the dreams, together with a modestly reassuring conclusion: "States of 'confusion,' loss of personality, apraxia, etc. so often taken to indicate cortical lesion or degeneration of dementic type, may be very superficial functional affections. In my own case the confusion was *foudroyante* — a state of consciousness unique and unparalleled in my 64 years . . . yet it alternated quickly with perfectly rational states, as this record shows. It seems, therefore, merely as if the threshold between the rational and the morbid state had, in my case, been temporarily lowered, and as if similar confusions might be very near the line of possibility in all of us."[17]

Like all of us, James had many sides. Like other uninhibited people, he had more layers and more life in him than most, and despite notable blindnesses, he was better acquainted with himself than most. He was always teetering on the brink of collapse, but had been able — so far — to catch himself and fall backward to safety at the last moment. The different parts of his personality never quite became different personalities; the parts held together in a kind of confederacy. The fundamental condition of his life was, now and always, torn-to-pieces-hood. But the pieces were never just thrown to the winds. They remained loosely if oddly clumped together, never completely unified, but all on the same shelf. Perhaps Leo Stein, the brother of Gertrude, said it best: "The world which [William James] perceived was a multitudinous one. He never lost the sense of the thing, and yet never lost himself in it. So he became the richest interpreter of that of which he was so rich a part."[18]

81. Earthquake

THE DAY AFTER the second flurry of dreams, James, still hobbled by gout and walking with crutches, went to San Francisco to meet Alice's train. A week later he gave a talk, "The Psychology of the War Spirit," to a Stanford student assembly. The assembly had been scheduled in response to a call, from the 1905 Lake Mohonk Conference on International Arbitration, for student meetings, to be held on or about George Washington's birthday, to agitate for arbitration as an alternative to war. In the *Varieties* James had proposed voluntary poverty as a moral equivalent for war. Now he underlined, as he always did, the plain fact of "the bellicose constitution of human nature" and pointed out that war was not about to just vanish. He proposed, citing Emerson, that students start by "speaking out as individuals whatever truth however unpopular is in you." He also said that "the wars of the future must be waged inside of every country, between the destructive and constructive ideals and forces."[1]

The Stanford semester hummed along. The big introductory class went well. James told friends, perhaps a bit defensively, he thought Stanford was getting its money's worth out of him. He told his son Harry, "I have lectured better than I ever did before."[2] He had accepted a salary of $5,000, the salary of a full professor for a year, to teach one course for one semester and build a philosophy department. He worked hard at both assignments, trying to get President Jordan to hire Ralph Barton Perry and writing Perry urging him to accept the offer. The generous salary also helps explain why James gave so many little talks around the Bay Area. His job, remember, was to "get Stanford on the map" in philosophy.

Early in March he began another course of lymph injections, and as often happened, he felt better almost at once. Two days after starting the shots, he was writing to Aleck (who, with his older brothers, was back in Cambridge) about its being a glorious day, similar to one of which his old friend Holmes had said it "looked as if God had just spit on his sleeve and polished up the universe till you could almost see your face reflected in it."[3]

Yet shadows intruded. Alice's migraines continued. Back in Cambridge, Nathaniel Shaler, whom James called "the best-loved man in our university," died. When James wrote his disconsolate widow, she returned the compliment, saying Shaler had always said James was "the dearest boy on the planet."[4] Shaler had taught geology but had been active in a dozen other fields. He wrote on earthquakes, whales, the moon, climate, hurricanes, mining metals, floods, red sunsets, altruism, the silver question, dreams, the Negro problem, and more. He was tall, erect, and active. "If he hears you call him old man," said one of his students, "he'll walk your damned legs off." He was one of the grand, outsize personalities James loved to be around. James called Shaler "a myriad minded and multiple personalitied embodiment of academic and extra-academic matters." When Shaler's Civil War poems were published posthumously, James felt, he said, "an epic wind of sadness" blowing all through the book.[5]

William and Alice spent a few days off in early April in Los Angeles, where Alice wrote Henry a long letter — her second — about a recent sitting with Mrs. Piper back in Cambridge, before Alice had left for California. A message had come through Mrs. Piper on January 29 for Henry from his (and William's) mother, Mary James, dead now for twenty-four years. Alice's first letter seems not to have survived, so we do not know what the message was. All we know is that Henry was strangely stirred by it. He explained to a friend that it was "an allusion to a matter known (so personal is it to myself) to no other individual in the world but *me* — not *possibly* either to the medium or to my sister-in-law, and an allusion so pertinent and *initiated* and tender and helpful, and yet so unhelped by any actual earthly knowledge on any one's part, that it quite astounds as well as deeply touches me."[6] Alice wrote Henry on April 6, going back over the incident, and saying, "William remains unmoved and unconvinced."

William could not let this stand quite so baldly, so he added a postscript to Alice's letter. "The episode of the message so exactly hitting your mental condition is very queer," he said, conceding that "there is *something* back there that shows that minds communicate." William went on to gently deprecate "the costume, so to speak, and the accessories of fact" as merely symbolic and "due to the medium's stock," but concluding nonetheless, "What it all means I don't know but it means at any rate that the world that our 'normal' consciousness makes use of is only a fraction of the whole world in which we have our being." And he carefully signed himself "your loving W.J."[7]

It may be too simple to say that Henry and Alice were the real believers in the messages from the discarnate. William cannot be described as just an opposed skeptic, but over and over it seems that Henry and Alice entered more fully, less reservedly, more emotionally into it than William, though he is the one whose name figures so prominently in the annals of psychical research.

By April 9 William and Alice were back in Stanford; James took up lecturing again, feeling himself "on the home stretch." Then on April 18 came the great earthquake. Alice Toklas was living with her widowed father and younger brother in a large house in San Francisco near the Presidio. The quake came, the chimney was demolished. Alice went to her father's bedroom. As James R. Mellow tells the story, "Ferdinand Toklas, incredibly, seemed to be asleep. Drawing the curtains aside and pushing up a window, Alice called to him, 'Do get up. The city is on fire.' Her father barely roused himself. 'That will give us a black eye in the East,' he said."[8] For William James it was a sort of message — in some uncanny way, a personality. "It was to my mind absolutely as a permanent Entity that had been holding back its activity all these months," William wrote his brother. William even made the earthquake speak German: "And on this exquisite early morning [it came] at last saying '*nun geht's los!* Now, *give* it to them.'"[9] As he said now to Henry, and later in the piece he wrote about the quake, it was "impossible not to feel it as animated by a will, so vicious was the expression of a temper displayed."

The devastation was appalling. Most of Stanford lay in ruins. James went into San Francisco and saw the "whole population in the streets, with what baggage they could rescue from their houses about to burn, while the flames and the dynamiting were steadily advancing and making everyone move farther. Every horse and vehicle was dragging property, every side-walk encumbered with trunks being dragged along by people, every vacant spot occupied by furniture and families."[10] The farther James got from the event, the more the destruction and suffering struck him; on May 24 he told Katharine Rodgers about the "big heritage of woe" the quake had left behind. But even though decent humanitarian feelings caught up with him later, and he sent money for the relief effort, there is no question that James's first, instinctual response was to greet the earthquake with a wild Olympian joy. There can be no real doubt that William James, in his heart of hearts, embraced and welcomed chaos, cataclysm, change, *Zerrissenheit*, impulse, and chance. He may have had a certain fellow feeling with the quake as a force for disorder.

He required himself to meet every demand made on him. Quite naturally he would read the human response to the quake as the calling up of heroic inner resources. James needed constant challenges and perpetual demands, if only to prove to himself that the inner well hadn't run dry. This mandatory — almost military — openness to experience, even to disastrous experience, is the key to the temperament that was now driving James's interest in radical empiricism, panpsychism, pluralism, and pragmatism. We may ignore no experience. As Joseph Conrad put it, "The unwearied self-forgetful attention to every phase of the living universe reflected in our consciousness may be our appointed task on this earth."[11]

82. *A General Theory of Human Action*

THE EARTHQUAKE ENERGIZED William James by some sort of kinetic empathy. When he wrote about it, he noted how the event had called up new energies in people. He also saw the quake as an opportunity for Stanford to reset its priorities, away from mere buildings and toward intellectual greatness — by which he meant raising professors' salaries. He warned the trustees and President Jordan that the faculty was underpaid, disaffected, and "almost demoralized." "Do you know that you are on a volcano here, and steering straight towards a first-class scandal?" he asked one trustee. If the university was to emerge from the quake into a new "stone-age" of bricks and mortar, James told Jordan, "I really think that a general *strike* on the part of the faculty . . . would be a not unnatural way of meeting such a policy." This was not, perhaps, the most diplomatic way to persuade administrators of the rightness of one's cause, and it is not surprising that James's challenging letters were received coolly by the Stanford authorities.[1]

James himself lived through the rest of 1906 on a cresting excitement, on a sort of spreading contagion of enthusiasm. Stanford was too badly damaged by the quake to continue, so the rest of the semester was canceled. William and Alice returned to Cambridge, arriving home on May 3. Almost at once they were caught up again in the psychical research enterprise. Richard Hodgson, a good and trusted friend of James's and the chief figure in the American branch of the Society for Psychical Research, had died back in December 1905. Now the American branch was being dissolved, and the new organization taking its place was being headed by James Hyslop, whose inclination for publicity and promotion impelled James to distance himself as much as he could from an undertaking to which he was still bound, as much by friendship and loyalty — Gurney, Sidgwick, Myers, and Hodgson were all dead now — as by active interest.

James attended at least three sittings with Leonora Piper, between May 8 and June 12, at which the medium told William and Alice she was in contact with — controlled by — the departed Hodgson. A long transcript of the sitting on May 21 survives in a 110-page report James drew up in 1909 on "Mrs. Piper's Hodgson-Control." James thought that this entire series of sittings was an "exceptionally bad" case study because of the long association Mrs. Piper had enjoyed with Hodgson when he was alive. The following excerpts bring us the voices of William and Alice in one of the sittings in which they spent what would for us be an uncomfortable amount of time.

The sitting opens with Hodgson speaking through Mrs. Piper: "Well, well, well, well! Well, well, well, that is — here I am. Good morning, good morning, Alice."

Mrs. W.J.: "Good morning, Mr. Hodgson."

Hodgson: "I am right here. Well, well, well! I am delighted!"

W.J.: "Hurrah! R.H.! Give us your hand!"

After much questioning and answering about names and places and details, Hodgson addresses William: "Now I want — William, I want one thing. I want you to get hold of the spiritual side of this thing and not only the physical side. I want you to feel intuitively and instinctively the spiritual truth, and when you do that you will be happy."

A little later, Alice puts in, "Mr. Hodgson, I am so glad to know that you can come at all."

Hodgson: "Well, you were always a great help to me, you always did see me, but poor William was blind. But we shall wholly straighten him out and put him on the right track." After this exchange Mrs. Piper reported that Hodgson had left.[2]

James had mixed feelings about the sittings, which never seemed to him to provide anything approaching proof, although he admitted that he sometimes felt as though some real, perhaps telepathic, communication had taken place. He recognized his inclination to believe, but he stubbornly held out for a respectable threshold of proof, which seemed never — or almost never — to be met.

But he was unambiguously enthusiastic this month about a different subject: the work the twenty-five-year-old Giovanni Papini and his circle of Italian pragmatists were doing. Papini was two years younger than James's oldest son, Harry; he wrote with fire-hose exuberance and a Nietzschean swagger. Papini titled the chapter on pragmatism in his autobiography "Toward a New World," and he described his conception of "a philosophy of action, a philosophy of doing, or rebuilding, transforming, creating . . . The *true* is the *useful,* to *know* is to *do.* Among many uncertain truths, choose the one best calculated to raise the tone of life and promising the most lasting rewards. If something is not true, but we wish it were true, we will *make* it true, by faith."[3]

"A gospel of power," Papini calls pragmatism. "A gospel of courage, a practical, an optimistic, an *American* gospel! Away with fear! Daring! Forward! A leap in the dark! Away with doubt! Every hundred dollar bill of theory must be convertible into the small change of particular fact, of desirable achievements! Away with metaphysics! Welcome to religions!"[4]

The William James who couldn't write without using italics responded joyfully to the Papini who couldn't write without exclamation marks. James hailed Papini's work as a "refreshing novelty," especially when he compared it with the work produced by the American Ph.D. students who "have all these years been accustomed to bore one another with the pedantry and technicality, formless, uncircumcised, unabashed and unrebuked, of their 'papers' and 'reports.'" (Such acid comments are the clear sign of a teacher who is ready to retire.) James praises Papini for his "cutting and untechnical phraseology," and calls him "the most enthusiastic pragmatist" of the whole Italian circle. James was always drawn to vivid expression of strong feelings. He notes approvingly the passion in both the preface and final chapter of Papini's *Il Crepuscolo dei filosofi,* and he embraces the "'good riddance,' which is Papini's cry of farewell to the past of philosophy" — his goodbye to its "exaggerated respect for universals and abstractions."[5]

The positive praise of Papini's pragmatism is in James's claim that it means an "unstiffening of all our theories and beliefs by attending to their *instrumental* value." In a superb short scheme, James lays out what Papini had helped him see about pragmatism, namely that it "incorporates and harmonizes various ancient tendencies, as:

"1. Nominalism . . . the appeal to the particular.
2. Utilitarianism, or the emphasizing of practical aspects and problems.
3. Positivism, or the disdain of verbal and useless questions.
4. Kantism, in so far as Kant affirms the primacy of practical reason.
5. Voluntarism, in the psychological sense, of the intellect's secondary position [to the will].
6. Fideism [the dependence of knowledge on faith] in its attitude toward religious questions."

By emphasizing that pragmatism "is thus only a collection of attitudes and methods," James is able to avoid characterizing it in terms of assumptions, doctrines, or goals, and is able instead to insist on pragmatism as an activity, an expansion of our means of action. James quotes with excited approval Papini's sudden enlargement of the subject: "The common denominator to which all the forms of human life can be reduced is this: *the quest of instruments to act with,* or, in other words, *the quest of power.*" For this quest, says James — catching fire from Papini — pragmatism is the best inspiration; that is, the most inspiriting attitude we can have. By adopting a pragmatic attitude, a philosophy or a philosopher can achieve "a *general theory of human action.*" In a giddy rush that James recognized as Nietzschean, he quickly sketches how far this general theory might reach. "Ends and means can here be studied together, in the abstractest most inclusive way, so that philosophy can resolve itself into a comparative discussion of all the possible programs for man's life when man is once for all regarded as a creative being." Regarded as creative — in other words, as acting — man becomes as God. This makes "of pragmatism a new militant form of religious or quasi-religious philosophy."[6]

James's short piece on Papini — the best, least guarded expression of James's hopes and ambitions for pragmatism — was written by mid-May. It reads as though a surge of energy had gone through James. On May 24 he began a new regimen of galvanizing, literally running electrical current through himself. Galvanism dated from the 1790s. With a small electrostatic generator, one could easily administer mild shocks to oneself. The treatment was thought helpful for nervous disorders. There were few things James wouldn't try. Three days later he was actively planning his coming Lowell Lectures, "Pragmatism in Recent Philosophy." In early June he accepted a long-standing invitation to lecture in Paris with the intention of doing pragmatism there too.

Also in June a letter arrived from a Clifford Beers, whom James had just met, together with the manuscript of a book Beers had written. Called *A Mind That Found Itself*, it was Beers's account of his own mental collapse and attempted suicide and of what happened to him subsequently in mental hospitals in Hartford and Middletown, Connecticut. Brilliantly written, full of vivid detail, Beers's was a blazingly sane indictment of the then standard use of "physical restraint" (straitjackets). It was and is a riveting book, a classic that was to be reprinted forty-one times by 1981.

Beers had many problems, some of which today would be called depression and delusional paranoia, but his main description of himself is as a neurasthenic. His writing has snap and tang. He says he exhibited a "seraphic passiveness" as a choirboy, "from which a reaction of some kind is to be expected immediately after a service or rehearsal." He tells a graphic story — which makes a reader hold his breath — about a vindictive restraint session during which he picked up, unnoticed, from the floor a fragment of broken glass and put it in his cheek before his keepers got him tied up. He held the glass sliver against his teeth with his tongue all night long, and when the doctor at long last showed up to see him the next morning, Beers put out his tongue with the glass sliver on it, to demonstrate to the doctor how, despite the straitjacket, he had retained the capacity to harm himself.

Beers recovered, wrote his book, and went on to found the mental hygiene movement, which was instrumental in reforming the care of the insane in America. James now read his manuscript and, in early July 1906, wrote Beers a warm letter praising the book as "the best written out 'case' that I have seen," and closing, "You speak of rewriting. Don't you do it. You can hardly improve your book." *A Mind That Found Itself* was a success story to which James could not help but respond. His letter, Beers said later, "came as a rescuing sun."[7]

If James got a boost from Beers's book, he also benefited from renewed efforts at self-help. He wrote Peggy, who was at Putnam Camp in the Adirondacks, on July 5, "I am feeling very well, owing to my having for the first time in my life practiced the mind-cure philosophy rather successfully." Other things went well. In France on July 13, after an extensive reinvestigation, Alfred Dreyfus, the Jewish army officer who had been convicted of treason in 1894, was cleared of all charges, restored to rank, and given the Legion of Honor medal. James wrote to his son Billy, who was painting at Giverny and associating with Monet and other artists, that he would have liked to be in Paris when the Dreyfus decision was announced.[8]

For summer jaunts James went twice in 1906 to Maine. The first time, in July, he went to Northeast Harbor and Mount Desert, and the second time, in August, to Penobscot Bay, Rockland, North Haven, Isle au Haut, and Swan's Island. But it was pragmatism that was on his mind. Between trips he wrote exultingly to Schiller that "things are drifting tremendously in our direction." Never hamstrung by modesty, James wrote, "It reminds me of the Protestant reformation!"[9]

There was one casualty of James's rush toward pragmatism: somewhere along the way he benched radical empiricism. On August 20, 1906, after his second trip to Maine and just before he set off for a month by himself at Putnam Camp, Keene Valley, and Chocorua, James deposited a collection of offprints of twelve articles by him on radical empiricism in the Harvard philosophy department library, and a similar collection in the university library. Each collection was subsequently bound and stamped "Radical Empiricism" on the spine, but the act of giving away these articles seems to mark the eclipse of radical empiricism as a separate concern of his. The subject, on which James had written so rapidly and extensively in 1904 and 1905 and which was the first subject on James's midterm exam in Philosophy 9 in 1905–06, simply disappears. The phrase does not even occur in the comprehensive forty-five-page printed syllabus for James's course at Stanford or on the very similar syllabus for what would be his last course at Harvard, in the fall of 1906.

Though many first-rate minds have ranked radical empiricism as James's greatest contribution to modern philosophy, the subject was no longer a preoccupation. Perhaps it was his turning away from what he scornfully called "technical" work, perhaps it was the force of "The Miller-Bode Objections," perhaps it had something to do with his fervid new interest in pragmatism. Whatever the reason, radical empiricism moved to the background as a program and a professional pursuit for William James, though it should be noted that the main ideas of radical empiricism — that consciousness is a process and only a process, that what we call objects are really bundles of relations, and that all we have to work with, think about, or live with is what we somehow experience — figure henceforth in James's thought and writing as settled notions, to be quietly taken for granted.[10]

If James's life was cresting toward something that might be thought of as fulfillment, he was himself in active revolt against what he took to be the characteristically American form of it, that "exclusive worship of the bitch-Goddess success." That worship, together "with the squalid cash interpretation put on the word success — is our national disease," James said. This outburst came in a letter to H. G. Wells, in which James thanks him for an article in which Wells criticized the American public for condoning official American injustices toward the English-born anarchist and labor organizer William McQueen. Instead of expressing outrage at illegal or unconstitutional behavior by the authorities, the ordinary citizen, James says bitterly, "begins to pooh-pooh and minimize and tone down the thing, and breed excuses from his general fund of optimism and respect for expediency." In other words, James is saying, we must not explain away indifference to justice as "pragmatism." Writing with unusual emphasis in an uncharacteristic defense of a general principle, James told Wells, "Exactly that callousness to abstract justice is *the* sinister feature . . . of our U.S. Civilization."[11]

The end of the summer and the start of the fall semester were fast approaching. He loved being at Putnam Camp, and despite catching a ferocious cold, he reveled in a vacation in which he could get his back "against a tree, or against mother-earth, and spend the entire day in the open air, with a good book as my companion." One of those books was Richard Jefferies's *Life of the Fields,* one piece of which, "The Pageant of Summer," was positively Whitmanesque in its "enumeration of all the details visible in the corner of an old field with a hedge and ditch." William wrote his brother, "Rightly taken in, it [Jefferies's book] is probably the highest flight of human genius in the direction of Nature-worship." Less rewarding was his involvement, probably at his wife's urging, in encouraging his former student Alfred Hodder's first wife and mother of his children, Jessie Hodder, to sue Alfred for bigamy when he married a Bryn Mawr colleague without divorcing Jessie. It turned out Alfred and Jessie had never been married in the first place.[12]

By the end of September the enthusiasm that had started with the earthquake was draining away. James was floundering physically, and he wrote President Eliot on September 23 that "for a year past my infirm 'heart' has been giving me trouble again, and within the past fortnight something like the bad symptoms of seven or eight years ago have broken loose." With the start of classes James prepared to shoulder his introduction to philosophy course one last time, but he wanted Eliot to be ready to appoint a backup instructor in case he had to quit midsemester. What he did not tell Eliot was that the thing he was most determined to carry out was not the college course but the public Lowell Lectures on pragmatism, scheduled for November and December.[13]

83. *Pragmatism*

ON OCTOBER 3 he began yet another course of lymph injections. They were, over the years and on the whole, the most successful treatment for his recurring nervous exhaustion. A few weeks later he began galvanic therapy again. Despite the usual blizzard of obligations — an Anti-Imperialist League lunch, a visit and a lecture by his old friend Pierre Janet, Charles Peirce's writing to say he was down to his last twenty-nine cents and could James lend him five dollars? — James stuck to his lecture preparation and on November 14 delivered the first of the pragmatism lectures to what he called a "splendid audience" of about five hundred people.

He prepared elaborate outlines for the lectures, but except for the opening lecture he did not write them out fully until after they were delivered, because he was trying to preserve as much spontaneity and directness as was consistent with intellectual clarity. "The whole lecture-business now-a-days," he had recently explained to Henry, "save where there is a stereopticon or exhibition of facts not presentable as 'reading-matter,' or where the lecturer is an artist in his line and speaks without notes, is doomed to second-rateness . . . A *read* lecture is doomed to inferiority — to really succeed the lecturer must *speak* and *command* his audience." By Thanksgiving he had delivered four lectures, but he had written out only one and half of another. His eighth and final talk was on December 8. On December 9 he noted that he had two lectures written out in full. The audience, "the intellectual elite of Boston," he called it in a letter to Henry, stayed at around five hundred. After the final lecture he was "called before the curtain."[1]

He had begun with the highly unconventional assertion that the history of philosophy is not so much a history of ideas as a history of a "certain clash of human temperaments." Philosophy for James is always *ad hominem*. This grounding of philosophy not just in feeling but in temperament enrages certain readers, but it seems to others the long-overdue light of common sense. Whether you are a rationalist, "meaning your devotee to abstract and eternal principles," or an empiricist, "meaning your lover of facts in all their crude variety," depends, says James, on your temperament, not your logical reasoning. He further sweeps it all up under two headings: the tender-minded, who are "rationalistic (going by 'principles'), intellectualistic, idealistic, optimistic, religious, free-willed, monistic and dogmatical," and the tough-minded, who are "empiricist (going by 'facts'), sensationalistic, materialistic, pessimistic, irreligious, fatalistic, pluralistic and skeptical." We can see in James himself a mostly tough-minded temperament, but with strong tender-minded leanings toward religion and a belief in free will. Perhaps we should not be surprised that James offers pragmatism as a mediating philosophy. Recognizing the "conflict between science and religion," James says, the ordinary person "wants facts; he wants science; but he also wants a religion."[2]

The opening lecture, like the original California talk "Philosophical Conceptions and Practical Results," frames the whole series in religious terms. "Empiricist writers give [the ordinary person] a materialism, rationalists give him something religious, but to that religion actual things are blank . . . I offer the oddly named thing pragmatism as a philosophy that can satisfy both kinds of demand." "Invent a vulgar (comparatively) and mercenary name for it," Henry advised him, "and don't, oh don't spell it heartbreakingly." Much as William James loved teaching, and as good as he was at it, he wanted a larger, more general audience. The pragmatism lectures have frequent references to the world beyond the college walls; democratic impulses were an essential part of James's temperament. Warming to the close of his first lecture, he said, "The finally victorious way of looking at things will be the most completely *impressive* way to the normal run of minds."[3]

He began the second lecture with "the principle of Peirce, the principle of pragmatism." He puts it a trifle austerely and abstractly. It will be the consequences of the principle, not the statement of it, that will really matter. "To attain perfect clearness in our thoughts of an object, then, we need only consider what conceivable effects of a practical kind the object may involve — what sensations we are to expect from it, and what reactions we must prepare. Our conception of these effects, whether immediate or remote, is then for us the whole of our conception of the object." Put more simply, "There can *be* no difference anywhere that doesn't *make* a difference elsewhere."[4]

Appealing again to temperament, to what he elsewhere calls the "massive cues of preference," James says, "A pragmatist turns his back resolutely and once for all upon a lot of inveterate habits dear to professional philosophers. He turns away from abstraction and insufficiency, from verbal solutions, from bad *a priori* reasons, from fixed principles, closed systems, and pretended absolutes and origins. He turns toward concreteness and adequacy, towards facts, towards action and towards power." Trying, despite his obvious enthusiasm, not to claim too much for it, he says pragmatism is, "first, a method; and second, a genetic theory of what is meant by truth." "True" is, as we have seen, more a verb than an adjective or noun for James. Truth happens to things and statements. "The true is the name of whatever proves itself to be good in the way of belief." Pragmatism's "only test of probable truth is what works best in the way of leading us, what fits every part of life best and combines with the collectivity of experience's demands, nothing being omitted."[5]

In the third lecture, James stops to exclaim over how completely Darwin's ideas have triumphed over the old rationalist argument from design. "Darwin," James says, "opens our minds to the power of chance happening to bring forth 'fit' results if only they have time to add themselves together." Pragmatism derives directly from Darwin. Variations that confer a benefit — an adaptive advantage — survive. A variation is judged entirely by its results; how it originates doesn't matter. Pragmatism is the recognition that activity and the consequences of activity are what matter.[6]

If pragmatism is a profoundly Darwinian philosophy, it is also, importantly, a literary one. James makes reference to or quotes from G. K. Chesterton, George Bernard Shaw, H. G. Wells, Dante, Wordsworth, and Browning. He quotes Walt Whitman extensively. This literary side of James's work is not a matter of ornament or showing off or name-dropping, nor is it just a gift for phrase and metaphor. John Dewey correctly perceived that James's "power of literary expression strikes one at first glance." In another context James said, "People's *sense of dramatic reality* is what they will certainly obey, no matter how much they pretend to follow nothing but points of evidence."

James understands his basic task of explaining how things are as in part a literary enterprise. Writing a friend, he said, "You bring vividly home to me the literary need of reconciling and mediating forms of expression." For James, writing was fundamentally about "taking it out of technical into real regions of persuasion." So James loved it when Walt Whitman said, "Who touches this book touches a man." He quotes these words, then adds, "The books of all the great philosophers are like so many men. Our sense of an essential personal flavor in each one of them . . . is the finest fruit of our own accomplished philosophic education." For James as for Whitman, real literature ran way deeper than fashionable literary language. "No one," said Whitman, "will get at my verses who insists upon viewing them as a literary performance." And James wrote, "I don't care how incorrect language may be if it only has fitness of epithet, energy, and clearness." Neither do most readers.[7]

James would call the book comprising the lectures *Pragmatism: A New Name for Some Old Ways of Thinking*, a staid title that hid the excitement he felt as the subject opened out in front of him. "I didn't know," he would write Flournoy in January 1907, with the lectures behind him, "until I came to prepare [them], how full of power to found a 'school' and to become a 'cause' the pragmatistic idea was. But now I am all aflame with it, as displacing all rationalistic systems."[8]

James had thought of dedicating *Pragmatism* to Dewey, Schiller, and Papini, his co-conspirators in the war of philosophical liberation against the imperial absolutists, but to do so would have left out Peirce. Besides, James really wanted to throw in his lot with the utilitarian tradition — since he was concentrating on the utility of pragmatism — so he dedicated the book to John Stuart Mill. Over and over in the eight lectures that comprise *Pragmatism*, James comes down firmly for philosophy as a guide to action. He believed now, as he always had, that any philosophy is good in vain if the reader tosses it aside, as Samuel Johnson had observed of certain works of literature. "True ideas," James says in lecture six, "are those that we can assimilate, validate, corroborate and verify. False ideas are those that we cannot." He took it a step further: "Verifiability . . . is as good as verification . . . Beliefs verified concretely by *somebody* are the posts of the whole superstructure." Truth, which James says "is simply a collective name for the verification-processes," is one of the "th" words. "Truth is *made*, just as health, wealth, and strength are made, in the course of experience."[9]

In James's final lecture, on December 8, it all comes down once again to action. "Our acts, our turning-places, where we seem to ourselves to make ourselves and grow, are the parts of the world to which we are closest, the parts of which our knowledge is the most intimate and complete. Why should we not take them at their face-value? Why may they not be the actual turning-places and growing-places which they seem to be, of the world — why not the workshop of being, where we catch fact in the making?" James makes his appeal to the reader's or hearer's own sense of dramatic reality. He appeals psychologically, philosophically, and literarily to what we feel and think of as the real situation. Pragmatism, says James, accepts the possibility that the world is various, pluralistic, "made up of a lot of eaches." It accepts, too, the possibility that all may not be at last right with the world. "I find myself," he says, "willing to take the universe to be really dangerous and adventurous, without therefore backing out and crying 'no play' . . . I am willing that there should be real losses and real losers, and no total preservation of all that is . . . When the cup is poured off, the dregs are left behind forever, but the possibility of what is poured off is sweet enough to accept."[10]

This is, when you get right down to it, a religious attitude, a way of facing final things, pragmatism's eschatology. "No fact in human nature," James had said in his Edinburgh lectures, "is more characteristic than its willingness to live on a chance." Now he said that the genuine pragmatist is one who "is willing to live on a scheme of uncertified possibilities."[11]

James's ambitions for pragmatism were breathtaking. When he compared the pragmatist movement to the Protestant Reformation, he was not being ironic. Just as he was launching the lectures in October 1906, he wrote to Giovanni Amendola, one of Papini's Italian pragmatists, "I think that pragmatism can be made — is not Papini tending to make it? — a sort of *surrogate* of religion, or if not that, it can combine with religious faith so as to be [a] surrogate for dogma." Saving his best shot for last, as he had in Edinburgh, he closed his pragmatism lectures by saying, "On pragmatistic principles, if the hypothesis of God works satisfactorily in the widest sense of the word, it is true." This is not the Protestant God, not the Christian God, not monotheism.

Saying it was too late to "start upon a whole theology at the end of this last lecture," he closed with one of his characteristic analogies, already quoted, but now bearing a whole new weight of meaning. "I firmly disbelieve, myself, that our human experience is the highest form of experience extant in the universe. I believe rather that we stand in much the same relation to the whole of the universe as our canine and feline pets do to the whole of human life. They inhabit our drawing-rooms and libraries. They take part in scenes of whose significance they have no inkling. They are merely tangent to curves of history the beginnings and ends and forms of which pass wholly beyond their ken. So," he ends grandly, "we are tangents to the wider life of things."[12]

84. The Energies of Men

THE PRAGMATISM LECTURES ended facing outward, away from the study, away from the college, to the wider world beyond. But the entire effort, an amazing one for a man in declining health, was underlaid and in some ways powered by a surge of inner energy. That surge was itself something James was interested in. "Whence is your power?" had been Emerson's question; now it was James's.

About a month after the San Francisco earthquake, James had given a talk to the psychology club at Harvard about how we occasionally work ourselves free of our inhibitions and "find we have *more resources than we thought*," and about how, "in great catastrophes and crises, folks astonish themselves." Then, in late 1906, a couple of weeks after the pragmatism lectures came to a close, James reworked this material into a talk, "The Energies of Men," for the annual December meeting, in New York, of the American Philosophical Association, of which he was the current president. Thus the work in pragmatism was bracketed — or contained, so to speak — by James's inquiry into "the *amount of energy available* for running one's mental and moral operations by."[1]

James considered this a problem in functional psychology. He firmly takes the clinicians' side against the analytical or laboratory psychologists, noting at the start that the concept of the amount of energy available to a person was something "never once mentioned or heard of in laboratory circles."[2]

He took as his starting point a feeling with which everyone is familiar: "Most of us feel as if we lived habitually with a sort of cloud weighing on us, below our highest notch of clearness in discernment, sureness in reasoning, or firmness in deciding. Compared with what we ought to be, we are only half awake. Our fires are damped, our drafts are checked." Whatever this subject should be called in clinical psychology — James called it dynamogenics — it is the long-standing American interest in awakening to new life and new power, the great theme of Thoreau and Emerson and Whitman, the great theme too of Jonathan Edwards, now carried to the new American century by William James.[3]

He starts, as he often does, with a common example: "The existence of reservoirs of energy that habitually are not tapped is most familiar to us in the phenomenon of 'second wind.'" It can be mental as well as physical.

"In exceptional cases, we may find, beyond the very extremity of fatigue-distress, amounts of ease and power that we never dreamed ourselves to own." What exactly enables us to reach this reservoir? James identifies three kinds of things: excitements, efforts, and ideas. Excitements that are capable of "carrying us over the usually effective dam" include love, anger, crowd contagion, despair, war, and shipwreck. He glancingly mentions the earthquake. "People must have been appalled lately in San Francisco to find the stores of bottled-up energy and endurance they possessed."[4]

Turning next to efforts, James cites heroic responses to unusual situations, but puts the most emphasis on how "the best practical knowers of the human soul have invented the thing known as methodical ascetic discipline to keep the deeper levels constantly in reach." James mentions the spiritual exercises of Ignatius Loyola, then quotes at length from his friend Lutoslawski's experience with hatha yoga, which James calls "the most venerable ascetic system and the one whose results ["strength of character, personal power, unshakability of soul"] have the most voluminous experimental corroboration." He quotes Lutoslawski's identification of hatha yoga with mind cure. "This is the truth at the bottom of all mind-cures," Lutoslawski had written James. "Our thoughts have a plastic" — i.e., a shaping, formative — "power over the body." Putting these together as "suggestive therapeutics" and as "methodical self-suggestion," James insists that "we habitually live inside our limits of power."[5]

Then James moves to the "third great dynamogenic agent," namely, ideas. Like excitements and efforts, ideas are triggers. "Ideas set free beliefs, and the beliefs set free our wills." He lists "Fatherland," "the Union," "Holy Church," the "Monroe Doctrine," "Truth," "Science," "Liberty," insisting shrewdly that "the social nature of all such phrases is an essential feature of their dynamic power." Moving to a strictly personal level, he cites "the idea of one's honor" and finally "conversions." "Conversions, whether they be political, scientific, philosophic, or religious, form another way in which bound energies are let loose. They unify, and put a stop to ancient mental interferences. The result is freedom and often a great enlargement of power."

As he speaks with evident personal interest about the "very copious unlocking of energies by ideas in the persons of those converted to 'New Thought,' 'Christian Science,' and 'Metaphysical Healing,'" it is hard to avoid at least the suggestion that James was, in his December address to the American Philosophical Association, giving a sort of account of the energies unleashed in him by his recent realization, taken from Papini, that his pragmatism was not just a new philosophy but a whole new conception of philosophy as "a *doctrine of action* in the widest sense, the study of all human powers and means."[6]

85. *The Harvard Elective System Applied to the Universe*

ALMOST IMMEDIATELY AFTER James's return to Cambridge from his "Energies of Men" talk in New York came the frantic visit of his student Henry Alsberg with the news that Charles Peirce was in an alarming — indeed starving — condition in a nearby rooming house. James's own energies were always mobilized by such an appeal, and he rushed off to save his old friend.

Three weeks after the rescue of Peirce, and just a week and a half after his sixty-fifth birthday, James gave the final lecture of his last course at Harvard. Philosophy D, with 130 students, met in the upstairs lecture room in Emerson Hall. On January 22, 1907, William James was defending pluralism, saying it "clings to certain appearances, as incompleteness, 'more,' uncertainty, insecurity, possibility, fact, novelty, compromise, remedy, success etc as being authentic realities." He called attention to the contrast between the philosophy classroom and the outside world of the street. "Your lecturer," he told the students, "chooses one world, that, namely, of which the street yields the type." He closed with a careful consideration of the relation between mind and matter, arguing at last that they might be "coextensive." "Matter might *everywhere* make mind conscious of what matter was doing, and mind might then everywhere either acquiesce in the performances, or encourage, hinder, or redirect them."[1]

At the close of a Harvard class, it is the custom for students to applaud. Sometimes the applause is polite, sometimes perfunctory. For William James's last class ever, it was a huge ovation. A deputation of students came down the aisle and presented James with a loving cup and a silver-mounted inkwell "from past and present undergraduates." Acknowledging the occasion, James thanked them all, observed how unprepared he was, and added, "As I am now on the point of dying, so to speak, as a Harvard

Professor of Philosophy, you are, at the moment strewing roses on my coffin. I may say it is deeply agreeable to me." Alice, who loved ceremonial moments, came and watched it all.[2]

Technically, this was retirement. But a week later James was off to New York to repeat the pragmatism lectures at Columbia. The first talk, scheduled for a room that held 250, had to be moved to the 1,100-seat chapel of Teachers College, which nearly filled. James attended four separate celebratory dinners for him at the Columbia Faculty Club. He dined, while in New York, not only with philosophers and students but with Charles Francis Adams, the statesman; Finley Peter Dunne, the satirist "Mr. Dooley"; Norman Hapgood, a reformer, writer, and friend; Nicholas Murray Butler, the president of Columbia; Horace Fletcher, the champion of chewing; John Jay Chapman, essayist and friend; John La Farge, the painter and an old friend; Mark Twain; and Admiral Mahon, the world's leading theorist of naval supremacy. James also rushed about the city, visiting the painting studio of his cousin Bay Emmett and calling on Pauline Goldmark. He made a quick trip to give a talk for Peggy and Bryn Mawr in between the first and second weeks of the Columbia lectures, and he made another quick visit to see Upton Sinclair's utopian community Helicon Hall in Englewood, New Jersey. It was all a whirl, a huge success. He tried to be modest about it, joked about hoping to be good but finding to his chagrin that he was merely "great," and admitted to Alice, "I enjoy being a lion." To Henry he wrote, "It was certainly the high tide of my existence, so far as *energizing* and being 'recognized' were concerned."[3]

His heart was troubling him again; he noted in his diary that "these devilish 'aortic' symptoms stop me short." He went to see Dr. Joseph Pratt on Jim Putnam's advice, but the findings were "heart of normal size, murmur with first sound very slight, and good strong action. Radial artery not badly sclerosed. No aortic enlargement detectable." Three days later a second examination by the same doctor found "total organic condition 'very fair': 'aortic' symptoms due to 'neurosis' [neuropathy] of heart." James continued to live, as much as he could, the active life he always had.[4]

In the weeks after his retirement he saw George Bernard Shaw's *Caesar and Cleopatra* and *Captain Brassbound's Conversion,* and he read Shaw's *Cashel Byron's Profession* and *An Unsocial Socialist.* He gave a dinner at 95 Irving Street for eleven "philosophical assistants and graduates." He read and admired Jane Addams's *Newer Ideals of Peace* (which cited his own views) and sent a copy to Shaw.[5] He had lunch with the muckraking journalist Ida Tarbell and dinner with a group of what he called in his diary "Russian Revolutionists."[6] He wrote to Bill in Paris about Bob James, now living in Concord, having given up smoking and drinking, and feeling rejuvenated by Christian Science. He worried about Aleck, who continued to have a hard time with schoolwork; James thought perhaps a year in Switzerland would help. At a philosophy department meeting there was considerable interest in trying to get John Dewey to come to Harvard to take James's place, but Harvard could find no money for a replacement for William James.[7]

But the main work of early 1907 was the preparation of the pragmatism talks for publication as a book. James was still in a state of euphoria as he wrote Henry on February 14 that *Pragmatism* "will be more original and (I believe) important than my previous works."[8] James had the manuscript ready for the printer by March 20. He seems to have made a deal with Longmans, Green similar to the one he had made for the *Varieties,* whereby he undertook the cost and the bother of physically producing the book and reaped the profits of publishing, while Longmans took a commission for handling advertising and sales. James had a wide audience in mind; the book was priced at a dollar, about a third of what the *Varieties* sold for.

Pragmatism appeared in June, just as James was elected a corresponding member of the British Academy. The preface pointedly distanced pragmatism from radical empiricism, saying that there was "no logical connection" between the two and asserting that radical empiricism "stands on its own feet. One may entirely reject it and still be a pragmatist." After James had handed over *Pragmatism* to the printer, he set out a rough table of contents, dated May 1907, for a book on radical empiricism. It was entirely in character for him to be racing ahead to the next project in the excitement of completing the one in hand.[9]

Pragmatism proved popular at once; four more printings were called for in the United States before the end of the year, and 1,940 copies were sold in England during the same time. But James was unprepared for the response of the philosophical community, which — apart from Dewey, Schiller, Papini, Bergson, and a few others — ranged from doubtful and grudging partial acceptance to derisive and hostile rejection.

There is something to be said for protective obfuscation, for the squid's squirting ink to hide behind. One problem with writing as clearly as James does is that people may understand you and decide they *really* don't approve of what you are up to. Shadworth Hodgson, an old friend of James's who had not yet read the copy of *Pragmatism* James sent him, wrote, "How can you dream of elevating the needs, the desires, the purposes of Man into a 'measure' of the universe?" James Seth, the Scottish philosopher and the brother of James's friend Andrew Seth Pringle-Pattison, wrote, "I find myself no nearer an agreement with you and your disciples . . . than I was before." Then he added, "I can see no reason for the present noise and hubbub!" Seth must have been an unusually unpleasant man, for he also dropped a sneering postscript: "I ought perhaps to have remembered that the lectures were to 'a Boston audience'!" In America, Arthur Lovejoy chopped it up into "The Thirteen Pragmatisms." Royce — who must be forgiven, since his son Christopher was on the edge of his final collapse — told James that "many see pragmatism as a joke, discrediting serious effort to deal with intellectual problems." John Jay Chapman wrote to tell James about the lady who called it "fragmentism," and who added, "Such a good name too." Someone at Yale concluded that pragmatism was "the Harvard elective system applied to the universe."[10]

As *Pragmatism* went to press, the Jameses had their yard in Cambridge dug up to a depth of eighteen inches and the soil hauled away. The idea was to improve the lawn by starting from scratch. A hundred and fifty double cartloads of loam and twenty-some double cartloads of manure were dumped around the James home. It turned out to have been an omen.

Pragmatism had been under fire for years before the book came out. One W. Caldwell, reviewing James's California talk for *Mind* in October 1900, wrote, "I am aware of the various epithets by which Prof. James's 'new ethical philosophy' and that of his intellectual associates have been stigmatized, such as Irrationalism, Romanticism, Disguised Scholasticism, The Philosophy of Reaction, or of Dogmatic Theology, The Philosophy of Authority or of Caprice, Dynamism, Voluntarism, or what not." Many philosophers seem to have felt James was saying a person could believe, and call true, anything he or she found convenient. Charles Peirce had an elegant answer "for people who say that pragmatism means believing anything one pleases. If one could believe what one pleased that would be true. But the fact is one cannot."[11]

James was surprised, then annoyed, and finally exasperated at the reception of *Pragmatism*. He complained to his brother that "no one seems rightly to understand [it] . . . representing it as a philosophy got up for the use of engineers, electricians and doctors, whereas it really grew up from a more subtle and delicate theoretic analysis of the function of knowing than previous philosophers had been willing to make." He came to regret the word "pragmatism" as "a very unlucky one. It suggests sordid practical interests, and all the critics take it to *exclude* logical ones." He even came to wonder if "the well-kept-up 'popular' style," of which he had been so proud, was not also a mistake, "a demerit in philosophy."[12]

A wider and far more generous view was also taking shape. In a talk delivered on August 25, 1911, before the Philosophical Union of the University of California at Berkeley, where James had launched pragmatism in 1898, George Santayana would invoke William James as "representing the genuine long silent American mind," and would credit James (and Walt Whitman) with overcoming what Santayana called the genteel tradition in American philosophy. That tradition, said Santayana, "forbids people to confess that they are unhappy," and therefore "serious poetry and profound religion are closed to them by that." James liberated himself from gentility. "The chief source of his liberty," Santayana said, "was his personal spontaneity, similar to that of Emerson, and his personal vitality, similar to that of nobody else. Convictions and ideas came to him, so to speak, from the subsoil. He had a prophetic sympathy with the dawning sentiments of the age, with the moods of the dumb majority. His scattered words caught fire in many parts of the world. His way of thinking and feeling represented the true America, and represented in a measure the whole ultramodern, radical world."[13]

James's heart condition worsened in June. He had gone to Chocorua to get the place ready for summer rental to the Goldmarks. When Pauline arrived with her dog Mowgli, James's dog Ryelie attacked it. "Since then," James noted glumly in his diary, "the angina has returned in full force."[14]

There were summer jaunts as always, but they were less wide-ranging than usual. James went to southern Maine (Old Orchard, Biddeford, and York), to Farmington, Connecticut, to Lincoln, Massachusetts, and to Keene Valley. The family was, generally speaking, flourishing. Harry was working, Bill abroad painting, Aleck in good spirits but still unable to pass exams. This year Peggy began a serious, intense friendship with a student at Bryn Mawr named Marianne Moore. Peggy had occasional headaches like her mother's, she was prone to spells of depression, but she could also be vivacious and entertaining. "Last evening," Alice wrote William, "she told me of college life, all sorts of things, and so entertainingly that I sat and listened till half past eleven o'clock! She was funny, graphic, indeed she was her father's own child and she looked so handsome and spirited. We don't half know her."[15]

Brother Bob seemed to have emerged into calm waters, while Henry was deeply engaged in the vast New York Edition of his writings. He was revising all the novels and stories he wished to keep and writing long prefaces for each of the projected twenty-three volumes. In May *The American Scene* had come out; William settled in to read it, writing Henry, "In its peculiar way [it] seems to me *supremely great*." But then he got off once again on a scolding critique of Henry's late style — the style of the splendid last novels *The Wings of the Dove, The Ambassadors,* and *The Golden Bowl.* "You know how opposed your whole 'third manner' of execution is to the literary ideals which animate my crude and Orson-like breast," William rumbled, "mine being to say a thing in one sentence as straight and explicit as it can be made, and then to drop it forever; yours being to avoid naming it straight, but by dint of breathing and sighing all round and round it, to arouse in the reader who may have had a similar perception already (Heaven help him if he hasn't!) the illusion of a solid object, made (like the 'ghost' at the Polytechnic) wholly out of impalpable materials, air, and the prismatic interferences of light, ingeniously focused by mirrors upon empty space." He tore on and on for page after page, seemingly unable to stop, until finally he burned out. "A truce, a truce! I had no idea, when I sat down, of pouring such a bath of my own subjectivity over you. Forgive! Forgive! And don't reply, don't at any rate in the sense of defending yourself, but only in that of attacking me, if you feel so minded."[16]

Despite the tirade, William was much taken with *The American Scene.* He told his wife what he didn't tell Henry, that the book "delivers its secret only to leisurely reading, with attention paid to every word — not a single word skipt — not to be read therefore in magazines nor amid the press of other occupations. And you can't read it straight along or 'through,' you must read *in* it, and *thus* it bears reading, I am sure, many times over."[17]

Henry took the high road, thanking William briefly for the "splendid critical" letter and returning to his usual comfortable retailing of family news. Then in early October William returned to the book while vacationing in the White Mountains. This time he wrote Henry with the genuine, slightly guilty enthusiasm of a person catching up on his reading: "I have just been reading to Mrs. B" — the wife of the diplomat and historian James Bryce — "with great gusto on her part and renewed gusto on mine, the first few pp. of your chapter on Florida in *The American Scene. Köstlich* [precious] stuff! I had just been reading to myself almost 50 pp. of the New England part of the book, and fairly melting with delight over the Chocorua portion. Evidently the book will last, and bear reading over and over again, few pp. at a time, which is the right way for 'literature' fitly so-called."[18]

William's problem with Henry's work was not, finally, with the style. As soon as Henry turned the late style on William's world, William was all admiration. *The American Scene* is, especially in its early parts, an extended elegiac meditation on places and people with which and with whom William was deeply familiar. The book leaps from the New Jersey seaside houses of the newly rich, with "their candid air of having cost as much as they knew how," to the idyllic Arcadian beauty of Chocorua and New Hampshire: "The apples are everywhere, and every interval, every old clearing, an orchard: they have 'run down' from neglect and shrunken from cheapness — you pick them up from under your feet but to bite into them, for fellowship, and throw them away, but as you catch their young brightness in the blue air . . . they seem to ask to be praised only by the cheerful shepherd and the oaten pipe." *The American Scene* is a complex paean to the two American worlds Henry shared with William, the world of twenty-five years ago and the world of the present.[19]

Henry responded joyfully to William's praise. If William had been slow to appreciate *The American Scene*, Henry was now eager to admit having been slow to acknowledge *Pragmatism*. "Why the devil I didn't write you after reading your *Pragmatism* — how I kept from it I can't now explain save by the very fact of the spell itself (of interest and enthrallment) that the book cast upon me . . . Then I was lost in the wonder of the extent to which all my life I have . . . unconsciously pragmatised. You are immensely and universally *right*."[20]

86. The True Race of Prophets

IN THE MIDDLE of November 1907, Josiah Royce began a series of public lectures that would be published the following year as *The Philosophy of Loyalty*. Though Royce explicitly intended for them to present a theory of truth and reality that was "opposed to the doctrines of recent pragmatism," his thought and language both now bore the marks of his long, friendly controversy with James. He agreed with James on the importance of experience. "Loyalty," said Royce, "is the Will to Believe in something eternal, and to express that belief in the practical life of a human being." Emphasizing the last clause, he added, "We can deal with no world which is out of relation to our experience." Ten days after Royce commenced the series, James cabled his acceptance of an offer to give a set of lectures at Oxford six months hence.[1]

The invitation came from Manchester College, which was located in the town of Oxford but was not then part of Oxford University. Only recently moved from the Midlands, Manchester was a "dissenting" school, meaning in this case Unitarian; it published a leading liberal periodical, the *Hibbert Journal*.[2] The college asked James for eight lectures, preferably on "the religious aspect of your Philosophy." James hesitated for only a week before accepting; he gave "The Present Situation in Philosophy" as a working title.[3]

Even though he would be lecturing in an ancient and famous university town, James seems to have considered the occasion a final chance to reach a general intellectual audience, not just a club of professional specialists. For one thing, he decided not to write the lectures out but to deliver them from detailed notes. The result, as it was eventually written out and printed, stands in marked contrast to the more tightly argued professional work he was doing at the same time on the meaning of truth.

As his decision to do the lectures came comparatively easily, so did the lectures themselves. His idea was to quickly trace the previous forty years in philosophy and "sum up by saying that idealism had displaced Theism, but that the issue that has defined itself more and more is that between a pluralistic and a monistic way of thinking." By "monism" James meant the absolute idealism of the Cairds and Royce; by "pluralism" he meant his own radical empiricism. He also thought of his project in these lectures as championing experience over intellectualism, prizing as he did "multifarious unfiltered nature" over "generalizing, simplifying, and subordinating." In a letter to Bergson, James said he was thinking of calling the book "Intellectualism and Reality."[4]

The lectures, which would eventually be published as *A Pluralistic Universe,* arose out of a pluralistic life. In the week before agreeing to the Oxford lectures, James attended Royce's last lecture on loyalty and began work on a lengthy report — it ran to 110 pages in print — on the séances in which Leonora Piper had professed to be in contact with the departed Richard Hodgson. He went to see *Lohengrin,* met for two hours with Clifford Beers about mental health reform, and had Mrs. Piper to dinner. As he worked on the lectures during the months ahead, he would give talks to professional groups on the meaning of truth, read and respond to Henry Adams's *Education,* and reread Fechner's *Zend-Avesta* as well as his brother's *Roderick Hudson* in the splendid New York Edition that was just coming out.

William had by now a printed card with which he could impersonally turn down invitations to speak. He reached out to Royce, who was shattered by the mental collapse of his son Christopher, who had to be institutionalized in January 1908. He began to sit for Bay Emmet as she started an oil portrait for the Harvard philosophy department. As winter turned into spring, he was down with colitis and vertigo, and by early April he was suffering "as bad nervous fatigue as I have ever been in my life." He hung on, took Trional in order to sleep, and kept pegging away at the lectures, sailing for England on April 21, 1908, "eager," as he wrote Henry, "for the scalp of the Absolute."[5]

Though he began with necessary distinctions — empiricism and absolutism, pluralism and monism — he had no faith in neat little systems and glib exclusionary categories; his deepest instinct was to sketch large circles of inclusion. "The most a philosophy can hope for," he said, superbly, in his opening talk, "is not to lock out any interest forever." The second lecture was a critique of "monistic idealism," lambasting the usual suspects (Bradley, Royce). The third lecture was a consideration of Hegel. James was willing now to concede that "merely as a reporter of certain empirical aspects of the actual, Hegel, then, is great and true." The trouble still, for James, was that "Hegel was dominated by the notion of a truth that should prove incontrovertible, binding on everyone, and certain, which should be *the* truth, one indivisible, eternal, objective, and necessary." James, of course, believed no such thing existed. Perhaps his most telling comment about Hegel is his asking his audience, If dialectical reasoning is so great, why don't scientists use it? "Doesn't it seem odd," he asked, "that in the greatest instance of rationalization mankind has known, in 'science,' namely, the dialectical method should never once have been tried?"[6]

By contrast, it was the scientific method, "hypotheses, and deductions from these, controlled by sense-observations and analogies with what we know elsewhere," which was the method of Fechner, to whose work James turns in lecture four. This chapter, innocuously titled "Concerning Fechner," is the high point of *A Pluralistic Universe,* the part of it James singled out for his friends' attention. What he chiefly admired in Fechner's writing was what Fechner called his *Tagenansicht,* his daylight view, the view that "the whole universe in its different spans and wave-lengths, exclusions and envelopments, is everywhere alive and conscious."[7]

Gustav Theodor Fechner was a man of Emerson's generation, born in

Saxony in 1801 and educated as a scientist at Leipzig, where he became a professor of physics. He is considered the founder of modern scientific psychology, owing to the publication, a year after Darwin's *Origin of Species*, of his *Elemente der Psychophysik*. Fechner's psychophysics aimed to "set up the proper operations by which numerical values could be assigned to psychological variables."[8]

But Fechner is more interesting than his psychomeasurements make him sound. His ideas were wide-ranging and imaginative. He wrote on aesthetics, and under the pseudonym Dr. Mises, he wrote satires; one was called "Proof That the Moon Is Made of Iodine." The Royal Saxon Secret Police maintained a file on Dr. Mises. Fechner was influenced by Schelling's *Naturphilosophie*, which he got to by reading Oken.[9] He moved in the best Leipzig circles, which included Felix Mendelssohn and the Schumanns. Clara Schumann, who would teach the young Alice Gibbens singing, was the stepdaughter of Fechner's sister.

In 1836, the same year as Emerson's *Nature* appeared, Fechner published *A Little Book of Life After Death,* the first English translation of which, in 1904, had (as we have seen) a short preface by William James. In 1839 Fechner underwent "a terrific attack of nervous prostration with painful hyperaesthesia of all the functions, from which he suffered for three years, cut off entirely from active life." Unable to bear light, he lived in a darkened room, going out only with metal cups he had made over his eyes, and communicating "with the family through a funnel shaped opening in the door." This illness, which struck Fechner at age thirty-eight, is similar in some ways to the experience James went through in America thirty years later. Fechner's recovery, as James tells it, seems eerily like James's own. "This illness," he writes, "bringing Fechner face to face with inner desperation made a great crisis in his life." "Had I not then clung to the faith," Fechner says, "that clinging to faith would somehow or other work its reward, *so hatte ich jene zeit nicht ausgehalten*" (I would not have gotten out of that time alive).[10]

By the time James wrote about Fechner for *A Pluralistic Universe,* he had known about him for a long time, had in fact learned, and then rejected as too mechanical, "Fechner's law" of psychophysical measurement. But he was drawn to the larger speculative themes that preoccupied Fechner after his recovery. The heart of Fechner's thought is more a point of view than anything else, the view that "inner experience is the reality, and that matter is but a form in which inner experiences may appear to one another when they affect each other from outside."

James had been excited since at least the summer of 1904 by the way he saw this giddy-seeming conclusion to be firmly based in physiological psychology. "The whole scheme, as the reader sees, is got from the fact that the span of our own inner life alternately contracts and expands."[11]

Fechner has a way of making the counterintuitive seem natural. James's account in the Oxford lecture is graphic: "The original sin, according to Fechner, of both our popular and our scientific thinking, is our inveterate habit of regarding the spiritual not as the rule, but as an exception in the midst of nature. Instead of believing our life to be fed at the breasts of the greater life, our individuality to be sustained by the greater individuality, which must necessarily have more consciousness and more independence than all that it brings forth, we habitually treat whatever lies outside of our life as so much slag and ashes of life only."

Fechner, as James presents him, looks back to the Plato of the *Timaeus* and forward to Jung and Teilhard de Chardin, the paleontologist and philosopher. "The vaster orders of mind go with the vaster orders of body. The entire earth on which we live must have, according to Fechner, its own collective consciousness. So must each sun, moon and planet; so must the whole solar system have its own wider consciousness, in which the consciousness of our earth plays one part. So has the entire starry system as such its consciousness; and if that starry system be not the sum of all that *is*, materially considered, then that whole system, along with whatever else may be, is the body of that absolutely totalized consciousness of the universe to which men give the name of God."[12]

The psychophysicist Fechner was also a visionary, just as was the physiological psychologist James, who recognized Fechner (in a letter to Bergson) as belonging to "the true race of prophets." Here is James's rendering of Fechner's account of how he came actively to understand that the earth is indeed alive:

> On a certain spring morning I went out to walk. The fields were green, the birds sang, the dew glistened, the smoke was rising, here and there a man appeared; a light as of transfiguration lay on all things. It was only a little bit of the earth: it was only one moment of her existence: and yet as my look embraced her more and more it seemed to me not only so beautiful an idea, but so true and clear a fact, that she is an angel, an angel so rich and fresh and flower-like, and yet going her round in the skies so firmly and so at one with herself, turning her whole living face to heaven, and carrying me along with her into that heaven, that I asked myself how the opinions of men could ever have so spun themselves away from life so far as to deem the earth only a dry clod, and to seek for angels above it or about it in the emptiness of the sky.[13]

It has been remarked that the person with a literal mind lives in a perpetual comedy of errors. William James escaped this fate. In his Fechner piece, James leaps to embrace what he calls Bain's definition of genius: "the power of seeing analogies." Analogies are to thinking what metaphor is to poetry — its inner life — but one must respect differences as much as samenesses. "Through his writing, Fechner makes difference and analogy walk abreast," says James, "and by his extraordinary power of noticing both, he converts what would ordinarily pass for objections to his conclusions into factors of their support."

The reader toils up the mountain after James, who toils after Fechner. The view from the top is "that the constitution of the world is identical throughout . . . The whole human and animal kingdoms come together as conditions of a consciousness of still wider scope . . . The more inclusive forms of consciousness are in part *constituted* by the more limited forms . . . We are closed against its [the earth soul's] world, but that world is not closed against us. It is as if the total universe of inner life had a sort of grain or direction." Finally, "Fechner likens our individual persons on the earth unto so many sense-organs of the earth's soul. We add to its perceptive life so long as our own life lasts." When we die, "it's as if an eye of the world were closed."[14] Perceptions from that eye may cease, but "the memories and conceptual relations that have spun themselves round the perceptions of that person remain in the larger earth-life as distinct as ever."

James is edging up on a notion of immortality here. He was thinking of more than his own. The day before he started lecturing at Oxford, he had been at Leamington, where his sister Alice had lived, and where he had so memorably rushed up to see her nineteen years before. Though it was raining, James made a point of looking up her old lodgings. What of Alice James might remain at 9 Halliburton Terrace?

87. A Pluralistic Universe

IF SOME HEARERS and readers found James's presentation of Fechner too much of a stretch, it should be noted that Ernst Mach wrote James to tell him his account of Fechner had succeeded where no German one had, that Henri Bergson was enthusiastic about it, and that even F. H. Bradley wrote to remind James that he, Bradley, had been influenced (a little) by Fechner.

James's lectures attracted such a crowd (about five hundred at the first) that later lectures were given not in the Manchester College library but in a large examination room in the center of town. The principal of the college reported that the talks "attracted an audience far larger, I believe, than any philosophical lectures ever given before in Oxford." After the lecture on Fechner, James gave one on "the compounding of consciousness," intending to supply technical, philosophical, and psychological support for the breathtaking views of Fechner.

James followed this with a lecture on Bergson, devoted mainly to drawing a sharp distinction between direct experience and the packaging and handling of experiences into concepts. James praised Bergson as *the* philosopher of direct experience and, by implication, of radical empiricism. "The essence of life is its continuously changing character," James said, "but our concepts are all discontinuous and fixed . . . The whole process of life is due to life's violation of our logical axioms . . . What really *exists* is not things made, but things in the making . . . What won't stay buried must have some genuine life. *Im anfang war die tat* ["In the beginning was the act" — *Faust*]; fact is a *first* to which all our conceptual handling comes as an inadequate second."

The "Bergson and Intellectualism" lecture is perhaps James's most persuasive attack on excessive rationalism, on vicious intellectualism, on the kind of conceptual thinking that ignores the ever-shifting quality of real-life experiences, and on formal logic considered as an adequate representation of how minds really function. "We are so subject," James concluded, "to the philosophic tradition which treats *logos* or discursive thought generally as the sole avenue to truth, that to fall back on raw unverbalized life as more of a revealer, and to think of concepts as the merely practical things which Bergson calls them, comes very hard."[1]

Not only is the whole world alive, but the various living parts are all connected, as James undertakes to show in the next lecture, called "The Continuity of Experience." "My present field of consciousness is a center," he says, "surrounded by a fringe that shades insensibly into a subconscious more." He is thinking, as he tells us, of the work of "Janet, Freud, Prince, Sidis and others," of what Erich Heller would later call the early twentieth century's discovery and colonization of inwardness. "I use three separate terms here to describe this fact," James goes on, "but I might as well use three hundred, for the fact is all shade and no boundaries. Which part of it properly is in my consciousness, which out? If I name what is out, it already has come in."[2]

The warrant for this connection lies in the fact, in the reality, of experiences we must ultimately recognize as religious experiences. "I think that they point," says James, "with reasonable probability to the continuity of our consciousness with a wider spiritual environment from which the ordinary prudential man (who is the only man that scientific psychology, so-called, takes cognizance of) is shut off."[3]

The final lecture, with which James was also somewhat pleased, makes two specific points about what he takes to be the most important religious experiences. The first is an affirmation of the reality of the experiences we usually and inadequately call conversion or second birth, experiences "of an unexpected life succeeding upon death. By this I don't mean immortality or the death of the body. I mean the death-like termination of certain mental processes within the individual's experience, processes that run to failure, and in some individuals, at least, eventuate in despair." He cites Luther's experience as the prototype, saying that such an experience — and here we must add Fechner's and James's experiences to Luther's — "brings all our naturalistic standards to bankruptcy. You are strong only by being weak, it shows. You cannot live on pride or self-sufficingness. There is a light in which all the naturally founded and currently accepted distinctions, excellences, and safeguards of our characters appear as utter childishness. Sincerely to give up one's conceit or hope of being good in one's own right is the only door to the universe's deeper reaches."[4]

Whether it be the classic example of Luther or the then fashionable mind cure and New Thought, the basic experience is the same. "The phenomenon is that of new ranges of life succeeding on our most despairing moments." What he had said in popular talks he now repeated in the most serious possible way in the final lecture at Oxford. "There are resources in us that naturalism . . . never recks of, possibilities that take our breath away, of another kind of happiness and power, based on giving up our own will and letting something higher work for us." Nothing is capitalized, nothing is necessarily Christian, but one feels that Henry James Sr. would have approved of the conclusion. "Here is a world in which all is well, *in spite* of certain forms of death, indeed *because* of certain forms of death — death of hope, death of strength, death of responsibility, of fear and worry, competency and desert, death of everything that paganism, naturalism and legalism pin their faith on and tie their trust to."[5]

A further, wider point is that religious experiences of this kind "suggest that our natural experience, our strictly moralistic and prudential experience, may be only a fragment of real human experience." One who has had such an experience "is continuous, to his own consciousness, at any rate, with a wider self from which saving experiences flow in." James concluded that "the drift of all the evidence we have seems to me to sweep us very strongly towards the belief in some form of superhuman life with which we may, unknown to ourselves, be co-conscious." He invoked, one last time, his favorite image of this condition: "We may be in the universe as dogs and cats are in our libraries, seeing the books and hearing the conversation, but having no inkling of the meaning of it all."[6]

The lectures went as well as James could have wished. The audiences remained large, "splendid and very attentive." The weather turned warm and fine; his health held up. Harry arrived from America; Peggy would come a few weeks later. As he looked about him, James found Oxford "simply delicious." He called on F. H. Bradley, who courteously showed him around Merton College. He received an honorary degree from Oxford and another, a month later, from Durham. He talked truth with Bertrand Russell, and when his lecturing came to a close, he set out on a glad round of travels and visits. At Newington House in Wallingford he saw Roger Fry and Logan Pearsall Smith and met Ottoline Morrell, the Bloomsbury hostess and protector of conscientious objectors, with whom he established a warm friendship. He and Harry went off to Wordsworth country, in the north of England, and Alice and Peggy traveled to Lincoln, Rye, and Harrow. While in the Lake District, dear to the English Romantic poets, James wrote day after day to Pauline Goldmark. The letters are full of reined-in feeling, of imperfectly suppressed longing for the *Rubáiyát* days of old in the Adirondacks. "Ah Pauline, Pauline," one letters ends. "God bless you! Your poor old W.J."[7]

Then, shaking off a cold, William went down to Rye, to his brother's home, Lamb House. H. G. Wells was in the neighborhood with his wife; so were the Kiplings. G. K. Chesterton was staying in the inn next door to Lamb House. William was intensely curious to see Chesterton, so he put a ladder against Henry's garden wall one day and climbed up and peered over the wall to see if he could spot him. Henry objected strenuously: this sort of thing was just not done in England. At that moment the Wellses drove up, intending to take William and Peggy to Sandgate, a village on the Kent coast. Wells tells of meeting a "totally unnerved" Henry, who appealed to him to rule on whether or not William's behavior was permissible. "To Henry's manifest relief," Wells says, "I carried William off and in the road just outside the town we ran against the Chestertons who had been for a drive in Romney Marsh; Chesterton descended slowly but firmly; he was moist and steamy but cordial; we chatted in the road for a time and William got his coveted impression."

A few days later, after Alice and Peggy had left for Geneva, William visited Chesterton (then a comparatively young man of thirty-four) at his inn, where he drank port, and Hilaire Belloc, who also happened to be passing through, talked while Chesterton "gurgled and giggled" and showed no inclination whatever to shine himself. There is a Dickensian, Pickwickian gaiety about William's ramblings around England after the lectures this summer, and the whole scene at Rye resembled what Chesterton himself once said about *The Pickwick Papers,* that the book gave off "a sense of everlasting youth — a sense as of the gods gone wandering in England."[8]

88. *Psychical Researches Redux*

WHEN JAMES RETURNED to the United States in mid-October 1908, it was to a scene of changes, disappointments, discouragements, and losses. He had stayed abroad through the summer and early fall, traveling and working on the four lecture-chapters of *A Pluralistic Universe* he had promised as articles for the *Hibbert Journal.* The book was to be held back until April 1909 to allow these pieces to appear first. James debarked in Boston and passed through East Boston and East Cambridge to get home; the trip "suggested a country fallen into irremediable decay."[1]

He went immediately to Chocorua, where he found the New England autumn "heartbreaking in its sentimentality." He described for Henry "the smoky haze, the windless heat, the litter of the leaves on the ground in their rich colors, with enough remaining on the trees to make the whole scene red and yellow, the penury and shabbiness of everything human." James was struck by the stark contrast between the sense of dearth in the American scenery and the "robust fullness" of England's. The American sky and earth he found empty compared with England's, though he thought the American sky made up for it by its "spiritual profundity and saturation of color at sunset." But comparisons were finally pointless, he told Henry; there were no common denominators. To Pauline he wrote, after a long descriptive complaint, "All I know is this, that my *heart* is american."[2]

Charles Eliot Norton died on October 21, five days after James got home. The resignation five days later of Charles W. Eliot as president of Harvard signaled the end of an era. No other single person before or after Eliot has had a comparable influence on the school. He was its president for forty years, and when he went to his last faculty meeting, everyone in the room had been appointed by him.[3] One thing William did not know, though the repercussions would soon affect him, was that in October Henry James got word from his publisher that from the point of view of sales, the New York Edition was a distinct failure.[4]

William repeated his *Pluralistic Universe* lectures in Cambridge starting in early November. The initial audience of six hundred declined to two hundred; James felt he was talking to "inert listeners" compared with those at Oxford. Within a week of starting the lectures, James's health and frame of mind were so bad that he began a complicated and expensive series of visits to a homeopathic physician, Dr. James R. Taylor, who had treated Alice's sister Mary with good results. James went to Dr. Taylor every day except Saturdays and Sundays for the next six months, 150 visits in all. The daily treatment consisted of "8 minutes of 'vibration' along the spine, in 6 minutes of 'high frequency' electricity, in 12 daily inhalations of a certain vapor, and in homeopathic pellets 6 times a day." James admitted to his brother that he had "no reason whatever to think that these things exert any effect beyond that of making me feel that something is being done." He also conceded Dr. Taylor to be "a poor talker, and a relatively uneducated man," but he was impressed by his persistent interest in "the 'pitch' at which a man lives." Taylor convinced James that the "unnecessarily high pitch" of his life, "by being indulged in all these years," was responsible for his present condition. "He has made me at last," William wrote Henry, "by his indefatigable talk, acutely conscious of my inferiority to my best possibilities, but it is hard to write down what I mean by this."

But he did write it down, and the result is a strangely moving self-portrait of the habitual temper — the pitch — of William James's life as he stood on the threshold of trying to change it. "Suffice it," he wrote, "that I have been racing too much, kept in a state of inner tension, anticipated the environment, braced myself to meet and resist it ere it was due (social environment chiefly here!), left the present act inattentively done because I was pre-occupied with the next act, failed to listen etc. because I was too eager to speak, kept *up* when I ought to have kept *down*, been jerky, angular, rapid, precipitate, let my mind run ahead of my body etc etc."

He had always been intensely active; now the intensity and activity both seemed to be the problem. Finding Taylor's sincerity effective, James accepted the likelihood of months and years of work devoted to "the serious remodeling of one's tissues," and he confessed with apparent relief that Taylor had "at last got his suggestive hook into my gills, and aroused my confidence, and it will be interesting to see what comes."[5]

What came was a period of concentrated philosophical writing, editing, and arranging of earlier articles. But even as he turned to grapple with four book-length projects simultaneously, he also, perhaps inevitably, immersed himself again in the psychic research enterprise on which he had lavished a woeful amount of time and energy over the years. There was, to begin with, the impending American visit of the famous Neapolitan medium Eusapia Paladino. Paladino was an uneducated woman, vigorous, vivacious, and high-strung. She had dark, lively eyes, and her hair, turning gray, had a single snow-white streak in the middle. She was fifty-five in 1910, and had been performing for scientists and investigators for more than fifteen years.

Despite her transparent willingness to cheat whenever possible, she still left investigators impressed and baffled. In semidarkened rooms, often before a dozen or more observers, Eusapia, as she was usually called, would have an investigator on either side of her, holding her hand. Other investigators lay on the floor, by her feet, half under the table. It all sounds hopelessly comical, but no matter what measures were taken, the table rose into the air, a mandolin played, visitors were struck or seized by solid though invisible hands, and a special "luminous hand" often appeared.[6]

At a séance attended by the flatly skeptical Hugo Münsterberg, a commotion occurred when an investigator grabbed hold of Eusapia's foot as she was, apparently, trying to raise the table with it. The episode was trumpeted by Münsterberg as a damning exposé. James, who had been impressed by accounts of Eusapia's "successes" with the Curies, Cesar Lombroso (the Italian criminologist), and others, but who was also disgusted by her "methods," kept his distance after this episode. Royce, another skeptic, circulated his view: "Eeny, meeny, miney mo. / Catch Eusapia by the toe. / If she hollers that will show / That James's theories are not so."[7]

A more serious, but in the end a no less dispiriting, enterprise was James's undertaking to write up for publication an account of numerous sittings by various persons with Leonora Piper, sittings that were all intended to make contact with the spirit of Richard Hodgson. If there was no dramatic exposure of Mrs. Piper, there was also, to James's mind, no positive clincher, no one sitting or moment that compelled belief. "My own poor stuff about R.H. is reaching its conclusion, amid sad interruptions," he wrote a fellow psychic researcher. "If I had to bet or take practical risks I should say of R.H.'s spirit *non-adest*" (it didn't come).[8]

During January 1909 James wrote and mailed off a piece called "Confidences of a Psychic Researcher." It was intended to sum up a lifetime of persistently hopeful though often disappointed interest in matters in which his wife and his brother Henry were at least as emotionally involved as he was. He told Henry he was working on the piece, observing, "It will be queer if after all these years I have *nothing* to say." In the article James confessed himself "baffled as to spirit return and as to many other special problems." But he accepted that there were "real natural types of phenomena ignored by orthodox science," and insisted that "one cannot get demonstrative proof here." He stated that he neither accepted nor rejected psychic phenomena, but was content with "waiting for more facts before concluding." He ended by insisting again that there is more in the world than we are able to take in, "that we with our lives are like islands in the sea, or like trees in the forest. The maple and the pine may whisper to each other with their leaves, and Conanicut and Newport hear each other's fog-horns. But the trees also commingle their roots in the darkness underground, and the islands also hang together through the ocean's bottom. Just so," he said, with a sweeping gesture, "there is a continuum of cosmic consciousness, against which our individuality builds but accidental fences, and into which our several minds plunge as into a mother-sea or reservoir."[9]

If we smile, albeit indulgently, at James's repeated assertions that it is better to believe too much than not enough, we need also to recognize how deeply his scientific skepticism really ran. Nothing in the annals of Mrs. Piper or Eusapia Paladino shows this as well as a single brief episode that occurred at Bar Harbor in early December 1908. A group of spiritualists, including George Dorr, a longtime friend of James's (and the man responsible for the creation of Acadia National Park), had been meeting weekly for a long time. The group had a table with a Ouija-board sort of alphabet and pointer built into it. The table had a brass ring around the edge, mounted on brass stems and collars that were screwed to the table. What happened on December 3, with William James present — he had made the difficult trip in winter weather — was that the brass rail moved all by itself, under brightly lighted conditions. James was quite clear that he saw the rail move, sliding six inches through the collars, and he was convinced that "I saw all there was to see." But what most amazed James was not "the sight of an *object moving without contact*," but his own response. "Since this is the crack in the levee of scientific routine through which the whole Mississippi of supernaturalism may pour in," he wrote his wife next day, "I am surprised that the spectacle hasn't moved my *feelings* more."

James's old friend Holmes had once accused James of turning down the lights so as to give magic a chance. This is not quite right. James no doubt wanted to turn down the lights, wanted the levee to break, but in the end, even with his extravagant investment of time and energy in psychic research — his habitual holding open the door, his insistent defense of one's right to believe — when it came down to it, he simply couldn't cross the line. His skeptical and scrupulous approach had become his conclusion. Even though he saw the brass rail move up there in Maine, he was no closer to being able or willing to seize upon it as proof of what he had hoped for all along. When he wrote up this incident for publication, he concluded, "I find, however, that I look on nature with unaltered eyes today, and that my orthodox habits tend to extrude this would-be leveebreaker. It forms too much of an exception."[10]

89. *The Meaning of Truth*

IN JANUARY 1909, three days after James's sixty-seventh birthday, Ellen Emerson, the older daughter of the poet and James's contemporary — she who had gone sailing with the Jameses in Newport when they were all young — died. Then, in early February, Henry sent bad news by letter from England: he had had "heart symptoms," for which he had been prescribed digitalis and strychnine. His condition, he confessed, had continued to worsen "in respect to panting, gasping [and] getting generally out of breath." Henry told of feeling "a little solitarily worried and depressed." Then his letter abruptly and strangely broke out in an epistolary wail. His previous good health had, he said, "suddenly, perversely, eccentrically led up to and *flowered into* a GRAVE trouble!"[1]

William cabled Henry at once, recommending a Dr. McKenzie; Henry duly went to see him. McKenzie found "absolutely nothing grave or ominous," and encouraged him to eat less and exercise more. Henry professed to be reassured, for the moment, though he privately suspected that his systematic Fletcherizing was the root cause of the trouble. He cabled William: "Stopped fletcherizing practically well."[2]

William's main energies for the early months of 1909 were directed toward his own writing. From the end of January to the end of March, the man who had taken twelve years to write his first book focused his attention on a range of projects that would eventually be published as four separate books. During the last days of January he put the finishing touches on *A Pluralistic Universe,* which now included, besides the Oxford lectures, two pieces that had previously been earmarked for his volume on radical empiricism. At the end of February he concentrated on his "nature of truth book." He may have been working on the book for some time; the surviving evidence is sketchy or inconclusive. At any rate, he quickly completed the book he called *The Meaning of Truth* on March 16.

When he worked on this book is unclear; how he assembled it is not. He took seven pieces he had previously written and published and then collated for the book to be called *Radical Empiricism* and transferred them, in whole or in part, to form the first two thirds of the new volume, *The Meaning of Truth.* The rest of the new volume consisted of six more pieces, on the pragmatic account of truth, which James had written and published between late 1907 and early 1909. Only the last two of the fifteen "chapters" were written at the time that he prepared the book for the printer.

If there was little that was new in *The Meaning of Truth,* there was much that was important. James had been widely attacked for what his critics considered his betrayal of the venerable Western — that is, Platonic — concept of truth and his substitution for it of a low standard of mere utility, expediency, or ungrounded personal preference, no better at last than whim. James defended himself again and again against this charge. The essence of his response is in a letter to Bertrand Russell of the previous May: "Instead of there being one universal relation *sui generis* called 'truth' between any reality and an idea, there are a host of particular relations varying according to special circumstances and constituted by the manner of 'working' or 'leading' of the idea through the surrounding experiences of which both the reality and the idea are part."[3]

Putting together *The Meaning of Truth* entailed what James's modern editors call the "dismemberment" of the radical-empiricism book project. It would be left to James's student Ralph Barton Perry to reconstitute the volume largely as James had originally planned it. *Essays in Radical Empiricism,* first published in 1912, has been part of the James canon ever since. But in March 1909 William James himself was moving in a different direction. After completing *The Meaning of Truth* in mid-March (it would appear in October), he took a few days off and then, as was his custom, he started immediately on the next big project. "I begin my Introduction to Philosophy," he noted in his diary for March 18, 1909.

This introduction to philosophy, edited by his student Horace Kallen and published in 1911 under the bland and self-effacing title *Some Problems of Philosophy*, grew out of James's teaching. A substantial part of the book follows the extensive forty-five-page syllabus James had printed for his Stanford course of 1906. The book covers the same topics as the syllabus, often with the same wording.[4]

Some Problems in Philosophy is written in straightforward, transparent prose, different from the vivid popular lecture style of *The Will to Believe, The Varieties of Religious Experience, Pragmatism,* and *A Pluralistic Universe,* which is a style meant for the educated nonspecialist. *Some Problems in Philosophy* differs, too, from the technical density of the professional papers of *Essays in Radical Empiricism* and *The Meaning of Truth.* And *Some Problems in Philosophy* does not follow the easy popular style of "The Energies of Men." The new book represents a fourth manner. It is clear exposition, directed to college students. The prose is sedate and classical, reminiscent at times of Edward Gibbon. "To know the chief rival attitudes towards life," James wrote, "as the history of human thinking has developed them, and to have heard some of the reasons they can give for themselves, ought surely to be considered an essential part of liberal education."[5]

In chapter 2, his list of big metaphysical questions begins: "What are 'thoughts' and what are 'things'? and how are they connected? What do we mean when we say 'truth'? Is there a common stuff out of which all facts are made? How comes there to be a world at all? And might it as well not have been?" Much of the book focuses on the distinction that had recently become central for James, that between percept and concept. Now he was ready to say emphatically, "The intellectual life of man consists almost wholly in his substituting a conceptual order for the perceptual order in which his experience originally comes."[6]

For this aspect of his later thinking, James has been called anti-intellectual. A better description of his real position would be anti-abstraction; best would be to recognize it as the culmination of a lifelong protest on behalf of experience. This is not a new position for James, of course. It is the same clear opposition to Plato, who denigrates perceptual knowledge as mere sense impressions, and contrasts them with ideas, which are true and eternal. James's life work had been to reverse this polarity, to answer Plato.

Daily life became more and more difficult; it was hard for him now to get to the college library, and all the household business fell to Alice and

Harry. He experienced, he told Flournoy, "violent pre-cordial pain whenever I exert myself strongly or rapidly, or whenever I get into any mental hesitation, trepidation or flurry." But as his life became more constricted and he was more and more limited to intellectual work, his outward-facing temperament kept him involved in the world. He was now double-tithing, giving 20 percent of his income away to good causes, such as Charley Peirce's pension, Clifford Beers's mental health crusade, Booker T. Washington's Tuskegee Institute, and promising young students.[7]

A Pluralistic Universe came out in April. The caterpillar of *Zerrissenheit* had been transformed into the butterfly of panpsychic pluralism, but not everyone saw it that way. When James sent Peirce advance proofs of an appendix of the book, Peirce replied, "I have laid awake several nights in succession in grief that you should be so careless of what you say." By mid-June, having received long, tedious critical letters from many colleagues, James felt the book was "almost unanimously rejected," though he continued to nurse hopes it would ultimately have some effect.[8]

Summer came back a little less for him this year. Up at Chocorua in early June, he stayed for a time at a place belonging to his brother-in-law. One morning he walked out at half past five through the brother-in-law's back pasture, "down to a little pond or lake ¾ of a mile away, the most secluded secret little garden of nature, like a pathway in a fairy tale, with the sky effulgent, the insects torpid with the morning cold and not biting, and all the wild flowers out at once in the carpet of foliage at one's feet." But such moments were now the exception, not the rule. "When I think that that was the staple of life with me in the summer, not many years ago, I feel as if things had changed," he wrote an acquaintance, "not wholly for the better."[9]

He was reading *Lives of the Noble Grecians and Romans,* the book in which Plutarch tried to make "of Hellenism a cult of civilization that could survive the loss of national sovereignty."[10] James found the book "more rammed with life than any book I know." The final two novels of Henry's New York Edition arrived, as did a letter from Henry about *A Pluralistic Universe.* "I read it while in town, with a more thrilled interest than I can say, with enchantment, with pride, and almost with comprehension. It may sustain and inspire you a little," wrote the loyal Henry, "to know that I'm *with* you, all along the line — and conceive of no sense in any philosophy that is not yours."[11]

With August 1909 came a plague of caterpillars (brown-tailed moths) that left whole forests in New England defoliated. There was also a severe drought. On August 22 James was at the Chocorua house. He noted, "To-day our spring of water (which has supplied the house for twenty years) [has] gone dry."

90. *Ever Not Quite*

JAMES RETURNED TO Cambridge in early September 1909. Going to Putman Camp was out of the question. Country walking meant too much struggling up hills; indeed, walking "at any angle" was difficult. Cambridge was bleak. All the elms had been attacked by leopard-moth caterpillars. "The College yard now contains nothing but butts of trees," he wrote Pauline Goldmark. "Most of the limbs having been killed and amputated."[1]

In mid-September he went to Worcester, Massachusetts, at Stanley Hall's invitation. Hall was celebrating the twentieth anniversary of Clark University with an international conference of psychologists. Sigmund Freud, who was fifty-three and beginning to be well known, was there. His book *The Interpretation of Dreams* had appeared, as had *The Psychopathology of Everyday Life* and *Three Essays on Sexuality,* though none had yet been translated into English. The psychoanalytic movement was in its earliest stages, the first international congress had been held in Salzburg in 1908, and the lectures Freud gave at Clark in 1909 would form the basis of his *Five Lectures on Psychoanalysis,* published in 1916. Accompanying Freud was a thirty-four-year-old Swiss psychologist, Carl Jung, who had met Freud three years earlier and who was now a favored, perhaps *the* favored, disciple. James went to Worcester "in order to see what Freud was like," but the one he hit it off with — up to a point — was Jung.

James was very ill but had lost none of his intellectual curiosity or his enthusiastic generosity. According to Freud's biographer Ernest Jones, James's "parting words, said with his arm round my [Jones's] shoulders," were "The future of psychology belongs to your work."[2] James's comment to his colleague Mary Calkins was less wholehearted. "I strongly suspect Freud with his dream-theory, of being a regular *halluciné*" (deluded one), he told her. "But I hope that he and his disciples will push it to its limits, as undoubtedly it covers some facts, and will add to our understanding of 'functional' psychology."[3] To his old friend Theodore Flournoy, about whom Jung had spoken warmly, James wrote ten days later that Freud "made on me personally the impression of a man obsessed by fixed ideas." James told Flournoy that Freud had given an interview to a Boston paper in which he "condemned the American religious therapy (which has had such extensive results) as very dangerous because so 'unscientific.' Bah!"[4]

Jung, on the other hand, "made a very pleasant impression" on James. James had two conversations with Jung, who noted that they "got along excellently with regard to the assessment of the religious factor in the psyche."[5] After his second conversation with James, Jung even found himself beginning to have doubts about certain aspects of Freud's work.[6]

After two days in Worcester, James was ready to go home. Freud accompanied him on the mile-and-a-half walk to the railroad station. "James stopped suddenly," Freud recalled, "handed me a bag he was carrying and asked me to walk on, saying that he would catch up as soon as he had got through an attack of angina pectoris which was just coming on. I have always wished that I could be as fearless as he was in the face of approaching death."[7]

In October *The Meaning of Truth* appeared. A grumpy thank-you note from brother Bob urged William, "For God's sake stop your research for truth (pragmatic or otherwise) and try and enjoy life." In November James found himself lying late in bed and doing just "a little writing." In the spirit of trying everything, he undertook a course of treatments, twenty-one over a month's time, with a Christian Science practitioner, Mr. Strang. In December he caught a cold, and the wretched business of Eusapia and Münsterberg unfolded.

James was increasingly limited physically, but as he turned sixty-eight, on January 11, 1910, he was keeping up an extensive correspondence, working on his introduction to philosophy, finishing and sending off several essays, sitting for his portrait by Bay Emmet, and preparing for and speaking at a banquet in his honor. He was able to work — write — an hour and a half a day. Late in January "The Moral Equivalent of War" was published. James had recast the argument, dropping the idea of voluntary poverty and proposing instead that young people be universally conscripted to work in coal and iron mines, on fishing boats, at road- and tunnel-building, in foundries, and on building construction. As John Dewey would remark, "An immense debt is due William James for the mere title of his essay."[8]

In February he published "A Suggestion Concerning Mysticism" (written in mid-December 1909). The suggestion was "that states of mystical intuition may be only very sudden and great extensions of the ordinary 'field of consciousness.'" Any sudden lowering of the threshold between conscious and unconscious "will . . . bring a mass of subconscious memories, conceptions, emotional feelings and perceptions of relation etc. into view all at once." In other words, the sudden enlargement *is* the mystical state. This seems to be an uncharacteristically reductive conclusion, but it does democratize the mystical state, and may indeed signal James's acceptance that he himself had had such states. One old friend wrote him, "But my dear *man!* — I could have described the general experience *years* ago and told you all about it — if you'd ever thought to ask me."[9]

Early in February further ominous signals came from England about Henry's state of mind, which made Alice want to go immediately to Rye to be with him. A letter from Henry of February 8, 1910, spoke of "the last dismal six weeks of persistent and depressing stomachic crisis," and of collapsing and going to bed. All this he summed up as "some rather depressing discouragements for a fortnight."

William's son Harry took ship at once to go to his uncle, who was glad to see him, but who then suffered a new and terrifying collapse. Harry described, in a letter home, how Henry James "panted and sobbed for two hours until the doctor arrived, and stammered in despair so eloquently and pathetically that as I write of it the tears flow down my cheeks again. He talked about Aunt Alice and his own end and I knew him to be facing not only the frustration of all his hopes and ambitions" — in October 1909 had come the second royalty report, with its grim word of the utter failure of the New York Edition — "but the vision looming close and threatening to his weary eyes, of a lingering illness such as hers; in sight of all that, he wanted to die."[10]

Then Henry himself wrote William. In an extraordinary letter he described his collapse of just before Harry's arrival and gave a vivid sense of his state of mind: "The week before he [Harry] came — arrived — was *all* collapse. It seems in fact *all* difficult and endlessly uphill — and I have a kind of terror of finding myself alone here again with my misery. This, I know, is the perfect platitude of weakness, but I long for you, and yearn for you, dearest William, Alice, and Peggy — and offer you all I have for your possible society. I would say to Harry '*Take me back to* THEM — ANY-how!'"[11]

That letter, of course, did it. A lifetime of Henry's reserve and self-control seemed to have simply evaporated. William and Alice determined to go to England at once. They had the eminent French philosopher Émile Boutroux staying with them at Irving Street. James's shortness of breath had become so severe he could barely speak to introduce Boutroux's lectures. As soon as Boutroux left, William — who now had trouble with any exertion whatever — took ship with Alice to be with Henry, who had obviously suffered a major nervous collapse, the worst such episode of his life.

William and Alice found Henry at Rye, where Alice now had two invalids on her hands. Henry was deeply depressed, though he had occasional short remissions. William was essentially housebound. Edith Wharton sent over a car and driver for ten days so they could get out. William kept at work, writing and sending off "A Pluralistic Mystic," on the life and work of Benjamin Paul Blood, whom he had admired for so long. The essay is a kind of coda to *A Pluralistic Universe.* Looking at Blood from a philosophical, not a religious, point of view, James is concerned with Blood's later mysticism, as it expresses itself in "a sort of 'left-wing' voice of defiance, and breaks into what to my ear has a radically pluralistic sound."[12]

James endorses Blood flamboyantly and generously, quoting extensively and with obvious approval. "Certainty is the root of despair," Blood had written. "The inevitable stales, while doubt and hope are sisters. Not unfortunately the universe is wild — game flavored as a hawk's wing. Nature is miracle all. She knows no laws; the same returns not, save to bring the different. The slow round of the engraver's lathe gains but the breadth of a hair, but the difference is distributed back over the whole curve, never an instant true — ever not quite."[13]

Blood's "ever not quite," which James has made famous, is another response to Plato. In the *Theaetetus,* when Socrates and his always-too-quickly-agreeing young men are making fun of Heraclitus, Socrates proposes that a good Heraclitean "oughtn't even to use the word 'so' because what's so wouldn't any longer be changing." All a good Heraclitean might be able to say, Socrates goes on, would be "not even so."[14] "Ever not quite," James said, "is fit to be pluralism's heraldic device." As with "certainty" so with "conclusions." "Let *my* last word, then, speaking in the name of intellectual philosophy, be *his* word: — 'There is no conclusion. What has been concluded, that we might conclude in regard to it? There are no fortunes to be told, and there is no advice to be given. — Farewell!'"[15]

Early in May, writing his son Harry, William gave his considered diagnosis of Henry's condition, which he called "typical melancholia" (that is, severe depression). He asked Harry not to "use the word melancholy but speak rather of a bad nervous breakdown." "Melancholia," he explained, "suggests insanity, which this is not." He added, "The inevitable course is to complete recovery." Henry, still convinced that his Fletcherizing was the real root of the problem, wanted to believe that his depression had an organic cause, while William was struggling to convince himself that his own all-too-organic symptoms had at least "an element of nervous hyperaesthesia," as he claimed in a letter to Dr. William Osler, the great Canadian physician who was now the Regius Professor of Medicine at Oxford. As he well knew, there was a possible advantage to his believing his trouble to be nervous, because with a change of attitude there might be a chance for improvement.[16]

James was well enough to go to Bad Nauheim by himself in May, stopping in Paris to see Henry Adams and Henri Bergson. In June Alice and the hard-to-move Henry joined him. Henry was still very much down. William wrote his mother-in-law that he was unable, and Henry unwilling, to do anything but sit and watch the time pass. Alice wrote in her diary, "William cannot walk and Henry cannot smile."[17]

Just as life had slowed almost to a halt, William finished reading Henry Adams's "Letter to American Teachers of History." This "letter," which fills 125 printed pages and which was later published as *The Degradation of the Democratic Dogma,* is Adams's grim extension of the second law of thermodynamics to the course of human history. William Thomson, later Lord Kelvin, had said in a paper of 1852, called "On a Universal Tendency in Nature to the Dissipation of Mechanical Energy," that the inevitable and irreversible running down of the earth's energy — defined as heat available for work — meant that the earth was headed for a "thermal death," that the earth would become "unfit for the habitation of man as at present constituted, unless operations have been, or are to be performed, which are impossible under the laws to which the known operations going on at present in the material world, are subject."[18] Seven years before the publication of Darwin's *Origin of Species,* Thomson had thus "tossed the universe into the ash-heap." Adams now interpreted the sixty years leading up to 1910 as a struggle not just between Darwin and Thomson, but between the application of Darwin to history (evolutionism) and the application of Thomson's idea (degradation of energy, or degradationism).

Adams had bitten deeply into the apple of entropy. The gloomy Spenglerian "Letter" James read presented with tacit approval the fevered predictions by the French astronomer Camille Flammarion of the eventual and inevitable approach of the terminal ice. "No longer will man live, no longer will he breathe — except in the equatorial zone, down to the last day when the last tribe, already expiring in cold and hunger, shall camp on the shores of the last sea in the rays of a pale sun which will henceforward illumine an earth that is only a wandering tomb, turning around a useless light and a barren heat."[19]

Adams had, in his *Education,* drawn attention to a leading feature of the new American world of the late nineteenth and early twentieth century — its love affair with energy — and he had proposed the dynamo or generator as the symbol of that energy. William James's life work was the discovery, retrieval, and harnessing of previously unused energies that lie dormant within us. So James was stirred, in June 1910, to rise in protest against the urbane and learned pessimism of his friend Adams's book-length funk. Finishing Adams's "Letter" in mid-June, James fired off a riposte. The beginning was jolly enough. Referring to the "Letter," James said, "To tell the truth it doesn't impress me at all, save by its wit and erudition, and I ask you whether an old man soon about to meet his maker can hope to save himself from the consequences of his life by pointing to the wit and learning he has shown in treating a tragic subject. No, sir, you can't do it, — can't *impress* God in that way."[20]

He then got down to cases. "I protest against your interpretation of some of the specifications of the great statistical drift downwards of the original high-level energy." Adams had neglected to remember, and James now reminded him, that history is "the course of things *before* that terminus," and in the course of things it was a question of what *use* was made of any given spoonful of energy.

> Physically a dinosaur's brain may show as much intensity of energy-exchange as a man's, but it can do infinitely fewer things, because as a force of detent it can only unlock the dinosaur's muscles, while the man's brain, by unlocking far feebler muscles, indirectly can by their means issue proclamations, write books, describe Chartres Cathedral etc. and guide the energies of the shrinking sun into channels which never would have been entered otherwise — in short *make* history. Therefore the man's brain and muscles are from the point of view of the historian, the more *important* place of energy-exchange, small as this may be, when measured in absolute physical units.

For this reason, James concluded, sweeping his hand across Adams's chessboard, "the 'second law' is wholly irrelevant to 'history.'"

It is impossible, after reading James for any length of time, to refrain from using italics oneself. But even italics fail to do justice to this magnificent outburst, the last stand of William James for the spirit of man. What can one *say* about the philosophical bravado, the cosmic effrontery, the sheer *panache* of this ailing philosopher with one foot in the grave talking down the second law of thermodynamics? It is a scene fit to set alongside the death of Socrates. The matchless incandescent *spirit* of the man!

The end came more quickly than anyone expected or imagined. By the end of June, Henry was beginning to emerge from his depression, but William had increasingly bad nights. On July 3 Bob James died of a heart attack in his sleep in Concord. "What a triumph, to slip out like that," William wrote his son Billy.[21] Early July was spent dragging about the Continent; William and Alice and Henry returned to Rye on the twenty-third. Henry was finally having some good days, but William was "worse and worse since leaving Nauheim." He wrote out instructions for Horace Kallen to follow in getting *Some Problems in Philosophy* ready for the press. "Say that I hoped by it to round out my system, which now is too much like an arch built only on one side."[22]

He was very weak, breathing became more difficult, but he still had moments of what he chose to call improvement. On August 10 he noted in his diary, "On the whole have gained strength and breathe better, but Lord, how little." Next day he left Rye with Alice and Henry, who was accompanying them back to America. William was so weak he had to be carried aboard the ship they took, not to Boston but to Quebec, because William wanted to see Chocorua again.

They arrived at Chocorua on August 19. Henry commented on the dreariness of the train trip, on "that flat desert of fir trees broken only here and there by a bit of prehistoric swamp."

"Better than anything in Europe, Henry," William replied. "Better than anything in England."[23]

He could no longer sit up; he was taking digitalis and morphine. They fed him milk every half hour. On the twenty-fourth he said to Alice, "I can't stand this again — cruel *cruel.*" He added, "It has come so rapidly, rapidly."[24] He made a "solemn request" that Alice "go to Henry when his time comes." On August 26, at two-thirty in the afternoon, with Alice holding his head, William James died. At the end there had been, Alice noted, "no pain and no consciousness."

EPILOGUE

ALICE NOTED IN HER DIARY that the autopsy showed "acute enlargement of the heart. He had worn himself out. They have laid him in the coffin and I can see his face no more." No one was harder hit than Henry, who, a week later, wrote to Tom Perry:

"I sit heavily stricken and in darkness — for from far back in dimmest childhood he had been my ideal Elder Brother, and I still, through all the years, saw in him, even as a small timorous boy yet, my protector, my backer, my authority and my pride. His extinction changes the face of life for me — besides the mere missing of his inexhaustible company and personality, originality, the whole unspeakably vivid and beautiful presence of him. And his noble intellectual vitality was still but at its climax — he had two or three ardent purposes and plans. He had cast them away, however, at the end — I mean that, dreadfully suffering, he wanted only to die."

To H. G. Wells, Henry wrote, "He did surely shed light to man, and *gave*, of his own great spirit and beautiful genius, with splendid generosity. Of my personal loss — the extinction of so shining a presence in my own life, and from so far back . . . I won't pretend to speak . . . I feel abandoned and afraid, even as a lost child. But he is a possession, of real magnitude, and I shall find myself still living upon him to the end."[1]

He would not be the only one.

CHRONOLOGY

JAMES FAMILY GENEALOGY

NOTES

PRINCIPAL SOURCES

INDEX

CHRONOLOGY

1842   William James born on January 11, Astor House, New York City.

1843   Brother Henry born on April 15. James family goes to London in October.

1844   Family goes to Paris, then Windsor, England. Father, Henry James Sr., has "vastation."

1845   Family returns to New York City. Brother Wilky (Garth Wilkinson) born on July 21.

1846   Brother Bob (Robertson) born on August 29.

1848   Sister, Alice, born on August 7.

1855   Family moves to London, then Geneva. William attends boarding school. Family returns to London in October.

1856   Family moves to Paris in June. William attends Fourierist school.

1857   Family moves to Boulogne-sur-Mer. William attends Collège Impériale.

1858   Family returns to America, moves to Newport. William takes up sketching in William Morris Hunt's studio.

1859   Family goes to Geneva. William studies science at Geneva Academy.

1860   Family returns to Newport in October. William studies painting with Hunt.

1861   Abandons painting to enter Lawrence Scientific School at Harvard in September. Studies chemistry with Charles W. Eliot. Meets Oliver Wendell Holmes Jr. and Charles S. Peirce.

1862   William at Lawrence School, Henry at Harvard Law School. Wilky enlists in 44th Massachusetts Regiment.

1863   Wilky transfers to 54th Massachusetts. Bob enlists, joins 55th Massachusetts. Wilky badly wounded at Fort Wagner on July 18. William continues at Lawrence School, begins studying under anatomist Jeffries Wyman.

1864   Enters Harvard Medical School. Family moves to Boston.

1865   Joins Agassiz's expedition to Brazil. Sails from New York on April 1.

1866   Returns to medical school in February. Family moves to Cambridge in November.

1867   Sails for Europe in April. Attends physiology lectures in Berlin starting in September.

1868   Adrift, visits Teplitz, Dresden, Heidelberg, Geneva, Paris. Returns to Cambridge in November.

1869   Takes M.D. degree in June.

1870   Minnie Temple (cousin) dies on March 22. William has crisis, probably in April, involving a vision of a green-skinned youth in an asylum.

1872   Appointed to teach physiology at Harvard College starting in spring 1873.

1873   Appointed to teach anatomy and physiology at Harvard. Postpones the appointment and sails for Europe in October.

1874   Returns to Cambridge, teaches comparative vertebrate anatomy. Becomes part of the new Metaphysical Club.

1876   Meets Alice Howe Gibbens. Teaches physiological psychology.

1877   Meets Josiah Royce.

1878   Gives "The Brain and the Mind" lectures at Johns Hopkins in February. Engaged to Alice Gibbens in May. Signs contract for book on psychology. Marries Alice on July 10 and honeymoons at Keene Valley, New York.

1879   Son Henry born on May 18.

1880   Spends summer in Europe. Appointed assistant professor of philosophy at Harvard.

1882   Mother dies on January 30. Son William born on June 17. Travels to Europe while wife and sons stay with her mother. Father dies on December 18.

1883   Returns to Cambridge in March. Wilky dies on November 15.

1884   Son Herman born on January 31. William edits and publishes *The Literary Remains of the Late Henry James.*

1885   Herman dies on July 9.

1886   Buys summer home in Chocorua, New Hampshire.

1887   Daughter, Peggy, born on March 24.

1889   Builds house at 95 Irving Street, Cambridge. Appointed Alford Professor of Psychology at Harvard. Reunion with sister Alice in England in July.

1890   Publishes *Principles of Psychology.* Son Aleck born on December 22.

1891   Trip to England to visit sister Alice in the fall. Sees dramatic adaptation of brother Henry's *The American* in London.

1892   Publishes *Psychology: Briefer Course.* Sister Alice dies on March 6. Goes abroad, with family, for sabbatical in May.

1893   Returns to Cambridge in August.

1896   Presents Lowell Lectures on exceptional mental states in Boston.

1897   Publishes *The Will to Believe.* In August, appointed professor of philosophy.

1898   *Walpurgisnacht* at Keene Valley. Overexertion and start of heart trouble. Travels to California, delivers "Philosophical Conceptions and Practical Results."

1899   Opposes American policy in the Philippines. Publishes *Talks to Teachers.* Goes to Bad Nauheim for heart treatments. Begins preparation for Gifford Lectures in Edinburgh.

1900   Lives abroad, works on Gifford Lectures.

1901   May–June, delivers Gifford Lectures. Returns to Cambridge on August 31.

1902   Sails for England on April 1. Presents second set of Gifford Lectures. Both sets published as *The Varieties of Religious Experience*. Sails for America on June 10.

1903   Gives talks on radical empiricism at Glenmore, in the Adirondacks.

1905   May–June, trip to Europe.

1906   January 8, arrives in California to teach at Stanford. February 21, first version of "The Moral Equivalent of War." April 18, San Francisco earthquake. End of April, returns to Cambridge.

1907   Resigns professorship at Harvard. Last lecture on January 22. *Pragmatism* published in June.

1908   Delivers Hibbert Lectures at Oxford in May.

1909   April, *A Pluralistic Universe* published. October, *The Meaning of Truth* published. September, meets Freud and Jung.

1910   March 29, sails to England with Alice to nurse brother Henry. August 18, returns to United States. August 30, dies at Chocorua.

James Family Genealogy

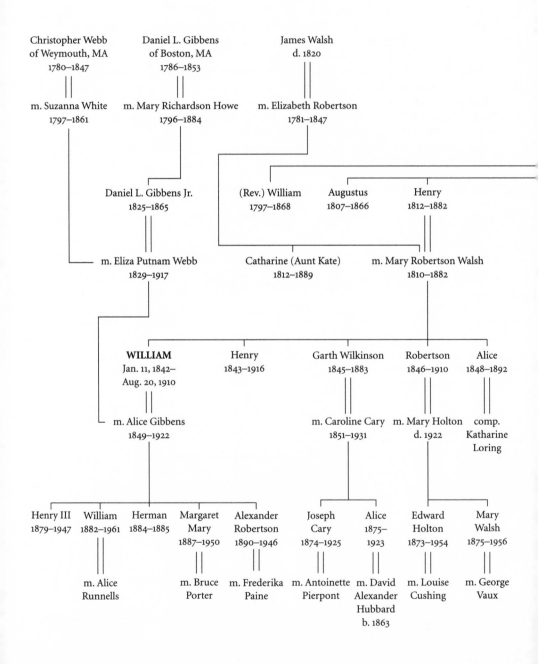

Christopher Webb
of Weymouth, MA
1780–1847

m. Suzanna White
1797–1861

Daniel L. Gibbens
of Boston, MA
1786–1853

m. Mary Richardson Howe
1796–1884

James Walsh
d. 1820

m. Elizabeth Robertson
1781–1847

Daniel L. Gibbens Jr.
1825–1865

(Rev.) William
1797–1868

Augustus
1807–1866

Henry
1812–1882

m. Eliza Putnam Webb
1829–1917

Catharine (Aunt Kate)
1812–1889

m. Mary Robertson Walsh
1810–1882

WILLIAM
Jan. 11, 1842–
Aug. 20, 1910

Henry
1843–1916

Garth Wilkinson
1845–1883

Robertson
1846–1910

Alice
1848–1892

m. Alice Gibbens
1849–1922

m. Caroline Cary
1851–1931

m. Mary Holton
d. 1922

comp.
Katharine
Loring

Henry III
1879–1947

William
1882–1961

Herman
1884–1885

Margaret
Mary
1887–1950

Alexander
Robertson
1890–1946

Joseph
Cary
1874–1925

Alice
1875–
1923

Edward
Holton
1873–1954

Mary
Walsh
1875–1956

m. Alice
Runnells

m. Bruce
Porter

m. Frederika
Paine

m. Antoinette
Pierpont

m. David
Alexander
Hubbard
b. 1863

m. Louise
Cushing

m. George
Vaux

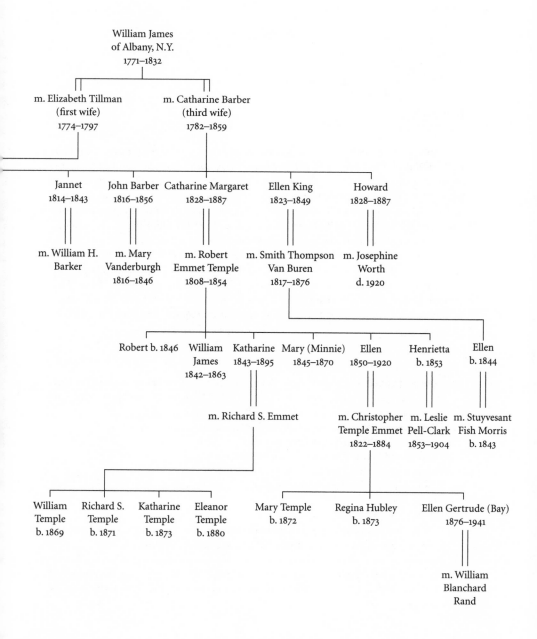

William James
of Albany, N.Y.
1771–1832

m. Elizabeth Tillman
(first wife)
1774–1797

m. Catharine Barber
(third wife)
1782–1859

Jannet
1814–1843

John Barber
1816–1856

Catharine Margaret
1828–1887

Ellen King
1823–1849

Howard
1828–1887

m. William H.
Barker

m. Mary
Vanderburgh
1816–1846

m. Robert
Emmet Temple
1808–1854

m. Smith Thompson
Van Buren
1817–1876

m. Josephine
Worth
d. 1920

Robert b. 1846

William
James
1842–1863

Katharine
1843–1895

Mary (Minnie)
1845–1870

Ellen
1850–1920

Henrietta
b. 1853

Ellen
b. 1844

m. Richard S. Emmet

m. Christopher
Temple Emmet
1822–1884

m. Leslie
Pell-Clark
1853–1904

m. Stuyvesant
Fish Morris
b. 1843

William
Temple
b. 1869

Richard S.
Temple
b. 1871

Katharine
Temple
b. 1873

Eleanor
Temple
b. 1880

Mary Temple
b. 1872

Regina Hubley
b. 1873

Ellen Gertrude (Bay)
1876–1941

m. William
Blanchard
Rand

NOTES

In quoting from William James's published writings I have followed the text of the Harvard edition of *The Writings of William James* (1975–1988). On occasion I have silently inserted or deleted a comma to conform to modern expectations. In quoting from his letters I have silently expanded ampersands to "and" and have normalized punctuation that would appear needlessly awkward now. Eccentricities that reveal the man himself have been left unretouched. Substantive departures from the published *Correspondence* — explanatory insertions mainly — are, of course, in square brackets.

In the notes, the Jameses are identified by their initials: WJ = William James; HJ = Henry James, the novelist; HJ Sr = Henry James Sr.; HJ III = William's son Henry; MJ = Mary Robertson James; AJ = Alice James; AGJ = Alice Howe Gibbens James (Mrs. William James); RJ = Robertson (Bob) James; GWJ = Garth Wilkinson (Wilky) James.

Abbreviations of works by WJ and short titles of frequently cited books are listed on pages 587–589.

Prologue

1. Gordon Thomas and Max Morgan Watts, *The San Francisco Earthquake* (New York: Stein and Day, 1971), 64. See also Philip Fradkin, *The Great Earthquake and Firestorms of 1906* (Berkeley: University of California Press, 2005).
2. Thomas and Watts, *The San Francisco Earthquake*, 65.
3. Thomas and Watts, *The San Francisco Earthquake*, 67.
4. Thomas and Watts, *The San Francisco Earthquake*, 70.
5. Thomas and Watts, *The San Francisco Earthquake*, 76.
6. "On Some Mental Effects of the Earthquake," in *EPs*, 333.
7. *EPs*, 331–32.
8. WJ Diary, 1906.
9. R.W.B. Lewis and Linda Simon have both remarked on the earthquake as the equivalent of a war experience for James. See Lewis, 553, and *WJ Rem*, 341.
10. *PU*, 27.
11. For Jeremy Bentham's idea that "each is to count for one and none for more than one," see Michael Pecter, "The Dangerous Philosopher," *The New Yorker*, Sept. 6, 1999, 48.

12. *PU*, 70. Fechner's idea of the infinitely full and variegated universe is in what has been called the tradition of liberal Platonism. See my article of that name in *Symbiosis* 1, no. 1, Apr. 1997.

13. *P*, 143–44.

14. George Eliot, *Middlemarch* (Boston: Houghton Mifflin, 1956), 194–95; *PU*, 9–10.

15. L. P. Jacks, "William James and His Letters," *Atlantic Monthly* 128, Aug. 1921, 198.

16. For the general influence of WJ on Bill W. (William Griffith Wilson), one of the founders of Alcoholics Anonymous, see Nan Robertson, *Getting Better: Inside AA* (New York: Morrow, 1988). The rebuilding project, the renovation, the sudden, dramatic, and significant change (in religious language, the conversion) to a better path begins, according to Wilson, with a feeling of hopelessness as regards a medical or psychological cure. Wilson's letter to Carl Jung of Jan. 23, 1961, details the beginning of Wilson's understanding of the process. A friend of Wilson's, Rowland H., had gone to seek Jung's help with his alcoholism. "First of all," Wilson wrote Jung, "you frankly told him of his hopelessness so far as any further medical or psychiatric treatment might be concerned. This candid and humble statement of yours was beyond doubt the first foundation stone upon which our society has since been built.

"Coming from you," Wilson continued, "one he so trusted and admired, the impact upon him was immense. When he asked you if there was any other hope, you told him there might be, provided he could become the subject of a spiritual or religious experience, in short a genuine conversion." Wilson then recounted how, after he heard of Rowland H's case, he went to Dr. William Silkworth, who treated him just as Jung had treated Rowland H. Shortly after his own conversion, Wilson read James's *Varieties,* and he told Jung, "This book gave me the realization that most conversion experiences, whatever their variety, do have a common denominator of ego collapse at depth." Wilson told Jung that AA "has made conversion experiences — nearly every variety reported by James — available on an almost wholesale basis." For the full text of Wilson's letter to Jung, see http://silkworth.net//aahistory. For Jung's reply, identifying alcoholism as in some sense a spiritual problem, see C. G. Jung, *Letters*, vol. 2, ed. Gerhard Adler and Aniella Jaffe, trans. R.F.C. Hall (Princeton, N.J.: Princeton University Press, 1975), 383–85. For Wilson's later saying "that James, though long in his grave, had been a founder of Alcoholics Anonymous," see *Pass It On: The Story of Bill Wilson* (New York: AA World Services, 1984), 124.

17. R. B. Perry, introduction to WJ's *Collected Essays and Reviews* (New York: Longmans, Green, 1920), ix.

18. Quoted in Cornel West, *The American Evasion of Philosophy* (Madison: University of Wisconsin Press, 1989), 55–56.

19. *PBC*, 142, 141.

20. *PBC*, 144.

21. *TT*, 113.

22. "On a Certain Blindness in Human Beings," in *TT*, 134–37.

23. Thomas and Watts, *The San Francisco Earthquake*, 77.

1. Art Is My Vocation

1. *Corr.* 4:36–37.

2. HJ Sr to Edmund Tweedy, July 24–30, 1860; Habegger, 411.

3. *Corr.* 4:39–40.
4. *Corr.* 4:33.
5. *Corr.* 4:21.
6. *Corr.* 4:23.
7. HJ Sr to ET, July 24–30, 1860; Habegger, 411.
8. WJ to AJ, June 1868.
9. *SBO,* 9; *NSB,* 134.
10. *SBO,* 259, 207.
11. *NSB,* 141; *SBO,* 253; *NSB,* 123; Perry, vol. 2, 679.
12. *Corr.* 4:14.
13. Quoted in Allen, 53; *HJ Letters,* vol. 1, 7.
14. WJ to K. Hillebrand, Aug. 10, 1883.
15. Perry, vol. 2, 285. The original French reads, "Pour moi je pense qu'il n'est pas dans l'universe d'intelligence supérieure a celle de l'homme."
16. *HJ Letters,* vol. 1, 19.
17. WJ Notebook 1. Most of these are translations of Hafiz, which WJ found in Emerson's essay "Persian Poetry."
18. AJ letter of Mar. 11, 1860, quoted in Perry, vol. 1, 188.
19. *Corr.* 4:27, 29.
20. *Corr.* 4:26; *Corr.* 4:31. William's letter is in French; he calls Goethe's *Werther* "un livre extraordinaire bien plus digne d'attention que je n'avais été porté à le croire."
21. *Corr.* 4:30. The French original says, "L'eau est toute jaune & le courant est si si rapide que cela fait l'effet le plus penible de le voir remonter par les bateaux a vapeur tant ils vont lentement."

2. Growing Up Zigzag

1. Habegger, 186–87.
2. HJ Sr to Catharine Barber James, May 1, 1844, quoted in *WJ Rem,* 33.
3. HJ Sr, *Society the Redeemed Form of Man* (Boston: Houghton, Osgood, 1879), 43f. A particularly detailed and nuanced view of this crucial episode in the life of HJ Sr is in Feinstein, 68–75.
4. *Corr.* 5:120.
5. *SBO,* 199–200.
6. *SBO,* 209.
7. Allen, 29; *SBO,* 266. Cole's painting is now in the Cleveland Museum of Art.
8. WJ to AJ, Nov. 19, 1867; *NSB,* 408; *SBO,* 159.
9. Captain Mayne Reid, *The Scalp Hunters* (New York: Hurst and Co., 1899), 5; WJ, "Philosophical Conceptions and Practical Results," in *Collected Essays and Reviews* (New York: Longmans, Green, 1920), 426.
10. Perry, vol. 1, 181.
11. *Corr.* 4:1, 2.
12. *SBO,* 327.
13. *SBO,* 343, 345. For an analysis of William's interest in Delacroix, see Feinstein, 110–12.
14. Lewis, 81; *NSB,* 122, 123; *Corr.* 4:17.
15. See Perry, vol. 2, 688, and *Corr.* 2:403 for the mescal story. The letter about alcohol was to Barrett Wendell, Dec. 1, 1904, and is in *Corr.* 10:508.

16. RJ to AJ, Feb. 24, 1898(?); Maher, 7; HJ Sr to Catharine Barber James, Oct. 15, 1857; Habegger, 393.

17. *SBO*, 301; WJ to Ed Van Winkle, May 26, 1858, *Corr.* 4:16.

3. Newport and the Jameses

1. WJ to RJ, June 11, 1876.

2. *WJ Rem*, 77.

3. It was William who, in a letter to his sister, described his brother Henry as "a native of the James family and has no other country." *Corr.* 6:517.

4. Lewis, 11; Habegger, 25. A portrait of William of Albany (Old Billy) hangs in the faculty lounge at Union College.

5. Allen, 67; *Life and Letters of Edwin Lawrence Godkin,* vol. 2, ed. Rollo Ogden (New York: Macmillan, 1907), 118.

6. Edward Waldo Emerson, *The Early Years of the Saturday Club* (Boston: Houghton Mifflin, 1918), 328; Ellen Tucker Emerson to her cousin John Haven Emerson, July 12–23, 1862, in *Letters of Ellen Tucker Emerson,* vol. 1, ed. Edith E. W. Gregg (Kent, Ohio: Kent State University Press, 1982), 291–92.

7. *NSB*, 62; Habegger, 3, 215.

8. *SBO*, 86; Habegger, 305, 456.

9. *New York Times,* Sept. 2, 1910, 8; Habegger, 453; WJ Notebook 1.

10. Habegger, 305, 487.

11. See, especially, Maher, 7. WJ's response to Kitty Temple is in *Corr.* 4:48.

12. WJ to AGJ, July 1889, *Corr.* 6:510.

4. The Father

1. Habegger, 307; WJ Notebook 1.

2. *Corr.* 2:30.

3. The story of HJ Sr's accident comes from Woolsey Rogers Hopkins, told in Habegger, 69. James Maraniss told me José Donoso took the title of his book *The Obscene Bird of Night* from this passage.

4. Habegger, 82.

5. HJ Sr, *Substance and Shadow* (Boston: Ticknor and Fields, 1863), 75; Habegger, 349, 50.

6. For the elder Henry James and his brother the Reverend William James, see Habegger, 121. Charles Hodge of Princeton had been a student of Tholuck, who had been a student of Neander, who was Schleiermacher's most eminent disciple. For Hodge and Henry James at Princeton, see Habegger, 132–33.

7. Habegger, 184.

8. Van Wyck Brooks, *The Flowering of New England* (New York: Dutton, 1936), 260–61.

9. HJ Sr to Joseph Henry, July 9, 1843, quoted in Habegger, 204.

10. Habegger, 378; HJ Sr, *The Secret of Swedenborg,* quoted in Lewis, 57. HJ Sr's vocabulary was often steamy. He called Whitman's poetry "stercoraceous." His phrases were hard to forgive and hard to forget. WJ remembered the phrase about the "invincibly squalid little corpus" all his life. See *Corr.* 12: 519.

11. *Collected Papers of Charles Sanders Peirce,* vol. 6, ed. Charles Hartshorne and Paul Weiss (Cambridge: Harvard University Press, 1931), 191.
12. Habegger, 235.

5. Newport and the Jameses, Continued

1. *SBO,* 2.
2. MJ to Emma Wilkinson, Nov. 29, 1846, quoted in Habegger, 249.
3. Habegger, 495.
4. *Diary of AJ,* 221; Strouse, 26. The dogma of the Immaculate Conception of Mary was dated Dec. 8, 1854. *NSB,* 177, 178; Strouse, 24, 5; letter of Jan. 23, 1874, in WJ Papers at Houghton.
5. MJ to HJ Sr, May 27, 1867, Houghton b Ms Am 1093.1 (59).
6. RJ to AGJ, Apr. 19, 1899; Maher, 7.
7. *NSB,* 33; *The Memoirs of Julian Hawthorne,* ed. E. G. Hawthorne (New York: Macmillan, 1938), 81.
8. RJ, unfinished autobiography, quoted in Maher, 3; Maher, 4; *The Memoirs of Julian Hawthorne,* 86, quoted in Maher, 19.
9. *Letters of Ellen Tucker Emerson,* vol. 1, ed. Edith E. W. Gregg (Kent, Ohio: Kent State University Press, 1982), 287–88.
10. Strouse, 23–57.
11. See the illustration and accompanying note in Strouse, between 80 and 81.
12. Sally Webster, *William Morris Hunt* (New York: Cambridge University Press, 1991), 13; *NSB,* 83; Webster, 55; Royal Cortissoz, *John La Farge* (Boston, 1911, repr. Da Capo Press, 1971).
13. Howard Feinstein has called attention to the qualities of energy and violence in WJ's early drawings. See Feinstein, 124f.
14. *NSB,* 91; Allen, 53; *NSB,* 85.
15. *NSB,* 17; Cortissoz, *John La Farge,* 117; *New York Times,* Sept. 2, 1910.
16. Allen, 70; *Corr.* 4:31; Allen, 71. By far the most detailed account of William and Henry James and the outbreak of the Civil War is Charles and Tess Hoffmann, "Henry James and the Civil War," *New England Quarterly* 62, Dec. 1989, 529–52.
17. *Letters of Ellen Tucker Emerson,* vol. 1, 291–92.

6. Harvard, 1861

1. Charles and Tess Hoffmann, "Henry James and the Civil War," *New England Quarterly* 62, Dec. 1989, 535, 536; HJ Sr to (probably) Christopher Cranch, quoted in Habegger, 430.
2. *Corr.* 4:19.
3. Morison 1, 311, 312.
4. HJ III, *Charles W. Eliot,* vol. 1 (Boston: Houghton Mifflin, 1930), 215, 222; Morison 1, 308.
5. HJ III, *Charles W. Eliot,* vol. 1, 94.
6. T. B. Macaulay, "The London University," in *Selected Writings of Thomas Babington Macaulay,* ed. John Clive and Thomas Pinney (Chicago: University of Chicago

Press, 1972), 29. Wolcott Gibbs, the chemist who brought European laboratory standards to Harvard, began teaching there in 1863.

7. Edward H. Cotton, *The Life of Charles W. Eliot* (Boston: Small, Maynard, 1926), 58; C. W. Eliot and F. H. Storer, *Manual of Inorganic Chemistry,* and Eliot and Storer's *A Compendious Manual of Qualitative Analysis* (Boston, 1868).

8. *Corr.* 4:43; *Corr.* 1:2. James's notebook for his 1861–62 course in qualitative analysis is in the Houghton Library, *57M-137. It consists entirely of detailed, scrupulously recorded lab notes made while testing substances for one or another element.

9. See James's rather sharp comments in *The Principles of Psychology* on the phosphorus craze of the time.

10. It is possible that the elegant fare James describes at the boarding house was a complete invention and that he was eating pork chops, potatoes, and no dessert every night. *Corr.* 4:42, 53. WJ's Account Book was begun on Sept. 4, 1861.

11. *Corr.* 4:56.

12. Charles S. Peirce, "Evolutionary Love," *The Monist* 3, 1893, 176–200.

13. *Corr.* 4:52.

14. *Corr.* 4:69–70.

7. Science and the Civil War

1. *Corr.* 1:2; Louis Agassiz, *Methods of Study in Natural History* (Boston: Houghton Mifflin, 1889), iii. "Germ" here means "source."

2. Agassiz, *Methods of Study,* 9, 102. Cuvier's *Tableau Élémentaire de l'Histoire Naturelle des Animaux* appeared in 1798.

3. *Corr.* 4:43.

4. Edward Waldo Emerson, "Jeffries Wyman," in *The Early Years of the Saturday Club* (Boston: Houghton Mifflin, 1918), 21–22; *Corr.* 4:43.

5. *Corr.* 4:72.

6. For the dates and a few details of WJ's visits to Wilky at Camp Meigs, see his Account Book.

7. See E. H. Hall, "Physics," in Morison 2.

8. For WJ on William Grove, see Notebook 3. The Faraday quotation, in the same notebook, is from Michael Faraday, *Experimental Researches in Chemistry and Physics* (1859), 450. The phrase about "matter is motion" is in *ECR,* 295, reprinted from *The Nation* 20, June 24, 1875.

9. HJ Sr to Dr. G. Wilkinson, Jan. 20, 1863.

10. For WJ's comments on his work at this time, see Notebook 3. John Dewey's comment is quoted in Matthiessen, 211.

11. For WJ's notes on Müller and Farrar, see Notebook 3.

12. For Pell's return, see Notebook 3. For the story about the party, see *Corr.* 8:3. Buckle's views are from Henry T. Buckle, "Mill on Liberty," in *Essays* (New York: Appleton, 1863), 3, 44, 71. For Balzac, see WJ's Notebook 3, 24. For a shrewd assessment of James and positivism, see David A. Hollinger, "James, Clifford, and the Scientific Conscience," in *The Cambridge Companion to William James,* ed. Ruth Anna Putnam (New York: Cambridge University Press, 1997), 69–83.

13. For WJ on Edwards, see Notebook 3, 24–25. The passage beginning "Surely all this being true" is on page 28 of the notebook.

14. HJ's review of Stoicism is in the *North American Review* 102, Apr. 1866, 599–606. William's early comments on Stoicism are from Notebook 3, 35.
15. HJ Sr's appearance at Holmes's is told by RJ and quoted in Habegger, 440.
16. Ferris Greenslet, *The Lowells and Their Seven Worlds* (Boston: Houghton Mifflin, 1946), 288–89.
17. The three hundred dollars — about six thousand dollars in today's money — needed to buy a substitute and thus get let out was, of course, a great deal of money for many working men; this was a good part of what fueled the draft riots that broke out in many northern cities in the summer of 1863. To compare the Civil War with World War I, it may be noted that in World War I more men went to war from Harvard, but fewer died: 11,319 Harvard men enlisted in the Great War; 375, or 3.3 percent, died or were killed. Morison 1, 303.
18. RJ, "Three Years Service," address in Concord, Mass., 1896, quoted in Maher, 59. RJ's account of his participation in the Boston riots has been called into question. See *Corr.* 11:128n.
19. GWJ, "Story of the War," *Milwaukee Sentinel*, Dec. 2, 1883, 16; Maher, 46.
20. *Corr.* 4:90.

8. Comparative Anatomy and Medical School

1. Maher, 61–62.
2. *Corr.* 4:83–84.
3. *Corr.* 4:81.
4. WJ Notebook 3; Charles Darwin, *Origin of Species,* chap. 14, paras. 4, 14.
5. C. Hartley Grattan, *The Three Jameses* (London: Longmans, Green, 1932), 71–72. For my account of HJ Sr's theology, I am greatly indebted to Grattan's excellent analysis.
6. HJ Sr's respect for science and his eagerness to extend it to his own thinking led him to correspond with his old teacher Joseph Henry and to seek out Michael Faraday, who was, like HJ Sr, a Sandemanian. It might be argued for HJ Sr, as it has been argued for Emerson by Eric Wilson, that he was alert to the earliest stirrings of the idea that there is no such thing finally as "matter." Everything is fields of force, or energy.
7. Smith would have known that *avena* can also mean "wild oats." The oatmeal motto was rejected for the heavier and rather ominous *Judex condemnatur et nocens absolvitur* (The judges are to be condemned and the innocent absolved). The definition of "association of ideas" is from Robert M. Young, "Association of Ideas," in *Dictionary of the History of Ideas,* ed. P. Wiener et al.; on metaphysics, see Sydney Smith, *Elementary Sketches of Moral Philosophy* (London: Longman, Brown, Green, and Longmans, 1850), 4 (the book prints lectures first given between 1804 and 1806); for Pyrro, see Smith, 7.
8. For habit, see Smith, *Elementary Sketches of Moral Philosophy,* 392 (quoting Lord Kames), 416–17, 423; for stubborn realities, see Smith, 7.
9. *Corr.* 4:87. Henry's story "A Tragedy of Error" was first published in the *Continental Monthly,* no. 5, Feb. 1864.
10. For entrance fees, see H. K. Beecher and M. D. Altschule, *Medicine at Harvard: The First 300 Years* (Hanover, N.H.: University Press of New England, 1977), 87. For Holmes

on medical visits, see HJ III, *Charles W. Eliot*, vol. 1 (Boston: Houghton Mifflin, 1930), 280. For medical student literacy, see Edward H. Cotton, *The Life of Charles W. Eliot* (Boston: Small, Maynard, 1926), 127, 132.

11. HJ III, *Charles W. Eliot*, vol. 1, 275; Morison 1, 339.

12. Abraham Flexner, *Medical Education in the United States and Canada* (New York: Carnegie Foundation for the Advancement of Teaching, 1910), 9; Feinstein was the first to suggest this explanation of James's pursuit of a medical degree.

13. *Corr.* 4:88; for WJ's notes on leeches, see his Notebook 26, "Bo."

14. *Corr.* 4:92.

15. *ECR*, 197, 198, 203.

16. This notebook is called Index Rerum.

17. *ECR*, 207, 208. We know James wrote this because his handwritten manuscript survives among his papers.

9. The Gulls at the Mouth of the Amazon

1. *A Journey in Brazil by Professor and Mrs. Louis Agassiz* (Boston: Ticknor and Fields, 1867), 9. Henry Thoreau's work "The Dispersion of Seeds," as he called it, has been brilliantly edited from manuscript by Bradley Dean and published as *Faith in a Seed* (Washington, D.C.: Island Press, 1993). Other accounts of the Brazilian expedition are in Menand, 117–48 (this superb account was published separately as a pamphlet, *William James in Brazil*, by the University of Nebraska Press in 2000), and in Louise Hall Tharp, *Adventurous Alliance: The Story of the Agassiz Family of Boston* (Boston: Little, Brown, 1959), 160–90. There is also excellent material in *Four Papers Presented in the Institute for Brazilian Studies* (Nashville: Vanderbilt University Press, 1951).

2. *A Journey in Brazil*, 33.

3. *Corr.* 4:99, 100, 101.

4. James's notes on Agassiz's shipboard lectures are in the Brazilian Diary at Harvard's Museum of Comparative Zoology.

5. *Corr.* 4:101–2.

6. *Corr.* 1:6.

7. *Corr.* 4:106, 117. On forcing talent, he wrote home, "Ne forcons point notre talent" ("We cannot force our talent"), *Corr.* 4:107, a view that Feinstein rightly calls romantic and Ruskinian. It was enough for James now, but was a view he would come to repudiate. *Corr.* 4:108. The description of Agassiz's house is by David Starr Jordan and Jessie K. Jordan in *Dictionary of American Biography* (New York: Scribner, 1926–1937).

8. *Corr.* 4:111.

9. *Corr.* 4:115.

10. Lucy Allen Paton, *Life of Elizabeth Cary Agassiz* (Boston: Houghton Mifflin, 1919), 88; letter of Sept. 8, 1865. Howard Feinstein has noted how WJ's drawings during this trip show a new, calmer mood; see Feinstein, 177. *Corr.* 4:126, 111.

11. *Corr.* 4:112.

12. "Louis Agassiz," in *ECR*, 49.

13. *Corr.* 4:125.

14. *A Journey in Brazil*, 201–2, 241–42.

15. Letter of Oct. 27, 1865.
16. Letter of Oct. 27, 1865; *Corr.* 4:118, 128, 120, 102, 117.
17. One of James's Amazon narratives is "A Month on the Solimoens," in *MEN*, 354–57. This is a transcript of Houghton b Ms Am 1092.9 (4531). The other is in James's Notebook 4, Brazilian Diary and Sketchbook, which James originally called Notebook Z.
18. "Louis Agassiz," in *ECR*, 47; *Corr.* 4:122.
19. Louis Agassiz to WJ, Dec. 8, 1865, Houghton b Ms Am 1092 (11).
20. *Corr.* 4:316; *Corr.* 10:169.
21. *Corr.* 4:432.

10. Tea Squalls and a Life According to Nature

1. Trouble hung over many of these young women. Clover Hooper would marry Henry Adams in 1872, then commit suicide in 1885. Her sister Ellen Sturgis Hooper married Ephraim Gurney; she suffered periodic mental breakdowns and died in 1887 at forty-nine. Clover's cousin Mary Louisa Shaw (called Loulie) died young in 1874. Ellen Tappan was the daughter of Caroline Sturgis Tappan, with whom Emerson had once been smitten.
2. The Temple sisters were first cousins of William's. Mary (Minnie), Katharine (Kitty), and Ellen (Ellie) were daughters of Henry James Sr.'s sister Catharine and Robert Emmet Temple. Catharine and Robert died in 1854, leaving six children, who were brought up by Edmund and Mary Tweedy in Newport and elsewhere. Ellie Van Buren was also a first cousin. Her mother, another sister of HJ Sr, was Ellen King James. She married Smith Thompson Van Buren. Ellie Van Buren married a physician, Stuyvesant Fish Morris; the couple lived till 1925.
3. *Corr.* 4:135. Ellen Washburn would die before 1877. Fanny Dixwell would marry Oliver Wendell Holmes Jr. Amelia Holmes's letter to her son is of July 3, 1866, quoted in Liva Baker, *The Justice from Beacon Hill* (New York: HarperCollins, 1991), 181.
4. *Corr.* 4:151, 594.
5. WJ Microscope Notebook.
6. *Corr.* 4:148.
7. For the young Holmes, see Menand, especially chaps. 2 and 3. For Holmes at Harvard and for Holmes and Emerson, see Baker, *The Justice from Beacon Hill,* 80–82, 85–90.
8. Baker, *The Justice from Beacon Hill,* 155.
9. Baker, *The Justice from Beacon Hill,* 60, 6.
10. Baker, *The Justice from Beacon Hill,* 60, 142.
11. *Corr.* 4:137, 302.
12. *Corr.* 4:157; Charles S. Peirce, "Evolutionary Love," *The Monist* 3, 1893, 176–200; Gerd Gigerenzer et al., *The Empire of Chance* (New York: Cambridge University Press, 1989), 68.
13. *Corr.* 4:139, 140.
14. *Corr.* 4:140–41.
15. "Inner sepulcher," quoted in Strouse, 97; "turns of hysteria," quoted in Strouse, 118;

Ruth Bernard Yeazell, ed., *The Death and Letters of Alice James* (Berkeley: University of California Press, 1981), 10.

16. *Corr.* 4:197. This is a letter to Ward of Sept. 1867, but it gives a detailed account of the onset of WJ's back problems in Nov. 1866.

17. *Corr.* 4:197. The letter WJ requested was to Herman Grimm, an author and critic, a friend of Emerson's, and the son of one of the famed brothers Grimm.

11. We Must Be Our Own Providence

1. *Corr.* 4:158.

2. *Corr.* 4:160.

3. *Corr.* 4:160; *Corr.* 1:18.

4. Notes on Goethe, Houghton b Ms Am 1092.9 (4533).

5. *Corr.* 4:185–86 (my translation); *Corr.* 4:189.

6. Marilynne Robinson's comment is in an essay called "Diminished Creatures," in *The Eleventh Draft,* ed. Frank Conroy (New York: HarperCollins, 2000), 156. *Corr.* 4:194.

7. *Corr.* 4:248.

8. Habegger, 349, 182, 348–49. The image of the waiter is from "Mr. Dooley" (Finley Peter Dunne).

9. *Corr.* 4:203, 221.

10. This is not entirely fair to Bob, who spent a good deal of time later on the study of Swedenborg in an effort to understand his father.

11. *Corr.* 4:221.

12. A Dead and Drifting Life

1. For "many social selves," see *PP,* vol. 1, 294; for WJ's choice of words, see *Corr.* 4:228, 294, 295, 336; for his complaints, see *Corr.* 4:197, 243, 245.

2. *Corr.* 4:195, 201.

3. See Claire Salomon-Bayet, "Bacteriology and Nobel Prize Selection, 1901–1920," in *Science, Technology, and Society in the Time of Alfred Nobel,* ed. Carl Gustaf Bernhard, Elisabeth Crawford, and Per Sörborn (Oxford: Pergamon Press, 1982).

4. Physiologists in Berlin at this time included Heinrich du Bois-Raymond and Isidore Rosenthal. James may have heard both.

5. *Corr.* 4:226.

6. *Corr.* 4:243, 255.

7. *Corr.* 4:244, 255.

8. *Corr.* 1:27; *ECR,* 215.

9. There is a kind of depression recognized by some in the medical profession that can be accompanied by a paradoxical but real gain in insight. It must be clear, of course, that this does not apply to severe clinical depression. This disclaimer is indeed the first sentence of Dr. Jonathan Zuess's *Wisdom of Depression* (New York: Harmony Books, 1998). I have tried, in this narrative of James's life, to avoid imposing modern diagnoses backward on him, but it may be helpful to note that his condition seems best described as "depressive mixed states, which while not specifically characterized in the *Diagnostic and Statistical Manual of Mental Disorders,* 4th ed., are best re-

garded as intrusions of hypomanic symptoms or hyperthymic traits into a retarded major depressive episode . . . The clinical picture consists of irritability, pressure of speech against a background of retardation, extreme fatigue, guilty ruminations, free-floating anxiety, panic attacks, intractable insomnia, increased libido, histrionic appearance yet genuine expressions of depressive suffering and, in the extreme, suicidal obsessions and impulses" (*Merck Manual*, 17th ed., 1540).

10. *ECR*, 238. HJ Sr's siblings mostly died young: Robert at twenty-four, Ellen at twenty-two, Ellen King at twenty-six, Jannet at twenty-eight, John Barber at forty, Edward at thirty-eight, Catharine at thirty-three.

11. *Corr.* 1:42.

12. WJ Diary 1, Apr. 13, 1868.

13. WJ Diary 1, 21.

14. WJ Diary 1, 32.

15. *Corr.* 4:306, 307. "Without ceasing" is a reference to Goethe's personal motto, "Ohne hast aber ohne rast" ("Without haste but without rest").

16. Goethe, *Faust,* part 1, ll. 1224–37.

17. *Corr.* 4:300.

18. WJ Diary 1, May 22, 1868.

19. WJ Diary 1, July 22, 1868.

20. Leon Edel's idea that Henry and William had a long, antagonistic, Jacob-and-Esau relationship is based in part on Edel's observation that Henry generally flourished when William was away, and got sick when he was near. There were many times, however — and the fall of 1868 is one of those times — when this was not the case.

21. *Corr.* 1:58.

22. *Corr.* 4:342. James apparently read Schultz's *Commentary* in French; see *Corr.* 4:229.

13. Minnie Temple

1. *Corr.* 4:342, 350.

2. *Corr.* 4:361. The *Journal of Speculative Philosophy,* edited by W. T. Harris, was founded in 1867, nine years before the English journal *Mind.* For an overview of the *JSP,* see the excellent introduction by James A. Good to *The Journal of Speculative Philosophy, 1867–1893* (Bristol, U.K.: Thoemmes Continuum, 2002), v–xx.

3. Introduction to *Writings of Charles S. Peirce: A Chronological Edition,* vol. 2 (1867–1871), ed. Max H. Fisch (Bloomington: Indiana University Press, 1984), xxvii.

4. From a letter of Edward L. Youmans, reporting a visit with Clifford, in John Fisk's *Edward Livingston Youmans* (New York: Appleton, 1894), 340, quoted in *Writings of Charles S. Peirce.*

5. O. W. Holmes Jr., *The Common Law* (Boston: Little, Brown, 1881), 1.

6. *NSB*, 462.

7. *NSB*, 492.

8. *NSB*, 455. Minnie Temple's letters to John Gray are in Houghton b Ms Am 1092.12 (4 folders). These are copies of the originals made by AGJ and her daughter, Peggy, before they sent the originals to Henry James, who used them for his portrait of Minnie in *NSB*, then destroyed the letters. For HJ's editing of Minnie's letters, see

Alfred Habegger, "Henry James's Rewriting of Minnie Temple's Letters," *American Literature* 58, no. 2, May 1986.

9. *NSB*, 401–2.
10. *NSB*, 455.
11. *NSB*, 477.
12. *NSB*, 463. Harry's remark was apropos of Minnie's having gone to hear Phillips Brooks and come away disappointed.
13. HJ to WJ, Mar. 29, 1870.
14. Minnie Temple to John Gray, Jan. 7, 1869, in Habegger, "Henry James's Rewriting of Minnie Temple's Letters," 168.
15. Minnie Temple to John Gray, Jan. 27, 1869.
16. See the list of missing papers in Lyndall Gordon's valuable *Private Life of Henry James* (New York: Norton, 1998), 446–47; Alfred Habegger, "New Light on William James and Minnie Temple," *New England Quarterly* 60, 1987, 32–33.
17. *Corr.* 1:129.
18. *Corr.* 1:64, 69.
19. D. F. Strauss, "Worte des Andenkens an Fr. Wilhelm Strauss," in *Kleine Schriften*, 1866, trans. Charles Ritter in *Essais d'Histoire Religieuse et Mélanges Littéraires de Strauss* (Paris: M. Lévy Frères, 1872). WJ read this in the French of his old Genevan school chum (see *Corr.* 4:368). My translation.
20. *Corr.* 4:370.
21. *ECR*, 4. The "planchette" of the title is a Ouija piece, a small movable board supported by two casters and a vertical pencil. James's fundamental view of psychic phenomena was at this time much like that of William Chambers, author of the protoevolutionist *Vestiges of Creation*. Chambers wrote in the late 1860s to Alfred Russel Wallace: "My idea is that the term 'supernatural' is a gross mistake. We have only to enlarge our conception of the natural and all will be right." Quoted in Randal Keynes, *Darwin, His Daughter, and Human Evolution* (New York: Penguin Putnam, 2002), 280.

14. William James, M.D.

1. *Corr.* 4:370–71.
2. Morison 1. Morison got the phrase about shirks and stragglers from Charles W. Eliot's "The New Education," *Atlantic Monthly*, Feb. 1869, 220.
3. Eliot, "The New Education," 207, 208.
4. Eliot, "The New Education," 205, 204, 210.
5. See Merle Curti, *The Growth of American Thought* (New York: Harper and Bros., 1943), chap. 23.
6. HJ III, *Charles W. Eliot*, vol. 1 (Boston: Houghton Mifflin, 1930), 275. For the Harvard Medical School at this time, see also Edward H. Cotton, *The Life of Charles W. Eliot* (Boston: Small, Maynard, 1926), and F. C. Shattuck and J. L. Bremer, "The Medical School," in Morison 2.
7. There are several versions of James's final exam at medical school. Mine is drawn from WJ's letter to H. P. Bowditch of Aug. 12, 1869, in *Corr.* 4:383, and his letter to his son William Junior of June 18, 1903, in *Corr.* 10:271.

15. Treading Water

1. *Corr.* 4:384. Minnie's comment is in her letter of July 29, 1869, to John Gray, Houghton b Ms Am 1092.12, folder 2.
2. *Corr.* 4:384, 385.
3. *ECR*, 248, 250.
4. *ECR*, 251, 253, 255.
5. *Corr.* 1:100.
6. Wilkie Collins, *The Woman in White* (New York: Penguin, 1974), 61.
7. *Corr.* 1:116, 104, 105, 106, 119. Colchicum is meadow saffron, which had been used to treat gout and rheumatism since the eighteenth century.
8. Habegger, 444, quoting HJ Sr, *Substance and Shadow;* C. Hartley Grattan, *The Three Jameses* (London: Longmans, Green, 1932), 257; Habegger, 257; Grattan, 93.
9. Habegger, 232.
10. In addition to *The Secret of Swedenborg*, this fall WJ was also reading his father's *Moralism and Christianity* and his *Lectures and Miscellanies.*
11. *Corr.* 1:102. It is reassuring to be informed by Peirce, himself a ferociously intelligent thinker with a difficult writing style, that he found reading *The Secret of Swedenborg* "terribly difficult." C. S. Peirce, "James's Secret of Swedenborg," *North American Review* 110, Apr. 1870, reprinted in *Writings of Charles S. Peirce*, vol. 2 (1867–1871), ed. Max H. Fisch (Bloomington: Indiana University Press, 1984), 437.
12. *Corr.* 1:125, 120.

16. The End of Youth

1. Minnie's letter to HJ of Nov. 7, 1869, refers to the first trip; WJ's letter to HJ of Dec. 5, 1869, refers to Minnie's second visit.
2. For the argument that Bob was engaged to Catharine Barber Van Buren, see Maher, 110.
3. Minnie Temple to Ellen Emmet, quoted in Alfred Habegger, "New Light on William James and Minnie Temple," *New England Quarterly* 60, 1987, 34.
4. Minnie Temple to John Gray, quoted in Habegger, "New Light on William James and Minnie Temple," 34, 42.
5. Lyndall Gordon, *The Private Life of Henry James* (New York: Norton, 1998), 321.
6. Charles Eliot Norton, "Nicholas's Quatrains de Kheyam," *North American Review* 109, Oct. 1869, 576. See Minnie Temple to John Gray of Jan. 25, 1870, Houghton b Ms Am 1092.12, folder 4.
7. WJ Diary 1; *Corr.* 4:396.
8. *Corr.* 4:401.
9. AGJ to HJ, Mar. 14, 1914, quoted in Gordon, *The Private Life of Henry James*, 354.
10. Chloral, or chloral hydrate, is a colorless, bitter sleeping potion; it was later called a Mickey Finn.
11. Minnie Temple to John Gray, Jan. 25, 1870; *NSB*, 511, quoted in Habegger, "New Light on William James and Minnie Temple," *New England Quarterly* 60, 1987.
12. WJ Diary 1.
13. *Corr.* 4:402, 403.

14. WJ Diary 1, Mar. 22, 1870. Italics added.
15. The Sanskrit scholar Wendy Doniger, Mircea Eliade Professor of Religion at the University of Chicago, says of WJ's use of this phrase in his apostrophe to Minnie, "I think he means that death is insignificant since ultimately we dissolve back into the world soul that is consubstantial with our individual souls." E-mail to author, Mar. 1, 2000. See also the Chandogya Upanishad, in *The Principal Upanishads*, ed. S. Radhakrishnan (New York: Harper, 1953), 458.

17. Hitting Bottom

1. WJ Diary 1.
2. *VRE*, 134–35. WJ confessed that the anonymous experience reported in *VRE* was his own in a letter to his French translator, Frank Abauzit; see *Corr.* 10:619.
3. *VRE*, 135.
4. Letter to Frank Abauzit of June 1, 1904, *Corr.* 10:619, quoted in *VRE*, 447. An excellent extended treatment of this episode is in Feinstein, 241–50. Feinstein dates WJ's vastation as the fall of 1872, but most biographers have concluded that it took place in the spring of 1870.
5. G. M. Beard, *A Practical Treatise on Nervous Exhaustion (Neurasthenia)*, 5th ed. (New York: E. B. Treat, 1905), 23.
6. Beard argued that neurasthenia was not generally recognized because Americans are "so blind in our deference to Europe, so fearful are we of making our own independent, original observations of the maladies peculiar to this land." Beard thought that neurasthenia could be the effect of "wasting fevers, exhausting wounds, parturition, protracted confinement, dyspepsia, phthisis, morbus Brightii [Bright's disease] and so forth." In other words, it could be caused by almost anything. He further thought neurasthenia could in turn cause "dyspepsia, headaches, paralysis, insomnia, anaesthesia, neuralgia, rheumatic gout, spermatorrhea in the male and menstrual irregularities in the female." Neurasthenia was, said Beard, often mistaken for anemia, but the specific symptoms of neurasthenia included "cerebrasthenia [exhaustion of the brain], myelasthenia [exhaustion of the spinal cord], sick headache [migraine], physical hysteria, hay fever, cerebral irritation and morbid fear." See G. M. Beard, "Neurasthenia or Nervous Exhaustion," *Boston Medical and Surgical Journal* 3, no. 13, Apr. 29, 1869, 217, and Beard's *Practical Treatise on Nervous Exhaustion*, 23–24.
7. WJ Diary 1, Apr. 30, 1870.
8. *Corr.* 4:342; Charles Renouvier, *L'Année Philosophique*, 1867, 13.
9. Renouvier, *L'Année Philosophique*, 101, 107.
10. WJ Diary 1, Apr. 30, 1870.
11. WJ Diary 1, Apr. 30, 1870. The last sentence of this diary entry was convincingly reconstructed by HJ III in *The Letters of William James* (Boston: Atlantic Monthly Press, 1920), 1, 148. In the manuscript diary, the page is torn just at this place, removing most of the letters that make up the words "be built." Because WJ usually dotted his *i*'s, and no dot appears here, it is probable that the missing word is "on."
12. Erik Erikson, *Identity, Youth, and Crisis* (New York: Norton, 1968), 154.
13. Erikson, *Identity, Youth, and Crisis*, 169.

18. The Turn to Physiology

1. WJ to HJ, May 7, 1870, *Corr.* 1:157, 158; Henry Adams, *The Education of Henry Adams* (New York: Library of America, 1983), 726.
2. *Corr.* 4:408–9.
3. These Pomfret principles were printed and discussed by Ralph Barton Perry; see Perry, vol. 1, 301–2. Perry dated them in the summer of 1869. But the Jameses also spent the summer of 1870 at Pomfret, and the language of resistance in the principles is so closely connected with James's thought and writing in the spring of 1870 (see, for example, *Corr.* 4:409) that I have redated the Pomfret sheets to summer 1870.
4. Perry, vol. 1, 301.
5. Perry, vol. 1, 301.
6. James's echo of the Margaret Fuller line ("I accept the universe") is no accident; he was reading the *Memoirs of Margaret Fuller Ossoli* in 1870. See WJ Diary 1.
7. Perry, vol. 1, 301–2.
8. HJ to Grace Norton, Sept. 26, 1870, *HJ Letters*, vol. 1, 243.
9. WJ to Tom Ward, Dec. 17, 1870.
10. WJ's reading for 1870 and 1871 is listed in Diary 1.
11. Many of these titles appear in Diary 1 as part of the second 1870 list. The date is WJ's mistake, as can be seen by the fact that the titles occur in his 1871 correspondence. The Griesinger title, for example, appears in the correspondence for April 1871.
12. *Corr.* 4:418.
13. Fielding H. Garrison, "Henry Bowditch," in *Dictionary of American Biography* (New York: Scribner, 1926–1937).
14. *Corr.* 4:419.
15. *Corr.* 4:416.

19. The Metaphysical Club and Chauncey Wright

1. Quoted in Philip Wiener, *Evolution and the Founders of Pragmatism* (New York: Harper, 1965, orig. 1949), v.
2. The questioner was a Miss Shattuck; the incident is reported in Edward H. Madden, *Chauncey Wright and the Foundations of Pragmatism* (Seattle: University of Washington Press, 1963). I am much indebted to this excellent book for my portrait of Wright.
3. In the still indispensable *Evolution and the Founders of Pragmatism*, Philip Wiener notes that it was Peirce who later talked and wrote about the Metaphysical Club and about the term "pragmatism." Wiener was bothered that "none of the members, including James, and none of their friends ever recorded the name of the Club which looms so large in Peirce's accounts of the genesis of Pragmatism" (22). After Wiener's book appeared, the *Letters of Henry James*, ed. Leon Edel (Cambridge: Belknap/Harvard University Press, 1974–1984), shows Henry referring explicitly, twice, to the Metaphysical Club and to his brother's part in it, once in a letter of Jan. 24, 1872, to Lizzie Boott, and once in a letter of Feb. 4, 1872, to Charles Eliot Norton. WJ also mentions the club by name in a letter of Feb. 1876 (*Corr.* 4:532). The best ac-

count of the club and its importance to American thought is Louis Menand's splendid *The Metaphysical Club.*

4. J. B. Thayer, *Letters of Chauncey Wright* (Cambridge: John Wilson and Son, 1878), 121, quoted in Madden, *Chauncey Wright and the Foundations of Pragmatism.*

5. Chauncey Wright, *Philosophical Discussions* (New York: H. Holt, 1877), xvii–xviii.

6. "Holmes-Cohen Correspondence," ed. Felix S. Cohen, *Journal of the History of Ideas* 9, 1948, 35; letter from Oliver Wendell Holmes Jr. to Cohen, Sept. 14, 1923, quoted in Wiener, *Evolution and the Founders of Pragmatism,* 276.

7. Catherine Drinker Bowen, *Yankee from Olympus* (Boston: Little, Brown, 1944), 222.

8. Chauncey Wright, *Philosophical Discussions,* xviii.

9. *ECR,* 15.

10. *ECR,* 15, 16, 17.

11. *ECR,* 153; quoted in Perry, vol. 2, 718.

12. Madden, *Chauncey Wright and the Foundations of Pragmatism,* citing *The Life and Letters of Charles Darwin,* vol. 2, ed. Francis Darwin (New York: Appleton, 1887), 343.

13. *North American Review,* Apr. 1873, 250.

14. *ECR,* 17; HJ quoted in Perry, vol. 1, 520f.

20. Charles Peirce

1. Brent, 36.

2. Brent, 38, 43.

3. *Corr.* 4:43.

4. Brent, 40–41.

5. Brent, 15.

6. James attended Peirce's Nov. 13, 1866, lecture.

7. Peirce's "On a New List of Categories" was published in the *Proceedings of the Academy of Arts and Sciences* 7, 1868, 287–98.

8. From Peirce's seventh Lowell Lecture of 1866, in *Writings of Charles S. Peirce,* vol. 1 (1857–1866), ed. Max H. Fisch (Bloomington: Indiana University Press, 1982), 457.

9. WJ Index Rerum, "Re."

10. Charles S. Peirce, "How to Make Our Ideas Clear," in *The Essential Peirce,* vol. 1 (1867–1893), ed. Nathan Houser and Christian Kloesel (Bloomington: Indiana University Press, 1992), 129.

11. Quoted in Brent, 72.

12. Charles S. Peirce, "Evolutionary Love," *The Monist* 3, 1893, 176–200, collected in *The Essential Peirce,* vol. 1, 352–71.

13. Charles S. Peirce, "Some Consequences of Four Incapacities," in *The Collected Papers of Charles Sanders Peirce,* vol. 5, ed. Charles Hartshone and Paul Weiss (Cambridge: Harvard University Press, 1934), 157, para. 265.

14. Peirce, "How to Make Our Ideas Clear," 121.

15. Max Fisch, "Was There a Metaphysical Club in Cambridge?" in *Studies in the Philosophy . . . ,* ed. E. C. Moore and R. S. Robin (Amherst: University of Massachusetts Press, 1964), 11.

16. Peirce, "Evolutionary Love," in *The Essential Peirce,* vol. 1, 362; Nathan Houser, "James, William," in Supplement to the *Encyclopedia of Philosophy,* 392.

17. Brent, 17, 60.

18. Peirce, "How to Make Our Ideas Clear," 132.
19. Quoted in Houser, "James, William."
20. Brent, 2.
21. Brent, 33.
22. Brent, 33, quoting *The Century Dictionary.*
23. Quoted in Brent, 2; *Corr.* 8:17.
24. Muriel Rukeyser, *Willard Gibbs* (Garden City, N.Y.: Doubleday, Doran, 1942), 378, quoted in Brent, 303.
25. Brent, 319.
26. J. H. Cotton, *Royce on the Human Self* (Cambridge: Harvard University Press, 1954), 204–5, quoted in Compton, 72.
27. WJ put these lines on the front of Notebook 3.

21. Cambridge and Harvard, 1872

1. Van Wyck Brooks, *New England: Indian Summer, 1865–1915* (New York: Dutton, 1940), 23.
2. Morison 1, 314.
3. *HJ Letters,* vol. 1, 243; Henry Adams, *The Education of Henry Adams* (New York: Library of America, 1983), 1000.
4. Robley Dunglison, *A Dictionary of Medical Science,* rev. ed. (Philadelphia: Henry C. Lea, 1874).
5. F. C. Shattuck and J. L. Bremer, "The Medical School," in Morison 2, 555.

22. Teaching

1. *Corr.* 1:162.
2. *Corr.* 4:422.
3. *Corr.* 4:422.
4. *Corr.* 4:425–26.
5. *Corr.* 4:427; *Corr.* 1:166.
6. *ECR,* 262.
7. In his introduction to Taine's book, Daniel Robinson says, "What is attempted in *On Intelligence* is the utter elimination of transcendentalism from psychology, the installation of naturalism and the scientific method as the reigning perspectives in matters of the mind." Hippolyte Taine, *On Intelligence,* trans. T. D. Haye (New York: Holt and Williams, 1871), xxi–xxii.
8. Preface to Taine, *On Intelligence,* vii; see Alfred North Whitehead, *Science and the Modern World* (orig. Lowell Lectures, 1925) (New York: Free Press, 1967), 54–55.
9. Taine, *On Intelligence,* vii.
10. Taine, *On Intelligence,* ix, 37, 45.
11. Taine, *On Intelligence,* 226.
12. *ECR,* 262.
13. *Corr.* 4:426; *Corr.* 1:167.
14. *Corr.* 4:427.
15. *Corr.* 1:165, 173.
16. *Corr.* 1:166.

17. *Corr.* 4:430. The letter is in French. James wrote, "Je commence à renaître à la vie morale."
18. *Corr.* 1:175.
19. *Corr.* 4:432.
20. *WJ Rem,* 267.
21. Perry, vol. 1, 335.
22. *Corr.* 4:506; WJ to HJ, Feb. 13–14, 1873; Perry, vol. 1, 339.
23. *Corr.* 1:192.
24. Perry, vol. 1, 339–40.
25. WJ Diary 1.
26. *ECR,* 7.

23. To Europe and Back

1. WJ Diary 1, Feb. 10, 1873.
2. *Corr.* 1:194.
3. WJ Diary 1.
4. *Corr.* 1:203.
5. *Corr.* 1:210, 215.
6. *Corr.* 1:219.
7. *Corr.* 4:449.
8. *Corr.* 4:451.
9. *Corr.* 4:452, 458, 462, 455.
10. James would mention three physiological articles by Schiff in *The Principles of Psychology;* see *PP,* 85, 67.
11. WJ Florence Notebook (T).
12. *HJ Letters,* vol. 1, 430.
13. *Corr.* 4:475–76, 465, 473; *HJ Letters,* vol. 1, 431.
14. *Corr.* 1:225; *Corr.* 4:489.
15. *Corr.* 1:183, 190; *Corr.* 4:486.
16. *Corr.* 4:496.

24. Emerson, Mill, and Blood

1. *Corr.* 1:229–30.
2. *SBO,* 8; HJ, *The American Scene* (New York: Horizon Press, 1967), 265.
3. Tom Perry to Van Wyck Brooks, Apr. 7, 1924, quoted in Virginia Harlow, *Thomas Sergeant Perry* (Durham, N.C.: Duke University Press, 1950), 9. Perry also noted that he was "brought up among Philistines who scoffed whenever the name Emerson was mentioned."
4. WJ Notebook 3; *Corr.* 4:246.
5. *Corr.* 4:274.
6. James's copy of Emerson's *Miscellanies* is the Boston, 1868, edition. It is preserved in the Houghton Library, with James's signature and his marking of this passage.
7. *Corr.* 4:493, 494.
8. Van Wyck Brooks, *The Flowering of New England* (New York: E. P. Dutton, 1936), 214.

9. Emerson's categories are enumerated in "Experience," in his *Essays, Second Series.* Aristotle held that everything that could meaningfully be said about something would fall into one or more of these ten categories: substance, quantity, quality, relation, where, when, position, having, acting on, affected by.

10. *Corr.* 4:496.

11. James refers to "Mill on Comte" in his Index Rerum. In James's usage, this kind of notation can refer to either a book or a piece in a magazine.

12. James owned the third edition of Mill's *Examination of Sir William Hamilton's Philosophy;* the fourth appeared in 1872. James was discussing the book in his own work by 1875. See *ECR,* 289.

13. John Stuart Mill, *Autobiography,* ed. John M. Robson (London: Penguin, 1989), 50.

14. Mill, *Autobiography,* 112.

15. Editor's note in Mill, *Autobiography,* 68.

16. Mill, *Autobiography,* 117, 118, 121.

17. Mill, *Autobiography,* 147–48.

18. James's review is in *ECR,* 285–88.

19. See Perry, vol. 2, 228.

20. Perry, vol. 2, 228, 229.

21. *ECR,* 286.

22. *ECR,* 286.

23. *ECR,* 287.

24. *ECR,* 287–88.

25. *Corr.* 8:42.

26. Perry, vol. 2, 229, 234, 235.

27. George Santayana, *Winds of Doctrine: Studies in Contemporary Opinion* (New York: Scribner, 1913), 205, quoted in Compton.

28. Jane Revere Burke, *Let Us In* (New York: Dutton, 1931). There are at least eight books claiming to have been written by James after his death. In addition to those listed in Skrupskelis, 197, see Susy Smith, *Ghost Writers in the Sky* (Vision Press, 1990), and Jane Roberts, *After Life* (Prentice Hall, n.d.). I am far from being a dogmatic skeptic, but it must be conceded that if these are authentic, James's prose style declined after his death.

25. From Physiology to Physiological Psychology

1. *Corr.* 4:505.

2. *ECR,* 9, 7.

3. *WJ Rem,* 141.

4. Bainbridge Bunting, *Harvard: An Architectural History* (Cambridge: Belknap/Harvard University Press, 1985), 87.

5. *Corr.* 4:503–4.

6. *ECR,* 115. For the exchange on self-reflection, see *Corr.* 1:247, 253.

7. *ECR,* 115, 116.

8. *ECR,* 284. James repeats what he learned from Agassiz in his review of *Physiology for Practical Use,* ed. James Hinton.

9. *ECR,* 11; *The Nation,* Feb. 25, 1875.

10. *Corr.* 4:510–11; *ECR,* 12.

11. B. Stewart and P. G. Tait, *The Unseen Universe*, 2nd ed. (New York: Macmillan, 1875), ix.
12. Stewart and Tait, *The Unseen Universe*, 146.
13. Hint: the thesis statement uses the letter *a* eight times, the letter *c* three times, and so on.
14. *ECR*, 291.
15. *ECR*, 292; A. S. Eddington, *The Nature of the Physical World* (New York: Macmillan, 1931). Gifford Lectures for 1927.
16. *ECR*, 293.
17. *Corr.* 4:517.
18. *PBC*, 79.
19. *HJ Letters*, vol. 1, 484.
20. *Corr.* 4:526, 527.

26. Days of Rapture and Heartbreak

1. I depart from the commonly repeated story that it was Henry Senior who identified William's future wife on the authority of Henry James III, the eldest son of William and Alice, who wrote in his 1938 unpublished biography of his mother that it was Davidson who introduced them. R. B. Perry agrees. Alice's son acknowledges that there is a different story, which he identifies as that published by Mrs. Glendower Evans ("William James and His Wife"), but he insists, "I am sure I have the matter right." See HJ III, "Alice Howe Gibbens (Mrs. William James)," Ms Life of AGJ, 34. The description of the Radical Club is that of Allen, 215. Allen had access to Alice Gibbens's diary, and I have followed his good account of Alice in several places.
2. HJ III, Ms Life of AGJ, 11.
3. HJ III, Ms Life of AGJ, 12.
4. HJ III, Ms Life of AGJ, 15.
5. For the story of Dr. Gibbens, see Lewis, Appendix A, "The Strange Death of Daniel Gibbens."
6. I owe the phrase "the wreck of arrival" to the Newfoundland novelist Wayne Johnston.
7. Whittier's gift to Alice is known only from an advertisement in MacDonnell Rare Book Catalog, no. 20, 1997, item 120.
8. According to the Harvard University Library Charging Records, p. 92, James borrowed *Les Fleurs du Mal* and *Petits Poèmes* on Nov. 23, 1875.
9. The poem was a bit of light social satire, called "The Radical Club: A Poem," by Katherine S. B. McDowell (Boston: Times Publishing, 1876). See *Corr.* 4:535.
10. *Corr.* 4:543.
11. The Jameses were great letter burners. Henry James tells of big fires at Lamb House; Henry III read the correspondence between his mother and father and then burned most of it, perhaps because it was so personal that William had once burst out in a letter, "No third eye should ever fall upon them [the letters]." In one letter to her mother, Alice assures her that she burns her mother's letters after reading them, probably because they were full of frank and lively gossip. The burners didn't get everything, however, and enough remains of Alice's letters to give us a clear impression of her as a lively correspondent. There are, for example, eighteen letters from Alice to William, written in 1892 and 1893, printed and calendared in *Corr.* 7.

12. HJ III, Ms Life of AGJ, 35.
13. *Corr.* 4:545, 547.
14. HJ III, Ms Life of AGJ, 35.
15. *Corr.* 4:548.
16. HJ III, Ms Life of AGJ, 35.
17. *Corr.* 4:552.
18. *Corr.* 4:558.
19. *Corr.* 4:571.
20. *Corr.* 4:574–75. I follow the printed text of this fragmentary letter, but there is a good chance that the letter originally ended with "will condemn me . . . Devotedly" and the signature. Later, James turned the paper sideways and wrote "(20 hours later) . . ." and ended with the passage beginning "If so, Amen!"
21. *Corr.* 11:447.
22. WJ to Alice Howe Gibbens, Mar. 4, 1888, in Ms Life of AGJ, 43.
23. Alice Howe Gibbens to WJ, in Ms Life of AGJ, 44.
24. Allen, 220.
25. *Corr.* 10:247.
26. HJ III, Ms Life of AGJ, 45.

27. The Trouble with Herbert Spencer

1. *ECR*, 320.
2. *ECR*, 325.
3. Liva Baker, *The Justice from Beacon Hill* (New York: HarperCollins, 1991), 210.
4. *Corr.* 1:269.
5. *Corr.* 4:541.
6. Perry, vol. 1, 476.
7. Perry, vol. 1, 477–78.
8. *ECR*, 333.
9. Perry, vol. 1, 482.
10. Perry, vol. 1, 476.
11. *Corr.* 4:580.
12. Hocking in *Dictionary of American Biography.*
13. *Corr.* 4:573.
14. *Corr.* 4:570–71.
15. *Journal of Speculative Philosophy,* no. 2, 1878, 1–18.
16. *EPh*, 8.
17. *EPh*, 8.
18. *EPh*, 12, 13.
19. *EPh*, 14.
20. *EPh*, 18, 20, 21.

28. The Action of Consciousness

1. *EPh*, 32, 33.
2. "Brute and Human Intellect," in *EPs*, 4.

3. *EPh*, 37.

4. *EPh*, 36, 37, 41.

5. *EPh*, 52. The colleague was John Watson, a contemporary of James's and not the twentieth-century behaviorist.

6. *EPh*, 60, 62–63.

7. *EPs*, 19–20.

8. *EPs*, 25.

9. *ML*, 4.

10. *Corr.* 5:3.

11. Quoted in R. V. Hine, *Josiah Royce: From Grass Valley to Harvard* (Norman: University of Oklahoma Press, 1992), 44.

12. Clendenning, 61.

13. Clendenning, 65.

14. Quoted in Compton, 71.

15. *Corr.* 5:59.

16. *Corr.* 5:20, 22, 19. Dr. James Jackson Putnam was a lifelong friend and colleague of William James. He also corresponded with Freud and was the central figure in what has been identified as the American school of psychoanalysis by Nathan Hale. See *James Jackson Putnam and Psychoanalysis*, ed. Nathan G. Hale Jr. (Cambridge: Harvard University Press, 1971).

29. Spaces

1. Strouse, 188.

2. Strouse, 182.

3. Strouse, 183.

4. Strouse, 186.

5. *The Diary of Alice James*, ed. Leon Edel (New York: Dodd, Mead, 1964), 230.

6. *ML*, 31.

7. *ML*, 23.

8. *ML*, 26.

9. *ML*, 26.

10. Concerning this point, Louis Menand remarks, superbly, that "the real lesson of *On the Origin of Species* for James . . . was that natural selection has produced, in human beings, organisms gifted with the capacity to make choices incompatible with 'the survival of the fittest . . .' It was our good luck that, somewhere along the way, we acquired minds. They released us from the prison of biology." Menand, 146.

11. *ML*, 30.

12. See J. E. Cabot, "Some Considerations on the Notion of Space," *Journal of Speculative Philosophy* 12, July 1878, 225–36.

13. *EPs*, 64, 66, 74, 755.

14. T. H. Huxley, *Science Culture and Other Essays* (London: Macmillan, 1881), 234–35, 239.

15. *EPs*, 38.

16. *EPs*, 40–41.

17. *EPs*, 46.

30. The Heart Wants Its Chance

1. HJ III, Ms Life of AGJ, 1–3.
2. "Rationality, Activity, and Faith" can be a little difficult to find. It originally appeared in *Princeton Review* 10 (4th series), July 1882, which is the version I quote from. Later James took part of the essay and combined it with part of "The Sentiment of Rationality" and published it under the latter title. In effect, James used that title for two different essays; see *EP*, 249. A few other pages from "Rationality, Activity, and Faith" were used in *PP*, vol. 2, 3, 12–15.
3. WJ, "Rationality, Activity, and Faith," 58, 59.
4. WJ, "Rationality, Activity, and Faith," 64, 65.
5. WJ, "Rationality, Activity, and Faith," 65, 66.
6. Whitehead said, "In western literature there are four great thinkers, whose services to civilized thought rest upon their achievements in philosophical assemblage; though each of them made important contributions to the structure of philosophic system. These men are Plato, Aristotle, Leibniz and William James." *Modes of Thought* (New York: Free Press, 1938), 3. For more on liberal Platonism, see R. D. Richardson, "Liberal Platonism and Transcendentalism: Shaftesbury, Schleiermacher, Emerson," *Symbiosis* 1, no. 1, 1997, 1–20, and R. D. Richardson, "Schleiermacher and Transcendentalism," in *Transient and Permanent* (Boston: Massachusetts Historical Society, 1999). WJ, "Rationality, Activity, and Faith," 68. Robert Baird has pointed out to me that Luther seems a poor fit in this list of men, as he deeply distrusted our "natural" faculties.
7. WJ, "Rationality, Activity, and Faith," 69.
8. WJ, "Rationality, Activity, and Faith," 70–71.
9. WJ, "Rationality, Activity, and Faith," 73, 74, 75. For parallels between James's thought here and that of Kierkegaard, see Myers, 389, 487.
10. WJ, "Rationality, Activity, and Faith," 78, 79.
11. WJ, "Rationality, Activity, and Faith," 86.

31. The Feeling of Effort

1. *Corr.* 1:319; see chap. 30, n. 2.
2. *Corr.* 5:70. J. J. Putnam to "Cousins," Oct. 19, 1879, ms letter at Countway Library, Harvard Medical School, HMS c.4.1., folder "JJ Putnam to Frances Rollins Morse et al."
3. Robert M. Young, "Association of Ideas," in *Dictionary of the History of Ideas*, vol. 1, 112, 113, 115; *PP*, vol. 1, 553.
4. *Corr.* 5:91; J. K. Ochsner, *Henry Hobson Richardson: Complete Architectural Works* (Cambridge: MIT Press, 1987), 277; *Corr.* 5:91.
5. *EPs*, 84, 85, 101, 102.
6. *EPs*, 103.
7. *EPs*, 111, 115, 124.
8. *Corr.* 5:93, 95; Sydney Ahlstrom and Robert B. Mullin, *The Scientific Theist: A Life of Francis Ellingwood Abbot* (Macon, Ga.: Mercer, 1987), 154.
9. *Corr.* 5:126, 96.
10. *Corr.* 5:105.

11. *Corr.* 5:107, 111, 107–8.

12. *Corr.* 5:114, 127, 128.

13. "Great Men, Great Thoughts, and the Environment," in *WB*, 226; *Corr.* 5:140.

32. Hegel in Cambridge

1. Palmer's comment on James and the Hegel seminar is in Perry, vol. 1, 713. Good general accounts of St. Louis Hegelianism include Flower and Murphey, and H. Pochmann, *New England Transcendentalism and St. Louis Hegelianism* (New York: Haskell House, 1970, orig. 1948).

2. G.W.F. Hegel, "Introduction to the Philosophy of History," in *Prose Writers of Germany*, 2nd ed., ed. F. H. Hedge (Philadelphia: Carey and Hart, 1849), 452.

3. My account of both Brokmeyer and Harris draws heavily on Pochmann, *New England Transcendentalism.*

4. See Merle Curti, *The Growth of American Thought* (New York: Harper and Bros., 1943), chap. 23.

5. Pochmann, *New England Transcendentalism,* 13; P. R. Anderson and M. H. Fisch, *Philosophers in America from the Puritans to James* (New York, 1939), 473, quoted in H. Schneider, *History of American Philosophy,* 2nd ed. (New York: Columbia University Press, 1963), 164.

6. In 1878 Hiram Jones, a Platonist from Jacksonville, Illinois, came with some friends from Quincy, Illinois, to visit Bronson Alcott. The Concord School of Philosophy was born out of this meeting. It opened the following summer, 1879, with fifty lectures crammed into five weeks. The previous spring Samuel Emery, who would be the director of the Concord School, moved to Boston from Quincy, and on July 15, 1879, the first session began with Harris as one of the five main lecturers. The second session was held in the summer of 1880, by which time Harris, too, had moved east.

   Hegel played a substantial role in the school. Here is Howison's account, delivered as part of a talk there on modern German thought, of Hegel's absolute idealism. It is, says Howison, "the doctrine of a one and only Infinite Person manifesting his eternal consciousness in an incessant system of persons, the complete expression of whose conscious lives into definite and adequate particularity forms the sensible universe of experience and the world of moral order that is perpetually being inorbed therein." G. H. Howison, "Present Aspects of Philosophy in Germany," in *Concord Lectures in Philosophy,* collected and arranged by R. L. Bridgman (Cambridge: Moses King, 1883), 30.

7. Perry, vol. 1, 725–26. James also owned vols. 2–5 and 11–15 of the 1839–1844 Berlin edition of Hegel's *Werke.* Volume 5 is the third volume of *Wissenschaft der Logik.*

8. *Corr.* 5:64.

9. *Corr.* 5:84, 145, 148, 149.

10. *Corr.* 5:164, 165.

11. *WB*, 216–17.

12. *WB*, 218.

13. *WB*, 220.

14. *WB*, 221; Perry, vol. 1, 727.

15. Perry, vol. 1, 725.

16. Perry noted that while Henry Senior had attacked Hegel in, for example, his review of John Stirling's *Secret of Hegel,* in *North American Review* 102, 1866, the philosophy of the elder James, "in its dialectic movement and in its assimilation of partial evil to total good, was not dissimilar to that of Hegel." Perry, vol. 1, 725.
17. "Reflex Action and Theism," in *WB,* 116.
18. "Reflex Action and Theism," 113, 115, 116, 125.
19. "Reflex Action and Theism," 127.

33. Death of a Mother

1. *HJ Letters,* vol. 2, Feb. 3, 1882, 376.
2. *The Complete Notebooks of Henry James,* ed. Leon Edel and L. H. Powers (New York: Oxford University Press, 1987), 229.
3. Letters from Mary Robertson James, Houghton b Ms Am 1093.1 (20, 21, 22, 23, 25, 26, 59, 62).
4. *HJ Letters,* vol. 2, 376; *The Complete Notebooks of Henry James,* 229.
5. Edel, vol. 3, 21, 41, 28, 33.
6. Maher, 139.
7. Maher, 138.
8. *Corr.* 5:168.
9. Strouse, 200.
10. *Corr.* 5:120.

34. Goodbye, My Sacred Old Father

1. Matthiessen, 448; John J. McAleer, in *Days of Encounter* (Boston: Little, Brown, 1984), 663, places William at Emerson's funeral.
2. HJ III, Ms Life of AGJ, 1.
3. *Corr.* 5:220.
4. *Corr.* 5:285. Stumpf was later involved in the investigation of the famous "Clever Hans," a horse that seemed able to read minds but was shown to be detecting slight, even unintended physical cues from his trainer. Hans could "count" by striking his hoof, but he couldn't get the number of strikes right if his trainer was out of his sight.
5. *Corr.* 5:285–86.
6. Ernst Mach, *Die Mechanik in ihrer Entwicklung,* English trans. T. J. McCormack (Leipzig, 1883, 4th ed. 1919).
7. M. Schlick, "Ernst Mach and the Fortunes of Positivism," in *Science and Anti-Science,* ed. Gerald Holton (Cambridge: Harvard University Press, 1993).
8. Quoted in Gerald Holton, *Einstein, History, and Other Passions* (Reading, Mass.: Addison-Wesley, 1996), 200.
9. *Corr.* 5:290, 298.
10. *Corr.* 5:302.
11. *Corr.* 1:336–37.
12. *Corr.* 5:300–301, 302.
13. *Corr.* 1:336, 337; *Corr.* 5:293, 294, 313, 314.

14. *Corr.* 5:320.
15. *Corr.* 5:320, 323, 329.
16. *Corr.* 1:340–41; *Corr.* 5:336.
17. *Corr.* 1:342. William's last letter to his father is in *Corr.* 5:227–28.

35. The Wonderful Stream of Our Consciousness

1. AGJ to WJ, Dec. 22, 1882, quoted in Maher, 149, and see 82. A rule of thumb for estimating the value of money is to regard one 1900 dollar as worth twenty in 2000. A
   more precise equivalency can be worked out with the help of a historical price index, such as John J. McCusker's in *What Is That in Real Money?* (Worcester, Mass.:
   American Antiquarian Society, 1992), and a current *Statistical Abstract of the United
   States.*
2. The fact that Harry was appointed executor, although William was the eldest, the father's favorite, and the one who lived in the United States, suggests that the will was
   drawn up when William was too depressed to function effectively, at least in the eyes
   of his parents.
3. *Corr.* 1:358.
4. *Corr.* 1:350, 352.
5. *Corr.* 1:355–56, 354, 349, 355.
6. *Corr.* 5:378, 379.
7. *Corr.* 5:394, 405, 406.
8. *Corr.* 1:344, 5:379.
9. *Corr.* 1:345.
10. The other members of the Scratch Eight were Frederick Pollard, a professor of law
    at London University; James Sully, a psychologist and philosopher; Frederick W.
    Maitland, a professor of law at Cambridge; and Carveth Read, who had written a
    book on logic. *Corr.* 5:362.
11. *Corr.* 5:390, 404, 408, 414–15.
12. *EPs,* 143, 144.
13. *EPs,* 145, 146, 152.
14. *EPs,* 154.
15. *EPs,* 160; *Corr.* 5:428.

36. Not a Simple Temperament

1. John J. Chapman, "William James," in *WJ Rem,* 56; George Santayana, "William
   James," in *WJ Rem,* 92; John E. Boodin, "William James as I Knew Him," in *WJ Rem,*
   210; James J. Putnam, "William James," in *WJ Rem,* 14. The supper with absinthe was
   on the ship *Parisien* in Sept. 1882; *Corr.* 7:374.
2. WJ to AGJ, Dec. 5, 1882; *Corr.* 6:13; *Corr.* after Apr. 19, 1875.
3. *Corr.* 6:522–23.
4. The telegram to Alice was sent on Aug. 9, 1889.
5. HJ III, Ms Life of AGJ, 37, 41, 37–38.
6. Santayana, "William James," 92.

7. Perry, vol. 1, 476; *PP,* 398; Santayana, "William James," 105; Chapman, "William James," 54.

8. Letter to Grace Norton, Dec. 28, 1892.

9. Quoted in Ludwig Lewisohn, *Expression in America* (New York: Harper and Bros., 1932), 331–36.

10. A similar temperament would lead Italo Calvino to project six lectures, to be given at Harvard, on lightness, quickness, exactitude, visibility, multiplicity, and consistency. Calvino died before he could finish the last one.

11. Huxley's comment is quoted in Geoff Dyer, *Out of Sheer Rage* (London: Little, Brown, 1997), 33; Richard Holmes, *Coleridge: Darker Reflections* (New York: Pantheon, 2000), 165.

37. What Is an Emotion?

1. The James family apartment was at 19 Rue d'Angoulême (now Rue de la Boétie); *Corr.* 5:429, 420; see "The Sense of Dizziness in Deaf-Mutes," *American Journal of Otology* 4, 1882, 239–54, reprinted in *EPs.*

2. *Corr.* 5:443, 446.

3. *Corr.* 5:447.

4. Howison delivered "Hume's Aim and Method" to the Concord School of Philosophy on July 19, 1883; *Corr.* 5:451, 453.

5. *Corr.* 5:477; HJ to S. Whitman, Aug. 21, 1883; *Corr.* 5:476, ed. note; *Phantasms of the Living* did not appear until 1886.

6. *Corr.* 5:465, 466–67, 468.

7. *EPs,* 170.

8. C. V. Calhoun and R. C. Solomon, *What Is an Emotion?* (New York: Oxford University Press, 1984), 126.

9. Oliver Sacks has emphasized, apropos the history every physician takes down, the importance of narrative to medicine. See also Melanie Thernstrom, "The Writing Cure," *New York Times Magazine,* Apr. 18, 2004.

10. *EPs,* 178.

38. The Literary Remains of Henry James Sr.

1. WJ to Carl Stumpf, Jan. 9, 1884; see Ernst Mach, *Beitrage zur Analyse der Empfindungen* (*Contributions to the Analysis of Feelings*); *Corr.* 5:568; Perry, vol. 1, 588; the French translation of "Some Omissions" is in *Revue Philosophique,* no. 17, Feb. 1884, 235–37.

2. See *WJ Rem,* 187, on this curious choice of a name.

3. For "balance of burdens," see Maher, 169.

4. See Norman Green's Apr. 28, 1998, interview with Singer at Salon.com.

5. *WB,* 115, 125.

6. *WB,* 123, 119.

7. *WB,* 136.

8. *ERE,* 137, 140, 143.

9. *The Literary Remains of Henry James,* ed. and with an introduction by William James (Boston: Osgood, 1885), 9.

10. *The Literary Remains of Henry James,* 16.

11. *The Literary Remains of Henry James,* 10, 12, 15.

12. HJ Sr, *Substance and Shadow* (Boston: Ticknor and Fields, 1863) 75; *The Literary Remains of Henry James,* 49–50.

13. *The Literary Remains of Henry James,* 17.

14. *The Literary Remains of Henry James,* 19.

15. There are several brilliant and distinguished treatments of HJ Sr; the most useful and detailed is Alfred Habegger, *The Father.* Other notable assessments include Hartley Grattan, *The Three Jameses* (1932); Austin Warren, *The Elder Henry James* (1934); and F. H. Young, *The Philosophy of Henry James Sr.* (1951).

16. *The Literary Remains of Henry James,* 25.

17. *The Literary Remains of Henry James,* 72.

18. *The Literary Remains of Henry James,* 118. Note how the phrasing of this passage echoes the description of the green-skinned idiot in *VRE;* see chap. 17.

19. *The Literary Remains of Henry James,* 119.

20. *Corr.* 5:513.

21. There is also a letter from WJ to C. A. Strong of Sept. 17, 1907, saying this essay was the *fons et origo* of all his pragmatism as a theory of truth. See *MT,* 205.

22. *MT,* 15, 25, 29–30. Pound's "Canto 2" begins, "Hang it all, Robert Browning / There can be but one "Sordello" / But Sordello and my Sordello? / Lo Sordels si fo di Mantovana."

39. The Death of Herman

1. Leon Edel notes that Harry twice used the word "abandoned" in letters to William's wife at the time. See Edel, vol. 3, 46.

2. *Corr.* 1:379, 380.

3. This is WJ's summary of Royce's argument; see *ECR,* 386.

4. *ECR,* 386–87.

5. See R. V. Hine, *Josiah Royce: From Grass Valley to Harvard* (Norman: University of Oklahoma Press, 1992). The social consequences of Royce's new allegiance to the Absolute are striking. "We thus must see ourselves as little members of a vast body, as little fragments of a mighty temple, as single workers whose work has importance only by reason of its relations to the whole." Quoted in Hine, 125.

6. *Corr.* 6:23.

7. *Corr.* 2:14.

8. Of this amount, $128.50 was Harry's share of some Syracuse rental income from buildings Old Billy James had acquired; the rest was a loan to be repaid "whenever you are able." *Corr.* 2:19.

9. *Corr.* 6:32.

10. *Corr.* 6:44, 67.

11. *Corr.* 2:21.

12. *VRE,* 137.

13. *P,* 50.

40. Mrs. Piper

1. *Corr.* 6:70.
2. Eliza was a frequent visitor to the house on Beacon Hill, where the maid was a sister of Mrs. Piper's maid. See Alta L. Piper, *The Life and Works of Mrs. Piper* (London: Kegan Paul, Trench, Trubner, 1929), 21.
3. *EPR*, 79, 80, 15–16.
4. *EPR*, 80, 81.
5. *Corr.* 6:33.
6. Piper, *The Life and Works of Mrs. Piper*, 12.
7. Piper, *The Life and Works of Mrs. Piper*, 13.
8. *EPR*, 398.
9. *EPR*, 436.
10. *EPR*, 131. James's phrase about white crows became so well known that R. Lawrence Moore could title his 1977 book *In Search of White Crows* (New York: Oxford University Press).
11. *Corr.* 6:65, 35.
12. Introduction to *The Writings of Andrew Jackson Davis*, ed. J. L. Moore (Boston: Christopher House, 1930), 13. For a serious treatment of Davis and spiritualism, see Ann Braude, *Radical Spirits*, 2nd ed. (Bloomington: Indiana University Press, 2001), and Catherine L. Albanese, "The Subtle Energies of Spirit," *Journal of the American Academy of Religion* 67, June 1999, 305–25.
13. Free Religious Association, *Freedom and Fellowship in Religion* (Boston: Roberts Brothers, 1875), 223–64.
14. Sydney E. Ahlstrom and Robert Bruce Mullin, *The Scientific Theist: A Life of Francis Ellingwood Abbot* (Macon, Ga.: Mercer, 1987), 130.
15. Francis Ellingwood Abbot, *Scientific Theism*, 3rd ed. (Boston: Little, Brown, 1888), 218.
16. *Corr.* 6:101.
17. *Corr.* 6:137.
18. See "Report of the Committee on Mediumistic Phenomena," *Proceedings of the American Society for Psychical Research* 1, July 1886, 102–6, reprinted in *EPR*, 14–18.
19. *Corr.* 6:125.
20. *Corr.* 6:105–6.
21. *Corr.* 2:34, 44. The fitness equipment William sent Harry is in an illustrated brochure filed with the letter, in Houghton b Ms Am 1092.9 (2628).

41. My Only Absolutely Satisfying Companion

1. *EPR*, 437; *Corr.* 2:35.
2. HJ III, Ms Life of AGJ, 66. This scrap is all we know about an incident that sounds a little like Henry's great story "The Turn of the Screw."
3. HJ III, Ms Life of AGJ, 66–67.
4. This list, which sheds light on those interests of William James to which his wife wished to direct the attention of posterity, also includes several other works on hypnosis: "George M. Beard, M.D., Study of muscle-reading Transc. state in Inebriety, *Archives of Electrology and Neurology* no 1, May 1875, II, May 1875, neurasthenia (ner-

vous exhaustion) as a cause of inebriety; Dr. Christian Baumler [*Der Sogenaunte*] *animalische Magnetismus [oder Hypnotismus*, Leipzig: F.C.W. Vogel, 1881]; [Albert P.] Schrenck-Notzing, *Ueber Spaltung der Personlichkeit* [Vienna: Holder, 1896]; G. H. Schneider *Die Psychologische* [*Ursache der Hypnotischen Erscheinungen*, Leipzig: A. Abel, 1880]; Hans Kaan (2 copies) *Ueber Beziehungen zwischen Hypnotismus und cerebraler Blutfullung* [Wiesbaden: J. F. Bergmann, 1885]; Dr Rudolf Heidenhain *Der sogenante thierische Magnetismus* . . . and a review of it in the *Nation* from Breslau by W. J. [Leipzig: Breitkopf und Hartel, 1880; no review by WJ is included in *ECR*]; [Emile] Boirac *L'hypothese du magnetism Animal* [Paris: Librairie de la Nouvelle Revue, 1895]; Dr S[amson] Landmann, *Die mehrkeit Geistiger Personlichkeiten in einem individuum* [Stuttgart: F. Enke, 1894]." There are English editions with varying titles. For the entire list, see b Ms Am 1092.9 (4581).

5. *Corr.* 5:311.
6. MacDonnell Rare Book Catalog, no. 20, 1997, item 120.
7. HJ III, Ms Life of AGJ, 40.
8. *Corr.* 5:195.
9. *Corr.* 6:70.
10. *Corr.* 11:50; *Corr.* 8:573; *Corr.* 7:545; *Corr.* 9:281; WJ to HJ III, July 20, 1904; *Corr.* 10:577.
11. *Corr.* 5:416.
12. *Corr.* 2:16.
13. *Corr.* 11:256.
14. *Corr.* 6:330.
15. *Corr.* 5:381, 376.
16. *Corr.* 5:320–21.
17. *Corr.* 9:381.
18. *Corr.* 6:131.
19. HJ III, Ms Life of AGJ, 84.
20. *Corr.* 6:357.
21. *Corr.* 5:317.

42. Hypnotism and Summers at Chocorua

1. *Corr.* 6:126.
2. WJ mentions Braid in his 1868 review of Liébeault, in his 1886 report of the Committee on Hypnotism (*EPs*, 190), and in his 1889 report on automatic writing (*EPR*, 45). J. K. Mitchell, father of S. Weir Mitchell, took the same view. James knew J. K. Mitchell's work because Mitchell's son sent him his father's work; see *Corr.* 6:91–92.
3. *ECR*, 246.
4. *EPs*, 192.
5. *ECR*, 241.
6. *Corr.* 2:32.
7. *Corr.* 2:51; *Corr.* 6:124, 156, 168.
8. *Corr.* 6:166.
9. HJ III, Ms Life of AGJ, 18. James bought the Savage Farm from Adam Leppere in the early fall of 1886. My information on early days at Chocorua comes from Lydia and Alan Smith, *Chocorua Recalled* (n.p., 1996); F. G. Balch, *Reminiscences;* Frank Bolles,

At the North of Bearcamp Water (Cambridge: Riverside Press, 1893); and Marjorie G. Harkness, *The Tamworth Narrative* (Freeport, Me.: Bond Wheelwright Co., 1958).

10. Robertson typeset the first half of the chapter on the self, then held it. Eventually it became chap. 10 of *PP.*

11. *PP,* 574, 603.

12. "Edmund Gurney's Death," in *ECR,* 26.

13. *Corr.* 6:147.

14. Review of *Phantasms of the Living,* in *EPR,* 27.

15. John Dewey, *Psychology* (Carbondale: Southern Illinois University Press, 1967), 174, 212.

43. Instinct and Will

1. *Corr.* 6:200. The Dressers, Annetta and Julius and their son, Horatio, were ardent defenders of Quimby. Whereas Mary Baker Eddy added a strong Christian strain to Quimby's ideas and then denied his influence on her, the Dressers told Quimby's side of the story and stuck to it for decades. WJ never showed any interest in Christian Science, though one of the books he was supposed to have dictated from "the other side," Jane Revere Burke's *Messages on Healing* (n.p., 1936), has him saying, "I told you before that Mary Baker Eddy had become a great friend of mine" (15). On this side, however, James was clearly in the camp of the Dressers. See Annetta G. Dresser, *The Philosophy of P. P. Quimby,* 3rd ed. (Boston: C .H. Ellis, 1899, orig. 1895); Julius A. Dresser, *The True History of Mental Science* (Boston: A. Mudge and Son, 1887); and Horatio W. Dresser, ed., *The Quimby Manuscripts* (New York: Crowell, 1921), the first edition of which has letters between Quimby and Mrs. Eddy, which are missing in later editions.

2. *Corr.* 2:59, 63; *Corr.* 6:204.

3. *ECR,* 400. In his review of Ladd, James somewhat confusingly used the word "spiritualistic" to mean idealistic.

4. In a letter of Apr. 8, 1887, to Alice, William gave a list of names he thought suitable, with the clear inference that the final choice was not his. In HJ III, Ms Life of AGJ, her son reports that Alice thought baby Herman's name was a "hair shirt" for him and that she longed to have it off him.

5. *Corr.* 6:213. William attributes this description to Alice. Whether it was his or hers, it says as much about the parental expectations of the times as it does about the baby itself. Still, times were changing. Alice had the services of a female doctor, Emma Call, for her lying-in.

6. *PP,* 1004, 1005, 1020.

7. *PP,* 1004, 1010, 1023, 1024, 1035.

8. *PP,* 1040. Young Harry's and young Willy's ages do not fit for 1887. James may have been remembering an incident, or, given the fact that he was indeed introducing the boys to Homer this year, he may have changed the ages for protection — or conceivably the story is about some other children.

9. *PP,* 1056.

10. *Corr.* 2:63.

11. *Corr.* 6:236.

12. *Corr.* 6:238–39, 265; *Corr.* 2:69.

13. *EPs,* 217.
14. *EPs,* 218, 220, 221.
15. *EPs,* 220.
16. *PBC,* chap. 26 and p. 372; *EPs,* 231.
17. *EPs,* 233–34.
18. *Corr.* 6:281–82.
19. *Corr.* 6:311.
20. Clendenning, 152.
21. Call is a neglected figure. Her *Power Through Repose* remains an appealing, unpretentious self-help book.
22. *TT,* 136.

44. Santayana at Harvard

1. *Corr.* 6:420.
2. *Corr.* 6:371.
3. *WJ Rem,* 116; *Corr.* 2:87, 89.
4. *Corr.* 6:395, 420; *Corr.* 6:425.
5. Flower and Murphey, vol. 2, 774.
6. See, for example, Santayana 1 and 2, as well as his "Genteel Tradition in American Philosophy" (1911), repr. in *Winds of Doctrine* (1913), and "Three American Philosophers," *American Scholar* 22, Summer 1953, 281–84.
7. G. W. Howgate, *George Santayana* (New York: A. S. Barnes, 1961, orig. 1938), 3.
8. Santayana 2, 389.
9. See George P. Adams and Wm. P. Montague, eds., *Contemporary American Philosophy: Personal Statements,* vol. 2 (New York: Macmillan, 1932), 251, quoted in Howgate, *George Santayana;* George Santayana, "William James," in *WJ Rem,* 93.
10. *Corr.* 6:483, 468; Santayana 2, 390, 234, 238, 239.

45. The Psychology of Belief

1. *PP,* 913.
2. *PP,* 914, 915.
3. *PP,* 918, 923, 924, 925.
4. *PP,* 926, 928, 932.
5. *PP,* 935, 936, 937.
6. *PP,* 940, 942, 943, 945.
7. *PP,* 948, 949.
8. *PP,* 948, 949n.
9. *Corr.* 2:102.
10. One sees how welcome Aunt Kate's legacy must have been when one notes that William had borrowed $2,000 from his mother-in-law, $1,000 from a sister-in-law, $1,688 from his banker (an advance, no doubt, on his Syracuse rents from the buildings that were part of Old Billy's empire), and $4,000 from a savings bank.

46. Reunion with Alice: The Hidden Self

1. *Corr.* 6:487, 490, 496, 499.
2. *Corr.* 6:502.
3. *Corr.* 6:503, 508, 511.
4. *Corr.* 2:108, 109; *Diary of AJ*, 51; *Corr.* 6:510.
5. *Diary of AJ*, 51–52.
6. *Corr.* 6:510, 511; *Diary of AJ*, 51.
7. *Corr.* 6:516, 517.
8. *Corr.* 6:524; *EPs*, 245.
9. *Corr.* 6:527.
10. R. V. Hine, *Josiah Royce: From Grass Valley to Harvard* (Norman: University of Oklahoma Press, 1992), 140.
11. "The Hidden Self" could not be incorporated into *The Principles of Psychology* as written, so James broke it up, with a few pages going into the *Principles* and the opening used in "What Psychic Research Has Accomplished," in *WB*. The balance was only rarely reprinted in its entirety, until the 1983 *EPs*.
12. *EPs*, 247. Dissociative personality disorder is still in the medical books. The description in the 1999 *Merck Manual of Diagnosis and Therapy*, ed. M. H. Beers and R. Berkow (Whitehouse Station, N.J.: Merck Research Laboratories), 1522–24, uses terms quite close to some used by Janet.
13. *EPs*, 258, 259, 263.
14. *EPs*, 262, 264; *Merck Manual*, 1522.
15. *Diary of AJ*, 149.
16. *Corr.* 6:552–53.
17. *Corr.* 2:129; *Corr.* 7:19.
18. WJ to HJ, Mar. 10, 1887; WJ to Renouvier, Aug. 5, 1883; WJ to Kitty Prince, Aug. 11, 1885; WJ to AJ, Oct. 19, 1885; *Corr.* 7:53.
19. WJ to Sarah Whitman, July 24, 1890.
20. *Corr.* 7:24.

47. Response to Principles and the Moral Philosopher

1. *Corr.* 7:45; *Corr.* 2:144, 146, 142, 148.
2. *Corr.* 7:86–87.
3. Barzun, 35; see the chapter called "The Masterpiece."
4. Santayana's assessment is in his "Character and Opinion in the United States," in *WJ Rem*, 93.
5. Perry, vol. 2, 92.
6. *Principles* sold for six dollars a copy. James's royalty was 18 percent, or 33⅓ cents per copy. A number had been given away, so James's receipts for the fifteen months were slightly under $600. As he told his brother, he had himself bought $450 worth of presentation copies, so his net income from the book was "not likely to be immense." *Corr.* 2:150.
7. *Corr.* 7:113, 578; *The Nation* 53, 1891, 15, quoted in Perry, vol. 1, 105. On impressionism as a breakthrough, see John J. McDermott, *The Culture of Experience* (New York: NYU Press, 1976), 29–34. Baldwin's review was in *Science* 16, Oct. 10, 1890, 207–8. The

attribution to Baldwin is in Perry, vol. 2, 104. Hall's review is in *American Journal of Psychology* 3, 1891, 585–91, quoted in Perry, vol. 2, 109. Dewey's comment is quoted in Perry, vol. 2, 104.

8. The group's comment is quoted in Myers, 485.

9. Barbara Ross, "William James: Spoiled Child of American Psychology," in *Portraits of Pioneers in Psychology,* ed. G. A. Kimble, M. Wertheimer, and C. White (Washington, D.C.: American Psychological Association, 1991), 24. Ross credits J. R. Angell's 1911 editorial in *Psychological Review,* no. 5, 1911, 78–79, where Angell lists six of the points, naming habit, emotion, instinct, the vague, the pathological, and space perception.

10. Josiah Royce, "A New Study of Psychology," *International Review of Ethics* 1, Jan. 1891, 143–69; précis from Skrupskelis, 5.

11. P. A. Schilp, *The Philosophy of John Dewey* (New York: Tudor, 1939), 23.

12. John Wild, *The Radical Empiricism of William James* (Garden City, N.Y.: Doubleday, 1969), vii; Alfred North Whitehead, *Modes of Thought* (New York: Free Press, 1938), 3.

13. George Santayana, *Atlantic Monthly* 67, Apr. 1891, 553; *WJ Rem,* 93.

14. Rebecca West, *Henry James* (New York: Holt, 1916), 11.

15. Quoted in Myers, 43.

16. Howells's review is in *Harper's Magazine,* no. 83, 1891, 314–16.

17. *PP,* 1180–81.

18. *"Will you or won't you have it so"* was the favorite James passage of a colleague of mine, Hope Weissman, who taught at Wesleyan in the 1990s and who had a wasting disease from which she knew she would die early. *PP,* 1182.

19. Student papers from WJ's Philosophy 2 class for 1890–91 are in the Harvard University Archives, call no. HUG 1466.406.

20. This not very heavily annotated copy (in the Houghton Library, call no. AC85.J2376.890p) is the basis for the new Harvard edition of 1981, incorporating WJ's later thoughts on the book. All earlier editions had been printed from the original plates, with only the most minor corrections that did not affect pagination.

21. *Corr.* 7:75, 100n.

22. Lewis has a good account of Alexander James (see 625); *Corr.* 2:162, 163.

23. Hutchins Hapgood, *A Victorian in the Modern World* (New York: Harcourt, Brace, 1939), 78.

24. *WB,* 141.

25. *WB,* 144.

26. Hapgood, *A Victorian in the Modern World,* 78.

27. *WB,* 148, 149, 153, 155.

28. *WB,* 161, 162.

48. Flooded by the Deep Life

1. *ECR,* 32.

2. *ECR,* 37, 40.

3. *ECR,* 417, 418.

4. *Corr.* 7:163, 177.

5. *Corr.* 7:177–78.

6. Alice's reply is in Ruth Bernard Yeazell, *The Death and Letters of Alice James* (Berkeley: University of California Press, 1981), 185–88.

7. *Corr.* 7:181.

8. *PBC,* 448n; Perry, vol. 2, 90.

9. Perry, vol. 2, 125. Gerald Myers recently chose this eminently readable volume over the longer *Principles of Psychology* for inclusion in the Library of America edition of the writings of WJ.

10. The anonymous story of James and the O. Henry student is in James's faculty file in the Harvard University Archives, call no. HUG 300 William James.

11. Quoted in Suzanne Smith, "Calkins, Mary Whiton," in *Women in World History,* vol. 3, ed. Anna Commire (Waterford, Conn.: Yorkin Publications, 1999), 305.

12. Marion Cannon Schlesinger, *Snatched from Oblivion* (Boston: Little, Brown, 1979), 45–46.

13. W.E.B. Du Bois, *Dusk of Dawn* (New York: Harcourt, Brace, 1940), 33, 38.

14. W.E.B. Du Bois, *The Autobiography of W.E.B. Du Bois* (New York: International Publishers, 1968), 133; Du Bois, *Dusk of Dawn,* 37.

15. *Corr.* 5:444.

16. Hutchins Hapgood, *A Victorian in the Modern World* (New York: Harcourt, Brace, 1939), 70.

17. Quoted in James R. Mellow, *Charmed Circle* (New York: Praeger, 1974), 49–50.

18. Hapgood, *A Victorian in the Modern World,* 69.

19. Esther Lanigan Stineman, *Mary Austin* (New Haven: Yale University Press, 1989), 60–61.

49. The Death of Alice James

1. *ECR,* 133; letter to Grace Ashburner, Aug. 25, 1891, Houghton b Ms Am 1092.9 (724).

2. *ECR,* 134.

3. *TT,* 132, 133, 134.

4. *Corr.* 7:198.

5. *Corr.* 7:203, 205.

6. Edel, vol. 3, 297.

7. *Corr.* 7:206.

8. Helen Keller, *Midstream: My Later Life* (Garden City, N.Y.: Doubleday, Duran, 1929), 316–18.

9. *ECR,* 136.

10. The two sources for this story are WJ's letter to AJ of Feb. 1885 (*Corr.* 6:2–3) and the account by Logan Pearsall Smith in his *Unforgotten Years* (Boston: Little, Brown, 1939), 116–20.

11. *Corr.* 7:232.

12. G. H. Palmer, "Münsterberg," in *The Development of Harvard University,* ed. S. E. Morison (Cambridge: Harvard University Press, 1930), 17.

13. *Corr.* 7:25, 286–87.

14. *Corr.* 7:243, 264.

15. The address given on Feb. 10, 1892, was edited for publication in *Forum* 13, 1892, 727–42, and is reprinted in *EPR.* Parts of it were combined with "The Hidden Self" and published in *WB* as "What Psychical Research Has Accomplished."

16. *EPR,* 91, 99.
17. *EPR,* 98.
18. *Corr.* 2:200, 203, 204n, 205.
19. Dante, *Paradiso,* trans. Allen Mandelbaum (Berkeley: University of California Press, 1982), 10:128.
20. *Corr.* 2:259.

50. European Sabbatical

1. AGJ to Eliza Gibbens, June 9, 1892, Houghton b Ms Am 1092.11.
2. AGJ to Eliza Gibbens, May 29, 1892.
3. *Corr.* 7:325; AGJ to Eliza Gibbens, Aug. 13, 1892.
4. *Corr.* 2:222, 250; *Corr.* 7:396, 399. The Tennyson passage is from "The Two Greetings," which is part one of *De Profundis.* HJ III, introduction to "Counsels of Courage."
5. *Corr.* 2:222, 236; *Corr.* 7:396; *Corr.* 2:254.
6. *Corr.* 7:418; *Corr.* 2:246; AGJ to Eliza Gibbens, June 8, 1892.
7. *Corr.* 7:441; letter of June 3, 1893; *Corr.* 7:421.
8. AGJ to Eliza Gibbens, June 27, 1892; *Corr.* 7:417–18.
9. *Corr.* 7:296, 355; *Corr.* 2:248.
10. *Corr.* 7:381; HJ III to Elizabeth Glendower Evans, May 25, 1931, ms. in Schlesinger Library, Cambridge.
11. *Corr.* 7:143; *Corr.* 2:202, 217, 232.
12. *Corr.* 2:244; *Corr.* 7:397.
13. *Corr.* 7:385.
14. *EPs,* 270, 272.
15. *EPs,* 273.
16. "A Plea for Psychology," in *EPs,* 270–77.

51. Abnormal Psych 1

1. Ahlstrom, 814. On the rise of modern fundamentalism, see George Marsden, *Fundamentalism and American Culture* (New York: Oxford University Press, 1980).
2. Richard Hughes Seager, ed., *The Dawn of Religious Pluralism: Voices from the World's Parliament of Religions* (La Salle, Ill.: Open Court, 1993), xiii.
3. WJ to HJ, Oct. 1, 1893; *Corr.* 2:292; *Corr.* 7:466, 469, 474. The word "melancholy" had for James the force that "depression" has for us. See his letter to his son in *Corr.* 12:487.
4. *Corr.* 7:468.
5. *Corr.* 7:454.
6. *Corr.* 7:472.
7. Ellenberger, v.
8. *Corr.* 2:299–300, 303–4. For the relationship between HJ and Constance Woolson, see Lyndall Gordon's excellent and suggestive book, *The Private Life of Henry James* (New York: Norton, 1998).
9. *Corr.* 7:486.
10. The visitor was Harry Kozol, quoted by Ellenberger in "Pierre Janet and His Ameri-

can Friends," in *Psychoanalysis, Psychotherapy, and the New England Medical Scene, 1894–1944*, ed. Geo E. Gifford Jr. (New York: Science History Press, 1978), 71.

11. *ECR*, 470, 471, 472; Ellenberger, 406.

12. See editor's introduction, by James Strachey, to Josef Breuer and Sigmund Freud, *Studies on Hysteria* (New York: Basic Books, 1957).

13. This article, "Über den Psychischen Mechanismus Hysterischer Phänomene," appeared in *Neurologisches Centralblatt*, Jan. 1 and 15, 1893, and was republished immediately in *Weiner Medizinische Blatter*, Jan. 19 and 26, 1893.

14. *ECR*, 515, 474, 474–75.

15. *Corr.* 7:609.

16. For the Brown-Sequard elixir, see S. W. Mitchell, *Fat and Blood: An Essay on the Treatment of Certain Forms of Neurasthenia and Hysteria*, 8th ed. (Philadelphia: Lippincott, 1905), 213–14.

17. Mitchell, *Fat and Blood*, 215.

18. See *Corr.* 7:474 and *Corr.* 9:270–71, where WJ says that Miss Clarke's treatments were "absolutely no use to me," and that he went "solely to pacify Alice."

19. *Corr.* 7:496; *ECR*, 145–50.

20. *Corr.* 2:302, 307, 311.

21. Alice's diary was not properly published until Leon Edel's edition in 1964. The best edition is that reissued by Northeastern University Press in 1999, with a fine introduction by Linda Simon. For an account of the long, slow process by which Alice's work became known, see Strouse, 319–26.

22. *Diary of AJ*, 59, 60, 66, 77, 55. Alice's comments on pain are quoted in French from a source I have not identified. My translation.

23. *ECR*, 507, 508, 513.

24. HJ III, *Charles W. Eliot*, vol. 2 (Boston: Houghton Mifflin, 1930), 98.

25. *Corr.* 7:503, 504, 524.

52. Talks to Teachers

1. *Corr.* 7:530; *EPs*, 315, 317, 321.

2. *Corr.* 7:539, 538; *EPh*, 87–89.

3. *Corr.* 7:541, 542, 544; *Corr.* 8:48; *Corr.* 2:403.

4. Stevenson wrote *The Wrecker* in collaboration with Lloyd Osbourne, the second son of his wife Fanny's first marriage.

5. *TT*, 14, 15, 19, 24, 26.

6. *TT*, 33, 30, 36, 47, 48.

7. *TT*, 55, 57, 62.

8. *TT*, 66, 68, 74.

9. *TT*, 87.

10. *TT*, 101, 102.

11. *TT*, 113.

53. Abnormal Psych 2

1. James Pope-Hennessy, *Robert Louis Stevenson* (London: Jonathan Cape, 1974), 96.

2. *Corr.* 2:337, 338.

3. *Corr.* 8:17.
4. *ML,* 50, 51.
5. George Santayana, *Persons and Places,* vol. 2, *The Middle Span* (New York: Scribner, 1944–1953), 166.
6. Herbert B. Adams, *The Study of American History in American Colleges and Universities* (Washington, D.C., 1887), quoted in Sheldon M. Stern, "William James and the New Psychology," in *Social Sciences at Harvard, 1860–1920,* ed. Paul Buck (Cambridge: Harvard University Press, 1965).
7. *ML,* 56, 63.
8. Taylor, 7.
9. *ML,* 71.
10. *ML,* 72.
11. Eugene Taylor has shown that WJ took this book out of the college library. See Taylor, 193–94.
12. Account given in the *Boston Herald,* Nov. 15, 1896, 9, quoted in Taylor, 149, 202n.
13. *ML,* 81.
14. *ML,* 82, 83.
15. *ML,* 76.

54. Sarah, Rosina, and Pauline

1. *Letters of Sarah Wyman Whitman* (Cambridge: Riverside Press, 1907), v, viii.
2. *Letters of Sarah Wyman Whitman,* 20–21.
3. *Corr.* 8:41; *Letters of Sarah Wyman Whitman,* 117.
4. *Corr.* 2:328.
5. *Corr.* 2:355, 356; letter of Aug. 11, 1897; *Corr.* 2:360.
6. *Corr.* 2:331, 364.
7. Letter of Apr. 18, 1899; letter to F.C.S. Schiller, May 19, 1899. Pauline was the daughter of a celebrated beauty, Regina Wehle Goldmark. See Josephine Goldmark, *Pilgrims of '48* (New Haven: Yale University Press, 1930).
8. Josephine Goldmark, "An Adirondack Friendship," *Atlantic Monthly* 154, Sept. 1934, 266.
9. Letter of Sept. 14, 1901. Pauline Goldmark had a long and productive career with the National Consumers League. She wrote a 184-page report, *Women and Children in the Canning Industry,* in 1908, a study called *Boyhood and Lawlessness* in 1914, and studies of longshoremen and public utilities and franchises. With Mary Hopkins she edited *The Gypsy Trail: An Anthology for Campers.*
10. Henry's living off Minnie Temple and Constance Woolson, emotionally speaking, is the subject of Lyndall Gordon's *Private Life of Henry James* (New York: Norton, 1998).
11. *Corr.* 8:79.

55. Is Life Worth Living?

1. *WB,* 35.
2. *WB,* 36, 37–38.
3. *WB,* 39.

4. *WB,* 40–41, 43.
5. *WB,* 48, 52, 53, 55.
6. *WB,* 55.

56. The Gospel of Relaxation

1. *Corr.* 8:60, 62, 65; *Corr.* 2:372, 374.
2. *Corr.* 8:85, 86, 87.
3. *ECR,* 151; *Corr.* 8:109, 111, 112.
4. *Corr.* 8:114; *Letters of Theodore Roosevelt,* vol. 1, ed. Elting E. Morison et al. (Cambridge: Harvard University Press, 1951–1954), 504–5.
5. *ECR,* 153.
6. *TT,* 123.
7. *TT,* 126, 127, 128, 131; *Corr.* 8:131.
8. *TT,* 118.
9. *TT,* 118, 129, 130, 131.

57. The Right to Believe

1. *Corr.* 8:146.
2. *WB,* 13, 14, 15.
3. *WB,* 16, 18. For an excellent discussion of James and Clifford, see David A. Hollinger, "James, Clifford, and the Scientific Conscience," in *The Cambridge Companion to William James,* ed. Ruth Anna Putnam (New York: Cambridge University Press, 1997), 69–83.
4. *WB,* 17, 24, 25.
5. *WB,* 25, 26, 27.
6. *WB,* 29.
7. *WB,* 29, 30.
8. *WB,* 31.
9. *Corr.* 8:162. *The Will to Believe* was also turned down by Houghton Mifflin.
10. *WB,* 3, 7.
11. *WB,* 5, 6.
12. *Corr.* 8:122.
13. *Corr.* 8:155.
14. *Corr.* 8:227–28.

58. High Tide

1. *Corr.* 2:353.
2. *Corr.* 2:403.
3. *Corr.* 8:171, 177.
4. *Corr.* 8:191.
5. *Corr.* 8:201, 205.
6. Edward Holton James, "Tangent," *Harvard Monthly* 21, Dec. 1895, 107–17; E. H.

James, "Cloistered," *Harvard Monthly* 21, Jan. 1896, 151–63; Rosina Hubley Emmet, "Alternating Currents," *Harper's Weekly* 40, Dec. 5, 1896, 1199–1200; HJ III, "Above the Trail," *Harvard Advocate* 62, Jan. 5, 1897.

7. Josiah Royce, *The World and the Individual* (New York: Macmillan, 1900), vii. Royce gave the Aberdeen Giffords in 1899 and 1900.

8. *Corr.* 3:8, 9.

9. *Corr.* 8:244, 246.

10. *Corr.* 8:253, 254.

11. *Corr.* 8:599.

12. *Corr.* 8:284, 288.

13. *ERM,* 79.

14. *Corr.* 8:322.

15. *Corr.* 8:339.

16. Charles Bakewell, "The Philosophy of George Herbert Palmer," in *George Herbert Palmer, 1842–1933: Memorial Addresses* (Cambridge: Harvard University Press, 1935), 3–43.

17. AGJ to HJ, quoted in *VRE*, 522.

59. Walpurgisnacht

1. *Corr.* 8:360.

2. *Corr.* 8:373.

3. *Corr.* 8:373.

4. *Corr.* 8:380, 383.

5. *The Journal of George Fox* (London: J. M. Dent, 1924), 6.

6. *Corr.* 3:64.

7. *Corr.* 8:390.

8. Corr. 8:390, 390–91.

9. *Corr.* 8:390, 391.

10. This comment by Henry James III was first noticed among the James papers at Harvard by Saul Rosenzweig and is printed in his *Historic Expedition to America (1909),* 2nd rev. ed. (St. Louis: Rana House, 1954), 186, and n. 6. *Corr.* 8:391.

60. California

1. *Corr.* 8:403, 405, 406; *Corr.* 3:36.

2. McDermott, 346.

3. *P,* 258, 259, 260.

4. *P,* 264.

5. *P,* 264–65.

6. *P,* 265, 266.

7. Edwin Starbuck, *The Psychology of Religion* (London: Walter Scott, 1899), 16.

8. *Corr.* 8:428.

9. *Corr.* 3:39, 40.

61. A Certain Blindness

1. *Corr.* 8:439.
2. There is some question as to when and where this lecture was first given. In a letter of Oct. 20, 1898, quoted in *TT*, 244, James writes of delivering the talk at the Episcopal Theological School in Cambridge, though the letter makes it sound like a repeat of a talk already given. The blindness theme is strongly present in WJ's "Human Immortality" and in "Philosophical Conceptions."
3. *ERM*, 99n.
4. *Corr.* 8:517, 522.
5. *TT*, 4.
6. The contract for *VRE* has not survived, but see *Corr.* 10:205 for a sense of the financial success of the book, and see *Corr.* 11:89 for James's comments on Longmans, Green's approach to consignment.
7. *Corr.* 8:460, 539; *Corr.* 3:59.
8. Albert J. Beveridge, campaign speech, Sept. 16, 1898, in *Modern Eloquence*, vol. 9, ed. Thomas B. Reed (Philadelphia: J. D. Morris, 1903), 224–43.
9. *ECR*, 154, 155.
10. *ECR*, 156, 157.
11. *Corr.* 8:523.
12. *Corr.* 8:546. For a shrewd analysis of James on bigness, see R. Posnock, "The Influence of William James on American Culture," in *The Cambridge Companion to William James*, ed. Ruth Anna Putnam (New York: Cambridge University Press, 1997), 326–27.

62. The Logic of the Absolute

1. James M. Baldwin, *Dictionary of Philosophy and Psychology*, new ed., vol. 1 (New York: Macmillan, 1918), 3.
2. Clendenning, 259; WJ to AGJ, Feb. 29, 1888; *Corr.* 7:83; Clendenning, 212.
3. Josiah Royce, *California: A Study of American Character* (Boston: Houghton Mifflin, 1886), 501.
4. "Words of Prof. Royce at the Walton Hotel in Philadelphia, Dec. 29, 1915," *Philosophical Review* 25, 1916, 510, 511.
5. Herbert Wallace Schneider, *A History of American Philosophy*, 2nd ed. (New York: Columbia University Press, 1963), 417.
6. Clendenning, 211, 212.
7. I owe this summary of Hegel on the Absolute to Jere Surber of the University of Denver.
8. Josiah Royce, *The Conception of God* (New York: Macmillan, 1897). Clendenning reports the student gossip.
9. Josiah Royce, *The World and the Individual* (New York: Macmillan, 1900), ix.
10. Perry, vol. 2, 728, 729.
11. *Corr.* 8:553, 555.
12. *Corr.* 9:34.
13. *Corr.* 9:4, 34.
14. Lithaemia: an excess of lithic or uric acid in the blood (*OED*).

63. Religion Is Real

1. *Corr.* 9:104–5, 111; Linda H. Davis, *Badge of Courage: The Life of Stephen Crane* (Boston: Houghton Mifflin, 1998), 316. WJ's account sounds firsthand, but I have found no proof that he was there.
2. The full title of the most recent English translation of Flournoy's extraordinary book is *From India to the Planet Mars: A Case of Multiple Personality with Imaginary Languages.* The 1994 Princeton University Press edition has particularly helpful commentary. *Corr.* 9:99.
3. *Corr.* 9:138–39.
4. *Corr.* 9:105. James considered a variety of titles for the first set of lectures, including "The Phenomena of Religious Experience," "A Discussion of Religious Experience," "The Demands of Religious Experience," and "Types of Religious Experience." He listed similar alternatives in his notes for the volume on religious philosophy.
5. *Corr.* 9:136, 166, 185–86.
6. *VRE*, 12, 14, 480. James is a proto-existentialist as well as a proto-phenomenologist. See John Wild, *The Radical Empiricism of William James.* For James and phenomenology, see Myers, 504; for James and existentialism, see Myers, 584.
7. *VRE*, 150. It is hard not to see an Emersonian strain here, a reflection of the opening of *Nature.*
8. *VRE*, 17.
9. *VRE*, 23.
10. *VRE*, 25, 26.
11. *VRE*, 30, 31.
12. *VRE*, 33, 32; see lecture four of Schleiermacher's *Talks on Religion to Its Cultured Despisers.* For a modern quarrel with James, see Stanley Hauerwas, *With the Grain of the Universe,* a brilliant and deeply informed account of James's failure to start from the given of the Christian Trinity. It is difficult to get away from James; even Hauerwas's title echoes a phrase of James's in "Concerning Fechner."
13. *VRE*, 34. James clearly seems to have understood that all the major American transcendentalists believed not in a transcendent deity but in an immanent one.
14. *VRE*, 46.

64. The Religion of Healthy-Mindedness

1. *Corr.* 9:149. Behind the domestic turmoil at Hyères was a tragic story. Fred Myers had once had an affair with his cousin Annie Marshall, who drowned herself in Ullswater in September 1875. During the last three years of his life (he died in 1901), Myers had some 150 sittings with Mrs. Thompson. "He was undoubtedly convinced that he had made contact with the spirit of Annie Marshall, and persisted in this conviction until the week of his death." See Alan Gauld, *The Founders of Psychical Research* (London: Routledge and Kegan Paul, 1968), 117–24, and James Webb's introduction to F.W.H. Myers, *The Subliminal Consciousness* (New York: Arno Press, 1967).
2. *VRE*, 67.
3. *VRE*, 61; this is James Russell Lowell speaking.
4. *VRE*, 67, 68.
5. *Corr.* 9:215, 216; *Corr.* 3:120.

6. *VRE,* 72, 73, 75, 115.

7. *VRE,* 78–79, 81, 83, 84, 92.

8. In the opening lecture of *On Heroes, Hero-Worship, and the Heroic in History* (University of Nebraska Press, 1966), 4, Carlyle remarks that all the "isms" "had a truth in them or men would not have taken them up."

9. *VRE,* 97, 99, 104. For a thoughtful treatment of WJ and religion in the context of mind cure, see Martin Marty, *Pilgrims in Their Own Land: 500 Years of American Religion* (Boston: Little, Brown, 1984), 331–35.

65. The Sick Soul: Slouching Toward Edinburgh

1. *VRE,* 112, 115, 116, 117, 119, 120. The "old poet" is Lucretius.

2. *VRE,* 122, 134. In a letter of June 1, 1904, to Frank Abauzit, the French translator of the *Varieties,* James wrote, referring to the book's original edition, "The document on page 160 is my own case — acute neurasthenic attack with phobia. I naturally disguised the provenance!" *VRE,* 508.

3. *VRE,* 135–36.

4. *VRE,* 136–37.

5. *Corr.* 9:274, 275, 276.

6. *Corr.* 9:382; *Corr.* 3:134; *Corr.* 9:366.

7. *Corr.* 9:365; *Corr.* 3:153.

8. *Corr.* 9:412; see also WJ's letter to Flournoy, Jan. 18, 1901, Houghton b Ms Am 1505 (27); Munthe's description of Myers's death is in *The Story of San Michele,* illus. ed. (New York: Dutton, 1936, orig. 1929), 280–82.

9. *Corr.* 9:626 and Houghton b Ms Am 1092.1 (letter from WJ to Eveleen Myers, Apr. 9, 1901); for the neuralgia, see letter to Giulio Cesare Ferrari, Apr. 1, 1901; for his equilibrium, see *Corr.* 3:167.

66. The Twice-Born

1. *Corr.* 9:485.

2. *Corr.* 9:484.

3. *VRE,* 146, 155, 157.

4. *VRE,* 153, 154, 156.

5. *VRE,* 161, 162.

6. *VRE,* 163, 165, 166–68. The letter by William G. Wilson to Carl Jung, Jan. 23, 1961, is reproduced at http://silkworth.net/aahistory/billw_carljung 012361. Jung's fascinating reply is also reproduced in facsimile. See note 16 in the Prologue for a fuller account of this point.

7. *VRE,* 139, 173.

8. *VRE,* 189, 193, 200, 202, 208.

9. *Corr.* 9:501.

10. *Corr.* 9:503, 504, 505, 632.

67. Voluntary Poverty

1. *Corr.* 9:507.

2. *Corr.* 9:539.

3. *Corr.* 9:508, 540, 560.

4. *Corr.* 9:464, 515, 558.

5. *Corr.* 9:339, 494, 566. The story of WJ watching baseball is from a clipping of an article by Sidney Lovett in James's faculty folder in the Harvard Archives, Pusey Library, call no. HUG 300 William James. *Corr.* 3:180, 184.

6. *VRE,* 213n; *Corr.* 9:550.

7. *VRE,* 210, 219, 220.

8. H. D. Thoreau, *Walden* (Boston: Houghton Mifflin, 1893), 206, abridged by WJ and quoted in *VRE,* 222.

9. *VRE,* 253, 256, 254, 259–60.

10. *VRE,* 292.

11. *VRE,* 293, 294.

68. The Mystical Center

1. *VRE,* 301, 302, 303.

2. *VRE,* 303, 304, 307, 308, 310n, 330, 332, 333. In an e-mail to the author, Professor Wendy Doniger provided the key to James's use of this Sanskrit phrase to refer to things that were, for him, almost beyond words, such as his love for Minnie Temple.

3. *VRE,* 336, 338.

4. *VRE,* 353, 354, 359.

5. *Corr.* 10:33; *VRE,* 376, 377.

6. The letter to Billy was dated Apr. 9, 1902. The phrase about "absolute addition" occurs in lecture two, *VRE,* 46, and is used here only as a summary of what the last chapter says in detail.

7. *VRE,* 400, 408, 414.

69. William James at Sixty

1. The description of the older WJ is from observations by Winifred Smith Rieber, who painted a group portrait of the Harvard philosophy department. See Myers, 41. Santayana's description is in *WJ Rem,* 92–93.

2. *Corr.* 8:31; WJ to Frank Thilly, an American philosopher; Robert C. Le Clair, ed., *The Letters of William James and Théodore Flournoy* (Madison: University of Wisconsin Press, 1966), 129. James here was, as he noted to Flournoy, borrowing a line from Whistler. When an admirer had said there were only two painters, Whistler and Velázquez, Whistler said, "Why drag in Velázquez?"

3. HJ III, Ms Life of AGJ, 40–41.

4. Though any of these drugs could be harmful if taken too freely, all were standard treatments, and James was, of course, a physician. Chloral hydrate is still used as a soporific, and Veronal, or diethylbarbituric acid, was a common sedative in James's time. It tended to lose its effect if taken over a prolonged period.

5. *Corr.* 11:228, 35; see, on this subject, Frederick J. Ruf, *The Creation of Chaos* (Albany: State University of New York Press, 1991).

6. Clendenning, 296.

7. *Corr.* 10:11.

8. *Corr.* 10:129.

9. The journalist was Marion Hamilton Carter. Mach's response is in Perry, vol. 2, 341.

10. See Jaime Nubiola and Izaskun Martínez, "The Reception of William James in Spain and Unamuno's Reading of the *Varieties*," *Streams of William James* 5, no. 2, summer 2003, 7–9.

11. *Corr.* 10:110.

12. See Hendrika Vande Kemp, "The Gifford Lectures on Natural Theology," *Streams of William James* 4, no. 3, fall 1902, and S. L. Jaki, *Lord Gifford and His Lectures* (Macon, Ga.: Mercer University Press, 1986).

13. Today, that $10,000 would be worth around $200,000. See letter of Jan. 26, 1903, to Bill, for details. James's 1902 diary has a cryptic entry on July 14 headed, "Longmans account for *VRE*"; it reads, "2876. 8622 dollars." This works out pretty closely if the first number is copies, the second dollars.

14. *Corr.* 9:186.

15. Ahlstrom, 745.

16. Ahlstrom, 747–48.

17. It is interesting that the year of publication of *VRE* was also the year of the founding of the American Bible League, an event that led to the publication of *The Fundamentals* as pamphlets in 1910, the beginning of modern fundamentalism. See *The Fundamentals*, ed. R. A. Torrey and A. C. Dixon (Grand Rapids, Mich.: Baker House, 1917). The dates of this movement are not agreed upon. Clark Blaise, in *Time Lord* (New York: Pantheon, 2000), gives 1902 as the date when the first of the essays later known as *The Fundamentals* was published. In an e-mail, Blaise further noted that the first publication was in St. Catherine, Ontario.

18. *ML*, 88–90, 92, 97.

19. *ML*, 93, 94.

20. *Corr.* 10:105.

70. Bergson

1. *Corr.* 10:139, 153.

2. *Corr.* 10:112, 160.

3. *ML*, 267, 268, 272, 273.

4. See James Mark Baldwin, *Dictionary of Philosophy and Psychology*, 5th ed., vol. 2 (New York: Macmillan, 1920), 256.

5. *Corr.* 10:118. Psychasthenia is defined in George M. Gould, *Pocket Medical Dictionary* (1907), as "mental fatigue," an example as much as a definition of the subject.

6. *Corr.* 3:220.

7. *Corr.* 10:151.

8. For the whole sorry episode, see *TT*, 256–66.

9. *Corr.* 10:167.

10. See, for example, André Robinet, *Bergson et les Métamorphoses de la Durée* (Paris: P. Seghers, 1965), facing p. 65.

11. Henri Bergson, *Introduction to Metaphysics*, 2nd ed., trans. T. E. Hulme (New York: Bobbs Merrill, 1955), 54.

12. Henri Bergson to WJ, May 9, 1908, translated and printed in Perry, vol. 2, 622–24.

13. Irwin Edman, foreword to Henri Bergson, *Creative Evolution* (New York: Random House, 1944), xiii–xiv.

14. Robinet, *Bergson et les Métamorphoses de la Durée*, 9.
15. *MEN*, 216.
16. Bergson, *Introduction to Metaphysics*, 51, 53.
17. *Einfühlung* was coined in 1903 by Theodor Lipps, who thought that the perception of another person's emotional expression or gesture automatically activates the same emotion in the perceiver. WJ mentions Lipps as among "the more exciting to my imagination" of the people who were going to attend the International Congress of Arts and Sciences in St. Louis in 1904. See *Corr.* 10:356. The word "empathy" shortly thereafter appeared in English. Though the term is fairly new, the idea strongly resembles John Keats's notion of negative capability and Henry Thoreau's remark that "the highest we can attain to is not knowledge but sympathy with intelligence."
18. Bergson, *Introduction to Metaphysics*, 53.

71. The Ph.D. Octopus and Dewey's New School

1. *Corr.* 10:205; *Corr.* 3:228.
2. *Corr.* 3:225; *Corr.* 10:183, 185.
3. *Corr.* 10:182, 191.
4. "The Ph.D. Octopus," in *ECR*, 68, 69, 71, 73, 72. The incident with which James began his attack involved Alfred Hodder, a Harvard Ph.D., and his troubles at Bryn Mawr. James's account claims that Bryn Mawr refused to appoint Hodder, who was to teach English, until he had finished his Ph.D. in philosophy. A letter from President Thomas of Bryn Mawr to James, Apr. 4, 1903, disputes James's account of the facts. See *ECR*, 568. James's hostility to what he saw as the increasingly mandarin atmosphere in American colleges is a little ironic in that he had recently been chairman of a Harvard committee on academic robes. The committee report recommended such a complicated and subtly graded variety of insignia, such fastidious attention to sumptuary detail, that it was quietly ignored by the university.
5. Perry, vol. 2, 607–8.
6. *Corr.* 10:213.
7. *Corr.* 10:210, 215; *EPh*, 102.
8. *ECR*, 103, 104. The sentence beginning "Thought must reconfigure" is my paraphrase of James's account; see *EPh*, 104.
9. *EPh*, 104–5.
10. *Corr.* 10:324, 325.

72. Emerson

1. *Corr.* 10:240, 243.
2. *Corr.* 3:229. Alice was much attracted to Emerson's writings. One of her early gifts to William was a copy of Emerson's *Lectures and Biographical Sketches*. There is a small puzzle about the copy of this book Alice gave William. The front flyleaf says, "William James from his wife / Quincy Street Cambridge June 1879" in William's handwriting, but the volume is the 1884 Riverside Press edition, vol. 10 of *The Complete Works of Ralph Waldo Emerson*. Perhaps it was a replacement for a lost copy.
3. *Corr.* 10:252.

4. Ralph Waldo Emerson, *Essays: First Series* (Boston: Fields Osgood, 1869), 61. James's copy is in the Houghton Library, call no. AC 85.52376.Zz2869e.
5. Emerson, *Essays: First Series*, 40, 129.
6. Ralph Waldo Emerson, *Natural History of Intellect*, 38.
7. *ERM*, 109, 112, 115. Lawrence Buell, in his bicentennial *Emerson* (Cambridge: Harvard University Press, 2003), strikes the same note of individualism as the lasting heart of Emerson.
8. *Corr.* 3:234.

73. The True Harvard

1. Sharon Cameron's *Writing Nature: Henry Thoreau's "Journal"* (New York: Oxford University Press, 1985) makes this point persuasively.
2. Flower and Murphey, vol. 2, 774.
3. Logan Pearsall Smith, *Unforgotten Years* (Boston: Little, Brown, 1939), 103; Morison 1, 420, 422; *Corr.* 3:207.
4. "The True Harvard," in *ECR*, 74, 75–76, 77.

74. A Life of Interruptions

1. William James Jr., "Sport or Business?" *Harvard Graduates' Magazine* 12, Dec. 1903, 225–29.
2. *Corr.* 2:149; *Corr.* 10:289.
3. Lewis has a fine account of Peggy, which I have drawn on.
4. *Corr.* 10:270, 278, 279; *Corr.* 3:255.
5. *Corr.* 10:95.
6. *Corr.* 10:234; review of *Human Personality and Its Survival of Bodily Death*, in *EPR*, 203.
7. *ECR*, 170–76, for WJ's original piece, and *ECR*, 686–87, for a supplemental comment. Quotations are *ECR*, 170, 171, 172. For statistics on lynching, probably understated, see the NAACP pamphlet *30 Years of Lynching in the United States, 1889–1918* (1919).
8. *ECR*, 81, 83, 85.
9. *Corr.* 10:292; *MEN*, xix. James is quoting from *Moby Dick*.
10. *ML*, 304.

75. The Many and the One

1. *Corr.* 10:365.
2. *Corr.* 10:415.
3. Back in 1866, when Henry James was twenty-three, William Dean Howells observed him one day eating nothing "except a biscuit he crumbled in his pocket and fed himself after the prescription of a famous doctor then prevalent among people of indigestion." Quoted in Susan Goodman and Carl Dawson, *William Dean Howells: A Writer's Life* (Berkeley: University of California Press, 2005), 114.
4. *MEN*, 3, 4.
5. *Corr.* 10:295.

6. *MEN*, 5, 12, 11.
7. *MEN*, 4, 5, 6, 9.

76. The Modern Moment: Radical Empiricism

1. The best short treatment by far of the centrality of radical empiricism in James's thought is the introduction to McDermott. The Chicago edition of 1977 is especially valuable, including, as it does, the best bibliography of WJ's writings.
2. *ERM*, 117.
3. *ERM*, 118.
4. *Corr.* 10:416, 422, 424, 480.
5. *Corr.* 10:434.
6. "Letters of John Ruskin," *Atlantic Monthly* 94, July 1904, 12.
7. Bertrand Russell, *Philosophy* (New York: Norton, 1927), 210; *ERE*, 3, 4.
8. Russell, *Philosophy*, 210; *ERE*, 4, 19.
9. *ERE*, 22.
10. *ERE*, 29.
11. *ERE*, 34, 39.
12. *ERE*, 42.
13. *Corr.* 11:226; see WJ's letter to Howison of July 24, 1898. Speaking of the lecture he is going to give, he writes, "I wanted to make something entirely popular, and as it were emotional, for technicality seems to me to spell 'failure' in philosophy."
14. Bertrand Russell, *A History of Western Philosophy* (New York: Simon and Schuster, 1945), 812.
15. Alfred North Whitehead, *Science and the Modern World* (New York: Free Press, 1967), 143 (orig. Lowell Lectures, 1925).
16. "Selving" is McDermott's word. Compare the process here described by James with Marcel Mauss, "A Category of the Human Mind: The Notion of Person, the Notion of 'Self,'" in *Sociology and Psychology*, trans. Ben Brewster (London: Routledge and Kegan Paul, 1999), 59–94.
17. *ML*, 326.

77. Schiller versus Bradley versus James

1. HJ, *The American Scene* (New York: Horizon Press, 1967), 2; *Corr.* 10:475.
2. *Corr.* 10:443, 445, 476.
3. *Mind! A Unique Review of Ancient and Modern Philosophy*, ed. A. Troglodyte [F.C.S. Schiller] (London, 1901).
4. *Mind* 9 (new series), 1900, 458; letter to S. Ilsley, Sept. 23, 1897.
5. F.C.S. Schiller, *Humanism: Philosophical Essays* (London: Macmillan, 1903), xvi.
6. *Corr.* 10:392, 393, 430, 431.
7. *Corr.* 10:336, 446, 447, 455, 501, 533.
8. Sprigge says James and Bradley never met (xiii), but an entry in James's pocket diary for 1908 says he called on Bradley on May 9, 1908, while he, James, was giving his pluralistic-universe lectures and three days before receiving an honorary doctor-

ate from Oxford. "Very courteous," says James's note. "Showed me Merton College and Library."

9. F. H. Bradley, *Essays in Truth and Reality* (Oxford: Clarendon Press, 1968, orig. 1914), 469, quoted in Sprigge, 572. Eliot wrote at Merton College under the direction of a Bradley disciple, Harold Joachim. Peter Ackroyd says Eliot did not meet Bradley. Lyndall Gordon notes that "Bradley himself was almost inaccessible." See Gordon's *Eliot's Early Years* (Oxford: Oxford University Press, 1977), chap. 4.

10. Sprigge, 573, 575–76, 583.

11. WJ to F. H. Bradley, Jan. 3, 1898; Bradley to WJ, Feb. 24, 1898; *Corr.* 8:347; *Corr.* 10:431, 433, 434.

78. Royce: Pragmatic Stirrings

1. *Corr.* 10:527, 530, 547.

2. For WJ's use of the Dyaks' heads in his course, see *ML*, 332, 333, 341. The full description is from "A World of Pure Experience," in *ERE*, 24.

3. Josiah Royce, *The Philosophy of Loyalty* (New York: Macmillan, 1908), 344–45, quoted in Ralph Barton Perry, *In the Spirit of William James* (New Haven: Yale University Press, 1938), 34.

4. To help in charting the evolution of WJ's radical empiricism in detail, the following list of his nine articles on the subject includes both the first publication as an article and the name of the book in which it eventually came to reside. (1) "Humanism and Truth" was published in *Mind* in Oct. 1904 and later in *MT*. (2) "Does Consciousness Exist?" was first published in Sept. 1904 and in book form in *ERE*. (3) "A World of Pure Experience" was first published in Sept. 1904 and later in *ERE*. (4) "The Pragmatic Method" appeared in Dec. 1904 and was later incorporated into *P.* (5) "The Experience of Activity" came out first in Dec. 1904 and later appeared in both *ERE* and *PU*. (6) "The Thing and Its Relations" appeared in Nov. 1904 and in book form in both *ERE* and *PU*. (7) "How Two Minds Can Know the Same Thing" was written by Feb. 1905, published in March of that year, and eventually reprinted in *ERE*. (8) "Thomas Davidson: A Knight Errant of the Intellectual Life" appeared in Jan. 1905 and was collected in *Memories and Studies*. (9) "The Place of Affectional Facts" was finished and sent off in Feb. 1905, published in May of that year, and collected in *ERE*.

5. *Corr.* 10:554, 563.

6. John Ruskin, *Praeterita*, vol. 35 of *The Works of John Ruskin*, ed. E. T. Cook and A. Wedderburn (London: George Allen, 1908), 562.

7. The text of the last Wellesley lecture is in *P*, 283–85.

79. William and Henry

1. WJ Diary 4, Apr. 1905.

2. *Corr.* 10:574, 575.

3. *Corr.* 11:1, 2.

4. *Corr.* 11:8, 33; George Santayana, *The Life of Reason* (New York: Scribner, 1905), 13, 29; *Corr.* 11:28, 34.

5. French uses the feminine noun *conscience* for both "conscience" and "consciousness."

6. "The Notion of Consciousness" ("La Notion de Conscience"), trans. Salvatore Saladino, in *ERE*, 261, 271.

7. WJ Diary 4, May 28?, 1905; *Corr.* 11:21, 24, 42.

8. This was the same Bruce Porter who later married Peggy James.

9. *Corr.* 11:62, 63.

10. Henry James was listed in *Who's Who* at least as early as 1899, whereas William appears from 1904 on.

11. *Corr.* 3:304.

12. *Corr.* 11:77.

13. See *Corr.* 3:300 for a letter to HJ in which William talks about being done with lecturing in Philosophy 1a "for good."

14. *Corr.* 11:111.

15. WJ Diary 4, 1905.

16. *Corr.* 3:301.

17. *Corr.* 3:305.

18. *Corr.* 3:305–6.

19. "The Miller-Bode Objections" are in *MEN*, 65–129.

20. The way James posed the question raised by Bode and Miller comes at the start of the first notebook: "In my psychology I contended that each field of consciousness is entitatively a unit. But in my doctrine that the same 'pen' may be known by two knowers I seem to imply that an identical part can help to *constitute* two fields . . . The fields are not then entitative units. They are decomposable into 'parts' one of which at least is common to both, and my whole tirade against 'composition' in the psychology is belied by my own subsequent doctrine! How can I rescue the situation? Which doctrine must I stand by?" *MEN*, 65f.

21. *MEN*, 75n, 129.

22. *Corr.* 11:133.

80. California Dreaming

1. *Corr.* 11:135, 141, 143.

2. *Corr.* 11:147, 148, 239.

3. WJ Diary 5, 1906.

4. "Reason and Faith," in *ERM*, 125.

5. "Reason and Faith," 128.

6. "A Suggestion Concerning Mysticism," in *EPh*, 161.

7. Boris Sidis's letter to WJ of Oct. 9, 1905, in *Corr.* 11:101, mentions both Freud's *Psychopathology of Everyday Life* and *The Interpretation of Dreams*.

8. *EPh*, 161; McDermott's hint for getting at William James is to *pay attention to the italics*.

9. *EPh*, 161–62, 163.

10. Erikson made James a major figure in his book *Identity, Youth, and Crisis,* and while one hesitates to quarrel with the conclusions of such a splendid writer, it must be noted that he got a few basic details wrong in his account of this part of James's life. Erikson was under the impression that the dream occurred a few months before

James's death, when in fact it was four years before. Erikson himself might have been willing to reconsider his view in light of the biographical record. Nevertheless, his treatment of James as a primary example of the processes of identity formation is, in most respects, a brilliant and helpful analysis.

11. Henry A. Murray, "Morton Prince: Sketch of His Life and Work," *Journal of Abnormal Psychology* 52, 1956, 292.
12. The fullest account of James's understanding of Prince's work is S. Rosenzweig, "Sally Beauchamp's Career: A Psychoarchaeological Key to Morton Prince's Classic Case of Multiple Personality," *Genetic, Social, and General Psychology Monographs* 113, no. 1, Feb. 1987, 5–60.
13. Murray, "Morton Prince," 292.
14. Morton Prince, *The Dissociation of a Personality* (New York: Longmans, 1906), 523. The book was copyrighted in 1905 and James had a copy before he went to California.
15. Prince, *The Dissociation of a Personality*, 3. For Miss Beauchamp's different personalities and their different dreams, see chap. 20.
16. Perry, vol. 2, 699–701.
17. *EPh*, 163n.
18. Leo Stein, "William James," *American Scholar,* Apr. 17, 1948, 165, repr. from *American Mercury* 9, Sept. 1926, 68–70.

81. Earthquake

1. *ERM*, 251–52.
2. *Corr.* 11:192.
3. *Corr.* 11:187.
4. *Corr.* 11:200, 586.
5. See the description of Shaler in W. David and R. A. Daly, "Geology and Geography," in Morison 2, 310–21.
6. *HJ Letters*, vol. 4, 396–97.
7. *Corr.* 3:310.
8. James R. Mellow, *Charmed Circle: Gertrude Stein and Company* (Boston: Houghton Mifflin, 1974), 132.
9. *Corr.* 3:311.
10. Corr. 3:312.
11. Joseph Conrad, *A Personal Record* (New York: Doubleday, 1924), 92.

82. A General Theory of Human Action

1. *Corr.* 11:203, 204, 208.
2. *EPR*, 323, 336, 337.
3. Giovanni Papini, *The Failure* (*Un Uomo Finito*), trans. Virginia Pope (New York: Greenwood, 1972, orig. 1924), 204. The full sweep of Papini's vision is evident in his "Dall'Uomo a Dio," published in the periodical *Leonardo*, Feb. 1906, 6–15, and read by James around this time.
4. Papini, *The Failure*, 204.
5. *EPh*, 145, 146.

6. *EPh*, 146, 224n (for James's comparison of Papini to Nietzsche), 147, 148.
7. Clifford W. Beers, *A Mind That Found Itself*, 5th ed. (New York: Longmans, Green, 1921), 242.
8. *Corr.* 11:247, 252.
9. *Corr.* 11:253.
10. The bound volume of offprints James deposited in the philosophy department library in Emerson Hall may have been intended for the use of his students. The volume is now in the Robbins Library in Emerson Hall, cat. no. AJ465.54.11B. See *ERE*, 200–202.
11. *Corr.* 11:267. In a separate incident that year, James again felt impelled to apologize for his countrymen. He wrote the Russian writer Maxim Gorky to apologize for the way Gorky and his female traveling companion were ostracized in New York when it became known that the woman was not his wife. The letter was hearty and friendly, but it did no good. "James is a wonderful old man," the disgruntled Russian wrote, "but he is also an American. Oh, to hell with them." *Corr.* 11:271.
12. *Corr.* 11:257; *Corr.* 3:323. Linda Simon gives a full account of the Hodder affair in *Genuine Reality*, 345–46. Brenda Wineapple has a fine portrait of Hodder in her *Sister Brother* (New York: Putnam, 1996).
13. *Corr.* 11:271. The backup person James had in mind was Apthorpe Fuller.

83. Pragmatism

1. *Corr.* 3:258, 330.
2. *P*, 11, 12, 13, 15. The chapter on WJ in Carl Jung's *Psychological Types* is concerned with the distinction between the tough- and the tender-minded.
3. *P*, 22–23; *Corr.* 3:328; *P*, 25.
4. *P*, 29, 30.
5. *P*, 31, 37, 42, 44, 122. The last two clauses of the final sentence show the ever-present shadow of radical empiricism in the later James.
6. See Philip P. Wiener, *Evolution and the Founders of Pragmatism* (Cambridge: Harvard University Press, 1949). Charles Peirce proposes, in "Design and Chance," a lecture he gave at Johns Hopkins in January 1884, that chance may be an antientropic force. He specifically cites the "dissipation of energy" and the "death of the universe," then says, "But although no force can counteract this tendency, chance may and will have the opposite influence. Force is in the long run dissipative; chance is in the long run concentrative." In *The Essential Peirce*, vol. 1, ed. Nathan Houser and Christian Kloesel (Bloomington: Indiana University Press, 1992).
7. John Dewey, *Characters and Events*, vol. 1, ed. Joseph Ratner (New York: Holt, 1929), 109; letter to A. Johns, Aug. 26, 1907; *Corr.* 11:59; letter to Schiller, Oct. 26, 1904; Walt Whitman, "A Backward Glance," in *Prose Works 1892*, vol. 2, ed. F. Stovall (New York: NYU Press, 1964), 731; *Corr.* 7:375.
8. *Corr.* 11:299.
9. *P*, 97, 99–100, 104.
10. *P*, 138, 141, 142.
11. *VRE*, 526; *P*, 142.
12. *Corr.* 11:276; *P*, 143–44.

84. The Energies of Men

1. "The Energies of Men," in *ERM*, 199n, 130.
2. *ERM*, 130. Insofar as James's pragmatism sounds like functionalism, it owes more to Dewey than to Durkheim, whose great work on religion, *Les Formes Élémentaires de la Vie Religieuse*, appeared in 1915, five years after the death of WJ. Psychology did not become a separate department at Harvard until 1934.
3. *ERM*, 131.
4. *ERM*, 132, 134.
5. *ERM*, 136, 139.
6. *ERM*, 141, 143, 145.

85. The Harvard Elective System Applied to the Universe

1. *ML*, 426, 427, 428.
2. H. V. Kaltenborn, "William James at Harvard," *Harvard Illustrated Magazine* 8, no. 5, Feb. 1907, 1–2.
3. *Corr.* 11:315; *Corr.* 3:333.
4. WJ Diary 6, Feb. 15, 1907; *Corr.* 11:322. The text in *Corr.* reads "radial artery not badly stressed"; the diary entry, in James's handwriting, reads "sclerosed," not "stressed."
5. Jane Addams, *Newer Ideals of Peace* (New York: Macmillan, 1907), 24, mentions James's ideas about war.
6. WJ's Diary 6 lists "Copeland, Tchaikowsky [not the composer], Alladin, Hurlbut, Bloomfield, Garland and other Russian revolutionists." Feb. 24, 1907.
7. *Corr.* 3:333.
8. *Corr.* 3:333.
9. *P*, 6.
10. *Corr.* 11:379, 389, 613, 614 (paraphrase), 397, 392–94, 423–28, 614, 604. G. W. Pierson, *Yale College* (New Haven: Yale University Press, 1952), 11. McDermott says Lovejoy, "The Thirteen Pragmatisms," is the best contemporary critique of *Pragmatism*.
11. *Mind* 9, no. 36, Oct. 1900, 436; Charles Peirce to WJ, Dec. 6, 1904.
12. *Corr.* 3:344; *Corr.* 11:410, 419.
13. George Santayana, "The Genteel Tradition in American Philosophy," in *Winds of Doctrine* (New York: Scribner, 1926).
14. WJ Diary 6, June 27, 1907.
15. *Corr.* 11:436.
16. *Corr.* 3:337–38, 339.
17. *Corr.* 11:358–59.
18. *Corr.* 3:341, 346.
19. HJ, *The American Scene* (New York: Horizon Press, 1967), 17, 77.
20. *Corr.* 3:347.

86. The True Race of Prophets

1. Josiah Royce, *The Philosophy of Loyalty* (New York: Macmillan, 1908), 357.
2. Manchester, now Harris Manchester College, was founded in 1786, moved to Ox-

ford in 1889, and became part of Oxford University in 1996. The college, on its Web site, suggests that it is still uneasy about having invited William James, noting that it is especially strong in the idealist tradition and putting ironic quotation marks around James's "great success."

3. *PU*, 214.

4. *PU*, 214–15. Edward Caird's Gifford Lectures of 1890–91 and 1891–92 were published as *The Evolution of Religion* (Glasgow: James Maclehose and Sons, 1893). John Caird's Giffords, several years later, appeared as *The Fundamental Ideas of Christianity* (Glasgow: James Maclehose and Sons, 1899). WJ to Henri Bergson, May 8, 1908.

5. *Corr.* 12:2; *Corr.* 3:360. Trional was the trade name of a synthetic narcotic, another drug in the long list of James's remedies for sleeplessness.

6. *PU*, 19, 49, 50, 68.

7. *PU*, 68, 70.

8. See Helmut Adler, "Gustav Theodor Fechner: A German Gelehrter," in *Portraits of Pioneers of Psychology*, vol. 3, ed. G. A. Kimble et al. (Washington, D.C.: American Psychological Association, 1991), 8.

9. "Fechner," *Deutsche Biographische Enzyklopädie* (Munich: K. G. Saur, 1996).

10. *PU*, 69; Adler, "Gustav Theodor Fechner," 5; *PU*, 69.

11. "Introduction to Fechner," in *ERM*, 119.

12. *PU*, 70, 71.

13. *PU*, 76–77.

14. "The eye of the world" passage would seem to come directly from two lines in Shelley's "Hymn of Apollo," written in 1820 and published in 1824. "I am the eye with which the Universe / Beholds itself and knows itself divine."

87. A Pluralistic Universe

1. *PU*, 113, 115, 117, 118, 220, 121.

2. *PU*, 130, 134.

3. *PU*, 135.

4. *PU*, 137, 138.

5. *PU*, 138.

6. *PU*, 138, 139, 140.

7. *Corr.* 12:18–19, 45.

8. H. G. Wells, *Experiment in Autobiography* (New York: Macmillan, 1934), 453–54; *Corr.* 12:58–59. Chesterton's remark is quoted by Robert Patten in his introduction to Charles Dickens, *The Posthumous Papers of the Pickwick Club* (New York: Penguin, 1986), 19.

88. Psychical Researches Redux

1. *Corr.* 12:106.

2. *Corr.* 3:367; *Corr.* 12:110.

3. WJ's son Henry would write a two-volume *Life of C. W. Eliot*, which would win a Pulitzer Prize.

4. See HJ's letter to J. B. Pinker, Oct. 23, 1908, in *HJ Letters*, vol. 4, 497–98.

5. *Corr.* 3:386–87.

6. See the lively description of a Paladino sitting in the *New York Times,* Apr. 19, 1908.
7. Perry, vol. 2, 171.
8. *Corr.* 12:140–41.
9. *Corr.* 3:376; *EPR,* 371, 374.
10. *EPR,* 251; *Corr.* 12:127; *EPR,* 252.

89. The Meaning of Truth

1. *Corr.* 3:378–79.
2. William showed Henry's telegram to Fletcher, who, horrified, asked William not to make it public. See *Corr.* 3:383.
3. *Corr.* 12:18.
4. Ralph Barton Perry first noticed the close similarity. See Perry, vol. 2, 445. There are also close connections between the book and the syllabus for the fall 1906 course at Harvard and for other courses James gave. See *SPP,* 202.
5. *SPP,* 10. See the first sentence of chap. 15 of Gibbon, *Decline and Fall of the Roman Empire.*
6. *SPP,* 21, 33.
7. WJ Diary for Jan. 1909 shows him promising three hundred dollars a year for two years to a Morton Rosse.
8. *Corr.* 12:171, 260.
9. *Corr.* 12:261.
10. Moses Hadas, *Ancilla to Classical Reading* (New York: Columbia University Press, 1954), 309.
11. *Corr.* 3:393.

90. Ever Not Quite

1. *Corr.* 12:318, 319. The famous and devastating Dutch elm disease did not arrive in North America until the early 1930s.
2. Quoted in Allen, 466.
3. *Corr.* 12:331.
4. In the interview, by Adelbert Albrecht in the *Boston Evening Transcript,* Sept. 11, 1909, part 3, 3, Freud specifically attacked hypnotherapy and the Emmanuel movement, a precursor of modern clinical-pastoral counseling. The leaders of this Boston movement were Dr. Richard C. Cabot and the Reverend Elwood Worcester. The practitioners provided religious and psychological treatment for functional nervous disorders; treatment was sometimes done in groups. It was endorsed at the start by James's friend James J. Putnam, and James himself read and admired Worcester's book *The Living Word,* which was an explicitly and profoundly Fechnerian work. James's "Energies of Men" was published as pamphlet 3 by the Boston Emmanuel Church in 1908. *Corr.* 12:334.
5. Deirdre Bair, *Jung: A Biography* (Boston: Little, Brown, 2003), 167–68.
6. Bair says, "After his second conversation with James, Jung came to the realization — startling and troubling in equal parts — that Freud 'due to the narrowness of his intellectual horizon let himself be overwhelmed by the object.'" *Jung,* 167. The last part of the sentence quotes Jung.

7. Sigmund Freud, *An Autobiographical Study,* quoted in Allen, 467.

8. John Dewey, *Human Nature and Conduct* (New York: H. Holt, 1930), 112.

9. *EPh,* 157, 159. The correspondent was Marion Hamilton, who was very interested in psychic research. See *Corr.* 12:451.

10. Edel, vol. 5, 440.

11. *Corr.* 3:413–14.

12. *EPh,* 173.

13. *EPh,* 189.

14. Plato, *Theaetetus,* 183b, l. 5, trans. John McDowell (Oxford: Clarendon Press, 1973), 64. James had mentioned the *Theaetetus* as recently as Aug. 24, 1906.

15. *EPh,* 189–90.

16. *Corr.* 12:487.

17. *Diary of AGJ,* quoted in Edel, vol. 5, 442. The current whereabouts of this diary are unknown.

18. Henry Adams, *Degradation of the Democratic Dogma* (New York: Putnam, 1958), 137–38.

19. Adams, *Degradation of the Democratic Dogma,* 178–79.

20. *Corr.* 12:555–56.

21. *Corr.* 12:569.

22. *SPP,* 203.

23. Edel, vol. 5, 446.

24. *Diary of AGJ,* quoted in Allen.

Epilogue

1. *Diary of AGJ,* quoted in Allen, 491–92; *HJ Letters,* vol. 4, 561–62.

PRINCIPAL SOURCES

Chief Unpublished Manuscript Sources

WJ	Notebook 1, Geneva, 1859	Houghton	b Ms Am 1092.9 (4495)
WJ	Account Book, 1861–	Houghton	b Ms Am 1092.9 (4560)
WJ	Chemistry Notebook, Cambridge, 1861–62 (K)	Houghton	*57M-137
WJ	Notebook 2, Cambridge, 1862	Houghton	b Ms Am 1092.9 (4496)
WJ	Notebook 3, Cambridge, 1862–	Houghton	b Ms Am 1092.9 (4497)
WJ	Drawings, 1862– (includes 3 small notebooks)	Houghton	b Ms Am 1092.2
WJ	Index Rerum (Notebook 26) (U) 1864–	Houghton	b Ms Am 1092.9 (4520)
WJ	Notebook 4, Brazilian Diary and Sketchbook (Z), 1865	Houghton	b Ms Am 1092.9 (4498)
WJ	Brazilian Diary, 1865	Harvard Museum of Comparative Zoology	6MU 1556.41.4.1
WJ	Microscope Notebook, 1866	Houghton	b Ms Am 1092.9 (4499)
WJ	Medical School Notebook, 1866–67 (Y)	Countway Archives	CB 1869.42
WJ	Diary, 1868–73 (Diary 1)	Houghton	b Ms Am 1092.9 (4550)
WJ	Florence Notebook (T), 1873	Houghton	b Ms Am 1092.9 (4500)
WJ	Diary, 1883 (Diary 2)	Houghton	b Ms Am 1092.9 (4551)
WJ	Diary, 1901–02 (Diary 3)	Houghton	b Ms Am 1092.9 (4552)
WJ	Diary, 1905 (Diary 4)	Houghton	b Ms Am 1092.9 (4553)
WJ	Diary, 1906 (Diary 5)	Houghton	b Ms Am 1092.9 (4554)
WJ	Diary, 1906 (Diary 6)	Houghton	b Ms Am 1092.9 (4555)
WJ	Diary, 1907 (Diary 7)	Houghton	b Ms Am 1092.9 (4556)
WJ	Diary, 1908 (Diary 8)	Houghton	b Ms Am 1092.9 (4557)
WJ	Diary, 1909 (Diary 9)	Houghton	b Ms Am 1092.9 (4558)
WJ	Diary, 1910 (Diary 10)	Houghton	b Ms Am 1092.9 (4559)

WJ	Faculty folder	Harvard University Archives (Pusey)	HUG 300 Wm James
WJ	Student papers	Harvard University Archives (Pusey)	HUG 1466.406
WJ	*The Principles of Psychology* (4-vol. interleaved copy belonging to WJ)	Houghton	AC85.J2376.890p
(WJ)	Harvard University Library Charging Records, 1870–	Harvard University Archives (Pusey)	HUG III.50.15.60
AGJ	"Valuable and Much Prized by WJ," list of books and manuscripts in AGJ's hand	Houghton	b Ms Am 1092.9 (4581)
AGJ	Letters	Houghton	b Ms Am 1092.11 (1–23)
(AGJ)	Ms Life of AGJ, by Henry James III	Houghton	b Ms Am 1095.1* 1962
(AGJ)	Letters to AGJ from J. G. Whittier	Houghton	b Ms Am 1092.9 (4343–64)
	Letters to J. C. Gray from Minnie Temple (4 folders)	Houghton	b Ms Am 1092.12
	HJ Sr Letters	Houghton	b Ms Am 1093.1
	MJ Letters	Houghton	b Ms Am 1093.1
	J. J. Putnam Letters	Massachusetts Historical Society, Putnam Collection	
	J. J. Putnam Letters	Countway	HMS C4.1 fol. 2–6
	"Counsels of Courage," anthology of WJ's writings, with an introduction by HJ III	Houghton	*60M-90

Abbreviations of the Works of William James

ECR	*Essays, Comments, and Reviews.* Cambridge: Harvard University Press, 1987
EPh	*Essays in Philosophy.* Cambridge: Harvard University Press, 1978
EPR	*Essays in Psychical Research.* Cambridge: Harvard University Press, 1986
EPs	*Essays in Psychology.* Cambridge: Harvard University Press, 1983
ERE	*Essays in Radical Empiricism.* Cambridge: Harvard University Press, 1976
ERM	*Essays in Religion and Morality.* Cambridge: Harvard University Press, 1982
MEN	*Manuscript Essays and Notes.* Cambridge: Harvard University Press, 1988
ML	*Manuscript Lectures.* Cambridge: Harvard University Press, 1988
MT	*The Meaning of Truth.* Cambridge, Harvard University Press, 1975
P	*Pragmatism.* Cambridge: Harvard University Press, 1975
PBC	*Psychology: Briefer Course.* Cambridge: Harvard University Press, 1984
PP	*The Principles of Psychology,* 3 vols. Cambridge: Harvard University Press, 1981
PU	*A Pluralistic Universe.* Cambridge: Harvard University Press, 1977
SPP	*Some Problems in Philosophy.* Cambridge: Harvard University Press, 1979
TT	*Talks to Teachers on Psychology.* Cambridge: Harvard University Press, 1983
VRE	*The Varieties of Religious Experience.* Cambridge: Harvard University Press, 1985
WB	*The Will to Believe.* Cambridge: Harvard University Press, 1979

Short Titles of Frequently Cited Books

Ahlstrom   Sidney E. Ahlstrom, *A Religious History of the American People.* New Haven: Yale University Press, 1972

Allen   Gay Wilson Allen, *William James.* New York: Viking, 1967

Barzun   Jacques Barzun, *A Stroll with William James.* New York: Harper and Row, 1983

Bjork 1   Daniel W. Bjork, *The Compromised Scientist: William James in the Development of American Psychology.* New York: Columbia University Press, 1983

Bjork 2   Daniel W. Bjork, *William James: The Center of His Vision.* New York: Columbia University Press, 1988

Brent   Joseph L. Brent, *Charles Sanders Peirce: A Life.* Bloomington: Indiana University Press, 1993

Clendenning   John Clendenning, *The Life and Thought of Josiah Royce,* rev. ed. Nashville, Tenn.: Vanderbilt University Press, 1999

Compton   Charles H. Compton, *William James: Philosopher and Man.* New York: Scarecrow Press, 1957

Corr.   *The Correspondence of William James,* 12 vols. John J. McDermott, gen. ed.; Ignas K. Skrupskelis, Elizabeth Berkeley, and Frederick H. Burkhardt, eds. Charlottesville: University of Virginia Press, 1992–2004

Croce   Paul Jerome Croce, *Science and Religion in the Era of William James,* 2 vols. Chapel Hill: University of North Carolina Press, 1995

Diary of AJ   *The Diary of Alice James.* Leon Edel, ed. Boston: Northeastern University Press, 1999

Edel   *Henry James,* 5 vols. New York: Lippincott, 1953–1972

Ellenberger   Henri Ellenberger, *The Discovery of the Unconscious.* New York: Basic Books, 1970

Feinstein   Howard Feinstein, *Becoming William James.* Ithaca, N.Y.: Cornell University Press, 1984

Flower and   Elizabeth Flower and Murray G. Murphey, *A History of Philosophy in*
Murphey   *America.* New York: Capricorn Books, 1977

Habegger   Alfred Habegger, *The Father.* New York: Farrar, Straus and Giroux, 1994

HJ Letters   *Henry James Letters,* 4 vols. Cambridge: Harvard University Press, 1974–1984

Lewis   R.W.B. Lewis, *The Jameses.* New York: Farrar, Straus and Giroux, 1991

Maher   Jane Maher, *Biography of Broken Fortunes.* Hamden, Conn.: Shoestring Press, 1986

Matthiessen   F. O. Matthiessen, *The James Family.* New York: Knopf, 1961

McDermott   John J. McDermott, *The Writings of William James* (with annotated bibliography updated through 1977). Chicago: University of Chicago Press, 1977

Menand   Louis Menand, *The Metaphysical Club.* New York: Farrar, Straus and Giroux, 2001

Morison 1   Samuel Eliot Morison, *Three Centuries of Harvard.* Cambridge: Harvard University Press, 1936

Morison 2   Samuel Eliot Morison, *The Development of Harvard University, 1869–1927.* Cambridge: Harvard University Press, 1930

Myers	Gerald E. Myers, *William James: His Life and Thought*. New Haven: Yale University Press, 1986
NSB	Henry James, *Notes of a Son and Brother*. New York: Scribner, 1914
Perry	Ralph Barton Perry, *The Thought and Character of William James*, 2 vols. Boston: Little, Brown, 1935
Santayana 1	George Santayana, "William James," in *Character and Opinion in the United States*. London: Constable, 1920
Santayana 2	George Santayana, *Persons and Places: Fragments of Autobiography* Cambridge: MIT Press, 1986
SBO	Henry James, *A Small Boy and Others*. New York: Scribner, 1913
Simon	Linda Simon, *Genuine Reality: A Life of William James*. New York: Harcourt Brace, 1998
Skrupskelis	Ignas Skrupskelis, *William James: A Reference Guide*. Boston: G. K. Hall, 1977
Sprigge	T.L.S. Sprigge, *James and Bradley: American Truth and British Reality*. Chicago: Open Court, 1993
Strouse	Jean Strouse, *Alice James: A Biography*. Boston: Houghton Mifflin, 1980
Taylor	Eugene Taylor, *William James on Exceptional Mental States: The 1896 Lowell Lectures*. Amherst: University of Massachusetts Press, 1984
WJ Rem	Linda Simon, ed., *William James Remembered*. Lincoln: University of Nebraska Press, 1986

INDEX

Empathy, 427, 575

Empiricism
  and WJ, 148, 248, 258, 485 (*see also* Radical empiricism)
  Whitehead on, 466

"Energies of Men, The" (WJ), 91, 489–91, 512

Entropy (second law of thermodynamics), 518, 519

Environment
  and great men of history, 210
  and mind, 179, 185–86

Epictetus, 15, 53

Epistemology, WJ talk on, 340

Erckmann, Émile, 81, 125, 225

Erikson, Erik, 122, 471, 473, 579

Error, for Royce, 255

Essays in Radical Empiricism (WJ), 252–53, 302, 458, 511, 512

Ether (medical), 270

Ether (physics), 165

Ethical philosophy, WJ on, 308–10

Ethical skepticism, WJ opposed to, 309

Eugène, Prince, memoirs of, 126

Euphorion (Lee), 330

Europeans, The (HJ Jr), 220

Evans, Elizabeth Glendower, 381

Evil
  HJ Sr on, 29–30, 32–33, 53, 58, 83
  and WJ on, 53, 90, 349, 399–400, 455
  Tolstoy's perceptions of, 404

Evolution
  Agassiz on, 43
  Bowen against, 180
  and WJ, 167, 186, 204
    on consciousness, 186, 195, 196
  Spencer on, 179

"Evolution and Mind" (WJ lecture), 200

"Evolutionary Love" (Peirce), 32–33

Evolutionism, vs. Hegelianism (WJ), 214

"Evolution of Self-Consciousness" (Wright), 132

Examinations (academic), WJ on, 343

Experience
  Bergson's philosophy of, 428
    vs. concepts, 503
  Fechner on, 500
  and WJ, xiii–xiv, 449, 465–66, 512
    on conceptual thinking, 503
    and knowledge, 244
    openness to, 3, 477
    on universe, 4
    on validity of, 215
  and language or philosophy, 391
  mystical, 113, 209–10, 375, 406, 412–14, 415, 515–16

as primal material, 447, 448–49, 451

religious, 378, 379, 391–92, 414 (*see also* Religion)

Royce on, 386, 497

"Experiencing nature" (Alice Gibbens), 168

Experimental psychology, 128, 357–38

Experimental spirit, WJ accused of lacking (Hall), 303

Experimental work, WJ's disinclination toward, 95, 323, 357

Facts of Consciousness (Green), 127

Faith
  WJ on, 202–3, 281, 361–63, 369, 469, 480
  Tolstoy on, 414
  See also Belief

Fanaticism, Santayana on, 460

Faraday, Michael, 31, 51, 155, 536

Farrar, Frederic, 52

Fatalism, WJ on, 289

Faust, 92, 207, 248, 503

Fechner, Gustav Theodor, 4, 44, 110, 160, 177, 447, 458, 465, 498, 499–502, 503, 504

Feeling, and WJ, xiv–xv, 198–99, 252, 280, 419, 450
  religion founded in, 415
  See also Emotion

"Feeling of Effort, The" (WJ), 206, 294

Feinstein, Howard, 532, 534, 537

Felton, C. C., 42

Fergusson, Robert, 15

Ferrari, Giulio Cesare, 457

Feydeau, Ernest Aimé, 88

Fichte, Johann Gottlieb, 110, 202, 386

Fideism, 480

Fields, Annie, 27

54th Massachusetts Regiment, 54–55

55th Massachusetts Regiment, 55

Filipino Progress Association, 457

Finney, Charles Grandison, 30, 369, 405

Fishbaugh, Reverend, 261

Fisher, George, 140

Fishes of Brazil, The (Agassiz), 65

Fiske, John, 42, 130, 140, 204

Fitler, Charles Henry, 370

Fitzgerald, F. Scott, 436

Fixed idea, and hysteria (WJ), 346

Flammarion, Camille, 518

Flaubert, Gustave, 143

Fletcher, Horace, 160, 397, 444, 492

Fletcherism, 23, 444, 510, 517

Fleury, L.J.D., 95

Florence, 150, 169, 219, 327, 329

Flournoy, Theodore, 266, 390, 416, 453, 461, 487, 513, 514–15